GROB

BASIC ELECTRONICS

EIGHTH EDITION

Bernard Grob

Glencoe McGraw-Hill

New York, New York   Columbus, Ohio   Mission Hills, California   Peoria, Illinois

IN MEMORY OF RUTH

Photo credits appear on page 1008, which is hereby made part of this copyright page.

The Library of Congress has cataloged *Basic Electronics,* **Eighth Edition, as follows:**
Grob, Bernard.
   Basic electronics / Bernard Grob.—8th ed.
     p.   cm.
   Includes bibliographical references and index.
   ISBN 0-02-802253-X
   1. Electronics. I. Title.
TK7816.G75 1997
621.3—dc21   96-39669
                                       CIP

Glencoe/McGraw-Hill

*A Division of The **McGraw·Hill** Companies*

Basic Electronics, Eighth Edition, Book 1, Survey and Chapters 1 to 15

Copyright © 1997 by The McGraw-Hill Companies, Inc. All rights reserved. Copyright © 1992, 1989, 1984, 1977, 1971, 1965, 1959 by The McGraw-Hill Companies, Inc. All rights reserved. Printed in the United States of America. Except as permitted under the United States Copyright Act of 1976, no part of this publication may be reproduced or distributed in any form or by any means, or stored in a data base or retrieval system, without the prior written permission of the publisher.

Send all inquiries to:
Glencoe/McGraw-Hill
936 Eastwind Drive
Westerville, Ohio 43081

ISBN 0-02-802264-5

1 2 3 4 5 6 7 8 9 027 02 01 00 99 98 97

TO THE STUDENT

Basic Electronics, Eighth Edition, has been split into two convenient books. This set divides the original text into two logical parts. Book 1 contains the Survey chapter and Chapters 1 through 15, which cover all the material on direct current. Book 2 contains the remainder of the book—Chapters 16 to 32, which cover alternating current and an introduction to electronics.

For the convenience of the student, the glossary and appendixes are included in both Book 1 and Book 2. To facilitate reference to the supplemental materials and to maintain continuity between the volumes, the page numbering system has been kept as it appears in the single-volume textbook. For instance, the text of Book 1 is numbered through page 412, with the appendixes beginning on the next page, numbered 955. The text of Book 2 is numbered from page 414 through 954, and the appendixes continue on page 955.

CONTENTS

PREFACE

Basic Electronics, now in its eighth edition, is intended for students taking their first course in the fundamentals of electricity and electronics. The book is written for the beginning student, who is assumed to have no prior knowledge of the technical aspects of the subject. The prerequisites for using this book include an understanding of basic algebra and some trigonometry. In many schools, it will be possible to take a basic algebra-trigonometry course concurrently with the use of this book in a course covering the fundamental concepts of dc and ac theory.

The primary focus of this revision was a very careful review of its content and layout. Many additions, deletions, and reordering of topics have occurred as a direct result of an extensive survey sent to electronics instructors all across the country. For current users of the book, the additions and changes will be easy to identify throughout the book.

ORGANIZATION   The book begins with a chapter entitled "Survey of Electronics." This chapter provides a brief overview of the history of the development of electronics, describes a variety of career opportunities available in electronics, explains the most common components used in electronics, and identifies some of the most common types of equipment used by professionals in the electronics field. Following the "Survey of Electronics" chapter, the book provides complete and comprehensive coverage of the subjects which form the real fundamentals of basic electronics. Beginning with the atomic nature of electricity in Chapter 1, the topics progress through a study of resistors, Ohm's law, series and parallel circuits, series-parallel circuits, voltage and current dividers, dc meters, Kirchhoff's laws and network theorems, conductors and insulators, batteries, magnetism, magnetic units, electromagnetic induction, alternating voltage and current, capacitance, capacitive reactance, capacitive circuits, inductance, inductive reactance, inductive circuits, *RC* and *L/R* time constants, ac circuits, complex numbers, resonance, and filters.

Current users of the book will notice that the chapters on capacitance, capacitive reactance, and capacitive circuits now precede the chapters on inductance, inductive reactance, and inductive circuits. This change has been made as a result of the previously mentioned survey that was sent to electronics instructors. If they wish, instructors may choose to cover the chapters on inductance prior to those on capacitance.

In this edition, several changes have been made in Chapter 2, "Resistors." There is expanded coverage of both carbon and metal film resistors and the five-band resistor color code. Also new to this chapter is coverage of surface-mount resistors and zero-ohm resistors. These additions reflect the most state-of-the-art coverage available on resistors in any basic textbook covering dc and ac theory.

In Chapter 11, "Conductors and Insulators," more information on switches has been added. In Chapter 15, "Electromagnetic Induction," a new section on electromechanical relays has been added.

In Chapter 17, "Capacitance," new and updated material regarding the coding system used with a wide variety of types of capacitors has been added. Also new to this chapter is the coverage of surface-mount capacitors and the coding systems used with them. In Chapter 20, "Inductance," new material covers impedance matching and the many ratings associated with transformers. In Chapter 23, "*RC* and *L/R* Time Constants," new information on differentiation and integration is included. In Chapter 27, "Filters," a wealth of new information, on phase angles, calculating cutoff frequency and output voltage, decibels, and frequency response curves, now appears.

The last five chapters of the book provide a basic introduction to semiconductor theory, diodes, transistors, amplifiers, oscillators, modulation, rectifier circuits, circuit configurations, class of operation, troubleshooting, number systems, basic logic gates, Boolean algebra, flip-flops, counters, op amp characteristics, and op amp circuits. The coverage of op amp circuits has been expanded in response to the survey.

Following the text chapters are four appendixes: Appendix A, "Electrical Symbols and Abbreviations," Appendix B, "Solder and the Soldering Process," Appendix C, "Schematic Symbols," and Appendix D, "Using the Oscilloscope." The appendixes are followed by a glossary, answers to self-tests, answers to odd-numbered chapter problems and critical thinking problems, and an index.

CHAPTER LAYOUT   Each chapter begins with a brief introduction of the topic, a list of important terms, chapter objectives (new to this edition), and a list of the sections appearing within the chapter. Within each chapter, test-point questions are given at the end of each section. This provides the student with a quick means of checking his or her understanding of the material in that section. At the end of each chapter are the following items: summary, self-test, questions, problems, and critical thinking questions. Like the chapter objectives, the critical thinking questions are new to the eighth edition. It should be noted that new problems have been added to each chapter. The answers to the test-point questions appear at the end of each chapter.

Step-by-step solutions of typical problems dealing with a particular concept are generously provided in every chapter of the book. Where appropriate, typical calculator keystroke routines are provided as an additional aid to the student. The illustrative examples are highlighted so that students can access them more readily.

ANCILLARY PACKAGE   The following supplements are available to adopters of Grob *Basic Electronics*:

- *Problems in Grob Basic Electronics:* This book, written by Mitchel E. Schultz, provides students and instructors with a source of hundreds of practical problems for self-study, homework assignments, tests, and review. Each chapter contains a number of solved illustrative problems demonstrating, step-by-step, how representative problems on a particular topic are solved. Following the solved problems are sets of problems for the students to solve.

- *Experiments in Grob Basic Electronics:* This book, written by Frank Pugh and Wes Ponick, provides students and instructors with 67 easy-to-follow laboratory experiments. The experiments range from an introduction to laboratory equipment to an experiment on operational amplifiers. All experiments have been student-tested to ensure their effectiveness.

- *Mathematics for Grob Basic Electronics:* This book, written by Bernard Grob, provides students with the basic math skills needed to solve problems in the text, *Grob Basic Electronics.* Included are chapters on algebra, trigonometry, the basics of computer mathematics, and a new chapter on complex numbers for ac circuits.

- *Instructor's Productivity Center for Grob Basic Electronics, Eighth Edition:* This package includes a Windows-based test generator, a math tutorial, and a Power Point presentation for every chapter of the text. It also includes a graphics file of the circuits in the text. These files can be used for tests or presentations. The optional Group Instruction software, developed by HyperGraphics, can be accessed directly from the IPC. An optional Electronics Workbench file of the circuits in *Basic Electronics* is also available.

- *Instructor's Annotated Edition for Grob Basic Electronics, Eighth Edition:* This book includes teaching hints and scheduling suggestions for the instructor and career information for students. Much of this material has been given in the margin of this text for the instructor's ease of reference while teaching a class. Answers to test-point questions, which appear in the student's text, are also included in the margin of this version, produced especially for the instructor.

- *Instructor's Manual for Grob Basic Electronics, Eighth Edition:* This book provides the instructor with answers to all the questions and problems in the text and in its supplements, *Problems in Grob Basic Electronics, Experiments in Grob Basic Electronics,* and *Mathematics for Grob Basic Electronics.*

Bernard Grob

CREDITS AND ACKNOWLEDGMENTS

The author would like to thank those individuals who responded to the survey which was sent out long before this book was revised. Their comments and suggestions provided the information needed to make this the most up-to-date book available on electricity and electronics. The author would also like to thank the reviewers listed below who painstakingly examined every sentence, example, and problem for accuracy prior to the publication of the eighth edition.

In addition, the author would like to thank the highly professional staff at Glencoe in Columbus, Ohio—especially Brian Mackin for his patience, hard work, and understanding during the long period of the manuscript preparation. My thanks also go to Mitchel Schultz for his help on this project. Finally, it is a pleasure to thank my wife, Sylvia, for her help in preparing the manuscript.

Tim Beecher
Wisconsin Indianhead Technical College
Superior, WI

Jack Berger
ITT Technical Institute
Murray, UT

B. J. Tobias Boydell
Seva Electronics
Burford, Ontario, Canada

Patrick J. Chalmers
ITT Technical Institute
Matteson, IL

Michael Fairbanks
ITT Technical Institute
Nashville, TN

Richard L. Green
ITT Technical Institute
Maitland, FL

Rich Hassler
ITT Technical Institute
Youngstown, OH

William M. Hessmiller
QRS Corporation
Dunmore, PA

Barry Hoy
ITT Technical Institute
Norfolk, VA

Arnold Kroeger
Hillsborough Community College
Tampa, FL

James A. McQuoid
ITT Technical Institute
San Antonio, TX

Jim Myers
Wallace Community College
Selma, AL

Tony Richardson
ITT Technical Institute
Strongsville, OH

T. Randall Riggs
ITT Technical Institute
Tampa, FL

Gregg Richley
ITT Technical Institute
Youngstown, OH

Victor Rozeboom
Burlington, NC

John Ryan
ITT Technical Institute
Knoxville, TN

Dan Siddall
ITT Technical Institute
Boise, ID

Mike Siemion
Madison Area Technical College
Madison, WI

William H. Sims III
ITT Technical Institute
Jacksonville, FL

Pat Thomason
Patterson State Technical
College
Montgomery, AL

Bryon K. Van Beek
Courtesy Communications
Spokane, WA

SURVEY OF ELECTRONICS

The broad field of electronics encompasses radio, audio, television, computers, fiber optics, medical, industrial, automotive, and aerospace electronics. Although each of these areas represents a remarkable advance in technology, electronics can still be considered the practical applications of the general principles of electricity. For example, the same electric current produced by a battery to power a flashlight can also be used to power a calculator, a computer, a television, a videocassette recorder (VCR), or even an orbiting satellite. All applications of electronics are based on the fundamental laws of electricity and magnetism. An electric current will always produce magnetism. Furthermore, magnetism will always be produced by an electric current.

The study of the technology of electricity and electronics is, to say the least, very exciting and challenging. Whether your goal is to become an electronics technician or engineer, you will need a thorough understanding of the fundamental concepts presented in this book. Before we analyze the fundamentals of electricity, though, it can be interesting and helpful to look at the history of the development of electronics. We shall also take a look at some of the available career opportunities in electronics. And, finally, we will introduce some of the most common electronic components and test instruments used by electronics technicians and engineers.

CHAPTER OBJECTIVES

Upon completion of this chapter, you should be able to:

- *List* some milestones in the history of the development of electronics.
- *List* the names of famous scientists who contributed to the early development of electronics.
- *List* a variety of different career opportunities available in electronics.
- *List* the names of the most common electronic components and *describe* their main function.
- *List* the names of the most common pieces of electronic test equipment used by technicians and engineers and *describe* their main function.

IMPORTANT TERMS IN THIS CHAPTER

alternating current	DMM	power supply
capacitors	electronics	resistors
communications electronics	function generator	surface-mount technology
digital electronics	integrated circuit	transistors
direct current	oscilloscope	waveform

TOPICS COVERED IN THIS CHAPTER

S-1 A BRIEF HISTORY OF THE DEVELOPMENT OF ELECTRONICS

Modern electronics began with the pioneer days of radio communications. The development of radio, however, was preceded by earlier experiments in electricity and magnetism. The beginning of wireless transmission for radio communications arose from work done by Heinrich Hertz, a German physicist. In 1887 he demonstrated the effects of electromagnetic radiation through space. Even though the distance of transmission was only a few feet, Hertz's experiment proved that radio waves could travel from one place to another without the need for any connecting wires between the transmitting and receiving equipment. The experiment also proved that radio waves, although invisible, travel with the same velocity as light waves. In fact, radio waves and light waves are both examples of *electromagnetic radiation*. This form of energy combines the effects of electricity and magnetism, whereby an electromagnetic wave transmits electric energy through space.

The work of Hertz actually followed even earlier experiments. In 1820, a Danish physicist, Hans Christian Oersted, proved that an electric current produces magnetic effects. Then, in 1831, Michael Faraday, a British physicist, discovered that a magnet in motion can generate electricity. The motion meets the requirement of a change in the magnetic field. In 1864, another British physicist, James Clerk Maxwell, on the basis of earlier work in electricity and magnetism, predicted the electromagnetic waves demonstrated later by Hertz.

The importance of the work done by Hertz, Maxwell, Oersted, and Faraday can be judged by the fact that their names are used as the basic units of measurement in electricity. For example, the maxwell (Mx) and the oersted (Oe) are basic units of magnetism. Similarly, the hertz (Hz) is the basic unit of frequency, equal to one complete cycle of alternating voltage or alternating current (ac) each second. The farad (F), which is named after Michael Faraday, is the basic unit of capacitance, which indicates how much electric charge is stored in a component known as a capacitor. Other famous scientists for which electrical units are named include André Ampère, Georg Simon Ohm, Joseph Henry, James Prescott Joule, Wilhelm Eduard Weber, James Watt, and Werner von Siemens, to name a few. The ampere is the basic unit of electric current, the ohm is the basic unit of electrical resistance, the joule is the basic unit of electric energy, the weber is a unit of magnetic flux, the henry is the basic unit of inductance, the watt is the basic unit of electric power, and the siemens is the basic unit of conductance.

In 1895, Guglielmo Marconi used a long wire as an antenna in developing a practical radio system for very long distances. (An antenna is needed to provide efficient radiation of the radio waves.) Marconi succeeded in producing wireless communications across the Atlantic Ocean in 1901. Electronic communication remained limited, however, until Lee DeForest invented the audion tube in 1906. Further development of vacuum tubes allowed the field of electronic communications to develop rapidly. In 1920, regularly scheduled radio programs were broadcast by station KDKA. The first radio broadcasts used what is called amplitude modulation (AM) to transmit its program information. The first frequency-modulated (FM) broadcast occurred in 1939, and the first FM stereo broadcast became available to listeners in 1961. Commercial television broadcasting began officially in 1941 but did not become popular until 1945. Our present color television system was adopted in 1953.

Perhaps one of the most important milestones in the history of electronics was the invention of the transistor in 1948 by John Bardeen, Walter Brattain, and William Schockley, all of whom worked for Bell Telephone Laboratories at the time. The transistor (also called a solid-state device or semiconductor) eventually replaced the vacuum tube in radios and televisions. The transistor is much more efficient than the vacuum tube, since it does not have a heater. Other solid-state devices include diodes and integrated circuits. Figure S-1 shows several different solid-state devices. The development of solid-state devices has led to the continued miniaturization of all types of electronic equipment. Each month we learn of new technological advances that produce increasingly sophisticated circuitry in ever smaller integrated circuits. The primary reasons for this trend are improved reliability, lower costs, and increased speed due to the reduction in the length of the interconnecting wires.

FIG. S-1   Semiconductor devices for electronic equipment (not shown to actual size). (*a*) Transistor amplifiers. (*b*) Diode rectifiers. (*c*) Integrated circuit (IC) packages.

S-2 RADIO AND TELEVISION BROADCASTING

The word *broadcast* means to send out in all directions. In a radio or television broadcasting system the transmitter sends out electromagnetic radio waves from its antenna. At the receiving end, an antenna picks up or intercepts the transmitted signal. The receiver reproduces the transmitted information. Because there are many radio signals traveling in space from different transmitters, a receiver must be able to select or *tune* to the frequency of the station desired. All other stations must be tuned out. Figure S-2 illustrates a basic radio broadcasting system. Notice that it consists of a transmitter, a receiver, and two antennas. The distance of transmission for a wireless communication system can be less than a mile or as much as 5000 miles, depending on the type of service. There are many different services, such as the radio broadcasting of voice and music, television broadcasting, amateur ("ham") radio, and citizen's band (CB) radio. Other examples of radio communication include police and aircraft radios, cordless and cellular telephones, and satellite communications. All radio communication services in the United States are regulated by the Federal Communications Commission (FCC). The FCC assigns carrier frequencies to each type of service and also regulates the lawful use of each assigned service.

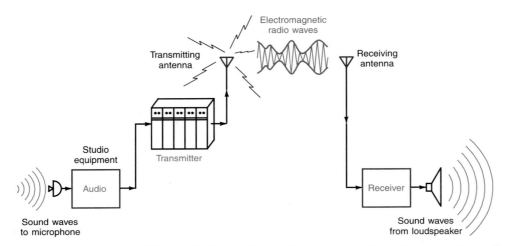

FIG. S-2 Radio broadcasting between transmitter and receiver. An amplitude-modulated (AM) carrier wave is shown here.

AM AND FM BROADCAST BANDS The AM broadcast band, which ranges from 540 to 1600 kilohertz (kHz), was the first system to be used for public broadcasting of program information such as news, weather, and music. Each station is assigned a carrier frequency by the FCC and is allotted a bandwidth of 10 kHz.

The FM broadcast band extends from 88 to 108 megahertz (MHz), with each station occupying a 200-kHz bandwidth. The FM system has several advantages over the AM system. Most important is the fact that it is inherently less noisy and is also capable of broadcasting a broader range of audio frequencies for better fidelity.

TELEVISION BROADCASTING *Television* (TV) means to see at a distance. Television is just another form of radio communication, but with video or picture information in addition to sound. Two separate carrier waves are used in the transmission of a television signal: one for the picture and one for the sound. The picture carrier signal is an AM signal, whereas the sound carrier signal is an FM signal. Each television station occupies a bandwidth of 6 MHz, which is 600 times more than an AM broadcast station and 30 times more than an FM broadcast station.

AMATEUR RADIO   Amateur radio is one of the largest noncommercial radio services in the world. Amateur operators, also called "hams," communicate with each other using Morse code, voice, radioteletype, slow-scan television, and digital communications. Public service is a large part of amateur radio. Hams often provide emergency communications in times of national disaster such as flooding, tornadoes, hurricanes, and earthquakes. Amateur radio operators have formed an organization known as the American Radio Relay League (ARRL). The ARRL was founded in 1914 and is headquartered in Newington, Connecticut.

CITIZEN'S BAND RADIO   Citizen's band (CB) radio is another noncommercial radio service which can be used by the general public. The CB band has forty 10-kHz channels extending from 26.965 MHz up to 27.405 MHz. The CB band allows a maximum power output of 4 watts (W). Unlike amateur radio, no license is required to operate a CB radio.

S-3 CAREER OPPORTUNITIES IN ELECTRONICS

Career opportunities in electronics continue to expand and become more varied with each passing year. It seems as if the career opportunities in electronics are almost limitless. The purpose of this section is to provide you, the newcomer to electronics, with some insight into the many possible career opportunities available to you.

CONSUMER ELECTRONICS TECHNICIAN   A consumer electronics technician is a person who repairs home entertainment equipment, such as stereos, televisions, VCRs, CD players, and camcorders. Electronic technicians who service these types of equipment can expect to encounter a wide variety of electronic circuits and mechanical devices. In this field, technicians often troubleshoot down to the component level rather than just the board level. A strong understanding of electronic theory and circuits is a must to be successful in this branch of electronics. With high-definition television (HDTV) and interactive television becoming more and more common, the opportunities awaiting the consumer electronics technician continue to look promising. One major advantage in choosing a career as a consumer electronics technician is that employment can be obtained just about anywhere in the United States.

COMPUTER REPAIR TECHNICIAN   With the use and applications of computers continuing to grow, the need for computer repair technicians is at an all-time high. To be a technician in this branch of electronics, you must have a thorough understanding of both the hardware and the software aspects of computer operation. The electronic, magnetic, and mechanical devices of a computer are referred to as the *hardware,* whereas the programs, which tell the computer what to do, are called the *software.*

Because computer technology is advancing so rapidly, it is hard to keep up with the latest developments, which may change on almost a week-to-week

ABOUT ELECTRONICS

Guglielmo Marconi is credited with sending the first radio transmission through the air using electromagnetic waves.

basis. Most computer repair technicians attend training schools on a regular basis in order to keep up to date.

INDUSTRIAL ELECTRONICS TECHNICIAN   An industrial electronics technician is a person who maintains, troubleshoots, and repairs a variety of industrial equipment, such as motors and motor controls, programmable logic controllers (PLCs), robots, and computer-controlled machine tools and fluid power systems. The industrial electronics technician may also be involved in the development and installation of equipment. With manufacturing on the rise in the United States, the need for industrial electronic technicians will continue to grow.

MEDICAL ELECTRONICS TECHNICIAN   A medical electronics technician is a person who works closely with nurses and physicians and other hospital staff to advise about and help maintain the wide range of electronic equipment used in medicine. As an electronic technician in this field you can expect to maintain, troubleshoot, and repair a variety of different types of medical equipment, such as computerized axial tomography (CAT) and magnetic resonance imaging (MRI) systems, surgical lasers, heart-lung bypass machines, dialysis machines, and electronic thermometers. Medical equipment manufacturers often provide training in the maintenance and repair of their products. As a technician in this branch of electronics you can expect to be under some stress. On the plus side, however, medical electronic technicians often make good to excellent wages and benefits, and the job is usually considered quite prestigious.

ABOUT ELECTRONICS

The unit of measure for capacitance, the farad, was named for Michael Faraday, an English chemist and physicist who discovered the principle of induction (1 F is the unit of capacitance that will store 1 C of charge when 1 V is applied).

COMMUNICATION ELECTRONICS TECHNICIAN   A communications electronics technician is a person who is trained to install, maintain, troubleshoot, and repair a variety of electronic communication equipment, such as FM communications transceivers, cellular phones, pagers, repeater systems, antenna systems, microwave systems, and AM and FM broadcasting equipment. Employment opportunities are exploding all across the country as a result of the rapid growth in this area. Wages and benefits are typically very good. The physical demands of this kind of work may range from climbing a 200-ft tower to install antennas, to sitting in an air-conditioned room troubleshooting equipment.

CABLE TELEVISION TECHNICIAN   A cable television technician is a person who is trained to install, test, maintain, troubleshoot, and repair cable television systems. In this branch of electronics an in-depth knowledge of electronic circuitry is helpful but not a necessity. This type of work is more likely to entail installing connectors on coaxial cable, testing coaxial lines for faults, and connecting and disconnecting customers to the cable system. Although this type of work often provides good wages, the physical demands of the job often make it less appealing than other career opportunities available in electronics.

OFFICE EQUIPMENT TECHNICIAN An office equipment technician is a person who maintains and repairs office equipment such as xerographic copiers, facsimile (FAX) machines, and laser printers. In this type of work, customer relation skills are extremely important, since the technician almost always travels to the customer's location. In many cases the job is more mechanical than it is electrical, since the moving parts within the equipment eventually wear out. Wages in this area are moderate to good, and jobs are plentiful.

S-4 A PREVIEW OF THE MOST COMMON ELECTRONIC COMPONENTS

Although there are an almost unlimited number of applications for electronics, all applications use basically the same types of electronic components. This section introduces the most common types found in all applications of electronics.

Electronic components are categorized as being either *passive* or *active*. Resistors, capacitors, and inductors are examples of passive components, whereas diodes, transistors, and vacuum tubes are examples of active components. Active components are capable of rectifying, amplifying, or changing energy from one form to another. Passive components, on the other hand, can control energy, but they cannot amplify or modify it. Both passive and active components generally are used together to form complete circuits in all types of electronic equipment. For the passive components, it may be surprising to learn that all electronic circuits use only three basic types: resistors, capacitors, and inductors.

RESISTORS Resistors are perhaps the most common component in electronic circuits. Their main function is to limit current flow or reduce the voltage in a circuit. The resistance may be either fixed or variable. Figure S-3 shows several different types of both fixed and variable resistors. Some fixed resistors are color coded to indicate their resistance value, while others have their resistance values printed right on the body. The basic unit of resistance is the ohm (Ω). Variable resistors usually have their maximum resistance stamped on them. Table S-1

FIG. S-3   Typical resistors for electronic circuits.

TABLE S-1 SCHEMATIC SYMBOLS FOR FIXED AND VARIABLE RESISTORS

TYPE	SCHEMATIC SYMBOL	NOTES
Fixed	*R*	Limits current and reduces voltage
Variable	*R*	Has three external connections Varies voltage
		Has two external connections Varies current

shows the schematic symbols for both fixed and variable resistors. All fixed resistors use the same symbol, but the symbol for a variable resistor may vary depending on how it is used in a circuit. Resistors are covered in Chap. 2.

CAPACITORS   A capacitor is a component that is able to hold or store an electric charge. Its physical construction consists of two metal plates separated by an insulator. In general, capacitors are used to block direct current (dc) but pass alternating current (ac). The basic unit of capacitance is the farad (F).

Like resistors, capacitors may be either fixed in value or variable. Figure S-4 shows several commonly used capacitors found in modern electronic circuitry. Some capacitors are coded using a special numbering system, whereas others have their value printed right on them. As you can see, capacitors come in a variety of different shapes and sizes. Table S-2 shows the schematic symbols for both fixed and variable capacitors. The symbol for an electrolytic capacitor (the one with polarity markings on its plates) indicates that polarity must be observed when connecting it into a circuit. Capacitors other than electrolytics can be connected into a circuit without concern for proper polarity. Capacitors are covered in detail in Chap. 17.

INDUCTORS   An inductor is a component whose physical construction is simply a coil of wire. For this reason inductors are often called *coils*. The function of an inductor is to provide opposition to a changing or varying current. Whenever a current change occurs within the coil windings, a voltage is induced across the ends of the coil. The polarity of the induced voltage is such that it

FIG. S-4   Typical small capacitors for electronic circuits. Length is ¼ to 1 in. without leads.

opposes the current change occurring within the coil. In more general terms, inductors are the opposite of capacitors in that they are able to pass a dc current and block an ac current. The basic unit of inductance is the henry (H).

Like resistors and capacitors, inductors may be either fixed or variable. Several different types are shown in Fig. S-5. When inductors are color coded, they can be distinguished from resistors by the fact that the first color band is always a wide silver band. The variable inductors frequently used in modern electronic equipment are adjusted by tuning a magnetic slug in and out of its core. The schematic symbols for both fixed and variable inductors are shown in Table S-3.

TABLE S-2	SCHEMATIC SYMBOLS FOR FIXED AND VARIABLE CAPACITORS	
TYPE	SCHEMATIC SYMBOL	NOTES
Fixed	C	Stores electric charge Blocks dc, passes ac
Electrolytic	C	Has large capacitance Must be connected with proper polarity Fixed values only
Variable	C	Used for tuning radios, TVs, and other electronic communications equipment

FIG. S-5   Typical inductors or coils for electronic circuits.

A transformer is another component that can technically be defined as a inductor, because it is constructed by placing two coils in close proximity to each other. One of the main applications of a transformer is to step up or step down an ac voltage. Transformers cannot step up or step down a dc voltage. Figure S-6 shows several modern transformers, whereas Table S-4 shows a typical transformer schematic symbol. Inductors and transformers are covered in Chap. 20.

FIG. S-6   Typical modern transformers.

DIODES   A diode is an electronic component which allows current to flow through it in one direction but not the other. A diode's main function is to change an ac voltage into a dc voltage. Figure S-7 shows a variety of different diodes found in modern electronic equipment. The end that is closest to the gray band

FIG. S-7   Typical diodes.

TABLE S-3	SCHEMATIC SYMBOLS FOR FIXED AND VARIABLE INDUCTORS	
TYPE	SCHEMATIC SYMBOL	NOTES
Air	L	Induces voltage when current changes Passes dc, limits ac
Iron core	L	Used for low frequencies
Variable	L	Used for tuning radios, TVs, and other electronic communications equipment

TABLE S-4   SCHEMATIC SYMBOL FOR TRANSFORMER

TYPE	SCHEMATIC SYMBOL	NOTES
Iron-core transformer	*T* Primary Secondary	Steps up or steps down ac voltages

identifies the lead known as the *cathode*. The other lead is called the *anode*. Although there are a wide variety of different diode types, Table S-5 shows the schematic symbols seen most frequently.

TABLE S-5   SCHEMATIC SYMBOLS FOR DIODES

TYPE	SCHEMATIC SYMBOL	NOTES
Semiconductor diode	Anode ▷ Cathode *D*	Passes current in only one direction
Zener diode	Anode ▷ Cathode	Regulates voltage

TRANSISTORS   A transistor is an electronic component that can be used to amplify small ac signals or switch a dc voltage. A wide variety of different types are available, so it is not practical to explain them all. However, Fig. S-8 shows some typical transistors, while Table S-6 shows the most common schematic symbols.

SURFACE-MOUNTED DEVICES   Surface-mounted devices (SMDs), also called *chip components,* have been in use for many years now, primarily where portability and compactness are needed or desired. All electronic components are available as SMDs. The widespread use of the SMD in portable electronic equipment such as camcorders, pagers, and hand-held communications transceivers has significantly reduced the cost of SMDs. Additional cost savings result from the fact that they require much less space than conventional components, and also that no holes need to be drilled to mount them. SMDs are soldered directly to the copper traces of a printed circuit board. SMDs do more than just save money and reduce the size of electronic equipment, however. They also improve a circuit's performance. This is due to the fact that with SMDs the components are all much closer together, which means shorter, more direct electric

FIG. S-8   Typical transistors.

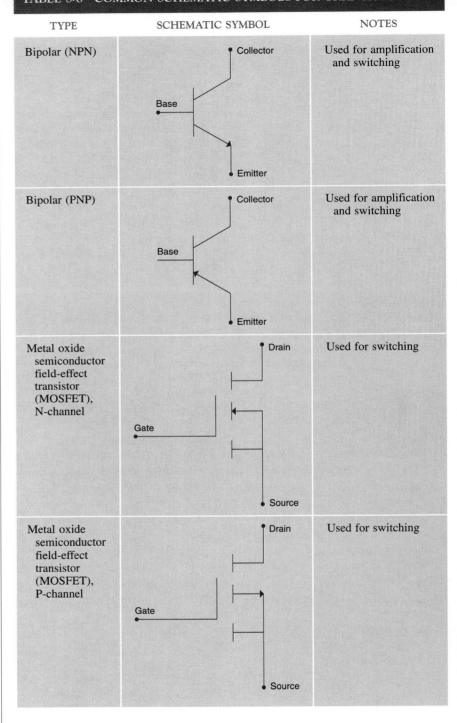

TABLE S-6 COMMON SCHEMATIC SYMBOLS FOR TRANSISTORS

TYPE	SCHEMATIC SYMBOL	NOTES
Bipolar (NPN)	Collector / Base / Emitter	Used for amplification and switching
Bipolar (PNP)	Collector / Base / Emitter	Used for amplification and switching
Metal oxide semiconductor field-effect transistor (MOSFET), N-channel	Drain / Gate / Source	Used for switching
Metal oxide semiconductor field-effect transistor (MOSFET), P-channel	Drain / Gate / Source	Used for switching

FIG. S-9 Typical surface-mounted devices.

connections, which in turn reduce the circuit's susceptibility to noise pickup. Figure S-9 shows a variety of different SMDs. In this book you will be introduced to passive surface-mount devices.

S-5 TOOLS OF THE TRADE

As an electronic technician or engineer, you can expect to encounter a wide variety of equipment when maintaining or troubleshooting electronic equipment. However, nearly all technicians use a digital multimeter (DMM), oscilloscope, power supply, and function generator. This section provides some basic information about the functions of each of these pieces of test equipment.

DIGITAL MULTIMETER A DMM is used to measure the voltage, current, or resistance in an electronic circuit. Most DMMs also have provisions for testing capacitors, diodes, and transistors. The meter may be either a hand-held or bench-top unit. Both types are shown in Fig. S-10. All digital meters have numerical readouts which indicate directly the value of voltage, current, or resistance being measured. Years ago, analog meters were used to make voltage, current, and resistance measurements. An analog meter uses a moving pointer and a printed scale. DMMs have replaced the older analog meters in almost all applications.

OSCILLOSCOPE The oscilloscope is a technician's most versatile piece of test equipment. Its basic function is to view and measure ac waveforms. Most oscilloscopes have dual-trace capabilities, which means they can display two waveforms at the same time. Figure S-11 shows a modern dual-trace oscilloscope.

POWER SUPPLY A power supply is a unit capable of supplying dc voltage and current to electronic circuits under test. Modern power supplies have regulated outputs. This means that their output voltage does not fluctuate as the load current varies. In most power supplies, a red jack is used for the positive terminal and a black jack is used for the negative terminal.

FUNCTION GENERATOR A function generator is a piece of test equipment capable of producing a number of different output waveforms. Function generators are used when designing, developing, and troubleshooting electronic equipment. All function generators have controls to adjust the amplitude, frequency, and shape of the output waveform.

(a)　　　　　　　　　　　　　　　　　(b)

FIG. S-10 Typical multimeters. (a) Hand-held. (b) Bench-top.

FIG. S-11 Dual-trace oscilloscope.

CHAPTER 1

ELECTRICITY

We see applications of electricity all around us, especially in electronics, but they are derived from more fundamental effects. Basically, electricity is an invisible force that can produce heat, light, and motion, as examples. The force for motion is an attraction or repulsion between electric charges. Specifically, electricity can be explained in terms of electric charge, current, and voltage.

Electric charge is the basic form for a quantity of electricity. The charge has an invisible field of force, extending outward in all directions, that can do the work of moving another charge.

Charge in motion provides an electric current. The practical unit of current is the ampere.

Two charges that are different in polarity provide a difference of potential with a net field of force that can move charges to produce current. This potential difference is indicated by the volt unit.

Electricity is often described as voltage or current but both are usually necessary and they are very different from each other. The closed path for the movement of charges is called a circuit. The circuit usually has resistance also, as a component to limit the amount of current. In short, the practical applications of electricity require the analysis of charge, current, and voltage with the components that make up the circuit.

CHAPTER OBJECTIVES

Upon completion of this chapter, you should be able to:

- *List* the two basic particles of electric charge.
- *Describe* the basic structure of the atom.
- *Define* the terms *conductor, insulator,* and *semiconductor* and give examples of each.
- *Define* the coulomb unit of electric charge.
- *Define* potential difference and voltage and list the unit of each.
- *Define* current and list its unit of measure.
- *Describe* the difference between voltage and current.
- *Define* resistance and conductance and list the unit of each.
- *List* three important characteristics of an electric circuit.
- *Define* the difference between electron flow and conventional current.
- *Describe* the difference between direct and alternating current.

IMPORTANT TERMS IN THIS CHAPTER

alternating current	electric field	open circuit
ampere unit	electron flow	polarity
circuit	hole charge	potential difference
conventional current	ion charge	proton
coulomb unit	insulator	short circuit
conductance	magnetic field	siemens unit
conductor	mho unit	static electricity
direct current	ohm unit	volt unit

TOPICS COVERED IN THIS CHAPTER

1-1 NEGATIVE AND POSITIVE POLARITIES

We see the effects of electricity in a battery, static charge, lightning, radio, television, and many other applications. What do they all have in common that is electrical in nature? The answer is basic particles of electric charge with opposite polarities. All the materials we know, including solids, liquids, and gases, contain two basic particles of electric charge: the *electron* and the *proton*. An electron is the smallest amount of electric charge having the characteristic called *negative polarity*. The proton is a basic particle with *positive polarity*.

Actually, the negative and positive polarities indicate two opposite characteristics that seem to be fundamental in all physical applications. Just as magnets have north and south poles, electric charges have the opposite polarities labeled negative and positive. The opposing characteristics provide a method of balancing one against the other to explain different physical effects.

It is the arrangement of electrons and protons as basic particles of electricity that determines the electrical characteristics of all substances. As an example, this paper has electrons and protons in it. There is no evidence of electricity, though, because the number of electrons equals the number of protons. In that case the opposite electrical forces cancel, making the paper electrically neutral. The neutral condition means that opposing forces are exactly balanced, without any net effect either way.

When we want to use the electrical forces associated with the negative and positive charges in all matter, work must be done to separate the electrons and protons. Changing the balance of forces produces evidence of electricity. A battery, for instance, can do electrical work because its chemical energy separates electric charges to produce an excess of electrons at its negative terminal and an excess of protons at its positive terminal. With separate and opposite charges at the two terminals, electric energy can be supplied to a circuit connected to the battery. Figure 1-1 shows a battery with its negative $(-)$ and positive $(+)$ terminals marked to emphasize the two opposite polarities.

FIG. 1-1 Positive and negative polarities for the voltage output of a typical battery.

TEST-POINT QUESTION 1-1

Answers at end of chapter.
a. Is the charge of an electron positive or negative?
b. Is the charge of a proton positive or negative?
c. Is it true or false that the neutral condition means equal positive and negative charges?

1-2 ELECTRONS AND PROTONS IN THE ATOM

Although there are any number of possible methods by which electrons and protons might be grouped, they assemble in specific atomic combinations for a stable arrangement. (An atom is the smallest particle of the basic elements which forms the physical substances we know as solids, liquids, and gases.) Each stable combination of electrons and protons makes one particular type of atom. For example, Fig. 1-2 illustrates the electron and proton structure of one atom of the gas hydrogen. This atom consists of a central mass called the *nucleus* and 1 electron outside. The proton in the nucleus makes it the massive and stable part of the atom because a proton is 1840 times heavier than an electron.

In Fig. 1-2, the 1 electron in the hydrogen atom is shown in an orbital ring around the nucleus. In order to account for the electrical stability of the atom, we can consider the electron as spinning around the nucleus, as planets revolve around the sun. Then the electrical force attracting the electrons in toward the nucleus is balanced by the mechanical force outward on the rotating electron. As a result, the electron stays in its orbit around the nucleus.

In an atom that has more electrons and protons than hydrogen, all the protons are in the nucleus, while all the electrons are in one or more outside rings. For example, the carbon atom illustrated in Fig. 1-3a has 6 protons in the nucleus and 6 electrons in two outside rings. The total number of electrons in the outside rings must equal the number of protons in the nucleus in a neutral atom.

FIG. 1-2 Electron and proton in hydrogen (H) atom.

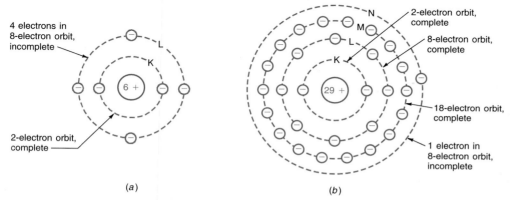

(a)   (b)

FIG. 1-3   Atomic structure showing the nucleus and its orbital rings of electrons. (a) Carbon (C) atom has 6 orbital electrons to balance 6 protons in nucleus. (b) Copper (Cu) atom with 29 protons in nucleus and 29 orbital electrons.

The distribution of electrons in the orbital rings determines the atom's electrical stability. Especially important is the number of electrons in the ring farthest from the nucleus. This outermost ring requires 8 electrons for stability, except when there is only one ring, which has a maximum of 2 electrons.

In the carbon atom in Fig. 1-3a, with 6 electrons, there are just 2 electrons in the first ring because 2 is its maximum number. The remaining 4 electrons are in the second ring, which can have a maximum of 8 electrons.

As another example, the copper atom in Fig. 1-3b has only 1 electron in the last ring, which can include 8 electrons. Therefore, the outside ring of the copper atom is less stable than the outside ring of the carbon atom.

When there are many atoms close together in a copper wire, the outermost orbital electrons are not sure which atoms they belong to. They can migrate easily from one atom to another at random. Such electrons that can move freely from one atom to the next are often called *free electrons*. This freedom accounts for the ability of copper to conduct electricity very easily. It is the movement of free electrons that provides electric current in a metal conductor.

The net effect in the wire itself without any applied voltage, however, is zero because of the random motion of the free electrons. When voltage is applied, it forces all the free electrons to move in the same direction to produce electron flow, which is an electric current.

CONDUCTORS, INSULATORS, AND SEMICONDUCTORS When electrons can move easily from atom to atom in a material, it is a *conductor.* In general, all the metals are good conductors, with silver the best and copper second. Their atomic structure allows free movement of the outermost orbital electrons. Copper wire is generally used for practical conductors because it costs much less than silver. The purpose of using conductors is to allow electric current to flow with minimum opposition.

The wire conductor is used only as a means of delivering current produced by the voltage source to a device that needs the current in order to function. As an example, a bulb lights only when current is made to flow through the filament.

A material with atoms in which the electrons tend to stay in their own orbits is an *insulator* because it cannot conduct electricity very easily. However, the insulators are able to hold or store electricity better than the conductors. An insulating material, such as glass, plastic, rubber, paper, air, or mica, is also called a *dielectric,* meaning it can store electric charge.

Insulators can be useful when it is necessary to prevent current flow. In addition, for applications requiring the storage of electric charge, as in capacitors, a dielectric material must be used because a good conductor cannot store any charge.

Carbon can be considered a semiconductor, conducting less than the metal conductors but more than the insulators. In the same group are germanium and silicon, which are commonly used for transistors and other semiconductor components. Practically all transistors are made of silicon.

ELEMENTS The combinations of electrons and protons forming stable atomic structures result in different kinds of elementary substances having specific characteristics. A few familiar examples are the elements hydrogen, oxygen, carbon, copper, and iron. An *element* is defined as a substance that cannot be decomposed any further by chemical action. The atom is the smallest particle of an element that still has the same characteristics as the element. *Atom* itself is a Greek word meaning a particle too small to be subdivided. As an example of the fact that atoms are too small to be visible, a particle of carbon the size of a pinpoint contains many billions of atoms. The electrons and protons within the atom are even smaller.

Table 1-1 lists some more examples of elements. These are just a few out of a total of 112. Notice how the elements are grouped. The metals listed across the top row are all good conductors of electricity. Each has an atomic structure with an unstable outside ring that allows many free electrons.

The semiconductors have 4 electrons in the outermost ring. This means they neither gain nor lose electrons but share them with similar atoms. The reason is that 4 is exactly halfway to the stable condition of 8 electrons in the outside ring.

The inert gas neon has a complete outside ring of 8 electrons, which makes it chemically inactive. Remember that 8 electrons in the outside ring is a stable structure.

MOLECULES AND COMPOUNDS A group of two or more atoms forms a molecule. For instance, two atoms of hydrogen (H) form a hydrogen molecule (H_2). When hydrogen unites chemically with oxygen, the result is water (H_2O),

TABLE 1-1 EXAMPLES OF THE CHEMICAL ELEMENTS

GROUP	ELEMENT	SYMBOL	ATOMIC NUMBER	ELECTRON VALENCE
Metal conductors, in order of conductance	Silver	Ag	47	+1
	Copper	Cu	29	+1*
	Gold	Au	79	+1*
	Aluminum	Al	13	+3
	Iron	Fe	26	+2*
Semiconductors	Carbon	C	6	±4
	Silicon	Si	14	±4
	Germanium	Ge	32	±4
Active gases	Hydrogen	H	1	±1
	Oxygen	O	8	−2
Inert gases	Helium	He	2	0
	Neon	Ne	10	0

*Some metals have more than one valence number in forming chemical compounds. Examples are cuprous or cupric copper, ferrous or ferric iron, and aurous or auric gold.

which is a compound. A compound, then, consists of two or more elements. The molecule is the smallest unit of a compound with the same chemical characteristics. We can have molecules for either elements or compounds. However, atoms exist only for the elements.

TEST-POINT QUESTION 1-2

Answers at end of chapter.
a. Which have more free electrons: metals or insulators?
b. Which is the best conductor: silver, carbon, or iron?
c. Which is a semiconductor: copper, silicon, or neon?

1-3 STRUCTURE OF THE ATOM

Although nobody has ever seen an atom, its hypothetical structure fits experimental evidence that has been measured very exactly. The size and electric charge of the invisible particles in the atom are indicated by how much they are deflected by known forces. Our present planetary model of the atom was proposed by Niels Bohr in 1913. His contribution was joining the new ideas of a nuclear atom developed by Lord Rutherford (1871–1937) with the quantum theory of radiation developed by Max Planck (1858–1947) and Albert Einstein (1879–1955).

As illustrated in Figs. 1-2 and 1-3, the nucleus contains protons for all the positive charge in the atom. The number of protons in the nucleus is equal to the number of planetary electrons. Then the positive and negative charges are balanced, as the proton and electron have equal and opposite charges. The orbits for the planetary electrons are also called *shells* or *energy levels*.

ATOMIC NUMBER This gives the number of protons or electrons required in the atom for each element. For the hydrogen atom in Fig. 1-2, the atomic number is 1, which means the nucleus has 1 proton balanced by 1 orbital electron. Similarly, the carbon atom in Fig. 1-3 with atomic number 6 has 6 protons in the nucleus and 6 orbital electrons. Also, the copper atom has 29 protons and 29 electrons because its atomic number is 29. The atomic number is listed for each of the elements in Table 1-1 to indicate the atomic structure.

ORBITAL RINGS The planetary electrons are in successive shells called K, L, M, N, O, P, and Q at increasing distances outward from the nucleus. Each shell has a maximum number of electrons for stability. As indicated in Table 1-2, these stable shells correspond to the inert gases, like helium and neon.

TABLE 1-2 SHELLS OF ORBITAL ELECTRONS IN THE ATOM		
SHELL	MAXIMUM ELECTRONS	INERT GAS
K	2	Helium
L	8	Neon
M	8 (up to calcium) or 18	Argon
N	8, 18, or 32	Krypton
O	8 or 18	Xenon
P	8 or 18	Radon
Q	8	—

The K shell, closest to the nucleus, is stable with 2 electrons, corresponding to the atomic structure for the inert gas helium. Once the stable number of electrons has filled a shell, it cannot take any more electrons. The atomic structure with all its shells filled to the maximum number for stability corresponds to an inert gas.

Elements with a higher atomic number have more planetary electrons. These are in successive shells, tending to form the structure of the next inert gas in the periodic table. (The periodic table is a very useful grouping of all elements according to their chemical properties.) After the K shell has been filled with 2 electrons, the L shell can take up to 8 electrons. Ten electrons filling the K and L shells is the atomic structure for the inert gas neon.

The maximum number of electrons in the remaining shells can be 8, 18, or 32 for different elements, depending on their place in the periodic table. The maximum for an outermost shell, though, is always 8.

To illustrate these rules, we can use the copper atom in Fig. 1-3*b* as an example. There are 29 protons in the nucleus balanced by 29 planetary electrons. This number of electrons fills the K shell with 2 electrons, corresponding to the helium atom, and the L shell with 8 electrons. The 10 electrons in these two shells correspond to the neon atom, which has an atomic number of 10. The remaining 19 electrons for the copper atom then fill the M shell with 18 electrons and 1 electron in the outermost N shell. These values can be summarized as follows:

$$K \text{ shell} = 2 \text{ electrons}$$
$$L \text{ shell} = 8 \text{ electrons}$$
$$M \text{ shell} = 18 \text{ electrons}$$
$$N \text{ shell} = 1 \text{ electron}$$
$$\text{Total} = 29 \text{ electrons}$$

For most elements, we can use the rule that the maximum number of electrons in a filled inner shell equals $2n^2$, where n is the shell number in sequential order outward from the nucleus. Then the maximum number of electrons in the first shell is $2 \times 1 = 2$; for the second shell $2 \times 2^2 = 8$, for the third shell $2 \times 3^2 = 18$, and for the fourth shell $2 \times 4^2 = 32$. These values apply only to an inner shell that is filled with its maximum number of electrons.

ELECTRON VALENCE   This value is the number of electrons in an incomplete outermost shell. A completed outer shell has a valence of zero. Copper, for instance, has a valence of 1, as there is 1 electron in the last shell, after the inner shells have been completed with their stable number. Similarly, hydrogen has a valence of 1, and carbon has a valence of 4. The number of outer electrons is considered positive valence, as these electrons are in addition to the stable shells.

Except for H and He, the goal of valence is 8 for all the atoms, as each tends to form the stable structure of 8 electrons in the outside ring. For this reason, valence can also be considered as the number of electrons in the outside ring needed to make 8. This value is the negative valence. As examples, the valence of copper can be considered $+1$ or -7; carbon has the valence of ± 4. The inert gases have 0 valence, as they all have a complete outer shell.

The valence indicates how easily the atom can gain or lose electrons. For instance, atoms with a valence of $+1$ can lose this 1 outside electron, especially to atoms with a valence of $+7$ or -1, which need 1 electron to complete the outside shell with 8 electrons.

SUBSHELLS   Although not shown in the illustrations, all the shells except K are divided into subshells. This subdivision accounts for different types of orbits in the same shell. For instance, electrons in one subshell may have elliptical orbits, while other electrons in the same main shell have circular orbits. The subshells indicate magnetic properties of the atom.

PARTICLES IN THE NUCLEUS   A stable nucleus, meaning it is not radioactive, contains protons and neutrons. The neutron is electrically neutral without any net charge. Its mass is almost the same as a proton.

A proton has the positive charge of a hydrogen nucleus. The charge is the same amount as that of an orbital electron but of opposite polarity. There are no electrons in the nucleus. Table 1-3 lists the charge and mass for these three basic particles in all atoms. The C in the charge column is for coulombs.

TABLE 1-3   STABLE PARTICLES IN THE ATOM

PARTICLE	CHARGE	MASS
Electron, in orbital shells	0.16×10^{-18} C, negative	9.108×10^{-28} g
Proton, in nucleus	0.16×10^{-18} C, positive	1.672×10^{-24} g
Neutron, in nucleus	None	1.675×10^{-24} g

TEST-POINT QUESTION 1-3

Answers at end of chapter.
a. An element with 14 protons and 14 electrons has what atomic number?
b. What is the electron valence of an element with atomic number 3?
c. The atomic number 32 indicates how many planetary electrons?

1-4 THE COULOMB UNIT OF ELECTRIC CHARGE

If you rub a hard rubber pen or comb on a sheet of paper, the rubber will attract a corner of the paper if it is free to move easily. The paper and rubber then give evidence of a static electric charge. The work of rubbing resulted in separating electrons and protons to produce a charge of excess electrons on the surface of the rubber and a charge of excess protons on the paper.

Because paper and rubber are dielectric materials, they hold their extra electrons or protons. As a result, the paper and rubber are no longer neutral, but each has an electric charge. The resultant electric charges provide the force of attraction between the rubber and the paper. This mechanical force of attraction or repulsion between charges is the fundamental method by which electricity makes itself evident.

Any charge is an example of *static electricity* because the electrons or protons are not in motion. There are many examples. When you walk across a wool rug, your body becomes charged with an excess of electrons. Similarly, silk, fur, and glass can be rubbed to produce a static charge. This effect is more evident in dry weather, because a moist dielectric does not hold its charge so well. Also, plastic materials can be charged easily, which is why thin, lightweight plastics seem to stick to everything.

The charge of many billions of electrons or protons is necessary for common applications of electricity. Therefore, it is convenient to define a practical unit called the *coulomb* (C) as equal to the charge of 6.25×10^{18} electrons or protons stored in a dielectric (see Fig. 1-4). The analysis of static charges and their forces is called *electrostatics*.

The symbol for electric charge is Q or q, standing for quantity. For instance, a charge of 6.25×10^{18} electrons* is stated as $Q = 1$ C. This unit is named after Charles A. Coulomb (1736–1806), a French physicist, who measured the force between charges.

NEGATIVE AND POSITIVE POLARITIES   Historically, the negative polarity has been assigned to the static charge produced on rubber, amber, and resinous materials in general. Positive polarity refers to the static charge produced on glass and other vitreous materials. On this basis, the electrons in all atoms are basic particles of negative charge because their polarity is the same as the charge on rubber. Protons have positive charge because the polarity is the same as the charge on glass.

CHARGES OF OPPOSITE POLARITY ATTRACT   If two small charged bodies of light weight are mounted so that they are free to move easily and are placed close to each other, one can be attracted to the other when the two charges have opposite polarity (Fig. 1-5a). In terms of electrons and protons, they tend to be attracted to each other by the force of attraction between opposite charges. Furthermore, the weight of an electron is only about $\frac{1}{1840}$ the weight of a proton. As a result, the force of attraction tends to make electrons move to protons.

CHARGES OF THE SAME POLARITY REPEL   In Fig. 1-5b and c, it is shown that when the two bodies have an equal amount of charge with the same polarity, they repel each other. The two negative charges repel in Fig. 1-5b, while two positive charges of the same value repel each other in Fig. 1-5c.

1 C of excess electrons in dielectric

(a)

1 C of excess protons in dielectric

(b)

FIG. 1-4   The coulomb (C) unit of electric charge. (*a*) Quantity of 6.25×10^{18} excess electrons for a negative charge of 1 C. (*b*) Same amount of protons for a positive charge of 1 C, caused by removing electrons from neutral atoms.

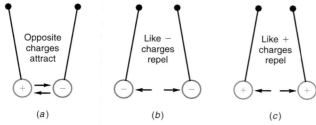

(a)   (b)   (c)

FIG. 1-5   Physical force between electric charges. (*a*) Opposite charges attract. (*b*) Two negative charges repel each other. (*c*) Two positive charges repel.

POLARITY OF A CHARGE   An electric charge must have either negative or positive polarity, labeled $-Q$ or $+Q$, with an excess of either electrons or protons. A neutral condition is considered zero charge. On this basis, consider the

---

*For an explanation of how to use powers of 10, see B. Grob, *Mathematics for Basic Electronics*, Glencoe/McGraw-Hill, Columbus, Ohio.

following examples, remembering that the electron is the basic particle of charge and the proton has exactly the same amount, although of opposite polarity.

Example

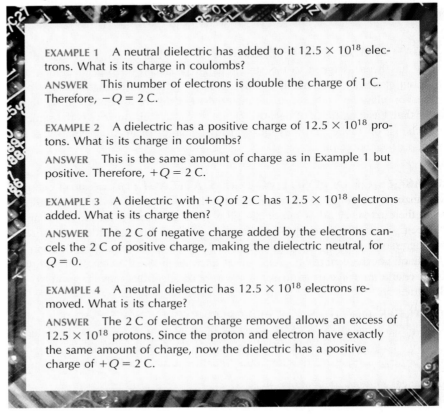

EXAMPLE 1   A neutral dielectric has added to it 12.5×10^{18} electrons. What is its charge in coulombs?

ANSWER   This number of electrons is double the charge of 1 C. Therefore, $-Q = 2$ C.

EXAMPLE 2   A dielectric has a positive charge of 12.5×10^{18} protons. What is its charge in coulombs?

ANSWER   This is the same amount of charge as in Example 1 but positive. Therefore, $+Q = 2$ C.

EXAMPLE 3   A dielectric with $+Q$ of 2 C has 12.5×10^{18} electrons added. What is its charge then?

ANSWER   The 2 C of negative charge added by the electrons cancels the 2 C of positive charge, making the dielectric neutral, for $Q = 0$.

EXAMPLE 4   A neutral dielectric has 12.5×10^{18} electrons removed. What is its charge?

ANSWER   The 2 C of electron charge removed allows an excess of 12.5×10^{18} protons. Since the proton and electron have exactly the same amount of charge, now the dielectric has a positive charge of $+Q = 2$ C.

Note that we generally consider the electrons moving, rather than the heavier protons. However, a loss of a given number of electrons is equivalent to a gain of the same number of protons.

CHARGE OF AN ELECTRON   Fundamentally, the quantity of any charge is measured by its force of attraction or repulsion. The extremely small force of an electron or proton was measured by Millikan* in experiments done from 1908 to 1917. Very briefly, the method consisted of measuring the charge on vaporized droplets of oil, by balancing the gravitational force against an electrical force that could be measured very precisely.

A small drop of oil sprayed from an atomizer becomes charged by friction. Furthermore, the charges can be increased or decreased slightly by radiation. These very small changes in the amount of charge were measured. The three

---

*Robert A. Millikan (1868–1953), an American physicist. Millikan received the Nobel prize in physics for this oil-drop experiment.

smallest values were 0.16×10^{-18} C, 0.32×10^{-18} C, and 0.48×10^{-18} C. These values are multiples of 0.16. In fact, all the charges measured were multiples of 0.16×10^{-18} C. Therefore, we conclude that 0.16×10^{-18} C is the basic charge from which all other values are derived. This ultimate charge of 0.16×10^{-18} C is the charge of 1 electron or 1 proton. Then

▶   1 electron or $Q_e = 0.16 \times 10^{-18}$ C

The reciprocal of 0.16×10^{-18} gives the number of electrons or protons in 1 C. Then

▶   1 C $= 6.25 \times 10^{18}$ electrons

Note that the factor 6.25 equals exactly $\frac{1}{0.16}$ and the 10^{18} is the reciprocal of 10^{-18}.

THE ELECTRIC FIELD OF A STATIC CHARGE   The ability of an electric charge to attract or repel another charge is actually a physical force. To help visualize this effect, lines of force are used, as shown in Fig. 1-6. All the lines form the electric field. The lines and the field are imaginary, since they cannot be seen. Just as the field of the force of gravity is not visible, however, the resulting physical effects prove the field is there.

Each line of force in Fig. 1-6 is directed outward to indicate repulsion of another charge in the field with the same polarity as Q, either positive or negative. The lines are shorter further away from Q to indicate that the force decreases inversely as the square of the distance. The larger the charge, the greater is the force. These relations describe Coulomb's law of electrostatics.

The electric field in the dielectric between two plates with opposite charges is the basis for the ability of a capacitor to store electric charge. More details are explained in Chap. 17, "Capacitance." In general, any charged insulator has capacitance. Practical capacitors, though, are constructed in a form that concentrates the electric field.

Electric lines
of force

FIG. 1-6   Arrows to indicate electric field around a stationary charge Q.

TEST-POINT QUESTION 1-4

Answers at end of chapter.
  a. How many electron charges are there in the practical unit of one coulomb?
  b. How much is the charge in coulombs for a surplus of 25×10^{18} electrons?
  c. Do opposite electric charges attract or repel each other?

1-5 THE VOLT UNIT OF POTENTIAL DIFFERENCE

Potential refers to the possibility of doing work. Any charge has the potential to do the work of moving another charge, by either attraction or repulsion. When we consider two unlike charges, they have a *difference of potential*.

A charge is the result of work done in separating electrons and protons. Because of the separation, there is stress and strain associated with opposite charges, since normally they would be balancing each other to produce a neutral condition. We could consider that the accumulated electrons are drawn tight and are straining themselves to be attracted toward protons in order to return to the neutral condition. Similarly, the work of producing the charge causes a condition of stress in the protons, which are trying to attract electrons and return to the neutral condition. Because of these forces, the charge of electrons or protons has potential, as it is ready to give back the work put into producing the charge. The force between charges is in the electric field.

POTENTIAL BETWEEN DIFFERENT CHARGES   When one charge is different from the other, there must be a difference of potential between them. For instance, consider a positive charge of 3 C, shown at the right in Fig. 1-7a. The charge has a certain amount of potential, corresponding to the amount of work this charge can do. The work to be done is moving some electrons, as illustrated.

Assume a charge of 1 C can move 3 electrons. Then the charge of +3 C can attract 9 electrons toward the right. However, the charge of +1 C at the opposite side can attract 3 electrons toward the left. The net result, then, is that 6 electrons can be moved toward the right to the more positive charge.

In Fig. 1-7b, one charge is 2 C, while the other charge is neutral with 0 C. For the difference of 2 C, again 2 × 3 or 6 electrons can be attracted to the positive side.

In Fig. 1-7c, the difference between the charges is still 2 C. The +1 C attracts 3 electrons to the right side. The −1 C repels 3 electrons to the right side also. This effect is really the same as attracting 6 electrons.

Therefore, the net number of electrons moved in the direction of the more positive charge depends on the difference of potential between the two charges. This difference corresponds to 2 C for all three cases in Fig. 1-7. Potential difference is often abbreviated PD.

The only case without any potential difference between charges is where they both have the same polarity and are equal in amount. Then the repelling and attracting forces cancel, and no work can be done in moving electrons between the two identical charges.

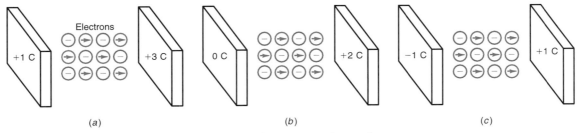

FIG. 1-7   The amount of work required to move electrons between two charges depends on their difference of potential. This potential difference (PD) is equivalent to the charge of 2 C for the examples in (a), (b), and (c).

THE VOLT UNIT OF POTENTIAL DIFFERENCE   This unit is named after Alessandro Volta (1754–1827). Fundamentally, the volt is a measure of the work needed to move an electric charge. When 0.7376 foot-pound (ft · lb) of work is required to move 6.25×10^{18} electrons between two points, each with its own charge, the potential difference is 1 V.

Note that 6.25×10^{18} electrons make up one coulomb. Therefore the definition of a volt is for a coulomb of charge.

Also, 0.7376 ft · lb of work is the same as 1 joule (J), which is the practical metric unit of work or energy. Therefore, we can say briefly that *one volt equals one joule of work per coulomb of charge,* or

▶ $$1 \text{ V} = \frac{1 \text{ J}}{1 \text{ C}}$$

The symbol for potential difference is *V* for voltage. In fact, the volt unit is used so often that potential difference is often called voltage. Remember, though, that voltage is the potential difference between two points. Two terminals are necessary to measure a potential difference.

Consider the 2.2-V lead-acid cell in Fig. 1-8. Its output of 2.2 V means that this is the amount of potential difference between the two terminals. The cell then is a voltage source, or a source of electromotive force (*emf*).

Sometimes the symbol *E* is used for emf, but the standard symbol is *V* for any potential difference. This applies either to the voltage generated by a source or to the voltage drop across a passive component, such as a resistor.

In a practical circuit, the voltage determines how much current can be produced.

(a)

(b)

FIG. 1-8   Chemical cell as a voltage source. (*a*) Voltage output is the potential difference between the two terminals. (*b*) Schematic symbol of any dc voltage source with constant polarity. Longer line indicates positive side.

TEST-POINT QUESTION 1-5

Answers at end of chapter.
a. How much potential difference is there between two identical charges?
b. Which applies a greater PD, a 1.5-V battery or a 12-V battery?

1-6 CHARGE IN MOTION IS CURRENT

When the potential difference between two charges forces a third charge to move, the charge in motion is an *electric current.* To produce current, therefore, charge must be moved by a potential difference.

In solid materials, such as copper wire, the free electrons are charges that can be forced to move with relative ease by a potential difference, since they require relatively little work to be moved. As illustrated in Fig. 1-9, if a potential difference is connected across two ends of a copper wire, the applied voltage forces the free electrons to move. This current is a drift of electrons, from the point of negative charge at one end, moving through the wire, and returning to the positive charge at the other end.

To illustrate the drift of free electrons through the wire shown in Fig. 1-9, each electron in the middle row is numbered, corresponding to a copper atom to

FIG. 1-9   Potential difference across two ends of wire conductor causes drift of free electrons throughout the wire to produce electric current.

which the free electron belongs. The electron at the left is labeled S to indicate that it comes from the negative charge of the source of potential difference. This one electron S is repelled from the negative charge $-Q$ at the left and is attracted by the positive charge $+Q$ at the right. Therefore, the potential difference of the voltage source can make electron S move toward atom 1. Now atom 1 has an extra electron. As a result, the free electron of atom 1 can then move to atom 2. In this way, there is a drift of free electrons from atom to atom. The final result is that the one free electron labeled 8 at the extreme right in Fig. 1-9 moves out from the wire to return to the positive charge of the voltage source.

Considering this case of just one electron moving, note that the electron returning to the positive side of the voltage source is not the electron labeled S that left the negative side. All electrons are the same, however, and have the same charge. Therefore, the drift of free electrons resulted in the charge of one electron moving through the wire. This charge in motion is the current. With more electrons drifting through the wire, the charge of many electrons moves, resulting in more current.

The current is a continuous flow of electrons. Only the electrons move, not the potential difference. For ordinary applications, where the wires are not long lines, the potential difference produces current instantaneously through the entire length of wire. Furthermore, the current must be the same at all points of the wire at any time.

POTENTIAL DIFFERENCE IS NECESSARY TO PRODUCE CURRENT   The number of free electrons that can be forced to drift through the wire to produce the moving charge depends upon the amount of potential difference across the wire. With more applied voltage, the forces of attraction and repulsion can make more free electrons drift, producing more charge in motion. A larger amount of charge moving during a given period of time means a higher value of current. Less applied voltage across the same wire results in a smaller amount of charge in motion, which is a smaller value of current. With zero potential difference across the wire, there is no current.

Two cases of zero potential difference and no current can be considered in order to emphasize the important fact that potential difference is needed to produce current. Assume the copper wire to be by itself, not connected to any voltage source, so that there is no potential difference across the wire. The free electrons in the wire can move from atom to atom, but this motion is random, without any organized drift through the wire. If the wire is considered as a whole, from one end to the other, the current is zero.

As another example, suppose that the two ends of the wire have the same potential. Then free electrons cannot move to either end, because both ends have the same force, and there is no current through the wire. A practical example of this case of zero potential difference would be to connect both ends of the wire to just one terminal of a battery. Each end of the wire would have the same potential, and there would be no current. The conclusion, therefore, is that two connections to two points at different potentials are needed in order to produce the current.

THE AMPERE OF CURRENT   Since current is the movement of charge, the unit for stating the amount of current is defined in rate of flow of charge. When the charge moves at the rate of 6.25×10^{18} electrons flowing past a given point per second, the value of the current is one *ampere* (A). This is the same as one coulomb of charge per second. The ampere unit of current is named after André M. Ampère (1775–1836).

Referring back to Fig. 1-9, note that if 6.25×10^{18} free electrons move past p_1 in 1 second (s), the current is 1 A. Similarly, the current is 1 A at p_2 because the electron drift is the same throughout the wire. If twice as many electrons moved past either point in 1 s, the current would be 2 A.

The symbol for current is I or i for intensity, since the current is a measure of how intense or concentrated the electron flow is. Two amperes of current in a copper wire is a higher intensity than 1 A; a greater concentration of moving electrons results because of more electrons in motion. Sometimes current is called *amperage*. However, the current in electronic circuits is usually in smaller units, milliamperes and microamperes.

HOW CURRENT DIFFERS FROM CHARGE   Charge is a quantity of electricity accumulated in a dielectric, which is an insulator. The charge is static electricity, at rest, without any motion. When the charge moves, usually in a conductor, the current I indicates the intensity of the electricity in motion. This characteristic is a fundamental definition of current:

▶ $$I = \frac{Q}{T}$$ (1-1)

where I is the current in amperes, Q is in coulombs, and the time T is in seconds. It does not matter whether the moving charge is positive or negative. The only question is how much charge moves and what its rate of motion is.

In terms of practical units,

▶ $$1\ A = \frac{1\ C}{1\ s}$$ (1-2)

One ampere of current results when one coulomb of charge moves past a given point in 1 s.

Example

EXAMPLE 5   The charge of 12 C moves past a given point every second. How much is the intensity of charge flow?

ANSWER $I = \dfrac{Q}{T} = \dfrac{12 \text{ C}}{1 \text{ s}}$

$I = 12 \text{ A}$

EXAMPLE 6   The charge of 5 C moves past a given point in 1 s. How much is the current?

ANSWER $I = \dfrac{Q}{T} = \dfrac{5 \text{ C}}{1 \text{ s}}$

$I = 5 \text{ A}$

The fundamental definition of current can also be used to consider the charge as equal to the product of the current multiplied by the time. Or

▶ $Q = I \times T$ **(1-3)**

In terms of practical units,

▶ $1 \text{ C} = 1 \text{ A} \times 1 \text{ s}$ **(1-4)**

One coulomb of charge results when one ampere of current accumulates charge during the time of one second. The charge is generally accumulated in the dielectric of a capacitor, or at the electrodes of a battery.

For instance, we can have a dielectric connected to conductors with a current of 0.4 A. If the current can deposit electrons for the time of 0.2 s, the accumulated charge in the dielectric will be

$$Q = I \times T = 0.4 \text{ A} \times 0.2 \text{ s}$$
$$Q = 0.08 \text{ C}$$

The formulas $Q = IT$ for charge and $I = Q/T$ for current illustrate the fundamental nature of Q as an accumulation of static charge in an insulator, while I measures the intensity of moving charges in a conductor. Furthermore, current I is different from voltage V. You can have V without I, but you cannot have current without an applied voltage.

THE GENERAL NATURE OF CURRENT   The moving charges that provide current in metal conductors like a copper wire are the free electrons of the copper atoms. In this case, the moving charges have negative polarity. The direction of motion between two terminals for this *electron current,* therefore, is toward the more positive end. It is important to note, however, that there are examples of positive charges in motion. Common applications include current in liquids, gases, and semiconductors. For the case of current resulting from the motion of positive charges, its direction is opposite from the direction of electron flow. Whether negative or positive charges move, though, the current is still defined fundamentally as Q/T. Note also that the current is provided by free charges, which are easily moved by an applied voltage.

TYPES OF ELECTRIC CHARGES FOR CURRENT   See Table 1-4. The most common charge is the electron. In metal conductors and solid materials in general, free electrons in the atoms can be forced to move by applying a potential difference. Therefore current is produced. The direction of electron flow is from the negative terminal of the voltage source, through the external circuit, and returning to the positive source terminal. Also, electrons are released by thermionic emission from the heated cathode in a vacuum tube. Finally, N-type semiconductors such as silicon and germanium have unbound electrons as a result of doping with impurity elements that can provide valence electrons from the added atoms.

For P-type semiconductors, the silicon and germanium are doped with impurity elements that cause a deficiency of electrons in the bonds between atoms. Each vacant space where an electron is missing is called a *hole charge*. The polarity is positive, opposite from the electron, but the amount of charge is exactly the same. In short, a hole charge is a deficiency of one valence electron in semiconductors. When hole charges move in a P-type semiconductor, they provide hole current. The direction of flow for the positive charges is from the positive terminal of the voltage source, through the external circuit, and returning to the negative source terminal.

An ion is an atom that has either lost or gained one or more valence electrons to become electrically charged. Therefore, the ion charge may be either positive or negative. The amount may be the charge of 1 electron Q_e, $2Q_e$, $3Q_e$, etc. Ions can be produced by applying voltage to liquids and gases to produce ionization of the atoms. The ions are much less mobile than electrons or hole charges because an ion includes a complex atom with its nucleus.

Note that protons are not included as charge carriers for current in Table 1-4. The reason is that the protons are bound in the nucleus. They cannot be released except by nuclear forces. Therefore, a current of positive charges is a flow of either hole charges or positive ions. The hole charge has the same amount of charge as the proton, which is the same amount as an electron. However, the positive hole charge is in the valence structure of the atoms, not in the nucleus.

TABLE 1-4 TYPES OF ELECTRIC CHARGES FOR CURRENT				
TYPE OF CHARGE	AMOUNT OF CHARGE	POLARITY	TYPE OF CURRENT	APPLICATIONS
Electron	$Q_e = 0.16 \times 10^{-18}$ C	Negative	Electron flow	In wire conductors, vacuum tubes, and N-type semiconductors
Ion	Q_e or multiples of Q_e	Positive or negative	Ion current	In liquids and gases
Hole	$Q_e = 0.16 \times 10^{-18}$ C	Positive	Hole current	In P-type semiconductors

MAGNETIC FIELD AROUND AN ELECTRIC CURRENT   When any current flows, it has an associated magnetic field. Figure 1-10 shows how iron filings line up in a circular field pattern corresponding to the magnetic lines of force. The magnetic field is in a plane perpendicular to the current. It should be noted that the iron filings are just a method of making the imaginary lines of force visible. The filings become magnetized by the magnetic field. Both magnetic and electric fields can do the physical work of attraction or repulsion.

The magnetic field of any current is the basis for many electromagnetic applications, including magnets, relays, loudspeakers, transformers, and coils in general. Winding the conductor in the form of a coil concentrates the magnetic field. More details of electromagnetism and magnetic fields are explained in Chap. 15, "Electromagnetic Induction."

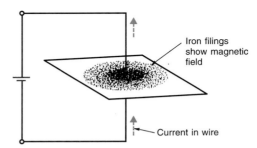

Iron filings show magnetic field

Current in wire

FIG. 1-10   Magnetic field around an electric current. Arrow for current indicates direction of electron flow.

TEST-POINT QUESTION 1-6

Answers at end of chapter.
a. The flow of 2 C/s of electron charges is how many amperes of current?
b. The flow of 2 C/s of hole charges is how many amperes of current?
c. How much is the current with zero potential difference?

1-7 RESISTANCE IS OPPOSITION TO CURRENT

The fact that a wire conducting current can become hot is evidence of the fact that the work done by the applied voltage in producing current must be accomplished against some form of opposition. This opposition, which limits the amount of current that can be produced by the applied voltage, is called *resistance*. Conductors have very little resistance; insulators have a large amount of resistance.

The atoms of a copper wire have a large number of free electrons, which can be moved easily by a potential difference. Therefore, the copper wire has little opposition to the flow of free electrons when voltage is applied, corresponding to a low value of resistance.

Carbon, however, has fewer free electrons than copper. When the same amount of voltage is applied to the carbon as to the copper, fewer electrons will flow. It should be noted that just as much current can be produced in the carbon by applying more voltage. For the same current, though, the higher applied voltage means that more work is necessary, causing more heat. Carbon opposes the current more than copper, therefore, and has a higher value of resistance.

THE OHM   The practical unit of resistance is the *ohm*. A resistance that develops 0.24 calorie of heat when one ampere of current flows through it for one second has one ohm of opposition. As an example of a low resistance, a good conductor like copper wire can have a resistance of 0.01 Ω for a 1-ft length. The resistance-wire heating element in a 600-W 120-V toaster has a resistance of 24 Ω, and the tungsten filament in a 100-W 120-V light bulb has a resistance of 144 Ω. The ohm unit is named after Georg Simon Ohm (1747–1854), a German physicist.

Figure 1-11*a* shows a wire-wound resistor. Resistors also are made with powdered carbon. They can be manufactured with a value from a few ohms to millions of ohms.

The symbol for resistance is *R*. The abbreviation used for the ohm unit is the Greek letter *omega,* written as Ω. In diagrams, resistance is indicated by a zigzag line, as shown by *R* in Fig. 1-11*b*.

(a)   (b)

FIG. 1-11   (*a*) Wire-wound type of resistor with cement coating for insulation. (*b*) Schematic symbol for any type of fixed resistor.

CONDUCTANCE   The opposite of resistance is conductance. The lower the resistance, the higher the conductance. Its symbol is *G*, and the unit is the *siemens* (S), named after Ernst von Siemens, a European inventor. (The old unit name for conductance is *mho,* which is *ohm* spelled backward.)

Specifically, *G* is the reciprocal of *R*, or $G = 1/R$. For example, 5 Ω of resistance is equal to ⅕ or 0.2 S of conductance. Also, $R = 1/G$. Therefore,

▶ $$R = \frac{1}{0.2\ \text{S}} = 5\ \Omega$$

Whether to use *R* or *G* for components is usually a matter of convenience. In general, *R* is easier to use in series circuits, because the series voltages are proportional to the resistances. However, *G* can be more convenient in parallel circuits, because the parallel currents are proportional to the conductances. (Series and parallel circuits are explained in Chaps. 4 and 5.)

Answers at end of chapter.
a. Which has more resistance, carbon or copper?
b. With the same voltage applied, which resistance will allow more current, 4.7 Ω or 5000 Ω?
c. What is the conductance value in siemens units for a 10-Ω R?

1-8 THE CLOSED CIRCUIT

In applications requiring the use of current, the components are arranged in the form of a circuit, as shown in Fig. 1-12. A circuit can be defined as a path for current flow. The purpose of this circuit is to light the incandescent bulb. The bulb lights when the tungsten-filament wire inside is white hot, producing an incandescent glow.

By itself the tungsten filament cannot produce current. A source of potential difference is necessary. Since the battery produces a potential difference of 1.5 V across its two output terminals, this voltage is connected across the filament of the bulb by means of the two wires so that the applied voltage can produce current through the filament.

In Fig. 1-12b the schematic diagram of the circuit is shown. Here the components are represented by shorthand symbols. Note the symbols for the battery and resistance. The connecting wires are shown simply as straight lines because their resistance is small enough to be neglected. A resistance of less than 0.01 Ω for the wire is practically zero compared with the 300-Ω resistance of the bulb. If the resistance of the wire must be considered, the schematic diagram includes it as additional resistance in the same current path.

It should be noted that the schematic diagram does not look like the physical layout of the circuit. The schematic shows only the symbols for the components and their electrical connections.

Any electric circuit has three important characteristics:

1. There must be a source of potential difference. Without the applied voltage, current cannot flow.
2. There must be a complete path for current flow, from one side of the applied voltage source, through the external circuit, and returning to the other side of the voltage source.
3. The current path normally has resistance. The resistance is in the circuit for the purpose of either generating heat or limiting the amount of current.

HOW THE VOLTAGE IS DIFFERENT FROM THE CURRENT It is the current that moves through the circuit. The potential difference does not move.

In Fig. 1-12 the voltage across the filament resistance makes electrons flow from one side to the other. While the current is flowing around the circuit, however, the potential difference remains across the filament to do the work of moving electrons through the resistance of the filament.

The circuit is redrawn in Fig. 1-13 to emphasize the comparison between V and I. The voltage is the potential difference across the two ends of the resistance. If you want to measure the PD, just connect the two leads of the voltmeter across the

FIG. 1-12 Example of an electric circuit with battery as voltage source connected to a light bulb as a resistance. (*a*) Wiring diagram of the closed path for current. (*b*) Schematic diagram of the circuit.

resistor. However, the current is the intensity of the electron flow past any one point in the circuit. Measuring the current is not as easy. You would have to break open the path, at any point, and then insert the current meter to complete the circuit.

The word *across* is used with voltage because it is the potential difference between two points. There cannot be a PD at one point. However, current can be considered at one point, as the motion of charges through that point.

To illustrate the difference between V and I another way, suppose the circuit in Fig. 1-12 is opened by disconnecting the bulb. Now no current can flow because there is no closed path. Still, the battery has its potential difference. If you measure across the two terminals, the voltmeter will read 1.5 V even though the current is zero.

FIG. 1-13 Comparison of voltage (V) across a resistance and the current (I) through R.

THE VOLTAGE SOURCE MAINTAINS THE CURRENT As current flows in the circuit, electrons leave the negative terminal of the cell or battery in Fig. 1-12, and the same number of free electrons in the conductor are returned to the positive terminal. As electrons are lost from the negative charge and gained by the positive charge, the two charges would tend to neutralize each other. The chemical action inside the battery, however, continuously separates electrons and protons to maintain the negative and positive charges on the outside terminals that provide the potential difference. Otherwise, the current would neutralize the charges, resulting in no potential difference, and the current would stop. Therefore, the battery keeps the current flowing by maintaining the potential difference across the circuit. The battery is the voltage source for the circuit.

THE CIRCUIT IS A LOAD ON THE VOLTAGE SOURCE We can consider the circuit as a means whereby the energy of the voltage source is carried by means of the current through the filament of the bulb, where the electric energy is used in producing heat energy. On this basis, the battery is the *source* in the circuit, since its voltage output represents the potential energy to be used. The part of the circuit connected to the voltage source is the *load resistance,* since it determines how much work the source will supply. In this case, the bulb's filament is the load resistance for the battery.

The resistance of the filament determines how much current the 1.5-V source will produce. Specifically, the current here is 0.005 A, equal to 1.5 V divided by 300 Ω. With more opposition, the same voltage will produce less current. For the opposite case, less opposition allows more current.

The current that flows through the load resistance is the *load current.* Note that a lower value of ohms for the load resistance corresponds to a higher load current. Unless noted otherwise, the term *load* by itself can be assumed generally to mean the load current. Therefore, a heavy or big load electrically means a high value of load current, corresponding to a large amount of work supplied by the source.

In summary, we can say that the closed circuit, normal circuit, or just a circuit is a closed path that has V to produce I with R to limit the amount of current. The circuit provides a means of using the energy of the battery as a voltage source. The battery has its potential difference V with or without the circuit. However, the battery alone is not doing any work in producing load current. The bulb alone has its resistance, but without current the bulb does not light. With the circuit, the voltage source is used for the purpose of producing current to light the bulb.

OPEN CIRCUIT   When any part of the path is open or broken, the circuit is open because there is no continuity in the conducting path. The open circuit can be in the connecting wires or in the bulb's filament as the load resistance. The resistance of an open circuit is infinitely high. The result is no current in an open circuit.

SHORT CIRCUIT   In this case, the voltage source has a closed path across its terminals, but the resistance is practically zero. The result is too much current in a short circuit. Usually, the short circuit is a bypass across the load resistance. For instance, a short across the conducting wires for a bulb produces too much current in the wires but no current through the bulb. Then the bulb is shorted out. The bulb is not damaged, but the wires can become hot enough to burn unless the line has a fuse as a safety precaution against too much current.

TEST-POINT QUESTION 1-8

Answers at end of chapter.

Answer True or False for the circuit in Fig. 1-12.
a. The bulb has a PD of 1.5 V across its filament only when connected to the voltage source.
b. The battery has a PD of 1.5 V across its terminals only when connected to the bulb.
c. The battery by itself, without the wires and the bulb, has a PD of 1.5 V.

1-9 DIRECTION OF THE CURRENT

Just as a voltage source has polarity, the current has a direction. The reference is with respect to the positive and negative terminals of the voltage source. What the direction is for the current depends on whether we consider the flow of negative electrons or the motion of positive charges in the opposite direction.

ELECTRON FLOW   As shown in Fig. 1-14a, the direction of electron drift for the current I is out from the negative side of the voltage source. The I flows through the external circuit with R and returns to the positive side of V. Note that this direction from the negative terminal applies to the external circuit connected to the output terminals of the voltage source. Electron flow is also shown in Fig. 1-14c with reversed polarity for V.

Inside the battery, the electrons move to the negative terminal because this is how the voltage source produces its potential difference. The battery is doing the work of separating charges, accumulating electrons at the negative terminal and protons at the positive terminal. Then the potential difference across the two output terminals can do the work of moving electrons around the external circuit. For the circuit outside the voltage source, however, the direction of the electron flow is from a point of negative potential to a point of positive potential.

CONVENTIONAL CURRENT The motion of positive charges, in the opposite direction from electron flow, is considered as conventional current. This direction is generally used for analyzing circuits in electrical engineering. The reason is based on some traditional definitions in the science of physics. By the definitions of force and work with positive values, a positive potential is considered above a negative potential. Then conventional current corresponds to a motion of positive charges "falling downhill" from a positive to a negative potential. The conventional current, therefore, is in the direction of positive charges in motion. An example is shown in Fig. 1-14*b*. The conventional *I* is out from the positive side of the voltage source, flows through the external circuit and returns to the negative side of *V*. Conventional current is also shown in Fig. 1-14*d*, with the voltage source in reverse polarity.

An example of positive charges in motion for conventional current is the current of hole charges in P-type semiconductors. Also a current of positive ions in liquids and gases moves in the opposite direction from electron flow. For instance, the current through the electrolyte in a battery is ionization current.

It should be noted that with semiconductors, the arrow symbols for *I* are shown in the direction of conventional current. This method is standardized by the Electronic Industries Association (EIA) for transistors, diodes, and all semiconductor devices.

Actually, either a negative or positive potential of the same value can do the same amount of work in moving a charge. Any circuit, therefore, can be analyzed either with electron flow for *I* or by conventional current. The two opposite directions with two opposite polarities for the voltage source are summarized by the four diagrams in Fig. 1-14.

In this book, the current is considered as electron flow in the applications where electrons are the moving charges. A dotted or dashed arrow, as in Fig. 1-14*a* and *c*, is used to indicate the direction of electron flow for *I*. In Fig. 14*b* and *d*, the solid arrow means the direction of conventional current. These arrows are used for the unidirectional current in dc circuits. For ac circuits, the direction of current can be considered either way because *I* reverses direction every half-cycle with the reversals in polarity for *V*.

(a)

(b)

(c)

(d)

FIG. 1-14 Direction of *I* in a closed circuit, shown for electron flow and conventional current. The circuit works the same way no matter which direction you consider. (*a*) Electron flow indicated with dashed arrow in diagram. (*b*) Conventional current indicated with solid arrow. (*c*) Electron flow as in (*a*) but with reversed polarity of voltage source. (*d*) Conventional *I* as in (*b*) but reversed polarity for *V*.

TEST-POINT QUESTION 1-9

Answers at end of chapter.
  a. Is electron flow out from the positive or negative terminal of the voltage source?
  b. Does conventional current return to the positive or negative terminal of the voltage source?
  c. Is it true or false that electron flow and conventional current are in opposite directions?

The electron flow illustrated for the circuit with a bulb in Fig. 1-12 is direct current because it has just one direction. The reason for the unidirectional current is that the battery maintains the same polarity of output voltage across its two terminals.

It is the flow of charges in one direction and the fixed polarity of applied voltage that are the characteristics of a dc circuit. Actually, the current can be a flow of positive charges, rather than electrons but the conventional direction of current does not change the fact that the charges are moving only one way.

Furthermore, the dc voltage source can change the amount of its output voltage but, with the same polarity, direct current still flows only in one direction. This type of source provides a fluctuating or pulsating dc voltage. A battery is a steady dc voltage source because it has fixed polarity and its output voltage is a steady value.

An alternating voltage source periodically reverses or alternates in polarity. The resulting alternating current, therefore, periodically reverses in direction. In terms of electron flow, the current always flows from the negative terminal of the voltage source, through the circuit, and back to the positive terminal, but when the generator alternates in polarity, the current must reverse its direction. The 60-cycle ac power line used in most homes is a common example. This frequency means that the voltage polarity and current direction go through 60 cycles of reversal per second.

The unit for 1 cycle per second is 1 hertz (Hz). Therefore 60 cycles per second is a frequency of 60 Hz.

The details of ac circuits are explained in Chap. 16. Direct-current circuits are analyzed first because they usually are simpler. However, the principles of dc circuits also apply to ac circuits. Both types are important, as most electronic circuits include ac voltages and dc voltages. A comparison of dc and ac voltages and their waveforms is illustrated in Figs. 1-15 and 1-16. Their uses are compared in Table 1-5. Note that transistors require dc electrode voltages in order to amplify an ac signal voltage.

FIG. 1-15   Steady dc voltage of fixed polarity, such as the output of a battery. Note schematic symbol at left.

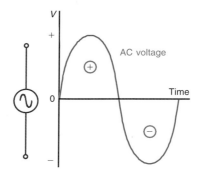

FIG. 1-16   Sine-wave ac voltage with alternating polarity, such as from an ac generator. Note schematic symbol at left. The ac line voltage in your home has this waveform.

TABLE 1-5 COMPARISON OF DC VOLTAGE AND AC VOLTAGE

DC VOLTAGE	AC VOLTAGE
Fixed polarity	Reverses in polarity
Can be steady or vary in magnitude	Varies between reversals in polarity
Steady value cannot be stepped up or down by a transformer	Can be stepped up or down for electric power distribution
Electrode voltages for transistor amplifiers	Signal input and output for amplifiers
Easier to measure	Easier to amplify
Heating effect is the same for direct or alternating current	

TEST-POINT QUESTION 1-10

Answers at end of chapter.

Answer True or False.

a. When the polarity of the applied voltage reverses, the direction of current flow also reverses.

b. A battery is a dc voltage source because it cannot reverse the polarity across its output terminals.

1-11 SOURCES OF ELECTRICITY

There are electrons and protons in the atoms of all materials, but to do useful work the charges must be separated to produce a potential difference that can make current flow. Some of the more common methods of providing electrical effects are listed here.

STATIC ELECTRICITY BY FRICTION   In this method, electrons in an insulator can be separated by the work of rubbing to produce opposite charges that remain in the dielectric.

CONVERSION OF CHEMICAL ENERGY   Wet or dry cells and batteries are the applications. Here a chemical reaction produces opposite charges on two dissimilar metals, which serve as the negative and positive terminals.

ELECTROMAGNETISM   Electricity and magnetism are closely related. Any moving charge has an associated magnetic field; also, any changing magnetic field can produce current. A motor is an example of how current can react with a magnetic field to produce motion; a generator produces voltage by means of a conductor rotating in a magnetic field.

DID YOU KNOW?

Electricity enables people to have healthier and longer lives, but more than half of available commercial energy is used by only a quarter of the world's population. In some developing nations, people without electricity lack basic services. Without access to health services, housing, clean water, and sewage treatment, life expectancy is low and infant mortality high.

PHOTOELECTRICITY   Some materials are photoelectric, meaning they can emit electrons when light strikes the surface. The element cesium is often used as a source of *photoelectrons*. Also, photovoltaic cells or solar cells use silicon to generate output voltage from the light input. In another effect, the resistance of the element selenium changes with light. When this is combined with a fixed voltage source, wide variations between *dark current* and *light current* can be produced. Such characteristics are the basis of many photoelectric devices, including television camera tubes, photoelectric cells, and phototransistors.

THERMAL EMISSION   Some materials when heated can "boil off" electrons from the surface. Then these emitted electrons can be controlled to provide useful applications of electric current. The emitting electrode is called a *cathode,* while an *anode* is used to collect the emitted electrons.

TEST-POINT QUESTION 1-11

Answers at end of chapter.
a. The excess charges at the negative terminal of a battery are _____.
b. The charges emitted from a heated cathode are _____.
c. The charges in a P-type semiconductor are _____.
d. In a liquid that is conducting current, the moving charges are _____.

1   SUMMARY AND REVIEW

- Electricity is present in all matter in the form of electrons and protons.
- The electron is the basic quantity of negative electricity, the proton of positive electricity. Both have the same amount of charge but opposite polarities. The charge of 6.25×10^{18} electrons or protons equals the practical unit of one coulomb.
- Charges of the same polarity tend to repel each other; charges of opposite polarities attract. There must be a difference of charges for any force of attraction or repulsion.
- Electrons tend to move toward protons because an electron has $\frac{1}{1840}$ the weight of a proton. Electrons in motion provide an electron current.
- The atomic number of an element gives the number of protons in the nucleus of its atom, balanced by an equal number of orbital electrons.
- The number of electrons in the outermost orbit is the valence of the element.
- Types of negative charges include electrons and negative ions. Types of positive charges include protons, positive ions, and hole charges.
- An electric circuit is a closed path for electron flow. Potential difference must be connected across the circuit to produce current. In the external circuit outside the voltage source, electrons flow from the negative terminal toward the positive terminal.
- Direct current has just one direction, as the dc voltage source has a fixed polarity. Alternating current periodically reverses in direction as the ac voltage source reverses its polarity.
- Table 1-6 summarizes the main features of electric circuits.

TABLE 1-6   ELECTRICAL CHARACTERISTICS

CHARACTERISTIC	SYMBOL	UNIT	DESCRIPTION
Charge	Q or q*	Coulomb (C)	Quantity of electrons or protons; $Q = I \times T$
Current	I or i*	Ampere (A)	Charge in motion; $I = Q/T$
Voltage	V or v*,†	Volt (V)	Potential difference between two unlike charges; makes charge move to produce I
Resistance	R or r‡	Ohm (Ω)	Opposition that reduces amount of current; $R = 1/G$
Conductance	G or g‡	Siemens (S)	Reciprocal of R, or $G = 1/R$

*Small letter q, i, or v is used for an instantaneous value of a varying charge, current, or voltage.
†E or e is sometimes used for a generated emf, but the standard symbol for any potential difference is V or v in the international system of units (SI).
‡Small letter r or g is used for internal resistance or conductance of transistors and tubes.

ANSWERS AT BACK OF BOOK.

Answer True or False.

1. All matter has electricity in the form of electrons and protons in the atom.
2. The electron is the basic unit of negative charge.
3. A proton has the same amount of charge as the electron but opposite polarity.
4. Electrons are repelled from other electrons but are attracted to protons.
5. The force of attraction or repulsion between charges is in their electric field.
6. The nucleus is the massive stable part of an atom, with positive charge.
7. Neutrons add to the weight of the atom's nucleus but not to its electric charge.
8. An element with atomic number 12 has 12 orbital electrons.
9. The element in question 8 has an electron valence of +2.
10. To produce current in a circuit, potential difference is connected across a closed path.
11. A dc voltage has fixed polarity, while ac voltage periodically reverses its polarity.
12. The coulomb is a measure of the quantity of stored charge.
13. If a dielectric has 2 C of excess electrons, removing 3 C of electrons will leave the dielectric with the positive charge of 1 C.
14. A charge of 5 C flowing past a point each second is a current of 5 A.
15. A 7-A current charging a dielectric will accumulate a charge of 14 C after a period of 2 s.
16. A voltage source has two terminals with different charges.
17. An ion is a charged atom.
18. The resistance of a few feet of copper wire is practically zero.
19. The resistance of the rubber or plastic insulation on wire is practically zero.
20. A resistance of 600 Ω has a conductance of 6 S.

QUESTIONS

1. Briefly define each of the following, giving its unit and symbol: charge, potential difference, current, resistance, and conductance.
2. Name two good conductors, two good insulators, and two semiconductors.
3. Explain briefly why there is no current in a light bulb unless it is connected across a source of applied voltage.
4. Give three differences between voltage and current.
5. In any circuit: (**a**) state two requirements for producing current; (**b**) give the direction of electron flow.

6. Show the atomic structure of the element sodium (Na), with atomic number 11. What is its electron valence?

7. Make up your own name for direct current and dc voltage to indicate how it differs from alternating voltage and current.

8. State the formulas for each of the following two statements: (a) Current is the time rate of change of charge. (b) Charge is current accumulated over a period of time.

9. Refer to Table 1-4 on page 31. (a) Name two types of moving charges that provide current in the direction of electron flow. (b) Name two types that provide conventional current.

10. Why is it that protons are not considered a source of moving charges for current flow?

11. Give one difference and one similarity in comparing electric and magnetic fields.

12. Give three methods of providing electric charges, and give their practical applications.

13. Give one way in which electricity and electronics are similar and one way in which they are different.

14. What kind of a meter would you use to measure the potential difference of a battery?

15. Give at least two voltage sources you have used and classify them as either dc or ac sources.

16. Compare the functions of a good conductor like copper wire with an insulator like paper, air, and vacuum.

17. How would you define *electromagnetism?*

18. Why is the characteristic of frequency used with alternating current and voltage?

PROBLEMS

ANSWERS TO ODD-NUMBERED PROBLEMS AT BACK OF BOOK.

1. A charge of 10 C flows past a given point every 2 s. How much is the current flow in amperes?

2. A charge of 5 C flows past a given point every 0.5 s. How much is the current flow in amperes?

3. A current of 3 A charges an insulator for 3 s. How much charge is accumulated?

4. If 31.25×10^{18} electrons are removed from a neutral dielectric, how much charge, in coulombs, is being stored?

5. If 18.75×10^{18} electrons are added to a neutral dielectric, how much charge, in coulombs, is being stored?

6. A dielectric has a charge Q of 6 C. To how many electrons does this correspond?

7. Show the atomic structure and determine the electron valence for the element silicon (Si), which has an atomic number of 14.

8. How long will it take a neutral dielectric to obtain a charge of $+4$ C if the charging current is 0.5 A?

9. How long will it take a neutral dielectric to obtain a charge of -20 C if the charging current is 2.5 A?

10. Calculate the resistance value in ohms for each of the following conductance values: (a) 0.001 S; (b) 0.01 S; (c) 0.1 S; (d) 1 S.

11. Calculate the resistance value in ohms for each of the following conductance values: (a) 0.002 S; (b) 0.004 S; (c) 0.00833 S; (d) 0.25 S.

12. Calculate the conductance value in siemens for each of the following resistance values: (a) 200 Ω; (b) 100 Ω; (c) 50 Ω; (d) 25 Ω.

13. Calculate the conductance value in siemens for each of the following resistance values: (a) 1 Ω; (b) 10,000 Ω; (c) 40 Ω; (d) 0.5 Ω.

14. Connect the components in Fig. 1-17 to form a complete electric circuit. Label the source voltage, with polarity, and the load resistance, R_L.

15. Calculate the voltage output of a battery if 15 J of energy is expended in moving 1.25 C of charge.

16. Calculate the voltage output of a battery if 3.6 J of energy is expended in moving 0.4 C of charge.

FIG. 1-17   Circuit components for Prob. 14.

CRITICAL THINKING

1. Suppose that 1000 electrons are removed from a neutral dielectric. How much charge, in coulombs, is stored in the dielectric?

2. How long will it take an insulator that has a charge of +5 C to charge to +30 C if the charging current is 2 A?

3. Assume that 6.25×10^{15} electrons flow past a given point in a conductor every 10 s. Calculate the current, I, in amperes.

4. The conductance of a wire at 100°C is one-tenth its value at 25°C. If the wire resistance equals 10 Ω at 25°C, calculate the resistance of the wire at 100°C.

1-1   **a.** negative
      b. positive
      c. true

1-2   **a.** metals
      b. silver
      c. silicon

1-3   **a.** 14
      b. 1
      c. 32

1-4   **a.** 6.25×10^{18}
      b. 4 C
      c. attract

1-5   **a.** zero
      b. 12 V

1-6   **a.** 2 A
      b. 2 A
      c. zero

1-7   **a.** carbon
      b. 4.7 Ω
      c. ¹⁄₁₀ S

1-8   **a.** T
      b. F
      c. T

1-9   **a.** negative
      b. negative
      c. true

1-10   **a.** T
       b. T

1-11   **a.** electrons
       b. electrons
       c. holes
       d. ions

CHAPTER 2

RESISTORS

Resistors are perhaps the most common component in electronic circuits. Their main function is to reduce the current I to the desired value, or to provide the desired voltage V in a circuit. A resistor is manufactured to have a specific value in ohms for its resistance R. The physical size of a resistor determines how much power it can dissipate in the form of heat. However, there is no direct correlation between a resistor's physical size and its resistance value. Resistors are manufactured in a variety of standard values and power ratings.

Resistors can be either fixed or variable in value. A fixed resistor has a resistance value that does not change, whereas a variable resistor has a resistance that can be varied over a range of values. Most fixed resistors have a four- or five-band color code that indicates their resistance value in ohms, but on larger resistors the resistance value may be printed right on the body. One important feature of resistance in general is that its effect is the same for both dc and ac circuits.

CHAPTER OBJECTIVES

Upon completion of this chapter, you should be able to:

• *List* five different types of resistors and describe the makeup of each type.
• *Interpret* the resistor color code to determine the resistance and tolerance of a resistor.
• *Explain* the difference between a potentiometer and a rheostat.
• *Explain* the significance of a resistor's power rating.
• *List* the most common troubles with resistors.
• *Explain* the precautions that must be observed when measuring a resistor with an ohmmeter.

IMPORTANT TERMS IN THIS CHAPTER

carbon-composition resistors
carbon-film resistors
chip resistor
color code
decade resistance box

metal-film resistors
noisy controls
potentiometer
preferred value
rheostat

surface-mount resistors
tapered control
tolerance
wire-wound resistors
zero-ohm resistor

TOPICS COVERED IN THIS CHAPTER

Molded
resistance element

Tinned leads

(a)

(b)

FIG. 2-1 Carbon-composition resistors. *(a)* Internal construction.
Length is ¾ in. without leads for
1-W power rating. Color stripes
give *R* in ohms. Tinned leads have
coating of solder. *(b)* Resistors
mounted on printed-circuit (PC)
board.

(a)

(b)

FIG. 2-3 Large wire-wound resistors with 50-W power rating.
(a) Fixed *R*, length of 5 in.
(b) Variable *R*, diameter of 2 in.

The two main characteristics of a resistor are its resistance *R* in ohms and its power rating *W* in watts. Resistors are available in a very wide range of *R* values, from a fraction of an ohm to many kilohms (kΩ) and megohms (MΩ). One kilohm is 1000 Ω, and one megohm is 1,000,000 Ω. More details of very small and large units are given in Chap. 3. The power rating for resistors may be as high as several hundred watts or as low as ⅒ W.

The *R* is the resistance value required to provide the desired current *I* or voltage. Also important is the wattage rating, because it specifies the maximum power the resistor can dissipate without excessive heat. Dissipation means that the power is wasted, since the resultant heat is not used. Too much heat can make the resistor burn. The wattage rating of the resistor is generally more than the actual power dissipation, as a safety factor.

Most common in electronic equipment are carbon resistors with a power rating of 1 W or less. The construction is illustrated in Fig. 2-1, while Fig. 2-2 shows a group of resistors mounted on a printed-circuit (PC) board. The resistors can be inserted automatically by machine.

FIG. 2-2 Carbon resistors commonly used on PC board. Typically, leads are cut and formed for insertion into holes with 0.5-in. spacing.

Resistors with higher *R* values usually have lower wattage ratings because they have less current. As an example, a common value is 1 MΩ at ¼ W, for a resistor only ½ in. long. The lower the power rating, the smaller the actual physical size of the resistor. However, the resistance value is not related to physical size.

WIRE-WOUND RESISTORS In this construction, a special type of wire called *resistance wire* is wrapped around an insulating core, as shown in Fig. 2-3.

The length of wire and its specific resistivity determine the R of the unit. Types of resistance wire include tungsten and manganin, as explained in Chap. 11, "Conductors and Insulators." The insulated core is commonly porcelain, cement, or just plain pressed paper. Bare wire is used, but the entire unit is generally encased in an insulating material.

Since they are generally for high-current applications with low resistance and appreciable power, wire-wound resistors are available in wattage ratings from 5 W up to 100 W or more. The resistance can be less than 1 Ω up to several thousand ohms.

In addition, wire-wound resistors are used where accurate, stable resistance values are necessary. Examples are precision resistors for the function of an ammeter shunt or a precision potentiometer to adjust for an exact amount of R.

For 2 W or less, carbon resistors are preferable because they are small and cost less. Between 2 and 5 W, combinations of carbon resistors can be used. Also, small wire-wound resistors are available in a 3- or 4-W rating.

CARBON-COMPOSITION RESISTORS This type of resistor is made of finely divided carbon or graphite mixed with a powdered insulating material as a binder, in the proportions needed for the desired R value. As shown in Fig. 2-1a, the resistor element is enclosed in a plastic case for insulation and mechanical strength. Joined to the two ends of the carbon resistance element are metal caps with leads of tinned copper wire for soldering the connections into a circuit. These are called *axial leads* because they come straight out from the ends.

Carbon resistors are commonly available in R values of 1 Ω to 20 MΩ. Examples are 10 Ω, 220 Ω, 4.7 kΩ, and 68 kΩ. The power rating is generally ¹⁄₁₀, ⅛, ¼, ½, 1, or 2 W.

FILM-TYPE RESISTORS There are two kinds of film-type resistors: carbon-film and metal-film resistors. The carbon-film resistor, whose construction is shown in Fig. 2-4, is made by depositing a thin layer of carbon on an insulated substrate. The carbon film is then cut in the form of a spiral to form the resistive element. The resistance value is controlled by varying the proportion of carbon to insulator. As compared to carbon-composition resistors, carbon-film resistors have the following advantages: tighter tolerances, less sensitivity to temperature changes and aging, and less noise generated internally.

Metal-film resistors are constructed in a manner similar to the carbon-film type. However, in a metal-film resistor a thin film of metal is sprayed onto a ceramic substrate and then cut in the form of a spiral. The construction of a metal-film resistor is shown in Fig. 2-5. The length, thickness, and width of the metal spiral determine the exact resistance value. Metal-film resistors have even more precise R values than do carbon-film resistors. Like carbon-film resistors, metal-film resistors are affected very little by temperature changes and aging. They also generate very little noise internally. In terms of overall performance, metal-film resistors are the best, carbon-film resistors are next, and carbon-composition resistors are last. Both carbon- and metal-film resistors can be distinguished from carbon-composition resistors by the fact that the diameters of the ends are a little larger than that of the body.

FIG. 2-4 Construction of carbon-film resistor.

FIG. 2-5 Construction of metal-film resistor.

SURFACE-MOUNT RESISTORS Surface-mount resistors, also called *chip resistors,* are constructed by depositing a thick carbon film on a ceramic base. The exact resistance value is determined by the composition of the carbon itself, as well as by the amount of trimming done to the carbon deposit. The resistance can vary from a fraction of an ohm to well over a million ohms. Power dissipation ratings are typically ⅛ to ¼ W. Figure 2-6 shows typical chip resistors. Electric connection to the resistive element is made via two leadless solder end electrodes (terminals). The end electrodes are C-shaped. The physical dimensions of a ⅛-W chip resistor are: 0.125 in. long by 0.063 in. wide and approximately 0.028 in. thick. This is many times smaller than a conventional resistor having axial leads. Chip resistors are very temperature-stable and also very rugged. The end electrodes are soldered directly to the copper traces of a circuit board, hence the name *surface-mount.*

FUSIBLE RESISTORS This type is a wire-wound resistor made to burn open easily when the power rating is exceeded. It then serves the dual functions of a fuse and a resistor to limit the current.

FIG. 2-6 Typical chip resistors.

TEST-POINT QUESTION 2-1

Answers at end of chapter.

Answer True or False.
a. An *R* of 10 Ω with a 10-W rating would be a wire-wound resistor.
b. A resistance of 10,000 Ω is the same as 10 kΩ.
c. Axial leads are not used for carbon resistors.
d. Which is more temperature stable, a carbon-composition or a metal-film resistor?
e. Which is larger physically, a 1000-Ω ½ W or a 1000-Ω 1 W carbon-film resistor?

2-2 RESISTOR COLOR CODING

Because carbon resistors are small physically, they are color-coded to mark their *R* value in ohms. The basis of this system is the use of colors for numerical values, as listed in Table 2-1. In memorizing the colors, note that the darkest col-

TABLE 2-1	COLOR CODE		
COLOR	VALUE	COLOR	VALUE
Black	0	Green	5
Brown	1	Blue	6
Red	2	Violet	7
Orange	3	Gray	8
Yellow	4	White	9

ors, black and brown, are for the lowest numbers, zero and one, whereas white is for nine. The color coding is standardized by the Electronic Industries Association (EIA).

RESISTANCE COLOR STRIPES

The use of bands or stripes is the most common system for color-coding carbon resistors, as shown in Fig. 2-7. Color stripes are printed at one end of the insulating body, which is usually tan. Reading from left to right, the first band closest to the edge gives the first digit in the numerical value of R. The next band marks the second digit. The third band is the decimal multiplier, which gives the number of zeroes after the two digits.

In Fig. 2-8a, the first stripe is red for 2 and the next stripe is green for 5. The red multiplier in the third stripe means add two zeroes to 25, or "this multiplier is 10^2." The result can be illustrated as follows:

Red	Green		Red	
↓	↓		↓	
2	5	×	100	= 2500

Therefore, this R value is 2500 Ω.

The example in Fig. 2-8b illustrates that black for the third stripe just means "do not add any zeroes to the first two digits." Since this resistor has red, green, and black stripes, the R value is 25 Ω.

RESISTORS UNDER 10 Ω

For these values, the third stripe is either gold or silver, indicating a fractional decimal multiplier. When the third stripe is gold, multiply the first two digits by 0.1. In Fig. 2-8c, the R value is

$$25 \times 0.1 = 2.5 \ \Omega$$

Silver means a multiplier of 0.01. If the third band in Fig. 2-8c were silver, the R value would be

$$25 \times 0.01 = 0.25 \ \Omega$$

It is important to realize that the gold and silver colors are used as decimal multipliers only in the third stripe. However, gold and silver are used most often as a fourth stripe to indicate how accurate the R value is.

RESISTOR TOLERANCE

The amount by which the actual R can be different from the color-coded value is the *tolerance,* usually given in percent. For instance, a 2000-Ω resistor with ±10 percent tolerance can have resistance 10 percent above or below the coded value. This R, therefore, is between 1800 and 2200 Ω. The calculations are as follows:

$$10 \text{ percent of } 2000 \text{ is } 0.1 \times 2000 = 200$$

For +10 percent, the value is

$$2000 + 200 = 2200 \ \Omega$$

For −10 percent, the value is

$$2000 - 200 = 1800 \ \Omega$$

FIG. 2-7   How to read color stripes on carbon resistors for R in ohms.

(a)

(b)

(c)

FIG. 2-8   Examples of color-coded R values, with percent tolerance.

As illustrated in Fig. 2-7, silver in the fourth band indicates a tolerance of ±10 percent; gold indicates ±5 percent. If there is no color band for tolerance, it is ±20 percent. The inexact value of carbon-composition resistors is a disadvantage of their economical construction. They usually cost only a few cents each, or less in larger quantities. In most circuits, though, a small difference in resistance can be tolerated.

FIVE-BAND CODE   Precision resistors often use a five-band code rather than the four-band code shown in Fig. 2-7. The purpose is to obtain more precise R values. With the five-band code, the first three color stripes indicate the first three digits, followed by the decimal multiplier in the fourth stripe and the tolerance in the fifth stripe. In the fifth stripe, the colors brown, red, green, blue, and violet represent the following tolerances:

Brown	±1%
Red	±2%
Green	±0.5%
Blue	±0.25%
Violet	±0.1%

Orange
Blue
Green
Black
Green

FIG. 2-9   Color-coded resistor.

Example

EXAMPLE 1   What is the resistance indicated by the five-band color code in Fig. 2-9? Also, what ohmic range is permissible for the specified tolerance?

ANSWER   The first stripe is orange for the number 3, the second stripe is blue for the number 6, and the third stripe is green for the number 5. Therefore, the first three digits of the resistance are 3, 6, and 5, respectively. The fourth stripe, which is the multiplier, is black, which means add no zeros. The fifth stripe, which indicates the resistor tolerance, is green for ±0.5%. Therefore $R = 365 \ \Omega$ ±0.5%. The permissible ohmic range is calculated as 365 × 0.005 = ±1.825 Ω, or 363.175 to 366.825 Ω.

WIRE-WOUND-RESISTOR MARKING   Usually, wire-wound resistors are big enough physically to have the R value printed on the insulating case. The tolerance is generally ±5 percent, except for precision resistors, which have a tolerance of ±1 percent or less.

Some small wire-wound resistors may be color-coded with stripes, however, like carbon resistors. In this case, the first stripe is double the width of the others to indicate a wire-wound resistor. This type may have a wattage rating of 3 or 4 W.

PREFERRED RESISTANCE VALUES   In order to minimize the problem of manufacturing different R values for an almost unlimited variety of circuits, specific values are made in large quantities so that they are cheaper and more easily available than unusual sizes. For resistors of ±10 percent, the preferred values are 10, 12, 15, 18, 22, 27, 33, 39, 47, 56, 68, and 82 with their decimal multiples. As examples, 47, 470, 4700, and 47,000 are preferred values. In this way, there is a preferred value available within 10 percent of any *R* value needed in a circuit. See Appendix A for a listing of preferred resistance values for tolerances of ±20%, ±10%, and ±5%.

ZERO-OHM RESISTORS   Believe it or not, there is such a thing as a zero-ohm resistor. In fact, zero-ohm resistors are quite common. The zero-ohm value is denoted by the use of a single black band around the center of the resistor body, as shown in Fig. 2-10. Zero-ohm resistors are available in ⅛- or ¼-W sizes. The actual resistance of a so-called ⅛-W zero-ohm resistor is about 0.004 Ω, whereas a ¼-W zero-ohm resistor has a resistance of approximately 0.003 Ω.

But why are zero-ohm resistors used in the first place? The reason is that for most printed-circuit boards, the components are inserted by automatic insertion machines (robots) rather than by human hands. In some instances it may be necessary to short two points on the printed-circuit board, in which case a piece of wire has to be placed between the two points. Because the robot can handle only components such as resistors, and not wires, zero-ohm resistors are used. Before zero-ohm resistors were developed, jumpers had to be installed by hand, which was time-consuming and expensive. Zero-ohm resistors may need to be used as a result of an after-the-fact design change which requires new point connections in a circuit.

CHIP RESISTOR CODING SYSTEM   A chip resistor, shown in Fig. 2-11*a*, has the following identifiable features.

Body color: white or off-white
Dark film on one side only (usually black, but may also be dark gray or green)
End electrodes (terminals) are C-shaped
Three-digit marking on either the film or the body side (usually the film)

The resistance value of a chip resistor is determined from the three-digit number printed on the film or body side of the component. The three digits provide the same information as the first three color stripes on a four-band resistor. This is shown in Fig. 2-11*b*. The first two digits indicate the first two numbers in the numerical value of the resistance; the third digit indicates the multiplier. If a four-digit number is used, the first three digits indicate the first three numbers in the numerical value of the resistance, while the fourth digit indicates the multiplier. Figure 2-11*c* shows the symbol used to denote a zero-ohm chip resistor.

FIG. 2-10   A zero-ohm resistor is indicated by a single black color band around the body of the resistor.

FIG. 2-11   Typical chip resistor coding system.

562

FIG. 2-12 Chip resistor with number coding.

Example

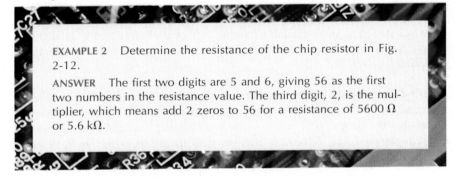

EXAMPLE 2 Determine the resistance of the chip resistor in Fig. 2-12.

ANSWER The first two digits are 5 and 6, giving 56 as the first two numbers in the resistance value. The third digit, 2, is the multiplier, which means add 2 zeros to 56 for a resistance of 5600 Ω or 5.6 kΩ.

TEST-POINT QUESTION 2-2

Answers at end of chapter.
a. Give the color for the number 4.
b. What tolerance does a silver stripe represent?
c. Give the multiplier for red in the third stripe.
d. Give R and the tolerance for a resistor coded with yellow, violet, brown, and gold stripes.
e. Assume that the chip resistor in Fig. 2-12 is marked 333. What is its resistance value in ohms?

2-3 VARIABLE RESISTORS

Variable resistors can be wire-wound, as in Fig. 2-3b, or the carbon type, illustrated in Fig. 2-13. Inside the metal case of Fig. 2-13a, the control has a circular disk, shown in Fig. 2-13b, that is the carbon-composition resistance element. It can be a thin coating on pressed paper or a molded carbon disk. Joined to the

FIG. 2-13 Construction of variable carbon resistance control. Diameter is ¾ in. (a) External view. (b) Internal view of circular resistance element.

two ends are the external soldering-lug terminals 1 and 3. The middle terminal is connected to the variable arm that contacts the resistor element by a metal spring wiper. As the shaft of the control is turned, the variable arm moves the wiper to make contact at different points on the resistor element. The same idea applies to the slide control in Fig. 2-14, except that the resistor element is straight instead of circular.

When the contact moves closer to one end, the R decreases between this terminal and the variable arm. Between the two ends, however, R is not variable but always has the maximum resistance of the control.

Carbon controls are available with a total R from 1000 Ω to 5 MΩ, approximately. Their power rating is usually $\frac{1}{2}$ to 2 W.

FIG. 2-14   Slide control for variable R. Length is 2 in.

TAPERED CONTROLS   The way R varies with shaft rotation is called the *taper* of the control. With a linear taper, one-half rotation changes R by one-half the maximum value. Similarly, all values of R change in direct proportion to rotation. For a nonlinear taper, though, R can change more gradually at one end, with bigger changes at the opposite end. This effect is accomplished by different densities of carbon in the resistance element. For the example of a volume control, its audio taper allows smaller changes in R at low settings. Then it is easier to make changes without having the volume too loud or too low.

DECADE RESISTANCE BOX   As shown in Fig. 2-15, the decade resistance box is a convenient unit for providing any one R within a wide range of values. It can be considered as test equipment for trying different R values in a circuit. Inside the box are six series strings of resistors, with one string for each dial switch.

FIG. 2-15   Decade resistance box for a wide range of R values.

The first dial connects in an R of 0 to 9 Ω. It is the *units* or $R \times 1$ dial.
The second dial has units of 10 from 0 to 90 Ω. It is the *tens* or $R \times 10$ dial.
The hundreds or $R \times 100$ dial has an R of 0 to 900 Ω.
The thousands or $R \times 1k$ dial has an R of 0 to 9000 Ω.
The ten-thousandths or $R \times 10k$ dial provides R values of 0 to 90,000 Ω.
The one-hundred thousandths or $R \times 100k$ dial provides R values of 0 to 900,000 Ω.

The six dial sections are connected internally so that their values add to one another. Then any value from 0 to 999,999 Ω can be obtained. Note the exact values that are possible. As an example, when all six dials are on 2, the total R equals 2 + 20 + 200 + 2,000 + 20,000 + 200,000 = 222,222 Ω.

TEST-POINT QUESTION 2-3

Answers at end of chapter.
a. In Fig. 2-13, which terminal provides variable R?
b. Is an audio taper linear or nonlinear?
c. In Fig. 2-15, how much is the total R if the $R \times 100k$ and $R \times 10k$ dials are set to 4 and 7, respectively, and all other dials are set to zero?

2-4 RHEOSTATS AND POTENTIOMETERS

These are variable resistances, either carbon or wire-wound, used to vary the amount of current or voltage for a circuit. The controls can be used in either dc or ac applications.

A rheostat is a variable R with two terminals connected in series with a load. The purpose is to vary the amount of current.

A potentiometer, generally called a *pot* for short, has three terminals. The fixed maximum R across the two ends is connected across a voltage source. Then the variable arm is used to vary the voltage division between the center terminal and the ends. This function of a potentiometer is compared with a rheostat in Table 2-2.

TABLE 2-2 POTENTIOMETERS AND RHEOSTATS

RHEOSTAT	POTENTIOMETER
Two terminals In series with load and V source Varies the I	Three terminals Ends are connected across V source Taps off part of V

RHEOSTAT CIRCUIT The function of the rheostat R_2 in Fig. 2-16 is to vary the amount of current through R_1. For instance, R_1 can be a small light bulb that requires a specified I. Therefore, the two terminals of the rheostat R_2 are connected in series with R_1 and the source V in order to vary the total resistance R_T in the circuit. When R_T changes, the I changes, as read by the meter.

In Fig. 2-16b, R_1 is 5 Ω and the rheostat R_2 varies from 0 to 5 Ω. With R_2 at its maximum of 5 Ω, then R_T equals $5 + 5 = 10$ Ω. The I equals 0.15 A or 150 mA. (The method for calculating I given R and V is covered in Chapter 3, "Ohm's Law.")

FIG. 2-16 Rheostat connected in series circuit to vary the current I. Symbol for current meter is A, for amperes. (*a*) Wiring diagram with digital meter for I. (*b*) Schematic diagram.

When R_2 is at its minimum value of 0 Ω, the R_T equals 5 Ω. Then I is 0.3 A or 300 mA for the maximum current. As a result, varying the rheostat changes the circuit resistance to vary the current through R_1. The I increases as R decreases.

It is important that the rheostat have a wattage rating high enough for the maximum I when R is minimum. Rheostats are often wire-wound variable resistors used to control relatively large values of current in low-resistance circuits for ac power applications.

POTENTIOMETER CIRCUIT   The purpose of the circuit in Fig. 2-17 is to tap off a variable part of the 100-V from the source. Consider this circuit in two parts:

1.   The applied V is input to the two end terminals of the potentiometer.
2.   The variable V is output between the variable arm and an end terminal.

FIG. 2-17   Potentiometer connected across voltage source to function as a voltage divider. (*a*) Wiring diagram. (*b*) Schematic diagram.

Two pairs of connections to the three terminals are necessary, with one terminal common to the input and output. One pair connects the source V to the end terminals 1 and 3. The other pair of connections is between the variable arm at the center terminal and one end. This end has double connections for input and output. The other end has only an input connection.

When the variable arm is at the middle value of the 500-kΩ R in Fig. 2-17, the 50 V is tapped off between terminals 2 and 1 as one-half the 100-V input. The other 50 V is between terminals 2 and 3. However, this voltage is not used for output.

As the control is turned up to move the variable arm closer to terminal 3, more of the input voltage is available between 2 and 1. With the control at its maximum R, the voltage between 2 and 1 is the entire 100 V. Actually, terminal 2 then is the same as 3.

When the variable arm is at minimum R, rotated to terminal 1, the output between 2 and 1 is zero. Now all the applied voltage is across 2 and 3, with no output for the variable arm. It is important to note that the source voltage is not short-circuited. The reason is that the maximum R of the pot is always across the applied V, regardless of where the variable arm is set. Typical examples of small potentiometers used in electronic circuits are shown in Fig. 2-18.

FIG. 2-18   Small potentiometers and trimmers often used for variable controls in electronic circuits. Terminal leads formed for insertion into a PC board.

POTENTIOMETER USED AS A RHEOSTAT Commercial rheostats are generally wire-wound high-wattage resistors for power applications. However, a small low-wattage rheostat is often needed in electronic circuits. One example is a continuous tone control in a receiver. The control requires the variable series resistance of a rheostat but dissipates very little power.

A method of wiring a potentiometer as a rheostat is to connect just one end of the control and the variable arm, using only two terminals. The third terminal is open, or floating, not connected to anything.

Another method is to wire the unused terminal to the center terminal. When the variable arm is rotated, different amounts of resistance are short-circuited. This method is preferable because there is no floating resistance.

Either end of the potentiometer can be used for the rheostat. The direction of increasing R with shaft rotation reverses, though, for connections at opposite ends. Also, the taper is reversed on a nonlinear control.

TEST-POINT QUESTION 2-4

Answers at end of chapter.
a. How many circuit connections to a potentiometer are needed?
b. How many circuit connections to a rheostat are needed?
c. In Fig. 2-17, with a 500-kΩ linear potentiometer, how much is the output voltage with 400 kΩ between terminals 1 and 2?

2-5 POWER RATING OF RESISTORS

In addition to having the required ohms value, a resistor should have a wattage rating high enough to dissipate the power produced by the current flowing through the resistance, without becoming too hot. Carbon resistors in normal operation are often quite warm, up to a maximum temperature of about 85°C, which is close to the 100°C boiling point of water. Carbon resistors should not be so hot, however, that they "sweat" beads of liquid on the insulating case. Wire-wound resistors operate at very high temperatures, a typical value being 300°C for the maximum temperature. If a resistor becomes too hot because of excessive power dissipation, it can change appreciably in resistance value or burn open.

The power rating is a physical property that depends on the resistor construction, especially physical size. Note the following:

1. A larger physical size indicates a higher power rating.
2. Higher-wattage resistors can operate at higher temperatures.
3. Wire-wound resistors are physically larger with higher wattage ratings than carbon resistors.

For approximate sizes, a 2-W carbon resistor is about 1 in. long with ¼ in. diameter; a ¼-W resistor is about 0.35 in. long with diameter of 0.1 in.

For both types, a higher power rating allows a higher voltage rating. This rating gives the highest voltage that may be applied across the resistor without internal arcing. As examples for carbon resistors, the maximum voltage is 500 V for a 1-W rating, 250 V for ¼-W, and 150 V for ⅛-W. In wire-wound resistors, excessive voltage can produce an arc between turns; in carbon resistors, the arc is between carbon granules.

SHELF LIFE   Resistors keep their characteristics almost indefinitely when not used. Without any current in a circuit to heat the resistor, it has practically no change with age. The shelf life of resistors is usually no problem, therefore.

TEST-POINT QUESTION 2-5

Answers at end of chapter.

Answer True or False.
a. The shelf life of a resistor is about 6 months.
b. Resistors should not operate above a temperature of 0°C.
c. Would a 10-W resistor be the wire-wound or carbon type?

2-6 SERIES AND PARALLEL COMBINATIONS OF RESISTORS

In some cases two or more resistors are combined to obtain a desired R value with a higher wattage rating. Several examples are shown in Fig. 2-19.

The total resistance R_T depends on the series or parallel connections. However, the combination has a power rating equal to the sum of the individual values, whether the resistors are in series or in parallel. The reason is that the total physical size increases with each added resistor. Equal resistors are generally used in order to have equal distribution of I, V, and P.

In general, series resistors add for a higher R_T. With parallel resistors, R_{EQ} is reduced. More details of series and parallel circuits are explained in Chaps. 4 and 5.

In Fig. 2-19a, the two equal resistors in series double the resistance for R_T. Also, the power rating of the combination is twice the rating for one resistor.

In Fig. 2-19b, the two equal resistors in parallel have one-half the resistance for R_T. However, the combined power rating is still twice the rating for one resistor.

In Fig. 2-19c, the series-parallel combination of four equal resistors makes R_T the same as each R. The total power rating, though, is four times the rating for one resistor.

TEST-POINT QUESTION 2-6

Answers at end of chapter.

Give R_T and the combined power rating of two 1-kΩ resistors rated at 2 W connected:
a. In series
b. In parallel
c. Do both methods provide the same power rating?

(a)

(b)

(c)

FIG. 2-19   Total resistance R_T and wattage rating for series and parallel circuits. Each R is 10 Ω with a 1-W rating. (a) For R_1 and R_2 in series, add wattage ratings; R_T is $2 \times R$. (b) For R_3 and R_4 in parallel, add wattage ratings; R_T is ½ R. (c) For this series-parallel combination, add all wattage ratings; R_T is equal to R.

2-7 RESISTOR TROUBLES

The most common trouble in resistors is an open. When the open resistor is a series component, there is no current in the entire series path.

NOISY CONTROLS   In applications such as volume and tone controls, carbon controls are preferred because the smoother change in resistance results in less noise when the variable arm is rotated. With use, however, the resistance element becomes worn by the wiper contact, making the control noisy. When a volume or tone control makes a scratchy noise as the shaft is rotated, it indicates a worn-out resistance element.

CHECKING RESISTORS WITH AN OHMMETER   Resistance measurements are made with an ohmmeter. The ohmmeter has its own voltage source so that it is always used without any external power applied to the resistance being measured. Separate the resistance from its circuit by disconnecting one lead of the resistor. Then connect the ohmmeter leads across the resistance to be measured.

An open resistor reads infinitely high ohms. For some reason, infinite ohms is often confused with zero ohms. Remember, though, that infinite ohms means an open circuit. The current is zero, but the resistance is infinitely high. Furthermore, it is practically impossible for a resistor to become short-circuited in itself. The resistor may be short-circuited by some other part of the circuit. However, the construction of resistors is such that the trouble they develop is an open circuit, with infinitely high ohms.

The ohmmeter must have an ohms scale capable of reading the resistance value, or the resistor cannot be checked. In checking a 10-MΩ resistor, for instance, if the highest R the ohmmeter can read is 1 MΩ, it will indicate infinite resistance, even if the resistor has its normal value of 10 MΩ. An ohms scale of 100 MΩ or more should be used for checking such high resistances.

To check resistors of less than 10 Ω, a low-ohms scale of about 100 Ω or less is necessary. Center scale should be 6 Ω or less. Otherwise, the ohmmeter will read a normally low resistance value as zero ohms.

When checking resistance in a circuit, it is important to be sure there are no parallel resistance paths. Otherwise, the measured resistance can be much lower than the actual resistor value, as illustrated in Fig. 2-20a. Here, the ohmmeter reads the resistance of R_2 in parallel with R_1. To check across R_2 alone, one end is disconnected, as in Fig. 2-20b.

For very high resistances, it is important not to touch the ohmmeter leads. There is no danger of shock, but the body resistance of about 50,000 Ω as a parallel path will lower the ohmmeter reading.

(a)   (b)

FIG. 2-20   Parallel R_1 can lower the ohmmeter reading for testing R_2. (a) The two resistances R_1 and R_2 are in parallel. (b) R_2 is isolated by disconnecting one end of R_1.

CHANGED VALUE OF R   In many cases, the value of a carbon-composition resistor can exceed its allowed tolerance, due to normal resistor heating over a long period of time. In most instances the value change is seen as an increase in R. This is known as *aging*. As you know, carbon-film and metal-film resistors age very little. Surface-mount resistors should never be rubbed or scraped, as this will remove some of the carbon deposit and cause its resistance to change.

TEST-POINT QUESTION 2-7

Answers at end of chapter.
a. What is the ohmmeter reading for a short circuit?
b. What is the ohmmeter reading for an open resistor?
c. Which has a higher R, an open or a short circuit?
d. Which is more likely to change in R value after many years of use, a metal-film or a carbon-composition resistor?

2 SUMMARY AND REVIEW

- The most common types of resistors include carbon-composition, carbon-film, metal-film, wire-wound, and surface-mount or chip resistors. Carbon-film and metal-film resistors are better than carbon-composition resistors because they have tighter tolerances, are less affected by temperature and aging, and generate less noise internally.
- Wire-wound resistors are typically used in high-current applications. Wire-wound resistors are available with wattage ratings of about 5 to 100 W.
- Resistors are usually color-coded to indicate their resistance value in ohms. Either a four-band or a five-band code is used. The five-band code is used for more precise R values. Chip resistors use a three- or four-digit code to indicate their resistance value.
- Zero-ohm resistors are used with automatic insertion machines when it is desired to short two points on a printed-circuit board. Zero-ohm resistors are available in ⅛- or ¼-W ratings.
- A potentiometer is a variable resistor with three terminals. It is used to vary the voltage in a circuit. A rheostat is a variable resistor with two terminals. It is used to vary the current in a circuit.
- The physical size of a resistor determines its wattage rating: the larger the physical size, the larger the wattage rating. There is no correlation between a resistor's physical size and its resistance value.
- Resistors can be combined in series, parallel, or series-parallel to obtain a higher overall power rating. The total power rating equals the sum of the individual wattage ratings of the resistors.
- The most common trouble in resistors is an open. An ohmmeter across the leads of an open resistor will read infinite, assuming there is no other parallel path across the resistor.

SELF-TEST

ANSWERS AT BACK OF BOOK.

Choose (a), (b), (c), or (d).

1. A carbon composition resistor having only three color stripes has a tolerance of (a) ±5%; (b) ±20%; (c) ±10%; (d) ±100%.
2. A resistor with a power rating of 25 W is most likely a (a) carbon-composition resistor; (b) metal-film resistor; (c) surface-mount resistor; (d) wire-wound resistor
3. When checked with an ohmmeter, an open resistor measures (a) infinite resistance; (b) its color-coded value; (c) zero resistance; (d) less than its color-coded value.
4. One precaution to observe when checking resistors with an ohmmeter is to (a) check high resistances on the lowest ohms range; (b) check low resistances on the highest ohms range; (c) disconnect all parallel paths; (d) make sure your fingers are touching each test lead.

5. A chip resistor is marked 394. Its resistance value is (*a*) 39.4 Ω; (*b*) 394 Ω; (*c*) 390,000 Ω; (*d*) 39,000 Ω.

6. A carbon-film resistor is color-coded with red, violet, black, and gold stripes. What are its resistance and tolerance? (*a*) 27 Ω ± 5%; (*b*) 270 Ω ± 5%; (*c*) 270 Ω ± 10%; (*d*) 27 Ω ± 10%.

7. A potentiometer is a (*a*) three-terminal device used to vary the voltage in a circuit; (*b*) two-terminal device used to vary the current in a circuit; (*c*) fixed resistor; (*d*) two-terminal device used to vary the voltage in a circuit.

8. A metal-film resistor is color-coded with brown, green, red, brown, and blue stripes. What are its resistance and tolerance? (*a*) 1500 Ω ± 1.25%; (*b*) 152 Ω ± 1%; (*c*) 1521 Ω ± 0.5%; (*d*) 1520 Ω ± 0.25%.

9. Which of the following resistors has the smallest physical size? (*a*) wire-wound resistors; (*b*) carbon-composition resistors; (*c*) surface-mount resistors; (*d*) potentiometers.

10. Which of the following statements is true? (*a*) Resistors always have axial leads. (*b*) Resistors are always made from carbon. (*c*) There is no correlation between the physical size of a resistor and its resistance value. (*d*) The shelf life of a resistor is about 1 year.

QUESTIONS

1. List five different types of fixed resistors.
2. List the advantages of using a metal-film resistor versus a carbon-composition resistor.
3. Draw the schematic symbols for a (*a*) fixed resistor; (*b*) potentiometer; (*c*) rheostat.
4. List the colors corresponding to the decimal digits 0 through 9.
5. How can a technician identify a wire-wound resistor that is color-coded?
6. Explain how the resistance of a carbon-film resistor can be controlled during the manufacturing process.
7. Explain an application where it may be desired to use a decade resistance box.
8. List the differences between a potentiometer and a rheostat.
9. For resistors using the four-band code, what are the values for gold and silver as decimal multipliers in the third band?
10. Give the color code for the following resistors using the four-band code: 1.2 Ω; 330 Ω; 2.2 MΩ; 680 kΩ; 1 kΩ; 10 kΩ; and 47 Ω. Each resistor has a tolerance of ±5%.
11. Give the color code for the following resistors using the five-band code: 3320 Ω ± 1%; 7.23 kΩ ± 0.1%; 333 kΩ ± 2%; and 47.5 Ω + 0.25%.
12. Briefly describe how you would check to see whether a 1-MΩ resistor is open or not. Give two precautions to make sure the test is not misleading.
13. Give at least two examples of variable resistors you have seen used for controls in electronic circuits.
14. Show how to connect three 1-kΩ resistors for a total R_T of 1.5 kΩ.
15. Show how to connect resistors for the following examples: (*a*) two 20-kΩ 1-W resistors for a total R_T of 10 kΩ with a power rating of 2 W; (*b*) two 20-kΩ 1-W resistors for an R_T of 40 kΩ and a power rating of 2 W; (*c*) four 20-kΩ 1-W resistors for an R_T of 20 kΩ and a power rating of 4 W.

ANSWERS TO ODD-NUMBERED PROBLEMS AT BACK OF BOOK.

1. Indicate the resistance and tolerance for each resistor shown in Fig. 2-21.
2. Indicate the resistance and tolerance for each resistor shown in Fig. 2-22.
3. Indicate the resistance for each chip resistor shown in Fig. 2-23.
4. Calculate the permissible ohmic range of a resistor whose resistance value and tolerance are (a) 3.9 kΩ ± 5%; (b) 100 Ω ± 10%; (c) 120 kΩ ± 2%; (d) 2.2 Ω ± 5%; (e) 75 Ω ± 1%.
5. Using the four-band code, indicate the colors of the bands for each of the following resistors: (a) 10 kΩ ± 5%; (b) 2.7 Ω ± 5%; (c) 5.6 kΩ ± 10%; (d) 1.5 MΩ ± 5%; (e) 0.22 Ω ± 5%.
6. Using the five-band code, indicate the colors of the bands for each of the following resistors: (a) 110 Ω ± 1%; (b) 34 kΩ ± 0.5%; (c) 82.5 kΩ ± 2%; (d) 62.6 Ω ± 1%; (e) 105 kΩ ± 0.1%.
7. Refer to Fig. 2-15 on page 55. Indicate the total resistance R_T for each of the different dial settings in Table 2-3.

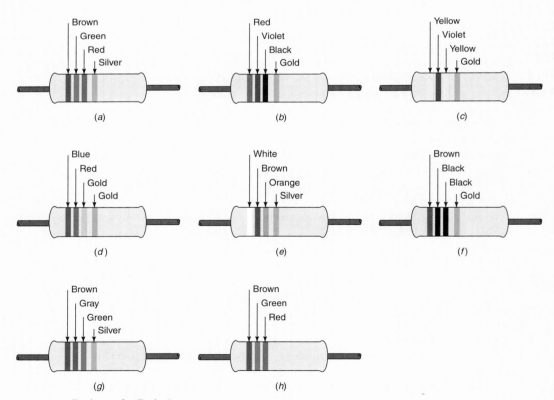

FIG. 2-21   Resistors for Prob. 1.

FIG. 2-22   Resistors for Prob. 2.

FIG. 2-23   Chip resistors for Prob. 3.

TABLE 2-3   DECADE RESISTANCE BOX (FIG. 2-15) DIAL SETTINGS FOR PROB. 7

	R × 100k	R × 10k	R × 1k	R × 100	R × 10	R × 1
(a)	6	8	0	2	2	5
(b)	0	0	8	2	5	0
(c)	0	1	8	5	0	3
(d)	2	7	5	0	6	0
(e)	0	6	2	9	8	4

8. Show how to wire two 100-Ω 5-W resistors for an R_T of 200 Ω and a total power rating of 10 W.

9. Show how to wire the resistors in Prob. 8 for an R_T of 50 Ω and a total power rating of 10 W.

10. Show two different ways to wire a potentiometer so it will work as a rheostat.

CRITICAL THINKING

1. A manufacturer of carbon-film resistors specifies a maximum working voltage of 250 V for all its ¼-W resistors. Exceeding 250 V causes internal arcing within the resistor. Above what minimum resistance will the maximum working voltage be exceeded before its ¼-W power dissipation rating is exceeded? **Hint:** The <u>maximum</u> voltage which produces the rated power dissipation can be calculated as $V_{max} = \sqrt{P \times R}$.

ANSWERS TO TEST-POINT QUESTIONS

2-1 a. T
    b. T
    c. F
    d. metal film
    e. 1000 Ω 1 W

2-2 a. yellow
    b. ±10 percent
    c. 100
    d. 470 Ω ±5 percent
    e. 33,000 Ω or 33 kΩ

2-3 a. terminal 2
    b. nonlinear
    c. 470,000 Ω or 470 kΩ

2-4 a. four connections to
       three terminals
    b. two
    c. 80 V

2-5 a. F
    b. F
    c. wire-wound

2-6 a. 2 kΩ 4 W
    b. 0.5 kΩ 4 W
    c. yes

2-7 a. 0 Ω
    b. infinite ohms
    c. open circuit
    d. carbon-composition resistor

CHAPTER 3

OHM'S LAW

When we have a circuit with voltage V applied and resistance R in the closed path, it is important to know how much the current I is in the circuit. This chapter explains how the amount of I increases with more applied voltage but is less with more resistance. Specifically, $I = V/R$, as determined in 1828 by the experiments of Georg Simon Ohm. If we know any two of the factors R, I, and V, the third can be calculated. As an example, when 6 V is applied across an R of 2 Ω, the I is 6 V/2 Ω = 3 A.

Ohm's law is also used to determine the amount of electric power P in the circuit. The P can be calculated as $V \times I$ or as $I^2 \times R$. All these relations derived from Ohm's law apply to both dc and ac circuits.

CHAPTER OBJECTIVES

Upon completion of this chapter, you should be able to:

- *List* the three forms of Ohm's law.
- *Use* Ohm's law to calculate the current, voltage, or resistance in a circuit.
- *List* the multiple and submultiple units of voltage, current, and resistance.
- *Explain* the difference between a linear and a nonlinear resistance.
- *Explain* the difference between work and power and list the units of each.
- *Calculate* the power in a circuit when the voltage and current, current and resistance, or voltage and resistance are known.
- *Understand* the shock hazards associated with working with electricity.
- *Explain* the difference between an open circuit and short circuit.

IMPORTANT TERMS IN THIS CHAPTER

volt	joule	mega
ampere	milli	linear graph
ohm	micro	power
watt	kilo	volt-ampere characteristic

TOPICS COVERED IN THIS CHAPTER

3-1 THE CURRENT $I = V/R$

If we keep the same resistance in a circuit but vary the voltage, the current will vary. The circuit in Fig. 3-1 demonstrates this idea. The applied voltage V can be varied from 0 to 12 V, as an example. The bulb has a 12-V filament, which requires this much voltage for its normal current to light with normal intensity. The meter I indicates the amount of current in the circuit for the bulb.

FIG. 3-1   Increasing the applied voltage V produces more current I to light the bulb with more intensity.

With 12 V applied, the bulb lights, indicating normal current. When V is reduced to 10 V, there is less light because of less I. As V decreases, the bulb becomes dimmer. For zero volts applied there is no current and the bulb cannot light. In summary, the changing brilliance of the bulb shows that the current is varying with the changes in applied voltage.

For the general case of any *V* and *R*, Ohm's law is

▶ $$I = \frac{V}{R} \qquad\qquad (3\text{-}1)$$

(handwritten: resistors are resistance)

where *I* is the amount of current through the resistance *R* connected across the source of potential difference *V*. With volts as the practical unit for *V* and ohms for *R*, the amount of current *I* is in amperes. Therefore,

▶ $$\text{Amperes} = \frac{\text{volts}}{\text{ohms}} \quad I = \frac{V}{R}$$

This formula says to simply divide the voltage across *R* by the ohms of resistance between the two points of potential difference to calculate the amperes of current through *R*. In Fig. 3-2, for instance, with 6 V applied across a 3-Ω resistance, by Ohm's law the amount of current *I* equals ⅔ or 2 A.

HIGH VOLTAGE BUT LOW CURRENT   It is important to realize that with high voltage, the current can have a low value when there is a very high resistance in the circuit. For example, 1000 V applied across 1,000,000 Ω results in a current of only ½₀₀₀ A. By Ohm's law,

$$I = \frac{V}{R}$$

$$I = \frac{1000 \text{ V}}{1,000,000 \text{ Ω}} = \frac{1}{1000}$$

$$I = 0.001 \text{ A}$$

(handwritten: Reduce to lowest; 1000 / 1,000,000; .001 / 1; I = current, V = volts, R = resistance)

*(handwritten: 6v = 2A * 3Ω; 3Ω = 6v/2A; I = 6v/3Ω; I = 2A)*

FIG. 3-2   Example of using Ohm's law. (*a*) Wiring diagram of a circuit with a 6-V battery for *V* applied across a load *R*. (*b*) Schematic diagram of the circuit with values for *I* and *R* calculated by Ohm's law.

The practical fact is that high-voltage circuits usually do have a small value of current in electronic equipment. Otherwise, tremendous amounts of power would be necessary.

LOW VOLTAGE BUT HIGH CURRENT   At the opposite extreme, a low value of voltage in a very low resistance circuit can produce a very high current. A 6-V battery connected across a resistance of 0.01 Ω produces 600 A of current:

$$I = \frac{V}{R}$$

$$= \frac{6 \text{ V}}{0.01 \text{ } \Omega}$$

$$I = 600 \text{ A}$$

LESS I WITH MORE R   Note the values of I in the following two examples also:

Example

EXAMPLE 1   A heater with a resistance of 8 Ω is connected across the 120-V power line. How much is the current I?

ANSWER $I = \dfrac{V}{R} = \dfrac{120 \text{ V}}{8 \text{ } \Omega}$

$I = 15$ A

EXAMPLE 2   A small light bulb with a resistance of 2400 Ω is connected across the same 120-V power line. How much is the current I?

ANSWER $I = \dfrac{V}{R} = \dfrac{120 \text{ V}}{2400 \text{ } \Omega}$

$I = 0.05$ A

Although both cases have the same 120 V applied, the current is much less in Example 2 because of the higher resistance.

To do a division problem like V/R in Example 2 on the calculator, punch in the number 120 for the numerator, then press the key ⊕ for division before punching in 2400 for the denominator. Finally, press the ⊜ key for the answer of 0.05 on the display. The numerator must be punched in first.

TYPICAL V AND I   Transistors and integrated circuits generally operate with a dc supply of 5, 6, 9, 12, 15, 24, or 50 V. The current is usually in millionths or thousandths of one ampere up to about 5 A.

TEST-POINT QUESTION 3-1

Answers at end of chapter.
  a. Calculate I for 24 V applied across 8 Ω.
  b. Calculate I for 12 V applied across 8 Ω.
  c. Calculate I for 24 V applied across 12 Ω.
  d. Calculate I for 6 V applied across 1 Ω.

3-2 THE VOLTAGE $V = IR$

Referring back to Fig. 3-2, the voltage across R must be the same as the source V because the resistance is connected directly across the battery. The numerical value of this V is equal to the product $I \times R$. For instance, the IR voltage in Fig. 3-2 is 2 A $\times$ 3 Ω, which equals the 6 V of the applied voltage. The formula is

▶ $V = IR$ (3-2)

With I in ampere units and R in ohms, their product V is in volts. Actually, this must be so because the I value equal to V/R is the amount that allows the IR product to be the same as the voltage across R.

To do a multiplication problem like $I \times R$ for this example on the calculator, punch in the factor 2, then press the $\otimes$ key for multiplication before punching in 3 for the other factor. Finally, press the $\ominus$ key for the answer of 6 on the display. The factors can be multiplied in any order.

Besides the numerical calculations possible with the IR formula, it is useful to consider that the IR product means voltage. Whenever there is current through a resistance, it must have a potential difference across its two ends equal to the IR product. If there were no potential difference, no electrons could flow to produce the current.

TEST-POINT QUESTION 3-2

Answers at end of chapter.
  a. Calculate V for 0.002 A through 1000 Ω.
  b. Calculate V for 0.004 A through 1000 Ω.
  c. Calculate V for 0.002 A through 2000 Ω.

3-3 THE RESISTANCE $R = V/I$

As the third and final version of Ohm's law, the three factors V, I, and R are related by the formula

▶ $R = \dfrac{V}{I}$ (3-3)

In Fig. 3-2, R is 3 Ω because 6 V applied across the resistance produces 2 A through it. Whenever V and I are known, the resistance can be calculated as the voltage across R divided by the current through it.

FIG. 3-3 The resistance R of any component is its V/I ratio.

Physically, a resistance can be considered as some material with elements having an atomic structure that allows free electrons to drift through it with more or less force applied. Electrically, though, a more practical way of considering resistance is simply as a V/I ratio. Anything that allows 1 A of current with 10 V applied has a resistance of 10 Ω. This V/I ratio of 10 Ω is its characteristic. If the voltage is doubled to 20 V, the current will also double to 2 A, providing the same V/I ratio of a 10-Ω resistance.

Furthermore, we do not need to know the physical construction of a resistance to analyze its effect in a circuit, so long as we know its V/I ratio. This idea is illustrated in Fig. 3-3. Here, a box with some unknown material in it is connected into a circuit where we can measure the 12 V applied across the box and the 3 A of current through it. The resistance is 12 V/3 A, or 4 Ω. There may be liquid, gas, metal, powder, or any other material in the box, but electrically it is just a 4-Ω resistance because its V/I ratio is 4.

TEST-POINT QUESTION 3-3

Answers at end of chapter.
a. Calculate R for 12 V with 0.003 A.
b. Calculate R for 12 V with 0.006 A.
c. Calculate R for 12 V with 0.001 A.

3-4 PRACTICAL UNITS

The three forms of Ohm's law can be used to define the practical units of current, potential difference, and resistance as follows:

▶
$$1 \text{ ampere} = \frac{1 \text{ volt}}{1 \text{ ohm}}$$

$$1 \text{ volt} = 1 \text{ ampere} \times 1 \text{ ohm}$$

$$1 \text{ ohm} = \frac{1 \text{ volt}}{1 \text{ ampere}}$$

One ampere is the amount of current through a one-ohm resistance that has one volt of potential difference applied across it.

One volt is the potential difference across a one-ohm resistance that has one ampere of current through it.

One ohm is the amount of opposition in a resistance that has a V/I ratio of 1, allowing one ampere of current with one volt applied.

In summary, the circle diagram in Fig. 3-4 for $V = IR$ can be helpful in using Ohm's law. Put your finger on the unknown quantity and the desired formula remains. The three possibilities are

Cover V and you have IR.
Cover I and you have V/R.
Cover R and you have V/I.

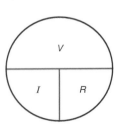

FIG. 3-4 A circle diagram to help in memorizing the Ohm's law formulas $V = IR$, $I = V/R$, and $R = V/I$. The V is always at the top.

Answers at end of chapter.

a. Calculate V for 0.007 A through 5000 Ω.
b. Calculate the amount of I for 12,000 V across 6,000,000 Ω.
c. Calculate R for 8 V with 0.004 A.

3-5 MULTIPLE UNITS

The basic units—ampere, volt, and ohm—are practical values in most electric power circuits, but in many electronics applications these units are either too small or too big. As examples, resistances can be a few million ohms, the output of a high-voltage supply in a television receiver is about 20,000 V, and current through tubes and transistors is generally thousandths or millionths of an ampere.

In such cases, it is helpful to use multiples of the basic units. These multiples are based on the decimal system of tens, hundreds, thousands, etc. The common conversions for V, I, and R are summarized at the end of this chapter, but a complete listing of all the prefixes is in App. A. Note that capital M is used for 10^6 to distinguish it from small m for 10^{-3}.*

Example

EXAMPLE 3 The I of 8 mA flows through a 5-kΩ R. How much is the IR voltage?

ANSWER $V = IR = 8 \times 10^{-3} \times 5 \times 10^3 = 8 \times 5$

$V = 40$ V

In general, milliamperes multiplied by kilohms results in volts for the answer, as 10^{-3} and 10^3 cancel.

EXAMPLE 4 How much current is produced by 60 V across 12 kΩ?

ANSWER $I = \dfrac{V}{R} = \dfrac{60}{12 \times 10^3} = 5 \times 10^{-3} = 5$ mA

Note that volts across kilohms produces milliamperes of current. Similarly, volts across megohms produces microamperes.

---

*The notations 10^6 and 10^{-3} are known as powers of 10. A detailed explanation of the uses and operations involving powers of 10 may be found in either B. Grob, *Mathematics for Basic Electronics*, or M. Schultz, *Problems in Basic Electronics*, Glencoe/McGraw-Hill, Columbus, Ohio.

In summary, common combinations to calculate the current I are

$$\frac{V}{k\Omega} = mA \quad \text{and} \quad \frac{V}{M\Omega} = \mu A$$

Also, common combinations to calculate IR voltage are

$$mA \times k\Omega = V$$
$$\mu A \times M\Omega = V$$

These relationships occur often in electronic circuits because the current is generally in units of milliamperes or microamperes. A useful relationship to remember is that 1 mA is equal to 1000 μA.

TEST-POINT QUESTION 3-5

Answers at end of chapter.
a. Change the following to basic units with powers of 10 instead of metric prefixes: 6 mA, 5 kΩ, and 3 μA.
b. Change the following powers of 10 to units with metric prefixes: 6×10^{-3} A, 5×10^3 Ω, and 3×10^{-6} A.
c. Which is larger, 2 mA or 20 μA?

3-6 THE LINEAR PROPORTION BETWEEN *V* AND *I*

The Ohm's law formula $I = V/R$ states that V and I are directly proportional for any one value of R. This relation between V and I can be analyzed by using a fixed resistance of 2 Ω for R_L, as in Fig. 3-5. Then when V is varied, the meter shows I values directly proportional to V. For instance, with 12 V, I equals 6 A; for 10 V, the current is 5 A; an 8-V potential difference produces 4 A.

All the values of V and I are listed in the table in Fig. 3-5*b* and plotted in the graph in Fig. 3-5*c*. The I values are one-half the V values because R is 2 Ω. However, I is zero with zero volts applied.

PLOTTING THE GRAPH   The voltage values for V are marked on the horizontal axis, called the *x axis* or *abscissa*. The current values I are on the vertical axis, called the *y axis* or *ordinate*.

Because the values for V and I depend on each other, they are variable factors. The independent variable here is V because we assign values of voltage and note the resulting current. Generally, the independent variable is plotted on the *x* axis, which is why the V values are shown here horizontally while the I values are on the ordinate.

The two scales need not be the same. The only requirement is that equal distances on each scale represent equal changes in magnitude. On the *x* axis here

Volts V	Ohms Ω	Amperes A
0	2	0
2	2	1
4	2	2
6	2	3
8	2	4
10	2	5
12	2	6

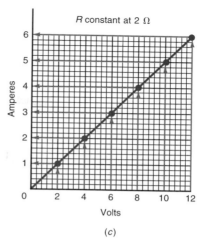

(a)   (b)   (c)

FIG. 3-5 Experiment to show that *I* increases in direct proportion to *V* with the same *R*. (*a*) Circuit with variable *V* but constant *R*. (*b*) Table of increasing *I* for higher *V*. (*c*) Graph of *V* and *I* values. This is a linear volt-ampere characteristic. It shows a direct proportion between *V* and *I*.

2-V steps are chosen, while the *y* axis has 1-A scale divisions. The zero point at the origin is the reference.

The plotted points in the graph show the values in the table. For instance, the lowest point is 2 V horizontally from the origin, and 1 A up. Similarly, the next point is at the intersection of the 4-V mark and the 2-A mark.

A line joining these plotted points includes all values of *I*, for any value of *V*, with *R* constant at 2 Ω. This also applies to values not listed in the table. For instance, if we take the value of 7 V, up to the straight line and over to the *I* axis, the graph shows 3.5 A for *I*.

VOLT-AMPERE CHARACTERISTIC The graph in Fig. 3-5*c* is called the volt-ampere characteristic of *R*. It shows how much current the resistor allows for different voltages. Multiple and submultiple units of *V* and *I* can be used, though. For transistors and tubes the units of *I* are often milliamperes or microamperes.

LINEAR RESISTANCE The straight-line graph in Fig. 3-5 shows that *R* is a linear resistor. A linear resistance has a constant value of ohms. Its *R* does not change with the applied voltage. Then *V* and *I* are directly proportional. Doubling the value of *V* from 4 to 8 V results in twice the current, from 2 to 4 A. Similarly, three or four times the value of *V* will produce three or four times *I*, for a proportional increase in current.

NONLINEAR RESISTANCE This type has a nonlinear volt-ampere characteristic. As an example, the resistance of the tungsten filament in a light bulb is nonlinear. The reason is that *R* increases with more current

ABOUT ELECTRONICS

The unit of measure for resistance (ohm) is named for German physicist Georg Simon Ohm. Ohm is also known for his development of Ohm's law: voltage = current × resistance.

as the filament becomes hotter. Increasing the applied voltage does produce more current, but I does not increase in the same proportion as the increase in V.

INVERSE RELATION BETWEEN I AND R Whether R is linear or not, the current I is less for more R, with the applied voltage constant. This is an inverse relation, meaning that I goes down as R goes up. Remember that in the formula $I = V/R$, the resistance is in the denominator. A higher value of R actually lowers the value of the complete fraction.

As an example, let V be constant at 1 V. Then I is equal to the fraction $1/R$. As R increases, the values of I decrease. For R of 2 Ω, I is ½ or 0.5 A. For a higher R of 10 Ω, I will be lower at ¹⁄₁₀ or 0.1 A.

TEST-POINT QUESTION 3-6

Answers at end of chapter.

Refer to the graph in Fig. 3-5c.
a. Are the values of I on the y or x axis?
b. Is this R linear or nonlinear?
c. If the voltage across a 5-Ω resistor increases from 10 V to 20 V, what happens to I?
d. The voltage across a 5-Ω resistor is 10 V. If R is doubled to 10 Ω, what happens to I?

3-7 ELECTRIC POWER

The unit of electric power is the *watt* (W), named after James Watt (1736–1819). One watt of power equals the work done in one second by one volt of potential difference in moving one coulomb of charge.

Remember that one coulomb per second is an ampere. Therefore power in watts equals the product of volts times amperes.

▶ Power in watts = volts × amperes
$$P = V \times I \tag{3-4}$$

When a 6-V battery produces 2 A in a circuit, for example, the battery is generating 12 W of power.

The power formula can be used in three ways:

▶ $P = V \times I$

$I = P \div V$ or $\dfrac{P}{V}$

$V = P \div I$ or $\dfrac{P}{I}$

Which formula to use depends on whether you want to calculate P, I, or V. Note the following examples:

Example

EXAMPLE 5 A toaster takes 10 A from the 120-V power line. How much power is used?

ANSWER $P = V \times I = 120 \text{ V} \times 10 \text{ A}$
$$P = 1200 \text{ W}$$

EXAMPLE 6 How much current flows in the filament of a 300-W bulb connected to the 120-V power line?

ANSWER $I = \dfrac{P}{V} = \dfrac{300 \text{ W}}{120 \text{ V}}$
$$I = 2.5 \text{ A}$$

EXAMPLE 7 How much current flows in the filament of a 60-W bulb connected to the 120-V power line?

ANSWER $I = \dfrac{P}{V} = \dfrac{60 \text{ W}}{120 \text{ V}}$
$$I = 0.5 \text{ A}$$

Note that the lower-wattage bulb uses less current.

WORK AND POWER Work and energy are essentially the same with identical units. Power is different, however, because it is the time rate of doing work.

As an example of work, if you move 100 lb a distance of 10 ft, the work is 100 lb × 10 ft or 1000 ft · lb, regardless of how fast or how slowly the work is done. Note that the unit of work is foot-pounds, without any reference to time.

However, power equals the work divided by the time it takes to do the work. If it takes 1 s, the power in this example is 1000 ft · lb/s; if the work takes 2 s, the power is 1000 ft · lb in 2 s, or 500 ft · lb/s.

Similarly, electric power is the time rate at which charge is forced to move by voltage. This is why the power in watts is the product of volts and amperes. The voltage states the amount of work per unit of charge; the current value includes the time rate at which the charge is moved.

WATTS AND HORSEPOWER UNITS A further example of how electric power corresponds to mechanical power is the fact that

▶ 746 W = 1 hp = 550 ft · lb/s

This relation can be remembered more easily as 1 hp equals approximately ¾ kilowatt (kW). One kilowatt = 1000 W.

PRACTICAL UNITS OF POWER AND WORK Starting with the watt, we can develop several other important units. The fundamental

ABOUT ELECTRONICS

The SI unit of measure for electrical energy is the joule, named for English physicist James Prescott Joule (1 J is equal to 1 volt-coulomb).

principle to remember is that power is the time rate of doing work, while work is power used during a period of time. The formulas are

$$\text{Power} = \frac{\text{work}}{\text{time}} \qquad \text{(3-5)}$$

and

$$\text{Work} = \text{power} \times \text{time} \qquad \text{(3-6)}$$

With the watt unit for power, one watt used during one second equals the work of one joule. Or one watt is one joule per second. Therefore, 1 W = 1 J/s. The joule is a basic practical unit of work or energy.

To summarize these practical definitions,

> 1 joule = 1 watt · second
> 1 watt = 1 joule/second

In terms of charge and current,

> 1 joule = 1 volt · coulomb
> 1 watt = 1 volt · ampere

Remember that the ampere unit includes time in the denominator, since the formula is 1 ampere = 1 coulomb/second.

ELECTRON VOLT (eV) This unit of work can be used for an individual electron, rather than the large quantity of electrons in a coulomb. An electron is charge, while the volt is potential difference. Therefore, 1 eV is the amount of work required to move an electron between two points that have a potential difference of one volt.

The number of electrons in one coulomb for the joule unit equals 6.25×10^{18}. Also, the work of one joule is a volt-coulomb. Therefore, the number of electron volts equal to one joule must be 6.25×10^{18}. As a formula,

> $1 \text{ J} = 6.25 \times 10^{18} \text{ eV}$

Either the electron volt or joule unit of work is the product of charge times voltage, but the watt unit of power is the product of voltage times current. The division by time to convert work to power corresponds to the division by time that converts charge to current.

KILOWATTHOURS This is a unit commonly used for large amounts of electrical work or energy. The amount is calculated simply as the product of the power in kilowatts multiplied by the time in hours during which the power is used. As an example, if a light bulb uses 300 W or 0.3 kW for 4 hours (h), the amount of energy is 0.3×4, which equals 1.2 kWh.

We pay for electricity in kilowatthours of energy. The power-line voltage is constant at 120 V. However, more appliances and light bulbs require more current because they all add in the main line to increase the power.

Suppose the total load current in the main line equals 20 A. Then the power in watts from the 120-V line is

$$P = 120 \text{ V} \times 20 \text{ A}$$
$$P = 2400 \text{ W or } 2.4 \text{ kW}$$

If this power is used for 5 h, then the energy or work supplied equals $2.4 \times 5 = 12$ kWh. If the cost of electricity is 6 cents/kWh, then 12 kWh of electricity will cost $0.06 \times 12 = 0.72$ or 72 cents. This charge is for a 20-A load current from the 120-V line during the time of 5 h.

TEST-POINT QUESTION 3-7

Answers at end of chapter.
a. An electric heater takes 15 A from the 120-V power line. Calculate the amount of power used.
b. How much is the load current for a 100-W bulb connected to the 120-V power line?
c. How many watts is the power of 200 J/s equal to?
d. How much will it cost to operate a 300-W light bulb for 48 h if the cost of electricity is 7 cents/kWh?

3-8 POWER DISSIPATION IN RESISTANCE

When current flows in a resistance, heat is produced because friction between the moving free electrons and the atoms obstructs the path of electron flow. The heat is evidence that power is used in producing current. This is how a fuse opens, as heat resulting from excessive current melts the metal link in the fuse.

The power is generated by the source of applied voltage and consumed in the resistance in the form of heat. As much power as the resistance dissipates in heat must be supplied by the voltage source; otherwise, it cannot maintain the potential difference required to produce the current.

The correspondence between electric power and heat is indicated by the fact that 1 W used during the time of 1 s is equivalent to 0.24 calorie of heat energy. The electric energy converted to heat is considered to be dissipated or used up because the calories of heat cannot be returned to the circuit as electric energy.

Since power is dissipated in the resistance of a circuit, it is convenient to express the power in terms of the resistance R. The formula $P = V \times I$ can be rearranged as follows:

Substituting IR for V,

▶ $$P = V \times I = IR \times I$$
$$P = I^2R \tag{3-7}$$

This is a common form for the power formula because of the heat produced by current in a resistance.

For another form, substitute V/R for I. Then

$$P = V \times I = V \times \frac{V}{R}$$

$$P = \frac{V^2}{R} \tag{3-8}$$

In all the formulas, V is the voltage across R in ohms, producing the current I in amperes, for power in watts.

Any one of the three formulas (3-4), (3-7), and (3-8) can be used to calculate the power dissipated in a resistance. The one to be used is just a matter of convenience, depending on which factors are known.

In Fig. 3-6, for example, the power dissipated with 2 A through the resistance and 12 V across it is $2 \times 12 = 24$ W.

FIG. 3-6 Calculating the electric power in a circuit as $P = V \times I$, $P = I^2R$, or $P = V^2/R$.

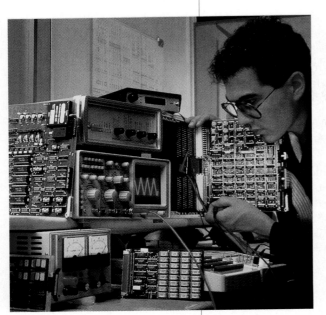

Or, calculating in terms of just the current and resistance, the power is the product of 2 squared, or 4, times 6, which equals 24 W.

Using the voltage and resistance, the power can be calculated as 12 squared, or 144, divided by 6, which also equals 24 W.

No matter which formula is used, 24 W of power is dissipated, in the form of heat. This amount of power must be generated continuously by the battery in order to maintain the potential difference of 12 V that produces the 2-A current against the opposition of 6 Ω.

In some applications, the electric power dissipation is desirable because the component must produce heat in order to do its job. For instance, a 600-W toaster must dissipate this amount of power to produce the necessary amount of heat. Similarly, a 300-W light bulb must dissipate this power to make the filament white-hot so that it will have the incandescent glow that furnishes the light. In other applications, however, the heat may be just an undesirable byproduct of the need to provide current through the resistance in a circuit. In any case, though, whenever there is current I in a resistance R, it dissipates the amount of power P equal to I^2R.

Example

EXAMPLE 8   Calculate the power in a circuit where the source of 100 V produces 2 A in a 50-Ω R.

ANSWER $P = I^2R = 2 \times 2 \times 50 = 4 \times 50$

$P = 200$ W

This means the source delivers 200 W of power to the resistance while the resistance dissipates 200 W in the form of heat.

EXAMPLE 9   Calculate the power in a circuit where the same source of 100 V produces 4 A in a 25-Ω R.

ANSWER $P = I^2R = 4^2 \times 25 = 16 \times 25$

$P = 400$ W

Note the higher power in Example 9 because of more I, even though R is less than in Example 8.

To use the calculator for a problem like Example 8 where I must be squared for $I^2 \times R$, use the following procedure:

Punch in the value of 2 for I.
Press the key marked (x^2) for the square of 2 equal to 4 on the display.
Next press the multiplication $(\times)$ key.
Punch in the value of 50 for R.
Finally, press the $(=)$ key for the answer of 200 on the display.

Be sure to square only the I value before multiplying by the R value.

Components that utilize the power dissipated in their resistance, such as light bulbs and toasters, are generally rated in terms of power. The power rating is given at normal applied voltage, which is usually the 120 V of the power line. For instance, a 600-W 120-V toaster has this rating because it dissipates 600 W in the resistance of the heating element when connected across 120 V.

Note this interesting point about the power relations. The lower the source voltage, the higher the current required for the same power. The reason is that $P = V \times I$. For instance, an electric heater rated at 240 W from the 120-V power line takes 240 W/120 V = 2 A of current from the source. However, the same 240 W from a 12-V source, as in a car or boat, requires 240 W/12 V = 20 A. More current must be supplied by a source with lower voltage, to provide a specified amount of power.

TEST-POINT QUESTION 3-8

Answers at end of chapter.

a. Current I is 2 A in a 5-Ω R. Calculate P.
b. Voltage V is 10 V across a 5-Ω R. Calculate P.
c. Resistance R has 10 V with 2 A. Calculate the values for P and R.

3-9 POWER FORMULAS

In order to calculate I or R for components rated in terms of power at a specified voltage, it may be convenient to use the power formulas in different forms. There are three basic power formulas, but each can be in three forms for nine combinations, as follows:

▶

$$P = VI \qquad P = I^2R \qquad P = \frac{V^2}{R}$$

$$\text{or} \quad I = \frac{P}{V} \quad \text{or} \quad R = \frac{P}{I^2} \quad \text{or} \quad R = \frac{V^2}{P}$$

$$\text{or} \quad V = \frac{P}{I} \quad \text{or} \quad I = \sqrt{\frac{P}{R}} \quad \text{or} \quad V = \sqrt{PR}$$

Example

EXAMPLE 10   How much current is needed for a 600-W 120-V toaster?

ANSWER $I = \dfrac{P}{V} = \dfrac{600}{120}$

$I = 5$ A

EXAMPLE 11   How much is the resistance of a 600-W 120-V toaster?

ANSWER $R = \dfrac{V^2}{P} = \dfrac{(120)^2}{600} = \dfrac{14,400}{600}$

$R = 24\ \Omega$

EXAMPLE 12   How much current is needed for a 24-Ω R that dissipates 600 W?

ANSWER $I = \sqrt{\dfrac{P}{R}} = \sqrt{\dfrac{600\ \text{W}}{24\ \Omega}} = \sqrt{25}$

$I = 5$ A

Note that all these formulas are based on Ohm's law $V = IR$ and the power formula $P = VI$. The following example with a 300-W bulb also illustrates this idea. The bulb is connected across the 120-V line. Its 300-W filament requires current of 2.5 A, equal to P/V. These calculations are

$$I = \frac{P}{V} = \frac{300\ \text{W}}{120\ \text{V}} = 2.5\ \text{A}$$

The proof is that the VI product then is 120×2.5, which equals 300 W.

3-12 OPEN-CIRCUIT AND SHORT-CIRCUIT TROUBLES

Ohm's law is useful for calculating I, V, and R in a closed circuit with normal values. However, an open circuit or a short circuit causes troubles that can be summarized as follows: An open circuit has zero I because R is infinitely high. It does not matter how much the V is. A short circuit has zero R, which causes excessively high I in the short-circuit path because of no resistance. These opposite troubles are compared in Figs. 3-9 and 3-10.

In Fig. 3-9a, the circuit is normal with I of 2 A produced by 10 V applied across R of 5 Ω. However, the resistor is shown open in Fig. 3-9b. Then the path for current has infinitely high resistance and there is no current in any part of the circuit. The trouble can be caused by an internal open in the resistor or a break in the wire conductors.

In Fig. 3-10a, the same normal circuit is shown with I of 2 A. In Fig. 3-10b, however, there is a short circuit path across R with zero resistance. The result is excessively high current in the short-circuit path, including the wire conductors. It may be surprising, but there is no current in the resistor itself because all the current is in the zero-resistance path around it.

Theoretically, the amount of current could be infinitely high with no R, but the voltage source can only supply a limited amount of I before it loses its ability to provide voltage output. Also, the wire conductors may become hot enough to burn open, which would open the circuit. Also, if there is any fuse in the circuit, it will open because of the excessive current produced by the short circuit.

It should be noted that the resistor itself is not likely to develop a short circuit, because of the nature of its construction. However, the wire conductors may touch or some other component in a circuit connected across the resistor may become short-circuited.

(a)

(b)

FIG. 3-9   Effect of an open circuit. (a) Normal circuit with current of 2 A for 10 V across 5 Ω. (b) Open circuit with no current and infinitely high resistance.

FIG. 3-10   Effect of a short circuit. (a) Normal circuit with current of 2 A for 10 V across 5 Ω. (b) Short circuit with zero resistance and excessively high current.

TEST-POINT QUESTION 3-12

Answers at end of chapter.

Answer True or False.

a. An open circuit has a zero current.

b. A short circuit has excessive current.

c. An open circuit and a short circuit have opposite effects on resistance and current.

3   SUMMARY AND REVIEW

- The three forms of Ohm's law are $I = V/R$, $V = IR$, and $R = V/I$.
- One ampere is the amount of current produced by one volt of potential difference across one ohm of resistance. This current of 1 A is the same as 1 C/s.
- With R constant, the amount of I increases in direct proportion as V increases. This linear relation between V and I is shown by the graph in Fig. 3-5.
- With V constant, the current I decreases as R increases. This is an inverse relation.
- Power is the time rate of doing work or using energy. The unit is the watt. One watt equals $1\ \text{V} \times 1\ \text{A}$. Also, watts = joules per second.
- The unit of work or energy is the joule. One joule equals $1\ \text{W} \times 1\ \text{s}$.
- The most common multiples and submultiples of the practical units are listed in Table 3-1.

TABLE 3-1   CONVERSION FACTORS

PREFIX	SYMBOL	RELATION TO BASIC UNIT	EXAMPLES
mega	M	1,000,000 or 1×10^6	5 MΩ (megohms) = 5,000,000 ohms = 5×10^6 ohms
kilo	k	1000 or 1×10^3	18 kV (kilovolts) = 18,000 volts = 18×10^3 volts
milli	m	0.001 or 1×10^{-3}	48 mA (milliamperes) = 48×10^{-3} ampere = 0.048 ampere
micro	μ	0.000 001 or 1×10^{-6}	15 μV (microvolts) = 15×10^{-6} volt = 0.000 015 volt

- Voltage applied across your body can produce a dangerous electric shock. Whenever possible, shut off the power and make resistance tests. If the power must be on, use only one hand. Do not let the other hand rest on a conductor.
- Table 3-2 summarizes the practical units used with Ohm's law.

TABLE 3-2   PRACTICAL UNITS OF ELECTRICITY

COULOMB	AMPERE	VOLT	WATT	OHM	SIEMENS
6.25×10^{18} electrons	$\dfrac{\text{coulomb}}{\text{second}}$	$\dfrac{\text{joule}}{\text{coulomb}}$	$\dfrac{\text{joule}}{\text{second}}$	$\dfrac{\text{volt}}{\text{ampere}}$	$\dfrac{\text{ampere}}{\text{volt}}$

• An open circuit has no current and infinitely high R. A short circuit has zero resistance and excessively high current.

ANSWERS AT BACK OF BOOK.

Fill in the missing answers.

1. With 10 V across 5-Ω R, the current I is _____ A.
2. When 10 V produces 2.5 A, R is _____ Ω.
3. With 8 A through a 2-Ω R, the IR voltage is _____ V.
4. The resistance of 500,000 Ω is _____ MΩ.
5. With 10 V across 5000-Ω R, the current I is _____ mA.
6. The power of 50 W = 2 A × _____ V.
7. The energy of 50 J = 2 C × _____ V.
8. The current drawn from the 120-V power line by a 1200-W toaster = _____ A.
9. The current of 400 μA = _____ mA.
10. With 12 V across a 2-Ω R, its power dissipation = _____ W.
11. A circuit has a 4-A I. If V is doubled and R is the same, I = _____ A.
12. A circuit has a 4-A I. If R is doubled and V is the same, I = _____ A.
13. A television receiver using 240 W from the 120-V power line draws current I = _____ A.
14. The rated current for a 100-W 120-V bulb = _____ A.
15. The resistance of the bulb in question 14 is _____ Ω.
16. The energy of 12.5 × 10^{18} eV = _____ J.
17. The current of 1200 mA = _____ A.
18. In an amplifier, the load resistor R_L of 5 kΩ has 15 V across it. Through R_L, then, the current = _____ mA.
19. In a transistor circuit, a 1-kΩ resistor R_1 has 200 μA through it. Across R_1, then, its voltage = _____ V.
20. In a transistor circuit, a 50-kΩ resistor R_2 has 6 V across it. Through R_2, then, its current = _____ mA.
21. A resistor is to be connected across a 45-V battery to provide 1 mA of current. The required resistance with a suitable wattage rating is (*a*) 4.5 Ω 1 W; (*b*) 45 Ω 10 W; (*c*) 450 Ω 2 W; (*d*) 45,000 Ω ¼ W.

1. State the three forms of Ohm's law relating V, I, and R.
2. (**a**) Why does higher applied voltage with the same resistance result in more current? (**b**) Why does more resistance with the same applied voltage result in less current?

3. Calculate the resistance of a 300-W bulb connected across the 120-V power line, using two different methods to arrive at the same answer.

4. State which unit in each of the following pairs is larger: (a) volt or kilovolt; (b) ampere or milliampere; (c) ohm or megohm; (d) volt or microvolt; (e) siemens or microsiemens; (f) electron volt or joule; (g) watt or kilowatt; (h) kilowatthour or joule; (i) volt or millivolt; (j) megohm or kilohm.

5. State two safety precautions to follow when working on electric circuits.

6. Referring back to the resistor shown in Fig. 1-11 in Chap. 1, suppose that it is not marked. How could you determine its resistance by Ohm's law? Show your calculations that result in the V/I ratio of 600 Ω. However, do not exceed the power rating of 10 W.

7. Give three formulas for electric power.

8. What is the difference between work and power? Give two units for each.

9. Prove that 1 kWh is equal to 3.6×10^6 J.

10. Give the metric prefixes for 10^{-6}, 10^{-3}, 10^3, and 10^6.

11. Which two units in Table 3-2 are reciprocals of each other?

12. A circuit has a constant R of 5000 Ω, while V is varied from 0 to 50 V in 10-V steps. Make a table listing the values of I for each value of V. Then draw a graph plotting these values of milliamperes vs. volts. (This graph should be similar to Fig. 3-5c.)

13. Give the voltage and power rating for at least two types of electrical equipment.

14. Which uses more current from the 120-V power line, a 600-W toaster or a 200-W television receiver?

15. Refer to the two resistors in series with each other in Fig. 4-1 in Chapter 4. How much would you guess is the current through R_2?

16. Consider the two resistors R_1 and R_2 shown before in Fig. 3-7. Would you say they are in one series path or separate parallel paths?

17. Give a definition for a short circuit and for an open circuit.

18. Compare the R of zero ohms and infinite ohms.

19. Derive the formula $P = I^2R$ from $P = IV$ by using an Ohm's-law formula.

20. Give two safety factors to consider for preventing an electric shock.

PROBLEMS

ANSWERS TO ODD-NUMBERED PROBLEMS AT BACK OF BOOK.

1. A 15-V dc source is connected across a 1-kΩ resistance. (a) Draw a schematic diagram. (b) Calculate the current I through the resistance. (c) How much current flows through the voltage source? (d) If the voltage of the source is doubled, how much is the current I in the circuit?

2. A 12-V battery is connected across a 3-Ω resistance. (a) Draw a schematic diagram. (b) Calculate the current I in the circuit. (c) How much power is dissipated in the resistance? (d) If the resistance is doubled to 6 Ω, how much power is dissipated by R?

3. A 240-Ω resistor is dissipating 5.4 W. Calculate: (a) the voltage across the resistor; (b) the current through the resistor.

4. Convert the following units: (a) 20 mA to amperes; (b) 3500 V to kilovolts; (c) 0.4 A to milliamperes; (d) 1.5 mA to microamperes; (e) 47,000 Ω to kilohms; (f) 2.2 MΩ to kilohms; (g) 2500 μA to milliamperes; (h) 16 kV to volts.

5. A current of 2 A flows through a 12-Ω resistance connected across a battery. (a) How much is the battery voltage? (b) How much power is dissipated by the resistance? (c) How much power is supplied by the battery?

6. A 560-kΩ resistor has a current of 30 μA. (a) How much voltage is across the resistor? (b) How much power is dissipated by the resistor?

7. Calculate the current I, in ampere (A) units, for each of the following examples: (a) 66 V across 220 kΩ; (b) 15 mV across 3 kΩ; (c) 24 V across 120 Ω; (d) 3 V across 10 kΩ; (e) 18 V across 18 kΩ; (f) 15 kV across 1 MΩ.

8. Calculate the IR voltage drop for each of the following examples: (a) 2 mA through 1 kΩ; (b) 60 μA through 120 kΩ; (c) 250 mA through 10 kΩ; (d) 330 μA through 2.2 MΩ; (e) 20 mA through 6.8 kΩ; (f) 0.4 mA through 12 kΩ.

9. Calculate the resistance R, in ohms, for each of the following examples: (a) 1 mA drawn from a 12-V source; (b) 4 mA drawn from a 15-V source; (c) 150 mW dissipated with 36 V applied; (d) 16.2 W dissipated with a current of 30 mA.

10. A 4-Ω resistor dissipates 16 W of power. (a) How much voltage is across the load? (b) How much current is flowing through the load?

11. A 1000-ft length of wire has a conductance G of 0.4 S. If the wire is carrying a current I of 10 A, calculate: (a) the resistance of the wire; (b) the IR voltage drop across the wire; (c) the power dissipated by the length of the wire.

12. Refer to Fig. 3-11. Draw a graph of the I and V values if (a) R = 2.5 Ω; (b) R = 5 Ω; (c) R = 10 Ω. In each case, the voltage source is to be varied in 5-V steps from 0 to 30 V.

13. Refer to Fig. 3-12. Draw a graph of the I and R values when R is varied in 2-Ω steps from 2 to 12 Ω. (V is constant at 12 V.)

FIG. 3-11   Circuit diagram for Prob. 12.

FIG. 3-12   Circuit diagram for Prob. 13.

14. How much will it cost to operate a 1500-W quartz heater for 36 h if the cost of electricity is 7 cents/kWh?

15. Calculate the hot resistance of a 60-W light bulb connected to the 120-V power line.

16. What is the maximum voltage that can be applied across a ½-W 10-kΩ resistor without exceeding its power dissipation rating?

17. What is the maximum current that can be allowed to flow through a 680-Ω ¼-W resistor without exceeding its power dissipation rating?

18. A 50-Ω load dissipates 100 W of power. Calculate: (a) the voltage across the load; (b) the current through the load.

19. How much current is drawn by a 2-W electric clock connected to the 120-V power line?
20. A 2.2-kΩ resistor is connected across a 9-V dc source. How much power is dissipated by the resistance?
21. A 1.8-kΩ resistor has a current of 25 mA. How much power is dissipated by the resistor?
22. What is the resistance of a 120-V 30-W soldering iron?
23. Determine the resistance and wattage ratings of a resistor to meet the following requirements: 5-V *IR* drop with a current *I* of 25 mA. When choosing the wattage rating, use a safety factor of 2.
24. How much current is drawn by a 6-W 12-V lamp?
25. What value of resistance dissipates 250 mW of power when its current equals 50 mA?

CRITICAL THINKING

1. The percent efficiency of a motor can be calculated as

$$\% \text{ efficiency} = \frac{\text{power out}}{\text{power in}} \times 100$$

where power out represents horsepower (hp). Calculate the current drawn by a 5-hp 240-V motor that is 72 percent efficient.

2. A ½-hp, 120-V motor draws 4.67 A when it is running. Calculate the motor's efficiency.

3. A ¾-hp motor with an efficiency of 75 percent runs 20 percent of the time over a 30-day period. If the cost of electricity is 7 cents/kwh, how much will it cost the user?

4. An appliance uses 14.4×10^6 J of energy for 1 day. How much will this cost the user if the cost of electricity is 6.5 cents/kwh?

5. A certain 1-kΩ resistor has a power rating of ½ W for temperatures up to 70°C. Above 70°C, however, the power rating must be reduced by a factor of 6.25 mW/°C. Calculate the maximum current that the resistor can allow at 120°C without exceeding its power dissipation rating at this temperature.

3-1   **a.** 3 A
      b. 1.5 A
      c. 2 A
      d. 6 A

3-2   **a.** 2 V
      b. 4 V
      c. 4 V

3-3   **a.** 4000 Ω
      b. 2000 Ω
      c. 12,000 Ω

3-4   **a.** 35 V
      b. 0.002 A
      c. 2000 Ω

3-5   **a.** See Prob. **b**
      b. See Prob. **a**
      c. 2 mA

3-6   **a.** *y* axis
      b. linear
      c. *I* doubles
      d. *I* is halved

3-7   **a.** 1.8 kW
      b. 0.83 A
      c. 200 W
      d. $1.01 (approx.)

3-8   **a.** 20 W
      b. 20 W
      c. 20 W and 5 Ω

3-9   **a.** 144 Ω
      b. 50 W
      c. 8 W

3-10   **a.** 1 W
       b. 4 mW
       c. 10 W

3-11   **a.** T
       b. T

3-12   **a.** T
       b. T
       c. T

CHAPTER 4

SERIES CIRCUITS

If two or more components are used with the voltage source, different types of circuits are possible. When the components are connected with only one path for current through all of them, the result is a series circuit. The series path is made by connecting an end of each component to an end of the next. Which end comes first does not matter with resistors. Since there is only one path for electron flow, the current I must be the same in all the series components.

The purpose of a series circuit is to connect different components that need the same current. However, the individual voltages across each of the series components can have different values. These principles of series connections apply to dc and ac circuits.

CHAPTER OBJECTIVES

Upon completion of this chapter, you should be able to:

• *Explain* why the current is the same in all parts of a series circuit.
• *Determine* the total resistance of a series circuit.
• *Determine* the individual resistor voltage drops in a series circuit.
• *Determine* the polarity of a resistor's *IR* voltage drop.
• *Calculate* the total power dissipated in a series circuit.
• *Determine* the net voltage of series-aiding and series-opposing voltage sources.
• *Solve* for the voltage, current, resistance, and power in a series circuit having random unknowns.
• *Describe* the effect of an open in a series circuit.
• *Describe* how series-connected switches can be used to describe the AND logic function.

IMPORTANT TERMS IN THIS CHAPTER

aiding voltages	open circuit	series string
AND gate	opposing voltages	total power
applied voltage	positive potential	total resistance
chassis ground	potential difference	voltage drop
IR drop	proportional parts	voltage polarity
negative potential	series components	

TOPICS COVERED IN THIS CHAPTER

4-1 WHY *I* IS THE SAME IN ALL PARTS OF A SERIES CIRCUIT

An electric current is a movement of charges between two points, produced by the applied voltage. When components are connected in successive order as in Fig. 4-1, they form a series circuit. The resistors R_1 and R_2 are in series with each other and the battery.

FIG. 4-1   A series circuit. (*a*) Pictorial wiring diagram. (*b*) Schematic diagram.

In Fig. 4-2*a*, the battery supplies the potential difference that forces electrons to drift from the negative terminal at A, toward B, through the connecting wires and resistances R_1, R_2, and R_3, back to the positive battery terminal at J. At the negative battery terminal, its negative charge repels electrons. Therefore, free electrons in the atoms of the wire at this terminal are repelled from A toward B. Similarly, free electrons at point B can then repel adjacent electrons, producing an electron drift toward C and away from the negative battery terminal.

At the same time, the positive charge of the positive battery terminal attracts free electrons, causing electrons to drift toward I and J. As a result, the free electrons in R_1, R_2, and R_3 are forced to drift toward the positive terminal.

The positive terminal of the battery attracts electrons just as much as the negative side of the battery repels electrons. Therefore, the motion of free electrons in the circuit starts at the same time and at the same speed in all parts of the circuit.

The electrons returning to the positive battery terminal are not the same electrons as those leaving the negative terminal. Free electrons in the wire are forced to move to the positive terminal because of the potential difference of the battery.

The free electrons moving away from one point are continuously replaced by free electrons flowing from an adjacent point in the series circuit. All electrons have the same speed as those leaving the battery. In all parts of the circuit, therefore, the electron drift is the same, with an equal number of electrons moving at one time with the same speed. That is why the current is the same in all parts of the series circuit.

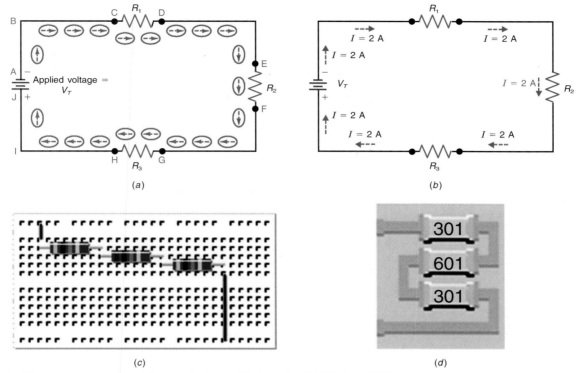

FIG. 4-2 There is only one current through R_1, R_2, and R_3 in series. (*a*) Electron drift is the same in all parts of a series circuit. (*b*) Current I is the same at all points in a series circuit. (*c*) Series circuit assembled on a lab prototype board, using axial-lead resistors. (*d*) Series circuit using surface-mount resistors assembled on a printed circuit board.

In Fig. 4-2*b*, when the current is 2 A, for example, this is the value of the current through R_1, R_2, R_3, and the battery at the same instant. Not only is the amount of current the same throughout, but in all parts of a series circuit the current cannot differ in any way because there is just one current path for the entire circuit. Figure 4-2*c* shows how to assemble resistors on a lab prototype board to form a series circuit. Figure 4-2*d* shows a series circuit using surface-mount resistors assembled on a printed circuit board.

The order in which components are connected in series does not affect the current. In Fig. 4-3*b*, resistances R_1 and R_2 are connected in reverse order compared with Fig. 4-3*a*, but in both cases they are in series. The current through each is the same because there is only one path for the electron flow. Similarly,

FIG. 4-3 Examples of series connections: R_1 and R_2 are in series in both (*a*) and (*b*); also, R_3, R_4, and R_5 are in series in (*c*), (*d*), and (*e*).

R_3, R_4, and R_5 are in series and have the same current for the connections shown in Fig. 4-3c, d, and e. Furthermore, the resistances need not be equal.

The question of whether a component is first, second, or last in a series circuit has no meaning in terms of current. The reason is that I is the same amount at the same time in all the series components.

In fact, series components can be defined as those in the same current path. The path is from one side of the voltage source, through the series components, and back to the other side of the applied voltage. However, the series path must not have any point where the current can branch off to another path in parallel.

TEST-POINT QUESTION 4-1

Answers at end of chapter.
a. In Fig. 4-2b, name five parts that have the I of 2 A.
b. In Fig. 4-3e, when I in R_5 is 5 A, then I in R_3 is _____ A.
c. In Fig. 4-4b, how much is the I in R_2?

4-2 TOTAL R EQUALS THE SUM OF ALL SERIES RESISTANCES

When a series circuit is connected across a voltage source, as shown in Fig. 4-3, the free electrons forming the current must drift through all the series resistances. This path is the only way the electrons can return to the battery. With two or more resistances in the same current path, therefore, the total resistance across the voltage source is the opposition of all the resistances.

Specifically, the total resistance R_T of a series string is equal to the sum of the individual resistances. This rule is illustrated in Fig. 4-4. In Fig. 4-4b, 2 Ω is added in series with the 3 Ω of Fig. 4-4a, producing the total resistance of 5 Ω. The total opposition of R_1 and R_2 limiting the amount of current is the same as though a 5-Ω resistance were used, as shown in the equivalent circuit in Fig. 4-4c.

(a)   (b)   (c)

FIG. 4-4 Series resistances are added for the total R_T. (a) R_1 alone is 3 Ω. (b) R_1 and R_2 in series total 5 Ω. (c) The R_T of 5 Ω is the same as one resistance of 5 Ω between points A and B.

SERIES STRING A combination of series resistances is often called a *string*. The string resistance equals the sum of the individual resistances. For instance, R_1 and R_2 in Fig. 4-4 form a series string having the R_T of 5 Ω. A string can have two or more resistors.

By Ohm's law, the amount of current between two points in a circuit equals the potential difference divided by the resistance between these points. As the entire string is connected across the voltage source, the current equals the voltage applied across the entire string divided by the total series resistance of the string. Between points A and B in Fig. 4-4, for example, 10 V is applied across 5 Ω in Fig. 4-4*b* and *c* to produce 2 A. This current flows through R_1 and R_2 in one series path.

SERIES RESISTANCE FORMULA In summary, the total resistance of a series string equals the sum of the individual resistances. The formula is

▶ $R_T = R_1 + R_2 + R_3 + \cdots + \text{etc.}$ **(4-1)**

where R_T is the total resistance and R_1, R_2, and R_3 are individual series resistances.

This formula applies to any number of resistances, whether equal or not, as long as they are in the same series string. Note that R_T is the resistance to use in calculating the current in a series string. Then Ohm's law is

▶ $I = \dfrac{V_T}{R_T}$ **(4-2)**

where R_T is the sum of all the resistances, V_T is the voltage applied across the total resistance, and I is the current in all parts of the string.

Example

EXAMPLE 1 Two resistances R_1 and R_2 of 5 Ω each and R_3 of 10 Ω are in series. How much is R_T?

ANSWER $R_T = R_1 + R_2 + R_3 = 5 + 5 + 10$

$\qquad\quad R_T = 20\ \Omega$

EXAMPLE 2 With 80 V applied across the series string of Example 1, how much is the current in R_3?

ANSWER $I = \dfrac{V_T}{R_T} = \dfrac{80\ \text{V}}{20\ \Omega}$

$\qquad\quad I = 4\ \text{A}$

This 4-A current is the same in R_3, R_2, R_1, or any part of the series circuit.

Note that adding series resistance reduces the current. In Fig. 4-4a the 3-Ω R_1 allows 10 V to produce $3\frac{1}{3}$ A. However, I is reduced to 2 A when the 2-Ω R_2 is added for a total series resistance of 5 Ω opposing the 10-V source.

TEST-POINT QUESTION 4-2

Answers at end of chapter.
a. The applied voltage is 10 V and R_1 is 5 kΩ, calculate I.
b. A 2-kΩ R_2 and 3-kΩ R_3 are added in series with R_1. Calculate R_T.
c. Calculate I in R_1, R_2, and R_3.

4-3 SERIES *IR* VOLTAGE DROPS

With current I through a resistance, by Ohm's law the voltage across R is equal to $I \times R$. This rule is illustrated in Fig. 4-5 for a string of two resistors. In this circuit, I is 1 A because the applied V_T of 10 V is across the total R_T of 10 Ω, equal to the 4-Ω R_1 plus the 6-Ω R_2. Then I is 10 V/10 Ω = 1 A.

For each *IR* voltage in Fig. 4-5, multiply each R by the 1 A of current in the series circuit. Then

$$V_1 = IR_1 = 1 \text{ A} \times 4 \ \Omega = 4 \text{ V}$$
$$V_2 = IR_2 = 1 \text{ A} \times 6 \ \Omega = 6 \text{ V}$$

FIG. 4-5 An example of *IR* voltage drops V_1 and V_2 in a series circuit.

The V_1 of 4 V is across the 4 Ω of R_1. Also, the V_2 of 6 V is across the 6 Ω of R_2. The two voltages V_1 and V_2 are in series.

The *IR* voltage across each resistance is called an *IR drop*, or a *voltage drop*, because it reduces the potential difference available for the remaining resistance in the series circuit. Note that the symbols V_1 and V_2 are used for the voltage drops across each resistor to distinguish them from the source V_T applied across both resistors.

DID YOU KNOW?

You may soon be able to find out what items in your home are using the most electricity. Some California residents are testing a system that allows them to see on TV how much their next electric bill will be, which appliances are using the most electricity, and when rates will be lowest during the day.

In Fig. 4-5, the V_T of 10 V is applied across the total series resistance of R_1 and R_2. However, because of the IR voltage drop of 4 V across R_1, the potential difference across R_2 is only 6 V. The negative potential drops from 10 V at point A, with respect to the common reference point at C, down to 6 V at point B with reference to point C. The potential difference of 6 V between B and the reference at C is the voltage across R_2.

Similarly, there is an IR voltage drop of 6 V across R_2. The negative potential drops from 6 V at point B with respect to point C, down to 0 V at point C with respect to itself. The potential difference between any two points on the return line to the battery must be zero because the wire has practically zero resistance and therefore no IR drop.

It should be noted that voltage must be applied by a source of potential difference such as the battery in order to produce current and have an IR voltage drop across the resistance. With no current through a resistor, the resistor has resistance only. There is no potential difference across the two ends of the resistor.

The IR drop of 4 V across R_1 in Fig. 4-5 represents that part of the applied voltage used to produce the current of 1 A through the 4-Ω resistance. Also, across R_2 the IR drop is 6 V because this much voltage allows 1 A in the 6-Ω resistance. The IR drop is more in R_2 because more potential difference is necessary to produce the same amount of current in the higher resistance. For series circuits, in general, the highest R has the largest IR voltage drop across it.

ABOUT ELECTRONICS

Among his many contributions to modern society is Benjamin Franklin's development of the concept of two types of electrical energy: positive and negative. Franklin concluded that like charged items repel one another and opposite types attract.

TEST-POINT QUESTION 4-3

Answers at end of chapter.

Refer to Fig. 4-5.
a. How much is the sum of V_1 and V_2?
b. Calculate I as V_T/R_T.
c. How much is I through R_1?
d. How much is I through R_2?

4-4 THE SUM OF SERIES *IR* DROPS EQUALS THE APPLIED V_T

The whole applied voltage is equal to the sum of its parts. For example, in Fig. 4-5, the individual voltage drops of 4 V and 6 V total the same 10 V produced by the battery. This relation for series circuits is given by the formula

▶ $$V_T = V_1 + V_2 + V_3 + \cdots + \text{etc.} \qquad (4\text{-}3)$$

where V_T is the applied voltage and V_1, V_2, V_3, . . . are the individual *IR* drops.

Example

EXAMPLE 3   A voltage source produces an *IR* drop of 40 V across a 20-Ω R_1, 60 V across a 30-Ω R_2, and 180 V across a 90-Ω R_3, all in series. How much is the applied voltage?

ANSWER $V_T = 40 + 60 + 180$

$V_T = 280$ V

Note that the *IR* drop across each *R* results from the same current of 2 A, produced by 280 V across the total R_T of 140 Ω.

EXAMPLE 4   An applied V_T of 120 V produces *IR* drops across two series resistors R_1 and R_2. If the drop across R_1 is 40 V, how much is the voltage across R_2?

ANSWER   Since V_1 and V_2 must total 120 V, and one is 40 V, the other must be the difference between 120 and 40 V. Or

$V_2 = V_T - V_1 = 120 - 40$

$V_2 = 80$ V

It really is logical that V_T is the sum of the series *IR* drops. The current *I* is the same in all the series components. For this reason, the total of all the series voltages V_T is needed to produce the same *I* in the total of all the series resistances R_T as the *I* that each resistor voltage produces in its *R*.

A practical application of voltages in a series circuit is illustrated in Fig. 4-6. In this circuit, two 120-V light bulbs are operated from a 240-V line. If one bulb were connected to 240 V, the filament would burn out. With the two bulbs in series, however, each has 120 V for proper operation. The two 120-V drops across the bulbs in series add to equal the applied voltage of 240 V.

FIG. 4-6   Series string of two 120-V light bulbs operating from a 240-V line. (*a*) Wiring diagram. (*b*) Schematic diagram.

Answers at end of chapter.

a. A series circuit has *IR* drops of 10 V, 20 V, and 30 V. How much is the applied voltage V_T of the source?

b. A 100-V source is applied across R_1 and R_2 in series. If V_1 is 25 V, how much is V_2?

c. A 120-V source is applied across three equal resistances in series. How much is each *IR* drop?

4-5 POLARITY OF *IR* VOLTAGE DROPS

When an *IR* voltage drop exists across a resistance, one end must be either more positive or more negative than the other end. Otherwise, without a potential difference no current could flow through the resistance to produce the *IR* drop. The polarity of this *IR* voltage can be associated with the direction of *I* through *R*. In brief, electrons flow into the negative side of the *IR* voltage and out the positive side (Fig. 4-7*a*).

If we want to consider conventional current, with positive charges moving in the opposite direction from electron flow, the rule is reversed for the positive charges. See Fig. 4-7*b*. Here the positive charges for *I* are moving into the positive side of the *IR* voltage.

However, for either electron flow or conventional current the actual polarity of the *IR* drop is the same. In both *a* and *b* of Fig. 4-7, the top end of *R* in the diagrams is negative since this is the negative terminal of the source producing the current. After all, the resistor does not know which direction of current we are thinking of.

A series circuit with two *IR* voltage drops is shown in Fig. 4-8. We can analyze these polarities in terms of electron flow. The electrons move from the negative terminal of the source V_T through R_1 from point C to D. Electrons move into C and out from D. Therefore C is the negative side of the voltage drop across R_1. Similarly, for the *IR* voltage drop across R_2, point E is the negative side, compared with point F.

A more fundamental way to consider the polarity of *IR* voltage drops in a circuit is the fact that between any two points the one nearer to the positive terminal of the voltage source is more positive; also, the point nearer to the negative terminal of the applied voltage is more negative. A point nearer to the terminal means there is less resistance in its path.

In Fig. 4-8 point C is nearer to the negative battery terminal than point D. The reason is that C has no resistance to A, while the path from D to A includes the resistance of R_1. Similarly, point F is nearer to the positive battery terminal than point E, which makes F more positive than E.

Notice that points D and E in Fig. 4-8 are marked with both plus and minus polarities. The plus polarity at D indicates that it is more positive than C. This polarity, however, is shown just for the voltage across R_1. Point D cannot be more positive than points F and B. The positive terminal of the applied voltage must be the most positive point because the battery is generating the positive potential for the entire circuit.

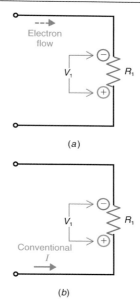

(a)

(b)

FIG. 4-7 Polarity of *IR* voltage drops. (*a*) Electrons flow into the negative side of V_1 across R_1. (*b*) Same polarity of V_1 with positive charges into positive side.

FIG. 4-8 Example of two *IR* voltage drops in series. Electron flow shown for direction of *I*.

Similarly, points A and C must have the most negative potential in the entire string, since point A is the negative terminal of the applied voltage. Actually, the plus polarity marked at D only means that this end of R_1 is less negative than C by the amount of voltage drop across R_1.

Consider the potential difference between E and D in Fig. 4-8, which is only a piece of wire. This voltage is zero because there is no resistance between these two points. Without any resistance here, the current cannot produce the *IR* drop necessary for a difference in potential. Points E and D are, therefore, the same electrically since they have the same potential.

When we go around the external circuit from the negative terminal of V_T, with electron flow, the voltage drops are drops in negative potential. For the opposite direction, starting from the positive terminal of V_T, the voltage drops are drops in positive potential. Either way, the voltage drop of each series R is its proportional part of the V_T needed for the one value of current in all the resistances.

TEST-POINT QUESTION 4-5

Answers at end of chapter.

Refer to Fig. 4-8.
a. Which point in the circuit is the most negative?
b. Which point in the circuit is the most positive?
c. Which is more negative, point D or F?

4-6 TOTAL POWER IN A SERIES CIRCUIT

The power needed to produce current in each series resistor is used up in the form of heat. Therefore, the total power used is the sum of the individual values of power dissipated in each part of the circuit. As a formula,

▶ $$P_T = P_1 + P_2 + P_3 + \cdots + \text{etc.} \qquad (4\text{-}4)$$

As an example, in Fig. 4-9, R_1 dissipates 40 W for P_1, equal to 20 V × 2 A for the *VI* product. Or, the P_1 calculated as I^2R is $(2 \times 2) \times 10 = 40$ W. Also, the P_1 is V^2/R, or $(20 \times 20)/10 = 40$ W.

FIG. 4-9 The sum of the individual powers P_1 and P_2 used in each resistance equals the total power P_T produced by the source.

Similarly, P_2 for R_2 is 80 W. This value is 40×2 for VI, $(2 \times 2) \times 20$ for I^2R, or $(40 \times 40)/20$ for V^2/R. The P_2 must be more than P_1 because R_2 is more than R_1 with the same current.

The total power dissipated by R_1 and R_2, then, is $40 + 80 = 120$ W. This power is generated by the source of applied voltage.

The total power can also be calculated as $V_T \times I$. The reason is that V_T is the sum of all the series voltages and I is the same in all the series components. In this case, then, $P_T = V_T \times I = 60 \times 2 = 120$ W.

The total power here is 120 W, calculated either from the total voltage or from the sum of P_1 and P_2. This is the amount of power produced by the battery. The voltage source produces this power, equal to the amount used by the resistors.

(a)

(b)

FIG. 4-10 Example of voltage sources V_1 and V_2 in series. (a) Note the connections for series-aiding polarities. Here 8 V + 6 V = 14 V for the total V_T. (b) Connections for series-opposing polarities. Now 8 V − 6 V = 2 V for V_T.

TEST-POINT QUESTION 4-6

Answers at end of chapter.
  a. Each of three equal resistances dissipates 2 W. How much P_T is supplied by the source?
  b. A 1-kΩ R_1 and 40-kΩ R_2 are in series with a 50-V source. Which R dissipates more power?

4-7 SERIES-AIDING AND SERIES-OPPOSING VOLTAGES

Series-aiding voltages are connected with polarities that allow current in the same direction. In Fig. 4-10a, the 6 V of V_1 alone could produce 3 A electron flow from the negative terminal, with the 2-Ω R. Also, the 8 V of V_2 could produce 4 A in the same direction. The total I then is 7 A.

Instead of adding the currents, however, the voltages V_1 and V_2 can be added, for a V_T of 6 + 8 = 14 V. This 14 V produces 7 A in all parts of the series circuit with a resistance of 2 Ω. Then I is 14/2 = 7 A.

Voltages are connected series-aiding when the plus terminal of one is connected to the negative terminal of the next. They can be added for a total equivalent voltage. This idea applies in the same way to voltage sources, such as batteries, and to voltage drops across resistances. Any number of voltages can be added, as long as they are connected with series-aiding polarities.

Series-opposing voltages are subtracted, as shown in Fig. 4-10b. Notice here that the positive terminals of V_1 and V_2 are connected. Subtract the smaller from the larger value, and give the net V the polarity of the larger voltage. In this example, V_T is 8 − 6 = 2 V. The polarity of V_T is the same as V_2 because its voltage is higher than V_1.

If two series-opposing voltages are equal, the net voltage will be zero. In effect, one voltage balances out the other. The current I also is zero, without any net potential difference.

Answers at end of chapter.
  a. Voltage V_1 of 40 V is series-aiding with V_2 of 60 V. How much is V_T?
  b. The same V_1 and V_2 are connected series-opposing. How much is V_T?

4-8 ANALYZING SERIES CIRCUITS

$V_1 = ?$
$P_1 = ?$

$R_1 = 14\ \Omega$

$V_T = 50\ V$

$R_2 = 6\Omega$ $V_2 = ?$
$P_2 = ?$

$I = ?$

FIG. 4-11 Analyzing a series circuit to find I, V_1, V_2, P_1, and P_2. See text for solution.

Refer to Fig. 4-11. Suppose that the source V_T of 50 V is known, with the 14-Ω R_1 and 6-Ω R_2. The problem is to find R_T, I, the individual voltage drops V_1 and V_2 across each resistor, and the power dissipated.

We must know the total resistance R_T to calculate I because the total applied voltage V_T is given. This V_T is applied across the total resistance R_T. In this example, R_T is $14 + 6 = 20\ \Omega$.

Now I can be calculated as V/R_T, or 50/20, which equals 2.5 A. This 2.5-A I flows through R_1 and R_2.

The individual voltage drops are

$$V_1 = IR_1 = 2.5 \times 14 = 35\ V$$
$$V_2 = IR_2 = 2.5 \times 6 = 15\ V$$

Note that V_1 and V_2 total 50 V, equal to the applied V_T.
  The calculations to find the power dissipated in each resistor are as follows:

$$P_1 = V_1 \times I = 35 \times 2.5 = 87.5\ W$$
$$P_2 = V_2 \times I = 15 \times 2.5 = 37.5\ W$$

These two values of dissipated power total 125 W. The power generated by the source equals $V_T \times I$ or 50×2.5, which is also 125 W.

GENERAL METHODS FOR SERIES CIRCUITS   For other types of problems with series circuits it is useful to remember the following:

1. When you know the I for one component, use this value for I in all the components, as the current is the same in all parts of a series circuit.
2. To calculate I, the total V_T can be divided by the total R_T, or an individual IR drop can be divided by its R. For instance, the current in Fig. 4-11 could be calculated as V_2/R_2 or 15/6, which equals the same 2.5 A for I. However, do not mix a total value for the entire circuit with an individual value for only part of the circuit.
3. When you know the individual voltage drops around the circuit, these can be added to equal the applied V_T. This also means that a known voltage drop can be subtracted from the total V_T to find the remaining voltage drop.

DID YOU KNOW?

Most electric cars need recharging, and this entails a risk of electrocution. A new GM car uses an inductive method that changes the way the batteries are charged. The driver parks the car and inserts a plastic card into the charge slot. An external charger generates a 120-kW magnetic field, energizing the car's converter to produce direct current for the batteries.

These principles are illustrated by the problem in Fig. 4-12. In this circuit R_1 and R_2 are known but not R_3. However, the current through R_3 is given as 3 mA.

With just this information, all values in this circuit can be calculated. The I of 3 mA is the same in all three series resistances. Therefore,

$$V_1 = 3 \text{ mA} \times 10 \text{ k}\Omega = 30 \text{ V}$$
$$V_2 = 3 \text{ mA} \times 30 \text{ k}\Omega = 90 \text{ V}$$

The sum of V_1 and V_2 is $30 + 90 = 120$ V. This 120 V plus V_3 must total 180 V. Therefore, V_3 is $180 - 120 = 60$ V.

With 60 V for V_3, equal to IR_3, then R_3 must be 60/0.003, equal to 20,000 Ω or 20 kΩ. The total circuit resistance is 60 kΩ, which results in the current of 3 mA with 180 V applied, as specified in the circuit.

Another way of doing this problem is to find R_T first. The equation $I = V_T/R_T$ can be inverted to calculate R_T.

$$R_T = \frac{V_T}{I}$$

With a 3-mA I and 180 V for V_T, the value of R_T must be 180 V/3 mA = 60 kΩ. Then R_3 is 60 kΩ − 40 kΩ = 20 kΩ.

The power dissipated in each resistance is 90 mW in R_1, 270 mW in R_2, and 180 mW in R_3. The total power is $90 + 270 + 180 = 540$ mW.

SERIES VOLTAGE-DROPPING RESISTORS   A common application of series circuits is to use a resistance to drop the voltage from the source V_T to a lower value, as in Fig. 4-13. The load R_L here represents a transistor radio that operates normally with a 9-V battery. When the radio is on, the dc load current with 9 V applied is 18 mA. Therefore, the requirements are 9 V, at 18 mA as the load.

To operate this radio from 12.6 V, the voltage-dropping resistor R_S is inserted in series to provide a voltage drop V_S that will make V_L equal to 9 V. The required voltage drop across V_S is the difference between V_L and the higher V_T. As a formula,

$$V_S = V_T - V_L = 12.6 - 9 = 3.6 \text{ V}$$

Furthermore, this voltage drop of 3.6 V must be provided with a current of 18 mA, as the current is the same through R_S and R_L. To calculate R_S,

$$R_S = \frac{3.6 \text{ V}}{18 \text{ mA}} = 0.2 \text{ k}\Omega = 200 \ \Omega$$

CIRCUIT WITH VOLTAGE SOURCES IN SERIES   See Fig. 4-14. Note that V_1 and V_2 are series-opposing, with + to + through R_1. Their net effect, then, is 0 V. Therefore, V_T consists only of V_3, equal to 4.5 V. The total R is $2 + 1 + 2 = 5$ kΩ for R_T. Finally, I is V_T/R_T or 4.5 V/5 kΩ, which is equal to 0.9 mA, or 900 μA.

FIG. 4-12   Find the resistance of R_3. See text for analysis of this series circuit.

FIG. 4-13   Example of a series voltage-dropping resistor R_S used to drop V_T of 12.6 V to 9 V for R_L. See text for calculations.

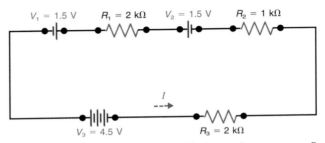

FIG. 4-14   Finding the I for this series circuit with three voltage sources. See text for solution.

TEST-POINT QUESTION 4-8

Answers at end of chapter.

Refer to Fig. 4-12.
a. Calculate V_1 across R_1.
b. Calculate V_2 across R_2.
c. How much is V_3?

4-9 EFFECT OF AN OPEN CIRCUIT IN A SERIES PATH

An open circuit is a break in the current path. The resistance of the open path is very high because an insulator like air takes the place of a conducting part of the circuit. Remember that the current is the same in all parts of a series circuit. Therefore, an open in any part results in no current for the entire circuit. As illustrated in Fig. 4-15, the circuit is normal in Fig. 4-15*a*, but in Fig. 4-15*b* there is no current in R_1, R_2, or R_3 because of the open in the series path.

The open between P1 and P2, or at any other point in the circuit, has practically infinite resistance because its opposition to electron flow is so great

(a)   (b)

FIG. 4-15   Effect of an open path in a series circuit. (*a*) Normal closed circuit with current of 1 A. (*b*) Open path in any part of the series path results in no current in the entire circuit.

compared with the resistance of R_1, R_2, and R_3. Therefore, the value of current is practically zero, although the battery produces its normal applied voltage of 40 V.

To take an example, suppose that the open circuit between P1 and P2 has a resistance of 40×10^9 Ω (40 gigaohms). The resistance of the entire circuit is essentially 40×10^9 Ω, since the resistance of R_1, R_2, and R_3 can then be neglected compared with the resistance of the open. Such a high resistance is practically infinite ohms.

By Ohm's law, the current that results from 40 V applied across 40×10^9 Ω is 1×10^{-9} A, which is practically zero. This is the value of current in all parts of the series circuit. With practically no current, the IR voltage drop is practically zero across the 25 Ω of R_1, the 10 Ω of R_2, and the 5 Ω of R_3.

In summary, with an open in any part of a series circuit, the current is zero in the entire circuit. There is no IR voltage drop across any of the series resistances, although the voltage source still maintains its output voltage.

THE CASE OF ZERO *IR* DROP   In Fig. 4-15b, each of the resistors in the open circuit has an IR drop of zero. The reason is that current of practically zero is the value in all the series components. Each R still has its resistance. However, with zero current the IR voltage is zero.

THE SOURCE VOLTAGE V_T IS STILL PRESENT WITH ZERO I
The open circuit in Fig. 4-15b illustrates another example of how V and I are different forms of electricity. There is no current with the open circuit because there is no complete path outside the battery between its two terminals. However, the battery has a potential difference across the positive and negative terminals. This source voltage is present with or without current in the external circuit. If you measure V_T, the meter will read 40 V with the circuit closed or open.

The same idea applies to the 120-Vac voltage from the power line in the home. The 120-V potential difference is across the two terminals of the wall outlet. If you connect a lamp or appliance, current will flow in the circuit. When nothing is connected, though, the 120-V potential difference is still there at the outlet. If you should touch it, you would get an electric shock. The power company is maintaining the 120 V at the outlets as a source to produce current in any circuits that are plugged in.

THE APPLIED VOLTAGE IS ACROSS THE OPEN TERMINALS   It is useful to note that the entire applied voltage is present across the open circuit. Between P1 and P2 in Fig. 4-15b, there is 40 V. The reason is that essentially all the resistance of the series circuit is between P1 and P2. Therefore, the resistance of the open circuit develops all the IR voltage drop.

The extremely small current of one-billionth of an ampere is not enough to develop any appreciable IR drop across R_1, R_2, and R_3. Across the open, however, the resistance is 40×10^9 Ω. Therefore, the IR voltage across the open here is one-billionth of an ampere multiplied by 40×10^9 Ω, which equals 40 V.

We could also consider the open circuit as a proportional voltage divider. Since practically all the series resistance is between P1 and P2, all the applied voltage is across the open terminals.

The fact that the open terminals have the entire applied voltage indicates a good way to find an open component in a series string. If you measure the voltage across each good component, zero voltage will be normal. However, the component that has the full source voltage is the one that is open.

A practical example is a fuse in a circuit. A good fuse has the normal current, practically zero resistance, and zero voltage. If the fuse blows, the result is no current in the circuit but the applied voltage is across the open fuse.

Another example is illustrated in Fig. 4-16 to emphasize again the difference between voltage and current in a circuit. In Fig. 4-16a, the circuit is normal, with the switch closed to light the bulb. The 120 V of the source is across the bulb to produce the normal current of 0.833 A for the 100-W bulb. Across the switch, the voltage is zero because it has practically no resistance in the closed position. When the switch is opened in Fig. 4-16b, however, the results are: (1) There is no current to light the bulb; (2) there is no voltage across the bulb because the *IR* drop is zero without any current; and (3) the applied voltage of 120 V is across the open switch.

FIG. 4-16   Switching a light bulb on and off. (*a*) Switch S_1 is closed to light the bulb. The bulb has the applied voltage and normal current *I*. (*b*) Switch S_1 open. Now *I* is zero and the applied voltage is across the open switch.

Answers at end of chapter.
a. Which component has 120 V in Fig. 4-16*a*?
b. Which component has 120 V in Fig. 4-16*b*?
c. How much is the current in the bulb in Fig. 4-16*b*?

4-10 SERIES SWITCHES REPRESENT THE AND LOGIC FUNCTION

In Fig. 4-17*a*, two series-connected switches, *A* and *B*, are used to control whether a lamp is on or off. If either or both switches *A* and *B* are open, the lamp will not light. The reason is that the open switches provide a *break* or *open* in the current path. In order for the lamp to light, both switches *A* and *B* must be closed.

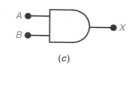

Switches		
A	B	Lamp
Open	Open	OFF
Open	Closed	OFF
Closed	Open	OFF
Closed	Closed	ON

(a)

(b)

(c)

$$A \cdot B = X$$

(d)

FIG. 4-17   Comparison of the AND logic gate to a series circuit and switches. (a) Series circuit with two switches, A and B. (b) Truth table with four possibilities for the switches. (c) Schematic symbol for the AND logic gate. (d) Boolean expression for the AND gate.

With both switches closed, current flows to light the lamp. Figure 4-17b is a table listing all of the possible combinations for switches A and B. As you can see from the table, both switches A and B must be closed in order for the lamp to be on. For the other three switch combinations the lamp is off. The table in Fig. 4-17b is often called a *truth table*.

The operation of the circuit in Fig. 4-17a is similar to that of the digital electronics circuit known as the AND logic gate. (It is important to note that the series circuit in Fig. 4-17a only illustrates the idea of the AND logic function; it is not the actual type of circuit used in digital electronic circuits.) With the actual digital AND logic gate, both inputs must have high voltages to produce a high voltage at the output. In digital circuits, 0 V and +5 V are representative of typical low and high voltages, respectively.

The schematic symbol for an AND logic gate is shown in Fig. 4-17c. The inputs are represented as A and B, whereas the output is represented as X. Figure 4-17d shows the mathematical expression which describes the operation of the AND logic gate. The dot between A and B represents the AND operation. The expression is read "A AND B equals X" rather than "A times B equals X." The expression can also be written as $AB = X$. It should be noted that an AND logic gate can have more than two inputs. Regardless of the number of inputs, however, the output is high only when all the inputs are high.

TEST-POINT QUESTION 4-10

Answers at end of chapter.

Answer True or False.
a. In Fig. 4-17a, the lamp is on only when switches A and B are both closed.
b. The mathematical expression for an AND gate with two inputs is $A \cdot B = X$.
c. When switches A and B are closed in Fig. 4-17a, the voltage across the lamp is 12 V.

- There is only one current I in a series circuit. $I = V_T/R_T$, where V_T is the voltage applied across the total series resistance R_T. This I is the same in all the series components.
- The total resistance R_T of a series string is the sum of the individual resistances.
- The applied voltage V_T equals the sum of the series IR voltage drops.
- The negative side of an IR voltage drop is where electrons flow in, attracted to the positive side at the opposite end.
- The sum of the individual values of power used in the individual resistances equals the total power supplied by the source.
- Series-aiding voltages are added; series-opposing voltages are subtracted.
- An open circuit results in no current in all parts of the series circuit.
- In an open circuit, the voltage across the two open terminals is equal to the applied voltage.
- The AND gate function corresponds to switches in series.

SELF-TEST

ANSWERS AT BACK OF BOOK.

Choose (a), (b), (c), or (d).

1. When two resistances are connected in series, (a) they must both have the same resistance value; (b) the voltage across each must be the same; (c) they must have different resistance values; (d) there is only one path for current through both resistances.
2. In Fig. 4-3c, if the current through R_5 is 1 A, then the current through R_3 must be (a) ⅓ A; (b) ½ A; (c) 1 A; (d) 3 A.
3. With a 10-kΩ resistance in series with a 2-kΩ resistance, the total R_T equals (a) 2 kΩ; (b) 8 kΩ; (c) 10 kΩ; (d) 12 kΩ.
4. With two 45-kΩ resistances in series across a 90-V battery, the voltage across each resistance equals (a) 30 V; (b) 45 V; (c) 90 V; (d) 180 V.
5. The sum of series IR voltage drops (a) is less than the smallest voltage drop; (b) equals the average value of all the voltage drops; (c) equals the applied voltage; (d) is usually more than the applied voltage.
6. Resistances R_1 and R_2 are in series with 90 V applied. If V_1 is 30 V, then V_2 must be (a) 30 V; (b) 90 V; (c) 45 V; (d) 60 V.
7. With a 4-Ω resistance and a 2-Ω resistance in series across a 6-V battery, the current (a) in the larger resistance is 1⅓ A; (b) in the smaller resistance is 3 A; (c) in both resistances is 1 A; (d) in both resistances is 2 A.

8. When one resistance in a series string is open, (a) the current is maximum in the normal resistances; (b) the current is zero in all the resistances; (c) the voltage is zero across the open resistance; (d) the current increases in the voltage source.

9. The resistance of an open series string is (a) zero; (b) infinite; (c) equal to the normal resistance of the string; (d) about double the normal resistance of the string.

10. A source of 100 V is applied across a 20-Ω R_1 and 30-Ω R_2 in series, and V_1 is 40 V. The current in R_2 is (a) 5 A; (b) 3⅓ A; (c) 1⅓ A; (d) 2 A.

QUESTIONS

1. Show how to connect two resistances in series with each other across a voltage source.
2. State three rules for the current, voltage, and resistance in a series circuit.
3. For a given amount of current, why does higher resistance have a larger voltage drop across it?
4. Two 300-W 120-V light bulbs are connected in series across a 240-V line. If the filament of one bulb burns open, will the other bulb light? Why? With the open circuit, how much is the voltage across the source and across each bulb?
5. Prove that if $V_T = V_1 + V_2 + V_3$, then $R_T = R_1 + R_2 + R_3$.
6. State briefly a rule for determining polarity of the voltage drop across each resistor in a series circuit.
7. Redraw the circuit in Fig. 4-12, marking the polarity of V_1, V_2, and V_3.
8. State briefly a rule to determine when voltages are series-aiding.
9. Derive the formula $P_T = P_1 + P_2 + P_3$ from the fact that $V_T = V_1 + V_2 + V_3$.
10. In a series string, why does the largest R dissipate the most power?
11. Give one application of series circuits.
12. Describe the function of the AND gate.

PROBLEMS

ANSWERS TO ODD-NUMBERED PROBLEMS AT BACK OF BOOK.

1. A circuit has 20 V applied across a 10-Ω resistance R_1. How much is the current in the circuit? How much resistance R_2 must be added in series with R_1 to reduce the current one-half? Show the schematic diagram of the circuit with R_1 and R_2.
2. Draw the schematic diagram of 20-, 30-, and 40-Ω resistances in series. (a) How much is the total resistance of the entire series string? (b) How much current flows in each resistance, with a voltage of 18 V applied across the series string? (c) Find the voltage drop across each resistance. (d) Find the power dissipated in each resistance.
3. An R_1 of 90 kΩ and an R_2 of 10 kΩ are in series across a 12-V source. (a) Draw the schematic diagram. (b) How much is V_2?

4. Draw a schematic diagram showing two resistances R_1 and R_2 in series across a 100-V source. (a) If the IR voltage drop across R_1 is 60 V, how much is the IR voltage drop across R_2? (b) Label the polarity of the voltage drops across R_1 and R_2. (c) If the current is 1 A through R_1, how much is the current through R_2? (d) How much is the resistance of R_1 and R_2? How much is the total resistance across the voltage source? (e) If the voltage source is disconnected, how much is the voltage across R_1 and across R_2?

5. In Fig. 4-18, calculate I, V_1, V_2, P_1, P_2, and P_T. (Note that R_1 and R_2 are in series even though V_T is shown at the right instead of the left.)

$R_1 = 2\ k\Omega$

$R_2 = 8\ k\Omega$

$V_T = 40\ V$

FIG. 4-18   Circuit diagram for Probs. 5 and 6.

6. If R_1 is increased to 8 kΩ in Fig. 4-18, what will be the new value of I?
7. Find the total R_T of the following resistances in series: 2 MΩ; 0.5 MΩ; 68 kΩ; 5 kΩ; and 470 Ω.
8. Referring to Fig. 4-13, calculate the power dissipated in the voltage-dropping resistor R_S.
9. Draw the circuit with values for three equal series resistances across a 90-V source, where each R has one-third the applied voltage and the current in the circuit is 5 mA.
10. A 100-W bulb normally takes 0.833 A, and a 200-W bulb takes 1.666 A from the 120-V power line. If these two bulbs were connected in series across a 240-V power line, prove that the current would be 1.111 A in both bulbs, assuming the resistances remain constant.
11. How much voltage V is needed for a 1.8-mA current through resistances R_1 of 4.7 kΩ and R_2 of 6.8 kΩ in series?
12. Three 10-Ω resistances are in series across a voltage source. Show the schematic diagram. If the voltage across each resistor is 10 V, how much is the applied voltage? How much is the current in each resistance?
13. How much resistance R_1 must be added in series with a 100-Ω R_2 to limit the current to 0.3 A with 120 V applied? Show the schematic diagram. How much power is dissipated in each resistance?
14. In Fig. 4-19, find resistance R_1. Why is the electron flow for I in the direction shown?
15. In Fig. 4-20, find the value of R_2.
16. Figure 4-21 shows the circuit for keeping a 12.6-V car battery charged from a 14.8-Vdc generator. Calculate current I and show the direction of electron flow for current between points A and B.
17. In Fig. 4-22, find voltage V_2. Show polarities for the voltage drops.
18. In Fig 4-23, calculate voltage V_T. Show polarities for the voltage drops and V_T.
19. Three resistors of 100, 200, and 300 Ω are in series across a 24-V source. (a) If the 200-Ω resistor shorts, how much voltage is across the 300-Ω resistor? (b) If the 300-Ω resistor opens, how much voltage is across the 100- and 200-Ω resistors?
20. A 1.5-kΩ resistor is in series with an unknown resistance. The applied voltage equals 36 V and the series current is 14.4 mA. Calculate the value of the unknown resistor.

FIG. 4-19 Circuit diagram for Prob. 14.

FIG. 4-20 Circuit diagram for Prob. 15.

FIG. 4-21 Circuit diagram for Prob. 16.

FIG. 4-22 Circuit diagram for Prob. 17.

FIG. 4-23 Circuit diagram for Prob. 18.

21. A 120-Ω resistor is in series with a resistor whose value is unknown. The voltage drop across the unknown resistance is 12 V, and the power dissipated by the 120-Ω resistor is 4.8 W. Calculate the value of the unknown resistance.

22. In Fig. 4-24, solve for the following unknown values: R_T, I, V_1, V_2, V_3, V_4, P_T, P_1, P_2, P_3, and P_4.

FIG. 4-24 Circuit diagram for Probs. 22 and 23.

23. In Fig. 4-24, assume R_2 opens. What are the values for V_1, V_2, V_3, and V_4?

24. In Fig. 4-25, solve for the following unknown values: R_T, I, V_1, V_2, V_3, V_4, V_5, P_T, P_1, P_2, P_3, P_4, and P_5.

FIG. 4-25   Circuit diagram for Prob. 24.

FIG. 4-26   Circuit diagram for Prob. 25.

25.   In Fig. 4-26, solve for the following unknown values: R_T, I, V_1, V_2, V_3, V_4, V_5, V_6, V_7, P_T, P_1, P_2, P_3, P_4, P_5, P_6, and P_7.

26.   In Fig. 4-27, solve for R_T, V_1, V_3, V_4, R_2, R_3, P_T, P_1, P_2, P_3, and P_4.

27.   In Fig. 4-28, solve for I, V_1, V_2, V_3, V_T, R_3, P_T, P_2, and P_3.

FIG. 4-27   Circuit diagram for Prob. 26.

FIG. 4-28   Circuit diagram for Prob. 27.

CRITICAL THINKING

1.   Three resistors in series have a total resistance R_T of 2.7 kΩ. If R_2 is twice the value of R_1 and R_3 is three times the value of R_2, what are the values of R_1, R_2, and R_3?

2.   Three resistors in series have an R_T of 7 kΩ. If R_3 is 2.2 times larger than R_1 and 1.5 times larger than R_2, what are the values of R_1, R_2, and R_3?

3.   A 100-Ω ⅛-W resistor is in series with a 330-Ω ½-W resistor. What is the maximum series current this circuit can handle without exceeding the wattage rating of either resistor?

4. A 1.5-kΩ ½-W resistor is in series with a 470-Ω ¼-W resistor. What is the maximum voltage that can be applied to this series circuit without exceeding the wattage rating of either resistor?

5. Refer to Fig. 4-29. Select values for R_1 and V_T so that when R_2 varies from 1 kΩ to 0 Ω, the series current varies from 1 to 5 mA. V_T and R_1 are to have fixed or constant values.

FIG. 4-29 Circuit diagram for Critical Thinking Problem 5.

ANSWERS TO TEST-POINT QUESTIONS

4-1 **a.** R_1, R_2, R_3, V_T and the wires
    b. $I = 5$ A
    c. 2 A

4-2 **a.** $I = 2$ mA
    b. $R = 10$ kΩ
    c. $I = 1$ mA

4-3 **a.** 10 V
    b. $I = 1$ A
    c. $I = 1$ A
    d. $I = 1$ A

4-4 **a.** 60 V
    b. 75 V
    c. 40 V

4-5 **a.** point A or C
    b. point B or F
    c. point D

4-6 **a.** $P = 6$ W
    b. R_2

4-7 **a.** 100 V
    b. 20 V

4-8 **a.** $V_1 = 30$ V
    b. $V_2 = 90$ V
    c. $V_3 = 60$ V

4-9 **a.** bulb
    b. switch
    c. zero

4-10 **a.** T
    b. T
    c. T

CHAPTER 5

PARALLEL CIRCUITS

Components in series have one common current, but parallel circuits are used where it is necessary to have one common voltage across all the components. A typical application is for the lights and appliances in a house, where they all need the same 120 V from the ac power line. As a definition, a parallel circuit is formed when two or more components are connected across one voltage source. The polarity of the connections does not matter for resistors. Each parallel path is then a branch circuit, with its own individual current.

Parallel circuits, therefore, have one common voltage across all the branches but separate branch currents that can be different. These characteristics are opposite from series circuits that have one common current but individual voltage drops. The principles of parallel or series connections apply to dc and ac circuits.

CHAPTER OBJECTIVES

Upon completion of this chapter, you should be able to:

- *Explain* why voltage is the same across all branches in a parallel circuit.
- *Calculate* the individual branch currents in a parallel circuit.
- *Calculate* the total current in a parallel circuit.
- *Calculate* the equivalent resistance of two or more resistors in parallel.
- *Explain* why the combined resistance of a parallel circuit is always less than the smallest branch resistance.
- *Calculate* the total conductance of a parallel circuit.
- *Calculate* the total power in a parallel circuit.
- *Solve* for the voltage, current, power, and resistance in a parallel circuit having random unknowns.
- *Describe* the effects of an open and short in a parallel circuit.
- *Describe* how parallel connected switches can be used to describe the OR logic function.

IMPORTANT TERMS IN THIS CHAPTER

inverse relation	parallel bank of resistors	short circuit
main-line current	parallel branch currents	total power
open branch	parallel conductances	
OR gate	reciprocal resistance formula	

TOPICS COVERED IN THIS CHAPTER

5-1 THE APPLIED VOLTAGE V_A IS THE SAME ACROSS PARALLEL BRANCHES

A parallel circuit is formed when two or more components are connected across a voltage source, as shown in Fig. 5-1. In this figure, R_1 and R_2 are in parallel with each other and a 1.5-V battery. In Fig. 5-1b, the points A, B, C, and E are really equivalent to a direct connection at the negative terminal of the battery because the connecting wires have practically no resistance. Similarly, points H, G, D, and F are the same as a direct connection at the positive battery terminal. Since R_1 and R_2 are directly connected across the two terminals of the battery, both resistances must have the same potential difference as the battery. It follows that the voltage is the same across components connected in parallel. The parallel circuit arrangement is used, therefore, to connect components that require the same voltage.

FIG. 5-1 Example of a parallel circuit with two resistors. (a) Wiring diagram. (b) Schematic diagram.

A common application of parallel circuits is typical house wiring to the power line, with many lights and appliances connected across the 120-V source (Fig. 5-2). The wall receptacle has the potential difference of 120 V across each pair of terminals. Therefore, any resistance connected to an outlet has the applied

FIG. 5-2 Light bulb and toaster connected in parallel with the 120-V line. (a) Wiring diagram. (b) Schematic diagram.

voltage of 120 V. The light bulb is connected to one outlet and the toaster to an-other outlet, but both have the same applied voltage of 120 V. Therefore, each operates independently of any other appliance, with all the individual branch circuits connected across the 120-V line.

TEST-POINT QUESTION 5-1

Answers at end of chapter.
a. In Fig. 5-1, how much is the common voltage across R_1 and R_2?
b. In Fig. 5-2, how much is the common voltage across the bulb and the toaster?
c. How many parallel branch circuits are connected across the voltage source in Figs. 5-1 and 5-2?

5-2 EACH BRANCH *I* EQUALS V_A/R

In applying Ohm's law, it is important to note that the current equals the voltage applied across the circuit divided by the resistance between the two points where that voltage is applied. In Fig. 5-3a, 10 V is applied across the 5 Ω of R_2, resulting in the current of 2 A between points E and F through R_2. The battery

(a)

(b)

(c)

FIG. 5-3   Parallel circuit. (a) The current in each parallel branch equals the applied voltage V_A divided by each branch resistance R. (b) Axial-lead resistors assembled on a lab prototype board, forming a parallel circuit. (c) Surface-mount resistors assembled on a printed circuit board, forming a parallel circuit. Note: 5R0 equals 5.0 Ω and 100 equals 10 Ω.

voltage is also applied across the parallel resistance of R_1, applying 10 V across 10 Ω. Through R_1, therefore, the current is 1 A between points C and D. The current has a different value through R_1, with the same applied voltage, because the resistance is different. These values are calculated as follows:

$$I_1 = \frac{V_A}{R_1} = \frac{10}{10} = 1 \text{ A}$$

$$I_2 = \frac{V_A}{R_2} = \frac{10}{5} = 2 \text{ A}$$

Figure 5-3b shows how to assemble axial-lead resistors on a lab prototype board to form a parallel circuit. Figure 5-3c shows surface-mount resistors assembled on a printed circuit board to form a parallel circuit.

Just as in a circuit with just one resistance, any branch that has less R allows more I. If R_1 and R_2 were equal, however, the two branch currents would have the same value. For instance, in Fig. 5-1b each branch has its own current equal to 1.5 V/5 Ω = 0.3 A.

The I can be different in parallel circuits that have different R because V is the same across all the branches. Any voltage source generates a potential difference across its two terminals. This voltage does not move. Only I flows around the circuit. The source voltage is available to make electrons move around any closed path connected to the terminals of the source. How much I is in each separate path depends on the amount of R in each branch.

TEST-POINT QUESTION 5-2

Answers at end of chapter.

Refer to Fig. 5-3.
a. How much is the voltage across R_1?
b. How much is I_1 through R_1?
c. How much is the voltage across R_2?
d. How much is I_2 through R_2?

5-3 THE MAIN-LINE I_T EQUALS THE SUM OF THE BRANCH CURRENTS

Components to be connected in parallel are usually wired directly across each other, with the entire parallel combination connected to the voltage source, as illustrated in Fig. 5-4. This circuit is equivalent to wiring each parallel branch directly to the voltage source, as shown in Fig. 5-1, when the connecting wires have essentially zero resistance.

The advantage of having only one pair of connecting leads to the source for all the parallel branches is that usually less wire is necessary. The pair of leads connecting all the branches to the terminals of the voltage source is the *main line*. In Fig. 5-4, the wires from G to A on the negative side and from B to F in the return path form the main line.

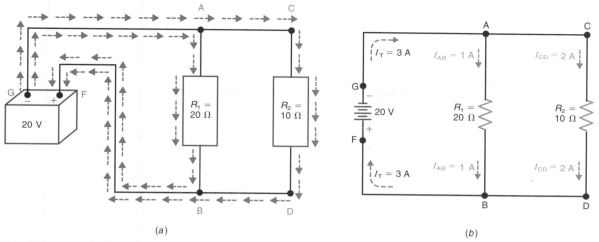

FIG. 5-4 The current in the main line equals the sum of the branch currents. Note that from G to A at the top of this diagram is the negative side of the main line, and from B to F at the bottom is the positive side. (*a*) Wiring diagram. Arrows inside the lines indicate current in the main line for R_1; arrows outside indicate current for R_2. (*b*) Schematic diagram. I_T is the total line current for both R_1 and R_2.

In Fig. 5-4*b*, with 20 Ω of resistance for R_1 connected across the 20-V battery, the current through R_1 must be 20 V/20 Ω = 1 A. This current is electron flow from the negative terminal of the source, through R_1, and back to the positive battery terminal. Similarly, the R_2 branch of 10 Ω across the battery has its own branch current of 20 V/10 Ω = 2 A. This current flows from the negative terminal of the source, through R_2, and back to the positive terminal, since it is a separate path for electron flow.

All the current in the circuit, however, must come from one side of the voltage source and return to the opposite side for a complete path. In the main line, therefore, the amount of current is equal to the total of the branch currents.

For example, in Fig. 5-4*b*, the total current in the line from point G to point A is 3 A. The total current at branch point A subdivides into its component branch currents for each of the branch resistances. Through the path of R_1 from A to B the current is 1 A. The other branch path ACDB through R_2 has a current of 2 A. At the branch point B, the electron flow from both parallel branches combines, so that the current in the main-line return path from B to F has the same value of 3 A as in the other side of the main line.

The formula for the total current I_T in the main line is

▶ $$I_T = I_1 + I_2 + I_3 + \cdots + \text{etc.} \qquad \textbf{(5-1)}$$

This rule applies for any number of parallel branches, whether the resistances in the branches are equal or unequal.

Example

EXAMPLE 1 An R_1 of 20 Ω, an R_2 of 40 Ω, and an R_3 of 60 Ω are connected in parallel across the 120-V power line. How much is the total line current I_T?

ANSWER Current I_1 for the R_1 branch is 120/20 or 6 A. Similarly, I_2 is 120/40 or 3 A, and I_3 is 120/60 or 2 A. The total current in the main line is

$$I_T = I_1 + I_2 + I_3 = 6 + 3 + 2$$
$$I_T = 11 \text{ A}$$

EXAMPLE 2 Two branches R_1 and R_2 across the 120-V power line draw a total line current I_T of 15 A. The R_1 branch takes 10 A. How much is the current I_2 in the R_2 branch?

ANSWER $I_2 = I_T - I_1 = 15 - 10$
$$I_2 = 5 \text{ A}$$

With two branch currents, one must equal the difference between I_T and the other branch current.

EXAMPLE 3 Three parallel branch currents are 0.1 A, 500 mA, and 800 μA. Calculate I_T.

ANSWER All values must be in the same units in order to be added. In this case, all units will be converted to milliamperes: 0.1 A = 100 mA and 800 μA = 0.8 mA. Then

$$I_T = 100 + 500 + 0.8$$
$$I_T = 600.8 \text{ mA}$$

You can convert the currents to A, mA, or μA units, as long as the same unit is used for adding all the currents.

TEST-POINT QUESTION 5-3

Answers at end of chapter.
a. Branch currents in a parallel circuit are 1 A for I_1, 2 A for I_2, and 3 A for I_3. How much is I_T?
b. Assume $I_T = 6$ A for three branch currents; I_1 is 1 A, and I_2 is 2 A. How much is I_3?
c. Branch currents in a parallel circuit are 1 A for I_1 and 200 mA for I_2. How much is I_T?

5-4 RESISTANCES IN PARALLEL

The combined equivalent resistance across the main line in a parallel circuit can be found by Ohm's law: *Divide the common voltage across the parallel resistances by the total current of all the branches.* Referring to Fig. 5-5a, note that the parallel resistance of R_1 with R_2, indicated by the equivalent resistance R_{EQ}, is the opposition to the total current in the main line. In this example, V_A/I_T is 60 V/3 A = 20 Ω for R_{EQ}.

FIG. 5-5   Resistances in parallel. (a) Combination of R_1 and R_2 is the total R_{EQ} for the main line. (b) Equivalent circuit showing R_{EQ} drawing the same 3-A I_T as the parallel combination of R_1 and R_2 in (a).

The total load connected to the source voltage is the same as though one equivalent resistance of 20 Ω were connected across the main line. This is illustrated by the equivalent circuit in Fig. 5-5b. For any number of parallel resistances of any value, therefore,

▶ $$R_{EQ} = \frac{V_A}{I_T} \qquad\qquad (5\text{-}2)$$

where I_T is the sum of all the branch currents and R_{EQ} is the equivalent resistance of all the parallel branches across the applied voltage source V_A.

The first step in solving for R_{EQ} is to add all the parallel branch currents to find the I_T being delivered by the voltage source. The voltage source thinks it is connected to a single resistance whose value allows I_T to flow in the circuit according to Ohm's law. This single resistance is R_{EQ}. An illustrative example of a circuit with two parallel branches will be used to show how R_{EQ} is calculated.

Example

EXAMPLE 4   Two branches, each with a 5-A current, are connected across a 90-V source. How much is the equivalent total resistance R_{EQ}?

ANSWER   The total line current I_T is 5 + 5 = 10 A. Then,

$$R_{EQ} = \frac{V_A}{I_T} = \frac{90}{10}$$
$$R_{EQ} = 9 \ \Omega$$

PARALLEL BANK   A combination of parallel branches is often called a *bank*. In Fig. 5-5, the bank consists of the 60-Ω R_1 and 30-Ω R_2 in parallel. Their combined parallel resistance R_{EQ} is the bank resistance, equal to 20 Ω in this example. A bank can have two or more parallel resistors.

When a circuit has more current with the same applied voltage, this greater value of I corresponds to less R because of their inverse relation. Therefore, the combination of parallel resistances R_{EQ} for the bank is always less than the smallest individual branch resistance. The reason is that I_T must be more than any one branch current.

WHY R_{EQ} IS LESS THAN ANY BRANCH R   It may seem unusual at first that putting more resistance into a circuit lowers the equivalent resistance. This feature of parallel circuits is illustrated in Fig. 5-6. Note that equal resistances of 30 Ω each are added across the source voltage, one branch at a time. The circuit in Fig. 5-6*a* has just R_1, which allows 2 A with 60 V applied. In Fig. 5-6*b* the R_2 branch is added across the same V_A. This branch also has 2 A. Now the parallel circuit has a 4-A total line current because of $I_1 + I_2$. Then the third branch, which also takes 2 A for I_3, is added in Fig. 5-6*c*. The combined circuit with three branches therefore requires a total load current of 6 A, which is supplied by the voltage source.

The combined resistance across the source, then, is V_A/I_T, which is 60/6 or 10 Ω. This equivalent resistance R_{EQ}, representing the entire load on the voltage source, is shown in Fig. 5-6*d*. More resistance branches reduce the combined resistance of the parallel circuit because more current is required from the same voltage source.

FIG. 5-6   How adding parallel branches of resistors increases I_T but decreases R_{EQ}. (*a*) One resistor. (*b*) Two branches. (*c*) Three branches. (*d*) Equivalent circuit of the three branches in (*c*).

RECIPROCAL RESISTANCE FORMULA   We can derive this formula from the fact that I_T is the sum of all the branch currents, or,

$$I_T = I_1 + I_2 + I_3 + \cdots + \text{etc.}$$

However, I_T is V/R_{EQ}. Also, each I is V/R. Substituting V/R_{EQ} for I_T on the left side of the formula and V/R for each branch I on the right side, the result is

$$\frac{V}{R_{EQ}} = \frac{V}{R_1} + \frac{V}{R_2} + \frac{V}{R_3} + \cdots + \text{etc.}$$

Dividing by V because the voltage is the same across all the resistances,

▶ $$\frac{1}{R_{EQ}} = \frac{1}{R_1} + \frac{1}{R_2} + \frac{1}{R_3} + \cdots + \text{etc.}$$ (5-3)

This reciprocal formula applies to any number of parallel resistances of any value. Using the values in Fig. 5-7a as an example,

$$\frac{1}{R_{EQ}} = \frac{1}{20} + \frac{1}{10} + \frac{1}{10} = \frac{1}{20} + \frac{2}{20} + \frac{2}{20} = \frac{5}{20}$$

$$R_{EQ} = \frac{20}{5} = 4\ \Omega$$

(a)   (b)

FIG. 5-7   Two methods of combining parallel resistances to find R_{EQ}. (a) Using the reciprocal resistance formula to calculate R_{EQ} as $4\ \Omega$. (b) Using the total line current method with an assumed line voltage of 20 V gives the same $4\ \Omega$ for R_{EQ}.

Notice that the value for $1/R_{EQ}$ must be inverted to obtain R_{EQ} when using Formula (5-3) because the formula gives the reciprocal of R_{EQ}.

When using the calculator to find a reciprocal such as $1/R$, choose either of two methods. Either divide the number 1 by the value of R, or use the reciprocal key labeled ⨀$1/x$. As an example, to find the reciprocal of $R = 20\ \Omega$ by division:

First punch in the number 1 on the key pad.
Then press the division ⨀÷ key.
Punch in 20 for the value of R.
Finally, press the equal ⨀= key for the quotient of 0.05 on the display.

To use the reciprocal key, first punch in 20 for R. Then press the ⨀$1/x$ key. This may be a second function on some calculators, requiring that you push the ⨀2ndF or ⨀SHIFT key before pressing ⨀$1/x$. The reciprocal equal to 0.05 is displayed without the need for the ⨀= key.

TOTAL-CURRENT METHOD Figure 5-7b shows how this same problem can be calculated in terms of total current instead of by the reciprocal formula, if it is easier to work without fractions. Although the applied voltage is not always known, any convenient value can be assumed because it cancels in the calculations. It is usually simplest to assume an applied voltage of the same numerical value as the highest resistance. Then one assumed branch current will automatically be 1 A and the other branch currents will be more, eliminating fractions less than 1 in the calculations.

In Fig. 5-7b, the highest branch R is 20 Ω. Therefore, assume 20 V for the applied voltage. Then the branch currents are 1 A in R_1, 2 A in R_2, and 2 A in R_3. Their sum is $1 + 2 + 2 = 5$ A for I_T. The combined resistance R_{EQ} across the main line is V_A/I_T, or 20 V/5 A = 4 Ω. This is the same value calculated with the reciprocal resistance formula.

SPECIAL CASE OF EQUAL R IN ALL BRANCHES If R is equal in all branches, the combined R_{EQ} equals the value of one branch resistance divided by the number of branches.

▶ $$R_{EQ} = \frac{R}{n}$$

where R is the resistance in one branch and n is the number of branches.

This rule is illustrated in Fig. 5-8, where three 60-kΩ resistances in parallel equal 20 kΩ.

The rule applies to any number of parallel resistances, but they must all be equal. As another example, five 60-Ω resistances in parallel have the combined resistance of 60/5, or 12 Ω. A common application is two equal resistors wired in a parallel bank for R_{EQ} equal to one-half R.

$$R_{EQ} = \frac{\text{value of one resistance}}{\text{number of resistances}} = \frac{60 \text{ kΩ}}{3}$$

FIG. 5-8 For the special case of all branches having the same resistance, just divide R by the number of branches to find R_{EQ}. Here, $R_{EQ} = 60$ kΩ/3 = 20 kΩ.

$$R_{EQ} = \frac{R_1 \times R_2}{R_1 + R_2} = \frac{2400}{100}$$

FIG. 5-9 For the special case of only two branch resistances, of any values, R_{EQ} equals their product divided by the sum. Here, $R_{EQ} = 2400/100 = 24 \, \Omega$.

SPECIAL CASE OF ONLY TWO BRANCHES   When there are two parallel resistances and they are not equal, it is usually quicker to calculate the combined resistance by the method shown in Fig. 5-9. This rule says that the combination of two parallel resistances is their product divided by their sum.

▶ $$R_{EQ} = \frac{R_1 \times R_2}{R_1 + R_2} \qquad\qquad (5\text{-}4)$$

where R_{EQ} is in the same units as all the individual resistances. For the example in Fig. 5-9,

$$R_{EQ} = \frac{R_1 \times R_2}{R_1 + R_2} = \frac{40 \times 60}{40 + 60} = \frac{2400}{100}$$
$$R_{EQ} = 24 \, \Omega$$

Each R can have any value, but there must be only two resistances. Note that this method gives R_{EQ} directly, not its reciprocal. If you use the reciprocal formula for this example, the answer will be $1/R_{EQ} = \frac{1}{24}$, which is the same value as $R_{EQ} = 24 \, \Omega$.

Formula (5-4) states a product over a sum. When using a calculator, group the R values in parentheses before adding. The reason is that the division bar is a mathematical sign of grouping for terms* to be added or subtracted. You must add $R_1 + R_2$ before dividing. By grouping R_1, and R_2 within parentheses, the addition will be done first before the division. The complete process is as follows. Multiply the R values in the numerator. Press the divide ⊝ key and then the left (or open) parentheses ⊙ key. Add the R values, $R_1 + R_2$, and press the right (or close) parentheses ⊙ key. Then press the equal ⊜ key for R_{EQ} on the display. Using the values in Fig. 5-9 as an example, multiply 40×60; press divide ⊝ and left parentheses ⊙ then 40 ⊕ 60 and the right parentheses ⊙. Finally, press ⊜ to display 24 as the answer.

SHORT-CUT CALCULATIONS   Figure 5-10 shows how these special rules can help in reducing parallel branches to a simpler equivalent circuit. In Fig. 5-10a, the 60-Ω R_1 and R_4 are equal and in parallel. Therefore, they are equivalent to the 30-Ω R_{14} in Fig. 5-10b. Similarly, the 20-Ω R_2 and R_3 are equivalent to the 10 Ω of R_{23}. The circuit in Fig. 5-10a is equivalent to the

---

*For definitions of terms and factors, see B. Grob, *Mathematics for Basic Electronics*, Glencoe/McGraw-Hill, Columbus, Ohio.

FIG. 5-10   An example of parallel resistance calculations with four branches. (*a*) Original circuit. (*b*) Resistors combined into two branches. (*c*) Equivalent circuit reduces to one R_{EQ} for all the branches.

simpler circuit in Fig. 5-10*b* with just the two parallel resistances of 30 and 10 Ω.

Finally, the combined resistance for these two equals their product divided by their sum, which is 300/40 or 7.5 Ω, as shown in Fig. 5-10*c*. This value of R_{EQ} in Fig. 5-10*c* is equivalent to the combination of the four branches in Fig. 5-10*a*. If you connect a voltage source across either circuit, the current in the main line will be the same for both cases.

The order of connections for parallel resistances does not matter in determining R_{EQ}. There is no question as to which is first or last because they are all across the same voltage source and receive their current at the same time.

FINDING AN UNKNOWN BRANCH RESISTANCE   In some cases with two parallel resistors, it is useful to be able to determine what size R_X to connect in parallel with a known R in order to obtain a required value of R_{EQ}. Then the factors can be transposed as follows:

▶
$$R_X = \frac{R \times R_{EQ}}{R - R_{EQ}}$$
(5-5)

This formula is just another way of writing Formula (5-4).

Example

EXAMPLE 5   What R_X in parallel with 40 Ω will provide an R_{EQ} of 24 Ω?

ANSWER $R_X = \dfrac{R \times R_{EQ}}{R - R_{EQ}} = \dfrac{40 \times 24}{40 - 24} = \dfrac{960}{16}$

$R_X = 60\ \Omega$

This problem corresponds to the circuit shown before in Fig. 5-9.

Note that Formula (5-5) for R_X has a product over a difference. The R_{EQ} is subtracted because it is the smallest R. Remember that both Formulas (5-4) and (5-5) can be used with only two parallel branches.

Example

EXAMPLE 6   What R in parallel with 50 kΩ will provide an R_{EQ} of 25 kΩ?

ANSWER $R = 50$ kΩ

Two equal resistances in parallel have R_{EQ} equal to one-half R.

TEST-POINT QUESTION 5-4

Answers at end of chapter.
a. Find R_{EQ} for three 4.7-MΩ resistances in parallel.
b. Find R_{EQ} for 3 MΩ in parallel with 2 MΩ.
c. Find R_{EQ} for two parallel 20-Ω resistances in parallel with 10 Ω.

5-5 CONDUCTANCES IN PARALLEL

Since conductance G is equal to $1/R$, the reciprocal resistance Formula (5-3) can be stated for conductance as

▶ $G_T = G_1 + G_2 + G_3 + \cdots + \text{etc.}$ **(5-6)**

With R in ohms, G is in siemens. For the example in Fig. 5-11, G_1 is $1/20 = 0.05$, G_2 is $1/5 = 0.2$, and G_3 is $1/2 = 0.5$. Then

$$G_T = 0.05 + 0.2 + 0.5 = 0.75 \text{ S}$$

FIG. 5-11   Conductances G_1, G_2, and G_3 in parallel are added for the total G_T.

Notice that adding the conductances does not require reciprocals. Actually, each value of G is the reciprocal of R.

The reason why parallel conductances are added directly can be illustrated by assuming a 1-V source across all the branches. Then calculating the values of $1/R$ for the conductances gives the same values as calculating the branch currents. These values are added for the total I_T or G_T.

Working with G may be more convenient than R in parallel circuits, since it avoids use of the reciprocal formula for R_{EQ}. Each branch current is directly proportional to its conductance. This idea corresponds to the fact that, in series circuits, each voltage drop is directly proportional to each of the series resistances. An example of the currents for parallel conductances is shown in Fig. 5-12. Note that the branch with G of 4 S has twice as much current as the 2-S branches because the branch conductance is doubled.

FIG. 5-12   Example of how parallel branch currents are directly proportional to each branch conductance G.

TEST-POINT QUESTION 5-5

Answers at end of chapter.
a. If G_1 is 2 S and G_2 in parallel is 4 S, calculate G_T.
b. If G_1 is 0.05 μS, G_2 is 0.2 μS, and G_3 is 0.5 μS, all in parallel, find G_T and its equivalent R_{EQ}.
c. If G_T is 4 μS for a parallel circuit, how much is R_{EQ}?

5-6 TOTAL POWER IN PARALLEL CIRCUITS

Since the power dissipated in the branch resistances must come from the voltage source, the total power equals the sum of the individual values of power in each branch. This rule is illustrated in Fig. 5-13. We can also use this circuit as an example of how to apply the rules of current, voltage, and resistance for a parallel circuit.

The applied 10 V is across the 10-Ω R_1 and 5-Ω R_2 in Fig. 5-13. The branch current I_1 then is V_A/R_1 or 10/10, which equals 1 A. Similarly, I_2 is 10/5, or 2 A. The total I_T is $1 + 2 = 3$ A. If we want to find R_{EQ}, it equals V_A/I_T or 10/3, which is $3\frac{1}{3}$ Ω.

The power dissipated in each branch R is $V_A \times I$. In the R_1 branch, I_1 is $10/10 = 1$ A. Then P_1 is $V_A \times I_1$ or $10 \times 1 = 10$ W.

FIG. 5-13 The sum of the power values P_1 and P_2 used in each branch equals the total power P_T produced by the source.

For the R_2 branch, I_2 is $10/5 = 2$ A. Then P_2 is $V_A \times I_2$ or $10 \times 2 = 20$ W. Adding P_1 and P_2, the answer is $10 + 20 = 30$ W. This P_T is the total power dissipated in both branches.

This value of 30 W for P_T is also the total power supplied by the voltage source by means of its total line current I_T. With this method, the total power is $V_A \times I_T$ or $10 \times 3 = 30$ W for P_T. The 30 W of power supplied by the voltage source is dissipated or used up in the branch resistances.

Note that in both parallel and series circuits the sum of the individual values of power dissipated in the circuit equals the total power generated by the source. This can be stated as a formula

$$P_T = P_1 + P_2 + P_3 + \cdots + \text{etc.} \qquad (5\text{-}7)$$

The series or parallel connections can alter the distribution of voltage or current, but power is the rate at which energy is supplied. The circuit arrangement cannot change the fact that all the energy in the circuit comes from the source.

TEST-POINT QUESTION 5-6

Answers at end of chapter.
a. Two parallel branches each have 2 A at 120 V. How much is P_T?
b. Three parallel branches of 10, 20, and 30 Ω have 60 V applied. How much is P_T?
c. Two parallel branches dissipate power of 15 W each. How much is P_T?

5-7 ANALYZING PARALLEL CIRCUITS

For many types of problems with parallel circuits it is useful to remember the following points:

1. When you know the voltage across one branch, this voltage is across all the branches. There can be only one voltage across branch points with the same potential difference.
2. If you know I_T and one of the branch currents I_1, you can find I_2 by subtracting I_1 from I_T.

The circuit in Fig. 5-14 illustrates these points. The problem is to find the applied voltage V_A and the value of R_3. Of the three branch resistances, only R_1 and R_2 are known. However, since I_2 is given as 2 A, the $I_2 R_2$ voltage must be $2 \times 60 = 120$ V.

FIG. 5-14   Analyzing a parallel circuit. What are the values for V_A and R_3? See solution in text.

Although the applied voltage is not given, this must also be 120 V. The voltage across all the parallel branches is the same 120 V that is across the R_2 branch.

Now I_1 can be calculated as V_A/R_1. This is $120/30 = 4$ A for I_1.

Current I_T is given as 7 A. The two branches take $2 + 4 = 6$ A. The third branch current through R_3 must be $7 - 6 = 1$ A for I_3.

Now R_3 can be calculated as V_A/I_3. This is $120/1 = 120\ \Omega$ for R_3.

TEST-POINT QUESTION 5-7

Answers at end of chapter.

Refer to Fig. 5-14.
a. How much is V_2 across R_2?
b. How much is I_1 through R_1?
c. How much is I_T in the voltage source?

5-8 EFFECT OF AN OPEN BRANCH IN PARALLEL CIRCUITS

An open in any circuit is an infinite resistance that results in no current. However, in parallel circuits there is a difference between an open circuit in the main line and an open circuit in a parallel branch. These two cases are illustrated in Fig. 5-15. In Fig. 5-15*a* the open circuit in the main line prevents any electron flow in the line to all the branches. The current is zero in every branch, therefore, and none of the bulbs can light.

However, in Fig. 5-15*b* the open is in the branch circuit for bulb 1. The open branch circuit has no current, then, and this bulb cannot light. The current in all the other parallel branches is normal, though, because each is connected to the voltage source. Therefore, the other bulbs light.

FIG. 5-15   Effect of an open in a parallel circuit. (*a*) Open path in the main line—no current and no light for all the bulbs. (*b*) Open path in any branch—bulb for that branch does not light, but the other two bulbs operate normally.

These circuits show the advantage of wiring components in parallel. An open in one component opens only one branch, while the other parallel branches have their normal voltage and current.

TEST-POINT QUESTION 5-8

Answers at end of chapter.
a. How much is the R of an open filament or heater?
b. In Fig. 5-15*b*, if only bulb 3 is open, which bulbs will light?
c. In Fig. 5-15*a*, which bulbs have no current?

5-9 EFFECT OF A SHORT CIRCUIT ACROSS PARALLEL BRANCHES

A short circuit has practically zero resistance. Its effect, therefore, is to allow excessive current in the shorted circuit. Consider the example in Fig. 5-16. In Fig. 5-16*a*, the circuit is normal, with 1 A in each branch and 2 A for the total line current. However, suppose the conducting wire at point H should accidentally contact the wire at point G, as shown in Fig. 5-16*b*. Since the wire is an excellent conductor, the short circuit results in practically zero resistance between

FIG. 5-16   Effect of a short circuit across parallel branches. (*a*) Normal circuit. (*b*) Short circuit across points H and G shorts out all the branches.

points H and G. These two points are connected directly across the voltage source. With no opposition, the applied voltage could produce an infinitely high value of current through this current path.

THE SHORT-CIRCUIT CURRENT Practically, the amount of current is limited by the small resistance of the wire. Also, the source usually cannot maintain its output voltage while supplying much more than its rated load current. Still, the amount of current can be dangerously high. For instance, the short-circuit current might be more than 100 A instead of the normal line current of 2 A in Fig. 5-16a. Because of the short circuit, excessive current flows in the voltage source, in the line to the short circuit at point H, through the short circuit, and in the line returning to the source from G. Because of the large amount of current, the wires can become hot enough to ignite and burn the insulation covering the wire. There should be a fuse that would open if there is too much current in the main line because of a short circuit across any of the branches.

THE SHORT-CIRCUITED COMPONENTS HAVE NO CURRENT For the short circuit in Fig. 5-16b, the I is 0 A in the parallel resistors R_1 and R_2. The reason is that the short circuit is a parallel path with practically zero resistance. Then all the current flows in this path, bypassing the resistors R_1 and R_2. Therefore R_1 and R_2 are short-circuited or *shorted out* of the circuit. They cannot function without their normal current. If they were filament resistances of light bulbs or heaters, they would not light without any current.

The short-circuited components are not damaged, however. They do not even have any current passing through them. Assuming that the short circuit has not damaged the voltage source and the wiring for the circuit, the components can operate again when the circuit is restored to normal by removing the short circuit.

ALL THE PARALLEL BRANCHES ARE SHORT-CIRCUITED If there were only one R in Fig. 5-16 or any number of parallel components, they would all be shorted out by the short circuit across points H and G. Therefore, a short circuit across one branch in a parallel circuit shorts out all the parallel branches.

This idea also applies to a short circuit across the voltage source in any type of circuit. Then the entire circuit is shorted out.

TEST-POINT QUESTION 5-9

Answers at end of chapter.

Refer to Fig. 5-16.
a. How much is the R of the short circuit between H and G?
b. How much is I_1 in R_1 with the short circuit across R_2?

5-10 PARALLEL SWITCHES REPRESENT THE OR LOGIC FUNCTION

Another common logic circuit found in digital electronics is the OR gate, which in one respect is opposite to the AND logic function described in Chap. 4. The parallel connected switches A and B in Fig. 5-17a illustrate the basic function of an OR gate. If either switch A or switch B or both is closed, the lamp will be on. The lamp is off only when both switches A and B are open. Figure 5-17b shows the truth table listing all possible combinations for switches A and B. With both switches open there is no complete current path and the lamp cannot light. With either or both switches closed, current flows to light the lamp.

It should be noted that the parallel-connected switches in Fig. 5-17a do not represent the actual type of circuit used to perform the OR logic function in digital circuits. However, the analogy of operation of an OR gate is identical to that of the parallel switches in Fig. 5-17a. Figure 5-17c shows the symbol used to represent the OR logic function in digital circuits. The inputs to the OR gate are applied to A and B and the output is taken from X. (An OR gate may have more than two inputs.) The mathematical expression describing the operation of the OR gate is shown in Fig. 5-17d. The statement is read "A or B equals X," rather than "A plus B equals X."

TEST POINT QUESTION 5-10

Answers at end of chapter.

Answer True or False.
a. In Fig. 5-17a, the lamp is on when both switches are open.
b. In Fig. 5-17a, the voltage across switch B is 12 V if switch A is closed and switch B is open.
c. The mathematical expression used to describe the circuit in Fig. 5-17a is $A + B = X$.
d. An OR gate can have more than two inputs.

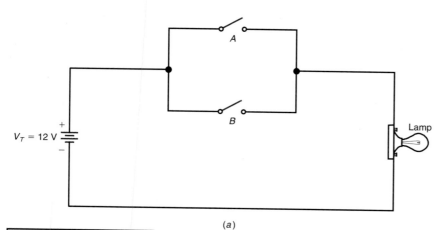

(a)

Switches		
A	**B**	**Lamp**
Open	Open	OFF
Open	Closed	ON
Closed	Open	ON
Closed	Closed	ON

(b)

(c)

$A + B = X$

(d)

FIG. 5-17 Comparison of the OR logic gate to a parallel circuit and switches. (a) Parallel circuit with two switches, A and B. (b) Truth table with four possibilities for the switches. (c) Schematic symbol for the OR logic gate. (d) Boolean expression for the OR gate.

5 SUMMARY AND REVIEW

- There is only one voltage V_A across all components in parallel.
- The current in each branch I_b equals the voltage V_A across the branch divided by the branch resistance R_b. Or $I_b = V_A/R_b$.
- The total line current equals the sum of all the branch currents. Or $I_T = I_1 + I_2 + I_3 + \cdots +$ etc.
- The equivalent resistance R_{EQ} of parallel branches is less than the smallest branch resistance, since all the branches must take more current from the source than any one branch.
- For only *two* parallel resistances of any value, $R_{EQ} = R_1 R_2/(R_1 + R_2)$.
- For any number of *equal* parallel resistances, R_{EQ} is the value of one resistance divided by the number of resistances.
- For the general case of any number of branches, calculate R_{EQ} as V_A/I_T or use the reciprocal resistance formula:

$$1/R_{EQ} = 1/R_1 + 1/R_2 + 1/R_3 + \cdots + \text{etc.}$$

- For any number of conductances in parallel, their values are added for G_T, in the same way as parallel branch currents are added.
- The sum of the individual values of power dissipated in parallel resistances equals the total power produced by the source.
- An open circuit in one branch results in no current through that branch, but the other branches can have their normal current. However, an open circuit in the main line results in no current for any of the branches.
- A short circuit has zero resistance, resulting in excessive current. When one branch is short-circuited, all the parallel paths are also short-circuited. The entire current is in the short circuit and no current is in the short-circuited branches.
- The OR gate function corresponds to switches in parallel.

SELF-TEST

ANSWERS AT BACK OF BOOK.

Choose (a), (b), (c), or (d).

1. With two resistances connected in parallel: (a) the current through each must be the same; (b) the voltage across each must be the same; (c) their combined resistance equals the sum of the individual values; (d) each must have the same resistance value.
2. With 100 V applied across ten 50-Ω resistances in parallel, the current through each resistance equals (a) 2 A; (b) 10 A; (c) 50 A; (d) 100 A.

3. With three 1-kΩ resistances connected in parallel, the combined equivalent resistance equals (*a*) ⅓ kΩ; (*b*) 1 kΩ; (*c*) 2 kΩ; (*d*) 3 kΩ.

4. A 1-Ω resistance in parallel with a 2-Ω resistance provides a combined equivalent resistance of (*a*) 3 Ω; (*b*) 1 Ω; (*c*) 2 Ω; (*d*) ⅔ Ω.

5. With resistances of 100, 200, 300, 400, and 500 Ω in parallel, R_{EQ} is (*a*) less than 100 Ω; (*b*) more than 1 MΩ; (*c*) about 500 Ω; (*d*) about 1 kΩ.

6. With two resistances connected in parallel, if each dissipates 10 W, the total power supplied by the voltage source equals (*a*) 5 W; (*b*) 10 W; (*c*) 20 W; (*d*) 100 W.

7. With eight 10-MΩ resistances connected in parallel across a 10-V source, the main-line current equals (*a*) 0.1 µA; (*b*) ⅛ µA; (*c*) 8 µA; (*d*) 10 µA.

8. A parallel circuit with 20 V applied across two branches has a total line current of 5 A. One branch resistance equals 5 Ω. The other branch resistance equals (*a*) 5 Ω; (*b*) 20 Ω; (*c*) 25 Ω; (*d*) 100 Ω.

9. Three 100-W light bulbs are connected in parallel across the 120-V power line. If one bulb opens, how many bulbs can light? (*a*) None; (*b*) one; (*c*) two; (*d*) all.

10. If a parallel circuit is open in the main line, the current (*a*) increases in each branch; (*b*) is zero in all the branches; (*c*) is zero only in the branch that has highest resistance; (*d*) increases in the branch that has lowest resistance.

QUESTIONS

1. Draw a wiring diagram showing three resistances connected in parallel across a battery. Indicate each branch and the main line.

2. State two rules for the voltage and current values in a parallel circuit.

3. Explain briefly why the current is the same in both sides of the main line that connects the voltage source to the parallel branches.

4. (**a**) Show how to connect three equal resistances for a combined equivalent resistance one-third the value of one resistance. (**b**) Show how to connect three equal resistances for a combined equivalent resistance three times the value of one resistance.

5. Why can the current in parallel branches be different when they all have the same applied voltage?

6. Why does the current increase in the voltage source as more parallel branches are added to the circuit?

7. Show how the formula

$$R_{EQ} = R_1R_2/(R_1 + R_2)$$

is derived from the reciprocal formula

$$\frac{1}{R_{EQ}} = \frac{1}{R_1} + \frac{1}{R_2}$$

8. Redraw Fig. 5-16 with five parallel resistors R_1 to R_5 and explain why they all would be shorted out with a short circuit across R_3.

9. State briefly why the total power equals the sum of the individual values of power, whether a series circuit or a parallel circuit is used.
10. Explain why an open in the main line disables all the branches, but an open in one branch affects only that branch current.
11. Give two differences between an open circuit and a short circuit.
12. List as many differences as you can in comparing series circuits with parallel circuits.
13. Why are household appliances connected to the 120-V power line in parallel instead of being in series?
14. Give one advantage and one disadvantage of parallel connections.
15. Describe the function of the OR gate.

PROBLEMS

1. A 6-Ω R_1 and a 12-Ω R_2 are connected in parallel across a 12-V battery. (a) Draw the schematic diagram. (b) How much is the voltage across R_1 and R_2? (c) How much is the current in R_1 and R_2? (d) How much is the main-line current? (e) Calculate R_{EQ}.
2. For the circuit in question 1, how much is the total power supplied by the battery?
3. A parallel circuit has three branch resistances of 20, 10, and 5 Ω for R_1, R_2, and R_3. The current through the 20-Ω branch is 1 A. (a) Draw the schematic diagram. (b) How much is the voltage applied across all the branches? (c) Find the current through the 10-Ω branch and the 5-Ω branch.
4. (a) Draw the schematic diagram of a parallel circuit with three branch resistances, each having 28 V applied and a 2-A branch current. (b) How much is I_T? (c) How much is R_{EQ}?
5. Referring to Fig. 5-13, assume that R_2 opens. (a) How much is the current in the R_2 branch? (b) How much is the current in the R_1 branch? (c) How much is the line current? (d) How much is the R_{EQ} of the circuit? (e) How much power is generated by the battery?
6. Two resistances R_1 and R_2 are in parallel across a 120-V source. The total line current is 10 A. The current I_1 through R_1 is 4 A. Draw a schematic diagram of the circuit, giving the values of currents I_1 and I_2 and resistances R_1 and R_2 in both branches. How much is the R_{EQ} of both branches across the voltage source?
7. Find the R_{EQ} for the following groups of branch resistances: (a) 10 Ω and 25 Ω; (b) five 10-kΩ resistances; (c) two 500-Ω resistances; (d) 100 Ω, 200 Ω, and 300 Ω; (e) two 5-kΩ and two 2-kΩ resistances; (f) four 40-kΩ and two 20-kΩ resistances.
8. Find R_3 in Fig. 5-18.
9. Find the total conductance in siemens for the following branches: $G_1 = 9000$ μS; $G_2 = 8000$ μS; $G_3 = 22,000$ μS.
10. Referring to Fig. 5-11, calculate R_{EQ} by combining resistances. Show that this R_{EQ} equals $1/G_T$, where G_T is 0.75 S.
11. How much parallel R_X must be connected across a 100-kΩ resistance to reduce R_{EQ} to (a) 50 kΩ; (b) 25 kΩ; (c) 10 kΩ?
12. In Fig. 5-19, (a) find each branch current and show the direction of electron flow; (b) calculate I_T; (c) calculate R_{EQ}; (d) calculate P_1, P_2, P_3, and P_T.
13. A 2.2-kΩ resistor R_1 and 3.9-kΩ resistor R_2 are in parallel. The current I_1 is 4 mA. Calculate V_1, V_2, and I_2.

FIG. 5-18   Circuit diagram for Prob. 8.

FIG. 5-19   Circuit diagram for Prob. 12.

14. Compare the combined resistance of a 5600-Ω R_1 and 8200-Ω R_2 connected in series and in parallel.

15. A 10-Ω R_1 is in parallel with a branch that has G_2 of 0.4 S. Calculate G_T and R_{EQ} for the two parallel branches.

16. What value of G_3 must be connected in parallel with G_1 of 1.62 S and G_2 of 1.34 S for a G_T of 4 S?

17. In Fig. 5-20, solve for I_1, I_2, I_3, I_T, R_{EQ}, P_1, P_2, P_3, and P_T.

18. In Fig. 5-20, what is R_{EQ} if R_2: (**a**) opens; (**b**) shorts?

19. In Fig. 5-21, solve for I_1, I_2, I_3, I_T, R_{EQ}, P_1, P_2, P_3, and P_T.

20. In Fig. 5-21, what is R_{EQ} if a 15-Ω resistor, R_4, is added in parallel with the other three resistors?

21. In Fig. 5-21, how is the branch current, I_1, affected if R_3 opens?

FIG. 5-20   Circuit diagram for Probs. 17 and 18.

FIG. 5-21   Circuit diagram for Probs. 19, 20, and 21.

22. In Fig. 5-22, solve for I_1, I_2, I_3, I_4, I_T, R_{EQ}, P_1, P_2, P_3, P_4, and P_T.

23. In Fig. 5-22, calculate R_{EQ} if V_A is doubled to 48 V.

24. In Fig. 5-23, calculate I_1, I_2, I_3, I_4, I_T, and R_{EQ}. Also, list the currents which will be indicated by meters M_1 and M_2.

25. In Fig. 5-23, how much current will be indicated by M_2 if: (**a**) R_4 opens; (**b**) R_2 opens?

26. In Fig. 5-24, calculate I_1, I_2, I_3, I_4, I_T, and R_{EQ}.

27. In Fig. 5-24, how much current will be indicated by M_1 if: (**a**) R_1 and R_4 open; (**b**) R_3 opens?

28. In Fig. 5-24, how much current will flow in M_2 if a 200-Ω resistor is added between points A and B?

29. In Fig. 5-25, find I_T, I_1, I_2, R_1, R_2, R_3, P_T, P_2, and P_3.

30. In Fig. 5-26, find I_T, I_1, I_2, I_4, R_3, R_4, P_T, P_1, P_2, P_3, and P_4.

31. In Fig. 5-27, find R_{EQ}, I_T, I_2, I_3, I_4, R_1, R_3, P_T, P_1, P_2, P_3, and P_4.

32. In Fig. 5-28, find V_A, I_T, I_1, I_2, R_3, P_T, P_1, P_2, and P_3.

FIG. 5-22   Circuit diagram for Probs. 22 and 23.

FIG. 5-23   Circuit diagram for Probs. 24 and 25.

FIG. 5-24   Circuit diagram for Probs. 26, 27, and 28.

FIG. 5-25   Circuit diagram for Prob. 29.

FIG. 5-26   Circuit diagram for Prob. 30.

FIG. 5-27 Circuit diagram for Prob. 31.

FIG. 5-28 Circuit diagram for Prob. 32.

CRITICAL THINKING

1. A 180-Ω ¼-W resistor is in parallel with a 1-kΩ ½-W and a 12-kΩ 2-W resistor. What is the maximum total current, I_T, that this parallel combination can have before the wattage rating of any resistor is exceeded?

2. A 470-Ω ⅛-W resistor is in parallel with a 1-kΩ ¼-W and a 1.5-kΩ ½-W resistor. What is the maximum voltage, V, that can be applied to this circuit without exceeding the wattage rating of any resistor?

3. Three resistors in parallel have a combined equivalent resistance, R_{EQ}, of 1 kΩ. If R_2 is twice the value of R_3 and three times the value of R_1, what are the values for R_1, R_2, and R_3?

4. Three resistors in parallel have a combined equivalent resistance, R_{EQ}, of 4 Ω. If the conductance, G_1, is one-fourth that of G_2 and one-fifth that of G_3, what are the values of R_1, R_2, and R_3?

5. A voltage source is connected across four resistors, R_1, R_2, R_3, and R_4, in parallel. The currents are labeled I_1, I_2, I_3, and I_4, respectively. If $I_2 = 2I_1$, $I_3 = 2I_2$, and $I_4 = 2I_3$, calculate the values for R_1, R_2, R_3, and R_4 if $R_{EQ} = 1$ kΩ.

ANSWERS TO TEST-POINT QUESTIONS

5-1 **a.** 1.5 V
    b. 120 V
    c. Two

5-2 **a.** 10 V
    b. 1 A
    c. 10 V
    d. 2 A

5-3 **a.** $I_T = 6$ A
    b. $I_3 = 3$ A
    c. $I_T = 1.2$ A

5-4 **a.** $R_{EQ} = 1.57$ MΩ
    b. $R_{EQ} = 1.2$ MΩ
    c. $R_{EQ} = 5$ Ω

5-5 **a.** $G_T = 6$ S
    b. $G_T = 0.75$ μS
        $R_{EQ} = 1.33$ MΩ
    c. $R_{EQ} = 0.25$ MΩ

5-6 **a.** 480 W
    b. 660 W
    c. 30 W

5-7 **a.** 120 V
    b. $I_1 = 4$ A
    c. 7 A

5-8 **a.** infinite ohms
    b. bulbs 1 and 2
    c. all

5-9 **a.** 0 Ω
    b. $I_1 = 0$ A

5-10 **a.** F
    b. F
    c. T
    d. T

CHAPTER 6

SERIES-PARALLEL CIRCUITS

Components in parallel with the voltage source V_A all have the same voltage, but what if they need a voltage less than V_A? The solution is to insert a voltage-dropping resistor in series with the parallel combination. The result is one type of series-parallel circuit. As another example, components in series have the same current but another component may need the same voltage that exists across one of the series components. Just connect the components in parallel for the same voltage for another type of series-parallel circuit.

In general, a series-parallel circuit is used when it is necessary to provide different amounts of voltage and current for the components using one source of applied voltage.

These principles are described for dc circuits in this chapter but they also apply to ac circuits, since resistors have the same value for direct or alternating current.

CHAPTER OBJECTIVES

Upon completion of this chapter, you should be able to:

- *Determine* the total resistance of a series-parallel circuit.
- *Calculate* the voltage, current, resistance, and power in a series-parallel circuit.
- *Calculate* the voltage, current, resistance, and power in a series-parallel circuit having random unknowns.
- *Explain* how a Wheatstone bridge can be used to determine the resistance of an unknown resistor.
- *Define* the term *chassis ground.*
- *Calculate* the voltage at a given point in a circuit with respect to chassis ground.
- *Describe* the effects of opens and shorts in series-parallel circuits.
- *Describe* how series-parallel switches can be used to describe the operation of a logic circuit containing AND and OR gates.

IMPORTANT TERMS IN THIS CHAPTER

balanced bridge	grounded tap	voltage divider
banks in series	strings in parallel	Wheatstone bridge
chassis-ground connections	voltage to chassis ground	

TOPICS COVERED IN THIS CHAPTER

6-1 FINDING R_T FOR SERIES-PARALLEL RESISTANCES

In Fig. 6-1, R_1 is in series with R_2. Also, R_3 is in parallel with R_4. However, R_2 is *not* in series with R_3 and R_4. The reason is the branch point A where the current through R_2 divides for R_3 and R_4. As a result, the current through R_3 must be less than the current through R_2. Therefore, R_2 and R_3 cannot be in series because they do not have the same current. For the same reason, R_4 also cannot be in series with R_2.

FIG. 6-1 Example of series-parallel circuit. (*a*) Wiring of a series-parallel circuit. (*b*) Schematic diagram of a series-parallel circuit. (*c*) Schematic with R_1 and R_2 in series added for $R_{1\text{-}2}$. (*d*) Schematic with R_3 and R_4 in parallel combined for $R_{3\text{-}4}$. (*e*) Axial-lead resistors assembled on a lab prototype board to form the series-parallel circuit shown in parts *a* and *b*. (*f*) Surface-mount resistors assembled on a printed circuit board to form the series-parallel circuit shown in parts *a* and *b*.

The wiring is shown in Fig. 6-1*a* with the schematic diagram in Fig. 6-1*b*. To find R_T, we add the series resistances and combine the parallel resistances.

In Fig. 6-1*c*, the 0.5-kΩ R_1 and 0.5-kΩ R_2 in series total 1 kΩ for $R_{1\text{-}2}$. The calculations are

$$0.5 \text{ k}\Omega + 0.5 \text{ k}\Omega = 1 \text{ k}\Omega$$

Also, the 1-kΩ R_3 in parallel with the 1-kΩ R_4 can be combined, for an equivalent resistance of 0.5 kΩ for $R_{3\text{-}4}$, as in Fig. 6-1*d*. The calculations are

$$\frac{1 \text{ } k\Omega}{2} = 0.5 \text{ } k\Omega$$

This parallel $R_{3\text{-}4}$ combination of 0.5 kΩ is then added to the series $R_{1\text{-}2}$ combination for the final R_T value of 1.5 kΩ. The calculations are

▶ $0.5 \text{ k}\Omega + 1 \text{ k}\Omega = 1.5 \text{ k}\Omega$

The 1.5 kΩ is the R_T of the entire circuit connected across the V_T of 1.5 V.

With R_T known to be 1.5 kΩ, we can find I_T in the main line produced by 1.5 V. Then

$$I_T = \frac{V_T}{R_T} = \frac{1.5 \text{ V}}{1.5 \text{ k}\Omega} = 1 \text{ mA}$$

This 1-mA I_T is the current through resistors R_1 and R_2 in Fig. 6-1*a* and *b* or $R_{1\text{-}2}$ in Fig. 6-1*c*.

At branch point A, at the top of the diagram in Fig. 6-1*b*, the 1 mA of electron flow for I_T divides into two branch currents for R_3 and R_4. Since these two branch resistances are equal, I_T divides into two equal parts of 0.5 mA each. At branch point B at the bottom of the diagram, the two 0.5-mA branch currents combine to equal the 1-mA I_T in the main line, returning to the source V_T.

Figure 6-1*e* shows axial-lead resistors assembled on a lab prototype board to form the series-parallel circuit shown in Fig. 6-1*a* and *b*. Figure 6-1*f* shows surface-mount resistors assembled on a printed circuit board to form the series-parallel circuit shown in Fig. 6-1*b*.

TEST-POINT QUESTION 6-1

Answers at end of chapter.

Refer to Fig. 6-1*b*.
a. Calculate the series R of R_1 and R_2.
b. Calculate the parallel R of R_3 and R_4.
c. Calculate R_T across the source V_T.

6-2 RESISTANCE STRINGS IN PARALLEL

More details about the voltages and currents in a series-parallel circuit are illustrated by the example in Fig. 6-2. Suppose there are four 120-V 100-W light bulbs to be wired, with a voltage source that produces 240 V. Each bulb needs

FIG. 6-2 Two identical series strings in parallel. All bulbs have 120-V 100-W rating. (a) Wiring diagram. (b) Schematic diagram.

120 V for normal brilliance. If the bulbs were connected across the source, each would have the applied voltage of 240 V. This would cause excessive current in all the bulbs that could result in burned-out filaments.

If the four bulbs were connected in series, each would have a potential difference of 60 V, or one-fourth the applied voltage. With too low a voltage, there would be insufficient current for normal operation and the bulbs would not operate at normal brilliance.

However, two bulbs in series across the 240-V line provide 120 V for each filament, which is the normal operating voltage. Therefore, the four bulbs are wired in strings of two in series, with the two strings in parallel across the 240-V source. Both strings have 240 V applied. In each string, two series bulbs divide the 240 V equally to provide the required 120 V for normal operation.

Another example is illustrated in Fig. 6-3. This circuit has just two parallel branches where one branch includes R_1 in series with R_2. The other branch has just the one resistance R_3. Ohm's law can be applied to each branch.

FIG. 6-3 Series string in parallel with another branch. (a) Schematic diagram. (b) Equivalent circuit.

BRANCH CURRENTS I_1 AND I_2 Each branch current equals the voltage applied across the branch divided by the total resistance in the branch. In branch 1, R_1 and R_2 total $8 + 4 = 12\ \Omega$. With 12 V applied, this branch current I_1 is $12/12 = 1$ A. Branch 2 has only the 6-Ω R_3. Then I_2 in this branch is $12/6 = 2$ A.

SERIES VOLTAGE DROPS IN A BRANCH   For any one resistance in a string, the current in the string multiplied by the resistance equals the IR voltage drop across that particular resistance. Also, the sum of the series IR drops in the string equals the voltage across the entire string.

Branch 1 is a string with R_1 and R_2 in series. The I_1R_1 drop equals 8 V, while the I_1R_2 drop is 4 V. These drops of 8 and 4 V add to equal the 12 V applied. The voltage across the R_3 branch is also the same 12 V.

CALCULATING I_T   The total line current equals the sum of the branch currents for all the parallel strings. Here I_T is 3 A, equal to the sum of 1 A in branch 1 and 2 A in branch 2.

CALCULATING R_T   The resistance of the total series-parallel circuit across the voltage source equals the applied voltage divided by the total line current. In Fig. 6-3, R_T equals 12 V/3 A, or 4 Ω. This resistance can also be calculated as 12 Ω in parallel with 6 Ω. Using the product divided by the sum formula, 72/18 = 4 Ω for the equivalent combined R_T.

APPLYING OHM'S LAW   There can be any number of parallel strings and more than two series resistances in a string. Still, Ohm's law can be used in the same way for the series and parallel parts of the circuit. The series parts have the same current. The parallel parts have the same voltage. Remember that for V/R the R must include all the resistance across the two terminals of V.

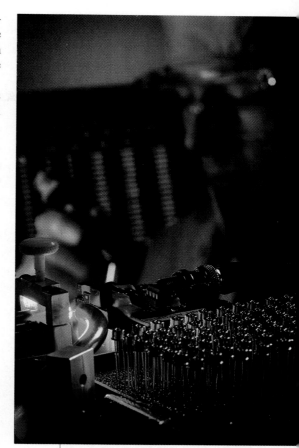

TEST-POINT QUESTION 6-2

Answers at end of chapter.

Refer to Fig. 6-3a.
a. How much is the voltage across R_3?
b. If I in R_2 were 6 A, what would I in R_1 be?
c. If the source voltage were 18 V, what would V_3 be across R_3?

6-3 RESISTANCE BANKS IN SERIES

In Fig. 6-4a, the group of parallel resistances R_2 and R_3 is a bank. This is in series with R_1 because the total current of the bank must go through R_1.

The circuit here has R_2 and R_3 in parallel in one bank so that these two resistances will have the same potential difference of 20 V across them. The source applies 24 V, but there is a 4-V drop across R_1.

The two series voltage drops of 4 V across R_1 and 20 V across the bank add to equal the applied voltage of 24 V. The purpose of a circuit like this is to pro-

FIG. 6-4 Parallel bank of R_2 and R_3 in series with R_1. (*a*) Original circuit. (*b*) Equivalent circuit.

vide the same voltage for two or more resistances in a bank, where the bank voltage must be less than the applied voltage by the amount of *IR* drop across any series resistance.

To find the resistance of the entire circuit, combine the parallel resistances in each bank and add the series resistance. As shown in Fig. 6-4*b*, the two 10-Ω resistances R_2 and R_3 in parallel are equivalent to 5 Ω. Since the bank resistance of 5 Ω is in series with 1 Ω for R_1, the total resistance is 6 Ω across the 24-V source. Therefore, the main-line current is 24 V/6 Ω, which equals 4 A.

The total line current of 4 A divides into two parts of 2 A each in the parallel resistances R_2 and R_3. Note that each branch current equals the bank voltage divided by the branch resistance. For this bank, 20/10 = 2 A for each branch.

The branch currents are combined in the line to provide the total 4 A in R_1. This is the same total current flowing in the main line, in the source, into the bank, and out of the bank.

There can be more than two parallel resistances in a bank and any number of banks in series. Still, Ohm's law can be applied the same way to the series and parallel parts of the circuit. The general procedure for circuits of this type is to find the equivalent resistance of each bank and then add all the series resistances.

TEST-POINT QUESTION 6-3

Answers at end of chapter.

Refer to Fig. 6-4*a*.
a. If V_2 across R_2 were 40 V, what would V_3 across R_3 be?
b. If I in R_2 were 4 A, with 4 A in R_3, what would I in R_1 be?
c. How much is V_1 across R_1 in Fig. 6-4*b*?

6-4 RESISTANCE BANKS AND STRINGS IN SERIES-PARALLEL

In the solution of such circuits, the most important fact to know is which components are in series with each other and what parts of the circuit are parallel branches. The series components must be in one current path without any branch points. A branch point such as point A or B in Fig. 6-5 is common to two or more current paths. For instance, R_1 and R_6 are *not* in series with each other. They do not have the same current, because the current in R_1 divides at point A into its two component branch currents. Similarly, R_5 is not in series with R_2, because of the branch point B.

FIG. 6-5   Reducing a series-parallel circuit to an equivalent series circuit to find the R_T. (a) Actual circuit. (b) R_3 and R_4 in parallel combined for the equivalent R_7. (c) R_7 and R_6 in series added for R_{13}. (d) R_{13} and R_5 in parallel combined for R_{18}. (e) The R_{18}, R_1, and R_2 in series are added for the total resistance of 50 Ω for R_T.

To find the currents and voltages in Fig. 6-5, first find R_T in order to calculate the main-line current I_T as V_T/R_T. In calculating R_T, start reducing the branch farthest from the source and work toward the applied voltage. The reason for following this order is that you cannot tell how much resistance is in series with R_1 and R_2 until the parallel branches are reduced to their equivalent resistance. If no source voltage is shown, R_T can still be calculated from the outside in toward the open terminals where a source would be connected.

To calculate R_T in Fig. 6-5, the steps are as follows:

1. The bank of the 12-Ω R_3 and 12-Ω R_4 in parallel in Fig. 6-5a is equal to the 6-Ω R_7 in Fig. 6-5b.
2. The 6-Ω R_7 and 4-Ω R_6 in series in the same current path total 10 Ω for R_{13} in Fig. 6-5c.
3. The 10-Ω R_{13} is in parallel with the 10-Ω R_5, across the branch points A and B. Their equivalent resistance, then, is the 5-Ω R_{18} in Fig. 6-5d.
4. Now the circuit in Fig. 6-5d has just the 15-Ω R_1, 5-Ω R_{18}, and 30-Ω R_2 in series. These resistances total 50 Ω for R_T, as shown in Fig. 6-5e.
5. With a 50-Ω R_T across the 100-V source, the line current I_T is equal to 100/50 = 2 A.

To see the individual currents and voltages, we can use the I_T of 2 A for the equivalent circuit in Fig. 6-5d. Now we work from the source V out toward the branches. The reason is that I_T can be used to find the voltage drops in the main line. The IR voltage drops here are

$$V_1 = I_T R_1 = 2 \times 15 = 30 \text{ V}$$
$$V_{18} = I_T R_{18} = 2 \times 5 = 10 \text{ V}$$
$$V_2 = I_T R_2 = 2 \times 30 = 60 \text{ V}$$

The 10-V drop across R_{18} is actually the potential difference between branch points A and B. This means 10 V across R_5 and R_{13} in Fig. 6-5c. The 10 V produces 1 A in the 10-Ω R_5 branch. The same 10 V is also across the R_{13} branch.

Remember that the R_{13} branch is actually the string of R_6 in series with the $R_3 R_4$ bank. Since this branch resistance is 10 Ω, with 10 V across it, the branch current here is 1 A. The 1 A through the 4 Ω of R_6 produces a voltage drop of 4 V. The remaining 6-V IR drop is across the $R_3 R_4$ bank. With 6 V across the 12-Ω R_3, its current is ½ A; the current is also ½ A in R_4.

Tracing all the current paths from the source, the main-line current through R_1 is 2 A. At the branch point A, this current divides into 1 A for R_5 and 1 A for the string with R_6. There is a 1-A branch current in R_6, but it subdivides in the bank, with ½ A in R_3 and ½ A in R_4. At the branch point B, the total bank current of 1 A combines with the 1 A through the R_5 branch, resulting in a 2-A total line current through R_2, the same as through R_1 in the opposite side of the line.

TEST-POINT QUESTION 6-4

Answers at end of chapter.

Refer to Fig. 6-5a.
a. Which R is in series with R_2?
b. Which R is in parallel with R_3?
c. Which R is in series with the $R_3 R_4$ bank?

6-5 ANALYZING SERIES-PARALLEL CIRCUITS

The circuits in Figs. 6-6 to 6-9 will be solved now. The following principles are illustrated:

1. With parallel strings across the main line, the branch currents and I_T can be found without R_T (see Figs. 6-6 and 6-7).
2. When parallel strings have series resistance in the main line, R_T must be calculated to find I_T, assuming no branch currents are known (see Fig. 6-9).
3. The source voltage is applied across the R_T of the entire circuit, producing an I_T that flows only in the main line.
4. Any individual series R has its own IR drop that must be less than the total V_T. In addition, any individual branch current must be less than I_T.

SOLUTION FOR FIG. 6-6   The problem here is to calculate the branch currents I_1 and $I_{2\text{-}3}$, total line current I_T, and the voltage drops V_1, V_2, and V_3. This order will be used for the calculations, because we can find the branch currents from the 90 V across the known branch resistances.

In the 30-Ω branch of R_1, the branch current is 90/30 = 3 A for I_1. The other branch resistance, with a 20-Ω R_2 and a 25-Ω R_3, totals 45 Ω. This branch current then is 90/45 = 2 A for $I_{2\text{-}3}$. In the main line, I_T is 3 A + 2 A, which is equal to 5 A.

For the branch voltages, V_1 must be the same as V_A, equal to 90 V. Or $V_1 = I_1 R_1$, which is 3 × 30 = 90 V.

In the other branch, the 2-A $I_{2\text{-}3}$ flows through the 20-Ω R_2 and the 25-Ω R_3. Therefore, V_2 is 2 × 20 = 40 V. Also, V_3 is 2 × 25 = 50 V. Note that these 40-V and 50-V series IR drops in one branch add to equal the 90-V source.

If we want to know R_T, it can be calculated as V_A/I_T. Then 90 V/5 A equals 18 Ω. Or R_T can be calculated by combining the branch resistances of 30 Ω in parallel with 45 Ω. Then, using the product-divided-by-sum formula, R_T is (30 × 45)/(30 + 45) or is 1350/75, which equals the same value of 18 Ω for R_T.

FIG. 6-6   Finding all the currents and voltages by calculating the branch currents first. See text for solution.

SOLUTION FOR FIG. 6-7   To find the applied voltage first, the I_1 branch current is given. This 3-A current through the 10-Ω R_1 produces a 30-V drop V_1 across R_1. The same 3-A current through the 20-Ω R_2 produces 60 V for V_2 across

FIG. 6-7 Finding the applied voltage V_A, then V_4 and R_4 from I_2 and the branch voltages. See text for the calculations.

R_2. The 30-V and 60-V drops are in series with each other across the applied voltage. Therefore, V_A equals the sum of $30 + 60$, or 90 V. This 90 V is also across the other branch combining R_3 and R_4 in series.

The other branch current I_2 in Fig. 6-7 must be 4 A, equal to the 7-A I_T minus the 3-A I_1. With 4 A for I_2, the voltage drop across the 12-Ω R_3 equals 48 V for V_3. Then the voltage across R_4 is $90 - 48$, or 42 V for V_4, as the sum of V_3 and V_4 must equal the applied 90 V.

Finally, with 42 V across R_4 and 4 A through it, this resistance equals 42/4, or 10.5 Ω. Note that 10.5 Ω for R_4 added to the 12 Ω of R_3 equals 22.5 Ω, which allows 90/22.5 or a 4-A branch current for I_2.

SOLUTION FOR FIG. 6-8 The division of branch currents also applies to Fig. 6-8, but the main principle here is that the voltage must be the same across R_1 and R_2 in parallel. For the branch currents, I_2 is 2 A, equal to the 6-A I_T minus the 4-A I_1. The voltage across the 10-Ω R_1 is 4×10, or 40 V. This same voltage is also across R_2. With 40 V across R_2 and 2 A through it, R_2 equals 40/2 or 20 Ω.

We can also find V_T in Fig. 6-8 from R_1, R_2, and R_3. The 6-A I_T through R_3 produces a voltage drop of 60 V for V_3. Also, the voltage across the parallel bank with R_1 and R_2 has been calculated as 40 V. This 40 V across the bank in series with 60 V across R_3 totals 100 V for the applied voltage.

SOLUTION FOR FIG. 6-9 In order to find all the currents and voltage drops, we need R_T to calculate I_T through R_6 in the main line. Combining resis-

FIG. 6-8 Finding R_2 in the parallel bank and its I_2. See text for solution.

FIG. 6-9 Finding all currents and voltages by calculating R_T and then I_T to find V_6 across R_6 in the main line.

tances for R_T, we start with R_1 and R_2 and work in toward the source. Add the 8-Ω R_1 and 8-Ω R_2 in series with each other for 16 Ω. This 16 Ω combined with the 16-Ω R_3 in parallel equals 8 Ω between points C and D. Add this 8 Ω to the series 12-Ω R_4 for 20 Ω. This 20 Ω with the parallel 20-Ω R_5 equals 10 Ω between points A and B. Add this 10 Ω in series with the 10-Ω R_6, to make R_T of 20 Ω for the entire series-parallel circuit.

Current I_T in the main line is V_T/R_T, or 80/20, which equals 4 A. This 4-A I_T flows through the 10-Ω R_6, producing a 40-V IR drop for V_6.

Now that we know I_T and V_6 in the main line, we use these values to calculate all the other voltages and currents. Start from the main line, where we know the current, and work outward from the source. To find V_5, the IR drop of 40 V for V_6 in the main line is subtracted from the source voltage. The reason is that V_5 and V_6 must add to equal the 80 V of V_T. Then V_5 is $80 - 40 = 40$ V.

Voltages V_5 and V_6 happen to be equal at 40 V each. They split the 80 V in half because the 10-Ω R_6 equals the combined resistance of 10 Ω between branch points A and B.

With V_5 known to be 40 V, then I_5 through the 20-Ω R_5 is $40/20 = 2$ A. Since I_5 is 2 A and I_T is 4 A, I_4 must be 2 A also, equal to the difference between I_T and I_5. At the branch point A, the 4-A I_T divides into 2 A through R_5 and 2 A through R_4.

The 2-A I_4 through the 12-Ω R_4 produces an IR drop equal to $2 \times 12 = 24$ V for V_4. It should be noted now that V_4 and V_3 must add to equal V_5. The reason is that both V_5 and the path with V_4 and V_3 are across the same two points AB or AD. Since the potential difference across any two points is the same regardless of the path, $V_5 = V_4 + V_3$. To find V_3 now, we can subtract the 24 V of V_4 from the 40 V of V_5. Then $40 - 24 = 16$ V for V_3.

With 16 V for V_3 across the 16-Ω R_3, its current I_3 is 1 A. Also I_{1-2} in the branch with R_1 and R_2 is equal to 1 A. The 2-A I_4 into branch point C divides into the two equal branch currents of 1 A each because of the equal branch resistances.

Finally, with 1 A through the 8-Ω R_2 and 8-Ω R_1, their voltage drops are $V_2 = 8$ V and $V_1 = 8$ V. Note that the 8 V of V_1 in series with the 8 V of V_2 add to equal the 16-V potential difference V_3 between points C and D.

All the answers for the solution of Fig. 6-9 are summarized below:

$R_T = 20\ \Omega$	$I_T = 4$ A	$V_6 = 40$ V
$V_5 = 40$ V	$I_5 = 2$ A	$I_4 = 2$ A
$V_4 = 24$ V	$V_3 = 16$ V	$I_3 = 1$ A
$I_{1-2} = 1$ A	$V_2 = 8$ V	$V_1 = 8$ V

Answers at end of chapter.
a. In Fig. 6-6, which R is in series with R_2?
b. In Fig. 6-6, which R is across V_A?
c. In Fig. 6-7, how much is I_2?
d. In Fig. 6-8, how much is V_3?

6-6 WHEATSTONE BRIDGE

A bridge circuit has four terminals, two for input voltage and two for output. The purpose is to have a circuit where the voltage drops can be balanced to provide zero voltage across the output terminals, with voltage applied across the input. In Fig. 6-10a the input terminals are C and D, with output terminals A and B.

(a)

(b)   (c)

FIG. 6-10   Wheatstone-bridge circuit. (a) Schematic diagram of a Wheatstone-bridge circuit. (b) A balanced Wheatstone bridge assembled using fixed resistors on a lab prototype board. (c) A balanced Wheatstone bridge assembled using surface-mount resistors on a printed circuit board.

The bridge circuit has many uses for comparison measurements. In the Wheatstone* bridge, an unknown resistance R_X is balanced against a standard accurate resistor R_S for precise measurement of resistance.

*Sir Charles Wheatstone (1802–1875), English physicist and inventor.

In Fig. 6-10a, S_1 applies battery voltage to the four resistors in the bridge. To balance the bridge, the value of R_S is varied. Balance is indicated by zero current in the galvanometer G. Finally, S_2 is a spring switch that is opened to disconnect R and increase the sensitivity of the meter for the bridge.

The reason for zero current in the meter can be seen by analysis of the voltage drops across the resistors. R_S in series with R_X divides the voltage across V_T; the parallel string of R_1 in series with R_2 is also a voltage divider across the same source. When the voltage divides in the same ratio for both strings, the voltage drop across R_S equals the voltage across R_2. Also, the voltage across R_X then equals the voltage across R_1. In this case, points A and B must be at the same potential. The difference of potential across the meter then must be zero, and there is no deflection of the meter's pointer.

At balance, the equal voltage ratios in the two branches of the Wheatstone bridge can be stated as

▶
$$\frac{I_A R_X}{I_A R_S} = \frac{I_B R_1}{I_B R_2} \quad \text{or} \quad \frac{R_X}{R_S} = \frac{R_1}{R_2}$$

Note that I_A and I_B cancel. Now, multiplying both sides of the equation by R_S,

▶
$$R_X = R_S \times \frac{R_1}{R_2} \qquad\qquad\qquad \textbf{(6-1)}$$

Usually, the total resistance of R_1 and R_2 is fixed, but any desired ratio can be chosen by moving point B on the ratio arm. The bridge is balanced by varying R_S for zero current in the meter. At balance, then, the value of R_X can be determined by multiplying R_S by the ratio of R_1/R_2. As an example, if the ratio is $\frac{1}{100}$ or 0.01 and R_S is 248 Ω, the value of R_X equals 248 × 0.01 = 2.48 Ω.

The balanced bridge circuit can be analyzed as simply two series resistance strings in parallel when the current is zero through the meter. Without any current between A and B, this path is effectively open. When current flows through the meter path, however, the bridge circuit must be analyzed by other methods as described in Chaps. 9 and 10.

Figure 6-10b shows a balanced Wheatstone bridge circuit assembled using fixed resistors on a lab prototype board. Figure 6-10c shows a balanced Wheatstone bridge circuit assembled using surface-mount resistors on a printed circuit board.

ABOUT ELECTRONICS

We want robots of the future to watch out and not bump into us. SensorSkin is designed to make robots aware that they're getting too close. The designer wrap is a flexible circuit board with proximity sensors.

TEST-POINT QUESTION 6-6

Answers at end of chapter.
a. A bridge circuit has how many *pairs* of terminals?
b. In Fig. 6-10a, how much is V_{AB} at balance?

6-7 CHASSIS-GROUND CONNECTIONS

In the wiring of practical circuits, one side of the voltage source is usually grounded. For the 120-Vac power line in residential wiring, the ground is actually the earth. The ground connection is usually made by driving copper rods into the ground and connecting the ground wire of the electrical system to these rods.

(a)

(b)

(c)

FIG. 6-11 Example of grounding one side of the voltage source. (a) The ac power line. (b) Negative side of a battery connected to a chassis ground. (c) Positive side of a battery connected to chassis ground.

In some cases, the incoming water pipe is used as the ground connection. For electronic equipment, the ground just indicates a metal chassis, which is used as a common return for connections to the source. With printed wiring on a plastic board instead of a metal chassis, a conducting path around the entire board is used as a common return for chassis ground. The chassis ground may or may not be connected to earth ground. In either case the grounded side is called the "cold side" or "low side" of the applied voltage, while the ungrounded side is the "hot side" or "high side."

GROUNDING ONE SIDE OF THE SOURCE VOLTAGE   Three examples are shown in Fig. 6-11. In Fig. 6-11a, one side of the 120-Vac power line is grounded. Note the symbol for earth ground. This symbol also indicates a chassis ground that is connected to one side of the voltage source. In electronic equipment, black wire is generally used for chassis ground returns and red wire for the high side of the voltage source. In residential wiring, green insulation denotes the grounding wire, whereas white insulation denotes the wire connected to the system's ground.

In Fig. 6-11b and c the 12-V battery is used as an example of a voltage source connected to chassis ground but not to earth. For instance, in an automobile one side of the battery is connected to the metal frame of the car. In Fig. 6-11b, the negative side is grounded, while in Fig. 6-11c the positive side is grounded. Some people have the idea that ground must always be negative, but this is not necessarily so.

The reason for connecting one side of the 120-Vac power line to earth ground is to reduce the possibility of electric shock. However, chassis ground in electronic equipment is mainly a common-return connection. Where the equipment operates from the power line, the metal chassis should be at ground potential, not connected to the hot side of the ac outlet. This connection reduces the possibility of electric shock from the chassis. Also, hum from the power line is reduced in audio, radio, and television equipment.

TEST-POINT QUESTION 6-7

Answers at end of chapter.
   a. In Fig. 6-11b, give the voltage to ground with polarity.
   b. Do the same for Fig. 6-11c.

6-8 VOLTAGES MEASURED TO CHASSIS GROUND

When a circuit has the chassis as a common return, we generally measure the voltages with respect to chassis. The circuit in Fig. 6-12a is called a voltage divider. Let us consider this circuit without any ground, and then analyze the effect of grounding different points on the divider. It is important to realize that this circuit operates the same way with or without the ground. The only factor that changes is the reference point for measuring the voltages.

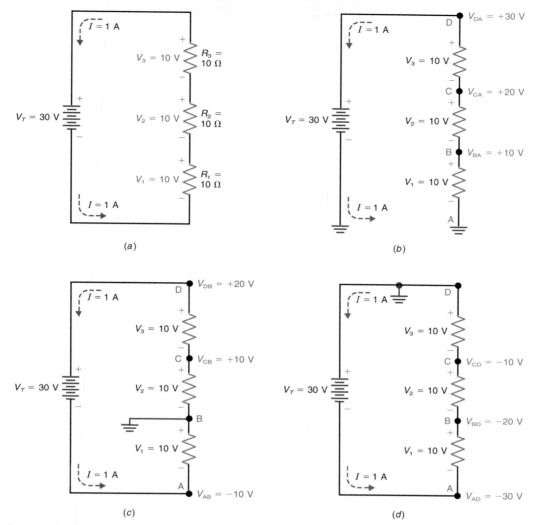

FIG. 6-12 An example of how to figure dc voltages to chassis ground. (a) Voltage divider without any ground connection. (b) Negative side of source V_T grounded to make all voltages positive with respect to ground. (c) Positive and negative voltages in the divider with respect to ground at point B. (d) With positive side of source grounded, all voltages are negative to chassis ground.

In Fig. 6-12a, the three 10-Ω resistances R_1, R_2, and R_3 divide the 30-V source equally. Then each voltage drop is 30/3 = 10 V for V_1, V_2, and V_3. The polarity is positive at the top and negative at the bottom, the same as V_T.

If we want to consider the current, I is 30/30 = 1 A. Each IR drop is 1 × 10 = 10 V for V_1, V_2, and V_3.

POSITIVE VOLTAGES TO NEGATIVE GROUND In Fig. 6-12b, the negative side of V_T is grounded and the bottom end of R_1 is also grounded to complete the circuit. The ground is at point A. Note that the individual voltages V_1, V_2, and V_3 are still 10 V each. Also the current is still 1 A. The direction is also the same, from the negative side of V_T, through the metal chassis, to the bottom end of R_1. The only effect of the chassis ground here is to provide a conducting path from one side of the source to one side of the load.

With the ground in Fig. 6-12b, though, it is useful to consider the voltages with respect to chassis ground. In other words, the ground at point A will now be the reference for all voltages. When a voltage is indicated for only one point in a circuit, generally the other point is assumed to be chassis ground. We must have two points for a potential difference.

Let us consider the voltages at points B, C, and D. The voltage at B to ground is V_{BA}. This double subscript notation shows that we measure at B with respect to A. In general, the first letter indicates the point of measurement and the second letter is the reference point.

Then V_{BA} is $+10$ V. The positive sign is used here to emphasize the polarity. The value of 10 V for V_{BA} is the same as V_1 across R_1 because points B and A are across R_1. However, V_1 as the voltage across R_1 really cannot be given any polarity without a reference point.

When we consider the voltage at C, then, V_{CA} is $+20$ V. This voltage equals $V_1 + V_2$. Also, for point D at the top, V_{DA} is $+30$ V for $V_1 + V_2 + V_3$.

POSITIVE AND NEGATIVE VOLTAGES TO A GROUNDED TAP

In Fig. 6-12c point B in the divider is grounded. The purpose is to have the divider supply negative and positive voltages with respect to chassis ground. The negative voltage here is V_{AB}, which equals -10 V. This value is the same 10 V as V_1, but V_{AB} is the voltage at the negative end A with respect to the positive end B. The other voltages in the divider are $V_{CB} = +10$ V and $V_{DB} = +20$ V.

We can consider the ground at B as a dividing point for positive and negative voltages. For all points toward the positive side of V_T, any voltage is positive to ground. Going the other way, at all points toward the negative side of V_T, any voltage is negative to ground.

NEGATIVE VOLTAGES TO POSITIVE GROUND

In Fig. 6-12d, point D at the top of the divider is grounded, which is the same as grounding the positive side of the source V_T. The voltage source here is *inverted*, compared with Fig. 6-12b, as the opposite side is grounded. In Fig. 6-12d, all the voltages on the divider are negative to ground. Here, $V_{CD} = -10$ V, while $V_{BD} = -20$ V and $V_{AD} = -30$ V. Any point in the circuit must be more negative than the positive terminal of the source, even when this terminal is grounded.

TEST-POINT QUESTION 6-8

Answers at end of chapter.

Refer to Fig. 6-12c and give the voltage and polarity for
a. A to ground.
b. B to ground.
c. D to ground.
d. V_{DA} across V_T.

6-9 OPENS AND SHORTS IN SERIES-PARALLEL CIRCUITS

A short circuit has practically zero resistance. Its effect, therefore, is to allow excessive current. An open circuit has the opposite effect because an open circuit has infinitely high resistance with practically zero current. Furthermore, in series-parallel circuits an open or short circuit in one path changes the circuit for the other resistances. For example, in Fig. 6-13, the series-parallel circuit in Fig. 6-13a becomes a series circuit with only R_1 when there is a short circuit between terminals A and B. As an example of an open circuit, the series-parallel circuit in Fig. 6-14a becomes a series circuit with just R_1 and R_2 when there is an open circuit between terminals C and D.

FIG. 6-13   Effect of a short circuit with series-parallel connections. (a) Normal circuit with S_1 open. (b) Circuit with short between points A and B when S_1 is closed; now R_2 and R_3 are short-circuited.

FIG. 6-14   Effect of an open path in a series-parallel circuit. (a) Normal circuit with S_2 closed. (b) Series circuit with R_1 and R_2 when S_2 is open. Now R_3 in the open path has no current and zero IR voltage drop.

EFFECT OF A SHORT CIRCUIT   We can solve the series-parallel circuit in Fig. 6-13a in order to see the effect of the short circuit. For the normal circuit, with S_1 open, R_2 and R_3 are in parallel. Although R_3 is drawn horizontally, both ends are across R_2. The switch S_1 has no effect as a parallel branch here because it is open.

The combined resistance of the 80-Ω R_2 in parallel with the 80-Ω R_3 is equivalent to 40 Ω. This 40 Ω for the bank resistance is in series with the 10-Ω R_1. Then R_T is 40 + 10 = 50 Ω.

In the main line, I_T is 100/50 = 2 A. Then V_1 across the 10-Ω R_1 in the main line is 2 × 10 = 20 V. The remaining 80 V is across R_2 and R_3 as a parallel bank. As a result, $V_2 = 80$ V and $V_3 = 80$ V.

Now consider the effect of closing switch S_1. A closed switch has zero resistance. Not only is R_2 short-circuited, but R_3 in the bank with R_2 is also short-circuited. The closed switch short-circuits everything connected between terminals A and B. The result is the series circuit shown in Fig. 6-13b.

Now the 10-Ω R_1 is the only opposition to current. I equals V/R_1, which is $100/10 = 10$ A. This 10 A flows through R_1, the closed switch, and the source. With 10 A through R_1, instead of its normal 2 A, the excessive current can cause excessive heat in R_1. There is no current through R_2 and R_3, as they are short-circuited out of the path for current.

EFFECT OF AN OPEN CIRCUIT Figure 6-14a shows the same series-parallel circuit as Fig. 6-13a, except that switch S_2 is used now to connect R_3 in parallel with R_2. With S_2 closed for normal operation, all currents and voltages have the values calculated for the series-parallel circuit. However, let us consider the effect of opening S_2, as shown in Fig. 6-14b. An open switch has infinitely high resistance. Now there is an open circuit between terminals C and D. Furthermore, because R_3 is in the open path, its 80 Ω cannot be considered in parallel with R_2.

The circuit with S_2 open in Fig. 6-14b is really the same as having just R_1 and R_2 in series with the 100-V source. The open path with R_3 has no effect as a parallel branch. The reason is that no current flows through R_3.

We can consider R_1 and R_2 in series as a voltage divider, where each IR drop is proportional to its resistance. The total series R is $80 + 10 = 90$ Ω. The 10-Ω R_1 is 10/90 or $\frac{1}{9}$ of the total R and the applied V_T. Then V_1 is $\frac{1}{9} \times 100$ V $= 11$ V and V_2 is $\frac{8}{9} \times 100$ V $= 89$ V, approximately. The 11-V drop for V_1 and 89-V drop for V_2 add to equal the 100 V of the applied voltage.

Note that V_3 is zero. Without any current through R_3, it cannot have any voltage drop.

Furthermore, the voltage across the open terminals C and D is the same 89 V as the potential difference V_2 across R_2. Since there is no voltage drop across R_3, terminal C has the same potential as the top terminal of R_2. Terminal D is directly connected to the bottom end of resistor R_2. Therefore, the potential difference from terminal C to terminal D is the same 89 V that appears across resistor R_2.

<hr>

TEST-POINT QUESTION 6-9

Answers at end of chapter.
a. In Fig. 6-13, the short circuit increases I_T from 2 A to what value?
b. In Fig. 6-14, the open branch reduces I_T from 2 A to what value?

6-10 SERIES-PARALLEL SWITCHES COMBINE THE AND AND OR LOGIC FUNCTIONS

Figure 6-15a shows how series-parallel switches can be connected to combine the AND and OR logic functions. If both switches A and B are closed or if switch C is closed, a complete path for current flow is provided and the lamp will be

Switches			
A	B	C	Lamp
Open	Open	Open	OFF
Open	Open	Closed	ON
Open	Closed	Open	OFF
Open	Closed	Closed	ON
Closed	Open	Open	OFF
Closed	Open	Closed	ON
Closed	Closed	Open	ON
Closed	Closed	Closed	ON

(a)

(c)

$$AB + C = X$$

(d)

(b)

FIG. 6-15 Series-parallel switches combine the AND and OR logic functions. (a) Circuit representing the logic function $AB + C = X$. (b) Truth table showing the eight possible combinations for switches A, B, and C. (c) Equivalent logic circuit using the AND and OR logic symbols. (d) Mathematical expression describing the AND and OR logic functions.

ON. However, if either switch A or switch B is open at the same time switch C is open, the lamp will be OFF. Figure 6-15b shows the truth table listing all of the possible combinations for switches A, B, and C. Notice in the last row of the truth table that the lamp is on when all three switches are closed.

Figure 6-15c shows the logic circuit corresponding to the series-parallel connection of switches in Fig. 6-15a. The AND logic symbol is used to represent the series switches A and B, whereas the OR logic symbol is used to represent the parallel connection of switch C. Figure 6-15d shows the mathematical expression describing both Figs. 6-15a and 6-15c. The statement is read: "A and B or C equals X."

TEST-POINT QUESTION 6-10

Answers at end of chapter.

Answer True or False.
a. In Fig. 6-15a, the lamp is ON when switches A and B are both open at the same time as switch C is closed.
b. In Fig. 6-15a, the lamp is OFF if either switch A or switch B is open at the same time switch C is open.

6   SUMMARY AND REVIEW

- Table 6-1 summarizes the main characteristics of series and parallel circuits. In circuits combining series and parallel connections, the components in one current path without any branch points are in series; the parts of the circuit connected across the same two branch points are in parallel.
- To calculate R_T in a series-parallel circuit with R in the main line, combine resistances from the outside back toward the source.
- Chassis ground is commonly used as a return connection to one side of the source voltage. Voltages measured to chassis ground can have either negative or positive polarity.
- When the potential is the same at the two ends of a resistance, its voltage is zero. If no current flows through a resistance, it cannot have any IR voltage drop.
- A Wheatstone bridge circuit has two input terminals and two output terminals. When balanced, the Wheatstone bridge can be analyzed as simply two series strings in parallel. The Wheatstone bridge finds many uses in applications where comparison measurements are needed.

TABLE 6-1   COMPARISON OF SERIES AND PARALLEL CIRCUITS

SERIES CIRCUIT	PARALLEL CIRCUIT
Current the same in all components	Voltage the same across all branches
V across each series R is $I \times R$	I in each branch R is V/R
$V_T = V_1 + V_2 + V_3 + \cdots +$ etc.	$I_T = I_1 + I_2 + I_3 + \cdots +$ etc.
$R_T = R_1 + R_2 + R_3 + \cdots +$ etc.	$G_T = G_1 + G_2 + G_3 + \cdots +$ etc.
R_T must be more than the largest individual R	R_{EQ} must be less than the smallest branch R
$P_T = P_1 + P_2 + P_3 + \cdots +$ etc.	$P_T = P_1 + P_2 + P_3 + \cdots +$ etc.
Applied voltage is divided into IR voltage drops	Main-line current is divided into branch currents
The largest IR drop is across the largest series R	The largest branch I is in the smallest parallel R
Open in one component causes entire circuit to be open	Open in one branch does not prevent I in other branches

SELF-TEST

ANSWERS AT BACK OF BOOK.

Choose (*a*), (*b*), (*c*), or (*d*).

1. In the series-parallel circuit in Fig. 6-1*b*: (*a*) R_1 is in series with R_3; (*b*) R_2 is in series with R_3; (*c*) R_4 is in parallel with R_3; (*d*) R_1 is in parallel with R_3.
2. In the series-parallel circuit in Fig. 6-2*b*: (*a*) R_1 is in parallel with R_3; (*b*) R_2 is in parallel with R_4; (*c*) R_1 is in series with R_2; (*d*) R_2 is in series with R_4.
3. In the series-parallel circuit in Fig. 6-5, the total of all the branch currents into branch point A and out of branch point B equals (*a*) ½ A; (*b*) 1 A; (*c*) 2 A; (*d*) 4 A.
4. In the circuit in Fig. 6-2 with four 120-V 100-W light bulbs, the resistance of one bulb equals (*a*) 72 Ω; (*b*) 100 Ω; (*c*) 144 Ω; (*d*) 120 Ω.
5. In the series-parallel circuit in Fig. 6-4*a*: (*a*) R_2 is in series with R_3; (*b*) R_1 is in series with R_3; (*c*) the equivalent resistance of the R_2R_3 bank is in parallel with R_1; (*d*) the equivalent resistance of the R_2R_3 bank is in series with R_1.
6. In a series circuit with unequal resistances: (*a*) the lowest R has the highest V; (*b*) the highest R has the highest V; (*c*) the lowest R has the most I; (*d*) the highest R has the most I.
7. In a parallel bank with unequal branch resistances: (*a*) the current is highest in the highest R; (*b*) the current is equal in all the branches; (*c*) the voltage is highest across the lowest R; (*d*) the current is highest in the lowest R.
8. In Fig. 6-14, with S_2 open, R_T equals (*a*) 90 Ω; (*b*) 100 Ω; (*c*) 50 Ω; (*d*) 10 Ω.
9. In Fig. 6-12*c*, V_{DA} equals (*a*) +10 V; (*b*) −20 V; (*c*) −30 V; (*d*) +30 V.
10. In the Wheatstone bridge of Fig. 6-10, at balance: (*a*) $I_A = 0$; (*b*) $I_B = 0$; (*c*) $V_2 = 0$; (*d*) $V_{AB} = 0$.

QUESTIONS

1. In a series-parallel circuit, how can you tell which resistances are in series with each other and which are in parallel?
2. Draw a schematic diagram showing two resistances in a bank that is in series with one resistance.
3. Draw a diagram showing how to connect three resistances of equal value so that the combined resistance will be 1½ times the resistance of one unit.
4. Draw a diagram showing two strings in parallel across a voltage source, where each string has three series resistances.
5. Explain why components are connected in series-parallel, showing a circuit as an example of your explanation.
6. Give two differences between a short circuit and an open circuit.
7. Explain the difference between voltage division and current division.
8. Where would a voltage be negative with respect to chassis ground.

9. Draw a circuit with nine 40-V 100-W bulbs connected to a 120-V source.
10. (a) Two 10-Ω resistors are in series with a 100-V source. If a third 10-Ω R is added in series, explain why I will decrease. (b) The same two 10-Ω resistors are in parallel with the 100-V source. If a third 10-Ω R is added in parallel, explain why I_T will increase.

PROBLEMS

ANSWERS TO ODD-NUMBERED PROBLEMS AT BACK OF BOOK.

1. Refer to Fig. 6-1. (a) Calculate the circuit's total resistance if all resistances are 10 Ω. (b) What is the main-line current if V_T equals 100 V?
2. In Fig. 6-2, calculate the total power supplied by the source for the four 100-W bulbs.
3. Refer to the diagram in Fig. 6-16. (a) Why is R_1 in series with R_3 but not with R_2? (b) Find the total circuit resistance across the battery.
4. Two 60-Ω resistances R_1 and R_2 in parallel require 60 V across the bank with 1 A through each branch. Show how to connect a series resistance R_3 in the main line to drop an applied voltage of 100 V to 60 V across the bank. (a) How much is the required voltage across R_3? (b) How much is the required current through R_3? (c) How much is the required resistance of R_3? (d) If R_3 opens, how much is the voltage across R_1 and R_2? (e) If R_1 opens, what are the voltages across R_2 and R_3?
5. Refer to the diagram in Fig. 6-17. (a) Calculate R across points AD. (b) How much is R across points AD with R_4 open?
6. Show how to connect four 100-Ω resistances in a series-parallel circuit with a combined resistance equal to 100 Ω. (a) If the combination is connected across a 100-V source, how much power is supplied by the source? (b) How much power is dissipated in each resistance?
7. In the Wheatstone-bridge circuit of Fig. 6-18, find each voltage, label the polarity, and calculate R_X. The bridge is balanced.
8. In Fig. 6-19, find each voltage V and current I for the four resistors with 30 V applied.
9. Calculate R_T for the series-parallel circuit in Fig. 6-20.
10. For the series-parallel circuit in Fig. 6-21, with 10 V applied, find voltage V_6 for the end resistor R_6.
11. Refer to Fig. 6-22. (a) Calculate V_2. (b) Find V_2 when R_3 is open.

FIG. 6-16 Circuit diagram for Prob. 3.

FIG. 6-17 Diagram for Prob. 5.

FIG. 6-18 Circuit diagram for Prob. 7.

FIG. 6-19 Circuit diagram for Prob. 8.

FIG. 6-20 Circuit diagram for Prob. 9.

FIG. 6-21 Circuit diagram for Prob. 10.

12. Refer to Fig. 6-23 with 12 V applied. (a) Find V_1, V_2, V_3, I_1, I_2, I_3, and I_T in the circuit with three resistors as shown. (b) Now connect point G to ground. Give the voltages, with polarity, at points A, B, and C with respect to ground. (c) Give the values of I_1, I_2, I_3, and I_T with point G grounded.

13. In Fig. 6-24, find I and V for the five resistors and calculate V_T. All the R values are given and the current I is 8 mA through R_1.

FIG. 6-22 Circuit diagram for Prob. 11.

FIG. 6-23 Circuit diagram for Prob. 12.

FIG. 6-24 Circuit diagram for Prob. 13.

FIG. 6-25 Circuit diagram for Prob. 14.

FIG. 6-26 Circuit diagram for Prob. 15.

FIG. 6-27 Circuit diagram for Probs. 16, 17, 18, and 19.

14. For the voltage divider in Fig. 6-25 with 28 V applied, give the voltages at points A, B, and C with polarity to ground when (**a**) point A is grounded; (**b**) point B is grounded; (**c**) point C is grounded.

15. In Fig. 6-26, calculate R_T, I_1, I_2, I_3, V_1, V_2, V_3, and V_{AB}.

16. In Fig. 6-27, calculate R_T, I_T, V_{R_1}, V_{AB}, V_{R_4}, I_2, and I_3.

17. Refer to Fig. 6-27. If R_3 opens, does V_{AB} increase, decrease, or stay the same? What about the currents, I_T, I_2, and I_3?

18. Refer to Fig. 6-27. If R_2 decreases to 25 Ω, does V_{AB} increase, decrease, or stay the same? What about the currents, I_T, I_2, and I_3?

19. Refer to Fig. 6-27. If R_3 shorts, does V_{AB} increase, decrease, or stay the same? What about the currents, I_T, I_2, and I_3?

20. In Fig. 6-28, solve for the following unknowns: R_T, I_1, I_2, I_3, I_4, I_5, I_6, I_7, V_1, V_2, V_3, V_4, V_5, V_6, and V_7.

21. In Fig. 6-29, calculate: R_T, I_1, I_2, I_3, I_4, I_5, I_6, I_7, I_8, I_9, V_1, V_2, V_3, V_4, V_5, V_6, V_7, V_8, and V_9.

FIG. 6-28   Circuit diagram for Prob. 20.

FIG. 6-29   Circuit diagram for Prob. 21.

CRITICAL THINKING

1. In Fig. 6-30, bulbs A and B each have an operating voltage of 28 V. If the wattage ratings for bulbs A and B are 1.12 W and 2.8 W respectively, calculate: **(a)** the required resistance of R_1; **(b)** the recommended wattage rating of R_1; **(c)** the total resistance R_T.
2. Refer to Fig. 6-31. How much voltage will be indicated by the voltmeter when the wiper arm of the linear potentiometer R_2 is set: **(a)** to point A; **(b)** to point B; **(c)** midway between points A and B.
3. Three switches, A, B, and C, are used to control whether a lamp is ON or OFF. The lamp is to be on only when switch A is closed at the same time as switch B or switch C (or both) is closed. **(a)** Draw the schematic diagram for the voltage source, three switches, and the lamp. **(b)** Write the mathematical expression which describes the operation of the series-parallel switches in controlling the lamp. **(c)** Draw the logic circuit, using the AND and OR logic symbols, which represents the operation of the series-parallel switches.

FIG. 6-30   Circuit diagram for Critical Thinking Prob. 1.

FIG. 6-31   Circuit diagram for Critical Thinking Prob. 2.

REVIEW: CHAPTERS 1 TO 6

SUMMARY

- The electron is the basic quantity of negative electricity; the proton is the basic quantity of positive electricity. Both have the same charge, but they have opposite polarities.
- A quantity of electrons is a negative charge; a deficiency of electrons is a positive charge. Like charges repel each other; unlike charges attract.
- Charge, Q, is measured in coulombs; 6.25×10^{18} electrons equals one coulomb of charge. Charge in motion is current. One coulomb of charge flowing past a given point each second equals one ampere of current.
- Potential difference, PD, is measured in volts. One volt produces one ampere of current against the opposition of one ohm of resistance.
- The main types of resistors are carbon-composition, carbon-film, metal-film, wire-wound, and surface-mount. Wire-wound resistors are used when the resistance must dissipate a lot of power, such as 5 W or more. Carbon-film and metal-film resistors are better than the older carbon-composition type because they have tighter tolerances, are less sensitive to temperature changes and aging, and generate less noise internally.
- Resistors having a power rating less than 2 W are often color-coded to indicate their resistance value. To review the color code, refer to Table 2-1 and Fig. 2-7.
- Surface-mount resistors (also called chip resistors) use a three-digit number printed on the body to indicate the resistance value in ohms. The first two digits indicate the first two digits in the numerical value of the resistance; the third digit is the multiplier. For example, a surface-mount resistor which is marked 103 has a resistance value of 10,000 Ω or 10 kΩ.
- A potentiometer is a variable resistor that has three terminals. It is used as a variable voltage divider. A rheostat is a variable resistor that has only two terminals. It is used to vary the current in a circuit.
- The most common trouble with resistors is that they develop an open and thus have an infinitely high resistance.
- The three forms of Ohm's law are $I = V/R$, $V = IR$, and $R = V/I$.
- The three power formulas are $P = VI$, $P = I^2R$, and $P = V^2/R$.
- The most common multiple and submultiples of the practical units are mega (M) for 10^6, micro (μ) for 10^{-6}, kilo (k) for 10^3, and milli (m) for 10^{-3}.
- For series resistances: (**1**) the current is the same in all resistances; (**2**) the IR drops can be different with unequal resistances; (**3**) the applied voltage equals the sum of the series IR drops; (**4**) the total resistance equals the sum of the individual resistances; (**5**) an open circuit in one resistance results in no current through the entire series circuit.

- For parallel resistances: (**1**) the voltage is the same across all resistances; (**2**) the branch currents can be different with unequal resistances; (**3**) the total line current equals the sum of the parallel branch currents; (**4**) the combined equivalent resistance, R_{EQ}, of parallel branches is less than the smallest resistance as determined by Formula (5-3); (**5**) an open circuit in one branch does not create an open in the other branches; (**6**) a short circuit across one branch short-circuits all the branches.
- In series-parallel circuits, the resistances in one current path without any branch points are in series; all the rules of series resistances apply. The resistances across the same two branch points are in parallel; all the rules of parallel resistances apply.
- Series-connected switches represent the AND logic function, whereas parallel-connected switches represent the OR logic function. Switches connected in a series-parallel manner combine the AND and OR logic functions.

REVIEW SELF-TEST

ANSWERS AT BACK OF BOOK.

Choose (*a*), (*b*), (*c*), or (*d*).

1. A carbon resistor is color-coded with brown, green, red, and gold stripes from left to right. Its value is (*a*) 1500 Ω ± 5 percent; (*b*) 6800 Ω ± 5 percent; (*c*) 10,000 Ω ± 10 percent; (*d*) 500,000 Ω ± 5 percent.

2. A metal-film resistor is color-coded with orange, orange, orange, red, and green stripes, reading from left to right. Its value is: (*a*) 3.3 kΩ ± 5 percent; (*b*) 333 kΩ ± 5 percent; (*c*) 33.3 kΩ ± 0.5 percent; (*d*) 333 Ω ± 0.5 percent.

3. With 30 V applied across two equal resistors in series, 10 mA of current flows. Typical values for each resistor to be used here are (*a*) 10 Ω 10 W; (*b*) 1500 Ω ½ W; (*c*) 3000 Ω 10 W; (*d*) 30 MΩ 2 W.

4. In which of the following circuits will the voltage source produce the most current? (*a*) 10 V across a 10-Ω resistance; (*b*) 10 V across two 10-Ω resistances in series; (*c*) 10 V across two 10-Ω resistances in parallel; (*d*) 1000 V across a 1-MΩ resistance.

5. Three 120-V 100-W bulbs are in parallel across the 120-V power line. If one bulb burns open: (*a*) the other two bulbs cannot light; (*b*) all three bulbs light; (*c*) the other two bulbs can light; (*d*) there is excessive current in the main line.

6. A circuit allows 1 mA of current to flow with 1 V applied. The conductance of the circuit equals (*a*) 0.002 Ω; (*b*) 0.005 μS; (*c*) 1000 μS; (*d*) 1 S.

7. If 2 A of current is allowed to accumulate charge for 5 s, the resultant charge equals (*a*) 2 C; (*b*) 10 C; (*c*) 5 A; (*d*) 10 A.

8. A potential difference applied across a 1-MΩ resistor produces 1 mA of current. The applied voltage equals (*a*) 1 μV; (*b*) 1 mV; (*c*) 1 kV; (*d*) 1,000,000 V.

9. A string of two 1000-Ω resistances is in series with a parallel bank of two 1000-Ω resistances. The total resistance of the series-parallel circuit equals (*a*) 250 Ω; (*b*) 2500 Ω; (*c*) 3000 Ω; (*d*) 4000 Ω.

10. In the circuit of Question 9, one of the resistances in the series string opens. Then the current in the parallel bank (a) increases slightly in both branches; (b) equals zero in one branch but is maximum in the other branch; (c) is maximum in both branches; (d) equals zero in both branches.

11. With 100 V applied across a 10,000-Ω resistance, the power dissipation equals (a) 1 mW; (b) 1 W; (c) 100 W; (d) 1 kW.

12. A source of 10 V is applied across R_1, R_2, and R_3 in series, producing 1 A in the series circuit. R_1 equals 6 Ω and R_2 equals 2 Ω. Therefore, R_3 equals (a) 2 Ω; (b) 4 Ω; (c) 10 Ω; (d) 12 Ω.

13. A 5-V source and a 3-V source are connected with series-opposing polarities. The combined voltage across both sources equals (a) 5 V; (b) 3 V; (c) 2 V; (d) 8 V.

14. In a circuit with three parallel branches, if one branch opens, the main-line current will be (a) more; (b) less; (c) the same; (d) infinite.

15. A 10-Ω R_1 and a 20-Ω R_2 are in series with a 30-V source. If R_1 opens, the voltage drop across R_2 will be (a) zero; (b) 20 V; (c) 30 V; (d) infinite.

16. A voltage V_1 of 40 V is connected series-opposing with V_2 of 50 V. The total voltage across both components is: (a) 10 V; (b) 40 V; (c) 50 V; (d) 90 V.

17. Two series voltage drops V_1 and V_2 total 100 V for V_T. When V_1 is 60 V, then V_2 must equal: (a) 40 V; (b) 60 V; (c) 100 V; (d) 160 V.

18. Two parallel branch currents I_1 and I_2 total 100 mA for I_T. When I_1 is 60 mA, then I_2 must equal: (a) 40 mA; (b) 60 mA; (c) 100 mA; (d) 160 mA.

19. A surface-mount resistor is marked 224. Its resistance is: (a) 224 Ω; (b) 220 kΩ; (c) 224 kΩ; (d) 22 kΩ.

20. If a variable voltage is connected across a fixed resistance: (a) I and V will vary in direct proportion; (b) I and V will be inversely proportional; (c) I will remain constant as V is varied; (d) none of the above.

21. If a fixed value of voltage is connected across a variable resistance: (a) I will vary in direct proportion to R; (b) I will be inversely proportional to R; (c) I will remain constant as R is varied; (d) none of the above.

REFERENCES

Cooke, N. M., H. F. R. Adams, and P. B. Dell: *Basic Mathematics for Electronics,* Glencoe/McGraw-Hill, Columbus, Ohio.

Grob, B.: *Mathematics for Basic Electronics,* Glencoe/McGraw-Hill, Columbus, Ohio.

Periodic Chart of the Atoms

Understanding Calculator Math, Texas Instruments Incorporated, Dallas.

Calculator instruction booklets.

CHAPTER 7

VOLTAGE DIVIDERS AND CURRENT DIVIDERS

Any series circuit is a voltage divider. The *IR* voltage drops are proportional parts of the applied voltage. Also, any parallel circuit is a current divider. Each branch current is part of the total line current, but in inverse proportion to the branch resistance.

Special formulas can be used for the voltage and current division as short cuts in the calculations. The voltage division formula gives the series voltages even when the current is not known. Also, the current division formula gives the branch currents even when the branch voltage is not known. Finally, we consider a series voltage divider with parallel branches that have load currents. The design of such a loaded voltage divider can be applied to the important case of different voltage taps from the power supply in electronic equipment.

CHAPTER OBJECTIVES

Upon completion of this chapter, you should be able to:

- *Calculate* the voltage drops in an unloaded voltage divider.
- *Explain* why resistor voltage drops are proportional to the resistor values in a series circuit.
- *Calculate* the branch currents in a parallel circuit.
- *Explain* why the branch currents are inversely proportional to the branch resistances in a parallel circuit.
- *Define* what is meant by the term *loaded voltage divider.*
- *Calculate* the voltage, current, and power values in a loaded voltage divider.

IMPORTANT TERMS IN THIS CHAPTER

bleeder current
current divider

load currents
loaded voltage

voltage divider

TOPICS COVERED IN THIS CHAPTER

The current is the same in all the resistances in a series circuit. Also, the voltage drops equal the product of I times R. Therefore, the IR voltages are proportional to the series resistances. A higher resistance has a greater IR voltage than a lower resistance in the same series circuit; equal resistances have the same amount of IR drop. If R_1 is double R_2, then V_1 will be double V_2.

The series string can be considered as a *voltage divider*. Each resistance provides an IR drop V equal to its proportional part of the applied voltage. Stated as a formula,

$$\blacktriangleright \quad V = \frac{R}{R_T} \times V_T \qquad\qquad (7\text{-}1)$$

Example

EXAMPLE 1 Three 50-kΩ resistors R_1, R_2, and R_3 are in series across an applied voltage of 180 V. How much is the IR voltage drop across each resistor?

ANSWER The voltage drop across each R is 60 V. Since R_1, R_2, and R_3 are equal, each has one-third the total resistance of the circuit and one-third the total applied voltage. Using the formula,

$$V = \frac{R}{R_T} \times V_T = \frac{50\ \text{k}\Omega}{150\ \text{k}\Omega} \times 180\ \text{V}$$

$$= \frac{1}{3} \times 180\ \text{V}$$

$$V = 60\ \text{V}$$

Note that R and R_T must be in the same units for the proportion. Then V is in the same units as V_T.

FIG. 7-1 Series string of resistors as a proportional voltage divider. Each V_R is R/R_T fraction of the total source voltage V_T.

TYPICAL CIRCUIT Figure 7-1 illustrates another example of a proportional voltage divider. Let the problem be to find the voltage across R_3. We can either calculate this voltage V_3 as IR_3 or determine its proportional part of the total applied voltage V_T. The answer is the same both ways. Note that R_T is $20 + 30 + 50 = 100\ \text{k}\Omega$.

PROPORTIONAL VOLTAGE METHOD Using Formula (7-1), V_3 equals 20/100 of the 200 V applied for V_T because R_3 is 20 kΩ and R_T is 100 kΩ. Then V_3 is 20/100 of 200 or $\frac{1}{5}$ of 200, which is equal to 40 V. The calculations are

$$V_3 = \frac{R_3}{R_T} \times V_T = \frac{20}{100} \times 200 \text{ V}$$
$$V_3 = 40 \text{ V}$$

In the same way, V_2 is 60 V. The calculations are

$$V_2 = \frac{R_2}{R_T} \times V_T = \frac{30}{100} \times 200 \text{ V}$$
$$V_2 = 60 \text{ V}$$

Also, V_1 is 100 V. The calculations are

$$V_1 = \frac{R_1}{R_T} \times V_T = \frac{50}{100} \times 200 \text{ V}$$
$$V_1 = 100 \text{ V}$$

The sum of V_1, V_2, and V_3 in series is $100 + 60 + 40 = 200$ V, which is equal to V_T.

To do a problem like this on the calculator, you can divide R_3 by R_T first and then multiply by V_T. For the values here, to find V_3, the procedure can be as follows:

Punch in the number 20 for R_3.
Push the ⊘ key, then 100 for R_T and press the ⊗ key for the quotient of 0.2 on the display.
Push the ⊗ key then 200 for V_T and press the ⊜ key to display the quotient of 40 as the answer for V_3.

As another method, you can multiply R_3 by V_T first and then divide by R_T, the answers will be the same for either method.

METHOD OF *IR* DROPS   If we want to solve for the current in Fig. 7-1, the I is V_T/R_T or 200 V/100 kΩ = 2 mA. This I flows through R_1, R_2, and R_3 in series. The IR drops are

$$V_1 = I \times R_1 = 2 \text{ mA} \times 50 \text{ k}\Omega = 100 \text{ V}$$
$$V_2 = I \times R_2 = 2 \text{ mA} \times 30 \text{ k}\Omega = 60 \text{ V}$$
$$V_3 = I \times R_3 = 2 \text{ mA} \times 20 \text{ k}\Omega = 40 \text{ V}$$

These voltages are the same values calculated by Formula (7-1) for proportional voltage dividers.

TWO VOLTAGE DROPS IN SERIES   For this case, it is not necessary to calculate both voltages. After you find one, subtract it from V_T to find the other.
As an example, assume V_T is 48 V across two series resistors R_1 and R_2. If V_1 is 18 V, then V_2 must be $48 - 18 = 30$ V.

THE LARGEST SERIES *R* HAS THE MOST *V*   The fact that series voltage drops are proportional to the resistances means that a very small R in series

DID YOU KNOW?

An experimental car dispenses with the transmission, differentials, and drivetrain. Instead, its wheels contain electric motors.

FIG. 7-2 Example of a very small R_1 in series with a large R_2; V_2 is almost equal to the whole V_T.

with a much larger R has a negligible IR drop. An example is shown in Fig. 7-2. Here the 1 kΩ of R_1 is in series with the much larger 999 kΩ of R_2. The V_T is 1000 V.

The voltages across R_1 and R_2 in Fig. 7-2 can be calculated by the voltage divider formula. Note that R_T is $1 + 999 = 1000$ kΩ.

$$\blacktriangleright \quad V_1 = \frac{R_1}{R_T} \times V_T = \frac{1}{1000} \times 1000 \text{ V} = 1 \text{ V}$$

$$V_2 = \frac{R_2}{R_T} \times V_T = \frac{999}{1000} \times 1000 \text{ V} = 999 \text{ V}$$

The 999 V across R_2 is practically the entire applied voltage. Also, the very high series resistance dissipates almost all the power.

Furthermore, the current of 1 mA through R_1 and R_2 in Fig. 7-2 is determined almost entirely by the 999 kΩ of R_2. The I for R_T is 1000 V/1000 kΩ, which equals 1 mA. However, the 999 kΩ of R_2 alone would allow 1.001 mA of current, which differs very little from the original I of 1 mA.

ADVANTAGE OF THE VOLTAGE DIVIDER METHOD   Using Formula (7-1), we can find the proportional voltage drops from V_T and the series resistances without knowing the amount of I. For odd values of R, calculating the I may be more troublesome than finding the proportional voltages directly. Also, in many cases we can approximate the voltage division without the need for any written calculations.

TEST-POINT QUESTION 7-1

Answers at end of chapter.

Refer to Fig. 7-1.
a. How much is R_T?
b. What fraction of the applied voltage is V_3?
c. If each resistance is doubled in value, how much is V_1?

7-2 CURRENT DIVIDER WITH TWO PARALLEL RESISTANCES

It is often necessary to find the individual branch currents in a bank from the resistances and I_T, but without knowing the voltage across the bank. This problem can be solved by using the fact that currents divide inversely as the branch resistances. An example is shown in Fig. 7-3. The formulas for the two branch currents are

$$\blacktriangleright \quad I_1 = \frac{R_2}{R_1 + R_2} \times I_T \qquad \qquad \textbf{(7-2)}$$

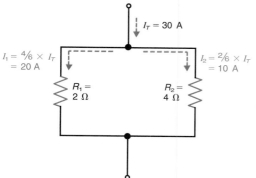

$I_1 = \frac{4}{6} \times I_T$
$= 20$ A

$I_T = 30$ A

$I_2 = \frac{2}{6} \times I_T$
$= 10$ A

$R_1 = 2\ \Omega$

$R_2 = 4\ \Omega$

FIG. 7-3 Current divider with two branch resistances. Each branch I is inversely proportional to its R. The smaller R has more I.

and

$$I_2 = \frac{R_1}{R_1 + R_2} \times I_T$$

Notice that the formula for each branch I has the opposite R in the numerator. The reason is that each branch current is inversely proportional to the branch resistance. The denominator is the same in both formulas, equal to the sum of the two branch resistances.

To calculate the currents in Fig. 7-3, with a 30-A I_T, a 2-Ω R_1, and a 4-Ω R_2,

$$I_1 = \frac{4}{2 + 4} \times 30 = \frac{4}{6} \times 30$$
$$I_1 = 20\ \text{A}$$

For the other branch,

$$I_2 = \frac{2}{2 + 4} \times 30 = \frac{2}{6} \times 30$$
$$I_2 = 10\ \text{A}$$

With all the resistances in the same units, the branch currents are in the units of I_T. For instance, kilohms of R and milliamperes of I can be used.

Actually, it is not necessary to calculate both currents. After one I is calculated, the other can be found by subtracting from I_T.

To use the calculator for a problem like this with current division between two branch resistances, as in Formula (7-2), there are several points to note. The numerator has the R of the branch opposite from the desired I. In adding R_1 and R_2, the parens keys ⊙ and ⊙ should be used. The reason is that both terms in the denominator must be added before the division. The procedure for calculating I_1 in Fig. 7-3 can be as follows:

Punch in 4 for R_2. Press the ⊙ key followed by the open parens key ⊙. Punch in 2 ⊕ 4 for R_1 and R_2 followed by the close parens key ⊙. The sum of 6 will be displayed. Press ⊗ and 30, then press ⊜ to display the answer 20 for I_1.

ABOUT
ELECTRONICS

A new "smart" car has an electronic steering wheel that interacts with a driver's palm perspiration and measures alcohol content. The car won't start if the driver is intoxicated or wearing gloves.

Notice that the division of branch currents in a parallel bank is opposite from the voltage division of resistance in a series string. With series resistances, a higher resistance develops a higher IR voltage proportional to its R; with parallel branches, a lower resistance takes more branch current, equal to V/R.

In Fig. 7-3, the 20-A I_1 is double the 10-A I_2 because the 2-Ω R_1 is one-half the 4-Ω R_2. This is an inverse relationship between I and R.

The inverse relation between I and R in a parallel bank means that a very large R has little effect with a much smaller R in parallel. As an example, Fig. 7-4 shows a 999-kΩ R_2 in parallel with a 1-kΩ R_1 dividing the I_T of 1000 mA. The branch currents are calculated as follows:

$$I_1 = \frac{999}{1000} \times 1000 \text{ mA} = 999 \text{ mA}$$

$$I_2 = \frac{1}{1000} \times 1000 \text{ mA} = 1 \text{ mA}$$

FIG. 7-4   Example of a very large R_2 in parallel with a small R_1. For the branch currents, the small R_1 has almost the entire total line current, I_T.

The 999 mA for I_1 is almost the entire line current of 1000 mA because R_1 is so small compared with R_2. Also, the smallest branch R dissipates the most power because it has the most I.

The current divider Formula (7-2) can be used only for two branch resistances. The reason is the inverse relation between each branch I and its R. In comparison, the voltage divider Formula (7-1) can be used for any number of series resistances because of the direct proportion between each voltage drop V and its R.

For more branches, it is possible to combine the branches in order to work with only two divided currents at a time. However, a better method is to use parallel conductances, because I and G are directly proportional, as explained in the next section.

TEST-POINT QUESTIONS 7-2

Answers at end of chapter.

Refer to Fig. 7-3.
a. What is the ratio of R_2 to R_1?
b. What is the ratio of I_2 to I_1?

7-3 CURRENT DIVISION BY PARALLEL CONDUCTANCES

Remember that the conductance G is $1/R$. Therefore, conductance and current are directly proportional. More conductance allows more current, for the same V. With any number of parallel branches, each branch current is

▶ $$I = \frac{G}{G_T} \times I_T \qquad\qquad (7\text{-}3)$$

where G is the conductance of one branch and G_T is the sum of all the parallel conductances. The unit for G is the siemens (S).

Note that Formula (7-3), for dividing branch currents in proportion to G, has the same form as Formula (7-1), for dividing series voltages in proportion to R. The reason is that both formulas specify a direct proportion.

TWO BRANCHES As an example of using Formula (7-3), we can go back to Fig. 7-3 and find the branch currents with G instead of R. For the 2 Ω of R_1, the G_1 is $1/2 = 0.5$ S. Also, the 4 Ω of R_2 has G_2 of $1/4 = 0.25$ S. Then G_T is $0.5 + 0.25 = 0.75$ S.

The I_T is 30 A in Fig. 7-3. For the branch currents,

$$I_1 = \frac{G_1}{G_T} \times I_T = \frac{0.50}{0.75} \times 30 \text{ A}$$

$$I_1 = 20 \text{ A}$$

This 20 A is the same I_1 calculated before.

For the other branch, I_2 is $30 - 20 = 10$ A. Also, I_2 can be calculated as $0.25/0.75$ or $\frac{1}{3}$ of I_T for the same 10-A value.

To calculate I_1 with a calculator, use the same procedure described before with Formula (7-1) for voltage dividers. Using Formula (7-3) for a proportional current divider with conductance, first divide G by G_T and then multiply the answer by I_T. The key strokes will be as follows: G ÷ G_T × I_T = . Remember that both Formulas (7-1) and (7-3) are mathematically similar as a direct proportion.

THREE BRANCHES A circuit with three branch currents is shown in Fig. 7-5. We can find G for the 10-Ω R_1, 2-Ω R_2, and 5-Ω R_3 as follows:

FIG. 7-5 Current divider with branch conductances G_1, G_2, and G_3, each equal to $1/R$. Note that S is the siemens unit for conductance. With conductance values, each branch I is directly proportional to the branch G.

$$G_1 = \frac{1}{R_1} = \frac{1}{10\ \Omega} = 0.1\ S$$

$$G_2 = \frac{1}{R_2} = \frac{1}{2\ \Omega} = 0.5\ S$$

$$G_3 = \frac{1}{R_3} = \frac{1}{5\ \Omega} = 0.2\ S$$

Remember that the siemens (S) unit is the reciprocal of the ohm (Ω) unit. The total conductance then is

$$G_T = G_1 + G_2 + G_3$$
$$= 0.1 + 0.5 + 0.2$$
$$G_T = 0.8\ S$$

The I_T is 40 mA in Fig. 7-5. To calculate the branch currents with Formula (7-3),

$$I_1 = 0.1/0.8 \times 40\ mA = 5\ mA$$
$$I_2 = 0.5/0.8 \times 40\ mA = 25\ mA$$
$$I_3 = 0.2/0.8 \times 40\ mA = 10\ mA$$

The sum is $5 + 25 + 10 = 40$ mA for I_T.

Although three branches are shown here, Formula (7-3) can be used to find the currents for any number of parallel conductances because of the direct proportion between I and G. The method of conductances is usually easier to use than the method of resistances for three or more branches.

TEST-POINT QUESTIONS 7-3

Answers at end of chapter.

Refer to Fig. 7-5.
a. What is the ratio of G_3 to G_1?
b. What is the ratio of I_3 to I_1?

7-4 SERIES VOLTAGE DIVIDER WITH PARALLEL LOAD CURRENT

The voltage dividers shown so far illustrate just a series string without any branch currents. Actually, though, a voltage divider is often used to tap off part of the applied voltage V_T for a load that needs less voltage than V_T. Then the added load is a parallel branch across part of the divider, as shown in Fig. 7-6. This example shows how the loaded voltage at the tap F is reduced below the potential it would have without the branch current for R_L.

(a)

(b)

(c)

FIG. 7-6 Effect of a parallel load in part of a series voltage divider. (*a*) R_1 and R_2 in series without any branch current. (*b*) Reduced voltage across R_2 and its parallel load R_L. (*c*) Equivalent circuit of the loaded voltage divider.

WHY THE LOADED VOLTAGE DECREASES   We can start with Fig. 7-6*a*, which shows an R_1R_2 voltage divider alone. Resistances R_1 and R_2 in series simply form a proportional divider across the 60-V source for V_T.

For the resistances, R_1 is 40 kΩ and R_2 is 20 kΩ, making R_T equal to 60 kΩ. Also, the current I is V_T/R_T or 60 V/60 kΩ = 1 mA. For the divided voltages in Fig. 7-6*a*,

$$V_1 = \frac{40}{60} \times 60 \text{ V} = 40 \text{ V}$$

$$V_2 = \frac{20}{60} \times 60 \text{ V} = 20 \text{ V}$$

Note that $V_1 + V_2$ is 40 + 20 = 60 V, which is the total applied voltage.

However, in Fig. 7-6*b* the 20-kΩ branch of R_L changes the equivalent resistance at tap F to ground. This change in the proportions of R changes the voltage division. Now the resistance from F to G is 10 kΩ, equal to the 20-kΩ R_2 and R_L in parallel. This equivalent bank resistance is shown as the 10-kΩ R_E in Fig. 7-6*c*.

Resistance R_1 is still the same 40 kΩ because it has no parallel branch. The new R_T for the divider in Fig. 7-6*c* is 40 kΩ + 10 kΩ = 50 kΩ. As a result, V_E from F to G in Fig. 7-6*c* becomes

$$V_E = \frac{R_E}{R_T} \times V_T = \frac{10}{50} \times 60 \text{ V}$$

$$V_E = 12 \text{ V}$$

Therefore, the voltage across the parallel R_2 and R_L in Fig. 7-6*b* is reduced to 12 V. This voltage is at the tap F for R_L.

Note that V_1 across R_1 increases to 48 V in Fig. 7-6*c*. Now V_1 is 40/50 $\times$ 60 V = 48 V. The V_1 increases here because there is more current through R_1.

The sum of $V_1 + V_E$ in Fig. 7-6*c* is 12 + 48 = 60 V. The IR drops still add to equal the applied voltage.

PATH OF CURRENT FOR R_L   All the current in the circuit must come from the source V_T. Trace the electron flow for R_L. It starts from the negative side of

V_T, through R_L, to the tap at F, and returns through R_1 in the divider to the positive side of V_T. This current I_L goes through R_1 but not R_2.

BLEEDER CURRENT   In addition, both R_1 and R_2 have their own current from the source. This current through all the resistances in the divider is bleeder current I_B. The electron flow for I_B is from the negative side of V_T, through R_2 and R_1, and back to the positive side of V_T.

The bleeder current is a steady drain on the source. However, I_B has the advantage of reducing variations in the total current in the voltage source for different values of load current.

In summary, then, for the three resistances in Fig. 7-6b, note the following currents:

1. Resistance R_L has just its load current I_L.
2. Resistance R_2 has only the bleeder current I_B.
3. Resistance R_1 has both I_L and I_B.

Note that only R_1 is in the path for both the bleeder current and the load current.

ABOUT

ELECTRONICS

Hearing aids should help the wearer listen to what's here, not there. So hearing aid electronics filter out the frequencies of background noise and amplify only higher frequencies, like speech, to the listener.

TEST-POINT QUESTION 7-4

Answers at end of chapter.

Refer to Fig. 7-6.
a. What is the proportion of R_2/R_T in Fig. 7-6a?
b. What is the proportion of R_E/R_T in Fig. 7-6c?

7-5 DESIGN OF A LOADED VOLTAGE DIVIDER

These principles can be applied to the design of a practical voltage divider, as shown in Fig. 7-7. This type of circuit is used for the output of a power supply in electronic equipment to supply different voltages at the taps, with different load currents. For instance, load D can represent the collector-emitter circuit for one or more power transistors that need $+100$ V for the collector supply. Also, the tap at E can be the 40-V collector supply for medium-power transistors. Finally, the 18-V tap at F can be for base-emitter bias current in the power transistors and collector voltage for smaller transistors.

Note the load specifications in Fig. 7-7. Load F needs 18 V from point F to chassis ground. When the 18 V is supplied by this part of the divider, a 36-mA branch current will flow through the load. Similarly, 40 V is needed at tap E for 54 mA of I_E in load E. Also, 100 V is available at D with a load current I_D of 180 mA. The total load current here is $36 + 54 + 180 = 270$ mA.

In addition, the bleeder current I_B through the entire divider is generally specified at about 10 percent of the load current. For the example here, I_B is taken as 30 mA to make a total line current I_T of $270 + 30 = 300$ mA from the source. Remember that the 30-mA I_B flows through R_1, R_2, and R_3.

$$I_T = I_B + I_F + I_E + I_D = 300 \text{ mA}$$

D

100 V 180 mA for load D

Load D

$$I_3 = I_B + I_F + I_E = 120 \text{ mA}$$

R_3

E

40 V 54 mA for load E

Load E

$V_T = 100 \text{ V}$
$I = 300 \text{ mA}$

$$I_2 = I_B + I_F = 66 \text{ mA}$$

R_2

F

18 V 36 mA for load F

$$I_1 = I_B = 30 \text{ mA}$$

$I_T = 300 \text{ mA}$

R_1

Load F

$I_F = 36 \text{ mA}$ $I_E = 54 \text{ mA}$ $I_D = 180 \text{ mA}$

G

FIG. 7-7   Voltage divider for different voltages and currents from the source V_T. See text for design calculations to find the values of R_1, R_2, and R_3.

The design problem in Fig. 7-7 is to find the values of R_1, R_2, and R_3 needed to provide the specified voltages. Each R is calculated as its ratio of V/I. However, the question is what are the correct values of V and I to use for each part of the divider.

FIND THE CURRENT IN EACH R   We start with R_1 because its current is only the 30-mA bleeder current I_B. No load current flows through R_1. Therefore I_1 through R_1 equals 30 mA.

The 36-mA current I_F for load F returns to the source through R_2 and R_3. Considering just R_2 now, its current is the I_F load current and the 30-mA bleeder current I_B. Therefore, I_2 through R_2 is $36 + 30 = 66$ mA.

The 54-mA current I_E for load E returns to the source through R_3 alone. However, R_3 also has the 36-mA I_F and the 30-mA I_B. Therefore I_3 through R_3 is $54 + 36 + 30 = 120$ mA. The values for I_1, I_2, and I_3 are given in Table 7-1.

Note that the load current I_D for load D at the top of the diagram does not flow through R_3 or any of the resistors in the divider. However, the I_D of 180 mA is the main load current through the source of applied voltage. The 120 mA of bleeder and load currents plus the 180-mA I_D load add to equal 300 mA for I_T in the main line of the power supply.

TABLE 7-1   DESIGN VALUES FOR VOLTAGE DIVIDER IN FIG. 7-7

	CURRENT, mA	VOLTAGE, V	RESISTANCE, Ω
R_1	30	18	600
R_2	66	22	333
R_3	120	60	500

CALCULATE THE VOLTAGE ACROSS EACH R   The voltages at the taps in Fig. 7-7 give the potential to chassis ground. However, we need the voltage across the two ends of each R. For R_1, the voltage V_1 is the indicated 18 V to ground because one end of R_1 is grounded. However, across R_2 the voltage is the difference between the 40-V potential at point E and the 18 V at F. Therefore V_2 is $40 - 18 = 22$ V. Similarly, V_3 is calculated as 100 V at point D minus the 40 V at E, or, V_3 is $100 - 40 = 60$ V. These values for V_1, V_2, and V_3 are summarized in Table 7-1.

CALCULATING EACH R   Now we can calculate the resistance of R_1, R_2, and R_3 as each V/I ratio. For the values listed in Table 7-1,

▶ $$R_1 = \frac{V_1}{I_1} = \frac{18 \text{ V}}{30 \text{ mA}} = 0.6 \text{ k}\Omega = 600 \text{ }\Omega$$

$$R_2 = \frac{V_2}{I_2} = \frac{22 \text{ V}}{66 \text{ mA}} = 0.333 \text{ k}\Omega = 333 \text{ }\Omega$$

$$R_3 = \frac{V_3}{I_3} = \frac{60 \text{ V}}{120 \text{ mA}} = 0.5 \text{ k}\Omega = 500 \text{ }\Omega$$

When these values are used for R_1, R_2, and R_3 and connected in a voltage divider across the source of 100 V, as in Fig. 7-7, each load will have the specified voltage at its rated current.

TEST-POINT QUESTION 7-5

Answers at end of chapter.

Refer to Fig. 7-7.
a. How much is the bleeder current I_B through R_1, R_2, and R_3?
b. How much is the voltage for load E at tap E to ground?
c. How much is V_2 across R_2?
d. If load D opens, how much voltage will be measured at tap F to ground?

7   SUMMARY AND REVIEW

- In a series circuit V_T is divided into IR voltage drops proportional to the resistances. Each $V_R = (R/R_T) \times V_T$, for any number of series resistances. The largest series R has the largest voltage drop.
- In a parallel circuit, I_T is divided into branch currents. Each I is inversely proportional to the branch R. The inverse division of branch currents is given by Formula (7-2), for two resistances only. The smaller branch R has the larger branch current.
- For any number of parallel branches, I_T is divided into branch currents directly proportional to each conductance G. Each $I = (G/G_T) \times I_T$.
- A series voltage divider is often tapped for a parallel load, as in Fig. 7-6. Then the voltage at the tap is reduced because of the load current.
- The design of a loaded voltage divider, as in Fig. 7-7, involves calculating each R. Find the I and potential difference V for each R. Then $R = V/I$.

SELF-TEST

ANSWERS AT BACK OF BOOK.

Answer True or False.

1. In a series voltage divider, each IR voltage is proportional to its R.
2. With parallel branches, each branch I is inversely proportional to its R.
3. With parallel branches, each branch I is directly proportional to its G.
4. Formula (7-2) for parallel current dividers can be used for three or more resistances.
5. Formula (7-3) for parallel current dividers can be used for five or more branch conductances.
6. In the series voltage divider of Fig. 7-1, V_1 is 2.5 times V_3 because R_1 is 2.5 times R_3.
7. In the parallel current divider of Fig. 7-3, I_1 is double I_2 because R_1 is one-half R_2.
8. In the parallel current divider of Fig. 7-5, I_2 is five times I_1 because G_2 is five times G_1.
9. In Fig. 7-6b, the branch current I_L flows through R_L, R_2, and R_1.
10. In Fig. 7-7, the bleeder current I_B flows through R_1, R_2, and R_3.

1. Define a series voltage divider.
2. Define a parallel current divider.
3. Give two differences between a series voltage divider and a parallel current divider.
4. Give three differences between Formula (7-2) for branch resistances and Formula (7-3) for branch conductances.
5. Define bleeder current.
6. What is the main difference between the circuits in Fig. 7-6a and b?
7. Referring to Fig. 7-1, why is V_1 series-aiding with V_2 and V_3 but in series opposition to V_T? Show polarity of each IR drop.
8. Show the derivation of Formula (7-2) for each branch current in a parallel bank of two resistances. [Hint: The voltage across the bank is $I_T \times R_{EQ}$ and R_{EQ} is $R_1 R_2 / (R_1 + R_2)$.]

PROBLEMS

ANSWERS TO ODD-NUMBERED PROBLEMS AT BACK OF BOOK.

1. A 100-Ω R_1 is in series with a 200-Ω R_2 and a 300-Ω R_3. The applied voltage is 18 V. Calculate V_1, V_2, and V_3.
2. A 10-kΩ R_1 is in series with a 12-kΩ R_2, a 4.7-kΩ R_3, and a 3.3-kΩ R_4. The applied voltage is 36 V. Calculate V_1, V_2, V_3, and V_4.
3. A 120-Ω R_1 is in parallel with a 60-Ω R_2. The total current I_T is 3 A. Calculate the branch currents I_1 and I_2.
4. A 10-Ω R_1 is in parallel with a 30-Ω R_2, a 60-Ω R_3, and a 20-Ω R_4. $I_T = 120$ mA. Calculate the branch currents I_1, I_2, I_3, and I_4.
5. In Fig. 7-8, calculate V_1, V_2, V_3, V_4, V_{CG}, V_{BG}, and V_{AG}.
6. In Fig. 7-9, calculate V_1, V_2, V_3, V_4, V_{DG}, V_{CG}, V_{BG}, and V_{AG}.
7. In Fig. 7-10, calculate I_1 and I_2.
8. In Fig. 7-11, calculate I_1, I_2, and I_3.
9. In Fig. 7-12, calculate I_1, I_2, I_3, and I_4.
10. In Fig. 7-12, find the voltage drop across the parallel bank.
11. In Fig. 7-13, calculate the required values for R_1, R_2, and R_3 if the bleeder current I_B (I_3) is chosen to equal 6 mA. Also, calculate the power dissipated by R_1, R_2, and R_3.
12. In Fig. 7-13, calculate the resistances of loads A, B, and C.
13. In Fig. 7-14, calculate the required values for R_1, R_2, and R_3 if $I_B = 15$ mA. Also, calculate the power dissipated by R_1, R_2, and R_3.
14. In Fig. 7-13, calculate the voltage across load B if load C develops an open.
15. In Fig. 7-13, calculate the voltage across load C if load B develops an open.
16. Select the values for R_1, R_2, R_3, R_4, and R_5 that will provide the specified voltages at points A, B, C, and D in Fig. 7-15. Use a series current I of 10 mA.

FIG. 7-8 Circuit diagram for Prob. 5.

FIG. 7-9 Circuit diagram for Prob. 6.

FIG. 7-10 Circuit diagram for Prob. 7.

FIG. 7-11 Circuit diagram for Prob. 8.

FIG. 7-12 Circuit diagram for Probs. 9 and 10.

FIG. 7-13   Circuit diagram for Probs. 11, 12, 14, and 15.

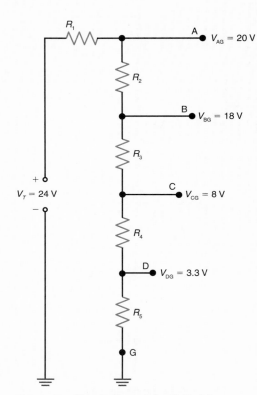

FIG. 7-15   Circuit diagram for Prob. 16.

FIG. 7-14   Circuit diagram for Prob. 13.

CRITICAL THINKING

1. Refer to Fig. 7-16. Select values for R_1 and R_3 that will allow the output voltage to vary between 6 V and 15 V.

2. Design a loaded voltage divider, using a 25-V supply, to meet the following requirements: load $A = 25$ V 10 mA; load $B = 15$ V 45 mA; load $C = 6$ V 5 mA; $I_B = 10$ percent of total load current. Draw the schematic diagram including all values.

3. Design a loaded voltage divider, using a 24-V supply, to meet the following requirements: load $A = 18$ V 10 mA; load $B = 12$ V 30 mA; load $C = 5$ V 6 mA; $I_B = 10$ percent of total load current. Draw the schematic diagram including all values.

4. Design a loaded voltage divider, using a 25-V supply, to meet the following requirements: load $A = 20$ V 25 mA; load $B = 12$ V 10 mA; load $C = -5$ V 10 mA; total current $I_T = 40$ mA. Draw the schematic diagram including all values.

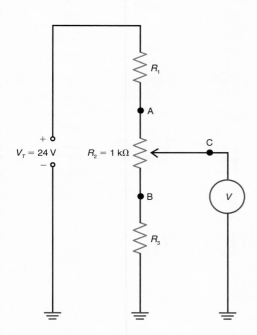

FIG. 7-16   Circuit diagram for Critical Thinking Prob. 1.

ANSWERS TO TEST-POINT QUESTIONS

7-1 **a.** $R_T = 100$ kΩ
  b. $V_3 = (^2/_{10}) \times V_T$
  c. $V_1 = 100$ V

7-2 **a.** 2 to 1
  b. 1 to 2

7-3 **a.** 2 to 1
  b. 2 to 1

7-4 **a.** ⅓
  b. ⅕

7-5 **a.** $I_B = 30$ mA
  b. $V_E = 40$ V
  c. $V_2 = 22$ V
  d. 18 V

CHAPTER 8

DIRECT-CURRENT METERS

Voltage, resistance, and current measurements are generally made with a combination volt-ohm-milliammeter (VOM) or the digital multimeter (DMM). They both have the same applications in measuring V, R, and I.

Meters with a printed scale and a moving pointer are called *analog* meters. Meters with numerical readouts are called *digital* meters.

To measure voltage, the test leads of the voltmeter are connected in parallel across the two points of potential difference. For dc voltages, observe the correct polarity. Otherwise, the pointer on the meter scale will move to the left instead of up-scale to the right.

Similarly, to measure R in ohms, the two leads of the ohmmeter are connected across the resistance to be measured, but power is off. No power is needed in the circuit being tested because the ohmmeter has its own internal battery. Polarity does not matter in checking the R of a resistor.

To measure current, make the meter a series component in the circuit. For direct current, the meter must be connected in the correct polarity to read up-scale. The circuit usually must be opened temporarily in order to insert the current meter in series. Thus, current measurements are not as convenient as testing V and R in troubleshooting.

Often, meters like the VOM and DMM are called *multimeters*. A multimeter is probably the most important type of test equipment in troubleshooting electronic equipment because it can check V, R, and I. The nondigital multitesters are basically dc meters. However, an internal rectifier is included to convert ac values to dc values for the meter measurement.

CHAPTER OBJECTIVES

Upon completion of this chapter, you should be able to:

- *Explain* the difference between an analog meter and a digital meter.
- *Explain* the construction and operation of a basic moving-coil meter.
- *Explain* how to use a meter to measure the current in a circuit.
- *Calculate* the value of shunt resistance required to extend the current range of a basic moving-coil meter.
- *Explain* how to use a meter to measure the voltage in a circuit.
- *Calculate* the value of multiplier resistance required to make a basic moving-coil meter capable of measuring voltage.
- *Explain* the importance of the ohms-per-volt rating of a voltmeter.
- *Explain* what is meant by *voltmeter loading.*
- *Explain* how a basic moving-coil meter can be used with a battery to construct an ohmmeter.
- *List* the main features of a digital multimeter.
- *Explain* how an ohmmeter can be used to check continuity.

IMPORTANT TERMS IN THIS CHAPTER

back-off ohmmeter scale	diode test	ohms-per-volt sensitivity
clamp probe	galvanometer	taut-band meter
continuity testing	loading effect of voltmeter	volt-ohm-milliammeter
D'Arsonval meter	meter shunt	(VOM)
decibel scale	multiplier resistor	zero-ohms adjustment
digital multimeter (DMM)	ohmmeter	

TOPICS COVERED IN THIS CHAPTER

Figure 8-1 shows two very typical types of multimeters used by electronics technicians. Figure 8-1*a* shows an analog volt-ohm-milliammeter, whereas Fig. 8-1*b* shows a digital multimeter. Both types are capable of measuring voltage, current, and resistance. It should be noted that a typical multimeter can measure dc or ac voltages but only dc values of current.

A moving coil meter movement, shown in Fig. 8-2, is generally used in an analog VOM. The construction consists essentially of a coil of fine wire on a drum mounted between the poles of a permanent magnet. When direct current flows in the coil, the magnetic field of the current reacts with the field of the magnet. The resultant force turns the drum with its pointer, winding up the restoring spring. When the current is removed, the pointer returns to zero. The amount of deflection indicates the amount of current in the coil. When the polarity is connected correctly, the pointer will read up-scale, to the right; the incorrect polarity forces the pointer off-scale, to the left.

The pointer deflection is directly proportional to the amount of current in the coil. If 100 μA is the current needed for full-scale deflection, 50 μA in the coil will produce half-scale deflection. The accuracy of the moving-coil meter mechanism is 0.1 to 2 percent.

The moving-coil principle is applied in several meter types which have different names. A *galvanometer* is an extremely sensitive instrument for measur-

(a)

(b)

FIG. 8-1 Typical multimeters used for measuring *V*, *I*, and *R*. (*a*) Analog VOM. (*b*) DMM.

Zero adjustment
for pointer

Restoring spring

Moving coil

Right pointer
stop

Pointer

Left pointer stop

Permanent
magnet

Iron core

Pole pieces

Moving coil terminal
(lower terminal not shown)

FIG. 8-2 Construction of a moving-coil meter. The diameter of the coil can be ½ to 1 in.

ing very small values of current. Laboratory-type galvanometers, which include a suspended moving coil with an optical system to magnify small deflection, can measure a small fraction of one microampere. A *ballistic galvanometer* is used for reading the value of a small momentary current, to measure electric charge. The moving-coil arrangement is often called a *D'Arsonval movement,* after its inventor, who patented this meter movement in 1881.

VALUES OF I_M   The full-scale deflection current I_M is the amount needed to deflect the pointer all the way to the right to the last mark on the printed scale. Typical values of I_M are from about 10 μA to 30 mA. In a VOM, the I_M is typically either 50 μA or 1 mA.

Refer to the analog VOM in Fig. 8-1a. Notice the mirror along the scale to eliminate reading errors. The meter is read when the pointer and its mirror reflection appear as one. This eliminates the optical error called *parallax* caused by looking at the meter from the side.

VALUES OF r_M   This is the internal resistance of the wire of the moving coil. Typical values range from 1.2 Ω for a 30-mA movement to 2000 Ω for a 50-μA movement. A movement with a smaller I_M has a higher r_M because many turns of fine wire are needed. An average value of r_M for a 1-mA movement is about 50 Ω. Figure 8-3 provides a close-up view of the basic components contained within a D'Arsonval meter movement. Notice that the moving coil is wound around a drum which will rotate when dc current flows through the wire of the moving coil.

TAUT-BAND METERS   The meter movement can be constructed with the moving coil and pointer suspended by a metal band, instead of the pivot and jewel design with a restoring spring. Both types of movements have similar operating characteristics. However, taut-band meters generally have lower values of r_M because a smaller coil can be used to force the pointer up-scale.

FIG. 8-3   Close-up view of a D'Arsonval moving coil meter movement.

TEST-POINT QUESTION 8-1

Answers at end of chapter.
a. Is a voltmeter connected in parallel or in series?
b. Is a milliammeter connected in parallel or in series?

8-2 MEASUREMENT OF CURRENT

Whether we are measuring amperes, milliamperes, or microamperes, two important facts to remember are:

1. The current meter must be in series in the circuit where the current is to be measured. The amount of deflection depends on the current through the meter. In a series circuit, the current is the same through all series components. Therefore, the current to be measured must be made to flow through the meter as a series component in the circuit.
2. A dc meter must be connected in the correct polarity for the meter to read up-scale. Reversed polarity makes the meter read down-scale, forcing the pointer against the stop at the left, which can bend the pointer.

HOW TO CONNECT A CURRENT METER IN SERIES

As illustrated in Fig. 8-4, the circuit must be opened at one point in order to insert the current meter in series in the circuit. Since R_1, R_2, R_3, and the meter are all in series, the current is the same in each and the meter reads the current in any part of the series circuit.

(a)　　　　　(b)　　　　　(c)

FIG. 8-4　Inserting a current meter in series. (a) Circuit without meter. (b) Connections opened between points B and C for the meter. (c) The meter is connected between R_1 and R_2 in series to read the common current I in the circuit.

In Fig. 8-4, V_T is 150 V with a total series resistance of 1500 Ω for the current of 0.1 A, or 100 mA. This value is the current in R_1, R_2, R_3, and the battery, as shown in Fig. 8-4a. Note that in Fig. 8-4b, the circuit is opened at the junction of R_1 and R_2 for insertion of the meter. In Fig. 8-4c, the meter completes the series circuit to read the current of 100 mA. The meter inserted in series at any point in the circuit would read the same current. Turn off the power to connect the current meter and then put the power back on to read the current.

HOW TO CONNECT A DC METER IN THE CORRECT POLARITY

A dc meter has its terminals marked for polarity, either with + and − signs or red for plus and black for minus. Electrons must flow into the negative side through the movement and out from the positive side for the meter to read upscale.

To have the meter polarity correct, always connect the negative terminal to the point in the circuit that has a path back to the negative side of the voltage source, *without going through the meter.* Similarly, the positive terminal of the meter returns to the positive terminal of the voltage source (Fig. 8-5). Here the negative terminal of the meter is joined to R_2 because this path with R_1 connects to the negative terminal of the battery. The positive meter terminal is connected to R_3. Electrons in the circuit will flow through R_1 and R_2 into the negative side of the meter, through the movement, and out from the meter and return through R_3 to the positive battery terminal.

FIG. 8-5　Correct polarity for a dc meter to read current.

A CURRENT METER SHOULD HAVE VERY LOW RESISTANCE

Referring back to Fig. 8-4a, the milliammeter reads 100 mA because its resistance is negligible compared with the total series R of 1500 Ω. Then I is the same with or without the meter.

In general, a current meter should have very low R compared with the circuit where the current is being measured. We take an arbitrary figure of $\frac{1}{100}$. For the circuit in Fig. 8-4, then, the meter resistance should be less than $1500/100 = 15\ \Omega$. Actually, a meter for 100 mA would have an internal R of about $1\ \Omega$ or less because of its internal shunt resistor. The higher the current range of the meter, the smaller its resistance.

An extreme case of a current meter with too much R is shown in Fig. 8-6. Here the series R_T is doubled when the meter is inserted in the circuit. The result is one-half the actual I in the circuit without the meter.

(a)   (b)

FIG. 8-6   An example of a current meter having too much R for accurate readings. (a) Circuit without meter has I of 50 μA. (b) Meter resistance reduces I to 25 μA.

TEST-POINT QUESTION 8-2

Answers at end of chapter.
a. In Fig. 8-4, how much will the milliammeter read when inserted at point A?
b. In Fig. 8-5, which R is connected to the positive side of the meter to make it read up-scale?
c. Should a current meter have very low or very high resistance?
d. Should a voltmeter have very high or very low resistance?

8-3 METER SHUNTS

A meter shunt is a precision resistor connected across the meter movement for the purpose of shunting, or bypassing, a specific fraction of the circuit's current around the meter movement. The combination then provides a current meter with an extended range. The shunts are usually inside the meter case. However, the schematic symbol for the current meter usually does not show the shunt.

In current measurements, the parallel bank of the movement with its shunt is still connected as a current meter in series in the circuit (Fig. 8-7). It should be noted that a meter with an internal shunt has the scale calibrated to take into account the current through both the shunt and the meter movement. Therefore, the scale reads total circuit current.

FIG. 8-7 Example of meter shunt R_S in bypassing current around the movement to extend range from 1 to 2 mA. (a) Wiring diagram. (b) Schematic diagram showing effect of shunt. With $R_S = r_M$ the current range is doubled. (c) Circuit with 2-mA meter to read the current.

RESISTANCE OF THE METER SHUNT   In Fig. 8-7b, the 1-mA movement has a resistance of 50 Ω, which is the resistance of the moving coil r_M. To double the range, the shunt resistance R_S is made equal to the 50 Ω of the movement. When the meter is connected in series in a circuit where the current is 2 mA, this total current into one terminal of the meter divides equally between the shunt and the meter movement. At the opposite meter terminal, these two branch currents combine to provide the 2 mA of the circuit current.

Inside the meter, the current is 1 mA through the shunt and 1 mA through the moving coil. Since it is a 1-mA movement, this current produces full-scale deflection. The scale is doubled, however, reading 2 mA, to account for the additional 1 mA through the shunt. Therefore, the scale reading indicates total current at the meter terminals, not just coil current. The movement with its shunt, then, is a 2-mA meter. Its internal resistance is 50 × ½ = 25 Ω.

Another example is shown in Fig. 8-8. In general, the shunt resistance for any range can be calculated with Ohm's law from the formula

$$ \blacktriangleright \qquad R_S = \frac{V_M}{I_S} \qquad\qquad (8\text{-}1) $$

where R_S is the resistance of the shunt and I_S is the current through it.

Voltage V_M is equal to $I_M \times r_M$. This is the voltage across both the shunt and the meter movement, which are in parallel.

CALCULATING I_S   This current through the shunt alone is the difference between the total current I_T through the meter and the divided current I_M through the movement. Or

$$ \blacktriangleright \qquad I_S = I_T - I_M \qquad\qquad (8\text{-}2) $$

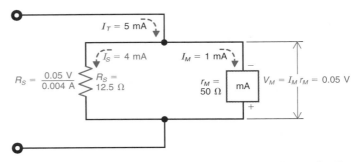

FIG. 8-8   Calculating the resistance of a meter shunt. R_S is equal to V_M/I_S. See text for calculations.

Use the values of current for full-scale deflection, as these are known. In Fig. 8-8,

$$I_S = 5 - 1 = 4 \text{ mA}, \quad \text{or} \quad 0.004 \text{ A}$$

CALCULATING R_S   The complete procedure for using the formula $R_S = V_M/I_S$ can be as follows:

1.   Find V_M. Calculate this for full-scale deflection as $I_M \times r_M$. In Fig. 8-8, with a 1-mA full-scale current through the 50-Ω movement,

$$V_M = 0.001 \times 50 = 0.05 \text{ V}$$

2.   Find I_S. For the values that are shown in Fig. 8-8,

$$I_S = 5 - 1 = 4 \text{ mA} = 0.004 \text{ A}$$

3.   Divide V_M by I_S to find R_S. For the final result,

$$R_S = 0.05/0.004 = 12.5 \text{ }\Omega$$

This shunt enables the 1-mA movement to be used for the extended range of 0 to 5 mA.

Note that R_S and r_M are inversely proportional to their full-scale currents. The 12.5 Ω for R_S equals one-fourth the 50 Ω of r_M because the shunt current of 4 mA is four times the 1 mA through the movement for full-scale deflection.

Example

EXAMPLE 1   A shunt extends the range of a 50-μA meter movement to 1 mA. How much is the current through the shunt at full-scale deflection?

ANSWER   All the currents must be in the same units for Formula (8-2). To avoid fractions, use 1000 μA for the 1-mA I_T. Then

$$I_S = I_T - I_M = 1000 \text{ }\mu\text{A} - 50 \text{ }\mu\text{A}$$
$$I_S = 950 \text{ }\mu\text{A}$$

DID YOU KNOW?

Three hours before the October 17, 1989, earthquake, Stanford University's electromagnetic wave detectors were bombarded with signals 300 times greater than normal. Earthquake waves are about 4 Hz.

EXAMPLE 2 A 50-μA meter movement has r_M of 1000 Ω. What R_S is needed to extend the range to 500 μA?

ANSWER The shunt current I_S is $500 - 50$, or 450 μA. Then

$$R_S = \frac{V_M}{I_S}$$

$$= \frac{50 \times 10^{-6}\ A \times 10^3\ \Omega}{450 \times 10^{-6}\ A} = \frac{50{,}000}{450}$$

$$R_S = 111.1\ \Omega$$

The shunts usually are precision wire-wound resistors. For very low values, a short wire of precise size can be used.

TEST-POINT QUESTION 8-3

Answers at end of chapter.

A 50-μA movement with a 900-Ω r_M has a shunt R_S for the range of 500 μA.
a. How much is I_S?
b. How much is V_M?
c. What is the size of R_S?

8-4 VOLTMETERS

Although a meter movement responds only to current in the moving coil, it is commonly used for measuring voltage by the addition of a high resistance in series with the movement (Fig. 8-9). The series resistance must be much higher than the coil resistance in order to limit the current through the coil. The combination of the meter movement with this added series resistance then forms a voltmeter. The series resistor, called a *multiplier*, is usually connected inside the voltmeter case.

Since a voltmeter has high resistance, it must be connected in parallel to measure the potential difference across two points in a circuit. Otherwise, the high-resistance multiplier would add so much series resistance that the current in the circuit would be reduced to a very low value. Connected in parallel, though, the high resistance of the voltmeter is an advantage. The higher the voltmeter resistance, the smaller the effect of its parallel connection on the circuit being tested.

The circuit is not opened to connect the voltmeter in parallel. Because of this convenience, it is common practice to make voltmeter tests in troubleshooting. The voltage measurements apply the same way to an *IR* drop or a generated emf.

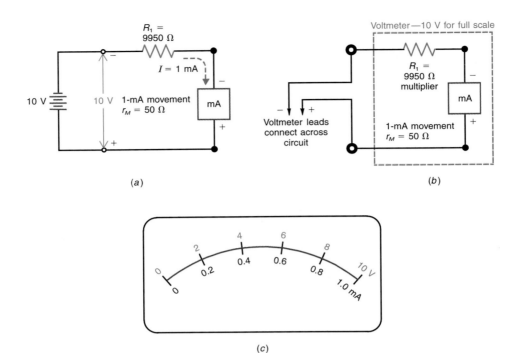

FIG. 8-9   Multiplier resistor R_1 added in series with meter movement to form a voltmeter. (*a*) Resistance of R_1 allows 1 mA for full-scale deflection on 1-mA movement with 10 V applied. (*b*) Internal multiplier R_1 forms a voltmeter. The test leads can be connected across a potential difference to measure 0 to 10 V. (*c*) 10-V scale of voltmeter and corresponding 1-mA scale of meter movement.

The correct polarity must be observed in using a dc voltmeter. Connect the negative voltmeter lead to the negative side of the potential difference being measured and the positive lead to the positive side.

MULTIPLIER RESISTANCE   Figure 8-9 illustrates how the meter movement and its multiplier R_1 form a voltmeter. With 10 V applied by the battery in Fig. 8-9*a*, there must be 10,000 Ω of resistance to limit the current to 1 mA for full-scale deflection of the meter movement. Since the movement has a 50-Ω resistance, 9950 Ω is added in series, resulting in a 10,000-Ω total resistance. Then I is 10 V/10 kΩ = 1 mA.

With 1 mA in the movement, the full-scale deflection can be calibrated as 10 V on the meter scale, as long as the 9950-Ω multiplier is included in series with the movement. It doesn't matter to which side of the movement the multiplier is connected.

If the battery is taken away, as in Fig. 8-9*b*, the movement with its multiplier forms a voltmeter that can indicate a potential difference of 0 to 10 V applied across its terminals. When the voltmeter leads are connected across a potential difference of 10 V in a dc circuit, the resulting 1-mA current through the meter movement produces full-scale deflection, and the reading is 10 V. In Fig. 8-9*c* the 10-V scale is shown corresponding to the 1-mA range of the movement.

If the voltmeter is connected across a 5-V potential difference, the current in the movement is ½ mA, the deflection is one-half of full scale, and the reading is 5 V. Zero voltage across the terminals means no current in the movement, and the voltmeter reads zero. In summary, then, any potential difference up to 10 V, whether an *IR* voltage drop or a generated emf, can be applied across the meter terminals. The meter will indicate less than 10 V in the same ratio that the meter current is less than 1 mA.

The resistance of a multiplier can be calculated from the formula

▶ $$R_{mult} = \frac{\text{full-scale } V}{\text{full-scale } I} - r_M \qquad (8\text{-}3)$$

Applying this formula to the example of R_1 in Fig. 8-9 gives

$$R_{mult} = \frac{10 \text{ V}}{0.001 \text{ A}} - 50 \text{ }\Omega = 10{,}000 - 50$$

$$R_{mult} = 9950 \text{ }\Omega$$

We can take another example for the same 10-V scale but with a 50-μA meter movement, which is commonly used. Now the multiplier resistance is much higher, though, because less *I* is needed for full-scale deflection. Let the resistance of the 50-μA movement be 2000 Ω. Then

$$R_{mult} = \frac{10 \text{ V}}{0.000\ 050 \text{ A}} - 2000 \text{ }\Omega = 200{,}000 - 2000$$

$$R_{mult} = 198{,}000 \text{ }\Omega$$

MULTIPLE VOLTMETER RANGES   Voltmeters often have several multipliers which are used with one meter movement. A range switch selects one multiplier for the required scale. The higher the voltage range is, the higher the multiplier resistance, in essentially the same proportion as the ranges.

Figure 8-10 illustrates two ranges. When the switch is on the 10-V range, multiplier R_1 is connected in series with the 1-mA movement. Then you read the 10-V scale on the meter face. With the range switch on 25 V, R_2 is the multiplier, and the measured voltage is read on the 25-V scale.

(a)   (b)

FIG. 8-10   Voltmeter with range of either 10 or 25 V. (*a*) Range switch selects scale by connecting either R_1 or R_2 as the series multiplier. (*b*) Both voltage scales on the meter.

Several examples of using these two scales are listed in Table 8-1. Note that voltages less than 10 V can be read on either scale. It is preferable, however, to have the pointer read on the middle third of the scale. That is why the scales are usually multiples of 10 and 2.5 or 3.

TABLE 8-1   MULTIPLE VOLTAGE-SCALE READINGS FOR FIG. 8-10

10-V SCALE, R_V* = 10,000 Ω			25-V SCALE, R_V* = 25,000 Ω		
METER, mA	DEFLECTION	SCALE READING, V	METER, mA	DEFLECTION	SCALE READING, V
0	0	0	0	0	0
0.5	½	5	0.2	²⁄₁₀	5
1.0	Full scale	10	0.4	⁴⁄₁₀	10
			0.5	½	12.5
			1.0	Full scale	25

*R_V is total voltmeter resistance of multiplier and meter movement.

FIG. 8-11   The range switch selects a multiplier for the voltage that can produce full-scale deflection of the meter movement. The reading shown here is 30 V on the 100-V range.

RANGE SWITCH   With multiple ranges, the setting of the selector switch is the voltage that produces full-scale deflection (Fig. 8-11). One scale is generally used for ranges that are multiples of 10. If the range switch is set for 250 V in Fig. 8-11, read the top scale as is. With the range switch at 25 V, however, the readings on the 250-V scale are divided by 10.

Similarly, the 100-V scale is used for the 100-V range and the 10-V range. In Fig. 8-11 the pointer indicates 30 V when the switch is on the 100-V range; this reading on the 10-V range is 3 V.

TYPICAL MULTIPLE VOLTMETER CIRCUIT   Another example of multiple voltage ranges is shown in Fig. 8-12, with a typical switching arrangement. Resistance R_1 is the series multiplier for the lowest voltage range of 2.5 V. When higher resistance is needed for the higher ranges, the switch adds the required series resistors.

FIG. 8-12   A typical voltmeter circuit with multiplier resistors for different ranges.

The meter in Fig. 8-12 requires 50 μA for full-scale deflection. For the 2.5-V range, a series resistance of $2.5/(50 \times 10^{-6})$, or 50,000 Ω, is needed. Since r_M is 2000 Ω, the value of R_1 is 50,000 − 2000, which equals 48,000 Ω or 48 kΩ.

For the 10-V range, a resistance of $10/(50 \times 10^{-6})$, or 200,000 Ω, is the value needed. Since $R_1 + r_M$ provides 50,000 Ω, R_2 is made 150,000 Ω, for a total of 200,000 Ω series resistance on the 10-V range. Similarly, additional resistors are switched in to increase the multiplier resistance for the higher voltage ranges. Note the separate jack and extra multiplier R_6 on the highest range for 5000 V. This method of adding series multipliers for higher voltage ranges is the circuit generally used in commercial multimeters.

VOLTMETER RESISTANCE   The high resistance of a voltmeter with a multiplier is essentially the value of the multiplier resistance. Since the multiplier is changed for each range, the voltmeter resistance changes.

Table 8-2 shows how the voltmeter resistance increases for the higher ranges. The middle column lists the total internal resistance R_V, including R_{mult} and r_M, for the voltmeter circuit in Fig. 8-12. With a 50-μA movement, R_V increases from 50 kΩ on the 2.5-V range to 20 MΩ on the 1000-V range. It should be noted that R_V has these values on each range whether you read full-scale or not.

TABLE 8-2	CHARACTERISTICS OF A VOLTMETER USING A 50-μA MOVEMENT	
FULL-SCALE VOLTAGE V_F	$R_V = R_{mult} + r_M$	OHMS PER VOLT $= R_V/V_F$
2.5	50 kΩ	20,000 Ω/V
10	200 kΩ	20,000 Ω/V
50	1 MΩ	20,000 Ω/V
250	5 MΩ	20,000 Ω/V
1000	20 MΩ	20,000 Ω/V

OHMS-PER-VOLT RATING   To indicate the voltmeter's resistance independently of the range, voltmeters are generally rated in ohms of resistance needed for 1 V of deflection. This value is the ohms-per-volt rating of the voltmeter. As an example, see the last column in Table 8-2. The values in the top row show that this meter needs 50,000 Ω R_V for 2.5 V of full-scale deflection. The resistance per 1 V of deflection then is 50,000/2.5, which equals 20,000 Ω/V.

The ohms-per-volt value is the same for all ranges. The reason is that this characteristic is determined by the full-scale current I_M of the meter movement. To calculate the ohms-per-volt rating, take the reciprocal of I_M in ampere units. For example, a 1-mA movement results in 1/0.001 or 1000 Ω/V; a 50-μA movement allows 20,000 Ω/V, and a 20-μA movement allows 50,000 Ω/V. The ohms-per-volt rating is also called the *sensitivity* of the voltmeter.

A high ohms-per-volt value means a high voltmeter resistance R_V. In fact R_V can be calculated as the product of the ohms-per-volt rating and the full-scale voltage of each range. For instance, across the second row in Table 8-2, on the 10-V range with a 20,000 Ω/V rating,

$$R_V = 10 \text{ V} \times \frac{20,000 \ \Omega}{\text{volts}}$$

$$R_V = 200,000 \ \Omega$$

These values are for dc volts only. The sensitivity for ac voltage is made lower, generally, to prevent erratic meter deflection produced by stray magnetic fields before the meter leads are connected into the circuit. Usually the ohms-per-volt rating of a voltmeter is printed on the meter face.

The sensitivity of 1000 Ω/V with a 1-mA movement used to be common for dc voltmeters, but 20,000 Ω/V with a 50-μA movement is generally used now. Higher sensitivity is an advantage, not only for less voltmeter loading, but because lower voltage ranges and higher ohmmeter ranges can be obtained.

TEST-POINT QUESTION 8-4

Answers at end of chapter.

Refer to Fig. 8-12.
a. Calculate the voltmeter resistance R_V on the 2.5-V range.
b. Calculate the voltmeter resistance R_V on the 50-V range.
c. Is the voltmeter multiplier resistor in series or parallel with the meter movement?
d. Is a voltmeter connected in series or parallel with the potential difference to be measured?
e. How much is the total R of a voltmeter with a sensitivity of 20,000 Ω/V on the 25-V scale?

8-5 LOADING EFFECT OF A VOLTMETER

When the voltmeter resistance is not high enough, connecting it across a circuit can reduce the measured voltage, compared with the voltage present without the voltmeter. This effect is called *loading down* the circuit, since the measured voltage decreases because of the additional load current for the meter.

LOADING EFFECT   Voltmeter loading can be appreciable in high-resistance circuits, as shown in Fig. 8-13. In Fig. 8-13a, without the voltmeter, R_1 and R_2 form a voltage divider across the applied voltage of 120 V. The two equal resistances of 100 kΩ each divide the applied voltage equally, with 60 V across each.

When the voltmeter in Fig. 8-13b is connected across R_2 to measure its potential difference, however, the voltage division changes. The voltmeter resistance R_V of 100 kΩ is the value for a 1000-ohms-per-volt meter on the 100-V range. Now the voltmeter in parallel with R_2 draws additional current and the equivalent resistance between the measured points 1 and 2 is reduced from 100,000 to 50,000 Ω. This resistance is one-third the total circuit resistance, and the measured voltage across points 1 and 2 drops to 40 V, as shown in Fig. 8-13c.

(a)   (b)   (c)

FIG. 8-13   How loading effect of the voltmeter can reduce the voltage reading.
(a) High-resistance series circuit without voltmeter. (b) Connecting voltmeter across one
of the series resistances. (c) Reduced R and V between points 1 and 2 caused by the
voltmeter as a parallel branch across R_2. The R_{2V} is the equivalent of R_2 and R_V in
parallel.

As additional current drawn by the voltmeter flows through the other series
resistance R_1, this voltage goes up to 80 V.

Similarly, if the voltmeter were connected across R_1, this voltage would go
down to 40 V, with the voltage across R_2 rising to 80 V. When the voltmeter is
disconnected, the circuit returns to the condition in Fig. 8-13a, with 60 V across
both R_1 and R_2.

The loading effect is minimized by using a voltmeter with a resistance much
greater than the resistance across which the voltage is measured. As shown in
Fig. 8-14, with a voltmeter resistance of 10 MΩ, the loading effect is negligible.
Because R_V is so high, it does not change the voltage division in the circuit. The
10 MΩ of the meter in parallel with the 100,000 Ω for R_2 results in an equivalent resistance practically equal to 100,000 Ω.

With multiple ranges on a VOM, the voltmeter resistance changes with the
range selected. Higher ranges require more multiplier resistance, increasing the
voltmeter resistance for less loading. As examples, a 20,000-ohms-per-volt meter on the 250-V range has an internal resistance R_V of 20,000 × 250, or 5 MΩ.
However, on the 2.5-V range the same meter has an R_V of 20,000 × 2.5, which
is only 50,000 Ω.

(a)   (b)

FIG. 8-14   Negligible loading effect with a high-resistance voltmeter. (a) High-resistance series circuit without voltmeter, as in Fig. 8-13a. (b) Same voltages in circuit with
voltmeter connected, because R_V is so high.

On any one range, though, the voltmeter resistance is constant whether you read full-scale or less than full-scale deflection. The reason is that the multiplier resistance set by the range switch is the same for any reading on that range.

CORRECTION FOR LOADING EFFECT   The following formula can be used:

$$\underset{\downarrow}{Actual\ reading} + \underset{\downarrow}{correction}$$

$$V = V_M + \frac{R_1 R_2}{R_V(R_1 + R_2)} V_M \tag{8-4}$$

Voltage V is the corrected reading the voltmeter would show if it had infinitely high resistance. Voltage V_M is the actual voltage reading. Resistances R_1 and R_2 are the voltage-dividing resistances in the circuit without the voltmeter resistance R_V. As an example, in Fig. 8-13,

$$V = 40\ V + \frac{100\ k\Omega \times 100\ k\Omega}{100\ k\Omega \times 200\ k\Omega} \times 40\ V = 40 + \frac{1}{2} \times 40 = 40 + 20$$

$$V = 60\ V$$

The loading effect of a voltmeter causes the voltage reading to be too low because R_V is too low as a parallel resistance. This corresponds to the case of a current meter reading too low because r_M is too high as a series resistance. Both of these effects illustrate the general problem of trying to make any measurement without changing the circuit being measured.

It should be noted that the digital multimeter (DMM) has practically no loading effect as a voltmeter. The input resistance is usually 10 MΩ or 20 MΩ, the same on all ranges.

TEST-POINT QUESTION 8-5

Answers at end of chapter.

With the voltmeter across R_2 in Fig. 8-13, what is the value for
a. V_1?
b. V_2?

8-6 OHMMETERS

Basically, an ohmmeter consists of an internal battery, the meter movement, and a current-limiting resistance, as illustrated in Fig. 8-15. For measuring resistance, the ohmmeter leads are connected across the external resistance to be measured. Power in the circuit being tested must be off. Then only the ohmmeter battery produces current for deflecting the meter movement. Since the amount of current through the meter depends on the external resistance, the scale can be calibrated in ohms.

The amount of deflection on the ohms scale indicates the measured resistance directly. The ohmmeter reads up-scale regardless of the polarity of the leads because the polarity of the internal battery determines the direction of current through the meter movement.

FIG. 8-15 How meter movement M can be used as an ohmmeter with a 1.5-V battery. (a) Equivalent closed circuit with R_1 and the battery when ohmmeter leads are short-circuited for zero ohms of external R. (b) Internal ohmmeter circuit with test leads open, ready to measure an external resistance.

SERIES OHMMETER CIRCUIT   In Fig. 8-15a, the circuit has 1500 Ω for $(R_1 + r_M)$. Then the 1.5-V cell produces 1 mA, deflecting the moving coil full scale. When these components are enclosed in a case, as in Fig. 8-15b, the series circuit forms an ohmmeter. Note that M indicates the meter movement.

If the leads are short-circuited together or connected across a short circuit, 1 mA flows. The meter movement is deflected full scale to the right. This ohmmeter reading is 0 Ω.

When the ohmmeter leads are open, not touching each other, the current is zero. The ohmmeter indicates infinitely high resistance or an open circuit across its terminals.

Therefore, the meter face can be marked zero ohms at the right for full-scale deflection and infinite ohms at the left for no deflection. In-between values of resistance result when less than 1 mA flows through the meter movement. The corresponding deflection on the ohms scale indicates how much resistance is across the ohmmeter terminals.

BACK-OFF OHMMETER SCALE   Table 8-3 and Fig. 8-16 illustrate the calibration of an ohmmeter scale in terms of meter current. The current equals V/R_T. Voltage V is the fixed applied voltage of 1.5 V supplied by the internal battery.

TABLE 8-3   CALIBRATION OF OHMMETER IN FIG. 8-16

EXTERNAL R_X, Ω	INTERNAL $R_i = R_1 + r_M$, Ω	$R_T = R_X + R_i$, Ω	$I = V/R_T$, mA	DEFLECTION	SCALE READING, Ω
0	1500	1500	1	Full scale	0
750	1500	2250	$\frac{2}{3} = 0.67$	$\frac{2}{3}$ scale	750
1500	1500	3000	$\frac{1}{2} = 0.5$	$\frac{1}{2}$ scale	1500
3000	1500	4500	$\frac{1}{3} = 0.33$	$\frac{1}{3}$ scale	3000
150,000	1500	151,500	0.01	$\frac{1}{100}$ scale	150,000
500,000	1500	501,500	0	None	∞

(a)

(b)

FIG. 8-16   Back-off ohmmeter scale with R readings increasing from right to left. (a) Series ohmmeter circuit for the unknown external resistor R_X to be measured. (b) Ohms scale has higher R readings to the left of the scale as more R_X decreases I_M. The R and I values are listed in Table 8-3.

Resistance R_T is the total resistance of R_X and the ohmmeter's internal resistance. Note that R_X is the external resistance to be measured.

The ohmmeter's internal resistance R_i is constant at $50 + 1450$, or $1500\ \Omega$ here. If R_X also equals $1500\ \Omega$, for example, R_T equals $3000\ \Omega$. The current then is $1.5\ \text{V}/3000\ \Omega$, or 0.5 mA, resulting in half-scale deflection for the 1-mA movement. Therefore, the center of the ohms scale is marked for $1500\ \Omega$. Similarly, the amount of current and meter deflection can be calculated for any value of the external resistance R_X.

Note that the ohms scale increases from right to left. This arrangement is called a *back-off scale,* with ohms values increasing to the left as the current backs off from full-scale deflection. The back-off scale is a characteristic of any ohmmeter where the internal battery is in series with the meter movement. Then more external R_X decreases the meter current.

A back-off ohmmeter scale is expanded at the right near zero ohms and crowded at the left near infinite ohms. This nonlinear scale results from the relation of $I = V/R$ with V constant at 1.5 V. Specifically, the back-off ohms scale represents the graph of a hyperbolic curve for a reciprocal function $y = 1/x$, where y is I and x is R.

The highest resistance that can be indicated by the ohmmeter is about 100 times its total internal resistance. Therefore, the infinity mark on the ohms scale, or the "lazy eight" symbol ∞ for infinity, is only relative. It just means that the measured resistance is infinitely greater than the ohmmeter resistance.

For instance, if a 500,000-Ω resistor in good condition were measured with the ohmmeter in Fig. 8-16, it would indicate infinite resistance because this ohmmeter cannot measure as high as $500,000\ \Omega$. To read higher values of resistance, the battery voltage can be increased to provide more current, or a more sensitive meter movement is necessary to provide deflection with less current.

MULTIPLE OHMMETER RANGES   Commercial multimeters provide for resistance measurements from less than $1\ \Omega$ up to many megohms, in several ranges. The range switch in Fig. 8-17 shows the multiplying factors for the ohms scale. On the $R \times 1$ range, for low-resistance measurements, read the ohms scale directly. In the example here, the pointer indicates $12\ \Omega$. When the range switch

FIG. 8-17   Multiple ohmmeter ranges with just one ohms scale. The ohms reading is multiplied by the factor set on the range switch.

is on $R \times 100$, multiply the scale reading by 100; this reading would then be 12×100 or $1200 \ \Omega$. On the $R \times 10,000$ range, the pointer would indicate $120,000 \ \Omega$.

A multiplying factor, instead of full-scale resistance, is given for each ohms range because the highest resistance is infinite on all the ohms ranges. This method for ohms should not be confused with the full-scale values for voltage ranges. For the ohmmeter ranges, always multiply the scale reading by the $R \times$ factor. On voltage ranges, you may have to multiply or divide the scale reading to match the full-scale voltage with the value on the range switch.

TYPICAL OHMMETER CIRCUIT   For high-ohms ranges a sensitive meter is necessary to read the low values of I with the high values of R_X. For the case of low ohms, however, less sensitivity is needed for the higher currents. These opposite requirements are solved by using a meter shunt across the meter movement and changing the shunt resistance for the multiple ohmmeter ranges. In Fig. 8-18, R_S is the meter shunt.

FIG. 8-18   Typical ohmmeter circuit, illustrated for $R \times 1$ range. (*a*) Circuit with test leads open. (*b*) Test leads short-circuited to adjust for zero ohms. (*c*) Ohmmeter measurement with test leads across external R_X of $12 \ \Omega$. This value results in half-scale deflection, as shown on the ohms scale in Fig. 8-17.

To analyze the ohmmeter circuit in Fig. 8-18, three conditions are shown. All are for the $R \times 1$ range with 12-Ω R_S. Figure 8-18a shows the internal circuit before the ohmmeter is adjusted for zero ohms. In Fig. 8-18b the test leads are short-circuited. Then there are two paths for branch current produced by the battery V. One branch is R_S. The other branch includes R_b, R_A, and the meter movement. The 1.5 V is across both branches.

To allow 50 μA through the meter, R_A is adjusted to 5000 Ω. Then the total resistance in this branch is 23 kΩ + 5 kΩ + 2 kΩ, which equals 30 kΩ. With 30 kΩ across 1.5 V, I_M equals 50 μA. Therefore, R_A is adjusted for full-scale deflection to read zero ohms with the test leads short-circuited.

In Fig. 8-18c assume that a resistance R_X being measured is 12 Ω, equal to R_S. Then the meter current is practically 25 μA for half-scale deflection. The center ohms reading on the $R \times 1$ scale, therefore, is 12 Ω. For higher values of R_X, the meter current decreases to indicate higher resistances on the back-off ohms scale.

For higher ohms ranges, the resistance of the R_S branch is increased. The half-scale ohms reading on each range is equal to the resistance of the R_S branch. A higher battery voltage can also be used for the highest ohms range.

On any range, R_A is adjusted for full-scale deflection to read zero ohms with the test leads short-circuited. This variable resistor is the *ohms adjust* or *zero-ohms* adjustment.

ZERO-OHMS ADJUSTMENT   To compensate for lower voltage output as the internal battery ages, an ohmmeter includes a variable resistor such as R_A in Fig. 8-18, to calibrate the ohms scale. A back-off ohmmeter is always adjusted for zero ohms. With the test leads short-circuited, vary the ZERO OHMS control on the front panel of the meter until the pointer is exactly on zero at the right edge of the ohms scale. Then the ohms readings are correct for the entire scale.

This type of ohmmeter must be zeroed again every time you change the range. The reason is that the internal circuit is changed.

When the adjustment cannot deflect the pointer all the way to zero at the right edge, it usually means the battery voltage is too low and the internal dry cells must be replaced. Usually, this trouble shows up first on the $R \times 1$ range, which takes the most current from the battery.

<hr>

TEST-POINT QUESTION 8-6

Answers at end of chapter.
a. The ohmmeter reads 40 Ω on the $R \times 10$ range. How much is R_X?
b. A voltmeter reads 40 V on the 300-V scale, but with the range switch on 30 V. How much is the measured voltage?

8-7 MULTIMETERS

Multimeters are also called *multitesters,* and they are used to measure voltage, current, or resistance. Table 8-4 compares the features of the main types of mul-

TABLE 8-4 COMPARISON OF VOM WITH DMM

VOM	DMM
Analog pointer reading	Digital readout
DC voltmeter R_V changes with range	R_V is 10 or 22 MΩ, the same on all ranges
Zero-ohms adjustment changed for each range	No zero-ohms adjustment
Ohms ranges up to $R \times 10,000\ \Omega$, as a multiplying factor	Ohms ranges up to 20 MΩ; each range is the maximum

timeters, which are the volt-ohm-milliammeter (VOM), in Fig. 8-19, and the digital multimeter (DMM), in Fig. 8-20. The DMM is explained in more detail in the next section.

Because it is simple, compact, and portable, the VOM is a very common basic instrument. The cost of a typical VOM is less than for a DMM.

Besides its digital readout, an advantage of the DMM is its high input resistance R_V, as a dc voltmeter. The R_V is usually 10 MΩ, the same on all ranges, which is high enough to prevent any loading effect by the voltmeter in most circuits. Some types have R_V of 22 MΩ. Many modern DMMs are autoranging; that is, the internal circuitry selects the proper range for the meter and indicates the range as a readout.

For either a VOM or a DMM, it is important to have a low-voltage dc scale with resolution good enough to read 0.2 V or less. The range of 0.2 to 0.6 V, or 200 to 600 mV, is needed for measuring dc bias voltages in transistor circuits.

LOW-POWER OHMS (LPΩ)   Another feature needed for transistor measurements is an ohmmeter that does not have enough battery voltage to bias a semiconductor junction into the ON or conducting condition. The limit is 0.2 V or less. The purpose is to prevent any parallel conduction paths in the transistor amplifier circuit, which can lower the ohmmeter reading.

DECIBEL SCALE   Most analog multimeters have an ac voltage scale calibrated in decibel (dB) units, for measuring ac signals. The decibel is a logarithmic unit used for comparisons of power levels or voltage levels. The mark of 0 dB on the scale indicates the reference level, which is usually 0.775 V for 1 mW across 600 Ω. Positive decibel values, above the zero mark, indicate ac voltages above the reference of 0.775 V; negative decibel values are less than the reference level.

FIG. 8-19   Analog VOM that combines a function selector and range switch.

FIG. 8-20 Portable digital multimeter (DMM).

AMP-CLAMP PROBE The problem of opening a circuit to measure I can be eliminated by using a probe with a clamp that fits around the current-carrying wire. Its magnetic field is used to indicate the amount of current. An example is shown in Fig. 8-21. The clamp probe measures just ac amperes, generally for the 60-Hz power line.

HIGH-VOLTAGE PROBE An accessory probe can be used with a multimeter to measure dc voltages up to 30 kV. This probe is often referred to as a high-voltage probe. One application is measuring the high voltage of 20 to 30 kV at the anode of the color picture tube in a television receiver. The probe is basically just an external multiplier resistance for the dc voltmeter. The required R for a 30-kV probe is 580 MΩ with a 20-kΩ/V meter on the 1000-V range.

FIG. 8-21 DMM with amp clamp accessory.

Answers at end of chapter.
  a. How much is R_V on the 1-V range for a VOM with a sensitivity of 20 kΩ/V?
  b. If R_V is 10 MΩ for a DMM on the 100-V range, how much is R_V on the 200-mV range?
  c. The low-power ohms function (LPΩ) does not require an internal battery. True or false?

8-8 DIGITAL MULTIMETER (DMM)

The digital multimeter has become a very popular test instrument because the digital value of the measurement is displayed automatically with decimal point, polarity, and the unit for V, A, or Ω. Digital meters are generally easier to use because they eliminate the human error that often occurs in reading different scales on an analog meter with a pointer. Examples of the portable DMM are shown in Figs. 8-20 and 8-22.

The basis of the DMM operation is the use of an analog-to-digital (A/D) converter circuit. It converts analog voltage values in the input to an equivalent binary form. These values are processed by digital circuits to be shown on a liquid-crystal display (LCD) with decimal values.

VOLTAGE MEASUREMENTS   The A/D converter requires a specific range of voltage input, typical values being −200 mV to +200 mV. For DMM input voltages that are higher, the voltage is divided down. When the input voltage is too low, it is increased by a dc amplifier circuit. The measured voltage can then be compared to a fixed reference voltage in the meter by a comparator circuit. Actually, all the functions in the DMM depend on the voltage measurements by the converter and comparator circuits.

The input resistance of the DMM is in the range of 10 to 20 MΩ, shunted by 50 pF of capacitance. This R is high enough to eliminate the problem of voltmeter loading in most transistor circuits. Not only does the DMM have high input resistance, but the R is the same on all ranges.

With ac measurements, the ac input is converted to dc voltage for the A/D converter. The DMM has an internal diode rectifier that serves as an ac converter.

FIG. 8-22   Typical digital multimeter (DMM) described in text.

***R* MEASUREMENT**   As an ohmmeter, the internal battery supplies I through the measured R for an IR drop measured by the DMM. The battery is usually the small 9-V type commonly used in portable equipment. A wide range of R values can be measured, from a fraction of an ohm to more than 30 MΩ. Remember that power must be off in the circuit being tested with an ohmmeter.

A DMM ohmmeter usually has an open-circuit voltage across the meter leads, which is much too low to turn on a semiconductor junction. The result is low-power ohms operation.

_I_ MEASUREMENTS   To measure current, internal resistors provide a proportional _IR_ voltage. The display shows the _I_ values. Note that the DMM still must be connected as a series component in the circuit when current is measured.

DIODE TEST   The DMM usually has a setting for testing semiconductor diodes, either silicon or germanium. Current is supplied by the DMM for the diode to test the voltage across its junction. Normal values are 0.7 V for silicon or 0.3 V for germanium. A short-circuited junction will read 0 V. The voltage across an open diode reads much too high. Most diodes are silicon.

RESOLUTION   This term for a DMM specifies how many places can be used to display the digits 0 to 9, regardless of the decimal point. For example, 9.99 V is a three-digit display. Also 9.999 V would be a four-digit display. Most portable units, however, compromise with a 3½-digit display. This means that the fourth digit at the left for the most significant place can only be a 1. If not, then the display has three digits. As examples, a 3½ digit display can show 19.99 V but 29.99 V would be read as 30.0 V. It should be noted that better resolution with more digits can be obtained with more expensive meters, especially the larger DMM units for bench mounting. Actually, though, 3½ digit resolution is enough for practically all measurements made in troubleshooting electronic equipment.

RANGE OVERLOAD   The DMM selector switch has specific ranges. Any value higher than the selected range is an overload. An indicator on the display warns that the value shown is not correct. Then a higher range is selected. Some units have an _autorange function,_ where the meter automatically shifts to a higher range as soon as an overload is indicated.

TYPICAL DMM   The unit in Fig. 8-22 can be used as an example. On the front panel, the two jacks at the bottom right are for the test leads. The lower jack is the common, with a black lead, used for all measurements. Above is the jack for the "hot" lead, usually red, used for most measurements of _V_, _R_, and _I_, either dc or ac values. The two jacks at the bottom left side are for the red lead with very high _I_ values up to 10 A or very low values below 300 mA.

Consider each function of the large selector switch at the center in Fig. 8-22. The first position at the top, after the switch is turned clockwise from the OFF position, is used to measure ac volts, as indicated by the sine wave. No ranges are given as this meter has autorange function. In operation, the meter has the ranges of 0 to 3.2 V, 32 V, 320 V, and, as a maximum, 750 V.

If the autorange function is not desired, press the range button at the top, to the right of the front panel, to hold the range. Each touch of the button will change the range. Hold the button down to return to autorange operation.

The next position on the function switch is for dc volts. Polarity can be either positive or negative as indicated by the solid and dashed lines next to the _V_. The ranges of dc voltages that can be measured are 0 to 3.2 V, 32 V, 320 V, and 1000 V as a maximum. Values of 300 mV or less are measured on this position of the function switch.

For an ohmmeter, the function switch is set to the position with the Ω symbol. The ohms values are from 0 to 32 MΩ in six ranges. Remember that power must be off in the circuit being measured, or the ohmmeter will read the wrong value.

Next on the function switch is the position for testing semiconductor diodes, as shown by the diode symbol. The lines next to the symbol indicate the meter produces a beep tone. Maximum diode test voltage is 2 V.

The last two positions on the function switch are for current measurements, in the range of 0 to 320 mA. For larger or smaller current values, the special jacks at the lower left are used.

In measuring ac values, either for V or I, the frequency range of the meter is limited to 45 to 1000 Hz, approximately. For amplitudes at higher frequencies, such as RF measurements, special meters are necessary. However, this meter can be used for V and I at the 60-Hz power-line frequency and the 400-Hz test frequency often used for audio equipment.

ANALOG DISPLAY   The bar at the bottom of the display in Fig. 8-22 is used only to show the relative magnitude of the input compared to the full-scale value of the range in use. This function is convenient when adjusting a circuit for a peak value or a minimum (null). The operation is comparable to watching the needle on a VOM for either a maximum or a null adjustment.

TEST-POINT QUESTION 8-8

Answers at end of chapter.

Answer True or False.

a. Typical resistance of a DMM voltmeter is 10 MΩ.

b. The ohmmeter on a portable DMM does not need an internal battery.

c. A DMM voltmeter with 3½ digit resolution can read the value of 3.5555 V.

8-9 METER APPLICATIONS

Table 8-5 summarizes the main points to remember in using a voltmeter, ohmmeter, or milliammeter. These rules apply whether the meter is a single unit or one function on a multimeter. Also, the voltage and current tests apply to either dc or ac circuits.

TABLE 8-5   DIRECT-CURRENT METERS

VOLTMETER	MILLIAMMETER OR AMMETER	OHMMETER
Power on in circuit	Power on in circuit	Power off in circuit
Connect in parallel	Connect in series	Connect in parallel
High internal R	Low internal R	Has internal battery
Has internal series multipliers; higher R for higher ranges	Has internal shunts; lower resistance for higher current ranges	Higher battery voltage and more sensitive meter for higher ohms ranges

To avoid excessive current through the meter, it is good practice to start on a high range when measuring an unknown value of voltage or current. It is very important not to make the mistake of connecting a current meter in parallel, because usually this mistake ruins the meter. The mistake of connecting a voltmeter in series does not damage the meter, but the reading will be wrong.

If the ohmmeter is connected to a circuit where power is on, the meter can be damaged, besides giving the wrong reading. An ohmmeter has its own internal battery, and the power must be off in the circuit being tested. When testing R with an ohmmeter, it may be necessary to disconnect one end of R from the circuit, to eliminate parallel paths.

CONNECTING A CURRENT METER IN THE CIRCUIT   In a series-parallel circuit, the current meter must be inserted in a branch to read branch current. In the main line, the meter reads the total current. These different connections are illustrated in Fig. 8-23. The meters are shown by dashed lines to illustrate the different points at which a meter could be connected to read the respective currents.

If the circuit is opened at point A to insert the meter in series in the main line here, the meter will read total line current I_T through R_1. A meter at B or C will read the same line current.

In order to read the branch current through R_2, this R must be disconnected from its junction with the main line at either end. A meter inserted at D or E, therefore, will read the R_2 branch current I_2. Similarly, a meter at F or G will read the R_3 branch current I_3.

FIG. 8-23   How to insert a current meter in different parts of a series-parallel circuit to read the desired current I. At point A, B, or C the meter reads I_T; at D or E the meter reads I_2; at F or G the meter reads I_3.

CALCULATING I FROM MEASURED VOLTAGE   The inconvenience of opening the circuit to measure current can often be eliminated by the use of Ohm's law. The voltage and resistance can be measured without opening the circuit and the current calculated as V/R. In the example in Fig. 8-24, when the voltage across R_2 is 15 V and its resistance is 15 Ω, the current through R_2 must be

FIG. 8-24   With 15 V measured across a known R of 15 Ω, the I can be calculated as V/R or 15 V/15 Ω = 1 A.

1 A. When values are checked during troubleshooting, if the voltage and resistance are normal, so is the current.

This technique can also be convenient for determining I in low-resistance circuits where the resistance of a microammeter may be too high. Instead of measuring I, measure V and R and calculate I as V/R.

Furthermore, if necessary, we can insert a known resistance R_S in series in the circuit, temporarily, just to measure V_S. Then I is calculated as V_S/R_S. The resistance of R_S, however, must be small enough to have little effect on R_T and I in the series circuit.

This technique is often used with oscilloscopes to produce a voltage waveform of IR which has the same waveform as the current in a resistor. The oscilloscope must be connected as a voltmeter because of its high input resistance.

CHECKING FUSES   Turn the power off or remove the fuse from the circuit to check with an ohmmeter. A good fuse reads 0 Ω. A blown fuse is open, which reads infinity on the ohmmeter.

A fuse can also be checked with the power on in the circuit by using a voltmeter. Connect the voltmeter across the two terminals of the fuse. A good fuse reads 0 V because there is practically no IR drop. With an open fuse, though, the voltmeter reading is equal to the full value of the applied voltage. Having the full applied voltage seems to be a good idea, but it should not be across the fuse.

VOLTAGE TESTS FOR AN OPEN CIRCUIT   Figure 8-25 shows four equal resistors in series with a 100-V source. A ground return is shown here because voltage measurements are usually made to chassis ground. Normally, each resistor would have an IR drop of 25 V. Then, at point B the voltmeter to ground should read $100 - 25 = 75$ V. Also, the voltage at C should be 50 V, with 25 V at D, as shown in Fig. 8-25a.

However, the circuit in Fig. 8-25b has an open in R_3, toward the end of the series string of voltages to ground. Now when you measure at B, the reading is 100 V, equal to the applied voltage. This full voltage at B shows that the series circuit is open, without any IR drop across R_1. The question is, however, which R has the open? Continue the voltage measurements to ground until you find 0 V. In this example, the open is in R_3, between the 100 V at C and 0 V at D.

The points that read the full applied voltage have a path back to the source of voltage. The first point that reads 0 V has no path back to the high side of the source. Therefore, the open circuit must be between points C and D in Fig. 8-25b.

FIG. 8-25   Voltage tests to localize an open circuit. (a) Normal circuit with voltages to chassis ground. (b) Reading of 0 V at point D shows R_3 is open.

Answers at end of chapter.
a. Which type of meter requires an internal battery?
b. How much is the normal voltage across a good fuse?
c. How much is the voltage across R_1 in Fig. 8-25a?
d. How much is the voltage across R_1 in Fig. 8-25b?

8-10 CHECKING CONTINUITY WITH THE OHMMETER

A wire conductor that is continuous without a break has practically zero ohms of resistance. Therefore, the ohmmeter can be useful in testing for the continuity. This test should be done on the lowest ohms range. There are many applications. A wire conductor can have an internal break which is not visible because of the insulated cover, or the wire can have a bad connection at the terminal. Checking for zero ohms between any two points along the conductor tests continuity. A break in the conducting path is evident from a reading of infinite resistance, showing an open circuit.

As another application of checking continuity, suppose there is a cable of wires harnessed together as illustrated in Fig. 8-26, where the individual wires cannot be seen, but it is desired to find the conductor that connects to terminal A. This is done by checking continuity for each conductor to point A. The wire that has zero ohms to A is the one connected to this terminal. Often the individual wires are color-coded, but it may be necessary to check the continuity of each lead.

FIG. 8-26 Continuity testing from point A to wire 3 shows this wire is connected.

An additional technique that can be helpful is illustrated in Fig. 8-27. Here it is desired to check the continuity of the two-wire line, but its ends are too far apart for the ohmmeter leads to reach. The two conductors are temporarily short-circuited at one end, however, so that the continuity of both wires can be checked at the other end.

In summary, then, the ohmmeter is helpful in checking the continuity of any wire conductor. This includes resistance-wire heating elements, like the wires in

FIG. 8-27 Temporary short circuit at one end of a long two-wire line to check continuity from the opposite end.

a toaster or the filament of an incandescent bulb. Their cold resistance is normally just a few ohms. Infinite resistance means that the wire element is open. Similarly, a good fuse has practically zero resistance; a burned-out fuse has infinite resistance, meaning it is open. Also, any coil for a transformer, solenoid, or motor will have infinite resistance if the winding is open.

TEST-POINT QUESTION 8-10

Answers at end of chapter.
a. On a back-off ohmmeter, is zero ohms at the left or the right end of the scale?
b. What is the ohmmeter reading for an open circuit?

- Direct current in a moving-coil meter deflects the coil in proportion to the amount of current.
- A current meter is a low-resistance meter connected in series to read the amount of current in the circuit.
- A meter shunt R_S in parallel with the meter movement extends the range of a current meter [see Formula (8-1)].
- A voltmeter consists of the meter movement in series with a high-resistance multiplier. The voltmeter with its multiplier is connected across two points to measure their potential difference in volts. The multiplier R can be calculated from Formula (8-3).
- The ohms-per-volt rating of a voltmeter with series multipliers specifies the sensitivity on all voltage ranges. It equals the reciprocal of the full-scale deflection current of the meter. A typical value is 20,000 Ω/V for a voltmeter using a 50-μA movement. The higher the ohms-per-volt rating, the better.
- Voltmeter resistance R_V is higher for higher ranges because of higher-resistance multipliers. Multiply the ohms-per-volt rating by the voltage range to calculate the R_V for each range.
- An ohmmeter consists of an internal battery in series with the meter movement. Power must be off in the circuit being checked with an ohmmeter. The series ohmmeter has a back-off scale with zero ohms at the right edge and infinity at the left. Adjust for zero ohms with the leads short-circuited each time the ohms range is changed.
- The VOM is a portable multimeter that measures volts, ohms, and milliamperes.
- The digital multimeter generally has an input resistance of 10 MΩ on all dc voltage ranges.
- In checking wire conductors, the ohmmeter reads 0 Ω or very low R for normal continuity and infinite ohms for an open.

SELF-TEST

ANSWERS AT BACK OF BOOK.

Choose (a), (b), (c), or (d).

1. To connect a current meter in series: (a) open the circuit at one point and use the meter to complete the circuit; (b) open the circuit at the positive and negative terminals of the voltage source; (c) short-circuit the resistance to be checked and connect the meter across it; (d) open the circuit at one point and connect the meter to one end.

2. To connect a voltmeter in parallel to read an *IR* drop: (a) open the circuit at one end and use the meter to complete the circuit; (b) open the circuit at two points and connect the meter

across both points; (c) allow the circuit to remain as is and connect the meter across the resistance; (d) allow the circuit to remain closed but disconnect the voltage source.

3. A shunt for a milliammeter (a) extends the range and reduces the meter resistance; (b) extends the range and increases the meter resistance; (c) decreases the range and the meter resistance; (d) decreases the range but increases the meter resistance.

4. For a 50-μA movement with 2000-Ω r_M, the voltage V_M at full-scale deflection is (a) 0.1 V; (b) 0.2 V; (c) 0.5 V; (d) 250 μV.

5. A voltmeter using a 20-μA meter movement has a sensitivity of (a) 1000 Ω/V; (b) 20,000 Ω/V; (c) 50,000 Ω/V; (d) 11 MΩ/V.

6. When using an ohmmeter, disconnect the applied voltage from the circuit being checked because: (a) the voltage source will increase the resistance; (b) the current will decrease the resistance; (c) the ohmmeter has its own internal battery; (d) no current is needed for the meter movement.

7. A multiplier for a voltmeter is (a) a high resistance in series with the meter movement; (b) a high resistance in parallel with the meter movement; (c) usually less than 1 Ω in series with the meter movement; (d) usually less than 1 Ω in parallel with the meter movement.

8. To double the current range of a 50-μA 2000-Ω meter movement, the shunt resistance is (a) 40 Ω; (b) 50 Ω; (c) 2000 Ω; (d) 18,000 Ω.

9. With a 50-μA movement, a VOM has an input resistance of 6 MΩ on the dc voltage range of (a) 3; (b) 12; (c) 60; (d) 300.

10. For a 1-V range, a 50-μA movement with an internal R of 2000 Ω needs a multiplier resistance of (a) 1 kΩ; (b) 3 kΩ; (c) 18 kΩ; (d) 50 kΩ.

QUESTIONS

1. (a) Why is a milliammeter connected in series in a circuit? (b) Why should the milliammeter have low resistance?

2. (a) Why is a voltmeter connected in parallel in a circuit? (b) Why should the voltmeter have high resistance?

3. A circuit has a battery across two resistances in series. (a) Draw a diagram showing how to connect a milliammeter in the correct polarity to read current through the junction of the two resistances. (b) Draw a diagram showing how to connect a voltmeter in the correct polarity to read the voltage across one resistance.

4. Explain briefly why a meter shunt equal to the resistance of the moving coil doubles the current range.

5. Describe how to adjust the ZERO OHMS control on a back-off ohmmeter.

6. What is meant by a 3½-digit display on a DMM?

7. Give two advantages of the DMM in Fig. 8-20 compared with the conventional VOM in Fig. 8-19.

8. What does the zero ohms control in the circuit of a back-off ohmmeter do?

9. State two precautions to be observed when you use a milliammeter.

10. State two precautions to be observed when you use an ohmmeter.

11. The resistance of a voltmeter R_V is 300 kΩ on the 300-V range when measuring 300 V. Why is R_V still 300 kΩ when measuring 250 V on the same range?

12. Redraw the schematic diagram in Fig. 6-1*b*, in Chap. 6, showing a milliammeter to read line current through R_1 and R_2, a meter for R_3 branch current, and a meter for R_4 branch current. Label polarities on each meter.

13. Give a typical value of voltmeter resistance for a DMM.

14. Would you rather use a DMM or VOM in troubleshooting? Why?

PROBLEMS

ANSWERS TO ODD-NUMBERED PROBLEMS AT BACK OF BOOK.

1. Calculate the shunt resistance R_S that is needed to extend the range of a 50-Ω 1-mA movement to: **(a)** 2 mA; **(b)** 10 mA; **(c)** 25 mA; **(d)** 100 mA **(e)** In each case, how much current is indicated by half-scale deflection?

2. Refer to Fig. 8-28. **(a)** Calculate the values for the separate shunt resistances, R_{S_1}, R_{S_2}, and R_{S_3}. **(b)** Calculate the resistance of the meter (R_S in parallel with r_M) for each setting of the range switch.

3. Calculate the multiplier resistance, R_{mult}, for a 50-Ω 1-mA movement if the voltage ranges are: **(a)** 3 V; **(b)** 10 V; **(c)** 30 V; **(d)** 100 V; **(e)** 300 V. In each case, how much voltage is indicated by half-scale deflection?

4. Refer to Fig. 8-29. **(a)** Calculate the values for the multiplier resistors, R_1, R_2, R_3, R_4, R_5, and R_6. **(b)** Calculate the total voltmeter resistance R_V for each setting of the range switch.

5. Refer to Fig. 8-30. **(a)** Calculate the dc voltage that should exist across R_2 without a voltmeter present. **(b)** Calculate the dc voltage that would be measured across R_2 using the volt-

FIG. 8-28 Circuit diagram for Prob. 2.

FIG. 8-29   Circuit diagram for Prob. 4.

FIG. 8-30   Circuit diagram for Prob. 5.

meter of Fig. 8-29 set to the 10-V range. (**c**) Calculate the dc voltage that would be measured across R_2 using a DMM with an R_V of 10 MΩ on all of its dc voltage ranges.

6.   A certain voltmeter has an Ω/V rating of 25 kΩ/V. Calculate the total voltmeter resistance R_V for the following voltmeter ranges: (**a**) 2.5 V; (**b**) 10 V; (**c**) 25 V; (**d**) 100 V; (**e**) 250 V; (**f**) 1000 V; (**g**) 5000 V.

7.   Determine the Ω/V rating for the meter in Fig. 8-29.

8.   Refer to Fig. 8-30. Suppose a voltmeter having an Ω/V rating of 20 kΩ/V is connected across R_1 to measure its voltage drop. If the voltmeter reads 6 V when set on its 15-V range, use Formula (8-4) to determine the actual value of V_1 without the meter present.

9.   Refer to the series ohmmeter in Fig. 8-15b. What value of external resistance R_X across the ohmmeter leads will produce: (**a**) full-scale deflection; (**b**) one-quarter full-scale deflection; (**c**) one-third full-scale deflection; (**d**) one-half full-scale deflection; (**e**) two-thirds full-scale deflection; (**f**) three-fourths full-scale deflection?

10.   In Fig. 8-15b, assume that the battery voltage $V_b = 1.65$ V. What value of external resistance R_X across the ohmmeter leads will produce half-scale deflection?

11. In Fig. 8-15*b*, assume that the meter movement is shunted to become a 10-mA meter. Calculate the value of R_1 required to produce full-scale deflection when the ohmmeter leads are shorted.

12. Refer to Fig. 8-31. With the ohmmeter leads shorted, to what value must R_A be adjusted to provide full-scale deflection of the meter's pointer?

13. In Fig. 8-31, what value of resistance between the ohmmeter leads will produce half-scale deflection of the meter's pointer?

14. Assume that a 15-Ω resistor is connected across the ohmmeter leads in Fig. 8-31. How much current will flow in the meter movement?

15. In Fig. 8-31, what is the minimum battery voltage that will still provide full-scale deflection of the meter's pointer when the ohmmeter leads are shorted?

FIG. 8-31   Circuit diagram for Probs. 12, 13, 14, and 15.

CRITICAL THINKING

1. Figure 8-32 shows a universal-shunt current meter. Calculate the values for R_1, R_2, and R_3 which will provide current ranges of 2 mA, 10 mA, and 50 mA.

2. Design a series ohmmeter using a 2-kΩ 50-μA meter movement and a 1.5-V battery. The center-scale ohms reading is to be 150 Ω.

3. The voltmeter across R_2 in Fig. 8-33 shows 20 V. If the voltmeter is set on the 30-V range, calculate the Ω/V rating of the meter.

FIG. 8-32 Circuit diagram for Critical Thinking Prob. 1.

FIG. 8-33 Circuit diagram for Critical Thinking Prob. 3.

8-1 **a.** parallel
    b. series

8-2 **a.** $I = 100$ mA
    b. R_3
    c. low
    d. high

8-3 **a.** $I_S = 450 \ \mu A$
    b. $V_M = 0.045$ V
    c. $R_S = 100 \ \Omega$

8-4 **a.** $R_V = 50$ kΩ
    b. $R_V = 1$ MΩ
    c. series
    d. parallel
    e. $R = 500$ kΩ

8-5 **a.** $V_1 = 80$ V
    b. $V_2 = 40$ V

8-6 **a.** $R_X = 400 \ \Omega$
    b. $V = 4$ V

8-7 **a.** 20 kΩ
    b. 10 MΩ
    c. F

8-8 **a.** T
    b. F
    c. F

8-9 **a.** ohmmeter
    b. 0 V
    c. 25 V
    d. 0 V

8-10 **a.** right edge
    b. ∞ ohms

REVIEW: CHAPTERS 7 AND 8

- In a series voltage divider the IR drop across each resistance is proportional to its R. A larger R has a larger voltage drop. Each $V = (R/R_T) \times V_T$. In this way, the series voltage drops can be calculated from V_T without I.
- In a parallel current divider, each branch current is inversely related to its R. A smaller R has more branch current. For only two resistances, we can use the inverse relation

$$I_1 = [R_2/(R_1 + R_2)] \times I_T$$

In this way, the branch currents can be calculated from I_T without V.

- In a parallel current divider, each branch current is directly proportional to its conductance G. A larger G has more branch current. For any number of parallel resistances, each branch $I = (G/G_T) \times I_T$.
- A milliammeter or ammeter is a low-resistance meter connected in series in a circuit to measure current.
- Different current ranges are obtained by meter shunts in parallel with the meter.
- A voltmeter is a high-resistance meter connected across the voltage to be measured.
- Different voltage ranges are obtained by multipliers in series with the meter.
- An ohmmeter has an internal battery to indicate the resistance of a component across its two terminals, with external power off.
- In making resistance tests, remember that $R = 0\ \Omega$ for continuity or a short circuit, but the resistance of an open circuit is infinitely high.
- Figure 8-1 shows a VOM and DMM. Both types can be used for voltage, current, and resistance measurements.

REVIEW SELF-TEST

ANSWERS AT BACK OF BOOK.

Answer True or False.

1. The internal R of a milliammeter must be low to have minimum effect on I in the circuit.
2. The internal R of a voltmeter must be high to have minimum current through the meter.
3. Power must be off when checking resistance in a circuit because the ohmmeter has its own internal battery.

4. In the series voltage divider in Fig. 8-25, the normal voltage from point B to ground is 75 V.
5. In Fig. 8-25, the normal voltage across R_1, between A and B, is 75 V.
6. The highest ohms range is best for checking continuity with an ohmmeter.
7. With four equal resistors in a series voltage divider with V_T of 44.4 V, each IR drop is 11.1 V.
8. With four equal resistors in parallel with I_T of 44.4 mA, each branch current is 11.1 mA.
9. Series voltage drops divide V_T in direct proportion to each series R.
10. Parallel currents divide I_T in direct proportion to each branch R.
11. The VOM cannot be used to measure current.
12. The DMM can be used as a high-resistance voltmeter.

REFERENCES

Gilmore, C. M.: *Instruments and Measurements,* Glencoe/McGraw-Hill, Columbus, Ohio.

Prensky, S. D., and R. L. Castellucis: *Electronic Instrumentation,* Prentice-Hall Inc., Englewood Cliffs, N.J.

Zbar, P. B., and G. Rockmaker: *Basic Electricity: A Text-Lab Manual,* Glencoe/McGraw-Hill, Columbus, Ohio.

CHAPTER 9

KIRCHHOFF'S LAWS

Many types of circuits have components that are not in series, in parallel, or in series-parallel. For example, a circuit may have two voltages applied in different branches. Another example is an unbalanced bridge circuit. Where the rules of series and parallel circuits cannot be applied, more general methods of analysis become necessary. These methods include the application of Kirchhoff's laws, as described here, and the network theorems explained in Chap. 10.

All circuits can be solved by Kirchhoff's laws because they do not depend on series or parallel connections. Stated in 1847 by the German physicist Gustav R. Kirchhoff, the two basic rules for voltage and current are:

1. *The algebraic sum of the voltage sources and IR voltage drops in any closed path must total zero.*

2. *At any point in a circuit the algebraic sum of the currents directed in and out must total zero.*

Specific methods for applying these basic rules in dc circuits are explained in this chapter.

CHAPTER OBJECTIVES

Upon completion of this chapter, you should be able to:

- *State* Kirchhoff's current and voltage laws.
- *Use* the method of branch currents to solve for all voltages and currents in a circuit containing two or more voltage sources in different branches.
- *Use* node-voltage analysis to solve for the unknown voltages and currents in a circuit containing two or more voltage sources in different branches.
- *Use* the method of mesh currents to solve for the unknown voltages and currents in a circuit containing two or more voltage sources in different branches.

IMPORTANT TERMS IN THIS CHAPTER

current law	network	ΣV
loop	node voltage	voltage law
mesh current	simultaneous equations	

TOPICS COVERED IN THIS CHAPTER

The algebraic sum of the currents entering and leaving any point in a circuit must equal zero. Or stated another way: *The algebraic sum of the currents into any point of the circuit must equal the algebraic sum of the currents out of that point.* Otherwise, charge would accumulate at the point, instead of having a conducting path. An algebraic sum means combining positive and negative values.

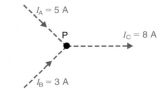

FIG. 9-1 Current I_C out from point P equals 5 A + 3 A into P.

ALGEBRAIC SIGNS In using Kirchhoff's laws to solve circuits it is necessary to adopt conventions that determine the algebraic signs for current and voltage terms. A convenient system for currents is: *Consider all currents into a branch point as positive and all currents directed away from that point as negative.*

As an example, in Fig. 9-1 we can write the currents as

$$I_A + I_B - I_C = 0$$

or

$$5\,A + 3\,A - 8\,A = 0$$

Currents I_A and I_B are positive terms because these currents flow into P, but I_C, directed out, is negative.

CURRENT EQUATIONS For a circuit application, refer to point C at the top of the diagram in Fig. 9-2. The 6-A I_T into point C divides into the 2-A I_3 and 4-A I_{4-5}, both directed out. Note that I_{4-5} is the current through R_4 and R_5. The algebraic equation is

$$I_T - I_3 - I_{4-5} = 0$$

Substituting the values for these currents,

$$6\,A - 2\,A - 4\,A = 0$$

FIG. 9-2 Series-parallel circuit to illustrate Kirchhoff's laws. See text for voltage and current equations.

For the opposite directions, refer to point D at the bottom of Fig. 9-2. Here the branch currents into D combine to equal the main-line current I_T returning to the voltage source. Now I_T is directed out from D, with I_3 and I_{4-5} directed in. The algebraic equation is

$$-I_T + I_3 + I_{4-5} = 0$$
$$-6 \text{ A} + 2 \text{ A} + 4 \text{ A} = 0$$

THE $I_{in} = I_{out}$ Note that at either point C or point D in Fig. 9-2, the sum of the 2-A and 4-A branch currents must equal the 6-A total line current. Therefore, Kirchhoff's current law can also be stated as: $I_{in} = I_{out}$. For Fig. 9-2, the equations of current can be written:

At point C: 6 A = 2 A + 4 A
At point D: 2 A + 4 A = 6 A

Kirchhoff's current law is really the basis for the practical rule in parallel circuits that the total line current must equal the sum of the branch currents.

TEST-POINT QUESTION 9-1

Answers at end of chapter.
a. With a 1-A I_1, 2-A I_2, and 3-A I_3 into a point, how much is I_{out}?
b. If I_1 into a point is 3 A and the I out of that point is 7 A, how much is I_2 into that point?

9-2 KIRCHHOFF'S VOLTAGE LAW (KVL)

The algebraic sum of the voltages around any closed path is zero. If you start from any point at one potential and come back to the same point and the same potential, the difference of potential must be zero.

ALGEBRAIC SIGNS In determining the algebraic signs for voltage terms in a KVL equation, first mark the polarity of each voltage as shown in Fig. 9-2. A convenient system then is: *Go around any closed path and consider any voltage whose negative terminal is reached first as a negative term and any voltage whose positive terminal is reached first as a positive term.* This method applies to *IR* voltage drops and voltage sources. The direction can be clockwise or counterclockwise.

Remember that electrons flowing into a resistor make that end negative with respect to the other end. For a voltage source, the direction of electrons returning to the positive terminal is the normal direction for electron flow, which means the source should be a positive term in the voltage equation.

When you go around the closed path and come back to the starting point, the algebraic sum of all the voltage terms must be zero. There cannot be any potential difference for one point.

If you do not come back to the start, then the algebraic sum is the voltage between the start and finish points.

You can follow any closed path. The reason is that the voltage between any two points in a circuit is the same regardless of the path used in determining the potential difference.

LOOP EQUATIONS   Any closed path is called a *loop*. A loop equation specifies the voltages around the loop.

Figure 9-2 has three loops. The outside loop, starting from point A at the top, through CEFDB, and back to A, includes the voltage drops V_1, V_4, V_5, and V_2 and the source V_T.

The inside loop ACDBA includes V_1, V_3, V_2, and V_T. The other inside loop, CEFDC with V_4, V_5, and V_3, does not include the voltage source.

Consider the voltage equation for the inside loop with V_T. In clockwise direction, starting from point A, the algebraic sum of the voltages is

$$-V_1 - V_3 - V_2 + V_T = 0$$

or

$$-30 \text{ V} - 120 \text{ V} - 90 \text{ V} + 240 \text{ V} = 0$$

Voltages V_1, V_3, and V_2 have the negative sign, because for each of these voltages the negative terminal is reached first. However, the source V_T is a positive term because its plus terminal is reached first, going in the same direction.

For the opposite direction, going counterclockwise in the same loop from point B at the bottom, V_2, V_3, and V_1 have positive values and V_T is negative. Then

$$V_2 + V_3 + V_1 - V_T = 0$$

or

$$90 \text{ V} + 120 \text{ V} + 30 \text{ V} - 240 \text{ V} = 0$$

When we transpose the negative term of -240 V, the equation becomes

$$90 \text{ V} + 120 \text{ V} + 30 \text{ V} = 240 \text{ V}$$

This equation states that the sum of the voltage drops equals the applied voltage.

$\Sigma V = V_T$ The Greek letter Σ means "sum of." In either direction, for any loop, the sum of the *IR* voltage drops must equal the applied voltage V_T. In Fig. 9-2, for the inside loop with the source V_T, going counterclockwise from point B:

$$90 \text{ V} + 120 \text{ V} + 30 \text{ V} = 240 \text{ V}$$

This system does not contradict the rule for algebraic signs. If 240 V were on the left side of the equation, this term would have a negative sign.

Stating a loop equation as $\Sigma V = V_T$ eliminates the step of transposing the negative terms from one side to the other to make them positive. In this form, the loop equations show that Kirchhoff's voltage law is really the basis for the practical rule in series circuits that the sum of the voltage drops must equal the applied voltage.

When a loop does not have any voltage source, the algebraic sum of the *IR* voltage drops alone must total zero. For instance, in Fig. 9-2, for the loop CEFDC without the source V_T, going clockwise from point C, the loop equation of voltages is

$$-V_4 - V_5 + V_3 = 0$$
$$-40 \ V - 80 \ V + 120 \ V = 0$$
$$0 = 0$$

Notice that V_3 is positive now, because its plus terminal is reached first by going clockwise from D to C in this loop.

Answers at end of chapter.

Refer to Fig. 9-2.
a. For partial loop CEFD, what is the total voltage across CD with −40 V for V_4 and −80 V for V_5?
b. For loop CEFDC, what is the total voltage with −40 V for V_4, −80 V for V_5, and including 120 V for V_3?

9-3 METHOD OF BRANCH CURRENTS

Now we can use Kirchhoff's laws to analyze the circuit in Fig. 9-3. The problem is to find the currents and voltages for the three resistors.

First, indicate current directions and mark the voltage polarity across each resistor consistent with the assumed current. Remember that electron flow in a resistor produces negative polarity where the current enters. In Fig. 9-3, we

FIG. 9-3 Application of Kirchhoff's laws to a circuit with two sources in different branches. See text for solution by finding the branch currents.

assume that the source V_1 produces electron flow from left to right through R_1, while V_2 produces electron flow from right to left through R_2.

The three different currents in R_1, R_2, and R_3 are indicated as I_1, I_2, and I_3. However, three unknowns would require three equations for the solution. From Kirchhoff's current law, $I_3 = I_1 + I_2$, as the current out of point C must equal the current in. The current through R_3, therefore, can be specified as $I_1 + I_2$.

With two unknowns, two independent equations are needed to solve for I_1 and I_2. These equations are obtained by writing two Kirchhoff's voltage law equations around two loops. There are three loops in Fig. 9-3, the outside loop and two inside loops, but we need only two. The inside loops are used for the solution here.

WRITING THE LOOP EQUATIONS For the loop with V_1, start at point B, at the bottom left, and go clockwise through V_1, V_{R_1}, and V_{R_3}. This equation for loop 1 is

$$84 - V_{R_1} - V_{R_3} = 0$$

For the loop with V_2, start at point F, at the lower right, and go counterclockwise through V_2, V_{R_2}, and V_{R_3}. This equation for loop 2 is

$$21 - V_{R_2} - V_{R_3} = 0$$

Using the known values of R_1, R_2, and R_3 to specify the IR voltage drops,

$$V_{R_1} = I_1 R_1 = I_1 \times 12 = 12I_1$$
$$V_{R_2} = I_2 R_2 = I_2 \times 3 = 3I_2$$
$$V_{R_3} = (I_1 + I_2)R_3 = 6(I_1 + I_2)$$

Substituting these values in the voltage equation for loop 1,

$$84 - 12I_1 - 6(I_1 + I_2) = 0$$

Also, in loop 2,

$$21 - 3I_2 - 6(I_1 + I_2) = 0$$

Multiplying $(I_1 + I_2)$ by 6 and combining terms and transposing, the two equations are

$$-18I_1 - 6I_2 = -84$$
$$-6I_1 - 9I_2 = -21$$

Divide the top equation by -6 and the bottom equation by -3 to reduce the equations to their simplest terms and to have all positive terms. The two equations in their simplest form then become

$$3I_1 + I_2 = 14$$
$$2I_1 + 3I_2 = 7$$

SOLVING FOR THE CURRENTS These two equations in the two unknowns I_1 and I_2 contain the solution of the network. It should be noted that the equations include every resistance in the circuit. Currents I_1 and I_2 can be calculated by any of the methods for the solution of simultaneous equations. Using the method of elimination, multiply the top equation by 3 to make the I_2 terms the same in both equations. Then

$$9I_1 + 3I_2 = 42$$
$$2I_1 + 3I_2 = 7$$

Subtract the bottom equation from the top equation, term by term, to eliminate I_2. Then, since the I_2 term becomes zero,

$$7I_1 = 35$$
$$I_1 = 5 \text{ A}$$

The 5-A I_1 is the current through R_1. Its direction is from A to C, as assumed, because the answer for I_1 is positive.

To calculate I_2, substitute 5 for I_1 in either of the two loop equations. Using the bottom equation for the substitution,

$$2(5) + 3I_2 = 7$$
$$3I_2 = 7 - 10$$
$$3I_2 = -3$$
$$I_2 = -1 \text{ A}$$

The negative sign for I_2 means this current is opposite to the assumed direction. Therefore, I_2 flows through R_2 from C to E instead of from E to C as was previously assumed.

WHY THE SOLUTION FOR I_2 IS NEGATIVE   In Fig. 9-3 (page 237), I_2 was assumed to flow from E to C through R_2 because V_2 produces electron flow in this direction. However, the other voltage source V_1 produces electron flow through R_2 in the opposite direction, from point C to E. This solution of -1 A for I_2 shows that the current through R_2 produced by V_1 is more than the current produced by V_2. The net result is 1 A through R_2 from C to E.

The actual direction of I_2 is shown in Fig. 9-4 with all the values for the solution of this circuit. Notice that the polarity of V_{R_2} is reversed from the assumed polarity in Fig. 9-3. Since the net electron flow through R_2 is actually from C to E, the end of R_2 at C is the negative end. However, the polarity of V_2 is the same in both diagrams because it is a voltage source, which generates its own polarity.

To calculate I_3 through R_3,

$$I_3 = I_1 + I_2 = 5 + (-1)$$
$$I_3 = 4 \text{ A}$$

The 4 A for I_3 is in the assumed direction from C to D. Although the negative sign for I_2 only means a reversed direction, its algebraic value of -1 must be used for substitution in the algebraic equations written for the assumed direction.

CALCULATING THE VOLTAGES   With all the currents known, the voltage across each resistor can be calculated as follows:

$$V_{R_1} = I_1 R_1 = 5 \times 12 = 60 \text{ V}$$
$$V_{R_2} = I_2 R_2 = 1 \times \ \ 3 = \ \ 3 \text{ V}$$
$$V_{R_3} = I_3 R_3 = 4 \times \ \ 6 = 24 \text{ V}$$

All the currents are taken as positive, in the correct direction, to calculate the voltages. Then the polarity of each IR drop is determined from the actual direction of current, with electron flow into the negative end (see Fig. 9-4). Notice that V_{R_3} and V_{R_2} have opposing polarities in loop 2. Then the sum of $+3$ V and -24 V equals the -21 V of V_2.

FIG. 9-4   Solution of circuit in Fig. 9-3 with all currents and voltages.

CHECKING THE SOLUTION   As a summary of all the answers for this problem, Fig. 9-4 shows the network with all the currents and voltages. The polarity of each V is marked from the known directions. In checking the answers, we can see whether Kirchhoff's current and voltage laws are satisfied:

At point C: 5 A = 4 A + 1 A
At point D: 4 A + 1 A = 5 A

Around the loop with V_1 clockwise from B:

$$84\ V - 60\ V - 24\ V = 0$$

Around the loop with V_2 counterclockwise from F:

$$21\ V + 3\ V - 24\ V = 0$$

It should be noted that the circuit has been solved using only the two Kirchhoff laws, without any of the special rules for series and parallel circuits. Any circuit can be solved just by applying Kirchhoff's laws for the voltages around a loop and the currents at a branch point.

TEST-POINT QUESTION 9-3

Answers at end of chapter.

Refer to Fig. 9-4.
a. How much is the voltage around partial loop CEFD?
b. How much is the voltage around loop CEFDC?

9-4 NODE-VOLTAGE ANALYSIS

In the method of branch currents, these currents are used for specifying the voltage drops around the loops. Then loop equations are written to satisfy Kirchhoff's voltage law. Solving the loop equations, we can calculate the unknown branch currents.

Another method uses the voltage drops to specify the currents at a branch point, also called a *node*. Then node equations of currents are written to satisfy Kirchhoff's current law. Solving the node equations, we can calculate the unknown node voltages. This method of node-voltage analysis often is shorter than the method of branch currents.

A node is simply a common connection for two or more components. A *principal node* has three or more connections. In effect, a principal node is just a junction or branch point, where currents can divide or combine. Therefore, we can always write an equation of currents at a principal node. In Fig. 9-5, points N and G are principal nodes.

However, one node must be the reference for specifying the voltage at any other node. In Fig. 9-5, point G connected to chassis ground is the reference node. Therefore, we need only write one current equation for the other node N. In general, the number of current equations required to solve a circuit is one less than the number of principal nodes.

FIG. 9-5   Method of node-voltage analysis for the same circuit as in Fig. 9-3. See text for solution by finding V_N across R_3 from the principal node N to ground.

WRITING THE NODE EQUATIONS   The circuit of Fig. 9-3, earlier solved by the method of branch currents, is redrawn in Fig. 9-5 to be solved now by node-voltage analysis. The problem here is to find the node voltage V_N from N to G. Once this voltage is known, all the other voltages and currents can be determined.

The currents in and out of node N are specified as follows: I_1 is the only current through the 12-Ω R_1. Therefore, I_1 is V_{R_1}/R_1 or $V_{R_1}/12\ \Omega$. Similarly, I_2 is $V_{R_2}/3\ \Omega$. Finally, I_3 is $V_{R_3}/6\ \Omega$.

Note that V_{R_3} is the node voltage V_N that we are to calculate. Therefore, I_3 can also be stated as $V_N/6\ \Omega$. The equation of currents at node N is

$$I_1 + I_2 = I_3$$

or

$$\frac{V_{R_1}}{12} + \frac{V_{R_2}}{3} = \frac{V_N}{6}$$

There are three unknowns here, but V_{R_1} and V_{R_2} can be specified in terms of V_N and the known values of V_1 and V_2. We can use Kirchhoff's voltage law, because the applied voltage V must equal the algebraic sum of the voltage drops. For the loop with V_1 of 84 V,

$$V_{R_1} + V_N = 84 \quad \text{or} \quad V_{R_1} = 84 - V_N$$

For the loop with V_2 of 21 V,

$$V_{R_2} + V_N = 21 \quad \text{or} \quad V_{R_2} = 21 - V_N$$

Now substitute these values of V_{R_1} and V_{R_2} in the equation of currents:

$$I_1 + I_2 = I_3$$
$$\frac{V_{R_1}}{R_1} + \frac{V_{R_2}}{R_2} = \frac{V_{R_3}}{R_3}$$

Using the value of each V in terms of V_N,

$$\frac{84 - V_N}{12} + \frac{21 - V_N}{3} = \frac{V_N}{6}$$

This equation has only the one unknown, V_N. Clearing fractions by multiplying each term by 12, the equation is

$$(84 - V_N) + 4(21 - V_N) = 2\,V_N$$
$$84 - V_N + 84 - 4\,V_N = 2\,V_N$$
$$-7\,V_N = -168$$
$$V_N = 24\ V$$

This answer of 24 V for V_N is the same as that calculated for V_{R_3} by the method of branch currents. The positive value means the direction of I_3 is correct, making V_N negative at the top of R_3 in Fig. 9-5.

CALCULATING ALL VOLTAGES AND CURRENTS   The reason for finding the voltage at a node, rather than some other voltage, is the fact that a node voltage must be common to two loops. As a result, the node voltage can be used for calculating all the voltages in the loops. In Fig. 9-5, with a V_N of 24 V, then V_{R_1} must be $84 - 24 = 60$ V. Also, I_1 is 60 V/12 Ω, which equals 5 A.

To find V_{R_2}, it must be $21 - 24$, which equals -3 V. The negative answer means that I_2 is opposite to the assumed direction and the polarity of V_{R_2} is the reverse of the signs shown across R_2 in Fig. 9-5. The correct directions are shown in the solution for the circuit in Fig. 9-4. The magnitude of I_2 is 3 V/3 Ω, which equals 1 A.

The following comparisons can be helpful in using node equations and loop equations. A node equation applies Kirchhoff's current law to the currents in and out of a node point. However, the currents are specified as V/R so that the equation of currents can be solved to find a node voltage.

A loop equation applies Kirchhoff's voltage law to the voltages around a closed path. However, the voltages are specified as IR so that the equation of voltages can be solved to find a loop current. This procedure with voltage equations is used for the method of branch currents explained before with Fig. 9-3 and for the method of mesh currents to be described next with Fig. 9-6.

TEST-POINT QUESTION 9-4

Answers at end of chapter.
a. How many principal nodes does Fig. 9-5 have?
b. How many node equations are necessary to solve a circuit with three principal nodes?

9-5 METHOD OF MESH CURRENTS

A mesh is the simplest possible closed path. The circuit in Fig. 9-6 has the two meshes ACDBA and CEFDC. The outside path ACEFDBA is a loop but not a mesh. Each mesh is like a single window frame. There is only one path without any branches.

A mesh current is assumed to flow around a mesh without dividing. In Fig. 9-6, the mesh current I_A flows through V_1, R_1, and R_3; mesh current I_B flows through V_2, R_2, and R_3. A resistance common to two meshes, such as R_3, has two mesh currents, which are I_A and I_B here.

The fact that a mesh current does not divide at a branch point is the difference between mesh currents and branch currents. A mesh current is an assumed current, while a branch current is the actual current. However, when the mesh currents are known, all the individual currents and voltages can be determined.

As an example, Fig. 9-6, which has the same circuit as Fig. 9-3, will now be solved by using the assumed mesh currents I_A and I_B. The mesh equations are

$$18I_A - 6I_B = 84 \text{ V} \qquad \text{in mesh A}$$
$$-6I_A + 9I_B = -21 \text{ V} \qquad \text{in mesh B}$$

WRITING THE MESH EQUATIONS The number of meshes equals the number of mesh currents, which is the number of equations required. Here two equations are used for I_A and I_B in the two meshes.

The assumed current is usually taken in the same direction around each mesh, in order to be consistent. Generally, the clockwise direction is used, as shown for I_A and I_B in Fig. 9-6.

FIG. 9-6 The same circuit as Fig. 9-3 analyzed as two meshes. See text for solution by calculating the assumed mesh currents I_A and I_B.

In each mesh equation, the algebraic sum of the voltage drops equals the applied voltage.

The voltage drops are added going around a mesh in the same direction as its mesh current. Any voltage drop in a mesh produced by its own mesh current is considered positive because it is added in the direction of the mesh current.

Since all the voltage drops of a mesh current in its own mesh must have the same positive sign, they can be written collectively as one voltage drop by adding all the resistances in the mesh. For instance, in the first equation, for mesh A, the total resistance equals $12 + 6$, or $18\ \Omega$. Therefore, the voltage drop for I_A is $18I_A$ in mesh A.

In the second equation, for mesh B, the total resistance is $3 + 6$, or $9\ \Omega$, making the total voltage drop $9I_B$ for I_B in mesh B. You can add all the resistances in a mesh for one R_T, because they can be considered in series for the assumed mesh current.

Any resistance common to two meshes has two opposite mesh currents. In Fig. 9-6, I_A flows down while I_B is up through the common R_3, with both currents clockwise. As a result, a common resistance has two opposing voltage drops. One voltage is positive for the current of the mesh whose equation is being written. The opposing voltage is negative for the current of the adjacent mesh.

In mesh A, the common 6-Ω R_3 has the opposing voltages $6I_A$ and $-6I_B$. The $6I_A$ of R_3 adds to the $12I_A$ of R_1 for the total positive voltage drop of $18I_A$ in mesh A. With the opposing voltage of $-6I_B$, then the equation for mesh A is $18I_A - 6I_B = 84$ V.

The same idea applies to mesh B. However, now the voltage $6I_B$ is positive because the equation is for mesh B. The $-6I_A$ voltage is negative here because I_A is for the adjacent mesh. The $6I_B$ adds to the $3I_B$ of R_2 for the total positive voltage drop of $9I_B$ in mesh B. With the opposing voltage of $-6I_A$, the equation for mesh B then is $-6I_A + 9I_B = -21$ V.

The algebraic sign of the source voltage in a mesh depends on its polarity. When the assumed mesh current flows into the positive terminal, as for V_1 in Fig. 9-6, it is considered positive for the right-hand side of the mesh equation. This direction of electron flow produces voltage drops that must add to equal the applied voltage.

With the mesh current into the negative terminal, as for V_2 in Fig. 9-6, it is considered negative. This is why V_2 is -21 V in the equation for mesh B. Then V_2 is actually a load for the larger applied voltage of V_1, instead of V_2 being the source. When a mesh has no source voltage, the algebraic sum of the voltage drops must equal zero.

These rules for the voltage source mean that the direction of electron flow is assumed for the mesh currents. Then electron flow is used to determine the polarity of the voltage drops. Note that considering the voltage source as a positive value with electron flow into the positive terminal corresponds to the normal flow of electron charges. If the solution for a mesh current comes out negative, the actual current for the mesh must be in the opposite direction from the assumed current flow.

SOLVING THE MESH EQUATIONS TO FIND THE MESH CURRENTS

The two equations for the two meshes in Fig. 9-6 are

$$18I_A - 6I_B = 84$$
$$-6I_A + 9I_B = -21$$

These equations have the same coefficients as in the voltage equations written for the branch currents, but the signs are different. The reason is that the directions of the assumed mesh currents are not the same as those of the branch currents.

The solution will give the same answers for either method, but you must be consistent in algebraic signs. Use either the rules for meshes with mesh currents or the rules for loops with branch currents, but do not mix the two methods.

To eliminate I_B and solve for I_A, divide the first equation by 2 and the second equation by 3. Then

$$9I_A - 3I_B = 42$$
$$-2I_A + 3I_B = -7$$

Add the equations, term by term, to eliminate I_B. Then

$$7I_A = 35$$
$$I_A = 5 \text{ A}$$

To calculate I_B, substitute 5 for I_A in the second equation:

$$-2(5) + 3I_B = -7$$
$$3I_B = -7 + 10 = 3$$
$$I_B = 1 \text{ A}$$

The positive solutions mean that the electron flow for both I_A and I_B is actually clockwise, as assumed.

FINDING THE BRANCH CURRENTS AND VOLTAGE DROPS   Referring to Fig. 9-6, the 5-A I_A is the only current through R_1. Therefore, I_A and I_1 are the same. Then V_{R_1} across the 12-Ω R_1 is 5 × 12, or 60 V. The polarity of V_{R_1} is marked negative at the left, with the electron flow into this side.

Similarly, the 1-A I_B is the only current through R_2. The direction of this electron flow through R_2 is from left to right. Note that this value of 1 A for I_B clockwise is the same as −1 A for I_2, assumed in the opposite direction in Fig. 9-3. Then V_{R_2} across the 3-Ω R_2 is 1 × 3 or 3 V, with the left side negative.

The current I_3 through R_3, common to both meshes, consists of I_A and I_B. Then I_3 is 5 − 1 or 4 A. The currents are subtracted because I_A and I_B are in opposing directions through R_3. When all the mesh currents are taken one way, they will always be in opposite directions through any resistance common to two meshes.

The direction of the net 4-A I_3 through R_3 is downward, the same as I_A, because it is more than I_B. Then, V_{R_3} across the 6-Ω R_3 is 4 × 6 = 24 V, with the top negative.

THE SET OF MESH EQUATIONS   The system for algebraic signs of the voltages in the mesh equations is different from the method used with branch currents, but the end result is the same. The advantage of mesh currents is the pattern of algebraic signs for the voltages, without the need for tracing any branch currents. This feature is especially helpful in a more elaborate circuit, such as the one in Fig. 9-7 that has three meshes. We can use Fig. 9-7 for more practice in writing mesh equations, without doing the numerical work of solving a set* of three equations. Each R is 2 Ω.

In Fig. 9-7, the mesh currents are shown with solid arrows to indicate conventional current, which is a common way of analyzing these circuits. Also, the volt-

---

*A set with any number of simultaneous linear equations, for any number of meshes, can be solved by determinants. This procedure is explained in B. Grob, *Mathematics for Basic Electronics*, Glencoe/McGraw-Hill, Columbus, Ohio.

FIG. 9-7   A circuit with three meshes. Each R is 2 Ω.
See text for mesh equations.

age sources V_1 and V_2 have the positive terminal at the top in the diagram. When the direction of conventional current is used, it is important to note that the voltage source is a positive value with mesh current into the negative terminal. This method corresponds to the normal flow of positive charges with conventional current.

For the three mesh equations in Fig. 9-7:

In mesh A: $\qquad 6I_A - 2I_B + 0 = 12$
In mesh B: $\qquad -2I_A + 8I_B - 2I_C = 0$
In mesh C: $\qquad 0 - 2I_B + 6I_C = -8$

The zero term in equations A and C represents a missing mesh current. Only mesh B has all three mesh currents. However, note that mesh B has a zero term for the voltage source because it is the only mesh with only IR drops.

In summary, the only positive IR voltage in a mesh is for the R_T of each mesh current in its own mesh. All other voltage drops for any adjacent mesh current across a common resistance are always negative. This procedure for assigning algebraic signs to the voltage drops is the same whether the source voltage in the mesh is positive or negative. It also applies even if there is no voltage source in the mesh.

TEST-POINT QUESTION 9-5

Answers at end of chapter.

Answer True or False.

a. A network with four mesh currents needs four mesh equations for a solution.

b. An R common to two meshes has opposing mesh currents.

9 SUMMARY AND REVIEW

- Kirchhoff's voltage law states that the algebraic sum of all voltages around any closed path must equal zero. Stated another way, the sum of the voltage drops equals the applied voltage.
- Kirchhoff's current law states that the algebraic sum of all currents directed in and out at any point in a closed path must equal zero. Stated another way, the current into a point equals the current out of that point.
- A closed path is a loop. The method of using algebraic equations for the voltages around the loops to calculate the branch currents is illustrated in Fig. 9-3.
- A principal node is a branch point where currents divide or combine. The method of using algebraic equations for the currents at a node to calculate each node voltage is illustrated in Fig. 9-5.
- A mesh is the simplest possible loop. A mesh current is assumed to flow around the mesh without branching. The method of using algebraic equations for the voltages around the meshes to calculate the mesh currents is illustrated in Fig. 9-6.

SELF-TEST

ANSWERS AT BACK OF BOOK.

Answer True or False.

1. The algebraic sum of all voltages around any mesh or any loop must equal zero.
2. A mesh with two resistors has two mesh currents.
3. With $I_1 = 3$ A and $I_2 = 2$ A directed into a node, the current I_3 directed out must equal 5 A.
4. In a loop without any voltage source, the algebraic sum of the voltage drops must equal zero.
5. The algebraic sum of $+40$ V and -10 V equals $+30$ V.
6. A principal node is a junction where branch currents can divide or combine.
7. In the node-voltage method, the number of equations of current equals the number of principal nodes.
8. In the mesh-current method, the number of equations of voltage equals the number of meshes.
9. When all mesh currents are clockwise or all counterclockwise, any resistor common to two meshes has two currents in opposite directions.
10. The rules of series voltages and parallel currents are based on Kirchhoff's laws.

QUESTIONS

1. State Kirchhoff's current law in two ways.
2. State Kirchhoff's voltage law in two ways.
3. What is the difference between a loop and a mesh?
4. What is the difference between a branch current and a mesh current?
5. Define a principal node.
6. Define a node voltage.
7. Use the values in Fig. 9-4 to show that the algebraic sum is zero for all voltages around the outside loop ACEFDBA.
8. Use the values in Fig. 9-4 to show that the algebraic sum is zero for all the currents into and out of node C and node D.

PROBLEMS

ANSWERS TO ODD-NUMBERED PROBLEMS AT BACK OF BOOK.

1. In Fig. 9-8, what is the value of: (**a**) I_3; (**b**) I_5; (**c**) I_6?
2. In Fig. 9-8, use KCL to write an equation for the currents entering and leaving: (**a**) point A; (**b**) point B; (**c**) point C.

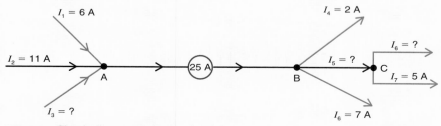

FIG. 9-8 Circuit diagram for Probs. 1 and 2.

3. In Fig. 9-9, calculate: (**a**) V_T, R_T, I, V_{R_1}, V_{R_2}, and V_{R_3}; (**b**) V_{AG}, V_{BG}, V_{CG}, and V_{DG}. Use KVL.
4. In Fig. 9-9, assume the polarity of V_2 is reversed. Calculate: (**a**) V_T, R_T, I, V_{R_1}, V_{R_2}, and V_{R_3}; (**b**) V_{AG}, V_{BG}, V_{CG}, and V_{DG}.
5. In Fig. 9-10, (**a**) calculate V_T, R_T, I, V_{R_1}, V_{R_2}, and V_{R_3}. (**b**) What voltage will be indicated by the voltmeter with the wiper arm of R_2 set to: point A, point B, and midway between points A and B? (Note: R_2 has a linear taper.)
6. In Fig. 9-10, assume R_2 is changed to a 10-kΩ potentiometer. (**a**) Calculate V_T, R_T, I, V_{R_1}, V_{R_2}, and V_{R_3}. (**b**) What voltage will be indicated by the voltmeter with the wiper arm of R_2 set to: point A, point B, and midway between points A and B?

FIG. 9-9　Circuit diagram for Probs. 3 and 4.

FIG. 9-10　Circuit diagram for Probs. 5 and 6.

7. In Fig. 9-11, use the method of branch currents to solve for I_1, I_2, and I_3. Once the currents have been calculated, determine the values for V_{R_1}, V_{R_2}, and V_{R_3}.

8. In Fig. 9-11, use KVL to prove that the algebraic sum of the voltages is zero in all three closed loops.

FIG. 9-11　Circuit diagram for Probs. 7, 8, and 9.

FIG. 9-12　Circuit diagram for Probs. 10, 11, and 12.

9. In Fig. 9-11, use node-voltage analysis to solve for V_{R_1}, V_{R_2}, V_{R_3}, I_1, I_2, and I_3.

10. In Fig. 9-12, use the method of branch currents to solve for I_1, I_2, I_3, V_{R_1}, V_{R_2}, and V_{R_3}.

11. In Fig. 9-12, use KVL to prove that the algebraic sum of the voltages is zero in all three closed loops.

12. In Fig. 9-12, use the method of mesh currents to solve for I_1, I_2, I_3, V_{R_1}, V_{R_2}, and V_{R_3}.

13. In Fig. 9-13, use the method of mesh currents to solve for I_1, I_2, I_3, V_{R_1}, V_{R_2}, and V_{R_3}.

14. In Fig. 9-13, use KVL to prove that the algebraic sum of the voltages is zero in all three closed loops.

FIG. 9-13   Circuit diagram for Probs. 13 and 14.

CRITICAL THINKING

1. In Fig. 9-14, determine the values for R_1 and R_3 which will allow the output voltage to vary between -5 V and $+5$ V.
2. Refer to Fig. 9-7. If all resistances are 10 Ω, calculate: (**a**) I_A, I_B, and I_C; (**b**) I_1, I_2, I_3, I_4, I_5, I_6, I_7, and I_8.

FIG. 9-14   Circuit diagram for Critical Thinking Prob. 1.

ANSWERS TO TEST-POINT QUESTIONS

9-1	**a.** 6 A	**9-3**	**a.** -24 V	**9-5**	**a.** T
	b. 4 A		**b.** 0 V		**b.** T
9-2	**a.** -120 V	**9-4**	**a.** two		
	b. 0 V		**b.** two		

CHAPTER 10

NETWORK THEOREMS

A network is just a combination of components, such as resistances, interconnected in a way as to achieve a particular end result. However, networks generally need more than the rules of series and parallel circuits for analysis. Kirchhoff's laws can always be applied for any circuit connections. The network theorems, though, usually provide shorter methods of solving the circuit.

Some theorems enable us to convert the network into a simpler circuit, equivalent to the original. Then the equivalent circuit can be solved by the rules of series and parallel circuits. Other theorems enable us to convert a given circuit into a form that permits easier solutions.

Only the applications are given here, although all the network theorems can be derived from Kirchhoff's laws. It should also be noted that resistance networks with batteries are shown as examples, but the theorems can also be applied to ac networks.

CHAPTER OBJECTIVES

Upon completion of this chapter, you should be able to:

- *Apply* the superposition theorem to find the voltage across two points in a circuit containing more than one voltage source.
- *State* the requirements for applying the superposition theorem.
- *Determine* the Thevenin and Norton equivalent circuits with respect to any pair of terminals in a complex network.
- *Apply* Thevenin's and Norton's theorems in solving for an unknown voltage or current.
- *Convert* a Thevenin equivalent circuit to a Norton equivalent circuit and vice versa.
- *Apply* Millman's theorem to find a common voltage across any number of parallel branches.
- *Simplify* the analysis of a bridge circuit by using delta to wye conversion formulas.

IMPORTANT TERMS IN THIS CHAPTER

active components
bilateral components
current source
delta (Δ) network
Δ-Y transformations
equivalent circuit
equivalent current source

linear components
Millman's theorem
nortonizing a circuit
Norton's theorem
passive components
pi (π) network
superposition

tee (T) network
Thevenin-Norton conversions
Thevenin's theorem
thevenizing a circuit
voltage source
wye (Y) network

TOPICS COVERED IN THIS CHAPTER

The superposition theorem is very useful because it extends the use of Ohm's law to circuits that have more than one source. In brief, we can calculate the effect of one source at a time and then superimpose the results of all the sources. As a definition, the superposition theorem states that: *In a network with two or more sources, the current or voltage for any component is the algebraic sum of the effects produced by each source acting separately.*

In order to use one source at a time, all other sources are "killed" temporarily. This means disabling the source so that it cannot generate voltage or current, without changing the resistance of the circuit. A voltage source such as a battery is killed by assuming a short circuit across its potential difference. The internal resistance remains.

VOLTAGE DIVIDER WITH TWO SOURCES   The problem in Fig. 10-1 is to find the voltage at P to chassis ground for the circuit in Fig. 10-1a. The method is to calculate the voltage at P contributed by each source separately, as in Fig. 10-1b and c, and then superimpose these voltages.

To find the effect of V_1 first, short-circuit V_2 as shown in Fig. 10-1b. Note that the bottom of R_1 then becomes connected to chassis ground because of the short circuit across V_2. As a result, R_2 and R_1 form a series voltage divider for the V_1 source.

Furthermore, the voltage across R_1 becomes the same as the voltage from P to ground. To find this V_{R_1} across R_1 as the contribution of the V_1 source, we use the voltage divider formula:

$$V_{R_1} = \frac{R_1}{R_1 + R_2} \times V_1 = \frac{60 \text{ k}\Omega}{30 \text{ k}\Omega + 60 \text{ k}\Omega} \times 24 \text{ V}$$

$$= \frac{60}{90} \times 24 \text{ V}$$

$$V_{R_1} = 16 \text{ V}$$

FIG. 10-1   Superposition theorem applied to a voltage divider with two sources V_1 and V_2. (*a*) Actual circuit with +13 V from point P to chassis ground. (*b*) V_1 alone producing +16 V at P. (*c*) V_2 alone producing −3 V at P.

Next find the effect of V_2 alone, with V_1 short-circuited as shown in Fig. 10-1c. Then point A at the top of R_2 becomes grounded. R_1 and R_2 form a series voltage divider again, but here the R_2 voltage is the voltage at P to ground.

With one side of R_2 grounded and the other side to point P, V_{R_2} is the voltage to calculate. Again we have a series divider, but this time for the negative voltage V_2. Using the voltage divider formula for V_{R_2} as the contribution of V_2 to the voltage at P,

$$V_{R_2} = \frac{R_2}{R_1 + R_2} \times V_2 = \frac{30 \text{ k}\Omega}{30 \text{ k}\Omega + 60 \text{ k}\Omega} \times -9 \text{ V}$$

$$= \frac{30}{90} \times -9 \text{ V}$$

$$V_{R_2} = -3 \text{ V}$$

This voltage is negative at P because V_2 is negative.

Finally, the total voltage at P is

$$V_P = V_1 + V_2 = 16 - 3$$

$$V_P = 13 \text{ V}$$

This algebraic sum is positive for the net V_P because the positive V_1 is larger than the negative V_2.

By means of superposition, therefore, this problem was reduced to two series voltage dividers. The same procedure can be used with more than two sources. Also, each voltage divider can have any number of series resistances. Note that in this case we were dealing with ideal voltage sources, that is, sources with zero internal resistance. If the source did have internal resistance, it would have been added in series with R_1 and R_2.

REQUIREMENTS FOR SUPERPOSITION   All the components must be linear and bilateral in order to superimpose currents and voltages. *Linear* means that the current is proportional to the applied voltage. Then the currents calculated for different source voltages can be superimposed.

Bilateral means that the current is the same amount for opposite polarities of the source voltage. Then the values for opposite directions of current can be combined algebraically. Networks with resistors, capacitors, and air-core inductors are generally linear and bilateral. These are also *passive components,* meaning they do not amplify or rectify. *Active components,* such as transistors, semiconductor diodes, and electron tubes, are never bilateral and often are not linear.

TEST-POINT QUESTION 10-1

Answers at end of chapter.
a. In Fig. 10-1b, which R is shown grounded at one end?
b. In Fig. 10-1c, which R is shown grounded at one end?

10-2 THEVENIN'S THEOREM

Named after M. L. Thevenin, a French engineer, Thevenin's theorem is very useful in simplifying the voltages in a network. By Thevenin's theorem, many sources and components, no matter how they are interconnected, can be represented by an equivalent series circuit with respect to any pair of terminals in the network. In Fig. 10-2 imagine that the block at the left contains a network connected to terminals A and B. Thevenin's theorem states that *the entire* network connected to A and B can be replaced by a single voltage source V_{TH} in series with a single resistance R_{TH}, connected to the same two terminals.

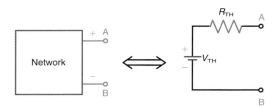

FIG. 10-2   Any network in the block at the left can be reduced to the Thevenin equivalent series circuit at the right.

Voltage V_{TH} is the open-circuit voltage across terminals A and B. This means, find the voltage that the network produces across the two terminals with an open circuit between A and B. The polarity of V_{TH} is such that it will produce current from A to B in the same direction as in the original network.

Resistance R_{TH} is the open-circuit resistance across terminals A and B, but with all the sources killed. This means, find the resistance looking back into the network from terminals A and B. Although the terminals are open, an ohmmeter across AB would read the value of R_{TH} as the resistance of the remaining paths in the network, without any sources operating.

THEVENIZING A CIRCUIT   As an example, refer to Fig. 10-3*a*, where we want to find the voltage V_L across the 2-Ω R_L and its current I_L. To use Thevenin's theorem, mentally disconnect R_L. The two open ends then become terminals A and B. Now we find the Thevenin equivalent of the remainder of the circuit that is still connected to A and B. In general, open the part of the circuit to be analyzed and "thevenize" the remainder of the circuit connected to the two open terminals.

Our only problem now is to find the value of the open-circuit voltage V_{TH} across AB and the equivalent resistance R_{TH}. The Thevenin equivalent always consists of a single voltage source in series with a single resistance, as in Fig. 10-3*d*.

The effect of opening R_L is shown in Fig. 10-3*b*. As a result, the 3-Ω R_1 and 6-Ω R_2 form a series voltage divider, without R_L.

Furthermore, the voltage across R_2 now is the same as the open-circuit voltage across terminals A and B. Therefore V_{R_2} with R_L open is V_{AB}. This is the V_{TH} we need for the Thevenin equivalent circuit. Using the voltage divider formula,

$$V_{R_2} = \frac{6}{9} \times 36 \text{ V} = 24 \text{ V}$$

$$V_{R_2} = V_{AB} = V_{TH} = 24 \text{ V}$$

This voltage is positive at terminal A.

FIG. 10-3 Application of Thevenin's theorem. (*a*) Actual circuit with terminals A and B across R_L. (*b*) Disconnect R_L to find that V_{AB} is 24 V. (*c*) Short-circuit V to find that R_{AB} is 2 Ω. (*d*) Thevenin equivalent circuit. (*e*) Reconnect R_L at terminals A and B to find that V_L is 12 V.

To find R_{TH}, the 2-Ω R_L is still disconnected. However, now the source V is short-circuited. So the circuit looks like Fig. 10-3*c*. The 3-Ω R_1 is now in parallel with the 6-Ω R_2, as they are both connected across the same two points. This combined resistance is

$$R_{TH} = \frac{18}{9} = 2 \ \Omega$$

Again, we assume an ideal voltage source whose internal resistance is zero.

As shown in Fig. 10-3*d*, the Thevenin circuit to the left of terminals A and B then consists of the equivalent voltage V_{TH}, equal to 24 V, in series with the equivalent series resistance R_{TH}, equal to 2 Ω. This Thevenin equivalent applies for any value of R_L because R_L was disconnected. We are actually thevenizing the circuit that feeds the open AB terminals.

To find V_L and I_L, we can finally reconnect R_L to terminals A and B of the Thevenin equivalent circuit, as shown in Fig. 10-3*e*. Then R_L is in series with R_{TH} and V_{TH}. Using the voltage divider formula for the 2-Ω R_{TH} and 2-Ω R_L, $V_L = 1/2 \times 24$ V = 12 V. To find I_L as V_L/R_L, the value is 12 V/2 Ω, which equals 6 A.

These answers of 6 A for I_L and 12 V for V_L apply to R_L in both the original circuit in Fig. 10-3*a* and the equivalent circuit in Fig. 10-3*e*. Note that the 6-A I_L also flows through R_{TH}.

The same answers could be obtained by solving the series-parallel circuit in Fig. 10-3*a*, using Ohm's law. However, the advantage of thevenizing the circuit is that the effect of different values of R_L can be calculated easily. Suppose that R_L were changed to 4 Ω. In the Thevenin circuit, the new value of V_L would be 4/6 × 24 V = 16 V. The new I_L would be 16 V/4 Ω, which equals 4 A. If we used Ohm's law in the original circuit, a complete new solution would be required each time R_L was changed.

LOOKING BACK FROM TERMINALS A AND B The way we look at the resistance of a series-parallel circuit depends on where the source is connected. In general, we calculate the total resistance from the outside terminals of the circuit in toward the source, as the reference.

When the source is short-circuited for thevenizing a circuit, terminals A and B become the reference. Looking back from A and B to calculate R_{TH}, the situation becomes reversed from the way the circuit was viewed to determine V_{TH}.

For R_{TH}, imagine that a source could be connected across AB, and calculate the total resistance working from the outside in toward terminals A and B. Actually an ohmmeter placed across terminals A and B would read this resistance.

This idea of reversing the reference is illustrated in Fig. 10-4. The circuit in Fig. 10-4a has terminals A and B open, ready to be thevenized. This circuit is similar to Fig. 10-3 but with the 4-Ω R_3 inserted between R_2 and terminal A. The interesting point is that R_3 does not change the value of V_{AB} produced by the source V, but R_3 does increase the value of R_{TH}. When we look back from terminals A and B, the 4 Ω of R_3 is in series with 2 Ω to make R_{TH} 6 Ω, as shown for R_{AB} in Fig. 10-4b and R_{TH} in Fig. 10-4c.

Let us consider why V_{AB} is the same 24 V with or without R_3. Since R_3 is connected to the open terminal A, the source V cannot produce current in R_3. Therefore, R_3 has no IR drop. A voltmeter would read the same 24 V across R_2 and from A to B. Since V_{AB} equals 24 V, this is the value of V_{TH}.

Now consider why R_3 does change the value of R_{TH}. Remember that we must work from the outside in to calculate the total resistance. Then, A and B are like the source terminals. As a result, the 3-Ω R_1 and 6-Ω R_2 are in parallel, for a combined resistance of 2 Ω. Furthermore, this 2 Ω is in series with the 4-Ω R_3 because R_3 is in the main line from terminals A and B. Then R_{TH} is 2 + 4 = 6 Ω. As shown in Fig. 10-4c, the Thevenin equivalent circuit consists of V_{TH} = 24 V and R_{TH} = 6 Ω.

FIG. 10-4 Thevenizing the circuit of Fig. 10-3 but with a 4-Ω R_3 in series with the A terminal. (*a*) V_{AB} is still 24 V. (*b*) Now the R_{AB} is 2 + 4 = 6 Ω. (*c*) Thevenin equivalent circuit.

TEST-POINT QUESTION 10-2

Answers at end of chapter.

Answer True or False.
a. For a Thevenin equivalent circuit, terminals A and B are open to find both V_{TH} and R_{TH}.
b. For a Thevenin equivalent circuit, the source voltage is short-circuited only to find R_{TH}.

10-3 THEVENIZING A CIRCUIT WITH TWO VOLTAGE SOURCES

The circuit in Fig. 10-5 has already been solved by Kirchhoff's laws, but we can use Thevenin's theorem to find the current I_3 through the middle resistance R_3. As shown in Fig. 10-5a, first mark the terminals A and B across R_3. In Fig. 10-5b, R_3 is disconnected. To calculate V_{TH}, find V_{AB} across the open terminals.

FIG. 10-5 Thevenizing a circuit with two voltage sources V_1 and V_2. (a) Original circuit with terminals A and B across the middle resistor R_3. (b) Disconnect R_3 to find V_{AB} is -33.6 V. (c) Short-circuit V_1 and V_2 to find R_{AB} is 2.4 Ω. (d) Thevenin equivalent with R_L reconnected to terminals A and B.

SUPERPOSITION METHOD With two sources we can use superposition to calculate V_{AB}. First short-circuit V_2. Then the 84 V of V_1 is divided between R_1 and R_2. The voltage across R_2 is between terminals A and B. To calculate this divided voltage across R_2,

$$V_{R_2} = \frac{R_2}{R_{1-2}} \times V_1 = \frac{3}{15} \times (-84)$$

$$V_{R_2} = -16.8 \text{ V}$$

This is only the contribution of V_1 to V_{AB}. The polarity is negative at terminal A.

To find the voltage that V_2 produces between A and B, short-circuit V_1. Then the voltage across R_1 is connected from A to B. To calculate this divided voltage across R_1,

$$V_{R_1} = \frac{R_1}{R_{1-2}} \times V_2 = \frac{12}{15} \times (-21)$$

$$V_{R_1} = -16.8 \text{ V}$$

Both V_1 and V_2 produce -16.8 V across the AB terminals with the same polarity. Therefore, they are added.

The resultant value of $V_{AB} = -33.6$ V, shown in Fig. 10-5b, is the value of V_{TH}. The negative polarity means that terminal A is negative with respect to B.

To calculate R_{TH}, short-circuit the sources V_1 and V_2, as shown in Fig. 10-5c. Then the 12-Ω R_1 and 3-Ω R_2 are in parallel across terminals A and B. Their combined resistance is 36/15, or 2.4 Ω, which is the value of R_{TH}.

The final result is the Thevenin equivalent in Fig. 10-5d with an R_{TH} of 2.4 Ω and a V_{TH} of 33.6 V, negative toward terminal A.

In order to find the current through R_3, it is reconnected as a load resistance across terminals A and B. Then V_{TH} produces current through the total resistance of 2.4 Ω for R_{TH} and 6 Ω for R_3:

$$\blacktriangleright \quad I_3 = \frac{V_{TH}}{R_{TH} + R_3} = \frac{33.6}{2.4 + 6} = \frac{33.6}{8.4} = 4 \text{ A}$$

This answer of 4 A for I_3 is the same value calculated before, using Kirchhoff's laws, in Fig. 9-4.

It should be noted that this circuit can be solved by superposition alone, without using Thevenin's theorem, if R_3 is not disconnected. However, opening terminals A and B for the Thevenin equivalent simplifies the superposition, as the circuit then has only series voltage dividers without any parallel current paths. In general, a circuit can often be simplified by disconnecting a component to open terminals A and B for Thevenin's theorem.

<hr>

TEST-POINT QUESTION 10-3

Answers at end of chapter.

In the Thevenin equivalent circuit in Fig. 10-5d,
a. How much is R_T?
b. How much is V_{R_L}?

10-4 THEVENIZING A BRIDGE CIRCUIT

As another example of Thevenin's theorem, we can find the current through the 2-Ω R_L at the center of the bridge circuit in Fig. 10-6a. When R_L is disconnected to open terminals A and B, the result is as shown in Fig. 10-6b. Notice how the circuit has become simpler because of the open. Instead of the unbalanced bridge in Fig. 10-6a which would require Kirchhoff's laws for a solution, the Thevenin equivalent in Fig. 10-6b consists of just two voltage dividers. Both the R_3R_4 divider and the R_1R_2 divider are across the same 30-V source.

Since the open terminal A is at the junction of R_3 and R_4, this divider can be used to find the potential at point A. Similarly the potential at terminal B can be found from the R_1R_2 divider. Then V_{AB} is the difference between the potentials at terminals A and B.

Note the voltages for the two dividers. In the divider with the 3-Ω R_3 and 6-Ω R_4, the bottom voltage V_{R_4} is 6/9 $\times$ 30 = 20 V. Then V_{R_3} at the top is 10 V because both must add up to equal the 30-V source. The polarities are marked negative at the top, the same as the source voltage V.

FIG. 10-6 Thevenizing a bridge circuit. (*a*) Original circuit with terminals A and B across middle resistor R_L. (*b*) Disconnect R_L to find V_{AB} of -8 V. (*c*) With source V short-circuited, R_{AB} is $2 + 2.4 = 4.4$ Ω. (*d*) Thevenin equivalent with R_L reconnected to terminals A and B.

Similarly, in the divider with the 6-Ω R_1 and 4-Ω R_2, the bottom voltage V_{R_2} is $4/10 \times 30 = 12$ V. Then V_{R_1} at the top is 18 V, as the two must add up to equal the 30-V source. The polarities are also negative at the top, the same as V.

Now we can determine the potentials at terminals A and B, with respect to a common reference in order to find V_{AB}. Imagine that the positive side of the source V is connected to a chassis ground. Then we would use the bottom line in the diagram as our reference for voltages. Note that V_{R_4} at the bottom of the R_3R_4 divider is the same as the potential of terminal A, with respect to ground. This value is -20 V, with terminal A negative.

Similarly, V_{R_2} in the R_1R_2 divider is the potential at B with respect to ground. This value is -12 V, with terminal B negative. As a result, V_{AB} is the difference between the -20 V at A and the -12 V at B, both with respect to the common ground reference.

The potential difference V_{AB} then equals

$$V_{AB} = -20 - (-12) = -20 + 12 = -8 \text{ V}$$

Terminal A is 8 V more negative than B. Therefore, V_{TH} is 8 V, with the negative side toward terminal A as shown in the Thevenin equivalent in Fig. 10-6d.

The potential difference V_{AB} can also be found as the difference between V_{R_3} and V_{R_1} in Fig. 10-6b. In this case V_{R_3} is 10 V and V_{R_1} is 18 V, both positive with respect to the top line connected to the negative side of the source V. The potential difference between terminals A and B then is $10 - 18$, which also equals -8 V. Note that V_{AB} must have the same value no matter which path is used to determine the voltage.

To find R_{TH}, the 30-V source is short-circuited while terminals A and B are still open. Then the circuit looks like Fig. 10-6c. Looking back from terminals A and B, the 3-Ω R_3 and 6-Ω R_4 are in parallel, for a combined resistance R_{T_A} of 18/9 or 2 Ω. The reason is that R_3 and R_4 are joined at terminal A, while their opposite ends are connected by the short circuit across the source V. Similarly, the 6-Ω R_1 and 4-Ω R_2 are in parallel, for a combined resistance R_{T_B} of 24/10 = 2.4 Ω. Furthermore, the short circuit across the source now provides a path that connects R_{T_A} and R_{T_B} in series. The entire resistance is $2 + 2.4 = 4.4$ Ω for R_{AB} or R_{TH}.

The Thevenin equivalent in Fig. 10-6d represents the bridge circuit feeding the open terminals A and B, with 8 V for V_{TH} and 4.4 Ω for R_{TH}. Now connect the 2-Ω R_L to terminals A and B in order to calculate I_L. The current is

$$I_L = \frac{V_{TH}}{R_{TH} + R_L} = \frac{8}{4.4 + 2} = \frac{8}{6.4}$$

$$I_L = 1.25 \text{ A}$$

This 1.25 A is the current through the 2-Ω R_L at the center of the unbalanced bridge in Fig. 10-6a. Furthermore, the amount of I_L for any value of R_L in Fig. 10-6a can be calculated from the equivalent circuit in Fig. 10-6d.

TEST-POINT QUESTION 10-4

Answers at end of chapter.

In the Thevenin equivalent circuit in Fig. 10-6d,
a. How much is R_T?
b. How much is V_{R_L}?

10-5 NORTON'S THEOREM

Named after E. L. Norton, a scientist with Bell Telephone Laboratories, Norton's theorem is used for simplifying a network in terms of currents instead of voltages. In many cases, analyzing the division of currents may be easier than voltage analysis. For current analysis, therefore, Norton's theorem can be used to reduce a network to a simple parallel circuit, with a current source. The idea of a current source is that it supplies a total line current to be divided among parallel branches, corresponding to a voltage source applying a total voltage to be divided among series components. This comparison is illustrated in Fig. 10-7.

EXAMPLE OF A CURRENT SOURCE   A source of electric energy supplying voltage is often shown with a series resistance which represents the internal resistance of the source, as in Fig. 10-7a. This method corresponds to showing an actual voltage source, such as a battery for dc circuits. However, the source may be represented also as a current source with a parallel resistance, as in Fig. 10-7b. Just as a voltage source is rated at, say, 10 V, a current source may be rated at 2 A. For the purpose of analyzing parallel branches, the concept of a current source may be more convenient than a voltage source.

If the current I in Fig. 10-7b is a 2-A source, it supplies 2 A no matter what is connected across the output terminals A and B. Without anything connected across A and B, all the 2 A flows through the shunt R. When a load resistance R_L is connected across A and B, then the 2-A I divides according to the current division rules for parallel branches.

Remember that parallel currents divide inversely to branch resistances but directly with conductances. For this reason it may be preferable to consider the current source shunted by the conductance G, as shown in Fig. 10-7c. We can always convert between resistance and conductance, because $1/R$ in ohms is equal to G in siemens.

The symbol for a current source is a circle with an arrow inside, as shown in Fig. 10-7b and c, to show the direction of current. This direction must be the same as the current produced by the polarity of the corresponding voltage source. Remember that a source produces electron flow out from the negative terminal.

An important difference between voltage and current sources is that a current source is killed by making it open, compared with short-circuiting a voltage source. Opening a current source kills its ability to supply current without affecting any parallel branches. A voltage source is short-circuited to kill its ability to supply voltage without affecting any series components.

(a)

(b)

(c)

FIG. 10-7   General forms for a voltage source or current source connected to a load R_L across terminals A and B. (a) Voltage source V with series R. (b) Current source I with parallel R. (c) Current source I with parallel conductance G.

THE NORTON EQUIVALENT CIRCUIT
As illustrated in Fig. 10-8, Norton's theorem states that the entire network connected to terminals A and B can be replaced by a single current source I_N in parallel with a single resistance R_N. The value of I_N is equal to the short-circuit current through the AB terminals. This means, find the current that the network would produce through A and B with a short circuit across these two terminals.

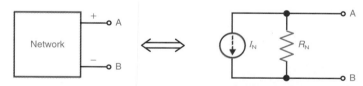

FIG. 10-8   Any network in the block at the left can be reduced to the Norton equivalent parallel circuit at the right.

The value of R_N is the resistance looking back from open terminals A and B. These terminals are not short-circuited for R_N but are open, as in calculating R_{TH} for Thevenin's theorem. Actually, the single resistor is the same for both the Norton and Thevenin equivalent circuits. In the Norton case, this value of R_{AB} is R_N in parallel with the current source; in the Thevenin case, it is R_{TH} in series with the voltage source.

NORTONIZING A CIRCUIT
As an example, let us recalculate the current I_L in Fig. 10-9a, which was solved before by Thevenin's theorem. The first step

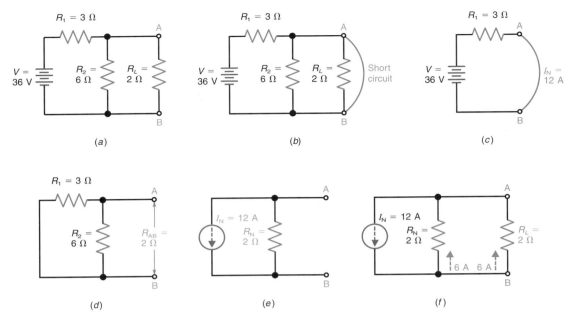

(a) (b) (c)

(d) (e) (f)

FIG. 10-9 Same circuit as in Fig. 10-3, but solved by Norton's theorem. (*a*) Original circuit. (*b*) Short circuit across terminals A and B. (*c*) The short-circuit current I_N is $36/3 = 12$ A. (*d*) Open terminals A and B but short-circuit V to find R_{AB} is 2 Ω, the same as R_{TH}. (*e*) Norton equivalent circuit. (*f*) R_L reconnected to terminals A and B to find I_L is 6 A.

in applying Norton's theorem is to imagine a short circuit across terminals A and B, as shown in Fig. 10-9*b*. How much current is flowing in the short circuit? Note that a short circuit across AB short-circuits R_L and the parallel R_2. Then the only resistance in the circuit is the 3-Ω R_1 in series with the 36-V source, as shown in Fig. 10-9*c*. The short-circuit current, therefore, is

$$I_N = \frac{36 \text{ V}}{3 \text{ }\Omega} = 12 \text{ A}$$

This 12-A I_N is the total current available from the current source in the Norton equivalent in Fig. 10-9*e*.

To find R_N, remove the short circuit across A and B and consider the terminals open, without R_L. Now the source V is considered to be short-circuited. As shown in Fig. 10-9*d*, the resistance seen looking back from terminals A and B is 6 Ω in parallel with 3 Ω, which equals 2 Ω for the value of R_N.

The resultant Norton equivalent is shown in Fig. 10-9*e*. It consists of a 12-A current source I_N shunted by the 2-Ω R_N.

The arrow on the current source shows the direction of electron flow from terminal B to terminal A, as in the original circuit.

Finally, to calculate I_L, replace the 2-Ω R_L between terminals A and B, as shown in Fig. 10-9f. The current source still delivers 12 A, but now that current divides between the two branches of R_N and R_L. Since these two resistances are equal, the 12-A I_N divides into 6 A for each branch, and I_L is equal to 6 A. This value is the same current we calculated in Fig. 10-3, by Thevenin's theorem. Also, V_L can be calculated as $I_L R_L$, or 6 A $\times$ 2 Ω, which equals 12 V.

LOOKING AT THE SHORT-CIRCUIT CURRENT   In some cases, there may be a question of which current is I_N when terminals A and B are short-circuited. Imagine that a wire jumper is connected between A and B to short-circuit these terminals. Then I_N must be the current that flows in this wire between terminals A and B.

Remember that any components directly across these two terminals are also short-circuited by the wire jumper. Then these parallel paths have no effect. However, any components in series with terminal A or terminal B are in series with the wire jumper. Therefore, the short-circuit current I_N also flows through the series components.

An example of a resistor in series with the short circuit across terminals A and B is shown in Fig. 10-10. The idea here is that the short-circuit I_N is a branch current, not the main-line current. Refer to Fig. 10-10a. Here the short circuit connects R_3 across R_2. Also, the short-circuit current I_N is now the same as the current I_3 through R_3. Note that I_3 is only a branch current.

To calculate I_3, the circuit is solved by Ohm's law. The parallel combination of R_2 with R_3 equals 72/18 or 4 Ω. The R_T is 4 + 4 = 8 Ω. As a result, the I_T from the source is 48 V/8 Ω = 6 A.

This I_T of 6 A in the main line divides into 4 A for R_2 and 2 A for R_3. The 2-A I_3 for R_3 flows through short-circuited terminals A and B. Therefore, this current of 2 A is the value of I_N.

To find R_N in Fig. 10-10b, the short circuit is removed from terminals A and B. Now the source V is short-circuited. Looking back from open terminals A and B, the 4-Ω R_1 is in parallel with the 6-Ω R_2. This combination is 24/10 = 2.4 Ω. The 2.4 Ω is in series with the 12-Ω R_3 to make R_{AB} = 2.4 + 12 = 14.4 Ω.

The final Norton equivalent is shown in Fig. 10-10c. Current I_N is 2 A because this branch current in the original circuit is the current that flows through R_3 and short-circuited terminals A and B. Resistance R_N is 14.4 Ω looking back from open terminals A and B with the source V short-circuited the same way as for R_{TH}.

(a)

(b)

(c)

FIG. 10-10   Nortonizing a circuit where the short-circuit current I_N is a branch current. (a) I_N is 2 A through short-circuited terminals A and B and R_3. (b) R_N = R_{AB} = 14.4 Ω. (c) Norton equivalent circuit.

Answers at end of chapter.

Answer True or False.
a. For a Norton equivalent circuit, terminals A and B are short-circuited to find I_N.
b. For a Norton equivalent circuit, terminals A and B are open to find R_N.

10-6 THEVENIN-NORTON CONVERSIONS

Thevenin's theorem says that any network can be represented by a voltage source and series resistance, while Norton's theorem says that the same network can be represented by a current source and shunt resistance. It must be possible, therefore, to convert directly from a Thevenin form to a Norton form and vice versa. Such conversions are often useful.

NORTON FROM THEVENIN Consider the Thevenin equivalent circuit in Fig. 10-11a. What is its Norton equivalent? Just apply Norton's theorem, the same as for any other circuit. The short-circuit current through terminals A and B is

$$I_N = \frac{V_{TH}}{R_{TH}} = \frac{15 \text{ V}}{3 \text{ } \Omega} = 5 \text{ A}$$

The resistance, looking back from open terminals A and B with the source V_{TH} short-circuited, is equal to the 3 Ω of R_{TH}. Therefore, the Norton equivalent consists of a current source that supplies the short-circuit current of 5 A, shunted by the same 3-Ω resistance that is in series in the Thevenin circuit. The results are shown in Fig. 10-11b.

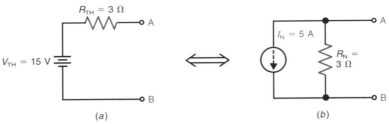

FIG. 10-11 Thevenin equivalent circuit in (a) corresponds to the Norton equivalent in (b).

THEVENIN FROM NORTON For the opposite conversion, we can start with the Norton circuit of Fig. 10-11b and get back to the original Thevenin circuit. To do this, apply Thevenin's theorem, the same as for any other circuit. First, we find the Thevenin resistance by looking back from open terminals A and B. An important principle here, though, is that while a voltage source is short-circuited to find R_{TH}, a current source is an open circuit. In general, a current source is killed by opening the path between its terminals. Therefore, we have just the 3-Ω R_N, in parallel with the infinite resistance of the open current source. The combined resistance then is 3 Ω.

In general, the resistance R_N always has the same value as R_{TH}. The only difference is that R_N is connected in parallel with I_N, but R_{TH} is in series with V_{TH}.

Now all that is required is to calculate the open-circuit voltage in Fig. 10-11b to find the equivalent V_{TH}. Note that with terminals A and B open, all the current of the current source flows through the 3-Ω R_N. Then the open-circuit voltage across the terminals A and B is

$$I_N R_N = 5 \text{ A} \times 3 \text{ } \Omega = 15 \text{ V} = V_{TH}$$

As a result, we have the original Thevenin circuit, which consists of the 15-V source V_{TH} in series with the 3-Ω R_{TH}.

CONVERSION FORMULAS   In summary, the following formulas can be used for these conversions:

Thevenin from Norton:

▶ $R_{TH} = R_N$
    $V_{TH} = I_N \times R_N$

Norton from Thevenin:

▶ $R_N = R_{TH}$
    $I_N = V_{TH}/R_{TH}$

Another example of these conversions is shown in Fig. 10-12.

(a)   (b)   (c)

FIG. 10-12   Example of Thevenin-Norton conversions. (*a*) Original circuit, the same as in Figs. 10-3*a* and 10-9*a*. (*b*) Thevenin equivalent. (*c*) Norton equivalent.

TEST-POINT QUESTION 10-6

Answers at end of chapter.

Answer True or False.
a. In Thevenin-Norton conversions, resistances R_N and R_{TH} are equal.
b. In Thevenin-Norton conversions, current I_N is V_{TH}/R_{TH}.
c. In Thevenin-Norton conversions, voltage V_{TH} is $I_N \times R_N$.

10-7 CONVERSION OF VOLTAGE AND CURRENT SOURCES

Norton conversion is a specific example of the general principle that any voltage source with its series resistance can be converted to an equivalent current source with the same resistance in parallel. In Fig. 10-13, the voltage source in Fig. 10-13a is equivalent to the current source in Fig. 10-13b. Just divide the source V by its series R to calculate the value of I for the equivalent current source shunted by the same R. Either source will supply the same current and voltage for any components connected across terminals A and B.

Conversion of voltage and current sources can often simplify circuits, especially those with two or more sources. Current sources are easier for parallel connections, where we can add or divide currents. Voltage sources are easier for series connections, where we can add or divide voltages.

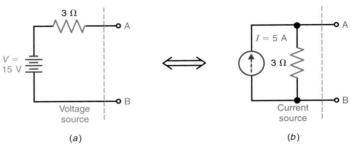

FIG. 10-13 The voltage source in (a) corresponds to the current source in (b).

TWO SOURCES IN PARALLEL BRANCHES Referring to Fig. 10-14a, assume that the problem is to find I_3 through the middle resistor R_3. Note that V_1 with R_1 and V_2 with R_2 are branches in parallel with R_3. All three branches are connected across terminals A and B.

When we convert V_1 and V_2 to current sources in Fig. 10-14b, the circuit has all parallel branches. Current I_1 is $^{84}/_{12}$ or 7 A, while I_2 is $^{21}/_3$, which also happens to be 7 A. Current I_1 has its parallel R of 12 Ω, while I_2 has its parallel R of 3 Ω.

Furthermore, I_1 and I_2 can be combined for the one equivalent current source I_T in Fig. 10-14c. Since both sources produce current in the same direction through R_L, they are added for $I_T = 7 + 7 = 14$ A.

The shunt R for the 14-A combined source is the combined resistance of the 12-Ω R_1 and the 3-Ω R_2 in parallel. This R equals $^{36}/_{15}$ or 2.4 Ω, as shown in Fig. 10-14c.

To find I_L, we can use the current divider formula for the 6- and 2.4-Ω branches, into which the 14-A I_T from the current source was split. Then

$$I_L = \frac{2.4}{2.4 + 6} \times 14 = 4 \text{ A}$$

The voltage V_{R_3} across terminals A and B is $I_L R_L$, which equals $4 \times 6 = 24$ V. These are the same values calculated for V_{R_3} and I_3 by Kirchhoff's laws in Fig. 9-4 and by Thevenin's theorem in Fig. 10-5.

(c)

FIG. 10-14   Converting two voltage sources in V_1 and V_2 in parallel branches to current sources I_1 and I_2 that can be combined. (*a*) Original circuit. (*b*) V_1 and V_2 converted to parallel current sources I_1 and I_2. (*c*) Equivalent circuit with one combined current source I_T.

TWO SOURCES IN SERIES   Referring to Fig. 10-15, assume that the problem is to find the current I_L through the load resistance R_L between terminals A and B. This circuit has the two current sources I_1 and I_2 in series with each other.

The problem here can be simplified by converting I_1 and I_2 to the series voltage sources V_1 and V_2 shown in Fig. 10-15*b*. The 2-A I_1 with its shunt 4-Ω R_1 is equivalent to 4×2, or 8 V, for V_1 with a 4-Ω series resistance. Similarly, the 5-A I_2 with its shunt 2-Ω R_2 is equivalent to 5×2, or 10 V, for V_2 with a 2-Ω series resistance. The polarities of V_1 and V_2 produce electron flow in the same direction as I_1 and I_2.

The series voltages can now be combined as in Fig. 10-15*c*. The 8 V of V_1 and 10 V of V_2 are added because they are series-aiding, resulting in the total V_T of 18 V. And, the resistances of 4 Ω for R_1 and 2 Ω for R_2 are added, for a

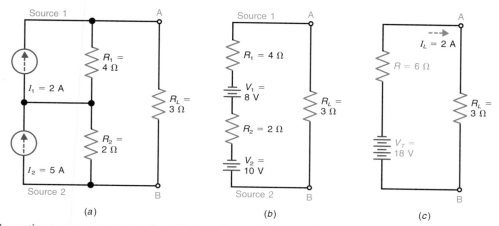

FIG. 10-15   Converting two current sources I_1 and I_2 in series to voltage sources V_1 and V_2 that can be combined. (*a*) Original circuit. (*b*) I_1 and I_2 converted to series voltage sources V_1 and V_2. (*c*) Equivalent circuit with one combined voltage source V_T.

combined R of 6 Ω. This is the series resistance of the 18-V source V_T connected across terminals A and B.

The total resistance of the circuit in Fig. 10-15c is R plus R_L, or $6 + 3 = 9\ \Omega$. With 18 V applied, $I_L = {}^{18}\!/_9 = 2$ A through R_L between terminals A and B.

TEST-POINT QUESTION 10-7

Answers at end of chapter.

A voltage source has 21 V in series with 3 Ω. For the equivalent current source,
a. How much is I?
b. How much is the shunt R?

10-8 MILLMAN'S THEOREM

Millman's theorem provides a shortcut for finding the common voltage across any number of parallel branches with different voltage sources. A typical example is shown in Fig. 10-16. For all the branches, the ends at point Y are connected to chassis ground. Furthermore, the opposite ends of all the branches are also connected to the common point X. The voltage V_{XY}, therefore, is the common voltage across all the branches.

FIG. 10-16   Example of Millman's theorem to find V_{XY}, the common voltage across branches with separate voltage sources.

Finding the value of V_{XY} gives the net effect of all the sources in determining the voltage at X with respect to chassis ground. To calculate this voltage

$$V_{XY} = \frac{V_1/R_1 + V_2/R_2 + V_3/R_3}{1/R_1 + 1/R_2 + 1/R_3} \ldots \text{etc.} \qquad (10\text{-}1)$$

This formula is derived from converting the voltage sources to current sources and combining the results. The numerator with V/R terms is the sum of the parallel current sources. The denominator with $1/R$ terms is the sum of the parallel conductances. The net V_{XY} then is the form of I/G or $I \times R$, which is in units of voltage.

CALCULATING V_{XY}   For the values in Fig. 10-16,

$$V_{XY} = \frac{32/4 + 0/2 - 8/4}{1/4 + 1/2 + 1/4}$$

$$= \frac{8 + 0 - 2}{1}$$

$$V_{XY} = 6 \text{ V}$$

Note that in branch 3, V_3 is considered negative because it would make point X negative. However, all the resistances are positive. The positive answer for V_{XY} means that point X is positive with respect to Y.

In branch 2, V_2 is zero because this branch has no voltage source. However, R_2 is still used in the denominator.

This method can be used for any number of branches, but they must all be in parallel, without any series resistances between the branches. In a branch with several resistances, they can be combined as one R_T. When a branch has more than one voltage source, they can be combined algebraically for one V_T.

APPLICATIONS OF MILLMAN'S THEOREM   In many cases, a circuit can be redrawn to show the parallel branches and their common voltage V_{XY}. Then with V_{XY} known the entire circuit can be analyzed quickly. For instance, Fig. 10-17 has been solved before by other methods. For Millman's theorem the common voltage V_{XY} across all the branches is the same as V_3 across R_3. This voltage is calculated with Formula (10-1), as follows:

$$V_{XY} = \frac{-84/12 + 0/6 - 21/3}{1/12 + 1/6 + 1/3} = \frac{-7 + 0 - 7}{7/12}$$

$$= \frac{-14}{7/12} = -14 \times \frac{12}{7}$$

$$V_{XY} = -24 \text{ V} = V_3$$

The negative sign means that point X is the negative side of V_{XY}.

With V_3 known to be 24 V across the 6-Ω R_3, then I_3 must be 24/6 = 4 A. Similarly, all the voltages and currents in this circuit can then be calculated. (See Fig. 9-4 in Chap. 9.)

FIG. 10-17   The same circuit as in Fig. 9-4 for Kirchhoff's laws, but shown with parallel branches to calculate V_{XY} by Millman's theorem.

As another application, the example of superposition in Fig. 10-1 has been redrawn in Fig. 10-18 to show the parallel branches with a common voltage V_{XY} to be calculated by Millman's theorem. Then

$$V_{XY} = \frac{24 \text{ V}/30 \text{ k}\Omega - 9 \text{ V}/60 \text{ k}\Omega}{1/(30 \text{ k}\Omega) + 1/(60 \text{ k}\Omega)} = \frac{0.8 \text{ mA} - 0.15 \text{ mA}}{3/(60 \text{ k}\Omega)}$$

$$= 0.65 \times \frac{60}{3} = \frac{39}{3}$$

$$V_{XY} = 13 \text{ V} = V_P$$

The answer of 13 V from point P to ground, using Millman's theorem, is the same value calculated before by superposition.

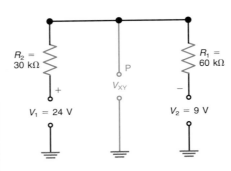

FIG. 10-18 Same circuit as in Fig. 10-1 for superposition, but shown with parallel branches to calculate V_{XY} by Millman's theorem.

TEST-POINT QUESTION 10-8

Answers at end of chapter.

For the example of Millman's theorem in Fig. 10-16,
a. How much is V_{R_2}?
b. How much is V_{R_3}?

10-9 CIRCUITS WITH CURRENT SOURCES

Examples are shown in Figs. 10-19 and 10-20 with multiple energy sources to illustrate how to simplify circuits with current sources. The general principles are as follows:

1. When current sources are in parallel, they can be combined. Add currents that produce I in the same direction through the load; subtract opposite currents.
2. When voltage sources are in series, they can be combined. Add voltages that produce I in the same direction through the load; subtract opposite voltages.
3. When current sources are in series, convert to voltage sources so that they can be combined. The polarity of the voltage must produce I in the same direction as the current source.

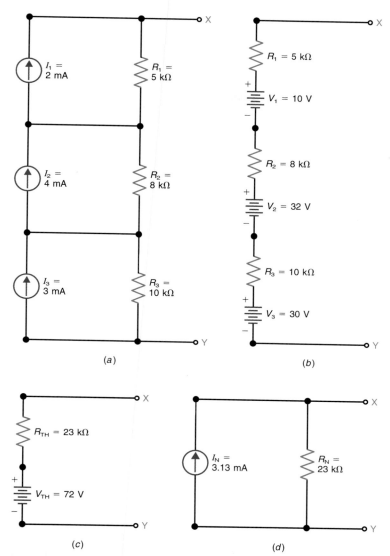

FIG. 10-19   Circuit with three current sources in series. I arrows shown for conventional current. See text for analysis that converts circuit to one Thevenin or Norton equivalent. (*a*) Original circuit. (*b*) I sources converted to V sources. (*c*) Thevenin equivalent. (*d*) Norton equivalent.

4. With voltage sources in parallel, convert to current sources so that they can be combined. The direction of I must be in the same direction through the load as would be produced by the voltage source.

The current sources in Figs. 10-19 and 10-20 are shown with solid arrows for the direction of conventional current, opposite from electron flow, although the circuits can be analyzed either way. In conversion, note that conventional I is out from the positive terminal of V and returns to the negative terminal. Also, these circuits have I of milliamperes and R of kilohms. Still, the IR product is in units of volts.

FIG. 10-20 Circuit with series-parallel I and V sources. I arrows shown for conventional current. See text for analysis that converts circuit to one Thevenin or Norton equivalent. (a) Original circuit. (b) V_1 and V_2 converted to one equivalent current source I_{12}. (c) The I_{12} converted to V_{12} and I_3 converted to V_3 for series circuit of voltage sources. (d) Thevenin equivalent. (e) Norton equivalent.

I SOURCES IN SERIES Refer to Fig 10-19a. The three current sources I_1, I_2, and I_3 are in series. They are converted to voltage sources in Fig 10-19b. The calculations are:

$$V_1 = I_1 \times R_1 \qquad V_2 = I_2 \times R_2 \qquad V_3 = I_3 \times R_3$$
$$= 2 \text{ mA} \times 5 \text{ k}\Omega \qquad = 4 \text{ mA} \times 8 \text{ k}\Omega \qquad = 3 \text{ mA} \times 10 \text{ k}\Omega$$
$$V_1 = 10 \text{ V} \qquad V_2 = 32 \text{ V} \qquad V_3 = 30 \text{ V}$$

The three voltage sources V_1, V_2, and V_3 in series in Fig. 10-19b are combined for one equivalent source V_{TH} in Fig. 10-19c, equal to $10 + 32 + 30 = 72$ V. Also, R_1, R_2, and R_3 in series total 23 kΩ.

The single voltage source of 72 V in Fig. 10-19c with series resistance of 23 kΩ is the Thevenin equivalent of the circuit in Fig. 10-19a. Any load connected across terminals X and Y will have the same V_L and I_L, for either circuit.

Finally, the circuit in Fig. 10-19d is the Norton equivalent of Fig. 10-19c. The I_N is 72 V/23 kΩ, which equals 3.13 mA. Also, R_N is the same 23 kΩ as R_{TH}.

SERIES-PARALLEL ENERGY SOURCES Refer to Fig. 10-20a. The first step is to convert V_1 and V_2 to current sources so that they can be combined in parallel for the single value of I_{12} in Fig. 10-20b. The calculations are

$$I_1 = V_1/R_1 \qquad I_2 = V_2/R_2 \qquad I_{12} = I_1 + I_2$$
$$= 4\ V/2\ k\Omega \qquad = 32\ V/8\ k\Omega \qquad = 2 + 4$$
$$I_1 = 2\ mA \qquad I_2 = 4\ mA \qquad I_{12} = 6\ mA$$

The equivalent resistance for R_{12} is the parallel combination of $(2 \times 8)/(2 + 8)$ or 16/10, which equals 1.6 kΩ.

Next, the current sources I_{12} and I_3 in Fig. 10-20b are converted to voltage sources in Fig. 10-20c, because of the series circuit. Then V_{12} becomes 6 mA $\times$ 1.6 kΩ = 9.6 V. The R_{12} is still 1.6 kΩ. Also, the current source I_3 is converted to V_3, equal to 3 mA $\times$ 2.4 kΩ = 7.2 V. The source resistance R_3 is still 2.4 kΩ.

In Fig. 10-20d, the series voltage sources are added for the single value of 9.6 + 7.2 = 16.8 V. This value is V_{TH}. The R_{TH} is 2.4 + 1.6 = 4 kΩ.

For the last step, the Thevenin circuit is converted to a Norton equivalent in Fig. 10-20e. The I_N is 16.8 V/4 kΩ, which equals 4.2 mA. Also, R_N is the same 4 kΩ as R_{TH}.

TEST-POINT QUESTION 10-9

Answers at end of chapter.

Answer True or False.

a. In Fig. 10-19, the current sources I_1, I_2, and I_3 are converted to voltage sources because they are in series.

b. In Fig. 10-20, the parallel bank of V_1 with R_1 and V_2 with R_2 is equivalent to one source of 9.6 V with series R of 1.6 kΩ.

10-10 T OR Y AND π OR Δ CONNECTIONS

The circuit in Fig. 10-21 is called a T (tee) or Y (wye) network, as suggested by the shape. They are different names for the same network; the only difference is that the R_2 and R_3 legs are shown at an angle in the Y.

The circuit in Fig. 10-22 is called a π (pi) or Δ (delta) network, as the shape is similar to these Greek letters. Both forms are the same network. Actually, the

FIG. 10-21 The form of a T or Y network.

FIG. 10-22 The form of a π or Δ network.

network can have the R_A arm shown at the top or bottom, as long as it is connected between R_B and R_C. In Fig. 10-22, R_A is at the top, as an inverted delta, to look like the π network.

The circuits in Figs. 10-21 and 10-22 are passive networks, without any energy sources. Also, they are three-terminal networks for two pairs of connections for input and output voltages, with one common. In Fig. 10-21, point B is the common terminal and point 2 is common in Fig. 10-22.

The Y and Δ forms are different ways to connect three resistors in a passive network. Note resistors in the Y are labeled with subscripts 1, 2, and 3, while the Δ has subscripts A, B, and C, in order to emphasize the different connections.

CONVERSION FORMULAS In the analysis of networks, it is often helpful to convert a Δ to Y or vice versa. Either it may be difficult to visualize the circuit without the conversion, or the conversion makes the solution simpler. The formulas for these transformations are given here. All are derived from Kirchhoff's laws. Note that letters are used as subscripts for R_A, R_B, and R_C in the Δ, while the resistances are numbered R_1, R_2, and R_3 in the Y.

▶ Conversions of Y to Δ, or T to π:

$$R_A = \frac{R_1R_2 + R_2R_3 + R_3R_1}{R_1}$$

$$R_B = \frac{R_1R_2 + R_2R_3 + R_3R_1}{R_2}$$ $$(10\text{-}2)$$

$$R_C = \frac{R_1R_2 + R_2R_3 + R_3R_1}{R_3}$$

or

▶ $$R_\Delta = \frac{\Sigma \text{ all cross products in Y}}{\text{opposite } R \text{ in Y}}$$

These formulas can be used to convert a Y network to an equivalent Δ, or a T network to π. Both networks will have the same resistance across any pair of terminals.

The three formulas have the same general form, indicated at the bottom as one basic rule. The symbol Σ is the Greek capital letter sigma, meaning "sum of."

For the opposite conversion:

▶ Conversion of Δ to Y or π to T:

$$R_1 = \frac{R_B R_C}{R_A + R_B + R_C}$$

$$R_2 = \frac{R_C R_A}{R_A + R_B + R_C}$$

(10-3)

$$R_3 = \frac{R_A R_B}{R_A + R_B + R_C}$$

or

▶ $$R_Y = \frac{\text{product of two adjacent } R \text{ in } \Delta}{\Sigma \text{ all } R \text{ in } \Delta}$$

As an aid in using these formulas, the following scheme is useful. Place the Y inside the Δ, as shown in Fig. 10-23. Notice that the Δ has three closed sides, while the Y has three open arms. Also note how resistors can be considered opposite each other in the two networks. For instance, the open arm R_1 is opposite the closed side R_A; R_2 is opposite R_B; and R_3 is opposite R_C.

Furthermore, each resistor in an open arm has two adjacent resistors in the closed sides. For R_1, its adjacent resistors are R_B and R_C; also R_C and R_A are adjacent to R_2, while R_A and R_B are adjacent to R_3.

In the formulas for the Y-to-Δ conversion, each side of the delta is found by first taking all possible cross products of the arms of the wye, using two arms at a time. There are three such cross products. The sum of the three cross products is then divided by the opposite arm to find the value of each side of the delta. Note that the numerator remains the same, the sum of the three cross products. However, each side of the delta is calculated by dividing this sum by the opposite arm.

For the case of the Δ-to-Y conversion, each arm of the wye is found by taking the product of the two adjacent sides in the delta and dividing by the sum of the three sides of the delta. The product of two adjacent resistors excludes the opposite resistor. The denominator for the sum of the three sides remains the same in the three formulas. However, each arm is calculated by dividing the sum into each cross product.

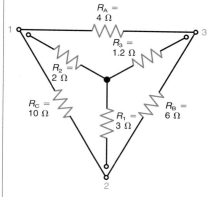

FIG. 10-23 Conversion between Y and Δ networks. See text for conversion formulas.

AN EXAMPLE OF CONVERSION

The values shown for the equivalent Y and Δ in Fig. 10-23 are calculated as follows: Starting with 4, 6, and 10 Ω for sides R_A, R_B, and R_C, respectively, in the delta, the corresponding arms in the wye are

$$R_1 = \frac{R_B R_C}{R_A + R_B + R_C} = \frac{6 \times 10}{4 + 6 + 10} = \frac{60}{20} = 3 \text{ Ω}$$

$$R_2 = \frac{R_C R_A}{20} = \frac{10 \times 4}{20} = \frac{40}{20} = 2 \text{ Ω}$$

$$R_3 = \frac{R_A R_B}{20} = \frac{4 \times 6}{20} = \frac{24}{20} = 1.2 \text{ Ω}$$

As a check on these values, we can calculate the equivalent delta for this wye. Starting with values of 3, 2, and 1.2 Ω for R_1, R_2, and R_3, respectively, in the wye, the corresponding values in the delta are:

$$R_A = \frac{R_1 R_2 + R_2 R_3 + R_3 R_1}{R_1} = \frac{6 + 2.4 + 3.6}{3} = \frac{12}{3} = 4 \ \Omega$$

$$R_B = \frac{12}{R_2} = \frac{12}{2} = 6 \ \Omega$$

$$R_C = \frac{12}{R_3} = \frac{12}{1.2} = 10 \ \Omega$$

These results show that the Y and Δ networks in Fig. 10-23 are equivalent to each other when they have the values obtained with the conversion formulas.

Note that the equivalent R values in the Y are less than in the equivalent Δ network. The reason is that the Y has two legs between the terminals, while the Δ has only one.

SIMPLIFYING A BRIDGE CIRCUIT As an example of the use of such transformations, consider the bridge circuit of Fig. 10-24. The total current I_T from the battery is desired. Therefore, we must find the total resistance R_T.

FIG. 10-24 Solving a bridge circuit by Δ-to-Y conversion. (*a*) Original circuit. (*b*) How the Y of $R_1 R_2 R_3$ corresponds to Δ of $R_A R_B R_C$. (*c*) The Y substituted for the Δ network. The result is a series-parallel circuit with the same R_T as the original bridge circuit. (*d*) R_T is 4.5 Ω between points P$_3$ and P$_4$.

One approach is to note that the bridge in Fig. 10-24a consists of two deltas connected between terminals P_1 and P_2. One of them can be replaced by an equivalent wye. We use the bottom delta with R_A across the top, in the same form as Fig. 10-23. We then replace this delta $R_A R_B R_C$ by an equivalent wye $R_1 R_2 R_3$, as shown in Fig. 10-24b. Using the conversion formulas,

▶
$$R_1 = \frac{R_B R_C}{R_A + R_B + R_C} = \frac{24}{12} = 2\ \Omega$$

$$R_2 = \frac{R_C R_A}{12} = \frac{12}{12} = 1\ \Omega$$

$$R_3 = \frac{R_A R_B}{12} = \frac{8}{12} = \frac{2}{3}\ \Omega$$

We next use these values for R_1, R_2, and R_3 in an equivalent wye to replace the original delta. Then the resistances form the series-parallel circuit shown in Fig. 10-24c. The combined resistance of the two parallel branches here is 4 × 6.67 divided by 10.67, which equals 2.5 Ω for R. Adding this 2.5 Ω to the series R_1 of 2 Ω, the total resistance is 4.5 Ω in Fig. 10-24d.

This 4.5 Ω is the R_T for the entire bridge circuit between P_3 and P_4 connected to source V. Then I_T is 30 V/4.5 Ω, which equals 6.67 A supplied by the source.

Another approach to finding R_T for the bridge circuit in Fig. 10-24a is to recognize that the bridge also consists of two T or Y networks between terminals P_3 and P_4. One of them can be transformed into an equivalent delta. The result is another series-parallel circuit but with the same R_T of 4.5 Ω.

BALANCED NETWORKS   When all the R values are equal in a network, it is balanced. Then the conversion is simplified, as R in the wye network is 1/3 the R in the equivalent delta. As an example, for $R_A = R_B = R_C$ equal to 6 Ω in the delta, the equivalent wye has $R_1 = R_2 = R_3$ equal to 6/3 or 2 Ω. Or, converting the other way, for 2-Ω R values in a balanced wye delta, the equivalent delta network has each R equal to 3 × 2 = 6 Ω. This example is illustrated in Fig. 10-25.

(a)   (b)

FIG. 10-25   Equivalent balanced networks. (a) Delta form. (b) Wye form.

<hr>

TEST-POINT QUESTION 10-10

Answers at end of chapter.

In the standard form for conversion,
a. Which resistor in the Y is opposite R_A in the Δ?
b. Which two resistors in the Δ are adjacent to R_1 in the Y?

10 SUMMARY AND REVIEW

- *Superposition theorem.* In a linear, bilateral network having more than one source, the current and voltage in any part of the network can be found by adding algebraically the effect of each source separately. All other sources are temporarily killed by short-circuiting voltage sources and opening current sources.
- *Thevenin's theorem.* Any network with two open terminals A and B can be replaced by a single voltage source V_{TH} in series with a single resistance R_{TH} connected to terminals A and B. Voltage V_{TH} is the voltage produced by the network across terminals A and B. Resistance R_{TH} is the resistance across open terminals A and B with all sources short-circuited.
- *Norton's theorem.* Any two-terminal network can be replaced by a single current source I_N in parallel with a single resistance R_N. The value of I_N is the current produced by the network through the short-circuited terminals. R_N is the resistance across the open terminals with all sources short-circuited.
- *Millman's theorem.* The common voltage across parallel branches with different V sources can be determined with Formula (10-1).
- A voltage source V with its series R can be converted to an equivalent current source I with parallel R. Similarly, a current source I with a parallel R can be converted to a voltage source V with a series R. The value of I is V/R, or V is $I \times R$. The value of R is the same for both sources. However, R is in series with V but in parallel with I.
- The comparison between delta and wye networks is illustrated in Fig. 10-23. To convert from one network to the other, Formula (10-2) or (10-3) is used.

SELF-TEST

ANSWERS AT BACK OF BOOK.

Answer True or False.

1. Voltage V_{TH} is an open-circuit voltage.
2. Current I_N is a short-circuit current.
3. Resistances R_{TH} and R_N have the same value.
4. A voltage source has series resistance.
5. A current source has parallel resistance.
6. A voltage source is killed by short-circuiting the terminals.
7. A current source is killed by opening the source.
8. A π network is the same as a T network.

QUESTIONS

1. State the superposition theorem, and discuss how to apply it.
2. State how to calculate V_{TH} and R_{TH} in Thevenin equivalent circuits.
3. State the method of calculating I_N and R_N for a Norton equivalent circuit.
4. How is a voltage source converted to a current source, and vice versa?
5. For what type of circuit is Millman's theorem used?
6. Draw a delta network and a wye network and give the six formulas needed to convert from one to the other.
7. Give two differences between a dc source and an ac source.

PROBLEMS

ANSWERS TO ODD-NUMBERED PROBLEMS AT BACK OF BOOK.

1. Refer to Fig. 10-26. Show the Thevenin equivalent and calculate V_L.
2. Show the Norton equivalent of Fig. 10-26 and calculate I_L.
3. In Fig. 10-26, convert V and R_1 to a current source and calculate I_L.
4. Use Ohm's law to solve Fig. 10-26 as a series-parallel circuit in order to calculate V_L and I_L. (Note: R_L is not opened for Ohm's law.)
5. Why is the value of V_L across terminals A and B in Prob. 4 not the same as V_{AB} for the Thevenin equivalent circuit in Prob. 1?
6. Refer to Fig. 10-27. Determine V_P by superposition.
7. Redraw Fig. 10-27 as two parallel branches to calculate V_P by Millman's theorem.
8. Refer to Fig. 10-28. Calculate V_L across R_L by Millman's theorem and also by superposition.
9. Show the Thevenin equivalent of Fig. 10-29, where terminals A and B are across the middle resistor R_2. Then calculate V_{R_2}.

FIG. 10-26   Circuit for Probs. 1, 2, 3, 4, and 5.

FIG. 10-27   Circuit for Probs. 6 and 7.

FIG. 10-28   Circuit for Prob. 8.

10. In Fig. 10-29, solve for V_{R_2} by superposition.
11. In Fig. 10-29, solve for V_{R_2} by Millman's theorem.
12. In Fig. 10-30, solve for all the currents by Kirchhoff's laws.
13. In Fig. 10-30, find V_3 by Millman's theorem.
14. Convert the T network in Fig. 10-31 to an equivalent π network.
15. Convert the π network in Fig. 10-32 to an equivalent T network.
16. Show the Thevenin and Norton equivalent circuits for the diagram in Fig. 10-33.
17. In Fig. 10-34, do the following: (a) convert the current sources, I_1 and I_2, into equivalent voltage sources, V_1 and V_2, in series with load R_L; (b) combine the individual voltage sources into one equivalent voltage source whose voltage and resistance values are identified as V_{TH} and R_{TH}, respectively; (c) calculate the load current I_L; (d) convert the Thevenin equivalent circuit in part (b) into its Norton equivalent. (The arrows in each current source indicate the direction of conventional current flow.)

FIG. 10-29   Circuit for Probs. 9, 10, and 11.

FIG. 10-30   Circuit for Probs. 12 and 13.

FIG. 10-31   Circuit for Prob. 14.

FIG. 10-32   Circuit for Prob. 15.

FIG. 10-33   Circuit for Prob. 16.

FIG. 10-34   Circuit for Prob. 17.

18. In Fig. 10-35, show the Thevenin equivalent circuit driving terminals A and B. Also, calculate the load current I_L.
19. Show the Thevenin equivalent circuit driving terminals A and B in Fig. 10-36. Also, calculate V_L.
20. In Fig. 10-36, show the Norton equivalent circuit driving terminals A and B. Also, calculate I_L.
21. In Fig. 10-37, show the Thevenin equivalent circuit driving terminals A and B. Also, calculate the values for I_L and V_L.
22. In Fig. 10-38, show the Thevenin equivalent circuit driving terminals A and B. Also, calculate I_L and V_L.
23. In Fig. 10-38, show the Norton equivalent circuit driving terminals A and B. Also, calculate I_L and V_L.

FIG. 10-35   Circuit for Prob. 18.

FIG. 10-36   Circuit for Probs. 19 and 20.

FIG. 10-37   Circuit for Prob. 21.

FIG. 10-38   Circuit for Probs. 22 and 23.

24.   In Fig. 10-39, show the Thevenin equivalent circuit driving terminals A and B. Also, calculate I_3 and V_{R_3}.

25.   In Fig. 10-39, use the superposition theorem to find currents I_1, I_2, I_3 and voltages V_{R_1}, V_{R_2}, and V_{R_3}.

FIG. 10-39   Circuit for Probs. 24 and 25.

CRITICAL THINKING

1.   Thevenize the circuit driving terminals A and B in Fig. 10-40. Show the Thevenin equivalent circuit and calculate the values for I_L and V_L.

2.   In Fig. 10-41, use the superposition theorem to solve for I_L and V_L.

3.   In Fig. 10-41, show the Thevenin equivalent circuit driving terminals A and B.

4.   Refer to Fig. 10-35. Remove R_2 from the circuit and show the Thevenin equivalent circuit driving the open terminals. Also, calculate the value of I_2 and V_{R_2}.

FIG. 10-40   Circuit for Critical Thinking Prob. 1.

FIG. 10-41   Circuit for Critical Thinking Probs. 2 and 3.

REVIEW: CHAPTERS 9 AND 10

SUMMARY

- Methods of applying Kirchhoff's laws include (**a**) equations of voltages using the branch currents in the loops to specify the voltages; (**b**) equations of currents at a node using the node voltages to specify the node currents; (**c**) equations of voltages using assumed mesh currents to specify the voltages.
- Methods of reducing a network to a simple equivalent circuit include (**a**) the superposition theorem using one source at a time; (**b**) Thevenin's theorem to convert the network to a series circuit with one source; (**c**) Norton's theorem to convert the network to a parallel circuit with one source; (**d**) Millman's theorem to find the common voltage across parallel branches with different sources; (**e**) delta (Δ) wye (Y) conversions to transform a network into a series-parallel circuit.

REVIEW TEST

ANSWERS AT BACK OF BOOK.

Answer True or False.

1. In Fig. 9-3, V_3 can be found by using Kirchhoff's laws with either branch currents or mesh currents.
2. In Fig. 9-3, V_3 can be found by superposition, thevenizing, or using Millman's theorem.
3. In Fig. 10-6, I_L cannot be found by delta-wye conversion because R_L disappears in the transformation.
4. In Fig. 10-6, I_L can be calculated with Kirchhoff's laws, using mesh currents for three meshes.
5. With superposition, we can use Ohm's law for circuits that have more than one source.
6. A Thevenin equivalent is a parallel circuit.
7. A Norton equivalent is a series circuit.
8. Either a Thevenin or a Norton equivalent of a network will produce the same current in any load across terminals A and B.
9. A Thevenin-to-Norton conversion means converting a voltage source to a current source.
10. The volts unit is equal to (volts/ohms) $\div$ siemens.
11. A node voltage is a voltage between current nodes.
12. A π network can be converted to an equivalent T network.

13. A 10-V source with 10-Ω series R will supply 5 V to a 10-Ω load R_L.
14. A 10-A source with 10-Ω parallel R will supply 5 A to a 10-Ω load R_L.
15. Current sources in parallel can be added when they supply current in the same direction through R_L.

REFERENCES

Hayt and Kemmerling: *Engineering Circuit Analysis,* McGraw-Hill, New York.

Kaufman and Seldman: *Handbook of Electronics Calculations for Engineers and Technicians,* McGraw-Hill, New York.

Nasar, S.: *3000 Solved Problems in Electric Circuits,* McGraw-Hill, New York.

CHAPTER 11

CONDUCTORS AND INSULATORS

Conductors have very low resistance. An R of 0.1 Ω or less for 10 ft of copper wire is a typical value. The function of the wire conductor is to connect a source of applied voltage to a load with minimum IR voltage drop in the conductor. Then practically all the applied voltage can produce current in the load.

At the opposite extreme, materials having a very high resistance of many megohms are insulators. Some common examples are air, paper, plastics, rubber, mica, glass, cotton, shellac or varnish, and wood. An insulator provides the equivalent of an open circuit with almost infinite R and practically zero I.

Between the extremes of conductors and insulators are semiconductor materials such as carbon (C), silicon (Si), and germanium (Ge). Carbon is used in the manufacture of carbon resistors. Si and Ge are used for transistors. Just about all semiconductor devices are made with silicon. It should be noted, though, that the medium resistance of Si and Ge is not so important as the fact their electrical characteristics can be altered to provide free charges to be controlled by a small applied voltage.

In a class by itself is the category of superconductors. As the name says, these materials have the superb characteristic of zero resistance. However, this very desirable feature can be provided only with special low-temperature conditions or unique ceramic materials.

CHAPTER OBJECTIVES

Upon completion of this chapter, you should be able to:

- *Explain* the main function of a conductor in an electric circuit.
- *Determine* the circular area of round wire when the wire diameter is known.
- *List* the advantages of using stranded wire versus solid wire.
- *List* several common types of connectors used with wire conductors.
- *Define* the terms *pole* and *throw* as they relate to switches.
- *Explain* the difference between a fast-acting and slow-blow fuse.
- *Calculate* the total resistance of a wire conductor whose length, cross-sectional area, and specific resistance are known.
- *Understand* what is meant by the *temperature coefficient of resistance*.
- *Explain* the difference between ion current and electron current.
- *List* three types of semiconductors.
- *Explain* the makeup of N-type and P-type semiconductor materials.
- *Explain* why insulators are sometimes called dielectrics.

IMPORTANT TERMS IN THIS CHAPTER

characteristic impedance	fuse types	RS-232 plug
circuit breaker	hole current	specific resistance
circular mil	hot resistance	superconductor
coaxial cable	ion current	switch types
corona effect	printed wiring	temperature coefficient of R
covalent bond	RCA plug	twin lead
cryogenics	resistance wire	wire gage sizes
F connector	ribbon cable	

TOPICS COVERED IN THIS CHAPTER

11-1 FUNCTION OF THE CONDUCTOR

In Fig. 11-1, the resistance of the two 10-ft lengths of copper-wire conductor is 0.08 Ω. This R is negligibly small compared with the 144-Ω R for the tungsten filament in the light bulb. When the current of 0.833 A flows in the bulb and the series conductors, the IR voltage drop of the conductors is only 0.07 V, with 119.93 V across the bulb. Practically all the applied voltage is across the bulb filament. Since the bulb then has its rated voltage of 120 V, approximately, it will dissipate the rated power of 100 W and light with full brilliance.

The current in the wire conductors and the bulb is the same, since they are in series. However, the IR voltage drop in the conductor is practically zero because its R is almost zero.

Also, the I^2R power dissipated in the conductor is negligibly small, allowing the conductor to operate without becoming hot. Therefore, the conductor delivers energy from the source to the load with minimum loss, by means of electron flow in the copper wires.

Although the resistance of wire conductors is very small, for some cases of high current the resultant IR drop can be appreciable. For example, suppose the 120-V power line is supplying 30 A of current to a load through two conductors, each of which has a resistance of 0.2 Ω. In this case, each conductor has an IR drop of 6 V, calculated as 30 A $\times$ 0.2 Ω = 6 V. With each conductor dropping 6 V, the load receives a voltage of only 108 V rather than the full 120 V. The lower-than-normal load voltage could result in the load not operating properly. Furthermore, the I^2R power dissipated in each conductor equals 180 W, calculated as $30^2 \times 0.2$ Ω = 180 W. The I^2R power loss of 180 W in the conductors is considered to be excessively high.

TEST-POINT QUESTION 11-1

Answers at end of chapter.

Refer to Fig. 11-1.
a. How much is R for the 20 ft of copper wire?
b. How much is the IR voltage drop for the wire conductors?
c. The voltage in **b** is what percent of the applied voltage?

11-2 STANDARD WIRE GAGE SIZES

Table 11-1 lists the standard wire sizes in the system known as the American Wire Gage (AWG), or Brown and Sharpe (B&S) gage. The gage numbers specify the size of round wire in terms of its diameter and cross-sectional area. Note the following:

1. As the gage numbers increase from 1 to 40, the diameter and circular area decrease. Higher gage numbers indicate thinner wire sizes.
2. The circular area doubles for every three gage sizes. For example, No. 10 wire has approximately twice the area of No. 13 wire.
3. The higher the gage number and the thinner the wire, the greater the resistance of the wire for any given length.

FIG. 11-1 The conductors should have minimum resistance to light the bulb with full brilliance. (*a*) Wiring diagram. (*b*) Schematic diagram. R_1 and R_2 represent the very small resistance of the wire conductors.

In typical applications, hookup wire for electronic circuits with current in the order of milliamperes is generally about No. 22 gage. For this size, 0.5 to 1 A is the maximum current the wire can carry without excessive heating.

House wiring for circuits where the current is 5 to 15 A is usually No. 14 gage. Minimum sizes for house wiring are set by local electrical codes, which

TABLE 11-1   COPPER-WIRE TABLE

GAGE NO.	DIAMETER, MILS	AREA, CIRCULAR-MILS	OHMS PER 1000 FT OF COPPER WIRE AT 25°C*	GAGE NO.	DIAMETER, MILS	AREA, CIRCULAR-MILS	OHMS PER 1000 FT OF COPPER WIRE AT 25°C*
1	289.3	83,690	0.1264	21	28.46	810.1	13.05
2	257.6	66,370	0.1593	22	25.35	642.4	16.46
3	229.4	52,640	0.2009	23	22.57	509.5	20.76
4	204.3	41,740	0.2533	24	20.10	404.0	26.17
5	181.9	33,100	0.3195	25	17.90	320.4	33.00
6	162.0	26,250	0.4028	26	15.94	254.1	41.62
7	144.3	20,820	0.5080	27	14.20	201.5	52.48
8	128.5	16,510	0.6405	28	12.64	159.8	66.17
9	114.4	13,090	0.8077	29	11.26	126.7	83.44
10	101.9	10,380	1.018	30	10.03	100.5	105.2
11	90.74	8234	1.284	31	8.928	79.70	132.7
12	80.81	6530	1.619	32	7.950	63.21	167.3
13	71.96	5178	2.042	33	7.080	50.13	211.0
14	64.08	4107	2.575	34	6.305	39.75	266.0
15	57.07	3257	3.247	35	5.615	31.52	335.0
16	50.82	2583	4.094	36	5.000	25.00	423.0
17	45.26	2048	5.163	37	4.453	19.83	533.4
18	40.30	1624	6.510	38	3.965	15.72	672.6
19	35.89	1288	8.210	39	3.531	12.47	848.1
20	31.96	1022	10.35	40	3.145	9.88	1069

*20° to 25°C or 68° to 77°F is considered average room temperature.

FIG. 11-2 American standard wire gage (AWG) for wire conductors.

are usually guided by the National Electrical Code published by the National Fire Protection Association. A gage for measuring wire size is shown in Fig. 11-2.

CIRCULAR MILS The cross-sectional area of round wire is measured in circular mils, abbreviated cmil. A mil is one-thousandth of an inch, or 0.001 in. One circular mil is the cross-sectional area of a wire with a diameter of 1 mil. The number of circular mils in any circular area is equal to the square of the diameter in mils.

Example

EXAMPLE 1 What is the area in circular mils of a wire with a diameter of 0.005 in.?

ANSWER We must convert the diameter to mils. Since 0.005 in. equals 5 mil,

$$\text{Circular mil area} = (5 \text{ mil})^2$$
$$\text{Area} = 25 \text{ cmil}$$

Note that the circular mil is a unit of area, obtained by squaring the diameter, while the mil is a linear unit of length, equal to one-thousandth of an inch. Therefore, the circular-mil area increases as the square of the diameter. As illustrated in Fig. 11-3, doubling the diameter quadruples the area. Circular mils are convenient for round wire because the cross section is specified without using the formula πr^2 or $\pi d^2/4$ for the area of a circle.

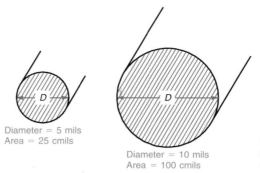

Diameter = 5 mils
Area = 25 cmils

Diameter = 10 mils
Area = 100 cmils

FIG. 11-3 Cross-sectional area for round wire. Doubling the diameter increases the circular area by four times.

TEST-POINT QUESTION 11-2

Answers at end of chapter.
a. How much is R for 1 ft of No. 22 wire?
b. What is the cross-sectional area in circular mils for wire with a diameter of 0.025 in.?
c. What is the wire gage size in Fig. 11-1?

11-3 TYPES OF WIRE CONDUCTORS

Most wire conductors are copper, although aluminum and silver are used sometimes. The copper may be tinned with a thin coating of solder, which gives it a silvery appearance. Tinned wire is easier to solder for connections. The wire can be solid or stranded, as shown in Fig. 11-4a and b.

Stranded wire is flexible, easier to handle and less likely to develop an open break. Sizes for stranded wire are equivalent to the sum of the areas for the individual strands. For instance, two strands of No. 30 wire correspond to solid No. 27 wire.

Very thin wire, such as No. 30, often has an insulating coating of enamel or shellac. It may look like copper, but the coating must be scraped off the ends to make a good connection. This type of wire is used for small coils.

Heavier wires generally are in an insulating sleeve, which may be rubber or one of many plastic materials. General-purpose wire for connecting electronic components is generally plastic-coated hookup wire of No. 20 gage. Hookup wire that is bare should be enclosed in a hollow insulating sleeve called *spaghetti*.

The braided conductor in Fig. 11-4c is used for very low resistance. It is wide for low R and thin for flexibility, and the braiding provides many strands. A common application is a grounding connection, which must have very low R.

WIRE CABLE Two or more conductors in a common covering form a cable. Each wire is insulated from the others. Cables often include two, three, ten, or many more pairs of conductors, usually color-coded to help identify the conductors at both ends of a cable.

The ribbon cable in Fig. 11-5 has multiple conductors but not in pairs. This cable is used for multiple connections to a computer and associated equipment.

(a) (b) (c)

(d) (e)

FIG. 11-4   Types of wire conductors. (a) Solid wire. (b) Stranded wire. (c) Braided wire for very low R. (d) Coaxial cable. Note braided wire for shielding the inner conductor. (e) Twin-lead cable.

FIG. 11-5   Ribbon cable with multiple conductors.

TRANSMISSION LINES Constant spacing between two conductors through the entire length provides a transmission line. Common examples are the coaxial cable in Fig. 11-4d and the twin lead in Fig 11-4e.

Coaxial cable with an outside diameter of ¼ in. is generally used for the signals in cable television. In construction, there is an inner solid wire, insulated from metallic braid that serves as the other conductor. The entire assembly is covered by an outer plastic jacket. In operation, the inner conductor has the desired signal voltage with respect to ground, while the metallic braid is connected to ground to shield the inner conductor against interference. Coaxial cable, therefore, is a shielded type of transmission line.

With twin-lead wire, two conductors are imbedded in plastic to provide constant spacing. This type of line is commonly used in television for connecting the antenna to the receiver. In this application, the spacing is ⅝ in. between wires of No. 20 gage size, approximately. This line is not shielded.

CHARACTERISTIC IMPEDANCE

The coaxial cable and twin-lead transmission lines are so common in television that they can be useful to consider an important characteristic that is usually reserved for more advanced ac theory. Because of the constant spacing, such line has a constant value of impedance between the two conductors. The term *impedance,* with the symbol Z, specifies an opposition to current that can include resistance, inductance, and capacitance.

Any transmission line has a constant value of impedance across the two conductors that is characteristic of the line, depending on the spacing, size of the conductors, and the insulation between the conductors. This value is specified as the *characteristic impedance,* with the symbol Z_0, for that type of transmission line. The Z_0 is constant for any length because it depends on the square root of the ratio for the inductance in the line to the capacitance between the conductors.

For ¼-in. coaxial cable, its characteristic impedance is approximately 75 Ω. This 75-Ω line is used in cable distribution systems for television. For twin-lead wire with ⅜-in. spacing between the two conductors in a plastic ribbon, the characteristic impedance is 300 Ω. This 300-Ω line is generally used for connecting an antenna to the receiver, either TV or FM radio.

The characteristic impedance is the same for any length of line because Z_0 depends mainly on the spacing between conductors and not at all on how long they are.

It is important to realize that Z_0 is an ac value that cannot be measured with an ohmmeter. However, you can check the continuity of each length of conductor with an ohmmeter. The R should be practically zero ohms for the wire in the line. If there is a break in the wire, an ohmmeter reading of infinity will show the open circuit.

TEST-POINT QUESTION 11-3

Answers at end of chapter.

Answer True or False.

a. The plastic coating on wire conductors has very high R.
b. Coaxial cable is a shielded transmission line.
c. The characteristic impedance of transmission lines cannot be measured with an ohmmeter.

11-4 CONNECTORS

Refer to Fig. 11-6 for different types. The spade lug in Fig. 11-6a is often used for screw-type terminals. In Fig. 11-6b, the alligator clip is convenient for a temporary connection. Alligator clips come in small and large sizes. The banana pins in Fig. 11-6c have spring-type sides that make a tight connection. In Fig. 11-6d, the terminal strip provides a block for multiple solder connections.

In Fig. 11-6e, the RCA-type plug is commonly used for shielded cables with audio equipment. The inner conductor of the coaxial cable is connected to the center pin of the plug and the cable braid to the shield. Both connections must be soldered.

The phone plug in Fig. 11-6f is still used in some applications, but in a smaller size. Note that the ring is insulated from the sleeve, to provide for two connections. There may be a separate tip, ring, and sleeve for three connections. The sleeve is usually the ground side.

The plug in Fig. 11-6g is called an *F connector*. It is universally used in cable television because of its convenience. The center conductor of the coaxial cable serves as the center pin of the plug, so that no soldering is needed. Also, the shield on the plug is press-fit onto the braid of the cable, underneath the plastic jacket.

All these are male-type plugs, with pins that fit the corresponding female-type socket. The connector that has the pins is male. However, the plug can be either male or female. The connector for power input usually is a female plug mating with a male socket on the equipment.

The multiple connector in Fig. 11-6h is shown with a ribbon cable. It has eight wires in a flat, plastic ribbon. This plug is a female type that mates with a male socket. The ribbon cable often has more than eight wires, as shown in Fig. 11-5a.

FIG. 11-6   Common types of connectors for wire conductors. (*a*) Spade lug. (*b*) Alligator clips. (*c*) Double banana-pin plug. (*d*) Terminal strip. (*e*) RCA-type plug for audio cables. (*f*) Phone plug. (*g*) F-type plug for cable TV. (*h*) Multiple-pin connector plug. (*i*) Spring-loaded metal hook as grabber for temporary connection in testing circuits.

The RS-232 plug is a standard connector for computer equipment. It has 25 pins. Each is assigned one function for data interface connections, as specified in standards of the Electronic Industries Association (EIA). The male pin plug is normally installed on the computer, the female connector being used for auxiliary equipment.

TEST-POINT QUESTION 11-4

Answers at end of chapter.

Answer True or False.
a. Cable television uses 75-Ω coaxial line.
b. The F-type connector is used with coaxial cable.
c. The RS-232 connector takes two pairs of 300-Ω twin-lead line.

11-5 PRINTED WIRING

Most electronic circuits are mounted on a plastic insulating board with printed wiring, as shown in Fig. 11-7. This is a printed-circuit (PC) or printed-wiring (PW) board. One side has the components, such as resistors, capacitors, coils, transistors, diodes, and integrated-circuit (IC) units. The other side has the conducting paths printed with silver or copper on the board, instead of using wires. On a double-sided board, the component side also has printed wiring. Sockets, small metal eyelets, or just holes in the board are used to connect the components to the wiring.

With a bright light on one side, you can see through to the opposite side to trace the connections. However, the circuit is usually drawn on the PC board.

It is important not to use too much heat in soldering or desoldering. Otherwise the printed wiring can be lifted off the board. Use a small iron of about 25

FIG. 11-7   Printed wiring board. (*a*) Component side with resistors, capacitors, and transistors. (*b*) Side with printed wiring for the circuit.

(*a*)   (*b*)

to 35 W rating. When soldering semiconductor diodes and transistors, hold the lead with pliers or connect an alligator clip as a heat sink to conduct heat away from the semiconductor junction.

For desoldering, use a solder-sucker tool, with a soldering iron, to clean each terminal. Another method is to use wire braid. Put the braid on the joint and heat it until the solder runs up into the braid. The terminal must be clean enough to lift out the component easily without damaging the PC board.

A small crack in the printed wiring acts like an open circuit preventing current flow. Cracks can be repaired by soldering a short length of bare wire over the open circuit. If a larger section of printed wiring is open, or if the board is cracked, you can bridge the open circuit with a length of hookup wire soldered at two convenient end terminals of the printed wiring.

TEST-POINT QUESTION 11-5

Answers at end of chapter.
a. Which is the best size iron to use to solder on a PC board, 25, 100, or 150 W?
b. How much is the resistance of a printed-wire conductor with a crack in the middle?

11-6 SWITCHES

A switch is a component which allows us to control whether the current is ON or OFF in a circuit. A closed switch has practically zero resistance, whereas an open switch has nearly infinite resistance. Figure 11-8 shows a switch in series with a voltage source and a light bulb. With the switch closed, as in Fig. 11-8a, a complete path for current is provided and the light is ON. Since the switch has a very low resistance when it is closed, all of the source voltage is across the load, with 0 V across the closed contacts of the switch. With the switch open, as in Fig. 11-8b, the path for current is interrupted and the bulb does not light. Since the switch has a very high resistance when it is open, all of the source voltage is across the open switch contacts, with 0 V across the load.

(a)   (b)

FIG. 11-8   Series switch used to open or close a circuit. (*a*) With the switch closed, current flows to light the bulb. The voltage drop across the closed switch is 0 V. (*b*) With the switch open, the light is OFF. The voltage drop across the open switch is 12 V.

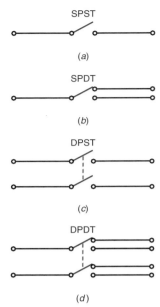

FIG. 11-9 Switches. (*a*) Single-pole, single-throw (SPST). (*b*) Single-pole, double-throw (SPDT). (*c*) Double-pole, single-throw (DPST). (*d*) Double-pole, double-throw (DPDT).

SWITCH RATINGS All switches have a current rating and a voltage rating. The current rating corresponds to the maximum allowable current the switch can carry when it is closed. The current rating is based on the physical size of the switch contacts as well as the type of metal used for the contacts. Many switches have gold- or silver-plated contacts to ensure a very low resistance when closed.

The voltage rating of a switch corresponds to the maximum voltage that can safely be applied across the open contacts without internal arcing. The voltage rating does not apply when the switch is closed, since the voltage drop across the closed switch contacts is practically zero.

SWITCH DEFINITIONS Toggle switches are usually described as having a certain number of poles and throws. For example, the switch in Fig. 11-8 is described as a *single-pole, single-throw* (SPST) switch. Other popular switch types include the *single-pole, double-throw* (SPDT), *double-pole, single-throw* (DPST), and *double-pole, double-throw* (DPDT). The schematic symbols for each type are shown in Fig. 11-9. Notice that the SPST switch has two connecting terminals, whereas the SPDT has three, the DPST has four, and the DPDT has six.

The term *pole* can be defined as the number of completely isolated circuits that can be controlled by the switch. The term *throw* can be defined as the number of closed contact positions that exist per pole. The SPST switch in Fig. 11-8 can only control the current in one circuit and there is only one closed contact position, hence the name single-pole, single-throw.

Figure 11-10 shows a variety of different switch applications. In Fig. 11-10*a*, a SPDT switch is being used to switch a 12-V dc source between one of two different loads. In Fig. 11-10*b*, a DPST switch is being used to control two completely separate circuits simultaneously. In Fig. 11-10*c*, a DPDT switch is being used to reverse the polarity of voltage across the terminals of a dc motor. (Reversing the polarity reverses the direction of the motor.) It is important to note that the dashed lines shown between the poles in Figs. 11-10*b* and 11-10*c* indicate that both sets of contacts within the switch are opened and closed simultaneously.

SWITCH TYPES Figure 11-11 shows a variety of different toggle switches. Although the toggle switch is a very popular type of switch, several other types are found in electronic equipment. Additional types include push-button switches, rocker switches, slide switches, rotary switches, and DIP switches.

Push-button switches are often spring-loaded switches that are either normally open (NO) or normally closed (NC). Figure 11-12 shows the schematic symbols for both types. For the normally open switch in Fig. 11-12*a*, the switch contacts remain open until the push button is depressed. When the push button is depressed, the switch closes, allowing current to pass. The normally closed switch in Fig. 11-12*b* operates just the opposite of the normally open switch in Fig. 11-12*a*. When the push button is depressed, the switch contacts open to interrupt current in the circuit. A typical push-button switch is shown in Fig. 11-13.

Figure 11-14 shows a DIP (dual-inline package) switch. Its construction consists of eight miniature rocker switches, where each switch can be set separately. A DIP switch has pin connections which fit into a standard IC socket.

Figure 11-15 shows another type of switch known as a rotary switch. As shown, its construction consists of three wafers or decks mounted on a common shaft.

(a)

(b)

(c)

FIG. 11-10 Switch applications. (*a*) SPDT switch used to switch a 12-V source between one of two different loads. (*b*) DPST switch controlling two completely isolated circuits simultaneously. (*c*) DPDT switch used to reverse the polarity of voltage across a dc motor.

TEST-POINT QUESTION 11-6

Answers at end of chapter.

a. How much is the IR voltage drop across a closed switch?
b. How many connections are there on an SPDT switch?
c. What is the resistance across the contacts of an open switch?
d. An SPST switch is rated at 10 A 250 V. Should the switch be used to turn a 120-V 1500-W heater ON and OFF?

FIG. 11-11 A variety of toggle switches.

11-7 FUSES

Many circuits have a fuse in series as a protection against an overload resulting from a short circuit. Excessive current melts the fuse element, blowing the fuse and opening the series circuit. The purpose is to let the fuse blow before the components are damaged. The blown fuse can easily be replaced by a new one, after the overload has been eliminated. A glass-cartridge fuse with holders is shown in Fig. 11-16. This is a type 3AG fuse, with a diameter of ¼ in. and length of 1¼ in. AG is an abbreviation of "automobile glass," since that was one of the first applications of fuses in a glass holder to make the wire link visible.

The metal fuse element may be made of aluminum, tin-coated copper, or nickel. Fuses are available with current ratings from ½₀₀ A to hundreds of amperes. The thinner the wire element in the fuse, the smaller its current rating. For example, a 2-in. length of No. 28 wire can serve as a 2-A fuse. As typical applications, the rating for plug fuses in each branch of house wiring is often 15 A; the high-voltage circuit in a television receiver is usually protected by a glass-

Normally open (NO)   Normally closed (NC)

(a)   (b)

FIG. 11-12 Push-button switch schematic symbols. (*a*) Normally open (NO) push-button switch. (*b*) Normally closed (NC) push-button switch.

where R is the total resistance, l the length, A the cross-sectional area, and ρ the specific resistance or *resistivity* of the conductor. The factor ρ then enables the resistance of different materials to be compared according to their nature without regard to different lengths or areas. Higher values of ρ mean more resistance. Note that ρ is the Greek letter *rho,* corresponding to r.

SPECIFIC RESISTANCE   Table 11-2 lists resistance values for different metals having the standard wire size of a 1-ft length with a cross-sectional area of 1 cmil. This rating is the *specific resistance* of the metal, in circular-mil ohms per foot. Since silver, copper, gold, and aluminum are the best conductors, they have the lowest values of specific resistance. Tungsten and iron have a much higher resistance.

Example

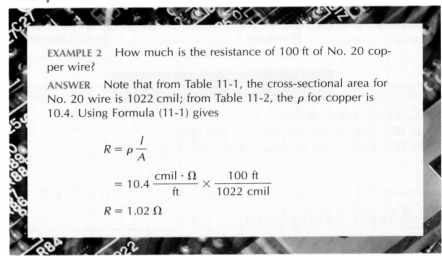

EXAMPLE 2   How much is the resistance of 100 ft of No. 20 copper wire?

ANSWER   Note that from Table 11-1, the cross-sectional area for No. 20 wire is 1022 cmil; from Table 11-2, the ρ for copper is 10.4. Using Formula (11-1) gives

$$R = \rho \frac{l}{A}$$

$$= 10.4 \frac{\text{cmil} \cdot \Omega}{\text{ft}} \times \frac{100 \text{ ft}}{1022 \text{ cmil}}$$

$$R = 1.02 \ \Omega$$

TABLE 11-2   PROPERTIES OF CONDUCTING MATERIALS*

MATERIAL	DESCRIPTION AND SYMBOL	SPECIFIC RESISTANCE (ρ) AT 20°C, cmil · Ω/ft	TEMPERATURE COEFFICIENT PER °C, α	MELTING POINT, °C
Aluminum	Element (Al)	17	0.004	660
Carbon	Element (C)	†	−0.0003	3000
Constantan	Alloy, 55% Cu, 45% Ni	295	0 (average)	1210
Copper	Element (Cu)	10.4	0.004	1083
Gold	Element (Au)	14	0.004	1063
Iron	Element (Fe)	58	0.006	1535
Manganin	Alloy, 84% Cu, 12% Mn, 4% Ni	270	0 (average)	910
Nichrome	Alloy 65% Ni, 23% Fe, 12% Cr	676	0.0002	1350
Nickel	Element (Ni)	52	0.005	1452
Silver	Element (Ag)	9.8	0.004	961
Steel	Alloy, 99.5% Fe, 0.5% C	100	0.003	1480
Tungsten	Element (W)	33.8	0.005	3370

*Listings approximate only, since precise values depend on exact composition of material.
†Carbon has about 2500 to 7500 times the resistance of copper. Graphite is a form of carbon.

All the units cancel except the ohms for R. Note that 1.02 Ω for 100 ft is approximately $\frac{1}{10}$ the resistance of 10.35 Ω for 1000 ft of No. 20 copper wire listed in Table 11-1, showing that the resistance is proportional to length.

Example

EXAMPLE 3   How much is the resistance of a 100-ft length of No. 23 copper wire?

ANSWER $R = \rho \dfrac{l}{A}$

$$= 10.4 \frac{\text{cmil} \cdot \Omega}{\text{ft}} \times \frac{100 \text{ ft}}{509.5 \text{ cmil}}$$

$$R = 2.04 \ \Omega$$

Note that a wire three gage sizes higher has half the circular area and double the resistance for the same wire length.

UNITS OF OHM-CENTIMETERS FOR ρ   Except for wire conductors, specific resistances are usually compared for the standard size of a 1-cm cube. Then ρ is specified in $\Omega \cdot$ cm for the unit cross-sectional area of 1 cm^2.

As an example, pure germanium has $\rho = 55 \ \Omega \cdot$ cm, as listed in Table 11-3. This value means that R is 55 Ω for a cube with a cross-sectional area of 1 cm^2 and length of 1 cm.

For other sizes, use Formula (11-1) with l in cm and A in cm^2. Then all the units of size cancel to give R in ohms.

Example

EXAMPLE 4   How much is the resistance for a slab of germanium 0.2 cm long with a cross-sectional area of 1 cm^2?

ANSWER $R = \rho \dfrac{l}{A}$

$$= 55 \ \Omega \cdot \text{cm} \times \frac{0.2 \text{ cm}}{1 \text{ cm}^2}$$

$$R = 11 \ \Omega$$

The same size slab of silicon would have R of 11,000 Ω. Note from Table 11-3 that ρ is 1000 times more for silicon than for germanium.

TABLE 11-3 COMPARISON OF RESISTIVITIES

MATERIAL	ρ, $\Omega \cdot$ cm, AT 25°C	DESCRIPTION
Silver	1.6×10^{-6}	Conductor
Germanium	55	Semiconductor
Silicon	55,000	Semiconductor
Mica	2×10^{12}	Insulator

TYPES OF RESISTANCE WIRE   For applications in heating elements, such as a toaster, an incandescent light bulb, or a heater, it is necessary to use wire that has more resistance than good conductors like silver, copper, or aluminum. Higher resistance is preferable so that the required amount of I^2R power dissipated as heat in the wire can be obtained without excessive current. Typical materials for resistance wire are the elements tungsten, nickel, or iron and alloys* such as manganin, Nichrome, and constantan. These types are generally called resistance wire because R is greater than for copper wire, for the same length.

TEST-POINT QUESTION 11-8

Answers at end of chapter.
a. Does Nichrome wire have less or more resistance than copper wire?
b. For 100 ft of No. 14 copper wire, R is 0.26 Ω. How much is R for 1000 ft?

11-9 TEMPERATURE COEFFICIENT OF RESISTANCE

This factor with the symbol alpha (α) states how much the resistance changes for a change in temperature. A positive value for α means R increases with temperature; with a negative α, R decreases; zero for α means R is constant. Some typical values of α, for metals and for carbon, are listed in Table 11-2 in the fourth column.

POSITIVE α   All metals in their pure form, such as copper and tungsten, have a positive temperature coefficient. The α for tungsten, for example, is 0.005. Although α is not exactly constant, an increase in wire resistance caused by a rise in temperature can be calculated approximately from the formula

$$R_t = R_0 + R_0(\alpha \Delta t) \tag{11-2}$$

---

*An *alloy* is a fusion of elements, without chemical action between them. Metals are commonly alloyed to alter their physical characteristics.

where R_0 is the resistance at 20°C, R_t is the higher resistance at the higher temperature, and Δt is the temperature rise above 20°C.

Example

EXAMPLE 5   A tungsten wire has a 14-Ω R at 20°C. Calculate its resistance at 120°C.

ANSWER   The temperature rise Δt here is 100°C; α is 0.005. Substituting in Formula (11-2),

$$R_t = 14 + 14(0.005 \times 100)$$
$$= 14 + 7$$
$$R_t = 21\ \Omega$$

The added resistance of 7 Ω increases the wire resistance by 50 percent because of the 100°C rise in temperature.

In practical terms, a positive α means that heat increases R in wire conductors. Then I is reduced, with a specified applied voltage.

NEGATIVE α   Note that carbon has a negative temperature coefficient. In general, α is negative for all semiconductors, including germanium and silicon. Also, all electrolyte solutions, such as sulfuric acid and water, have a negative α.

A negative value of α means less resistance at higher temperatures. The resistance of semiconductor diodes and transistors, therefore, can be reduced appreciably when they become hot with normal load current.

ZERO α   This means R is constant with changes in temperature. The metal alloys constantan and manganin, for example, have the value of zero for α. They can be used for precision wire-wound resistors, which do not change resistance when the temperature increases.

HOT RESISTANCE   Because resistance wire is made of tungsten, Nichrome, iron, or nickel, there is usually a big difference in the amount of resistance the wire has when hot in normal operation and when cold without its normal load current. The reason is that the resistance increases with higher temperatures, since these materials have a positive temperature coefficient, as shown in Table 11-2.

As an example, the tungsten filament of a 100-W 120-V incandescent bulb has a current of 0.833 A when the bulb lights with normal brilliance at its rated power, since $I = P/V$. By Ohm's law, the hot resistance is V/I, or 120 V/0.833 A, which equals 144 Ω. If, however, the filament resistance is measured with an ohmmeter when the bulb is not lit, the cold resistance is only about 10 Ω.

ABOUT ELECTRONICS

British physicist Lord Kelvin (1824–1907) was born William Thomson. He became Lord Kelvin when he was knighted by Queen Victoria for his scientific achievements. Perhaps his best-known accomplishment is the development of the Kelvin temperature scale, which begins the measurement of temperature at absolute zero (the total absence of thermal energy). Kelvin also developed the Kelvin absolute electrometer and the Kelvin balance.

The Nichrome heater elements in appliances and the tungsten heaters in vacuum tubes also become several hundred degrees hotter in normal operation. In these cases, only the cold resistance can be measured with an ohmmeter. The hot resistance must be calculated from voltage and current measurements with the normal value of load current. As a practical rule, the cold resistance is generally about one-tenth the hot resistance. In troubleshooting, however, the problem is usually just to check if the heater element is open. Then it reads infinite ohms on the ohmmeter.

SUPERCONDUCTIVITY   The effect opposite to hot resistance is to cool a metal down to very low temperatures to reduce its resistance. Near absolute zero, 0 K or −273°C, some metals abruptly lose practically all their resistance. As an example, when cooled by liquid helium, the metal tin becomes superconductive at 3.7 K. Tremendous currents can be produced, resulting in very strong electromagnetic fields. Such work at very low temperatures, near absolute zero, is called *cryogenics*.

New types of ceramic materials have been developed and are stimulating great interest in superconductivity because they provide zero resistance at temperatures much above absolute zero. One type is a ceramic pellet, with a 1-in. diameter, that includes yttrium, barium, copper, and oxygen atoms. The superconductivity occurs at a temperature of 93 K, equal to −160°C. This value is still far below room temperature, but the cooling can be done with liquid nitrogen, which is much cheaper than liquid helium. As research continues, it is likely that new materials will be discovered that are superconductive at even higher temperatures.

TEST-POINT QUESTION 11-9

Answers at end of chapter.

Answer True or False.
a. Metal conductors have more R at higher temperatures.
b. Tungsten can be used for resistance wire.
c. A superconductive material has practically zero resistance.

11-10 ION CURRENT IN LIQUIDS AND GASES

We usually think of metal wire for a conductor, but there are other possibilities. Liquids such as salt water or dilute sulfuric acid can also allow the movement of electric charges. For gases, consider the neon glow lamp, where neon serves as a conductor.

The mechanism may be different for conduction in metal wire, liquids, or gases, but in any case the current is a motion of charges. Furthermore, either positive or negative charges can be the carriers that provide electric current. The amount of current is Q/T. For one coulomb of charge per second, the current is one ampere.

In solid materials like the metals, the atoms are not free to move among each other. Therefore, conduction of electricity must take place by the drift of free electrons. Each atom remains neutral, neither gaining nor losing charge, but the metals are good conductors because they have plenty of free electrons that can be forced to drift through the solid substance.

In liquids and gases, however, each atom is able to move freely among all the other atoms because the substance is not solid. As a result, the atoms can easily take on electrons or lose electrons, particularly the valence electrons in the outside shell. The result is an atom that is no longer electrically neutral. Adding one or more electrons produces a negative charge; the loss of one or more electrons results in a positive charge. The charged atoms are called *ions*. Such charged particles are commonly formed in liquids and gases.

Na atom

(a)

Na⁺ ion

(b)

FIG. 11-19   Formation of ions. (a) Normal sodium (Na) atom. (b) Positively charged ion indicated as Na^+, missing one free electron.

THE ION   An ion is an atom, or group of atoms, that has a net electric charge, either positive or negative, resulting from a loss or gain of electrons. In Fig. 11-19a, the sodium atom is neutral, with 11 positive charges in the nucleus balanced by 11 electrons in the outside shells. This atom has only 1 electron in the shell farthest from the nucleus. When the sodium is in a liquid solution, this 1 electron can easily leave the atom. The reason may be another atom close by that needs 1 electron in order to have a stable ring of 8 electrons in its outside shell. Notice that if the sodium atom loses 1 valence electron, the atom will still have an outside ring of 8 electrons, as shown in Fig. 11-19b. This sodium atom now is a positive ion, with a charge equal to 1 proton. An ion still has the characteristics of the element because the nucleus is not changed.

CURRENT OF IONS   Just as in electron flow, opposite ion charges are attracted to each other, while like charges repel. The resultant motion of ions provides electric current. In liquids and gases, therefore, conduction of electricity results mainly from the movement of ions. This motion of ion charges is called *ionization current*. Since an ion includes the nucleus of the atom, the ion charge is much heavier than an electron charge and moves with less velocity. We can say that ion charges are less mobile than electron charges.

The direction of ionization current can be the same as electron flow or the opposite. When negative ions move, they are attracted to the positive terminal of an applied voltage, in the same direction as electron flow. However, when positive ions move, this ionization current is in the opposite direction, toward the negative terminal of an applied voltage.

For either direction, though, the amount of ionization current is determined by the rate at which the charge moves. If 3 C of positive ion charges move past a given point per second, the current is 3 A, the same as 3 C of negative ions or 3 C of electron charges.

IONIZATION IN LIQUIDS   Ions are usually formed in liquids when salts or acids are dissolved in water. Salt water is a good conductor because of ionization, but pure distilled water is an insulator. In addition, metals immersed in acids or alkaline solutions produce ionization. Liquids that are good conductors because of ionization are called *electrolytes*. In general, electrolytes have a negative value of α, as more ionization at higher temperatures lowers the resistance.

IONIZATION IN GASES   Gases have a minimum striking or ionization potential, which is the lowest applied voltage that will ionize the gas. Before ionization the gas is an insulator, but the ionization current makes the ionized gas a

DID YOU KNOW?

A ring of superconducting material will circulate a current forever, even after the source is removed. For example, high-field magnets using superconducting coils (cooled by helium) maintain themselves without huge amounts of electricity.

low resistance. An ionized gas usually glows. Argon, for instance, emits blue light when the gas is ionized. Ionized neon gas glows red. The amount of voltage needed to reach the striking potential varies with different gases and depends on the gas pressure. For example, a neon glow lamp for use as a night light ionizes at approximately 70 V.

IONIC BONDS   The sodium ion in Fig. 11-20 has a charge of $+1$ because it is missing 1 electron. If such positive ions are placed near negative ions with a charge of -1, there will be an electrical attraction to form an ionic bond.

A common example is the combination of sodium (Na) ions and chlorine (Cl) ions to form table salt (NaCl), as shown in Fig. 11-20. Notice that the 1 outer electron of the Na atom can fit into the 7-electron shell of the Cl atom. When these two elements are combined, the Na atom gives up 1 electron to form a positive ion, with a stable L shell having 8 electrons; also, the Cl atom adds this 1 electron to form a negative ion, with a stable M shell having 8 electrons. The two opposite types of ions are bound in NaCl because of the strong attractive force between opposite charges close together.

The ions in NaCl can separate in water to make salt water a conductor of electricity, while pure water is not. When current flows in salt water, then, the moving charges must be ions, as another example of ionization current.

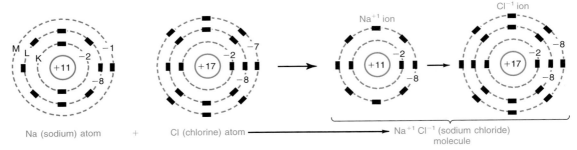

FIG. 11-20   Ionic bond between atoms of sodium (Na) and chlorine (Cl) to form a molecule of sodium chloride (NaCl).

TEST-POINT QUESTION 11-10

Answers at end of chapter.
a. How much is I for 2 C/s of positive ion charges?
b. Which have the greatest mobility, positive ions, negative ions, or electrons?
c. True or False? A dielectric material is a good conductor of electricity.

11-11 ELECTRONS AND HOLE CHARGES IN SEMICONDUCTORS

The semiconductor materials like germanium and silicon are in a class by themselves as conductors, because the charge carriers for current flow are neither ions nor free valence electrons. With a valence of ±4 for these elements, the tendency to gain or lose electrons to form a stable 8 shell is the same either way. As a result, these elements tend to share their outer electrons in pairs of atoms.

An example is illustrated in Fig. 11-21, for two silicon (Si) atoms, each sharing its 4 valence electrons with the other atom to form one Si_2 molecule. This type of combination of atoms sharing their outer electrons to form a stable molecule is called a *covalent bond*.

FIG. 11-21 Covalent bond between silicon (Si) atoms.

The covalent-bond structure in germanium and silicon is the basis for their use in transistors. This is because, although the covalent-bond structure is electrically neutral, it permits charges to be added by *doping* the semiconductor with a small amount of impurity atoms.

As a specific example, silicon, with a valence of 4, is combined with phosphorus, with a valence of 5. Then the doped silicon has covalent bonds with an excess of 1 electron for each impurity atom of phosphorus. The result is a negative, or N-type, semiconductor.

For the opposite case, silicon can be doped with aluminum, which has a valence of 3. Then covalent bonds formed with the impurity atoms have 7 outer electrons, instead of the 8 with a pair of silicon atoms.

The 1 missing electron for each covalent bond with an impurity atom corresponds to a positive charge called a *hole*. The amount of charge for each hole is 0.16×10^{-18} C, the same as for an electron, but of opposite polarity. This type of doping results in a P-type semiconductor with positive hole charges.

For either N- or P-type semiconductors the charges can be made to move by an applied voltage that produces current. When electrons move, the current direction is the same as for electron flow. When the positive hole charges move, the direction is opposite from electron current. For either electrons or hole charges, when 1 C moves past a given point in 1 s, the amount of current is 1 A. However, electrons have greater mobility than hole charges.

For semiconductor diodes, the P and N types are combined in a PN junction. It should be noted that this junction is just an electrical boundary between opposite types, but without any physical separation. In a PNP transistor, the N type is between two P types. The opposite case, a P type between two N types, results in the NPN transistor. The NPN and PNP types are junction transistors, with two junctions. More details of semiconductors in general, as important solid-state components, and transistors in particular, as commonly used for amplifier circuits, are given in Chaps. 28 and 29, which explain the operation of semiconductor diodes and transistors. Solid-state integrated circuits are discussed in Chap. 32.

Answers at end of chapter.
a. What is the polarity of the hole charges in P-type doped semiconductors?
b. What is the electron valence of silicon and germanium?
c. What are the charge carriers in N-type semiconductors?

11-12 INSULATORS

DID YOU KNOW?

High-temperature super-conductors require nitrogen; low-temperature ones require hydrogen. More research is now focused on superconductors that use nitrogen, because it is cheaper, easier to handle, and useful in refrigeration.

Substances that have very high resistance, of the order of many megohms, are classed as insulators. With such high resistance, an insulator cannot conduct appreciable current when voltage is applied. As a result, insulators can have either of two functions. One is to isolate conductors to eliminate conduction between them. The other is to store an electric charge when voltage is applied.

An insulator maintains its charge because electrons cannot flow to neutralize the charge. The insulators are commonly called *dielectric materials,* meaning that they can store a charge.

Among the best insulators, or dielectrics, are air, vacuum, rubber, wax, shellac, glass, mica, porcelain, oil, dry paper, textile fibers, and plastics such as Bakelite, Formica, and polystyrene. Pure water is a good insulator, but salt water is not. Moist earth is a fairly good conductor, while dry, sandy earth is an insulator.

For any insulator, a high enough voltage can be applied to break down the internal structure of the material, forcing the dielectric to conduct. This dielectric breakdown is usually the result of an arc, which ruptures the physical structure of the material, making it useless as an insulator. Table 11-4 compares several insulators in terms of dielectric strength, which is the voltage breakdown rating. The higher the dielectric strength, the better the insulator, since it is less likely to break down with a high value of applied voltage. The breakdown voltages in Table 11-4 are approximate values for the standard thickness of 1 mil, or 0.001 in. More thickness allows a higher breakdown-voltage rating. Note that the value of 20 V/mil for air or vacuum is the same as 20 kV/in.

TABLE 11-4	VOLTAGE BREAKDOWN OF INSULATORS		
MATERIAL	DIELECTRIC STRENGTH, V/MIL	MATERIAL	DIELECTRIC STRENGTH, V/MIL
Air or vacuum	20	Paraffin wax	200–300
Bakelite	300–550	Phenol, molded	300–700
Fiber	150–180	Polystyrene	500–760
Glass	335–2000	Porcelain	40–150
Mica	600–1500	Rubber, hard	450
Paper	1250	Shellac	900
Paraffin oil	380		

INSULATOR DISCHARGE CURRENT An insulator in contact with a voltage source stores charge, producing a potential on the insulator. The charge tends to remain on the insulator, but it can be discharged by one of the following methods:

1. Conduction through a conducting path. For instance, a wire across the charged insulator provides a discharge path. Then the discharged dielectric has no potential.
2. Brush discharge. As an example, high voltage on a sharp pointed wire can discharge through the surrounding atmosphere by ionization of the air molecules. This may be visible in the dark as a bluish or reddish glow, called the *corona effect.*
3. Spark discharge. This is a result of breakdown in the insulator because of a high potential difference that ruptures the dielectric. The current that flows across the insulator at the instant of breakdown causes the spark.

Corona is undesirable, as it reduces the potential by brush discharge into the surrounding air. In addition, the corona often indicates the beginning of a spark discharge. A potential of the order of kilovolts is usually necessary for corona, as the breakdown voltage for air is approximately 20 kV/in. To reduce the corona effect, conductors that have high voltage should be smooth, rounded, and thick. This equalizes the potential difference from all points on the conductor to the surrounding air. Any sharp point can have a more intense field, making it more susceptible to corona and eventual spark discharge.

TEST-POINT QUESTION 11-12

Answers at end of chapter.
a. Which has a higher voltage breakdown rating, air or mica?
b. Can 30 kV arc across an air gap of 1 in.?

11-13 TROUBLESHOOTING HINTS FOR WIRES AND CONNECTORS

For all types of electronic equipment, a common problem is an open circuit in the wire conductors, the connectors, and the switch contacts.

For conductors, both wires and printed wiring, you can check the continuity with an ohmmeter. A good conductor reads 0 Ω for continuity. An open reads infinite ohms.

Connectors can also be checked for continuity between the wire and the connector itself. Also, the connector may be tarnished, oxide coated, or rusted. Then it must be cleaned with either fine sandpaper or emery cloth. Sometimes, it helps just to pull out the plug and reinsert it to make sure of tight connections.

With a plug connector for cable, make sure the wires have continuity to the plug. Except for the F-type connector, most plugs require careful soldering to the center pin.

A switch with dirty or pitted contacts can produce intermittent operation. In most cases the switch cannot be disassembled for cleaning. Therefore, the switch must be replaced with a new one.

TEST-POINT QUESTION 11-13

Answers at end of chapter.

Answer True or False.
a. Printed wiring cannot be checked for continuity with an ohmmeter.
b. A tarnished or rusty connection will have a higher than normal resistance.

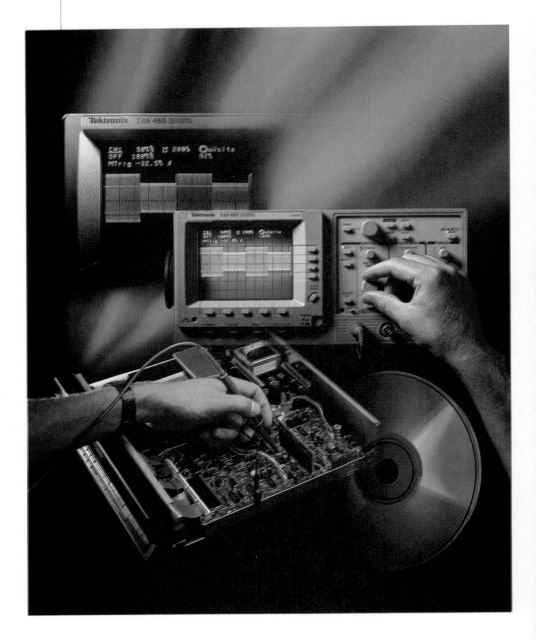

11   SUMMARY AND REVIEW

- A conductor has very low resistance. All the metals are good conductors, the best being silver, copper, and aluminum. Copper is generally used for wire conductors.
- The sizes for copper wire are specified by the American Wire Gage. Higher gage numbers mean thinner wire. Typical sizes are No. 22 gage hookup wire for electronic circuits and No. 12 and No. 14 for house wiring.
- The cross-sectional area of round wire is measured in circular mils. One mil is 0.001 in. The area in circular mils equals the diameter in mils squared.
- The resistance R of a conductor can be found using the formula $R = \rho(l/A)$. The factor ρ is specific resistance, l is length of the conductor, and A is the cross-sectional area of the conductor. Wire resistance increases directly with length l, but decreases inversely with the cross-sectional area A.
- A switch inserted in one side of a circuit opens the entire series circuit. When open, the switch has the applied voltage across it.
- A fuse protects the circuit components against overload, as excessive current melts the fuse element to open the entire series circuit. A good fuse has very low resistance and practically zero voltage across it.
- Ionization in liquids and gases produces atoms that are not electrically neutral. These are ions. Negative ions have an excess of electrons; positive ions have a deficiency of electrons. In liquids and gases, electric current is a result of movement of the ions.
- In the semiconductors, such as germanium and silicon, the charge carriers are electrons in N type and positive hole charges in P type. One hole charge is 0.16×10^{-18} C, the same as one electron, but with positive polarity.
- The resistance of pure metals increases with temperature. For semiconductors and liquid electrolytes, the resistance decreases at higher temperatures.
- An insulator has very high resistance. Common insulating materials are air, vacuum, rubber, paper, glass, porcelain, shellac, and plastics. Insulators are also called dielectrics.
- Superconductors have practically no resistance.
- A common circuit trouble is an open in wire conductors, dirty contacts in switches, and dirt, oxides, and corrosions on connectors and terminals.

Choose (*a*), (*b*), (*c*), or (*d*).

1. A 10-ft length of copper-wire conductor of No. 20 gage has a total resistance of (*a*) less than 1 Ω; (*b*) 5 Ω; (*c*) 10.4 Ω; (*d*) approximately 1 MΩ.
2. A copper-wire conductor with 0.2 in. diameter has an area of (*a*) 200 cmil; (*b*) 400 cmil; (*c*) 20,000 cmil; (*d*) 40,000 cmil.
3. If a wire conductor of 0.1 Ω resistance is doubled in length, its resistance becomes (*a*) 0.01 Ω; (*b*) 0.02 Ω; (*c*) 0.05 Ω; (*d*) 0.2 Ω.
4. If two similar wire conductors are connected in parallel, their total resistance is (*a*) double the resistance of one wire; (*b*) one-half the resistance of one wire; (*c*) the same as the resistance of one wire; (*d*) two-thirds the resistance of one wire.
5. The hot resistance of the tungsten filament in a bulb is higher than its cold resistance because the filament's temperature coefficient is (*a*) negative; (*b*) positive; (*c*) zero; (*d*) about 10 Ω per degree.
6. A closed switch has a resistance of (*a*) zero; (*b*) infinity; (*c*) about 100 Ω at room temperature; (*d*) at least 1000 Ω.
7. An open fuse has a resistance of (*a*) zero; (*b*) infinity; (*c*) about 100 Ω at room temperature; (*d*) at least 1000 Ω.
8. Insulating materials have the function of (*a*) conducting very large currents; (*b*) preventing an open circuit between the voltage source and the load; (*c*) preventing a short circuit between conducting wires; (*d*) storing very high currents.
9. An ion is (*a*) a free electron; (*b*) a proton; (*c*) an atom with unbalanced charges; (*d*) a nucleus without protons.
10. Ionization current in liquids and gases results from a flow of (*a*) free electrons; (*b*) protons; (*c*) positive or negative ions; (*d*) ions that are lighter in weight than electrons.

QUESTIONS

1. Name three good metal conductors in order of resistance. Describe at least one application.
2. Name four insulators. Give one application.
3. Name two semiconductors. Give one application.
4. Name two types of resistance wire. Give one application.
5. What is meant by the dielectric strength of an insulator?
6. Why does ionization occur more readily in liquids and gases, compared with the solid metals? Give an example of ionization current.

7. Define the following: ion, ionic bond, covalent bond, molecule.
8. Draw a circuit with two bulbs, a battery, and an SPDT switch that determines which bulb lights.
9. Why is it not possible to measure the hot resistance of a filament with an ohmmeter?
10. Give one way in which negative ion charges are similar to electron charges and one way in which they are different.
11. Define the following abbreviations for switches: SPST, SPDT, DPST, DPDT, NO, and NC.
12. Give two common circuit troubles with conductors and connector plugs.

PROBLEMS

ANSWERS TO ODD-NUMBERED PROBLEMS AT BACK OF BOOK.

1. A copper wire has a diameter of 0.032 in. (**a**) How much is its circular-mil area? (**b**) What is its AWG size? (**c**) How much is the resistance of a 100-ft length?
2. Draw the schematic diagram of a resistance in series with an open SPST switch and a 100-V source. (**a**) With the switch open, how much is the voltage across the resistance? Across the open switch? (**b**) With the switch closed, how much is the voltage across the switch and across the resistance? (**c**) Do the voltage drops around the series circuit add to equal the applied voltage in both cases?
3. Draw the schematic diagram of a fuse in series with the resistance of a 100-W 120-V bulb connected to a 120-V source. (**a**) What size fuse can be used? (**b**) How much is the voltage across the good fuse? (**c**) How much is the voltage across the fuse if it is open?
4. Compare the resistance of two conductors: 100 ft of No. 10 gage copper wire and 200 ft of No. 7 gage copper wire.
5. How much is the hot resistance of a 150-W 120-V bulb operating with normal load current?
6. How much is the resistance of a slab of silicon 0.1 cm long with a cross-sectional area of 1 cm^2?
7. A cable with two lengths of No. 10 copper wire is short-circuited at one end. The resistance reading at the open end is 10.35 Ω. What is the cable length in feet? (Temperature is 25°C.)
8. (**a**) How many hole charges are needed to equal 1 C? (**b**) How many electrons? (**c**) How many ions with a negative charge of 1 electron?
9. (**a**) If a copper wire has a resistance of 4 Ω at 25°C, how much is its resistance at 75°C? (**b**) If the wire is No. 10 gage, what is its length in feet?
10. A coil is wound with 1500 turns of No. 20 copper wire. If the average amount of wire in a turn is 4 in., how much is the total resistance of the coil? What will be its resistance if No. 30 wire is used instead? (Temperature is 25°C.)
11. Calculate the voltage drop across 1000 ft of No. 10 gage wire connected to a 3-A load.
12. What is the smallest size of copper wire that will limit the line drop to 5 V, with 120 V applied and a 6-A load? The total line length is 200 ft.

100 ft of No. 16 wire

120 V

R_L

$V_R = 95.4$ V

100 ft of No. 16 wire

FIG. 11-22   Circuit diagram for Probs. 13 and 14.

13. Refer to Fig. 11-22. Calculate the load current I for the IR drop of 24.6 V that reduces V_R to 95.4 V with the 120-V supply.

14. From Fig. 11-22, calculate the value of R_L.

15. An extension cord is made up of 26 strands of No. 28 gage copper wire for each of its two conductors. (**a**) What is the equivalent gage size of each conductor in solid wire (approximately)? (**b**) If the extension cord is 50 ft long, what is the total resistance of both conductors? (**c**) What is the resistance of each individual 50-ft strand of No. 28 gage wire?

16. Calculate the resistance of the following conductors: (**a**) 1000 ft of No. 14 gage copper wire; (**b**) 1000 ft of No. 14 gage aluminum wire; (**c**) 1000 ft of No. 14 gage steel wire.

17. A 100-ft pair of No. 12 gage copper wires connects a 15-A load to the 120-V power line. (**a**) What is the total length of No. 12 gage wire? (**b**) What is the resistance of the total length? (**c**) How much voltage is available at the load? (**d**) How much is the I^2R power loss in the conductors?

18. Calculate the resistance of 1000 ft of No. 23 gage aluminum wire. (**a**) What is the resistance if the length is doubled to 2000 ft? (**b**) What is the resistance if the length is cut in half to 500 ft? (**c**) What is the resistance of a 1000-ft length of No. 20 gage aluminum wire?

19. Draw the schematic symbol for a(n): (**a**) single-pole, triple-throw switch; (**b**) triple-pole, triple-throw switch.

20. A No. 16 gage copper wire has 20 Ω of resistance at 65°C. Calculate its length.

CRITICAL THINKING

1. Use two switches having the appropriate number of poles and throws to build a partial decade resistance box. The resistance is to be adjustable in 1-Ω and 10-Ω steps from 0 Ω to 99 Ω across two terminals identified as A and B. Draw the circuit showing all resistance values and switch connections.

2. Show how two SPDT switches can be wired to turn ON and OFF a light from two different locations. The voltage source is a 12-V battery.

11-1 **a.** 0.08 Ω
     b. 0.07 V
     c. 0.06 percent

11-2 **a.** 0.01646 Ω
     b. 625 cmil
     c. No. 16

11-3 **a.** T
     b. T
     c. T

11-4 **a.** T
     b. T
     c. F

11-5 **a.** 25 W
     b. infinite ohms

11-6 **a.** zero
     b. three
     c. infinite
     d. no

11-7 **a.** zero
     b. zero

11-8 **a.** more
     b. 2.6 Ω

11-9 **a.** T
     b. T
     c. T

11-10 **a.** $I = 2$ A
      b. electrons
      c. F

11-11 **a.** positive
      b. four
      c. electrons

11-12 **a.** mica
      b. yes

11-13 **a.** F
      b. T

CHAPTER 12

BATTERIES

A battery is a group of cells that generate energy from the internal chemical reaction. The cell itself consists of two different conducting materials as the electrodes that are immersed in an electrolyte. The chemical reaction between the electrodes and the electrolyte results in a separation of electric charges, in the form of ions and free electrons. Then the two electrodes have a difference of potential that provides voltage output from the cell.

The main types are the alkaline cell with an output of 1.5 V and the lead-sulfuric acid wet cell with 2.1 V for output. A common application for dry cells is the 9-V flat battery often used for transistor radios. It has six cells connected in series internally for an output of $6 \times 1.5 = 9$ V. Dry batteries are used for all types of portable electronic equipment, photographic equipment and toys.

The lead-sulfuric acid cell is the type almost always used for automobile batteries. Six cells are connected in series internally for 12-V as the nominal output.

The function of a battery is to provide a source of steady dc voltage of fixed polarity. Furthermore, the battery is a good example of a generator or energy source. The source supplies voltage for a circuit as the load to produce the desired load current. An important factor is the internal resistance r_i of the source, which affects the output voltage when a load is connected. In general, a low r_i means that the source can maintain a constant output voltage for different values of load current. For the opposite case, a high r_i makes the output voltage drop, but a constant value of load current can be maintained.

CHAPTER OBJECTIVES

Upon completion of this chapter, you should be able to:

- *Explain* the difference between a primary cell and a secondary cell.
- *Define* what is meant by the internal resistance of a cell.
- *List* several different types of voltaic cells.
- *Explain* how cells can be connected together to increase the voltage of a battery.
- *Explain* how cells can be connected together to increase the current capacity of a battery.
- *Explain* how cells can be arranged to increase both the voltage and the current ratings of a battery.
- *Explain* why the terminal voltage of a battery drops with more load current.
- *Understand* the difference between a voltage source and a current source.
- *Explain* the concept of maximum power transfer.

IMPORTANT TERMS IN THIS CHAPTER

alkaline cell	internal resistance	open-circuit voltage
ampere-hour capacity	lead-acid cell	primary cell
carbon-zinc cell	Leclanché cell	secondary cell
constant-current generator	lithium cell	solar cell
constant-voltage generator	matching the load	specific gravity
galvanic cell	mercury cell	storage cell
hydrometer	nickel-cadmium cell	

TOPICS COVERED IN THIS CHAPTER

A battery is a combination of cells. The chemical battery has always been important as a dc voltage source for the operation of radios and other electronic equipment. The reason is that a transistor amplifier needs dc operating voltages in order to conduct current. With current in the amplifier, the circuit can be used to amplify an ac signal. Originally, all radio receivers used batteries. Then rectifier power supplies were developed to convert the ac power-line voltage to dc output, eliminating the need for batteries. However, now batteries are used more than ever for all types of electronic portable equipment.

From the old days of radio, dry batteries are still called A, B, and C batteries, according to their original functions in vacuum-tube operation. The A battery was used to supply enough current to heat the filament for thermionic emission of electrons from a heated cathode. A typical rating is 4.5 V or 6 V with a load current of 150 mA or more. The C battery was used for a small negative dc bias voltage at the control grid, typically 1.5 V, with practically no current drain.

The A battery is seldom used any more, although a 6-V lantern battery has ratings like an A battery. However, the function of a B battery with medium voltage and current ratings is the same now as it always was. Transistors need a steady dc voltage for the collector electrode, which receives charges from the emitter through the base electrode. For an NPN transistor, positive voltage is needed at the collector or negative voltage at the emitter. With a PNP transistor, the polarities are reversed. The positive dc supply voltage is called B^+ or $+V_{cc}$. In a small transistor radio with a 9-V battery, as an example, the battery is the $+V_{cc}$ supply. The same requirements for dc supply voltage apply to integrated circuits, as the IC chip contains transistor amplifiers.

PRIMARY CELLS   This type cannot be recharged. After it has delivered its rated capacity, the primary cell must be discarded. The reason is that the internal chemical reaction cannot be restored. Figure 12-1 shows a variety of different dry cells and batteries, all of which are of the primary type. In Table 12-1 several different cells are listed by name. Each of the different cells is listed as being of either the primary or the secondary type. Notice the open circuit voltage for each of the cell types listed.

FIG. 12-1 Typical dry cells and batteries. These primary types cannot be recharged.

TABLE 12-1   CELL TYPES AND OPEN-CIRCUIT VOLTAGE

CELL NAME	TYPE	NOMINAL OPEN-CIRCUIT* VOLTAGE, Vdc
Carbon-zinc	Primary	1.5
Zinc chloride	Primary	1.5
Manganese dioxide (alkaline)	Primary or secondary	1.5
Mercuric oxide	Primary	1.35
Silver oxide	Primary	1.5
Lithium	Primary	3.0
Lead-acid	Secondary	2.1
Nickel-cadmium	Secondary	1.25
Nickel-iron (Edison cell)	Secondary	1.2
Silver-zinc	Secondary	1.5
Silver-cadmium	Secondary	1.1

*Open-circuit V is the terminal voltage without a load.

SECONDARY CELLS   This type can be recharged because the chemical action is reversible. When it supplies current to a load resistance, the cell is *discharging*, as the current tends to neutralize the separated charges at the electrodes. For the opposite case, the current can be reversed to re-form the electrodes as the chemical action is reversed. This action is *charging* the cell. The charging current must be supplied by an external dc voltage source, with the cell serving just as a load resistance. The discharging and recharging is called *cycling* of the cell. Since a secondary cell can be recharged, it is also called a *storage cell*. The most common type is the lead-acid cell generally used in automotive batteries (Fig. 12-2). In addition, the list in Table 12-1 indicates which are secondary cells.

FIG. 12-2   Example of a 12-V auto battery using six lead-acid cells in series. This is a secondary type, which can be recharged.

DRY CELLS   What we call a "dry cell" really has moist electrolyte. However, the electrolyte cannot be spilled and the cell can operate in any position.

SEALED RECHARGEABLE CELLS This type is a secondary cell that can be recharged, but it has a sealed electrolyte that cannot be refilled. These cells are capable of charge and discharge in any position.

TEST-POINT QUESTION 12-1

Answers at end of chapter.
a. How much is the output voltage of a carbon-zinc cell?
b. How much is the output voltage of a lead-acid cell?
c. Which type can be recharged, a primary or a secondary cell?

12-2 THE VOLTAIC CELL

When two different conducting materials are immersed in an electrolyte, as illustrated in Fig. 12-3a, the chemical action of forming a new solution results in the separation of charges. This method for converting chemical energy into electric energy is a voltaic cell. It is also called a *galvanic cell,* named after Luigi Galvani (1737–1798).

Referring to Fig. 12-3a, the charged conductors in the electrolyte are the electrodes or plates of the cell. They serve as the terminals for connecting the voltage output to an external circuit, as shown in Fig. 12-3b. Then the potential difference resulting from the separated charges enables the cell to function as a source of applied voltage. The voltage across the cell's terminals forces current to flow in the circuit to light the bulb.

DID YOU KNOW?

Doctors can sort sperm to favor the birth of either males or females by charging one positively and the other negatively. With this technology, parents carrying genetic diseases affecting only one sex can conceive healthy children.

FIG. 12-3 How a voltaic cell converts chemical energy into electrical energy. (a) Electrodes or plates in liquid electrolyte solution. (b) Schematic of a circuit with a voltaic cell as a dc voltage source V to produce current in load R_L, which is the light bulb.

CURRENT OUTSIDE THE CELL Electrons from the negative terminal of the cell flow through the external circuit with R_L and return to the positive terminal. The chemical action in the cell separates charges continuously to maintain the terminal voltage that produces current in the circuit.

The current tends to neutralize the charges generated in the cell. For this reason, the process of producing load current is considered discharging of the cell. However, the internal chemical reaction continues to maintain the separation of charges that produces the output voltage.

CURRENT INSIDE THE CELL   The current through the electrolyte is a motion of ion charges. Notice in Fig. 12-3b that the current inside the cell flows from the positive terminal to the negative terminal. This action represents the work being done by the chemical reaction to generate the voltage across the output terminals.

The negative terminal in Fig. 12-3a is considered to be the anode of the cell because it forms positive ions for the electrolyte. The opposite terminal of the cell is its cathode.

INTERNAL RESISTANCE   Any practical voltage source has internal resistance, indicated as r_i, which limits the current it can deliver. For a chemical cell, as in Fig. 12-3, the r_i is mainly the resistance of the electrolyte. For a good cell, r_i is very low, with typical values less than 1 Ω. As the cell deteriorates, though, r_i increases, preventing the cell from producing its normal terminal voltage when load current is flowing. The reason is that the internal voltage drop across r_i opposes the output terminal voltage. This factor is why you can often measure normal voltage on a dry cell with a voltmeter, which drains very little current, but the terminal voltage drops when the load is connected.

The voltage output of a cell depends on the elements used for the electrodes and the electrolyte. The current rating depends mostly on the physical size. Larger batteries can supply more current. Dry cells are generally rated up to 250 mA, while the lead-acid wet cell can supply current up to 300 A or more. Note that a smaller r_i allows a higher current rating.

ELECTROMOTIVE SERIES   The fact that the voltage output of a cell depends on its elements can be seen from Table 12-2. This list, called the *electrochemical series* or *electromotive series,* gives the relative activity in forming ion charges for some of the chemical elements. The potential for each element is the

TABLE 12-2   ELECTROMOTIVE SERIES OF ELEMENTS

ELEMENT	POTENTIAL, V
Lithium	−2.96
Magnesium	−2.40
Aluminum	−1.70
Zinc	−0.76
Cadmium	−0.40
Nickel	−0.23
Lead	−0.13
Hydrogen (reference)	0.00
Copper	+0.35
Mercury	+0.80
Silver	+0.80
Gold	+1.36

voltage with respect to hydrogen as a zero reference. The difference between the potentials for two different elements indicates the voltage of an ideal cell using these electrodes. It should be noted, though, that other factors, such as the electrolyte, cost, stability, and long life, are important for the construction of commercial batteries.

TEST-POINT QUESTION 12-2

Answers at end of chapter.

Answer True or False.
a. The negative terminal of a chemical cell has a charge of excess electrons.
b. The internal resistance of a cell limits the amount of output current.
c. Two electrodes of the same metal provide the highest voltage output.

12-3 CARBON-ZINC DRY CELL

The carbon-zinc dry cell is a very common type because of its low cost. It is also called the *Leclanché cell*, named after the inventor. Examples are shown in Fig. 12-1, while Fig. 12-4 illustrates internal construction for the D-size round cell. Voltage output for the carbon-zinc cell is 1.4 to 1.6 V, with a nominal value of 1.5 V. Suggested current range is up to 150 mA for the D size, which has a height of 2¼ in. and volume of 3.18 in.³. The C, A, AA, and AAA sizes are smaller, with lower current ratings. The larger No. 6 cell has a height of 6 in., a diameter of 2½ in., and a current range of up to 1500 mA.

The electrochemical system consists of a zinc anode and a manganese dioxide cathode in a moist electrolyte. The electrolyte is a combination of ammonium

FIG. 12-4 Cutaway view of carbon-zinc dry cell. This is size D, with height of 2¼ in.

chloride and zinc chloride dissolved in water. For the round-cell construction, a carbon rod is used down the center, as shown in Fig. 12-4. The rod is chemically inert. However, it serves as a current collector for the positive terminal at the top. The path for current inside the cell includes the carbon rod as the positive terminal, the manganese dioxide, the electrolyte, and the zinc can which is the negative electrode. As additional functions of the carbon rod, it prevents leakage of the electrolyte but is porous to allow the escape of gases which accumulate in the cell.

In operation of the cell, the ammonia releases hydrogen gas which collects around the carbon electrode. This reaction is called *polarization,* and it can reduce the voltage output. However, the manganese dioxide releases oxygen, which combines with the hydrogen to form water. The manganese dioxide functions as a *depolarizer.* Powdered carbon is also added to the depolarizer to improve conductivity and retain moisture.

Carbon-zinc dry cells are generally designed for an operating temperature of 70°F. Higher temperatures will enable the cell to provide greater output. However, temperatures of 125°F or more will cause rapid deterioration of the cell.

The chemical efficiency of the carbon-zinc cell increases with less current drain. Stated another way, the application should allow for the largest battery possible, within practical limits. In addition, performance of the cell is generally better with intermittent operation. The reason is that the cell can recuperate between discharges, probably by the effect of depolarization.

As an example of longer life with intermittent operation, a carbon-zinc D cell may operate for only a few hours with a continuous drain at its rated current. Yet the same cell could be used for a few months or even a year with intermittent operation of less than 1 hour at a time with smaller values of current.

TEST-POINT QUESTION 12-3

Answers at end of chapter.

Answer True or False.
a. A size D cell and a larger No. 6 carbon-zinc cell have the same voltage output of 1.5 V.
b. The zinc can of a carbon-zinc cell is the negative terminal.
c. Polarization at the carbon rod increases the voltage output.

12-4 ALKALINE CELL

Another popular type is the manganese-zinc cell shown in Fig. 12-5, which has an alkaline electrolyte. It is available either as a primary or secondary cell but the primary type is more common. Output is the same 1.5 V as a carbon-zinc cell but the alkaline cell lasts much longer.

The electrochemical system consists of a powdered zinc anode and a manganese dioxide cathode in an alkaline electrolyte. The electrolyte is potassium hydroxide, which is the main difference between the alkaline and Leclanché cells. Hydroxide compounds are alkaline with negative hydroxyl (OH) ions, while an acid electrolyte has positive hydrogen (H) ions. Voltage output from the alkaline cell is 1.5 V.

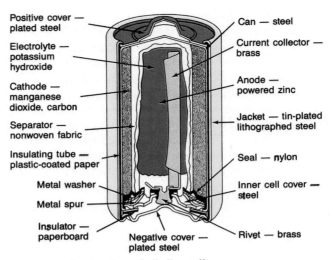

FIG. 12-5 Construction of alkaline cell.

The alkaline cell has many applications because of its ability to work with high efficiency with continuous high discharge rates. Depending on the application, an alkaline cell can provide up to seven times the service of a Leclanché cell. As examples, in a transistor radio an alkaline cell will normally have twice the service life of a general-purpose carbon-zinc cell; in toys the alkaline cell typically provides seven times more service.

The outstanding performance of the alkaline cell is due to its low internal resistance. Its r_i is low because of the dense cathode material, the large surface area of the anode in contact with the electrolyte, and the high conductivity of the electrolyte. In addition, alkaline cells will perform satisfactorily at low temperatures.

ZINC CHLORIDE CELLS   This type is actually a modified carbon-zinc cell with the construction illustrated in Fig. 12-4. However, the electrolyte contains only zinc chloride. The zinc chloride cell is often referred to as the "heavy duty" type. It can normally deliver more current over a longer period of time than the Leclanché cell. Another difference is that the chemical reaction in the zinc chloride cell consumes water along with the chemically active materials, so that the cell is nearly dry at the end of its useful life. As a result, liquid leakage is not a problem.

TEST-POINT QUESTION 12-4

Answers at end of chapter.

Answer True or False.
a. Alkaline cells have the same 1.5-V output as carbon-zinc cells.
b. They are used primarily for their ability to deliver a higher discharge rate than carbon-zinc cells.

12-5 ADDITIONAL TYPES OF PRIMARY CELLS

The miniature button construction shown in Fig. 12-6 is often used for the mercury cell and the silver-oxide cell. Diameter of the cell is ⅜ to 1 in.

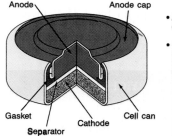

• Anodes are a gelled mixture of amalgamated zinc powder and electrolyte.

• Cathodes
  Silver cells: AgO_2, MnO_2, and conductor
  Mercury cells: HgO and conductor (may contain MnO_2)
  Manganese dioxide cells: MNO_2 and conductor

FIG. 12-6   Construction of miniature button type of primary cell. Diameter is ⅜ to 1 in. Note the chemical symbols AgO_2 for silver oxide, HgO for mercuric oxide, and MnO_2 for manganese dioxide.

MERCURY CELL   The electrochemical system consists of a zinc anode, a mercury compound for the cathode, and an electrolyte of potassium or sodium hydroxide. Mercury cells are available in flat, round cylinder, and miniature button shapes. It should be noted, though, that some round mercury cells have the top button as the negative terminal and the bottom terminal positive. The open-circuit voltage is 1.35 V when the cathode is mercuric oxide (HgO) and 1.4 V or more with mercuric oxide/manganese dioxide. The 1.35-V type is more common.

The mercury cell is used where a relatively flat discharge characteristic is required with high current density. Its internal resistance is low and essentially constant. These cells perform well at elevated temperatures, up to 130°F continuous or 200°F for short periods. One drawback of the mercury cell is its relatively high cost compared with a carbon-zinc cell.

SILVER OXIDE CELL   The electrochemical system consists of a zinc anode, a cathode of silver oxide (AgO_2) with small amounts of manganese dioxide, and an electrolyte of potassium or sodium hydroxide. It is commonly available in the miniature button shape shown in Fig. 12-6. The open-circuit voltage is 1.6 V, but the nominal output with a load is considered to be 1.5 V. Typical applications include hearing aids, cameras, and electronic watches, which use very little current.

TEST-POINT QUESTION 12-5

Answers at end of chapter.

Answer True or False.
a. The mercury cell has output of 2.6 V as a minimum.
b. Most miniature button cells can be recharged.

12-8 LEAD-ACID WET CELL

Where high values of load current are necessary, the lead-acid cell is the type most commonly used. The electrolyte is a dilute solution of sulfuric acid (H_2SO_4). In the application of battery power to start the engine in an automobile, for example, the load current to the starter motor is typically 200 to 400 A. One cell has a nominal output of 2.1 V, but lead-acid cells are often used in a series combination of three for a 6-V battery and six for a 12-V battery. Examples are shown in Figs. 12-2 and 12-8.

FIG. 12-8   Construction of lead-acid batteries. (*a*) 12-V type. (*b*) Individual plates of 6-V battery.

The lead-acid type is a secondary cell or storage cell, which can be recharged. The charge and discharge cycle can be repeated many times to restore the output voltage, as long as the cell is in good physical condition. However, heat with excessive charge and discharge currents shortens the useful life to about 3 to 5 years for an automobile battery. Of the different types of secondary cells, the lead-acid type has the highest output voltage, which allows less cells for a specified battery voltage.

CONSTRUCTION   Inside a lead-acid battery, the positive and negative electrodes consist of a group of plates welded to a connecting strap. The plates are immersed in the electrolyte, consisting of 8 parts of water to 3 parts of concentrated sulfuric acid. Each plate is a grid or framework, made of a lead-antimony alloy. This construction enables the active material, which is lead oxide, to be pasted into the grid. In manufacture of the cell, a forming charge produces the positive and negative electrodes. In the forming process, the active material in the positive plate is changed to lead peroxide (PbO_2). The negative electrode is spongy lead (Pb).

DID YOU KNOW?

Sony and Nissan are working on a car that runs on a high-current lithium battery that would provide triple the range of traditional batteries.

Automobile batteries are usually shipped dry from the manufacturer. The electrolyte is put in at the time of installation, then the battery is charged to form the plates. With maintenance-free batteries, little or no water need be added in normal service. Some types are sealed, except for a pressure vent, without provision for adding water.

CHEMICAL ACTION   Sulfuric acid is a combination of hydrogen and sulfate ions. When the cell discharges, lead peroxide from the positive electrode combines with hydrogen ions to form water and with sulfate ions to form lead sulfate. The lead sulfate is also produced by combining lead on the negative plate with sulfate ions. Therefore, the net result of discharge is to produce more water, which dilutes the electrolyte, and to form lead sulfate on the plates.

As discharge continues, the sulfate fills the pores of the grids, retarding circulation of acid in the active material. Lead sulfate is the powder often seen on the outside terminals of old batteries. When the combination of weak electrolyte and sulfation on the plate lowers the output of the battery, charging is necessary.

On charge, the external dc source reverses the current in the battery. The reversed direction of ions flowing in the electrolyte results in a reversal of the chemical reactions. Now the lead sulfate on the positive plate reacts with the water and sulfate ions to produce lead peroxide and sulfuric acid. This action re-forms the positive plate and makes the electrolyte stronger by adding sulfuric acid. At the same time, charging enables the lead sulfate on the negative plate to react with hydrogen ions; this also forms sulfuric acid while re-forming lead on the negative electrode.

As a result, the charging current can restore the cell to full output, with lead peroxide on the positive plates, spongy lead on the negative plate, and the required concentration of sulfuric acid in the electrolyte. The chemical equation for the lead-acid cell is

$$Pb + PbO_2 + 2H_2SO_4 \underset{\text{Discharge}}{\overset{\text{Charge}}{\rightleftarrows}} 2PbSO_4 + 2H_2O$$

On discharge, the Pb and PbO_2 combine with the SO_4 ions at the left side of the equation to form lead sulfate ($PbSO_4$) and water (H_2O) at the right side of the equation.

On charge, with reverse current through the electrolyte, the chemical action is reversed. Then the Pb ions from the lead sulfate on the right side of the equation re-form the lead and lead peroxide electrodes. Also the SO_4 ions combine with H_2 ions from the water to produce more sulfuric acid at the left side of the equation.

CURRENT RATINGS   Lead-acid batteries are generally rated in terms of how much discharge current they can supply for a specified period of time. The output voltage must be maintained above a minimum level, which is 1.5 to 1.8 V per cell. A common rating is ampere-hours (A·h) based on a specific discharge time, which is often 8 h. Typical values for automobile batteries are 100 to 300 A·h.

As an example, a 200 A·h battery can supply a load current of 200/8 or 25 A, based on 8 h discharge. The battery can supply less current for a longer time or more current for a shorter time. Automobile batteries may be rated for "cold cranking power," which is related to the job of starting the engine. A typical rating is 450 A for 30 s at a temperature of 0°F.

Note that the ampere-hour unit specifies coulombs of charge. For instance, 200 A·h corresponds to 200 A × 3600 s (1 h = 3600 s). This equals 720,000 A·s, or coulombs. One ampere-second is equal to one coulomb. Then the charge equals 720,000 or 7.2×10^5 C. To put this much charge back into the battery would require 20 h with a charging current of 10 A.

The ratings for lead-acid batteries are given for a temperature range of 77 to 80°F. Higher temperatures increase the chemical reaction, but operation above 110°F shortens the battery life. Low temperatures reduce the current capacity and voltage output. The ampere-hour capacity is reduced approximately 0.75 percent for each decrease of 1°F below normal temperature rating. At 0°F the available output is only 60 percent of the ampere-hour battery rating. In cold weather, therefore, it is very important to have an automobile battery up to full charge. In addition, the electrolyte freezes more easily when diluted by water in the discharged condition.

SPECIFIC GRAVITY The state of discharge for a lead-acid cell is generally checked by measuring the specific gravity of the electrolyte. Specific gravity is a ratio comparing the weight of a substance with the weight of water. For instance, concentrated sulfuric acid is 1.835 times as heavy as water for the same volume. Therefore, its specific gravity equals 1.835. The specific gravity of water is 1, since it is the reference.

In a fully charged automotive cell, the mixture of sulfuric acid and water results in a specific gravity of 1.280 at room temperatures of 70 to 80°F. As the cell discharges, more water is formed, lowering the specific gravity. When it is down to about 1.150, the cell is completely discharged.

Specific-gravity readings are taken with a battery hydrometer, such as the one in Fig. 12-9. Note that the calibrated float with the specific gravity marks will rest higher in an electrolyte of higher specific gravity. The decimal point is often omitted for convenience. For example, the value of 1.220 in Fig. 12-9c is simply read "twelve twenty." A hydrometer reading of 1260 to 1280 indicates full charge, approximately 1250 is half charge, and 1150 to 1200 indicates complete discharge.

The importance of the specific gravity can be seen from the fact that the open-circuit voltage of the lead-acid cell is approximately equal to

$$V = \text{specific gravity} + 0.84$$

(a)   (b)   (c)

FIG. 12-9 Hydrometer to check specific gravity of lead-acid battery. (*a*) Syringe to suck up electrolyte. (*b*) Float at specific gravity of 1.120. (*c*) Float is higher for higher reading of 1.220.

For the specific gravity of 1.280, the voltage is $1.280 + 0.84 = 2.12$ V, as an example. These values are for a fully charged battery.

CHARGING THE LEAD-ACID BATTERY

The requirements are illustrated in Fig. 12-10. An external dc voltage source is necessary to produce current in one direction. Also, the charging voltage must be more than the battery emf. Approximately 2.5 V per cell is enough to overcome the cell emf so that the charging voltage can produce current opposite to the direction of discharge current.

Note that the reversal of current is obtained just by connecting the battery V_B and charging source V_G with + to + and − to −, as shown in Fig. 12-10*b*. The charging current is reversed because the battery effectively becomes a load resistance for V_G when it is higher than V_B. In this example, the net voltage available to produce charging current is $15 - 12 = 3$ V.

A commercial charger for automobile batteries is shown in Fig. 12-11. This unit can also be used to test batteries and jump-start cars. The charger is essentially a dc power supply, rectifying input from the ac power line to provide dc output for charging batteries.

Float charging refers to a method in which the charger and the battery are always connected to each other for supplying current to the load. In Fig. 12-12, the charger provides current for the load and the current necessary to keep the battery fully charged. The battery here is an auxiliary source for dc power.

It may be of interest to note that an automobile battery is in a floating-charge circuit. The battery charger is an ac generator or alternator with rectifier diodes, driven by a belt from the engine. When you start the car, the battery supplies the

(a)

(b)

FIG. 12-10 Reversed directions for charge and discharge currents of a battery. The r_i is internal resistance. (*a*) V_B of battery discharges to supply load current for R_L. (*b*) Battery is load resistance for V_G, which is an external source of charging voltage.

FIG. 12-11   Charger for auto batteries.

FIG. 12-12   Circuit for battery in float-charge application.

cranking power. Once the engine is running, the alternator charges the battery. It is not necessary for the car to be moving. A voltage regulator is used in this system to maintain the output at approximately 13 to 15 V.

TEST-POINT QUESTION 12-8

Answers at end of chapter.
a. How many lead-acid cells in series are needed for a 12-V battery?
b. A battery is rated for 120 A·h at the 8-h rate at 77°F. How much discharge current can it supply for 8 h?
c. Which of the following is the specific gravity reading for a good lead-acid cell: 1070, 1170, or 1270?

12-9 ADDITIONAL TYPES OF SECONDARY CELLS

A secondary cell is a storage cell that can be recharged by reversing the internal chemical reaction. A primary cell must be discarded after it has been completely discharged. The lead-acid cell is the most common type of storage cell. However, other types of secondary cells are available. Some of these are described next.

NICKEL-CADMIUM (NiCd) CELL   This type is popular because of its ability to deliver high current and to be cycled many times for recharging. Also, the cell can be stored for a long time, even when discharged, without any damage. The NiCd cell is available in both sealed and nonsealed designs, but the sealed construction shown in Fig. 12-13 is common. Nominal output voltage is 1.25 V per cell. Applications include portable power tools, alarm systems, and portable radio or television equipment.

The chemical equation for the NiCd cell can be written as follows:

$$2\ Ni(OH)_3 + Cd \xrightleftharpoons[\text{Discharge}]{\text{Charge}} 2\ Ni(OH)_2 + Cd(OH)_2$$

The electrolyte is potassium hydroxide (KOH), but it does not appear in the chemical equation. The reason is that the function of this electrolyte is just to act as a conductor for the transfer of hydroxyl (OH) ions. Therefore, unlike the lead-acid cell, the specific gravity of the electrolyte in the NiCd cell does not change with the state of charge.

The NiCd cell is a true storage cell with a reversible chemical reaction for recharging that can be cycled up to 1000 times. Maximum charging current is equal to the 10-h discharge rate. It should be noted that a new NiCd battery may need charging before use.

FIG. 12-13 Examples of nickel-cadmium batteries. The output voltage for each is 1.25 V.

NICKEL-IRON (EDISON) CELL   Developed by Thomas Edison, this cell was once used extensively in industrial truck and railway applications. However, it has been replaced almost entirely by the lead-acid battery. New methods of construction for less weight, though, are making this cell a possible alternative in some applications.

The Edison cell has a positive plate of nickel oxide, a negative plate of iron, and an electrolyte of potassium hydroxide in water with a small amount of lithium hydroxide added. The chemical reaction is reversible for recharging. Nominal output is 1.2 V per cell.

NICKEL-ZINC CELL   This type has been used in limited railway applications. There has been renewed interest in it for use in electric cars, because of its high energy density. However, one drawback is its limited cycle life for recharging. Nominal output is 1.6 V per cell.

ZINC-CHLORINE (HYDRATE) CELL   This cell has been under development for use in electric vehicles. It is sometimes considered a zinc-chloride cell. This type has high energy density with a good cycle life. Nominal output is 2.1 V per cell.

LITHIUM-IRON SULFIDE CELL   This type is under development for commercial energy applications. Nominal output is 1.6 V per cell. The normal operating temperature is 800 to 900°F, which is high compared with the more popular types of cells.

SODIUM-SULFUR CELL   This is another type of cell being developed for electric vehicle applications. It has the potential of long life at low cost with high efficiency. The cell is designed to operate at temperatures between 550 and 650°F. Its most interesting feature is the use of a ceramic electrolyte.

PLASTIC CELLS   A recent development in battery technology is the rechargeable plastic cell made from a conductive polymer, which is a combination of organic chemical compounds. These cells could have ten times the power of the lead-acid type with one-tenth the weight and one-third the volume. In addition,

ABOUT ELECTRONICS

A Nobel prize was earned by researchers J. Bardeen, L. N. Cooper, and J. R. Schrieffer when they learned the secret of superconductivity—that pairs of linked electrons move within mercury without meeting obstacles.

the plastic cell does not require maintenance. One significant application could be for electric vehicles.

A plastic cell consists of an electrolyte between two polymer electrodes. Operation is similar to that of a capacitor. During charge, electrons are transferred from the positive electrode to the negative electrode by a dc source. On discharge, the stored electrons are driven through the external circuit to provide current in the load.

SOLAR CELLS   This type converts the sun's light energy directly into electric energy. The cells are made of semiconductor materials, which generate voltage output with light input. Silicon, with an output of 0.5 V per cell, is mainly used now. Research is continuing, however, on other materials, such as cadmium sulfide and gallium arsenide, that might provide more output. In practice, the cells are arranged in modules that are assembled into a large solar array for the required power.

In most applications, the solar cells are used in combination with a lead-acid cell specifically designed for this use. When there is sunlight, the solar cells charge the battery, as well as supplying power to the load. When there is no light, the battery supplies the required power.

TEST-POINT QUESTION 12-9

Answers at end of chapter.

Answer True or False.
a. The NiCd cell is a primary type.
b. Output of the NiCd cell is 1.25 V.
c. The Edison cell is a storage type.
d. Output of a solar cell is typically 0.5 V.

12-10 SERIES AND PARALLEL CELLS

An applied voltage higher than the emf of one cell can be obtained by connecting cells in series. The total voltage available across the battery of cells is equal to the sum of the individual values for each cell. Parallel cells have the same voltage as one cell but have more current capacity. The combination of cells is a *battery*.

SERIES CONNECTIONS   Figure 12-14 shows series-aiding connections for three dry cells. Here the three 1.5-V cells in series provide a total battery voltage of 4.5 V. Notice that the two end terminals A and B are left open to serve as the plus and minus terminals of the battery. These terminals are used to connect the battery to the load circuit, as shown in Fig. 12-14c.

In the lead-acid battery in Fig. 12-2, short, heavy metal straps connect the cells in series. The current capacity of a battery with cells in series is the same as for one cell because the same current flows through all the series cells.

FIG. 12-14   Cells connected in series for higher voltage. Current rating is the same as for one cell. (a) Wiring. (b) Schematic symbol for battery with three series cells. (c) Battery connected to load resistance R_L.

PARALLEL CONNECTIONS   For more current capacity, the battery has cells in parallel, as shown in Fig. 12-15. All the positive terminals are strapped together, as are all the negative terminals. Any point on the positive side can be the plus terminal of the battery, and any point on the negative side can be the negative terminal.

FIG. 12-15   Cells connected in parallel for higher current rating. (a) Wiring. (b) Schematic symbol for battery with three parallel cells. (c) Battery connected to load resistance R_L.

The parallel connection is equivalent to increasing the size of the electrodes and electrolyte, which increases the current capacity. The voltage output of the battery, however, is the same as for one cell.

Identical cells in parallel supply equal parts of the load current. For example, with three identical parallel cells producing a load current of 300 mA, each cell has a drain of 100 mA. Bad cells should not be connected in parallel with good cells, however, since the cells in good condition will supply more current, which may overload the good cells. In addition, a cell with lower output voltage will act as a load resistance, draining excessive current from the cells that have higher output voltage.

SERIES-PARALLEL CONNECTIONS   In order to provide higher output and more current capacity, cells can be connected in series-parallel combinations. Figure 12-16 shows four No. 6 cells connected in series-parallel to form a battery that has a 3-V output with a current capacity of ½ A. Two of the 1.5-V cells in series provide 3 V total output voltage. This series string has a current capacity of ¼ A, however, assuming this current rating for one cell.

To double the current capacity, another string is connected in parallel. The two strings in parallel have the same 3-V output as one string, but with a current capacity of ½ A instead of the ¼ A for one string.

(a)

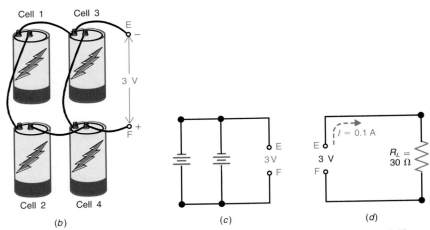

(b)   (c)   (d)

FIG. 12-16   Cells connected in series-parallel combinations. (a) Wiring two 3-V strings, each with two 1.5-V cells in series. (b) Wiring two 3-V strings in parallel. (c) Schematic symbol for the battery in (b) with output of 3 V. (d) Equivalent battery connected to load resistance R_L.

TEST-POINT QUESTION 12-10

Answers at end of chapter.
  a. How many carbon-zinc cells in series are required to obtain a 9-V dc output? How many lead-acid cells are required to obtain 12 Vdc?
  b. How many identical cells in parallel would be required to double the current rating of a single cell?
  c. How many cells rated 1.5 Vdc 300 mA would be required in a series-parallel combination which would provide a rating of 900 mA at 6 Vdc?

12-11 CURRENT DRAIN DEPENDS ON LOAD RESISTANCE

It is important to note that the current rating of batteries, or any voltage source, is only a guide to typical values permissible for normal service life. The actual amount of current produced when the battery is connected to a load resistance is equal to $I = V/R$, by Ohm's law.

Figure 12-17 illustrates three different cases of using the applied voltage of 1.5 V from a dry cell. In Fig. 12-17a, the load resistance R_1 is 7.5 Ω. Then I is 1.5/7.5 = ⅕ A or 200 mA.

A No. 6 carbon-zinc cell used as the voltage source could supply this load of 200 mA continuously for about 74 h at a temperature of 70°F before dropping to an end voltage of 1.2 V. If an end voltage of 1.0 V could be used, the same load would be served for approximately 170 h.

In Fig. 12-17b, a larger load resistance R_2 is used. The value of 150 Ω limits the current to 1.5/150 = 0.01 A or 10 mA. Again using the No. 6 carbon-zinc cell at 70°F, the load could be served continuously for 4300 h with an end voltage of 1.2 V. The two principles here are

1. The cell delivers less current for a higher resistance in the load circuit.
2. The cell can deliver a smaller load current for a longer time.

In Fig. 12-17c, the load resistance R_3 is reduced to 2.5 Ω. Then I is 1.5/2.5 = 0.6 A or 600 mA. The No. 6 cell could serve this load continuously for only 9 h for an end voltage of 1.2 V. The cell could deliver even more load current, but for a shorter time. The relationship between current and time is not linear. For any one example, though, the amount of current is determined by the circuit, not by the current rating of the battery.

(a)   (b)   (c)

FIG. 12-17   An example of how current drain from a battery used as a voltage source depends on R of the load resistance. Different values of I are shown for the same V of 1.5 V. (a) The V/R_1 equals I of 200 mA. (b) The V/R_2 equals I of 10 mA. (c) The V/R_3 equals I of 600 mA.

TEST-POINT QUESTION 12-11

Answers at end of chapter.

Answer True or False.
a. A cell rated at 250 mA will produce this current for any value of R_L.
b. A higher value of R_L allows the cell to operate with normal voltage for a longer time.

12-12 INTERNAL RESISTANCE OF A GENERATOR

Any source that produces voltage output continuously is a generator. It may be a cell separating charges by chemical action or a rotary generator converting mo-

The lower the internal resistance of a generator, the better it is in terms of being able to produce full output voltage when supplying current for a load. For example, the very low r_i, about 0.01 Ω, for a 12-V lead-acid battery is the reason it can supply high values of load current and maintain its output voltage.

For the opposite case, a higher r_i means that the terminal voltage of a generator is much less with load current. As an example, an old dry battery with r_i of 500 Ω would appear normal when measured by a voltmeter but be useless because of low voltage when normal load current flows in an actual circuit.

HOW TO MEASURE r_i   The internal resistance of any generator can be measured indirectly by determining how much the output voltage drops for a specified amount of load current. The difference between the no-load voltage and the load voltage is the amount of internal voltage drop $I_L r_i$. Dividing by I_L gives the value of r_i. As a formula,

$$r_i = \frac{V_{NL} - V_L}{I_L} \qquad \text{(12-1)}$$

Example

EXAMPLE 1   Calculate r_i if the output of a generator drops from 100 V with zero load current to 80 V when $I_L = 2$ A.

ANSWER $r_i = \dfrac{100 - 80}{2}$

$= \dfrac{20}{2}$

$r_i = 10$ Ω

A convenient technique for measuring r_i is to use a variable load resistance R_L. Vary R_L until the load voltage is one-half the no-load voltage. This value of R_L is also the value of r_i, since they must be equal to divide the generator voltage equally. For the same 100-V generator with the 10-Ω r_i used in Example 1, if a 10-Ω R_L were used, the load voltage would be 50 V, equal to one-half the no-load voltage.

You can solve this circuit by Ohm's law to see that I_L is 5 A with 20 Ω for the combined R_T. Then the two voltage drops of 50 V each add to equal the 100 V of the generator.

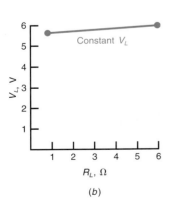

FIG. 12-21   Constant-voltage generator with low r_i. The V_L stays approximately the same 6 V as I varies with R_L. (a) Circuit. (b) Graph for V_L.

TEST-POINT QUESTION 12-13

Answers at end of chapter.

Answer True or False.

a. For Eq. (12-1), V_L must be more than V_{NL}.

b. For Eq. (12-1), when V_L is one-half V_{NL}, the r_i is equal to R_L.

12-14 CONSTANT-VOLTAGE AND CONSTANT-CURRENT SOURCES

A generator with very low internal resistance is considered to be a constant-voltage source. Then the output voltage remains essentially the same when the load current changes. This idea is illustrated in Fig. 12-21a for a 6-V lead-acid battery with an r_i of 0.005 Ω. If the load current varies over the wide range of 1 to 100 A, for any of these values, the internal Ir_i drop across 0.005 Ω is less than 0.5 V.

CONSTANT-CURRENT GENERATOR It has very high resistance, compared with the external load resistance, resulting in constant current, although the output voltage varies.

The constant-current generator shown in Fig. 12-22 has such high resistance, with an r_i of 0.9 MΩ, that it is the main factor determining how much current can be produced by V_G. Here R_L varies in a 3:1 range from 50 to 150 kΩ. Since the current is determined by the total resistance of R_L and r_i in series, however, I is essentially constant at 1.05 to 0.95 mA, or approximately 1 mA. This relatively constant I_I is shown by the graph in Fig. 12-22b.

Note that the terminal voltage V_L varies in approximately the same 3:1 range as R_L. Also, the output voltage is much less than the generator voltage because of the high internal resistance compared with R_L. This is a necessary condition, however, in a circuit with a constant-current generator.

A common practice is to insert a series resistance to keep the current constant, as shown in Fig. 12-23a (page 344). Resistance R_1 must be very high compared with R_L. In this example, I_L is 50 μA with 50 V applied, and R_T is practically equal to the 1 MΩ of R_1. The value of R_L can vary over a range as great as 10:1 without changing R_T or I_I appreciably.

The circuit with an equivalent constant-current source is shown in Fig. 12-23b. Note the arrow symbol for a current source. As far as R_L is concerned, its terminals A and B can be considered as receiving either 50 V in series with 1 MΩ or 50 μA in shunt with 1 MΩ.

(a)

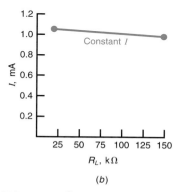

(b)

FIG. 12-22 Constant-current generator with high r_i. The I stays approximately the same 1 mA as V_L varies with R_L. (a) Circuit. (b) Graph for I.

TEST-POINT QUESTION 12-14

Answers at end of chapter.

Is the internal resistance high or low for:
a. A constant-voltage source?
b. A constant-current source?

12-15 MATCHING A LOAD RESISTANCE TO THE GENERATOR r_i

In the diagram in Fig. 12-24 (page 345), when R_L equals r_i the load and generator are matched. The matching is significant because the generator then produces maximum power in R_L, as verified by the values listed in Table 12-5.

MAXIMUM POWER IN R_L   When R_L is 100 Ω to match the 100 Ω of r_i, maximum power is transferred from the generator to the load. With higher resistance for R_L, the output voltage V_L is higher, but the current is reduced. Lower resistance for R_L allows more current, but V_L is less. When r_i and R_L both equal 100 Ω, this combination of current and voltage produces the maximum power of 100 W across R_L.

With generators that have very low resistance, however, matching is often impractical. For example, if a 6-V lead-acid battery with a 0.003-Ω internal resistance were connected to a 0.003-Ω load resistance, the battery could be damaged by excessive current as high as 1000 A.

MAXIMUM VOLTAGE ACROSS R_L   If maximum voltage, rather than power, is desired, the load should have as high a resistance as possible. Note that R_L and r_i form a voltage divider for the generator voltage, as illustrated in Fig. 12-24b. The values for IR_L listed in Table 12-5 show how the output voltage V_L increases with higher values of R_L.

MAXIMUM EFFICIENCY   Note also that the efficiency increases as R_L increases because there is less current, resulting in less power lost in r_i. When R_L equals r_i, the efficiency is only 50 percent, since one-half the total generated power is dissipated in r_i, the internal resistance of the generator. In conclusion, then, matching the load and generator resistances is desirable when the load requires maximum power rather than maximum voltage or efficiency, assuming that the match does not result in excessive current.

TEST-POINT QUESTION 12-15

Answers at end of chapter.

Answer True or False.
a. When $R_L = r_i$, the P_L is maximum.
b. The V_L is maximum when R_L is maximum.

(a)

(b)

FIG. 12-23   Voltage source in (a) equivalent to current source in (b) for load resistance R_L across terminals A and B.

FIG. 12-24 Circuit for varying R_L to match r_i. (a) Schematic diagram. (b) Equivalent voltage divider for voltage output across R_L. (c) Graph of power output P_L for different values of R_L. All values are listed in Table 12-5.

TABLE 12-5 EFFECT OF LOAD RESISTANCE ON GENERATOR OUTPUT*

	R_L, V	$I = V_G/R_T$, A	Ir_i, V	IR_L, V	P_L, W	P_i, W	P_T, W	EFFICIENCY = P_L/P_T, %
	1	1.98	198	2	4	392	396	1
	50	1.33	133	67	89	178	267	33
$R_L = r_i \rightarrow$	100	1	100	100	100	100	200	50
	500	0.33	33	167	55	11	66	83
	1,000	0.18	18	180	32	3.24	35.24	91
	10,000	0.02	2	198	4	0.04	4.04	99

*Values calculated approximately for circuit in Fig. 12-24, with $V_G = 200$ V and $r_i = 100$ Ω.

- A voltaic cell consists of two different conductors as electrodes immersed in an electrolyte. The voltage output depends only on the chemicals in the cell. The current capacity increases with larger sizes. A primary cell cannot be recharged. A secondary or storage cell can be recharged.
- A battery is a group of cells in series or in parallel. With cells in series, the voltages add, but the current capacity is the same as that of one cell. With cells in parallel, the voltage output is the same as that of one cell, but the total current capacity is the sum of the individual values.
- The carbon-zinc dry cell is the most common type of primary cell. Zinc is the negative electrode; carbon is the positive electrode. Its output voltage is approximately 1.5 V.
- The lead-acid cell is the most common form of storage battery. The positive electrode is lead peroxide; spongy lead is the negative electrode. Both are in a dilute solution of sulfuric acid for the electrolyte. The voltage output is approximately 2.1 V per cell.
- To charge a lead-acid battery, connect it to a dc voltage equal to approximately 2.5 V per cell. Connecting the positive terminal of the battery to the positive side of the charging source and the negative terminal to the negative side results in charging current through the battery.
- The mercury cell is a primary cell with an output of 1.35 or 1.4 V.
- The nickel-cadmium cell is rechargeable, with an output of 1.25 V.
- A constant-voltage generator has very low internal resistance. Output voltage is relatively constant with changing values of load because of the low internal voltage drop.
- A constant-current generator has a very high internal resistance. This determines the constant value of current in the generator circuit relatively independent of the load resistance.
- Any generator has an internal resistance r_i. With load current I_L, the internal $I_L r_i$ drop reduces the voltage across the output terminals. When I_L makes the terminal voltage drop to one-half the no-load voltage, the external R_L equals the internal r_i.
- Matching a load to a generator means making the R_L equal to the generator's r_i. The result is maximum power delivered to the load from the generator.

SELF-TEST

ANSWERS AT BACK OF BOOK.

Choose (a), (b), (c), or (d).

1. Which of the following is false? (a) A lead-acid cell can be recharged. (b) A primary cell has an irreversible chemical reaction. (c) A storage cell has a reversible chemical reaction. (d) A carbon-zinc cell has unlimited shelf life.
2. The output voltage of a lead-acid cell is (a) 1.25 V; (b) 1.35 V; (c) 2.1 V; (d) 6 V.

3. The current in a chemical cell is a movement of (*a*) positive hole charges; (*b*) positive and negative ions; (*c*) positive ions only; (*d*) negative ions only.

4. Cells are connected in series to (*a*) increase the voltage output; (*b*) decrease the voltage output; (*c*) decrease the internal resistance; (*d*) increase the current capacity.

5. Cells are connected in parallel to (*a*) increase the voltage output; (*b*) increase the internal resistance; (*c*) decrease the current capacity; (*d*) increase the current capacity.

6. Which of the following is a sealed secondary cell? (*a*) Edison cell; (*b*) carbon-zinc cell; (*c*) mercury cell; (*d*) nickel-cadmium cell.

7. When R_L equals the generator r_i, which of the following is maximum? (*a*) Power in R_L; (*b*) current; (*c*) voltage across R_L; (*d*) efficiency of the circuit.

8. Five carbon-zinc cells in series have an output of (*a*) 1.5 V; (*b*) 5.0 V; (*c*) 7.5 V; (*d*) 11.0 V.

9. A constant-voltage generator has (*a*) low internal resistance; (*b*) high internal resistance; (*c*) minimum efficiency; (*d*) minimum current capacity.

10. A generator has an output of 10 V on open circuit, which drops to 5 V with a load current of 50 mA and an R_L of 1000 Ω. The internal resistance r_i equals (*a*) 25 Ω; (*b*) 50 Ω; (*c*) 100 Ω; (*d*) 1000 Ω.

QUESTIONS

1. Draw a sketch illustrating the construction of a carbon-zinc dry cell. Indicate the negative and positive electrodes and the electrolyte.

2. Draw a sketch illustrating construction of the lead-acid cell. Indicate the negative and positive electrodes and the electrolyte.

3. Show the wiring for the following batteries: (**a**) six lead-acid cells for a voltage output of approximately 12 V; (**b**) six standard No. 6 dry cells for a voltage output of 4.5 V with a current capacity of ½ A. Assume a current capacity of ¼ A for one cell.

4. (**a**) What is the advantage of connecting cells in series? (**b**) What is connected to the end terminals of the series cells?

5. (**a**) What is the advantage of connecting cells in parallel? (**b**) Why can the load be connected across any one of the parallel cells?

6. How many cells are necessary in a battery to double the voltage and current ratings of a single cell? Show the wiring diagram.

7. Draw a diagram showing two 12-V lead-acid batteries being charged by a 15-V source.

8. Why is a generator with very low internal resistance called a constant-voltage source?

9. Why does discharge current lower the specific gravity in a lead-acid cell?

10. Would you consider the lead-acid battery a constant-current source or a constant-voltage source? Why?

11. List five types of chemical cells, giving two features of each.

12. Referring to Fig. 12-21*b*, draw the corresponding graph that shows how *I* varies with R_L.

13. Referring to Fig. 12-22*b*, draw the corresponding graph that shows how V_L varies with R_L.

14. Referring to Fig. 12-24*c*, draw the corresponding graph that shows how V_L varies with R_L.

ANSWERS TO ODD-NUMBERED PROBLEMS AT BACK OF BOOK.

1. A 1.5-V No. 6 carbon-zinc dry cell is connected across an R_L of 1000 Ω. How much current flows in the circuit?

2. Draw the wiring diagram for six No. 6 cells providing a 3-V output with a current capacity of $\frac{3}{4}$ A. Assume a current capacity of $\frac{1}{4}$ A for one cell. Draw the schematic diagram of this battery connected across a 10-Ω resistance. **(a)** How much current flows in the circuit? **(b)** How much power is dissipated in the resistance? **(c)** How much power is supplied by the battery?

3. A 6-V lead-acid battery has an internal resistance of 0.01 Ω. How much current will flow if the battery has a short circuit?

4. How much is the specific gravity of a solution with equal parts of sulfuric acid and water?

5. A lead-acid battery discharges at the rate of 8 A for 10 h. **(a)** How many coulombs of charge must be put back into the battery to restore the original charge, assuming 100 percent efficiency? **(b)** How long will this recharging take, with a charging current of 2 A?

6. The output voltage of a battery drops from 90 V at no load to 60 V with a load current of 50 mA. **(a)** How much is the internal r_i of the battery? **(b)** How much is R_L for this load current? **(c)** How much R_L reduces the load voltage to one-half the no-load voltage?

7. The output voltage of a source reads 60 V with a DMM. When a meter with 1000 Ω/V sensitivity is used, the reading is 50 V on the 100-V range. How much is the internal resistance of the source?

8. A 100-V source with an internal resistance of 10 kΩ is connected to a variable load resistance R_L. Tabulate I, V_L, and power in R_L for values of 1 kΩ, 5 kΩ, 10 kΩ, 15 kΩ, and 20 kΩ.

9. A generator has an open-circuit emf of 18 V. Its terminal voltage drops to 15 V with an R_L of 30 Ω. Calculate r_i.

10. Referring to Fig. 12-24, calculate P_L when R_L is 200 Ω. Compare this value with the maximum P_L at $R_L = r_i = 100$ Ω.

11. In Fig. 12-25, calculate I, V_L, P_L, P_T, and the percent efficiency $[(P_L/P_T) \times 100]$ for the following values of R_L: 1 Ω, 3 Ω, 5 Ω, 7 Ω, 10 Ω, 15 Ω, 45 Ω, and 100 Ω.

12. In Fig. 12-26, calculate: **(a)** the value of I_L for the following values of R_L: 0 Ω, 1 Ω, 10 Ω, 100 Ω, 1 kΩ, 10 kΩ, 100 kΩ, and 1 MΩ; **(b)** the value of R_L for which maximum power transfer will occur; **(c)** the power transferred to R_L when $R_L = r_i$.

13. Refer to Fig. 12-27. With S_1 in position 1, $V = 50$ V. With S_1 in position 2, $V = 37.5$ V. Calculate r_i.

FIG. 12-25   Circuit diagram for Prob. 11.

FIG. 12-26   Circuit diagram for Prob. 12.

14. A 1.5-V cell develops a terminal voltage of 1.35 V while delivering 150 mA to a load R_L. Calculate: **(a)** r_i; **(b)** R_L; **(c)** P_L; **(d)** P_T; **(e)** percent efficiency.

15. A 10-V generator has an internal resistance r_i of 50 Ω. Calculate the value of R_L which will provide an efficiency of 75 percent in the transfer of power to R_L.

FIG. 12-27   Circuit diagram for Prob. 13.

CRITICAL THINKING

1. In Fig. 12-28, calculate **(a)** V_L, **(b)** I_L, and **(c)** the current supplied to R_L by each separate voltage source.

2. In Fig. 12-29, calculate: **(a)** the value of R_L for which the maximum transfer of power occurs; **(b)** the maximum power delivered to R_L.

FIG. 12-28   Circuit diagram for Critical Thinking Prob. 1.

FIG. 12-29   Circuit diagram for Critical Thinking Prob. 2.

ANSWERS TO TEST-POINT QUESTIONS

12-1	**a.** 1.5 V	**12-3**	**a.** T	**12-6**	**a.** alkaline	**12-9**	**a.** F	**12-12**	**a.** T
	b. 2.1 V		**b.** T		**b.** mercury		**b.** T		**b.** T
	c. secondary		**c.** F		**c.** size C		**c.** T	**12-13**	**a.** F
12-2	**a.** T	**12-4**	**a.** T	**12-7**	**a.** T		**d.** T		**b.** T
	b. T		**b.** T		**b.** T	**12-10**	**a.** six	**12-14**	**a.** low
	c. F	**12-5**	**a.** F	**12-8**	**a.** six		**b.** two		**b.** high
			b. F		**b.** 15 A		**c.** twelve	**12-15**	**a.** T
					c. 1270	**12-11**	**a.** F		**b.** T
							b. T		

REVIEW: CHAPTERS 11 AND 12

SUMMARY

- A conductor is a material whose resistance is very low. Some examples of good conductors are silver, copper, and aluminum, with copper generally being used for wire. An insulator is a material whose resistance is very high. Some examples of good insulators include air, mica, rubber, porcelain, and plastics.
- The gage sizes for copper wires are listed in Table 11-1. As the gage sizes increase from 1 to 40, the diameter and circular area decrease. Higher gage numbers correspond to thinner wire.
- For switches, the term *pole* refers to the number of completely isolated circuits that can be controlled by the switch. The term *throw* refers to the number of closed-contact positions that exist per pole. A switch can have any number of poles and throws.
- A good fuse has very low resistance, with an *IR* voltage of practically zero. An open fuse has nearly infinite resistance. If an open fuse exists in a series circuit or in the main line of a parallel circuit, its voltage drop equals the applied voltage.
- The resistance of a wire is directly proportional to its length and inversely proportional to its cross-sectional area.
- All metals in their purest form have a positive temperature coefficient, which means that their resistance increases with an increase in temperature. Carbon has a negative temperature coefficient, which means that its resistance decreases as the temperature increases.
- An ion is an atom that has either gained or lost electrons. A negative ion is an atom with more electrons than protons. Conversely, a positive ion is an atom with more protons than electrons. Ions can move to provide electric current in liquids and gases. The motion of ions is called ionization current.
- A battery is a combination of individual voltaic cells. A primary cell cannot be recharged, whereas a secondary cell can be recharged several times. The main types of cells for batteries include alkaline, silver oxide, nickel cadmium, lithium, and lead-acid.
- With individual cells in series, the total battery voltage equals the sum of the individual cell voltages. This is assuming that the cells are connected in a series-aiding manner. The current rating of the series-aiding cells is the same as that for the cell with the lowest current rating.
- With individual cells in parallel, the voltage is the same as that across one cell. However, the current rating of the combination equals the sum of the individual current-rating values. Only cells that have the same voltage should be connected in parallel.
- All types of dc and ac generators have an internal resistance r_i. Physically, the value of r_i may be the resistance of the electrolyte in a battery or the wire in a rotary generator.
- When a generator supplies current to a load, the terminal voltage drops because some voltage is dropped across the internal resistance r_i.

- Matching a load to a generator means making R_L equal to r_i. When $R_L = r_i$, maximum power is delivered from the generator to the load.
- A constant-voltage source has a very low internal r_i, whereas a constant-current source has a very high internal r_i.

REVIEW SELF-TEST

ANSWERS AT BACK OF BOOK.

Choose (a), (b), (c), or (d).

1. Which of the following is the best conductor of electricity? (a) carbon; (b) silicon; (c) rubber; (d) copper.
2. Which of the following wires has the largest cross-sectional area? (a) No. 28 gage; (b) No. 23 gage; (c) No. 12 gage; (d) No. 16 gage.
3. The filament of a light bulb measures 2.5 Ω when cold. With 120 V applied across the filament, the bulb dissipates 75 W of power. What is the hot resistance of the bulb? (a) 192 Ω; (b) 0.625 Ω; (c) 2.5 Ω; (d) 47 Ω.
4. A DPST switch has how many terminal connections for soldering? (a) 3; (b) 1; (c) 4; (d) 6.
5. Which of the following materials has a negative temperature coefficient? (a) steel; (b) carbon; (c) tungsten; (d) nichrome.
6. The IR voltage across a good fuse equals: (a) the applied voltage; (b) one-half the applied voltage; (c) infinity; (d) zero.
7. A battery has a no-load voltage of 9 V. Its terminal voltage drops to 8.25 V when a load current of 200 mA is drawn from the battery. The internal resistance r_i equals: (a) 0.375 Ω; (b) 3.75 Ω; (c) 41.25 Ω; (d) 4.5 Ω.
8. When $R_L = r_i$: (a) maximum voltage is across R_L; (b) maximum power is delivered to R_L; (c) the efficiency is 100 percent; (d) the minimum power is delivered to R_L.
9. A constant-current source has a(n): (a) very high internal resistance; (b) constant output voltage; (c) very low internal resistance; (d) output voltage that is always zero.
10. Cells can be connected in series-parallel to: (a) increase the voltage above that of a single cell; (b) increase the current capacity above that of a single cell; (c) reduce the voltage and current rating below that of a single cell; (d) both (a) and (b).

REFERENCES

Adams, J. A., and G. Rockmaker: *Industrial Electricity—Principles and Practices,* Glencoe/McGraw-Hill, Columbus, Ohio.

Fowler, R. J.: *Electricity—Principles and Applications,* Glencoe/McGraw-Hill, Columbus, Ohio.

Richter, H. P.: *Practical Electrical Wiring,* McGraw-Hill, New York.

CHAPTER 13

MAGNETISM

Electrical effects exist in two forms, voltage and current. In terms of voltage, separated electric charges have the potential to do mechanical work in attracting or repelling charges. Similarly, any electric current has an associated magnetic field that can do the work of attraction or repulsion. Materials made of iron, nickel, and cobalt, particularly, concentrate their magnetic effects at opposite ends, where the magnetic material meets a nonmagnetic medium such as air.

The points of concentrated magnetic strength are called north and south poles. The opposite magnetic poles correspond to the idea of opposite polarities of electric charges. The name *magnetism* is derived from the iron oxide mineral *magnetite*. Ferromagnetism refers specifically to the magnetic properties of iron.

CHAPTER OBJECTIVES

Upon completion of this chapter, you should be able to:

- *Describe* the magnetic field surrounding a magnet.
- *Define* the units of magnetic flux and flux density.
- *Describe* how an iron bar is magnetized by induction.
- *Define* the term *relative permeability*.
- *Explain* the difference between a bar magnet and an electromagnet.
- *List* the three classifications of magnetic materials.
- *Explain* the electrical and magnetic properties of ferrites.
- *Describe* the Hall effect.

IMPORTANT TERMS IN THIS CHAPTER

air gap	gauss unit	permanent magnet
diamagnetic	Hall effect	relative permeability
electromagnet	keeper	shielding
ferrites	magnetic induction	tesla unit
ferromagnetic	magnetic poles	toroid
flux	maxwell unit	weber unit
flux density	paramagnetic	

TOPICS COVERED IN THIS CHAPTER

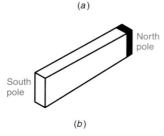

FIG. 13-1 Poles of a magnet. (*a*) Electromagnet (EM) produced by current from a battery. (*b*) Permanent magnet (PM) without any external source of current.

As shown in Fig. 13-1, the north and south poles of a magnet are the points of concentration of magnetic strength. The practical effects of this ferromagnetism result from the magnetic field of force between the two poles at opposite ends of the magnet. Although the magnetic field is invisible, evidence of its force can be seen when small iron filings are sprinkled on a glass or paper sheet placed over a bar magnet (Fig. 13-2*a*). Each iron filing becomes a small bar magnet. If the sheet is tapped gently to overcome friction so that the filings can move, they become aligned by the magnetic field.

Many filings cling to the ends of the magnet, showing that the magnetic field is strongest at the poles. The field exists in all directions but decreases in strength with increasing distance from the poles of the magnet.

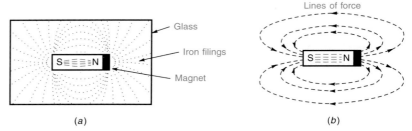

FIG. 13-2 Magnetic field of force around a bar magnet. (*a*) Field outlined by iron filings. (*b*) Field indicated by lines of force.

FIELD LINES In order to visualize the magnetic field without iron filings, we show the field as lines of force, as in Fig. 13-2*b*. The direction of the lines outside the magnet shows the path a north pole would follow in the field, repelled away from the north pole of the magnet and attracted to its south pole. Although we cannot actually have a unit north pole by itself, the field can be explored by noting how the north pole on a small compass needle moves.

The magnet can be considered as the generator for an external magnetic field, provided by the two opposite magnetic poles at the ends. This idea corresponds to the two opposite terminals on a battery as the source for an external electric field provided by opposite charges.

Magnetic field lines are unaffected by nonmagnetic materials such as air, vacuum, paper, glass, wood, or plastics. When these materials are placed in the magnetic field of a magnet, the field lines are the same as though the material were not there.

However, the magnetic field lines become concentrated when a magnetic substance like iron is placed in the field. Inside the iron, the field lines are more dense, compared with the field in air.

NORTH AND SOUTH MAGNETIC POLES The earth itself is a huge natural magnet, with its greatest strength at the north and south poles. Because of the earth's magnetic poles, if a small bar magnet is suspended so that it can turn easily, one end will always point north. This end of the bar magnet is defined as the *north-seeking pole,* as shown in Fig. 13-3. The opposite end is the

FIG. 13-3 Definition of north and south poles of bar magnet.

south-seeking pole. When polarity is indicated on a magnet, the north-seeking end is the north pole (N) and the opposite end is the south pole (S). It should be noted that the magnetic north pole deviates from true geographic north, the amount depending on location.

Similar to the force between electric charges is a force between magnetic poles causing attraction of opposite poles and repulsion between similar poles:

1. A north pole (N) and a south pole (S) tend to attract each other.
2. A north pole (N) tends to repel another north pole (N), while a south pole (S) tends to repel another south pole (S).

These forces are illustrated by the field of iron filings between opposite poles in Fig. 13-4*a* and between similar poles in Fig. 13-4*b*.

(*a*) (*b*)

FIG. 13-4 Magnetic field patterns produced by iron filings. (*a*) Field between opposite poles. The north and south poles could be reversed. (*b*) Field between similar poles. The two north poles could be south poles.

TEST-POINT QUESTION 13-1

Answers at end of chapter.

Answer True or False.
a. On a magnet, the north-seeking pole is labeled N.
b. Like poles have a force of repulsion.

13-2 MAGNETIC FLUX φ

The entire group of magnetic field lines, which can be considered to flow outward from the north pole of a magnet, is called *magnetic flux.* Its symbol is the

Greek letter ϕ (phi). A strong magnetic field has more lines of force and more flux than a weak magnetic field.

THE MAXWELL One maxwell (Mx) unit equals one magnetic field line. In Fig. 13-5, as an example, the flux illustrated is 6 Mx because there are 6 field lines flowing in or out for each pole. A 1-lb magnet can provide a magnetic flux ϕ of about 5000 Mx. This unit is named for James Clerk Maxwell (1831–1879), an important Scottish mathematical physicist who contributed much to electrical and field theory.

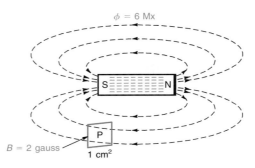

$\phi = 6$ Mx

$B = 2$ gauss

1 cm²

FIG. 13-5   Total flux ϕ is 6 lines or 6 Mx. Flux density B at point P is 2 lines per square centimeter or 2 G.

THE WEBER This is a larger unit of magnetic flux. One weber (Wb) equals 1×10^8 lines or maxwells. Since the weber is a large unit for typical fields, the microweber unit can be used. Then $1\ \mu\text{Wb} = 10^{-6}$ Wb. This unit is named for Wilhelm Weber (1804–1890), a German physicist.

To convert microwebers to lines, multiply by the conversion factor 10^8 lines per weber, as follows:

▶ $$1\ \mu\text{Wb} = 1 \times 10^{-6}\ \text{Wb} \times 10^8\ \frac{\text{lines}}{\text{Wb}}$$

$$= 1 \times 10^2\ \text{lines}$$

$$1\ \mu\text{Wb} = 100\ \text{lines or Mx}$$

Note that the conversion is arranged to make the weber units cancel, since we want maxwell units in the answer.

Even the microweber unit is larger than the maxwell unit. For the same 1-lb magnet producing the magnetic flux of 5000 Mx, it corresponds to 50 μWb. The calculations for this conversion of units are

$$\frac{5000\ \text{Mx}}{100\ \text{Mx}/\mu\text{Wb}} = 50\ \mu\text{Wb}$$

Note that the maxwell units cancel. Also, the $1/\mu$Wb becomes inverted from the denominator to μWb in the numerator.

SYSTEMS OF MAGNETIC UNITS The basic units in metric form can be defined in two ways:

1. The centimeter-gram-second system defines small units. This is the cgs system.

2. The meter-kilogram-second system is for larger units of a more practical size. This is the mks system.

Furthermore, the Système Internationale (SI) units provide a worldwide standard in mks dimensions. They are practical values based on the ampere of current.

With magnetic flux ϕ, the maxwell (Mx) is a cgs unit, while the weber (Wb) is an mks or SI unit. For science and engineering, the SI units are preferred values, but the cgs units are still used in many practical applications of magnetism.

TEST-POINT QUESTION 13-2

Answers at end of chapter.

The value of 2000 magnetic lines is how much flux in
a. Maxwell units?
b. Microweber units?

13-3 FLUX DENSITY *B*

As shown in Fig. 13-5, the flux density is the number of magnetic field lines per unit area of a section perpendicular to the direction of flux. As a formula,

▶
$$B = \frac{\phi}{A}$$

(13-1)

where ϕ is the flux through an area A, and the flux density is B.

THE GAUSS In the cgs system, this unit is one line per square centimeter, or 1 Mx/cm^2. As an example, in Fig. 13-5, the total flux ϕ is 6 lines, or 6 Mx. At point P in this field, however, the flux density B is 2 G because there are 2 lines per cm^2. The flux density has a higher value close to the poles, where the flux lines are more crowded.

As an example of flux density, B for a 1-lb magnet would be 1000 G at the poles. This unit is named for Karl F. Gauss (1777–1855), a German mathematician.

Example

EXAMPLE 1   With a flux of 10,000 Mx through a perpendicular area of 5 cm^2, what is the flux density in gauss?

ANSWER $B = \dfrac{\phi}{A} = \dfrac{10,000 \text{ Mx}}{5 \text{ cm}^2} = 2000 \dfrac{\text{Mx}}{\text{cm}^2}$

$B = 2000$ G

As typical values, B for the earth's magnetic field can be about 0.2 G; a large laboratory magnet produces B of 50,000 G. Since the gauss is so small, it is often used in kilogauss units, where 1 kG = 10^3 G.

THE TESLA   In SI, the unit of flux density B is webers per square meter (Wb/m^2). One weber per square meter is called a *tesla*, abbreviated T. This unit is named for Nikola Tesla (1857–1943), a Yugoslav-born American inventor in electricity and magnetism.

When converting between cgs and mks units, note that

▶   1 m = 100 cm or 1 × 10^2 cm
         1 m^2 = 10,000 cm^2 or 10^4 cm^2

These conversions are from the larger m and m^2 to smaller units of cm and cm^2. To go the opposite way,

▶   1 cm = 0.01 m or 1 × 10^{-2} m
         1 cm^2 = 0.0001 m^2 or 1 × 10^{-4} m^2

As an example, 5 cm^2 is equal to 0.0005 m^2 or 5 × 10^{-4} m^2. The calculations for the conversion are

$$5 \text{ cm}^2 \times \frac{0.0001 \text{ m}^2}{\text{cm}^2} = 0.0005 \text{ m}^2$$

In powers of 10, the conversion is

$$5 \text{ cm}^2 \times \frac{1 \times 10^{-4} \text{ m}^2}{\text{cm}^2} = 5 \times 10^{-4} \text{ m}^2$$

In both cases, note that the units of cm^2 cancel to leave m^2 for the desired unit.

Example

EXAMPLE 2   With the flux of 400 μWb through an area of 0.0005 m^2, what is the flux density B in tesla units?

ANSWER $B = \dfrac{\phi}{A} = \dfrac{400 \times 10^{-6} \text{ Wb}}{5 \times 10^{-4} \text{m}^2}$

$= \dfrac{400}{5} \times 10^{-2}$

$= 80 \times 10^{-2}$ Wb/m^2

$B = 0.80$ T

The tesla is a larger unit than the gauss, as

▶ $1 \text{ T} = 1 \times 10^4 \text{ G}$

For example, the flux density of 20,000 G is equal to 2 T. The calculations for this conversion are

$$\frac{20,000 \text{ G}}{1 \times 10^4 \text{ G/T}} = \frac{2 \times 10^4 \text{ T}}{1 \times 10^4} = 2 \text{ T}$$

Note that the G units cancel to leave T units for the desired answer. Also, the 1/T in the denominator becomes inverted to T units in the numerator.

COMPARISON OF FLUX AND FLUX DENSITY   Remember that the flux ϕ includes total area, while the flux density B is for a specified unit area. The difference between ϕ and B is illustrated in Fig. 13-6 with cgs units. The total area A here is 9 cm², equal to 3 cm × 3 cm. For one unit box of 1 cm², 16 lines are shown. Therefore, the flux density B is 16 lines or maxwells per cm², which equals 16 G. The total area includes nine of these boxes. Therefore, the total flux ϕ is 144 lines or maxwells, equal to 9 × 16 for $B \times A$.

For the opposite case, if the total flux ϕ is given as 144 lines or maxwells, the flux density is found by dividing 144 by 9 cm². This division of 144/9 equals 16 lines or maxwells per cm², which is 16 G.

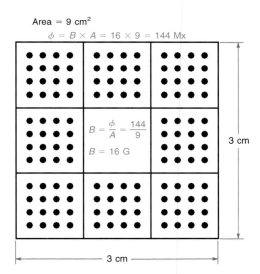

Area = 9 cm²
$\phi = B \times A = 16 \times 9 = 144$ Mx

$B = \dfrac{\phi}{A} = \dfrac{144}{9}$

$B = 16$ G

3 cm

3 cm

FIG. 13-6   Comparison of total flux ϕ and flux density B. Total area of 9 cm² has 144 lines or 144 Mx. For 1 cm² the flux density is 144/9 = 16 G.

TEST-POINT QUESTION 13-3

Answers at end of chapter.
a. The ϕ is 9000 Mx through 3 cm². How much is B in gauss units?
b. How much is B in tesla units for ϕ of 90 μWb through 0.0003 m²?

The electric or magnetic effect of one body on another without any physical contact between them is called *induction*. For instance, a permanent magnet can induce an unmagnetized iron bar to become a magnet, without the two touching. The iron bar then becomes a magnet, as shown in Fig. 13-7. What happens is that the magnetic lines of force generated by the permanent magnet make the internal molecular magnets in the iron bar line up in the same direction, instead of the random directions in unmagnetized iron. The magnetized iron bar then has magnetic poles at the ends, as a result of the magnetic induction.

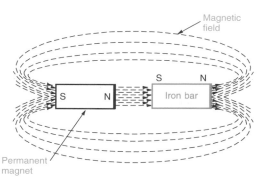

FIG. 13-7 Magnetizing an iron bar by induction.

Note that the induced poles in the iron have opposite polarity from the poles of the magnet. Since opposite poles attract, the iron bar will be attracted. Any magnet attracts to itself all magnetic materials by induction.

Although the two bars in Fig. 13-7 are not touching, the iron bar is in the magnetic flux of the permanent magnet. It is the invisible magnetic field that links the two magnets, enabling one to affect the other. Actually, this idea of magnetic flux extending outward from the magnetic poles is the basis for many inductive effects in ac circuits. More generally, the magnetic field between magnetic poles and the electric field between electric charges form the basis for wireless radio transmission and reception.

POLARITY OF INDUCED POLES Note that the north pole of the permanent magnet in Fig. 13-7 induces an opposite south pole at this end of the iron bar. If the permanent magnet were reversed, its south pole would induce a north pole. The closest induced pole will always be of opposite polarity. This is the reason why either end of a magnet can attract another magnetic material to itself. No matter which pole is used, it will induce an opposite pole, and the opposite poles are attracted.

RELATIVE PERMEABILITY Soft iron, as an example, is very effective in concentrating magnetic field lines, by induction in the iron. This ability to concentrate magnetic flux is called *permeability*. Any material that is easily magnetized has high permeability, therefore, as the field lines are concentrated because of induction.

DID YOU KNOW?

Some Chicago buses are emission-free because they run on hydrogen-generated electricity, which operates fuel cells.

Numerical values of permeability for different materials compared with air or vacuum can be assigned. For example, if the flux density in air is 1 G but an iron core in the same position in the same field has a flux density of 200 G, the relative permeability of the iron core equals 200/1, or 200.

The symbol for relative permeability is μ_r (mu), where the subscript r indicates relative permeability. Typical values for μ_r are 100 to 9000 for iron and steel. There are no units, because μ_r is a comparison of two flux densities and the units cancel. The symbol K_m may also be used for relative permeability, to indicate this characteristic of a material for a magnetic field, corresponding to K_ϵ for an electric field.

TEST-POINT QUESTION 13-4

Answers at end of chapter.

Answer True or False.
a. Induced poles always have opposite polarity from the inducing poles.
b. The relative permeability of air or vacuum is approximately 300.

13-5 AIR GAP OF A MAGNET

As shown in Fig. 13-8, the air space between poles of a magnet is its air gap. The shorter the air gap, the stronger the field in the gap for a given pole strength. Since air is not magnetic and cannot concentrate magnetic lines, a larger air gap only provides additional space for the magnetic lines to spread out.

Referring to Fig. 13-8a, note that the horseshoe magnet has more crowded magnetic lines in the air gap, compared with the widely separated lines around the bar magnet in Fig. 13-8b. Actually, the horseshoe magnet can be considered as a bar magnet bent around to place the opposite poles closer. Then the magnetic lines of the poles reinforce each other in the air gap. The purpose of a short air gap is to concentrate the magnetic field outside the magnet, for maximum induction in a magnetic material placed in the gap.

RING MAGNET WITHOUT AIR GAP When it is desired to concentrate magnetic lines within a magnet, however, the magnet can be formed as a closed magnetic loop. This method is illustrated in Fig. 13-9a by the two permanent horseshoe magnets placed in a closed loop with opposite poles touching. Since the loop has no open ends, there can be no air gap and no poles. The north and south poles of each magnet cancel as opposite poles touch.

Each magnet has its magnetic lines inside, plus the magnetic lines of the other magnet, but outside the magnets the lines cancel because they are in opposite directions. The effect of the closed magnetic loop, therefore, is maximum concentration of magnetic lines in the magnet with minimum lines outside.

The same effect of a closed magnetic loop is obtained with the *toroid* or ring magnet in Fig. 13-9b, made in the form of a doughnut. Iron is often used for the core. This type of electromagnet has maximum strength in the iron ring, with little flux outside. As a result, the toroidal magnet is less sensitive to induction from external magnetic fields and, conversely, has little magnetic effect outside the coil.

(a)

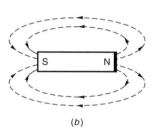

(b)

FIG. 13-8 The horseshoe magnet in (a) has a smaller air gap than the bar magnet in (b).

(a)

(b)

FIG. 13-9 Examples of a closed magnetic ring without any air gap. (*a*) Two PM horseshoe magnets with opposite poles touching. (*b*) Toroid magnet.

(a)   (b)

(c)

FIG. 13-10 Storing permanent magnets in a closed loop, with opposite poles touching. (*a*) Four bar magnets. (*b*) Two bar magnets. (*c*) Horseshoe magnet with iron keeper across air gap.

It should be noted that, even if the winding is over only a small part of the ring, practically all the flux is in the iron core because its permeability is so much greater than that of air. The small part of the field in the air is called *leakage flux.*

KEEPER FOR A MAGNET The principle of the closed magnetic ring is used to protect permanent magnets in storage. In Fig. 13-10*a*, four permanent-magnet bars are in a closed loop, while Fig. 13-10*b* shows a stacked pair. Additional even pairs can be stacked this way, with opposite poles touching. The closed loop in Fig. 13-10*c* shows one permanent horseshoe magnet with a soft-iron *keeper* across the air gap. The keeper maintains the strength of the permanent magnet as it becomes magnetized by induction to form a closed loop. Then any external magnetic field is concentrated in the closed loop without inducing opposite poles in the permanent magnet. If permanent magnets are not stored this way, the polarity can be reversed with induced poles produced by a strong external field from a dc source; an alternating field can demagnetize the magnet.

13-6 TYPES OF MAGNETS

The two broad classes are permanent magnets and electromagnets. An electromagnet needs current from an external source to maintain its magnetic field. With a permanent magnet, not only is its magnetic field present without any external current, but the magnet can maintain its strength indefinitely. Sharp mechanical shock as well as extreme heat, however, can cause demagnetization.

ELECTROMAGNETS Current in a wire conductor has an associated magnetic field. If the wire is wrapped in the form of a coil, as in Fig. 13-11, the current and its magnetic field become concentrated in a smaller space, resulting in a stronger field. With the length much greater than its width, the coil is called a *solenoid.* It acts like a bar magnet, with opposite poles at the ends.

More current and more turns make a stronger magnetic field. Also, the iron core concentrates magnetic lines inside the coil. Soft iron is generally used for the core because it is easily magnetized and demagnetized.

The coil in Fig. 13-11, with the switch closed and current in the coil, is an electromagnet that can pick up the steel nail shown. If the switch is opened, the magnetic field is reduced to zero, and the nail will drop off. This ability of an electromagnet to provide a strong magnetic force of attraction that can be turned on or off easily has many applications in lifting magnets, buzzers, bells or chimes, and relays. A relay is a switch with contacts that are opened or closed by an electromagnet.

Another common application is magnetic tape recording. The tape is coated with fine particles of iron oxide. The recording head is a coil that produces a magnetic field in proportion to the current. As the tape passes through the air gap of the head, small areas of the coating become magnetized by induction. On playback, the moving magnetic tape produces variations in electric current.

FIG. 13-11 Electromagnet holding nail when switch S is closed for current in coil.

PERMANENT MAGNETS   These are made of hard magnetic materials, such as cobalt steel, magnetized by induction in the manufacturing process. A very strong field is needed for induction in these materials. When the magnetizing field is removed, however, residual induction makes the material a permanent magnet. A common PM material is *alnico,* a commercial alloy of aluminum, nickel, and iron, with cobalt, copper, and titanium added to produce about 12 grades. The Alnico V grade is often used for PM loudspeakers (Fig. 13-12). In this application, a typical size of PM slug for a steady magnetic field is a few ounces to about 5 lb, with a flux ϕ of 500 to 25,000 lines or maxwells. One advantage of a PM loudspeaker is that only two connecting leads are needed for the voice coil, as the steady magnetic field of the PM slug is obtained without any field-coil winding.

Commercial permanent magnets will last indefinitely if they are not subjected to high temperatures, to physical shock, or to a strong demagnetizing field. If the magnet becomes hot, however, the molecular structure can be rearranged, resulting in loss of magnetism that is not recovered after cooling. The point at which a magnetic material loses its ferromagnetic properties is the *Curie temperature.* For iron, this temperature is about 800°C, when the relative permeability drops to unity. A permanent magnet does not become exhausted with use, as its magnetic properties are determined by the structure of the internal atoms and molecules.

CLASSIFICATION OF MAGNETIC MATERIALS   When we consider materials simply as either magnetic or nonmagnetic, this division is really based on the strong magnetic properties of iron. However, weak magnetic materials can be important in some applications. For this reason, a more exact classification includes the following three groups:

1. *Ferromagnetic materials.* These include iron, steel, nickel, cobalt, and commercial alloys such as alnico and Permalloy. They become strongly magnetized in the same direction as the magnetizing field, with high values of permeability from 50 to 5000. Permalloy has μ_r of 100,000 but is easily saturated at relatively low values of flux density.
2. *Paramagnetic materials.* These include aluminum, platinum, manganese, and chromium. The permeability is slightly more than 1. They become weakly magnetized in the same direction as the magnetizing field.
3. *Diamagnetic materials.* These include bismuth, antimony, copper, zinc, mercury, gold, and silver. The permeability is less than 1. They become weakly magnetized, but in the opposite direction from the magnetizing field.

The basis of all magnetic effects is the magnetic field associated with electric charges in motion. Within the atom, the motion of its orbital electrons generates a magnetic field. There are two kinds of electron motion in the atom. First is the electron revolving in its orbit. This motion provides a diamagnetic effect. However, this magnetic effect is weak because thermal agitation at normal room temperature results in random directions of motion that neutralize each other.

FIG. 13-12   Example of a PM loudspeaker.

More effective is the magnetic effect from the motion of each electron spinning on its own axis. The spinning electron serves as a tiny permanent magnet. Opposite spins provide opposite polarities. Two electrons spinning in opposite directions form a pair, neutralizing the magnetic fields. In the atoms of ferromagnetic materials, however, there are many unpaired electrons with spins in the same direction, resulting in a strong magnetic effect.

In terms of molecular structure, iron atoms are grouped in microscopically small arrangements called *domains*. Each domain is an elementary *dipole magnet,* with two opposite poles. In crystal form, the iron atoms have domains that are parallel to the axes of the crystal. Still, the domains can point in different directions, because of the different axes. When the material becomes magnetized by an external magnetic field, though, the domains become aligned in the same direction. With PM materials, the alignment remains after the external field is removed.

TEST-POINT QUESTION 13-6

Answers at end of chapter.

Answer True or False.
a. An electromagnet needs current to maintain its magnetic field.
b. A relay coil is an electromagnet.
c. Steel is a diamagnetic material.

13-7 FERRITES

Ferrites is the name for nonmetallic materials that have the ferromagnetic properties of iron. The ferrites have very high permeability, like iron. However, a ferrite is a nonconducting ceramic material, while iron is a conductor. The permeability of ferrites is in the range of 50 to 3000. The specific resistance is $10^5 \, \Omega \cdot$ cm, which makes the ferrite an insulator.

A common application is a ferrite core, usually adjustable, in the coils for RF transformers. The ferrite core is much more efficient than iron when the current alternates at a high frequency. The reason is that less I^2R power is lost by eddy currents in the core because of its very high resistance.

A ferrite core is used in small coils and transformers for signal frequencies up to 20 MHz, approximately. The high permeability means the transformer can be very small. However, the ferrites are easily saturated at low values of magnetizing current. This disadvantage means the ferrites are not used for power transformers.

Another application is in ferrite beads (Fig. 13-13). A bare wire is used as a string for one or more beads. The bead concentrates the magnetic field of the current in the wire. This construction serves as a simple, economical RF choke, instead of a coil. The purpose of the choke is to reduce the current just for an undesired radio frequency.

No. 22 wire Ferrite bead

1 in.

FIG. 13-13 Ferrite bead equivalent to coil with 20 μH of inductance at 10 MHz.

TEST-POINT QUESTION 13-7

Answers at end of chapter.
a. Which has more R, the ferrites or soft iron?
b. Which has more I^2R losses, an insulator or a conductor?

13-8 MAGNETIC SHIELDING

The idea of preventing one component from affecting another through their common electric or magnetic field is called *shielding*. Examples are the braided copper-wire shield around the inner conductor of a coaxial cable, a metal shield can that encloses an RF coil, or a shield of magnetic material enclosing a cathode-ray tube.

The problem in shielding is to prevent one component from inducing an effect in the shielded component. The shielding materials are always metals, but there is a difference between using good conductors with low resistance like copper and aluminum and using good magnetic materials like soft iron.

Magnetic field
B = 10 kG

InAs plate

I = 100 mA

v_H = 60 mV
(Hall voltage)

FIG. 13-14 The Hall effect. Hall voltage V_H generated across the element is proportional to the perpendicular flux density B.

A good conductor is best for two shielding functions. One is to prevent induction of static electric charges. The other is to shield against the induction of a varying magnetic field. For static charges, the shield provides opposite induced charges, which prevent induction inside the shield. For a varying magnetic field, the shield has induced currents that oppose the inducing field. Then there is little net field strength to produce induction inside the shield.

The best shield for a steady magnetic field is a good magnetic material of high permeability. A steady field is produced by a permanent magnet, a coil with steady direct current, or the earth's magnetic field. A magnetic shield of high permeability concentrates the magnetic flux. Then there is little flux to induce poles in a component inside the shield. The shield can be considered as a short circuit for the lines of magnetic flux.

TEST-POINT QUESTION 13-8

Answers at end of chapter.

Answer True or False.
a. Magnetic material with high permeability is a good shield for a steady magnetic field.
b. A conductor is a good shield against a varying magnetic field.

13-9 THE HALL EFFECT

FIG. 13-15 Gaussmeter to measure flux density, with probe containing indium arsenide element.

In 1879, E. H. Hall observed that a small voltage is generated across a conductor carrying current in an external magnetic field. The Hall voltage was very small with typical conductors, and little use was made of this effect. However, with the development of semiconductors, larger values of Hall voltage can be generated. The semiconductor material indium arsenide (InAs) is generally used. As illustrated in Fig. 13-14, the InAs element inserted in the magnetic field can generate 60 mV with B equal to 10 kG and an I of 100 mA. The applied flux must be perpendicular to the direction of current. With current in the direction of the length of conductor, the generated voltage is developed across the width.

The amount of Hall voltage v_H is directly proportional to the value of flux density B. This means that values of B can be measured by means of v_H. As an example, the gaussmeter in Fig. 13-15 uses an InAs probe in the magnetic field to generate a proportional Hall voltage v_H. This value of v_H is then read by the meter, which is calibrated in gauss. The original calibration is made in terms of a reference magnet with a specified flux density.

TEST-POINT QUESTION 13-9

Answers at end of chapter.
a. In Fig. 13-14, how much is the generated Hall voltage?
b. Does the gaussmeter in Fig. 13-15 measure flux or flux density?

13 SUMMARY AND REVIEW

- Iron, nickel, and cobalt are common examples of magnetic materials. Air, paper, wood, and plastics are nonmagnetic.
- The pole of a magnet that seeks the magnetic north pole of the earth is called a north pole; the opposite pole is a south pole.
- Opposite magnetic poles have a force of attraction; similar poles repel.
- An electromagnet needs current from an external source to provide a magnetic field. Permanent magnets retain their magnetism indefinitely.
- Any magnet has an invisible field of force outside the magnet, indicated by magnetic field lines. Their direction is from the north to the south pole.
- The open ends of a magnet where it meets a nonmagnetic material provide magnetic poles. At opposite open ends, the poles have opposite polarity.
- A magnet with an air gap has opposite poles with magnetic lines of force across the gap. A closed magnetic ring has no poles.
- Magnetic induction enables the field of a magnet to induce magnetic poles in a magnetic material without touching.
- Permeability is the ability to concentrate magnetic flux. A good magnetic material has high permeability.
- Magnetic shielding means isolating a component from a magnetic field. The best shield against a steady magnetic field is a material with high permeability.
- The Hall voltage is a small emf generated across the width of a conductor carrying current through its length, when magnetic flux is applied perpendicular to the current. This effect is generally used in the gaussmeter to measure flux density.
- Table 13-1 summarizes the units of magnetic flux ϕ and flux density B.

TABLE 13-1 MAGNETIC FLUX ϕ AND FLUX DENSITY B

NAME	SYMBOL	CGS UNITS	MKS OR SI UNITS
Flux, or total lines	$\phi = B \times \text{area}$	1 maxwell (Mx) = 1 line	1 weber (Wb) = 10^8 Mx
Flux density, or lines per unit area	$B = \dfrac{\phi}{\text{area}}$	$1 \text{ gauss (G)} = \dfrac{1 \text{ Mx}}{\text{cm}^2}$	$1 \text{ tesla (T)} = \dfrac{1 \text{ Wb}}{\text{m}^2}$

ANSWERS AT BACK OF BOOK.

Answer True or False.

1. Iron and steel are ferromagnetic materials with high permeability.
2. Ferrites are ferromagnetic but have high electrical resistance.
3. Air, vacuum, wood, paper, and plastics have no effect on magnetic flux.
4. Aluminum is ferromagnetic.
5. Magnetic poles exist on opposite sides of an air gap.
6. A closed magnetic ring has no poles and no air gap.
7. A magnet can pick up a steel nail by magnetic induction.
8. Induced poles are always opposite from the original field poles.
9. Soft iron concentrates magnetic flux by means of induction.
10. Without current, an electromagnet has practically no magnetic field.
11. The total flux ϕ of 5000 lines equals 5 Mx.
12. A flux ϕ of 5000 Mx through a cross-sectional area of 5 cm^2 has a flux density B of 1000 G or 1 kG.
13. The flux density B of 1000 G equals 1000 lines/cm^2.
14. A magnetic pole is a terminal where a magnetic material meets a nonmagnetic material.
15. High permeability for magnetic flux corresponds to high resistance for a current conductor.

QUESTIONS
---

1. Name two magnetic materials and three nonmagnetic materials.
2. Explain the difference between a permanent magnet and an electromagnet.
3. Draw a horseshoe magnet, with its magnetic field. Label the magnetic poles, indicate the air gap, and show the direction of flux.
4. Define: relative permeability, shielding, induction, Hall voltage.
5. Give the symbol, cgs unit, and SI unit for magnetic flux and for flux density.
6. How are the north and south poles of a bar magnet determined with a magnetic compass?
7. Referring to Fig. 13-11, why can either end of the magnet pick up the nail?
8. What is the difference between flux ϕ and flux density B?

PROBLEMS

ANSWERS TO ODD-NUMBERED PROBLEMS AT BACK OF BOOK.

1. A magnet produces 5000 field lines. Find ϕ in maxwells and webers.
2. If the area of the pole in Prob. 1 is 5 cm^2, calculate B in gauss units.

3. Calculate B in tesla units for a 200-μWb flux through an area of 5×10^{-4} m^2.
4. Convert 3000 G to tesla units.
5. For a flux density B of 3 kG at a pole with a cross-sectional area of 8 cm^2, how much is the total flux ϕ in maxwell units?
6. Convert 17,000 Mx to weber units.
7. The flux density is 0.002 T in the air core of an electromagnet. When an iron core is inserted, the flux density in the core is 0.6 T. How much is the relative permeability μ_r of the iron core?
8. Draw the diagram of an electromagnet operated from a 12-V battery, in series with a switch. (a) If the coil resistance is 60 Ω, how much is the current in the coil with the switch closed? (b) Why is the magnetic field reduced to zero when the switch is opened?
9. Derive the conversion of 1 μWb = 100 Mx from the fact that 1 μWb = 10^{-6} Wb and 1 Wb = 10^8 Mx.
10. Derive the relation 1 T = 10^4 G. (Note: 1 m^2 = 10,000 cm^2.)
11. Make the following conversions: (a) 50 T to kG; (b) 6000 μWb to Mx; (c) 2500 G to T; (d) 15,000 Mx to Wb; (e) 0.004 T to G.
12. A permanent magnet produces a flux ϕ of 100,000 Mx. How many weber units does this represent?
13. A flux ϕ of 500 μWb exists in an area A of 0.01 m^2. What is the flux density B in gauss units?
14. The flux density in an iron core is 0.5 T. If the area of the core is 10 cm^2, calculate the total number of flux lines in the core.
15. Calculate the flux density B, in teslas for a flux ϕ of 400 μWb in an area of 0.005 m^2.

CRITICAL THINKING

1. A flux ϕ of 25 μWb exists in an area of 0.25 in^2. What is the flux density B in: (a) gauss units; (b) teslas?
2. At the north pole of an electromagnet, the flux density B equals 5 T. If the area A equals 0.125 in^2, determine the total number of flux lines ϕ in: (a) maxwells; (b) webers.

ANSWERS TO TEST-POINT QUESTIONS

13-1 a. T	13-3 a. 3000 G	13-5 a. T	13-7 a. ferrites	13-9 a. 60 mV
b. T	b. 0.3 T	b. T	b. conductor	b. flux density
13-2 a. 2000 Mx	13-4 a. T	13-6 a. T	13-8 a. T	
b. 20 μWb	b. F	b. T	b. T	
		c. F		

CHAPTER 14

MAGNETIC UNITS

A magnetic field is always associated with charges in motion. Therefore, the magnetic units can be derived from the current that produces the field.

The current in a conductor and its magnetic flux through the medium outside the conductor are related as follows:

1. The current I supplies a magnetizing force, or magneto-motive force (mmf), that increases with the amount of I.
2. The mmf results in a magnetic field intensity H that decreases with the length of conductor, as the field is less concentrated with more length.
3. The field intensity H produces a flux density B that increases with the permeability of the medium.

CHAPTER OBJECTIVES

Upon completion of this chapter, you should be able to:

- *Describe* what is meant by the terms *magnetomotive force* and *field intensity* and *list* the units of each.
- *Define absolute permeability.*
- *Explain* the *B-H* magnetization curve.
- *Define* the term *saturation* as it relates to a magnetic core.
- *Understand* magnetic hysteresis.
- *Write* the three forms of Ohm's law for magnetic circuits.
- *Explain* the difference between electric and magnetic fields.

IMPORTANT TERMS IN THIS CHAPTER

ampere-turns	hysteresis	reluctance
ampere-turns/meter	International System of	saturation
Coulomb's law	Units (SI)	tesla unit
degaussing	magnetomotive force (mmf)	
demagnetization	permeability (μ or mu)	

TOPICS COVERED IN THIS CHAPTER

14-1 AMPERE-TURNS OF MAGNETOMOTIVE FORCE (mmf)

With a coil magnet, the strength of the magnetic field depends on how much current flows in the turns of the coil. The more current, the stronger the magnetic field. Also, more turns in a specific length concentrate the field. The coil serves as a bar magnet, with opposite poles at the ends, providing a magnetic field proportional to the ampere-turns. As a formula,

▶ Ampere-turns $= I \times N = $ mmf   (14-1)

where I is the current in amperes multiplied by the number of turns N. The quantity IN specifies the amount of *magnetizing force or magnetic potential,* which is the *magnetomotive force (mmf)*.

The practical unit is the ampere-turn. The SI abbreviation for ampere-turn is A, the same as for the ampere, since the number of turns in a coil usually is constant but the current can be varied. However, for clarity we shall use the abbreviation A · t.

As shown in Fig. 14-1, a solenoid with 5 turns and 2 amperes has the same magnetizing force as one with 10 turns and 1 ampere, as the product of the amperes and turns is 10 for both cases. With thinner wire, more turns can be used in a given space. The amount of current is determined by the resistance of the wire and the source voltage. How many ampere-turns are necessary depends on the required magnetic field strength.

$IN = 2 \times 5$
$= 10$ A · t

(a)

$IN = 1 \times 10$
$= 10$ A · t

(b)

FIG. 14-1 Two examples of equal ampere-turns for the same mmf. (a) IN is $2 \times 5 = 10$. (b) IN is $1 \times 10 = 10$.

Example

EXAMPLE 1   Calculate the ampere-turns of mmf for a coil with 2000 turns and a 5-mA current.

ANSWER   mmf $= I \times N = 2000 \times 5 \times 10^{-3}$
$= 10$ A · t

EXAMPLE 2   A coil with 4 A is to provide the magnetizing force of 600 A · t. How many turns are necessary?

ANSWER $N = \dfrac{A \cdot t}{I} = \dfrac{600}{4}$
$N = 150$ turns

EXAMPLE 3   A coil with 400 turns must provide 800 A · t of magnetizing force. How much current is necessary?

ANSWER $I = \dfrac{A \cdot t}{N} = \dfrac{800}{400}$
$I = 2$ A

EXAMPLE 4 The wire in a solenoid of 250 turns has a resistance of 3 Ω. (**a**) How much is the current with the coil connected to a 6-V battery? (**b**) Calculate the ampere-turns of mmf.

ANSWER

a. $I = \dfrac{V}{R} = \dfrac{6\text{ V}}{3\text{ }\Omega}$

$I = 2\text{ A}$

b. mmf $= I \times N = 2$ A $\times$ 250 t

$= 500$ A $\cdot$ t

The ampere-turn is an SI unit. It is calculated as *IN*, with the current in amperes.

The cgs unit of mmf is the *gilbert,** abbreviated Gb. One ampere-turn equals 1.26 Gb. The number 1.26 is approximately $4\pi/10$, derived from the surface area of a sphere, which is $4\pi r^2$.

To convert *IN* to gilberts, multiply the ampere-turns by the constant conversion factor 1.26 Gb/1 A · t. As an example, 1000 A · t is the same mmf as 1260 Gb. The calculations are

$$1000 \text{ A} \cdot \text{t} \times 1.26\,\frac{\text{Gb}}{1\text{ A} \cdot \text{t}} = 1260 \text{ Gb}$$

Note that the units of A · t cancel in the conversion.

TEST-POINT QUESTION 14-1

Answers at end of chapter.

a. If the mmf is 243 A · t, and *I* is doubled from 2 to 4 A with the same number of turns, how much is the new mmf?
b. Convert 500 A · t to gilberts.

14-2 FIELD INTENSITY (*H*)

The ampere-turns of mmf specify the magnetizing force, but the intensity of the magnetic field depends on how long the coil is. At any point in space, a specific value of ampere-turns must produce less field intensity for a long coil than for a

---

*William Gilbert (1540–1603) was an English scientist who investigated the magnetism of the earth.

short coil that concentrates the same mmf. Specifically, the field intensity H in mks units is

$$\blacktriangleright \quad H = \frac{\text{ampere-turns of mmf}}{l \text{ meters}} \qquad \text{(14-2)}$$

This formula is for a solenoid. The field intensity H is at the center of an air core. With an iron core, H is the intensity through the entire core. By means of units for H, the magnetic field intensity can be specified for either electromagnets or permanent magnets, since both provide the same kind of magnetic field.

The length in Formula (14-2) is between poles. In Fig. 14-2a, the length is 1 m between the poles at the ends of the coil. In Fig. 14-2b, also, l is 1 m between the ends of the iron core. In Fig. 14-2c, though, l is 2 m between the poles at the ends of the iron core, although the winding is only 1 m long.

The examples in Fig. 14-2 illustrate the following comparisons:

1. In all three cases, the mmf is 1000 A · t, with the same value of IN.
2. In Fig. 14-2a and b, H equals 1000 A · t/m. In a, this H is the intensity at the center of the air core; in b, this H is the intensity through the entire iron core.
3. In Fig. 14-2c, because l is 2 m, H is 1000/2, or 500 A · t/m. This H is the intensity in the entire iron core.

FIG. 14-2   Relation between ampere-turns of mmf and the resultant field intensity H for different cores. Note that H = mmf/length. (a) Intensity H is 1000 A · t/m with an air core. (b) H = 1000 A · t/m in an iron core of the same length as the coil. (c) H is 1000/2 = 500 A · t/m in an iron core twice as long as the coil.

UNITS FOR H   The field intensity is basically mmf per unit of length. In practical units, H is ampere-turns per meter. The cgs unit for H is the *oersted,** abbreviated Oe, which equals one gilbert of mmf per centimeter.

CONVERSION OF UNITS   To convert SI units of A · t/m to cgs units of Oe, multiply by the conversion factor 0.0126 Oe per 1 A · t/m. As an example, 1000 A · t/m is the same H as 12.6 Oe. The calculations are

$$1000 \, \frac{\text{A} \cdot \text{t}}{\text{m}} \times 0.0126 \, \frac{\text{Oe}}{1 \, \text{A} \cdot \text{t/m}} = 12.6 \, \text{Oe}$$

*H. C. Oersted (1777–1851), a Danish physicist, discovered electromagnetism.

Note that the units of A · t and m cancel. The m in the conversion factor becomes inverted to the numerator.

TEST-POINT QUESTION 14-2

Answers at end of chapter.
a. Suppose that H is 250 A · t/m. The length is doubled from 0.2 to 0.4 m for the same IN. How much is the new H?
b. Convert 500 A · t/m to oersted units.

14-3 PERMEABILITY (μ)

Whether we say H is 1000 A · t/m or 12.6 Oe, these units specify how much field intensity is available to produce magnetic flux. However, the amount of flux actually produced by H depends on the material in the field. A good magnetic material with high relative permeability can concentrate flux and produce a large value of flux density B for a specified H. These factors are related by the formula:

▶ $$B = \mu \times H \tag{14-3}$$

or

▶ $$\mu = \frac{B}{H} \tag{14-4}$$

Using SI units, B is the flux density in webers per square meter, or teslas; H is the field intensity in ampere-turns per meter. In the cgs system the units are gauss for B and oersted for H. The factor μ is the absolute permeability, not referred to any other material, in units of B/H.

In the cgs system the units of gauss for B and oersteds for H have been defined to give μ the value of 1 G/Oe, for vacuum, air, or space. This simplification means that B and H have the same numerical values in air and in vacuum. For instance, the field intensity H of 12.6 Oe produces the flux density of 12.6 G, in air.

Furthermore, the values of relative permeability μ_r are the same as those for absolute permeability in B/H units in the cgs system. The reason is that μ is 1 for air or vacuum, used as the reference for the comparison. As an example, if μ_r for an iron sample is 600, the absolute μ is also 600 G/Oe.

In SI, however, the permeability of air or vacuum is not 1. Specifically, this value is $4\pi \times 10^{-7}$, or 1.26×10^{-6}, with the symbol μ_0. Therefore, values of relative permeability μ_r must be multiplied by 1.26×10^{-6} for μ_0 to calculate μ as B/H in SI units.

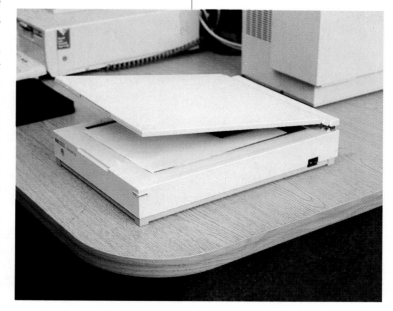

For an example of $\mu_r = 100$, the SI value of μ can be calculated as follows:

▶ $\mu = \mu_r \times \mu_0$

$= 100 \times 1.26 \times 10^{-6} \dfrac{\text{T}}{\text{A} \cdot \text{t/m}}$

$\mu = 126 \times 10^{-6} \dfrac{\text{T}}{\text{A} \cdot \text{t/m}}$

Example

EXAMPLE 5   A magnetic material has a μ_r of 500. Calculate the absolute μ as B/H **(a)** in cgs units, and **(b)** in SI units.

ANSWER

a. $\mu = \mu_r \times \mu_0$ in cgs units. Then

$= 500 \times 1 \dfrac{\text{G}}{\text{Oe}}$

$\mu = 500 \dfrac{\text{G}}{\text{Oe}}$

b. $\mu = \mu_r \times \mu_0$ in SI units. Then

$= 500 \times 1.26 \times 10^{-6} \dfrac{\text{T}}{\text{A} \cdot \text{t/m}}$

$\mu = 630 \times 10^{-6} \dfrac{\text{T}}{\text{A} \cdot \text{t/m}}$

EXAMPLE 6   For this example of $\mu = 630 \times 10^{-6}$ in SI units, calculate the flux density B that will be produced by the field intensity H equal to 1000 A · t/m.

ANSWER $B = \mu H = \left(630 \times 10^{-6} \dfrac{\text{T}}{\text{A} \cdot \text{t/m}} \right) \left(1000 \dfrac{\text{A} \cdot \text{t}}{\text{m}} \right)$

$= 630 \times 10^{-3} \text{ T}$

$B = 0.63 \text{ T}$

Note that the ampere-turns and meter units cancel, leaving only the tesla unit for the flux density B.

TEST-POINT QUESTION 14-3

Answers at end of chapter.
a. What is the value of μ_r for air, vacuum, or space?
b. An iron core has 200 times more flux density than air for the same field intensity H. How much is μ_r?
c. An iron core produces 200 G of flux density for 1 Oe of field intensity H. How much is μ?

14-4 *B-H* MAGNETIZATION CURVE

The *B-H* curve in Fig. 14-3 is often used to show how much flux density *B* results from increasing the amount of field intensity *H*. This curve is for soft iron, plotted for the values in Table 14-1, but similar curves can be obtained for all magnetic materials.

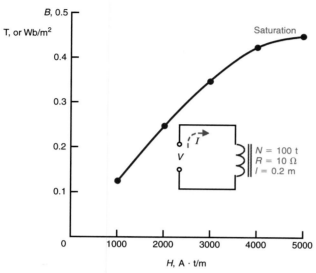

FIG. 14-3   *B-H* magnetization curve for soft iron. No values are shown near zero, where μ may vary with previous magnetization.

CALCULATING *H* AND *B*   The values in Table 14-1 are calculated as follows:

1. The current *I* in the coil equals *V/R*. For a 10-Ω coil resistance with 20 V applied, *I* is 2 A, as listed in the top row of Table 14-1. Increasing values of *V* produce more current in the coil.
2. The ampere-turns *IN* of magnetizing force increase with more current. Since the turns are constant at 100, the values of *IN* increase from 200 for 2 A in the top row to 1000 for 10 A in the bottom row.

TABLE 14-1   *B-H* VALUES FOR FIG. 14-3

V, VOLTS	R, Ω	$I = V/R$, AMPERES	N, TURNS	mmf, A·t	l, m	H, A·t/m	μ_R	$B = \mu \times H$, T
20	10	2	100	200	0.2	1000	100	0.126
40	10	4	100	400	0.2	2000	100	0.252
60	10	6	100	600	0.2	3000	100	0.378
80	10	8	100	800	0.2	4000	85	0.428
100	10	10	100	1000	0.2	5000	70	0.441

3. The field intensity H increases with higher IN. The values of H are in mks units of ampere-turns per meter. These values equal $IN/0.2$, as the length is 0.2 m. Therefore, each IN is just divided by 0.2, or multiplied by 5, for the corresponding values of H. Since H increases in the same proportion as I, sometimes the horizontal axis on a B-H curve is calibrated only in amperes, instead of in H units.

4. The flux density B depends on the field intensity H and permeability of the iron. The values of B in the last column are obtained by multiplying $\mu \times H$. However, with SI units the values of μ_r listed must be multiplied by 1.26×10^{-6} to obtain $\mu \times H$ in teslas.

SATURATION   Note that the permeability decreases for the highest values of H. With less μ, the iron core cannot provide proportional increases in B for increasing values of H. In the graph, for values of H above 4000 A · t/m, approximately, the values of B increase at a much slower rate, making the curve relatively flat at the top. The effect of little change in flux density when the field intensity increases is called *saturation*.

The reason is that the iron becomes saturated with magnetic lines of induction. After most of the molecular dipoles and the magnetic domains are aligned by the magnetizing force, very little additional induction can be produced. When the value of μ is specified for a magnetic material, it is usually the highest value before saturation.

TEST-POINT QUESTION 14-4

Answers at end of chapter.

Refer to Fig. 14-3.
a. How much is B, in tesla units, for 1500 A · t/m?
b. What value of H starts to produce saturation?

14-5 MAGNETIC HYSTERESIS

Hysteresis means "a lagging behind." With respect to the magnetic flux in an iron core of an electromagnet, the flux lags the increases or decreases in magnetizing force. The hysteresis results from the fact that the magnetic dipoles are not perfectly elastic. Once aligned by an external magnetizing force, the dipoles do not return exactly to their original positions when the force is removed. The effect is the same as if the dipoles were forced to move against an internal friction between molecules. Furthermore, if the magnetizing force is reversed in direction by reversal of the current in an electromagnet, the flux produced in the opposite direction lags behind the reversed magnetizing force.

HYSTERESIS LOSS   When the magnetizing force reverses thousands or millions of times per second, as with rapidly reversing alternating current, the hysteresis can cause a considerable loss of energy. A large part of the magnetizing force is then used just to overcome the internal friction of the molecular dipoles. The work done by the magnetizing force against this internal friction produces heat. This energy wasted in heat as the molecular dipoles lag the magnetizing force is called *hysteresis loss.* For steel and other hard magnetic materials, the hysteresis losses are much higher than in soft magnetic materials like iron.

When the magnetizing force varies at a slow rate, the hysteresis losses can be considered negligible. An example is an electromagnet with direct current that is simply turned on and off, or the magnetizing force of an alternating current that reverses 60 times per second or less. The faster the magnetizing force changes, however, the greater the hysteresis effect.

HYSTERESIS LOOP   To show the hysteresis characteristics of a magnetic material, its values of flux density B are plotted for a periodically reversing magnetizing force. See Fig. 14-4. This curve is the hysteresis loop of the material. The larger the area enclosed by the curve, the greater the hysteresis loss. The hysteresis loop is actually a *B-H* curve with an ac magnetizing force.

On the vertical axis, values of flux density B are indicated. The units can be gauss or teslas.

The horizontal axis indicates values of field intensity H. On this axis the units can be oersteds, ampere-turns per meter, ampere-turns, or just magnetizing current, as all factors are constant except I.

Opposite directions of current result in the opposite directions of $+H$ and $-H$ for the field lines. Similarly, opposite polarities are indicated for flux density as $+B$ or $-B$.

The current starts from zero at the center, when the material is unmagnetized. Then positive H values increase B to saturation at $+B_{max}$. Next H decreases to zero, but B drops to the value B_R, instead of to zero, because of hysteresis. When H becomes negative, B drops to zero and continues to $-B_{max}$, which is saturation in the opposite direction from $+B_{max}$ because of the reversed magnetizing current.

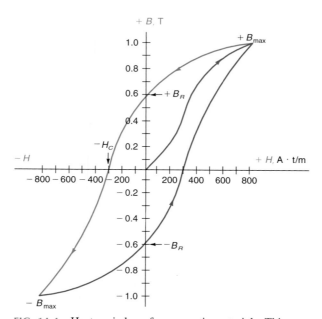

FIG. 14-4   Hysteresis loop for magnetic materials. This graph is a *B-H* curve like Fig. 14-3, but H alternates in polarity with alternating current.

Then, as the $-H$ values decrease, the flux density is reduced to $-B_R$. Finally, the loop is completed, with positive values of H producing saturation at B_{max} again. The curve does not return to the zero origin at the center because of hysteresis. As the magnetizing force periodically reverses, the values of flux density are repeated to trace out the hysteresis loop.

The value of either $+B_R$ or $-B_R$, which is the flux density remaining after the magnetizing force has been reduced to zero, is the *residual induction* of a magnetic material, also called its *retentivity*. In Fig. 14-4, the residual induction is 0.6 T, in either the positive or negative direction.

The value of $-H_C$, which equals the magnetizing force that must be applied in the reverse direction to reduce the flux density to zero, is the *coercive force* of the material. In Fig. 14-4, the coercive force $-H_C$ is 300 A · t/m.

DEMAGNETIZATION In order to demagnetize a magnetic material completely, the residual induction B_R must be reduced to zero. This usually cannot be accomplished by a reversed dc magnetizing force, because the material then would just become magnetized with opposite polarity. The practical way is to magnetize and demagnetize the material with a continuously decreasing hysteresis loop. This can be done with a magnetic field produced by alternating current. Then as the magnetic field and the material are moved away from each other, or the current amplitude is reduced, the hysteresis loop becomes smaller and smaller. Finally, with the weakest field, the loop collapses practically to zero, resulting in zero residual induction.

This method of demagnetization is also called *degaussing*. One application is degaussing the metal electrodes in a color picture tube, with a deguassing coil providing alternating current from the power line. Another example is erasing the recorded signal on magnetic tape by demagnetizing with an ac bias current. The average level of the erase current is zero, and its frequency is much higher than the recorded signal.

<hr>

TEST-POINT QUESTION 14-5

Answers at end of chapter.

Answer True or False.
a. Hysteresis loss increases with higher frequencies.
b. Degaussing is done with alternating current.

14-6 OHM'S LAW FOR MAGNETIC CIRCUITS

In comparison with electric circuits, the magnetic flux ϕ corresponds to current. The flux ϕ is produced by ampere-turns IN of magnetomotive force. Therefore, the mmf corresponds to voltage.

Opposition to the production of flux in a material is called its *reluctance*, comparable with resistance. The symbol for reluctance is $\mathcal{R}$. Reluctance is inversely proportional to permeability. Iron has high permeability and low reluctance. Air or vacuum has low permeability and high reluctance.

In Fig. 14-5, the ampere-turns of the coil produce magnetic flux throughout the magnetic path. The reluctance is the total opposition to the flux ϕ. In Fig. 14-5a, there is little reluctance in the closed iron path, and few ampere-turns are necessary. In Fig. 14-5b, however, the air gap has high reluctance, which requires many more ampere-turns for the same flux as in Fig. 14-5a.

The three factors—flux, ampere-turns of mmf, and reluctance—are related as follows:

▶ $$\phi = \frac{\text{mmf}}{\mathcal{R}}$$ (14-5)

which is known as Ohm's law for magnetic circuits, corresponding to $I = V/R$. The mmf is considered to produce flux ϕ in a magnetic material against the opposition of its reluctance $\mathcal{R}$. This relationship corresponds to emf or voltage producing current in a conducting material against the opposition of its resistance.

Remember that the units for the flux ϕ are maxwells and webers. These units measure total lines, as distinguished from flux density B, which equals lines per unit area.

There are no specific units for reluctance, but it can be considered as an mmf/ϕ ratio, just as resistance is a V/I ratio. Then $\mathcal{R}$ is ampere-turns per weber in SI units, or gilberts per maxwell in the cgs system.

The units for mmf are either gilberts in the cgs system or ampere-turns in SI.

Example

EXAMPLE 7 A coil has an mmf of 600 A · t and reluctance of 2 × 10^6 A · t/Wb. Calculate the total flux ϕ in microwebers.

ANSWER $\phi = \dfrac{\text{mmf}}{\mathcal{R}} = \dfrac{600 \text{ A} \cdot \text{t}}{2 \times 10^6 \text{ A} \cdot \text{t/Wb}}$

$\phi = 300 \times 10^{-6} \text{ Wb} = 300 \ \mu\text{Wb}$

EXAMPLE 8 A magnetic material has a total flux ϕ of 80 μWb with an mmf of 160 A · t. Calculate the reluctance in ampere-turns per weber.

ANSWER $\mathcal{R} = \dfrac{\text{mmf}}{\phi} = \dfrac{160 \text{ A} \cdot \text{t}}{80 \times 10^{-6} \text{ Wb}}$

$\mathcal{R} = 2 \times 10^6 \ \dfrac{\text{A} \cdot \text{t}}{\text{Wb}}$

Ampere-turns of mmf

Flux ϕ

(a)

$\phi = \dfrac{\text{mmf}}{\mathcal{R}}$

Ampere-turns of mmf

Air gap

(b)

FIG. 14-5 Two examples of a magnetic circuit. (*a*) Closed iron path with low reluctance that requires little mmf. (*b*) Higher-reluctance path with an air gap that requires more mmf.

TEST-POINT QUESTION 14-6

Answers at end of chapter.

Answer True or False.
a. Air has higher reluctance than soft iron.
b. More reluctance means more flux for a specified mmf.

The following examples show how the values of mmf, H, ϕ, B, and $\mathcal{R}$ depend on each other. These calculations are in SI units, which are generally used for magnetic circuits.

Example

EXAMPLE 9 For a coil having 50 turns and 2 A, how much is the mmf?

ANSWER $\quad$ mmf $= IN = 2 \times 50$

$\qquad$ mmf $= 100$ A $\cdot$ t

The value of 100 A $\cdot$ t is the mmf producing the magnetic field, with either an air core or an iron core.

EXAMPLE 10 If this coil is on an iron core with a length of 0.2 m, how much is the field intensity H throughout the iron?

ANSWER $\quad H = \dfrac{\text{mmf}}{l} = \dfrac{100 \text{ A} \cdot \text{t}}{0.2 \text{ m}}$

$\qquad H = 500$ A $\cdot$ t/m

This is an example of calculating the field intensity of the external magnetic field from the mmf of the current in the coil.

EXAMPLE 11 If the iron core in Example 10 has a relative permeability μ_r of 200, calculate the flux density B in teslas.

ANSWER $\quad B = \mu H = \mu_r \times 1.26 \times 10^{-6} \times H$

$$= 200 \times 1.26 \times 10^{-6} \frac{\text{T}}{\text{A} \cdot \text{t/m}} \times \frac{500 \text{ A} \cdot \text{t}}{\text{m}}$$

$\qquad B = 0.126$ T

EXAMPLE 12 The iron core in Example 11 has a cross-sectional area of 2×10^{-4} m². Calculate the amount of flux ϕ in the core.

ANSWER Use the relations between flux and density: $\phi = B \times$ Area. Since $B = 0.126$ T, or 0.126 Wb/m², then

$$\phi = B \times \text{Area} = 0.126 \frac{\text{Wb}}{\text{m}^2} \times 2 \times 10^{-4} \text{ m}^2$$

$$= 0.252 \times 10^{-4} \text{ Wb} = 25.2 \times 10^{-6} \text{ Wb}$$

$$\phi = 25.2 \ \mu\text{Wb}$$

EXAMPLE 13 With the mmf of 100 A $\cdot$ t for the coil in Fig. 14-5a and a value for ϕ of approximately 25×10^{-6} Wb in the iron core, calculate its reluctance $\mathcal{R}$.

ANSWER Using Ohm's law for magnetic circuits,

$$\mathcal{R} = \frac{\text{mmf}}{\phi} = \frac{100 \text{ A} \cdot \text{t}}{25 \times 10^{-6} \text{ Wb}}$$

$$\mathcal{R} = 4 \times 10^6 \text{ A} \cdot \text{t/Wb}$$

EXAMPLE 14 Refer to Fig. 14-5b. If the reluctance of the path (including the air gap) were 400×10^6 A · t/Wb, how much mmf would be required for the same flux of 25 μWb?

ANSWER

$$mmf = \phi \times \mathcal{R} = 25 \times 10^{-6}\, Wb \times 400 \times 10^6\, \frac{A \cdot t}{Wb}$$

$$mmf = 10{,}000\ A \cdot t$$

Notice that the 10,000 A · t of mmf here is 100 times more than the 100 A · t in Example 13, because of the higher reluctance with an air gap. This idea corresponds to the higher voltage needed to produce the same current in a higher resistance.

TEST-POINT QUESTION 14-7

Answers at end of chapter.

Answer True or False.
a. More I in a coil produces more mmf for a specified number of turns.
b. More length for the coil produces more field intensity H for a specified mmf.
c. Higher permeability of the core material produces more flux density B for a specified H.

14-8 COMPARISON OF MAGNETIC AND ELECTRIC FIELDS

As shown in Fig. 14-6a, there is an external field of lines of force between two electric charges, similar to the magnetic field between the magnetic poles in Fig. 14-6b. We cannot see the force of attraction and repulsion, just as the force of

FIG. 14-6 Comparison of electric and magnetic fields. (a) Electric field of attraction between static charges of opposite polarity. (b) Magnetic field of attraction between opposite magnetic poles.

gravity is invisible, but the force is evident in the work it can do. For both fields, the force tends to make opposite polarities attract and similar polarities repel.

The electric lines show the path an electron would follow in the field; the magnetic lines show how a north pole would move. The entire group of electric lines of force of the static charges is called *electrostatic flux*. Its symbol is the Greek letter ψ (psi), corresponding to ϕ for magnetic flux.

In general, magnetic flux is associated with moving charges, or current, while electrostatic flux is associated with the voltage between static charges. For electric circuits, the application of magnetic flux is often a coil of wire, which is the construction of an inductor. With current, the wire has a magnetic field. As a coil, the wire's magnetic flux is concentrated in the coil. Furthermore, when the magnetic field varies, the change in magnetic flux produces an induced voltage, as explained in Chap. 15, "Electromagnetic Induction," and Chap. 20, "Inductance."

For the case of an electric field, the application is often a dielectric between two conducting plates, which is the construction of a capacitor. With voltage across the dielectric, it has an electric field. As a capacitor, the dielectric's electric field is concentrated between the plates. Furthermore, when the electric field varies, the result is induced current through any conducting path connected to the capacitor. More details are explained in Chap. 17, "Capacitance."

COULOMB'S LAW The electric lines of force in Fig. 14-6a illustrate the force on an electron in the field. The amount of force between two charges is given by Coulomb's law:

$$F = 9 \times 10^9 \times \frac{q_1 q_2}{r^2} \tag{14-6}$$

where q_1 and q_2 are in coulomb units, F is in newtons, and r is the distance in meters between the charges. The constant factor 9×10^9 converts the values to SI units of newtons for the force in air or vacuum.

Coulomb's law states that the force increases with the amount of charge, but decreases as the square of the distance between charges. Typical values of q are in microcoulombs, since the coulomb is a very large unit of charge.

INTERNATIONAL SYSTEM OF UNITS In order to provide a closer relation between practical units for electricity and magnetism, these mks units were standardized in 1960 by international agreement. The abbreviation is SI, for *Système International*. Table 14-2 lists the magnetic SI units. The corresponding electrical SI units include the coulomb, which is used for both electric flux and charge, the ampere for current, the volt for potential, and the ohm for resistance. The henry unit for inductance and the farad unit for capacitance are also SI units.

In Table 14-2, note that the reciprocal of reluctance is *permeance*, corresponding to conductance as the reciprocal of resistance. The SI unit for conductance is the siemens (S), equal to $1/\Omega$. This unit is named after Ernst von Siemens, a European inventor.

As another comparison, the permeability μ of a magnetic material with magnetic flux corresponds to the electric *permittivity* ϵ of an insulator with electric flux. Just as permeability is the ability of a magnetic material to concentrate magnetic flux, permittivity is the ability of an insulator to concentrate electric flux. The symbol K_ϵ is used for relative permittivity, corresponding to K_m for relative permeability.

TABLE 14-2 INTERNATIONAL SYSTEM OF MKS UNITS (SI) FOR MAGNETISM

QUANTITY	SYMBOL	UNIT
Flux	ϕ	Weber (Wb)
Flux density	B	Wb/m^2 = tesla (T)
Potential	mmf	Ampere-turn (A · t)
Field intensity	H	Ampere-turn per meter (A · t/m)
Reluctance	$\mathcal{R}$	Ampere-turn per weber (A · t/Wb)
Permeance	$\rho = \dfrac{1}{\mathcal{R}}$	Weber per ampere-turn (Wb/A · t)
Relative μ	μ_r or K_m	None
Permeability	$\mu = \mu_r \times 1.26 \times 10^{-6}$	$\dfrac{B}{H} = \dfrac{\text{tesla (T)}}{\text{ampere-turn per meter (A · t/m)}}$

TEST-POINT QUESTION 14-8

Answers at end of chapter.

Give the SI units for the following:
a. Voltage potential.
b. Magnetic potential.
c. Electric current.
d. Magnetic flux.

14 SUMMARY AND REVIEW

- Table 14-2 summarizes the magnetic units and their definitions.

SELF-TEST

ANSWERS AT BACK OF BOOK.

Answer True or False.

1. A current of 4 A through 200 turns provides an mmf of $IN = 200$ A · t.
2. For the mmf of 200 A · t with 100 turns, a current of 2 A is necessary.
3. An mmf of 200 A · t across a flux path of 0.1 m provides a field intensity H of 2000 A · t/m.
4. A magnetic material with relative permeability μ_r of 100 has an absolute permeability μ of 126 G/Oe in cgs units.
5. There are no units for relative permeability μ_r.
6. Hysteresis losses are greater in soft iron than in air.
7. Magnetic saturation means that flux density B does not increase in proportion to increases in field intensity H.
8. The units for a B-H curve can be teslas plotted against ampere-turns.
9. In Ohm's law for magnetic circuits, reluctance $\mathcal{R}$ is the opposition to flux ϕ.
10. Ampere-turns of mmf between magnetic poles do not depend on the length of the coil.
11. The ampere-turn is a unit of magnetomotive force.
12. The tesla is an SI unit.

QUESTIONS

1. In Ohm's law for magnetic circuits, what magnetic quantities correspond to V, I, and R?
2. Why can reluctance and permeability be considered opposite characteristics?
3. Give the SI magnetic unit and symbol for each of the following: (**a**) flux; (**b**) flux density; (**c**) field intensity; (**d**) absolute permeability.
4. What cgs units correspond to the following SI units? (**a**) weber; (**b**) tesla; (**c**) ampere-turn; (**d**) ampere-turn per meter.
5. Define the following: (**a**) saturation; (**b**) relative permeability; (**c**) relative permittivity.

6. Explain briefly how to demagnetize a metal object that has become temporarily magnetized.
7. Draw a *B-H* curve with μ, *N*, *I*, and *V* the same as in Fig. 14-3, but with a coil resistance of 5 Ω.
8. Give the formula for Coulomb's law for the force between electrostatic charges, with SI units.
9. What is meant by magnetic hysteresis? Why can hysteresis cause losses in an iron core with a reversing field produced by alternating current?

PROBLEMS

ANSWERS TO ODD-NUMBERED PROBLEMS AT BACK OF BOOK.

1. A coil of 2000 turns with a 100-mA current has a length of 0.4 m. (**a**) Calculate the mmf in ampere-turns. (**b**) Calculate the field intensity *H* in ampere-turns per meter.
2. If the current in the coil of Prob. 1 is increased to 400 mA, calculate the increased values of mmf and *H*.
3. An iron core has a flux density *B* of 3600 G with an *H* of 12 Oe. Calculate (**a**) the permeability μ in cgs units; (**b**) the permeability μ in SI units; (**c**) the relative permeability μ_r of the iron core.
4. A coil of 250 turns with a 400-mA current is 0.2 m long with an iron core of the same length. Calculate the following in mks units: (**a**) mmf; (**b**) *H*; (**c**) *B* in the iron core with a μ_r of 200; (**d**) *B* with an air core instead of the iron core.
5. Referring to the *B-H* curve in Fig. 14-3, calculate the μ in SI units for the iron core at an *H* of: (**a**) 3000 A · t/m; (**b**) 5000 A · t/m.
6. Referring to the hysteresis loop in Fig. 14-4, give the values of (**a**) residual induction B_R, and (**b**) coercive force $-H_C$.
7. A battery is connected across a coil of 100 turns and a 20-Ω *R*, with an iron core 0.2 m long. (**a**) Draw the circuit diagram. (**b**) How much battery voltage is needed for 200 A · t? (**c**) Calculate *H* in the iron core in ampere-turns per meter. (**d**) Calculate *B* in teslas in the iron core if its μ_r is 300. (**e**) Calculate ϕ in webers at each pole with an area of 8×10^{-4} m². (**f**) How much is the reluctance $\mathcal{R}$ of the iron core, in ampere-turns per weber?
8. In cgs units, how much is the flux density *B* in gauss, for a field intensity *H* of 24 Oe, with μ of 500?
9. Calculate the force, in newtons, between two 4-μC charges separated by 0.1 m in air or vacuum.
10. Make the following conversions: (**a**) 250 A · t to Gb; (**b**) 150 Gb to A · t; (**c**) 400 A · t/m to Oe; (**d**) 1260 Oe to A · t/m.
11. Calculate the relative permeability μ_r of an iron core when a field intensity *H* of 750 A · t/m produces a flux density *B* of 0.126 T.
12. Find *H* in A · t/m units when *B* = 50.4 T and μ_r = 200.
13. A coil with an iron core has a field intensity *H* of 5 A · t/m. If the relative permeability μ_r equals 300, calculate the flux density *B* in teslas.
14. A magnetic material has a total flux ϕ of 300 μWb with an mmf of 12 A · t. Calculate the reluctance in A · t/Wb units.

15. A coil has an mmf of 1000 A · t and a reluctance of 0.1×10^6 A · t/Wb. Calculate the total flux in webers.
16. If the reluctance of a material is 0.5×10^6 A · t/Wb, how much mmf is required to produce a flux ϕ of 600 μWb?

CRITICAL THINKING

1. Derive the value of 1.26×10^{-6} T/(A · t/m) for μ_0 from $\mu = B/H$.
2. What is the relative permeability (μ_r) of a piece of soft iron whose permeability (μ) equals 3.0×10^{-3} T/(A · t/m)?

ANSWERS TO TEST-POINT QUESTIONS

14-1 a. 486 A · t
   b. 630 Gb
14-2 a. 125 A · t/m
   b. 6.3 Oe

14-3 a. 1
   b. 200
   c. 200 G/Oe
14-4 a. 0.2 T
   b. 4000 A · t/m
14-5 a. T
   b. T

14-6 a. T
   b. F
14-7 a. T
   b. F
   c. T

14-8 a. volt
   b. ampere-turn
   c. ampere
   d. weber

CHAPTER 15

ELECTRO-MAGNETIC INDUCTION

The link between electricity and magnetism was discovered in 1824 by Oersted, who found that current in a wire could move a magnetic compass needle. A few years later the opposite effect was discovered: A magnetic field in motion forces electrons to move, producing current. This important effect was studied by the English physicist and pioneer in electromagnetism, Michael Faraday (1791–1867); the American physicist, Joseph Henry (1797–1878); and the Russian physicist, H. F. E. Lenz (1804–1865).

The henry unit of inductance is named after Joseph Henry. The farad unit of capacitance is named after Michael Faraday, who did important work in electrostatics as well as electromagnetism. There is no unit named after Lenz, but Lenz' law explains many important electromagnetic effects with a varying electric current.

Electromagnetism combines the effect of an electric current and magnetism. Electrons in motion, or any current, always have an associated magnetic field. For the opposite effect, when a magnetic field is in motion, the work put into this action forces electrons to move in any conductor within the field, producing current. These electromagnetic effects have many practical applications that are the basis for motors and generators. More fundamentally, these effects explain why a coil of wire has special characteristics in a circuit when the current is changing in value.

CHAPTER OBJECTIVES

Upon completion of this chapter, you should be able to:

- *Describe* the magnetic field associated with an electric current.
- *Determine* the magnetic polarity of a coil by using the left-hand rule.
- *Explain* what is meant by motor action between two magnetic fields.
- *Understand* how a magnetic flux cutting across a conductor can produce an induced current.
- *State* Lenz' law.
- *Calculate* the amount of induced voltage across the ends of a conductor by using Faraday's law.
- *Understand* the construction and operation of a basic relay.
- *List* and *explain* some important relay ratings.

IMPORTANT TERMS IN THIS CHAPTER

attraction	induced current and voltage	pickup current
chatter	left-hand rule	relay chatter
Faraday's law of induced voltage	Lenz' law	repulsion
field intensity	magnetic flux	solenoid
generator action	magnetic polarity	switching contacts
holding current	make and break	time rate of change
	motor action	torque

TOPICS COVERED IN THIS CHAPTER

15-1 MAGNETIC FIELD AROUND AN ELECTRIC CURRENT

In Fig. 15-1, the iron filings aligned in concentric rings around the conductor show the magnetic field of the current in the wire. The iron filings are dense next to the conductor, showing that the field is strongest at this point. Furthermore, the field strength decreases inversely as the square of the distance from the conductor. It is important to note the following two factors about the magnetic lines of force:

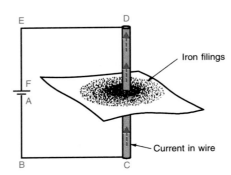

FIG. 15-1 How iron filings can be used to show the invisible magnetic field around the electric current in a wire conductor.

1. The magnetic lines are circular, as the field is symmetrical with respect to the wire in the center.
2. The magnetic field with circular lines of force is in a plane perpendicular to the current in the wire.

From points C to D in the wire, its circular magnetic field is in the horizontal plane because the wire is vertical. Also, the vertical conductor between points EF and AB has the associated magnetic field in the horizontal plane. Where the conductor is horizontal, as from B to C and D to E, the magnetic field is in a vertical plane.

These two requirements of a circular magnetic field in a perpendicular plane apply to any charge in motion. Whether electron flow or a motion of positive charges is considered, the associated magnetic field must be at right angles to the direction of current.

In addition, the current need not be in a wire conductor. As an example, the beam of moving electrons in the vacuum of a cathode-ray tube has an associated magnetic field. In all cases, the magnetic field has circular lines of force in a plane perpendicular to the direction of motion of the electric charges.

CLOCKWISE AND COUNTERCLOCKWISE FIELDS   With circular lines of force, the magnetic field would tend to move a magnetic pole in a circular path. Therefore, the direction of the lines must be considered as either clockwise or counterclockwise. This idea is illustrated in Fig. 15-2, showing how a north pole would move in the circular field.

The directions are tested with a magnetic compass needle. When the compass is in front of the wire, the north pole on the needle points up. On the opposite side, the compass points down. If the compass were placed at the top, its

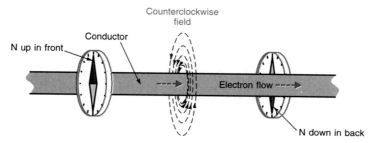

FIG. 15-2   Rule for determining direction of circular field around straight conductor. Field is counterclockwise for direction of electron flow shown here. Circular field is clockwise for conventional current.

needle would point toward the back of the wire; below the wire, the compass would point forward.

When all these directions are combined, the result is the circular magnetic field shown, with counterclockwise lines of force. This field has the magnetic lines upward at the front of the conductor and downward at the back.

Instead of testing every conductor with a magnetic compass, however, we can use the following rule to determine the circular direction of the magnetic field: *If you look along the wire in the direction of electron flow, the magnetic field is counterclockwise.* In Fig. 15-2, the line of electron flow is from left to right. Facing this way, you can assume the circular magnetic flux in a perpendicular plane has lines of force in the counterclockwise direction.

The opposite direction of electron flow produces a reversed field. Then the magnetic lines of force have clockwise rotation. If the charges were moving from right to left in Fig. 15-2, the associated magnetic field would be in the opposite direction, with clockwise lines of force.

FIELDS AIDING OR CANCELING   When the magnetic lines of two fields are in the same direction, the lines of force aid each other, making the field stronger. With magnetic lines in opposite directions, the fields cancel.

In Fig. 15-3 the fields are shown for two conductors with opposite directions of electron flow. The dot in the middle of the field at the left indicates the tip of an arrowhead to show current up from the paper. The cross symbolizes the back of an arrow to indicate electron flow into the paper.

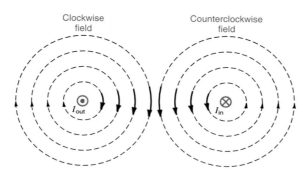

FIG. 15-3   Magnetic fields aiding between parallel conductors with opposite directions of current.

ABOUT ELECTRONICS

Terrorists may have met their match in the InVision CTX 5000 luggage scanner, which can find military explosives hidden behind a circuit board, concealed plastic-sheet explosives, and commercial explosives like dynamite and powders. Although it costs a million dollars, many airports use it already.

Notice that the magnetic lines *between the conductors* are in the same direction, although one field is clockwise and the other counterclockwise. Therefore, the fields aid here, making a stronger total field. On either side of the conductors, the two fields are opposite in direction and tend to cancel each other. The net result, then, is to strengthen the field in the space between the conductors.

TEST-POINT QUESTION 15-1

Answers at end of chapter.

Answer True or False.
a. Magnetic field lines around a conductor are circular in a perpendicular cross section of the conductor.
b. In Fig. 15-3, the field is strongest between the conductors.

15-2 MAGNETIC POLARITY OF A COIL

FIG. 15-4 Magnetic poles of a current loop.

Bending a straight conductor into the form of a loop, as shown in Fig. 15-4, has two effects. First, the magnetic field lines are more dense inside the loop. The total number of lines is the same as for the straight conductor, but inside the loop the lines are concentrated in a smaller space. Furthermore, all the lines inside the loop are aiding in the same direction. This makes the loop field effectively the same as a bar magnet with opposite poles at opposite faces of the loop.

SOLENOID AS A BAR MAGNET A coil of wire conductor with more than one turn is generally called a *solenoid*. An ideal solenoid, however, has a length much greater than its diameter. Like a single loop, the solenoid concentrates the magnetic field inside the coil and provides opposite magnetic poles at the ends. These effects are multiplied, however, by the number of turns as the magnetic field lines aid each other in the same direction inside the coil. Outside the coil, the field corresponds to a bar magnet with north and south poles at opposite ends, as illustrated in Fig. 15-5.

(a)   (b)

FIG. 15-5 Magnetic poles of a solenoid. (*a*) Coil winding. (*b*) Equivalent bar magnet.

MAGNETIC POLARITY   To determine the magnetic polarity, use the *left-hand rule* illustrated in Fig. 15-6: *If the coil is grasped with the fingers of the left hand curled around the coil in the direction of electron flow, the thumb points to the north pole of the coil.* The left hand is used here because the current is electron flow.

The solenoid acts like a bar magnet whether it has an iron core or not. Adding an iron core increases the flux density inside the coil. In addition, the field strength then is uniform for the entire length of the core. The polarity is the same, however, for air-core and iron-core coils.

The magnetic polarity depends on the direction of current flow and the direction of winding. The current is determined by the connections to the voltage source. Electron flow is from the negative side of the voltage source, through the coil, and back to the positive terminal.

The direction of winding can be over and under, starting from one end of the coil, or under and over with respect to the same starting point. Reversing either the direction of winding or the direction of current reverses the magnetic poles of the solenoid. See Fig. 15-7. With both reversed, though, the polarity is the same.

FIG. 15-6   Left-hand rule for north pole of a coil with current *I*. The *I* is electron flow here.

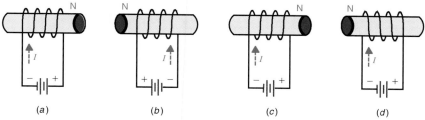

FIG. 15-7   Examples for determining the magnetic polarity of a coil with direct current *I*. The *I* is electron flow here. The polarities are reversed in (*a*) and (*b*) because the battery is reversed to reverse the direction of current. Also, (*d*) is the opposite of (*c*) because of the reversed winding.

Answers at end of chapter.
a. In Fig. 15-5, if the battery is reversed, will the north pole be at the left or the right?
b. If one end of a solenoid is a north pole, is the opposite end a north or a south pole?

15-3 MOTOR ACTION BETWEEN TWO MAGNETIC FIELDS

The physical motion resulting from the forces of magnetic fields is called *motor action*. One example is the simple attraction or repulsion between bar magnets.

We know that like poles repel and unlike poles attract. It can also be considered that fields in the same direction repel and opposite fields attract.

Consider the repulsion between two north poles, illustrated in Fig. 15-8. Similar poles have fields in the same direction. Therefore, the similar fields of the two like poles repel each other.

A more fundamental reason for motor action, however, is the fact that the force in a magnetic field tends to produce motion from a stronger field toward a weaker field. In Fig. 15-8, note that the field intensity is greatest in the space between the two north poles. Here the field lines of similar poles in both magnets reinforce in the same direction. Farther away the field intensity is less, for essentially one magnet only. As a result there is a difference in field strength, providing a net force that tends to produce motion. The direction of motion is always toward the weaker field.

To remember the directions, we can consider that the stronger field moves to the weaker field, tending to equalize the field intensity. Otherwise, the motion would make the strong field stronger and the weak field weaker. This must be impossible, because then the magnetic field would multiply its own strength without any work being added.

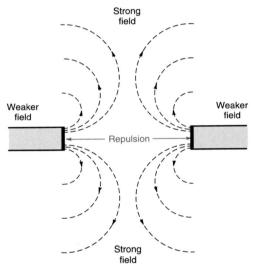

FIG. 15-8   Repulsion between similar poles of two bar magnets. The motion is from the stronger field to the weaker field.

FORCE ON A STRAIGHT CONDUCTOR IN A MAGNETIC FIELD

Current in a conductor has its associated magnetic field. When this conductor is placed in another magnetic field from a separate source, the two fields can react to produce motor action. The conductor must be perpendicular to the magnetic field, however, as shown in Fig. 15-9. This way, the perpendicular magnetic field produced by the current then is in the same plane as the external magnetic field.

Unless the two fields are in the same plane, they cannot affect each other. In the same plane, however, lines of force in the same direction reinforce to make a stronger field, while lines in the opposite direction cancel and result in a weaker field.

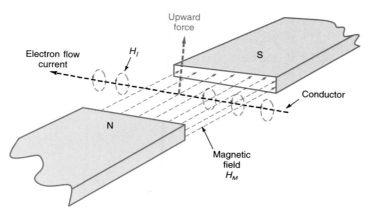

FIG. 15-9 Motor action of current in a straight conductor when it is in an external magnetic field. The H_I is the circular field of the current. The H_M indicates field lines between the north and south poles of the external magnet.

To summarize these directions:

1. With the conductor at 90°, or perpendicular to the external field, the reaction between the two magnetic fields is maximum.
2. With the conductor at 0°, or parallel to the external field, there is no effect between them.
3. When the conductor is at an angle between 0 and 90°, only the perpendicular component is effective.

In Fig. 15-9, electrons flow in the wire conductor in the plane of the paper, from the bottom to the top of the page. This flow provides the counterclockwise field H_I around the wire, in a perpendicular plane cutting through the paper. The external field H_M has lines of force from left to right in the plane of the paper. Then lines of force in the two fields are parallel above and below the wire.

Below the conductor, its field lines are left to right in the same direction as the external field. Therefore, these lines reinforce to produce a stronger field. Above the conductor the lines of the two fields are in opposite directions, causing a weaker field. As a result, the net force of the stronger field makes the conductor move upward out of the page, toward the weaker field.

If electrons flow in the reverse direction in the conductor, or if the external field is reversed, the motor action will be in the opposite direction. Reversing both the field and the current, however, results in the same direction of motion.

ROTATION OF A CURRENT LOOP IN A MAGNETIC FIELD   With a loop of wire in the magnetic field, opposite sides of the loop have current in opposite directions. Then the associated magnetic fields are opposite. The resulting forces are upward on one side of the loop and downward on the other side, making it rotate. This effect of a force in producing rotation is called *torque*.

The principle of motor action between magnetic fields producing rotational torque is the basis of all electric motors. Also, the moving-coil meter described in Sec. 8-1 is a similar application. Since the torque is proportional to current, the amount of rotation indicates how much current flows through the coil.

Answers at end of chapter.

Answer True or False.
a. In Fig. 15-8, the field is strongest between the two north poles.
b. In Fig. 15-9, if both the magnetic field and the current are reversed, the motion will still be upward.

15-4 INDUCED CURRENT

B Field *H*

Magnet moves down

*µ*A

Microammeter

FIG. 15-10 Induced current produced by magnetic flux cutting across a conductor. Direction of *I* here is for electron flow.

Just as electrons in motion provide an associated magnetic field, when magnetic flux moves, the motion of magnetic lines cutting across a conductor forces free electrons in the conductor to move, producing current. This action is called *induction* because there is no physical connection between the magnet and the conductor. The induced current is a result of generator action as the mechanical work put into moving the magnetic field is converted into electric energy when current flows in the conductor.

Referring to Fig. 15-10, let the conductor AB be placed at right angles to the flux in the air gap of the horseshoe magnet. Then, when the magnet is moved up or down, its flux cuts across the conductor. The action of magnetic flux cutting across the conductor generates current. The fact that current flows is indicated by the microammeter.

When the magnet is moved downward, current flows in the direction shown. If the magnet is moved upward, current will flow in the opposite direction. Without motion, there is no current.

DIRECTION OF MOTION   Motion is necessary in order to have the flux lines of the magnetic field cut across the conductor. This cutting can be accomplished by motion of either the field or the conductor. When the conductor is moved upward or downward, it cuts across the flux. The generator action is the same as moving the field, except that the relative motion is opposite. Moving the conductor upward, for instance, corresponds to moving the magnet downward.

CONDUCTOR PERPENDICULAR TO EXTERNAL FLUX   In order to have electromagnetic induction, the conductor and the magnetic lines of flux must be perpendicular to each other. Then the motion makes the flux cut through the cross-sectional area of the conductor. As shown in Fig. 15-10, the conductor is at right angles to the lines of force in the field *H*.

The reason the conductor must be perpendicular is to make its induced current have an associated magnetic field in the same plane as the external flux. If the field of the induced current does not react with the external field, there can be no induced current.

HOW INDUCED CURRENT IS GENERATED   The induced current can be considered the result of motor action between the external field *H* and the magnetic field of free electrons in every cross-sectional area of the wire. Without an external field, the free electrons move at random without any specific direction, and they have no net magnetic field. When the conductor is in the magnetic field H, there still is no induction without relative motion, since the magnetic fields for the free electrons are not disturbed. When the field or conductor moves, however, there must be a reaction opposing the motion. The reaction is a flow of free electrons resulting from motor action on the electrons.

Referring to Fig. 15-10, for example, the induced current must flow in the direction shown because the field is moved downward, pulling the magnet away from the conductor. The induced current of electrons then has a clockwise field, with lines of force aiding H above the conductor and canceling H below. With motor action between the two magnetic fields tending to move the conductor toward the weaker field, the conductor will be forced downward, staying with the magnet to oppose the work of pulling the magnet away from the conductor.

The effect of electromagnetic induction is increased where a coil is used for the conductor. Then the turns concentrate more conductor length in a smaller area. As illustrated in Fig. 15-11, moving the magnet into the coil enables the flux to cut across many turns of conductors.

FIG. 15-11   Induced current produced by magnetic flux cutting across turns of wire in a coil. Direction of I here is for electron flow.

TEST-POINT QUESTION 15-4

Answers at end of chapter.

Answer True or False.
a. Refer to Fig. 15-10. If the conductor is moved up, instead of the magnet down, the induced current will flow in the same direction.
b. Refer to Fig. 15-10. The electron flow through the meter is from terminal A to B.

15-5 LENZ' LAW

Lenz' law is the basic principle that is used to determine the direction of an induced voltage or current. Based on the principle of conservation of energy, the law simply states that the direction of the induced current must be such that its own magnetic field will oppose the action that produced the induced current.

In Fig. 15-11, for example, the induced current has the direction that produces a north pole at the left to oppose the motion by repulsion of the north pole being moved in. This is why it takes some work to push the permanent magnet into the coil. The work expended in moving the permanent magnet is the source of energy for the current induced in the coil.

Using Lenz' law, we can start with the fact that the left end of the coil in Fig. 15-11 must be a north pole to oppose the motion. Then the direction of the induced current is determined by the left-hand rule for electron flow. If the fingers coil around the direction of electron flow shown, under and over the winding, the thumb will point to the left for the north pole.

For the opposite case, suppose that the north pole of the permanent magnet in Fig. 15-11 is moved away from the coil. Then the induced pole at the left end of the coil must be a south pole, by Lenz' law. The induced south pole will attract the north pole to oppose the motion of the magnet being moved away. For a south pole at the left end of the coil, then, the electron flow will be reversed from the direction shown in Fig. 15-11. We could actually generate an alternating current in the coil by moving the magnet periodically in and out.

TEST-POINT QUESTION 15-5

Answers at end of chapter.

Refer to Fig. 15-11.
a. If the north end of the magnet is moved away from the coil, will its left side be north or south?
b. If the south end of the magnet is moved in, will the left end of the coil be north or south?

15-6 GENERATING AN INDUCED VOLTAGE

Consider the case of magnetic flux cutting a conductor that is not in a closed circuit, as shown in Fig. 15-12. The motion of flux across the conductor forces free electrons to move, but with an open circuit, the displaced electrons produce opposite electric charges at the two open ends.

For the directions shown, free electrons in the conductor are forced to move to point A. Since the end is open, electrons accumulate here. Point A then develops a negative potential.

At the same time, point B loses electrons and becomes charged positive. The result is a potential difference across the two ends, provided by the separation of electric charges in the conductor.

The potential difference is an electromotive force (emf), generated by the work of cutting across the flux. You can measure this potential difference with a voltmeter. However, a conductor cannot store electric charge. Therefore, the voltage is present only while the motion of flux cutting across the conductor is producing the induced voltage.

INDUCED VOLTAGE ACROSS A COIL   With a coil, as in Fig. 15-13a, the induced emf is increased by the number of turns. Each turn cut by flux adds to the induced voltage, since they all force free electrons to accumulate at the negative end of the coil, with a deficiency of electrons at the positive end.

The polarity of the induced voltage follows from the direction of induced current. The end of the conductor to which the electrons go and at which they

FIG. 15-12 Voltage induced across open ends of conductor cut by magnetic flux.

Motion in

S N

N [coil] S

I

A V_{ind} B

Excess   Deficiency
electrons   of electrons

(a)

Coil

+

V

(b)

Coil

+

V

I R_L

(c)

FIG. 15-13   Voltage induced across coil cut by magnetic flux. (*a*) Motion of flux generating voltage across coil. (*b*) Induced voltage acts in series with coil. (*c*) Induced voltage is a source that can produce current in an external load resistor R_L connected across
coil.

accumulate is the negative side of the induced voltage. The opposite end, with a
deficiency of electrons, is the positive side. The total emf across the coil is the
sum of the induced voltages, since all the turns are in series.

Furthermore, the total induced voltage acts in series with the coil, as illustrated by the equivalent circuit in Fig. 15-13*b*, showing the induced voltage as a separate generator. This generator represents a voltage source with a
potential difference resulting from the separation of charges produced by electromagnetic induction. The source *v* then can produce current in an external
load circuit connected across the negative and positive terminals, as shown in
Fig. 15-13*c*.

The induced voltage is in series with the coil because current produced by
the generated emf must flow through all the turns. An induced voltage of 10 V,
for example, with R_L equal to 5 Ω, results in a current of 2 A, which flows through
the coil, the equivalent generator *v*, and the load resistance R_L.

The direction of current in Fig. 15-13*c* shows electron flow around the circuit. Outside the source *v*, the electrons move from its negative terminal, through
R_L, and back to the positive terminal of *v* because of its potential difference.

Inside the generator, however, the electron flow is from the + terminal to
the − terminal. This direction of electron flow results from the fact that the left
end of the coil in Fig. 15-13*a* must be a north pole by Lenz' law, to oppose the
north pole being moved in.

Notice how motors and generators are similar in using the motion of a magnetic field, but with opposite applications. In a motor, current is supplied so that
an associated magnetic field can react with the external flux to produce motion
of the conductor. In a generator, motion must be supplied so that the flux and
conductor can cut across each other to induce voltage across the ends of the conductor.

TEST-POINT QUESTION 15-6

Answers at end of chapter.

Refer to Fig. 15-13.
a. Is terminal A or B the negative side of the induced voltage?
b. Is the bottom of R_L the negative side of V_{R_L}?

The voltage induced by magnetic flux cutting the turns of a coil depends upon the number of turns and how fast the flux moves across the conductor. Either the flux or the conductor can move. Specifically, the amount of induced voltage is determined by the following three factors:

1. *Amount of flux.* The more magnetic lines of force that cut across the conductor, the higher the amount of induced voltage.
2. *Number of turns.* The more turns in a coil, the higher the induced voltage. The v_{ind} is the sum of all the individual voltages generated in each turn in series.
3. *Time rate of cutting.* The faster the flux cuts a conductor, the higher the induced voltage. Then more lines of force cut the conductor within a specific period of time.

These factors are of fundamental importance in many applications. Any conductor with current will have voltage induced in it by a change in current and its associated magnetic flux.

The amount of induced voltage can be calculated by Faraday's law:

▶ $$v_{ind} = N \frac{d\phi \text{ (webers)}}{dt \text{ (seconds)}}$$ **(15-1)**

where N is the number of turns and $d\phi/dt$ specifies how fast the flux ϕ cuts across the conductor. With $d\phi/dt$ in webers per second, the induced voltage is in volts.

As an example, suppose that magnetic flux cuts across 300 turns at the rate of 2 Wb/s.

To calculate the induced voltage,

▶ $$v_{ind} = N \frac{d\phi}{dt}$$
$$= 300 \times 2$$
$$v_{ind} = 600 \text{ V}$$

It is assumed that all the flux links all the turns, which is true with an iron core.

TIME RATE OF CHANGE   The symbol d in $d\phi$ and dt is an abbreviation for *change*. The $d\phi$ means a change in the flux ϕ, and dt means a change in time. In mathematics, dt represents an infinitesimally small change in time, but in this book we are using the d to mean rate of change in general. The results are exactly the same for the practical changes used here because the rate of change is constant.

As an example, if the flux ϕ is 4 Wb one time but then changes to 6 Wb, the change in flux $d\phi$ is 2 Wb. The same idea applies to a decrease as well as an increase. If the flux changed from 6 to 4 Wb, $d\phi$ would still be 2 Wb. However, an increase is usually considered a change in the positive direction, with an upward slope, while a decrease has a negative slope downward.

Similarly, dt means a change in time. If we consider the flux at a time 2 s after the start and at a later time 3 s after the start, the change in time is $3 - 2$, or 1 s for dt. Time always increases in the positive direction.

Combining the two factors of $d\phi$ and dt, we can say that for magnetic flux increasing by 2 Wb in 1 s, $d\phi/dt$ equals 2/1, or 2 Wb/s. This states the time rate of change of the magnetic flux.

As another example, suppose that the flux increases by 2 Wb in the time of ½ or 0.5 s. Then

▶ $$\frac{d\phi}{dt} = \frac{2 \text{ Wb}}{0.5 \text{ s}} = 4 \text{ Wb/s}$$

ANALYSIS OF INDUCED VOLTAGE AS $N(d\phi/dt)$ This fundamental concept of voltage induced by a change in flux is illustrated by the graphs in Fig. 15-14, for the values listed in Table 15-1. The linear rise in Fig. 15-14a shows values of flux ϕ increasing at a uniform rate. In this case, the curve goes up 2 Wb for every 1-s interval of time. The slope of this curve, then, equal to $d\phi/dt$, is 2 Wb/s. Note that, although ϕ increases, the rate of change is constant because the linear rise has a constant slope.

For induced voltage, only the $d\phi/dt$ factor is important, not the actual value of flux. To emphasize this basic concept, the graph in Fig. 15-14b shows the $d\phi/dt$ values alone. This graph is just a straight horizontal line for the constant value of 2 Wb/s.

The induced-voltage graph in Fig. 15-14c is also a straight horizontal line. Since $v_{ind} = N(d\phi/dt)$, the graph of induced voltage is just the $d\phi/dt$ values mul-

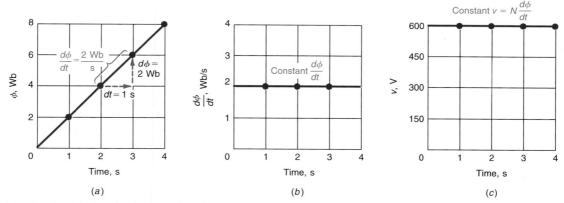

FIG. 15-14   Graphs of induced voltage produced by magnetic flux changes in a coil. (a) Linear increase of flux ϕ. (b) Constant rate of change for $d\phi/dt$ at 2 Wb/s. (c) Constant induced voltage of 600 V, for a coil with 300 turns.

TABLE 15-1   INDUCED-VOLTAGE CALCULATIONS FOR FIG. 15-14

ϕ, Wb	$d\phi$, Wb	t, s	dt, s	$d\phi/dt$, Wb/s	N, TURNS	$N(d\phi/dt)$, v
2	2	1	1	2	300	600
4	2	2	1	2	300	600
6	2	3	1	2	300	600
8	2	4	1	2	300	600

tiplied by the number of turns. The result is a constant 600 V, with 300 turns cut by flux changing at the constant rate of 2 Wb/s.

The example illustrated here can be different in several ways without changing the basic fact that the induced voltage is equal to $N(d\phi/dt)$. First, the number of turns or the $d\phi/dt$ values can be greater than the values assumed here, or less. More turns will provide more induced voltage, while fewer turns mean less voltage. Similarly, a higher value for $d\phi/dt$ results in more induced voltage.

Note that two factors are included in $d\phi/dt$. Its value can be increased by a higher value of $d\phi$ or a smaller value of dt. As an example, the value of 2 Wb/s for $d\phi/dt$ can be doubled by either increasing $d\phi$ to 4 Wb or reducing dt to ½ s. Then $d\phi/dt$ is 4/1 or 2/0.5, which equals 4 Wb/s in either case. The same flux changing within a shorter time means a faster rate of flux cutting the conductor, resulting in a higher value of $d\phi/dt$ and more induced voltage.

For the opposite case, a smaller value of $d\phi/dt$, with less flux or a slower rate of change, results in a lower value of induced voltage. As $d\phi/dt$ decreases, the induced voltage will reverse polarity.

Finally, it should be noted that the $d\phi/dt$ graph in Fig. 15-14b has the constant value of 2 Wb/s because the flux is increasing at a linear rate. However, the flux need not have a uniform rate of change. Then the $d\phi/dt$ values will not be constant. In any case, though, the values of $d\phi/dt$ at all instants of time will determine the values of the induced voltage equal to $N(d\phi/dt)$.

POLARITY OF THE INDUCED VOLTAGE   The polarity is determined by Lenz' law. Any induced voltage has the polarity that opposes the change causing the induction. Sometimes this fact is indicated by using a negative sign for v_{ind} in Formula (15-1). However, the absolute polarity depends on whether the flux is increasing or decreasing, the method of winding, and which end of the coil is the reference.

When all these factors are considered, v_{ind} has the polarity such that the current it produces and the associated magnetic field will oppose the change in flux producing the induced voltage. If the external flux increases, the magnetic field of the induced current will be in the opposite direction. If the external field decreases, the magnetic field of the induced current will be in the same direction as the external field to oppose the change by sustaining the flux. In short, the induced voltage has the polarity that opposes the change.

TEST-POINT QUESTION 15-7

Answers at end of chapter.
  a. The magnetic flux of 8 Wb changes to 10 Wb in 1 s. How much is $d\phi/dt$?
  b. The flux of 8 μWb changes to 10 μWb in 1 μs. How much is $d\phi/dt$?

15-8 RELAYS

A relay is an electromechanical device which operates on the basis of electromagnetic induction. It uses either an ac- or a dc-actuated electromagnet to open or close one or more sets of contacts. Relay contacts which are open when the relay is not energized are called *normally open* (NO) contacts. Conversely, relay contacts which are closed when the relay is not energized are called *normally closed* (NC) contacts. Relay contacts are held in their resting or normal position either by a spring or by some type of gravity-actuated mechanism. In most cases, an adjustment of the spring tension is provided to set the restraining force on the normally open and normally closed contacts to some desired level based on predetermined circuit conditions.

Figure 15-15 shows the schematic symbols that are commonly used to represent relay contacts. Figure 15-15*a* shows the symbols used to represent normally open contacts, whereas Fig. 15-15*b* shows the symbols used to represent normally closed contacts. When normally open contacts close, they are said to *make*, whereas when normally closed contacts open they are said to *break*. Like mechanical switches, the switching contacts of a relay can have any number of poles and throws.

Figure 15-16 shows the basic parts of an SPDT armature relay. Terminal connections 1 and 2 provide connection to the electromagnet, and terminal connections 3, 4, and 5 provide connections to the SPDT relay contacts which open or close when the relay is energized. A relay is said to be *energized* when NO contacts close and NC contacts open. The movable arm of an electromechanical relay is called the *armature*. The armature is magnetic and has contacts which make or break with other contacts when the relay is energized. For example, when terminals 1 and 2 are connected to a dc source in Fig. 15-16, current flows in the relay coil and an electromagnet is formed. If there is sufficient current in the relay coil, contacts 3 and 4 close (make) and contacts 4 and 5 open (break). The armature is attracted whether the electromagnet produces a north or a south pole on the end adjacent to the armature. Figure 15-17 shows a photo of a typical relay.

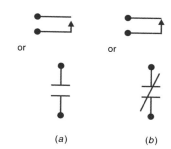

FIG. 15-15 Schematic symbols commonly used to represent relay contacts. (*a*) Symbols used to represent normally open (NO) contacts. (*b*) Symbols used to represent normally closed (NC) contacts.

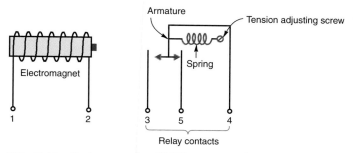

FIG. 15-16 Basic parts of an SPDT armature relay. Terminal connections 1 and 2 provide connection to the electromagnet, and terminal connections 3, 4, and 5 provide connections to the SPDT relay contacts which open or close when the relay is energized.

RELAY SPECIFICATIONS Manufacturers of electromechanical relays always supply a specification sheet for each of their relays. The specification sheet contains voltage and current ratings for both the relay coil and its switching contacts. The specification sheet also includes information regarding the location of the relay coil and switching contact terminals. And finally, the specification sheet will indicate whether the relay can be energized from either an ac or dc source. The following is an explanation of a relay's most important ratings.

FIG. 15-17 Typical relay.

Pickup voltage. The minimum amount of relay coil voltage necessary to energize or operate the relay.

Pickup current. The minimum amount of relay coil current necessary to energize or operate the relay.

Holding current. The minimum amount of current required to keep a relay energized or operating. (The holding current is less than the pickup current.)

Dropout voltage. The maximum relay coil voltage at which the relay is no longer energized.

Contact voltage rating. The maximum voltage the relay contacts are capable of switching safely.

Contact current rating. The maximum current the relay contacts are capable of switching safely.

Contact voltage drop. The voltage drop across the closed contacts of a relay when operating.

Insulation resistance. The resistance measured across the relay contacts in the open position.

RELAY APPLICATIONS Figure 15-18 shows schematic diagrams for two different relay systems. The diagram in Fig. 15-18a represents an open-circuit system. With the control switch S_1 open, the SPST relay contacts are open and the load is inoperative. Closing S_1 energizes the relay. This closes the NO relay contacts and makes the load operative.

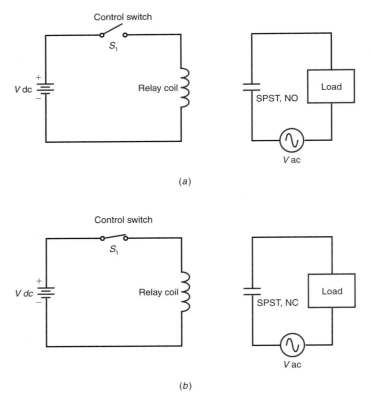

FIG. 15-18 Schematic diagrams for two relay systems. (*a*) Open-circuit system. (*b*) Closed-circuit system.

Figure 15-18b represents a closed-circuit system. In this case, the relay is energized by the control switch S_1, which is closed during normal operation. With the relay energized, the normally closed relay contacts are open and the load is inoperative. When it is desired to operate the load, the control switch S_1 is opened. This returns the relay contacts to their normally closed position, thereby activating the load.

It is important to note that a relay can be energized using a low-voltage, low-power source. However, the relay contacts can be used to control a circuit whose load consumes much more power at a much higher voltage than the relay coil circuit. In fact, one of the main advantages of using a relay is its ability to switch or control very high power loads with a relatively low amount of input power. In remote-control applications, a relay can control a high power load a long distance away much more efficiently than a mechanical switch can.

COMMON RELAY TROUBLES   If the relay coil develops an open, the relay cannot be energized. The reason is simple. With an open relay coil the current is zero and no magnetic field is set up by the electromagnet to attract the armature. An ohmmeter can be used to check for the proper relay coil resistance. Since it is usually not practical to repair an open relay coil, the entire relay must be replaced.

A common problem with relays is dirty switching contacts. The switching contacts develop a thin carbon coating after extended use as a result of arcing across the contact terminals when they are opened and closed. Dirty switching contacts usually produce intermittent operation of the load being controlled—for example, a motor. In some cases the relay contacts may chatter (vibrate) if they are dirty.

One final point: The manufacturer of a relay usually indicates its life expectancy in terms of the number of times the relay can be energized (operated). A typical value is 5 million operations.

TEST-POINT QUESTION 15-8

Answers at end of chapter.

Answer True or False.
a. A relay is energized if a set of NC contacts are opened.
b. The pickup current is the minimum relay coil current required to keep a relay energized.
c. The voltage drop across a set of closed relay contacts carrying 1 A of current is very low.
d. An open relay coil measures 0 Ω with an ohmmeter.

- Current in a straight conductor has an associated magnetic field with circular lines of force in a plane perpendicular to the conductor. The direction of the circular field is counterclockwise when you look along the conductor in the direction of electron flow.
- With two fields in the same plane, produced by either current or a permanent magnet, lines of force in the same direction aid each other to provide a stronger field. Lines of force in opposite directions cancel, resulting in a weaker field.
- A solenoid is a long, narrow coil of wire which concentrates the conductor and its associated magnetic field. Because the fields for all turns aid inside the coil and cancel outside, a solenoid has a resultant electromagnetic field like a bar magnet with north and south poles at opposite ends.
- The left-hand rule for polarity of an electromagnet says that when your fingers curl around the turns in the direction of electron flow, the thumb points to the north pole.
- Motor action is the motion that results from the net force of two fields that can aid or cancel each other. The direction of the resultant force is always from the stronger field to the weaker field.
- Generator action refers to induced voltage. For N turns, $v_{ind} = N(d\phi/dt)$, where $d\phi/dt$ stands for the change in flux (ϕ) with time (t). The change is given in webers per second. There must be a change in the flux to produce induced voltage.
- Lenz' law states that the polarity of the induced voltage will produce I with a magnetic field that opposes the change in magnetic flux causing the induction.
- The faster the flux changes, the higher the induced voltage.
- When the flux changes at a constant rate, the induced voltage is constant.
- The switching contacts of an electromechanical relay may be either normally open (NO) or normally closed (NC). The contacts are held in their normal or resting positions by springs or some gravity-actuated mechanism.
- The movable arm on a relay is called the armature. The armature is magnetic and has contacts which open or close with other contacts when the relay is energized.
- The pickup current of a relay is the minimum amount of relay coil current which will energize the relay. The holding current is the minimum relay coil current required to keep a relay energized.
- The main advantage of a relay over an ordinary mechanical switch is that it can control a high-power load a long distance away with very low I^2R power losses in the wire conductors. The relay is energized using a low-power source. The switching contacts are used to turn on and off the high-power load.

ANSWERS AT BACK OF BOOK.

Answer True or False.

1. A vertical wire with electron flow into this page has an associated magnetic field counter-clockwise in the plane of the paper.
2. Lines of force of two magnetic fields in the same direction aid each other to produce a stronger resultant field.
3. Motor action always tends to produce motion toward the weaker field.
4. In Fig. 15-6, if the battery connections are reversed, the magnetic poles of the coil will be reversed.
5. A solenoid is a coil that acts as a bar magnet only when current flows.
6. A torque is a force tending to cause rotation.
7. In Fig. 15-9, if external poles are reversed, motor action will be downward.
8. In Fig. 15-10, if the conductor is moved down, instead of the magnet, the induced current flows in the opposite direction.
9. An induced voltage is produced only while the flux is changing.
10. Faraday's law determines the amount of induced voltage.
11. Lenz' law determines the polarity of an induced voltage.
12. Induced voltage increases with a faster rate of flux cutting.
13. An induced voltage is effectively in series with the turns of the coil in which the voltage is produced.
14. A decrease in flux will induce a voltage of opposite polarity from an increase in flux, with the same direction of field lines in both cases.
15. The flux of 1000 lines increasing to 1001 lines in 1 s produces a flux change $d\phi/dt$ of 1 line per s.
16. The pickup voltage of a relay is the maximum voltage the relay contacts can switch safely.
17. The switching contacts of a relay are always open when the relay is not energized.
18. The movable arm on a relay is called the armature.
19. One difference between a standard mechanical switch and a relay is that relay contacts never get dirty.

QUESTIONS

1. Draw a diagram showing two conductors connecting a battery to a load resistance through a closed switch. (**a**) Show the magnetic field of the current in the negative side of the line and in the positive side. (**b**) Where do the two fields aid? Where do they oppose?
2. State the rule for determining the magnetic polarity of a solenoid. (**a**) How can the polarity be reversed? (**b**) Why are there no magnetic poles when the current through the coil is zero?
3. Why does the motor action between two magnetic fields result in motion toward the weaker field?

4. Why does current in a conductor perpendicular to this page have a magnetic field in the plane of the paper?
5. Why must the conductor and the external field be perpendicular to each other in order to have motor action or to generate induced voltage?
6. Explain briefly how either motor action or generator action can be obtained with the same conductor in a magnetic field.
7. Assume that a conductor being cut by the flux of an expanding magnetic field has 10 V induced with the top end positive. Now analyze the effect of the following changes: (a) The magnetic flux continues to expand, but at a slower rate. How does this affect the amount of induced voltage and its polarity? (b) The magnetic flux is constant, neither increasing nor decreasing. How much is the induced voltage? (c) The magnetic flux contracts, cutting across the conductor with the opposite direction of motion. How does this affect the polarity of the induced voltage?
8. Redraw the graph in Fig. 15-14c for 500 turns, with all other factors the same.
9. Redraw the circuit with the coil and battery in Fig. 15-6, showing two different ways to reverse the magnetic polarity.
10. Referring to Fig. 15-14, suppose that the flux decreases from 8 Wb to zero at the same rate as the increase. Tabulate all the values as in Table 15-1 and draw the three graphs corresponding to those in Fig. 15-14.
11. Assume you have in your possession a relay whose pickup and holding current values are unknown. Explain how you can determine their values experimentally.

PROBLEMS

ANSWERS TO ODD-NUMBERED PROBLEMS AT BACK OF BOOK.

1. A magnetic flux of 800 Mx cuts across a coil of 1000 turns in 1 μs. How much is the voltage induced in the coil? (1 Mx = 10^{-8} Wb)
2. Refer to Fig. 15-13. (a) Show the induced voltage here connected to a load resistance R_L of 50 Ω. (b) If the induced voltage is 100 V, how much current flows in R_L? (c) Give one way to reverse the polarity of the induced voltage.
3. Calculate the constant rate of flux change with time ($d\phi/dt$) in webers per second for the following: (a) 6 Wb increasing to 8 Wb in 1 s; (b) 8 Wb decreasing to 6 Wb in 1 s.
4. Calculate the voltage induced in 400 turns by each of the flux changes in Prob. 3.
5. Draw a circuit with a 20-V battery connected to a 100-Ω coil of 400 turns with an iron core 0.2 m long. Using SI magnetic units, calculate (a) I; (b) ampere-turns of mmf; (c) field intensity H; (d) flux density B in a core with a μ_r of 500; (e) total flux ϕ at each pole with an area of 6×10^{-4} m^2. (f) Show the direction of winding and magnetic polarity of the coil.
6. For the coil in Prob. 5: (a) If the iron core is removed, how much will the flux be in the air-core coil? (b) How much induced voltage would be produced by this change in flux while the core is being moved out in 1 s? (c) How much is the induced voltage after the core is removed?
7. A magnetic field cuts across a coil, which has 500 turns, at the rate of 2000 μWb/s. Calculate the value of induced voltage, v_{ind}.

8. A coil that has 250 turns has an induced voltage v_{ind} of 10 V. Calculate the rate of flux change, $d\phi/dt$, in Wb/s.

9. A coil has an induced voltage v_{ind} of 40 V when the rate of flux change equals 25,000 μWb/s. How many turns are in the coil?

10. A magnetic field cuts across a coil that has 2000 turns at the rate of 2500 μWb/s. Calculate the induced voltage v_{ind}.

CRITICAL THINKING

1. Refer to Fig. 15-19a. Calculate: (**a**) the total wire resistance R_W of the No. 12 gage copper wires; (**b**) the total resistance R_T of the circuit; (**c**) the voltage available across the load R_L; (**d**)

FIG. 15-19 Circuit diagram for Critical Thinking Probs. 1 and 2. (*a*) Mechanical switch controlling a high-power load a long distance away. (*b*) Relay controlling a high-power load a long distance away.

the I^2R power loss in the wire conductors; (e) the load power P_L; (f) the total power P_T consumed by the circuit; (g) the efficiency of the system calculated as $(P_L/P_T) \times 100$.

2. Refer to Fig. 15-19b. Calculate: (a) the total wire resistance R_W of the No. 20 gage copper wires; (b) the total resistance R_T of the relay coil circuit; (c) the voltage across the relay coil; (d) the I^2R power loss in the No. 20 gage copper wires in the relay coil circuit; (e) the total wire resistance R_W of the 10-ft length of No. 12 gage copper wires which connect the 16-Ω load, R_L to the 240-V_{ac} power line; (f) the voltage available across the load R_L; (g) the I^2R power loss in the 10-ft length of the No. 12 gage copper wire; (h) the load power P_L; (i) the total power P_T consumed by the load side of the circuit; (j) the percent efficiency of the system calculated as $(P_L/P_T) \times 100$.

3. Explain the advantage of using a relay rather than an ordinary mechanical switch when controlling a high-power load a long distance away. Use your solutions from Critical Thinking Probs. 1 and 2 to support your answer.

ANSWERS TO TEST-POINT QUESTIONS

15-1 **a.** T
    b. T

15-2 **a.** left
    b. south pole

15-3 **a.** T
    b. T

15-4 **a.** T
    b. T

15-5 **a.** south
    b. south

15-6 **a.** A
    b. yes

15-7 **a.** 2 Wb/s
    b. 2 Wb/s

15-8 **a.** T
    b. F
    c. T
    d. F

ELECTRICAL SYMBOLS AND ABBREVIATIONS

Table A-1 summarizes the letter symbols used as abbreviations for electrical characteristics and their basic units. All the metric prefixes for multiple and fractional values are listed in Table A-2. In addition, Table A-3 shows electronic symbols from the Greek alphabet. Table A-4 shows the preferred values for resistors having tolerances of ± 20 percent, ± 10 percent, and ± 5 percent.

TABLE A-1   ELECTRICAL CHARACTERISTICS

QUANTITY	SYMBOL*	BASIC UNIT
Current	I or i	ampere (A)
Charge	Q or q	coulomb (C)
Power	P	watt (W)
Voltage	V or v	volt (V)
Resistance	R	ohm (Ω)
Reactance	X	ohm (Ω)
Impedance	Z	ohm (Ω)
Conductance	G	siemens (S)
Admittance	Y	siemens (S)
Susceptance	B	siemens (S)
Capacitance	C	farad (F)
Inductance	L	henry (H)
Frequency	f	hertz (Hz)
Period	T	second (s)

*Capital letters for I, Q, and V are generally used for peak, rms, or dc value; small letters are used for instantaneous values. Small r and g are used for internal values, such as r_p and g_m of a tube.

TABLE A-2   MULTIPLES AND SUBMULTIPLES OF UNITS*

VALUE	PREFIX	SYMBOL	EXAMPLE
$1\,000\,000\,000\,000 = 10^{12}$	tera	T	$THz = 10^{12}\ Hz$
$1\,000\,000\,000 = 10^{9}$	giga	G	$GHz = 10^{9}\ Hz$
$1\,000\,000 = 10^{6}$	mega	M	$MHz = 10^{6}\ Hz$
$1\,000 = 10^{3}$	kilo	k	$kV = 10^{3}\ V$
$100 = 10^{2}$	hecto	h	$hm = 10^{2}\ m$
$10 = 10$	deka	da	$dam = 10\ m$
$0.1 = 10^{-1}$	deci	d	$dm = 10^{-1}\ m$
$0.01 = 10^{-2}$	centi	c	$cm = 10^{-2}\ m$
$0.001 = 10^{-3}$	milli	m	$mA = 10^{-3}\ A$
$0.000\,001 = 10^{-6}$	micro	μ	$\mu V = 10^{-6}\ V$
$0.000\,000\,001 = 10^{-9}$	nano	n	$ns = 10^{-9}\ s$
$0.000\,000\,000\,001 = 10^{-12}$	pico	p	$pF = 10^{-12}\ F$

*Additional prefixes are exa $= 10^{18}$, peta $= 10^{15}$, femto $= 10^{-15}$, and atto $= 10^{-18}$.

TABLE A-3   GREEK LETTER SYMBOLS*

NAME	LETTER CAPITAL	LETTER SMALL	USES
Alpha	A	α	α for angles, transistor characteristic
Beta	B	β	β for angles, transistor characteristic
Gamma	Γ	γ	
Delta	Δ	δ	Small change in value
Epsilon	E	ϵ	ϵ for permittivity; also base of natural logarithms
Zeta	Z	ζ	
Eta	H	η	
Theta	Θ	θ	Phase angle
Iota	I	ι	
Kappa	K	κ	
Lambda	Λ	λ	λ for wavelength
Mu	M	μ	μ for prefix micro, permeability, amplification factor
Nu	N	ν	
Xi	Ξ	ξ	
Omicron	O	o	
Pi	Π	π	π is 3.1416 for ratio of circumference to diameter of a circle
Rho	P	ρ	ρ for resistivity
Sigma	Σ	σ	Summation
Tau	T	τ	Time constant
Upsilon	Y	υ	
Phi	Φ	ϕ	Magnetic flux, angles
Chi	X	χ	
Psi	Ψ	ψ	Electric flux
Omega	Ω	ω	Ω for ohms; ω for angular velocity

*This table includes the complete Greek alphabet, although some letters are not used for electronic symbols.

TABLE A-4   PREFERRED VALUES* FOR RESISTORS

TOLERANCE 20%	TOLERANCE 10%	TOLERANCE 5%	TOLERANCE 20%	TOLERANCE 10%	TOLERANCE 5%
10	10	10			36
		11		39	39
	12	12			43
		13	47	47	47
15	15	15			51
		16		56	56
	18	18			62
		20	68	68	68
22	22	22			75
		24		82	82
	27	27			91
		30	100	100	100
33	33	33			

*Numbers and decimal multiples for ohms.

APPENDIX B

SOLDER AND THE SOLDERING PROCESS*

FROM SIMPLE TASK TO FINE ART

Soldering is the process of joining two metals together by the use of a low-temperature melting alloy. Soldering is one of the oldest known joining techniques, first developed by the Egyptians in making weapons such as spears and swords. Since then, it has evolved into what is now used in the manufacturing of electronic assemblies. Soldering is far from the simple task it once was; it is now a fine art, one that requires care, experience, and a thorough knowledge of the fundamentals.

The importance of having high standards of workmanship cannot be overemphasized. Faulty solder joints remain a cause of equipment failure, and because of that, soldering has become a *critical skill.*

The material contained in this appendix is designed to provide the student with both the fundamental knowledge and the practical skills needed to perform many of the high-reliability soldering operations encountered in today's electronics.

Covered here the fundamentals of the soldering process, the proper selection, and the use of the soldering station.

The key concept in this appendix is *high-reliability soldering.* Much of our present technology is vitally dependent on the reliability of countless, individual soldered connections. High-reliability soldering was developed in response to early failures with space equipment. Since then the concept and practice have spread into military and medical equipment. We have now come to expect it in everyday electronics as well.

THE ADVANTAGE OF SOLDERING

Soldering is the process of connecting two pieces of metal together to form a reliable electrical path. Why solder them in the first place? The two pieces of metal could be put together with nuts and bolts, or some other kind of mechanical fastening. The disadvantages of these methods are twofold. First, the reliability of the connection cannot be assured because of vibration and shock. Second, because oxidation and corrosion are continually occurring on the metal surfaces, electrical conductivity between the two surfaces would progressively decrease.

A soldered connection does away with both of these problems. There is no movement in the joint and no interfacing surfaces to oxidize. A continuous conductive path is formed, made possible by the characteristics of the solder itself.

---

*This material is provided courtesy of PACE, Inc., Laurel, Maryland.

THE NATURE OF SOLDER

Solder used in electronics is a low-temperature melting alloy made by combining various metals in different proportions. The most common types of solder are made from tin and lead. When the proportions are equal, it is known as 50/50 solder—50 percent tin and 50 percent lead. Similarly, 60/40 solder consists of 60 percent tin and 40 percent lead. The percentages are usually marked on the various types of solder available; sometimes only the tin percentage is shown. The chemical symbol for tin is Sn; thus Sn 63 indicates a solder which contains 63 percent tin.

Pure lead (Pb) has a melting point of 327°C (621°F); pure tin, a melting point of 232°C (450°F). But when they are combined into a 60/40 solder, the melting point drops to 190°C (374°F)—lower than either of the two metals alone.

Melting generally does not take place all at once. As illustrated in Fig. B-1, 60/40 solder begins to melt at 183°C (361°F), but it has not fully melted until the temperature reaches 190°C (374°F). Between these two temperatures, the solder exists in a plastic (semiliquid) state—some, but not all, of the solder has melted.

The plastic range of solder will vary, depending on the ratio of tin to lead, as shown in Fig. B-2. Various ratios of tin to lead are shown across the top of this figure. With most ratios, melting begins at 183°C (361°F), but the full melting temperatures vary dramatically. There is one ratio of tin to lead that has no plastic state and is known as *eutectic solder.* This ratio is 63/37 (Sn 63) and it fully melts and solidifies at 183°C (361°F).

FIG. B-1 Plastic range of 60/40 solder. Melt begins at 183°C (361°F) and is complete at 190°C (374°F).

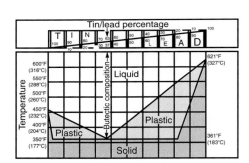

FIG. B-2 Fusion characteristics of tin/lead solders.

The solder most commonly used for hand soldering in electronics is the 60/40 type, but because of its plastic range, care must be taken not to move any elements of the joint during the cool-down period. Movement may cause a disturbed joint. Characteristically, this type of joint has a rough, irregular appearance and looks dull instead of bright and shiny. It is unreliable and therefore one of the types of joints that is unacceptable in high-reliability soldering.

In some situations, it is difficult to maintain a stable joint during cooling, for example, when wave soldering is used with a moving conveyor line of circuit boards during the manufacturing process. In other cases it may be necessary to use minimal heat to avoid damage to heat-sensitive components. In both of these situations, eutectic solder is the preferred choice, since it changes from a liquid to a solid during cooling with no plastic range.

THE WETTING ACTION

To someone watching the soldering process for the first time, it looks as though the solder simply sticks the metals together like a hot-melt glue, but what actually happens is far different.

A chemical reaction takes place when the hot solder comes into contact with the copper surface. The solder dissolves and penetrates the surface. The molecules of solder and copper blend together to form a new metal alloy, one that is part copper and part solder and that has characteristics all its own. This reaction is called *wetting* and forms the intermetallic bond between the solder and copper (Fig. B-3).

Proper wetting can occur only if the surface of the copper is free of contamination and from oxide films that form when the metal is exposed to air. Also, the solder and copper surfaces need to have reached the proper temperature.

Even though the surface may look clean before soldering, there may still be a thin film of oxide covering it. When solder is applied, it acts like a drop of water on an oily surface because the oxide coating prevents the solder from coming into contact with the copper. No reaction takes place, and the solder can be easily scraped off. For a good solder bond, surface oxides must be removed during the soldering process.

FIG. B-3   The wetting action. Molten solder dissolves and penetrates a clean copper surface, forming an intermetallic bond.

THE ROLE OF FLUX

Reliable solder connections can be accomplished only on clean surfaces. Some sort of cleaning process is essential in achieving successful soldered connections, but in most cases it is insufficient. This is due to the extremely rapid rate at which oxides form on the surfaces of heated metals, thus creating oxide films which prevent proper soldering. To overcome these oxide films, it is necessary to utilize materials, called *fluxes,* which consist of natural or synthetic rosins and sometimes additives called activators.

It is the function of flux to remove surface oxides and keep them removed during the soldering operation. This is accomplished because the flux action is very corrosive at or near solder melt temperatures and accounts for the flux's ability to rapidly remove metal oxides. It is the fluxing action of removing oxides and carrying them away, as well as preventing the formation of new oxides, that allows the solder to form the desired intermetallic bond.

Flux must activate at a temperature lower than solder so that it can do its job prior to the solder flowing. It volatilizes very rapidly; thus it is mandatory that the flux be activated to flow onto the work surface and not simply be volatilized by the hot iron tip if it is to provide the full benefit of the fluxing action.

There are varieties of fluxes available for many applications. For example, in soldering sheet metal, acid fluxes are used; silver brazing (which requires a much higher temperature for melting than that required by tin/lead alloys) uses a borax paste. Each of these fluxes removes oxides and, in many cases, serves additional purposes. The fluxes used in electronic hand soldering are the pure rosins, rosins combined with mild activators to accelerate the rosin's fluxing

FIG. B-4 Types of cored solder, with varying solder-flux percentages.

capability, low-residue/no-clean fluxes, or water-soluble fluxes. Acid fluxes or highly activated fluxes should never be used in electronic work. Various types of flux-cored solder are now in common use. They provide a convenient way to apply and control the amount of flux used at the joint (Fig. B-4).

SOLDERING IRONS

In any kind of soldering, the primary requirement, beyond the solder itself, is heat. Heat can be applied in a number of ways—conductive (e.g., soldering iron, wave, vapor phase), convective (hot air), or radiant (IR). We are mainly concerned with the conductive method, which uses a soldering iron.

Soldering stations come in a variety of sizes and shapes, but consist basically of three main elements: a resistance heating unit; a heater block, which acts as a heat reservoir; and the tip, or bit, for transferring heat to the work. The standard production station is a variable-temperature, closed-loop system with interchangeable tips and is made with ESD-safe plastics.

CONTROLLING HEAT AT THE JOINT

Controlling tip temperature is not the real challenge in soldering; the real challenge is to control the *heat cycle* of the work—how fast the work gets hot, how hot it gets, and how long it stays that way. This is affected by so many factors that, in reality, tip temperature is not that critical.

The first factor that needs to be considered is the *relative thermal mass* of the area to be soldered. This mass may vary over a wide range.

Consider a single land on a single-sided circuit board. There is relatively little mass, so the land heats up quickly. But on a double-sided board with plated-through holes, the mass is more than doubled. Multilayered boards may have an even greater mass, and that's before the mass of the component lead is taken into consideration. Lead mass may vary greatly, since some leads are much larger than others.

Further, there may be terminals (e.g., turret or bifurcated) mounted on the board. Again, the thermal mass is increased, and will further increase as connecting wires are added.

Each connection, then, has its particular thermal mass. How this combined mass compares with the mass of the iron tip, the "relative" thermal mass, determines the time and temperature rise of the work.

With a large work mass and a small iron tip, the temperature rise will be slow. With the situation reversed, using a large iron tip on a small work mass, the temperature rise of the work will be much more rapid—even though the *temperature of the tip is the same.*

Now consider the capacity of the iron itself and its ability to sustain a given flow of heat. Essentially, irons are instruments for generating and storing heat, and the reservoir is made up of both the heater block and the tip. The tip comes in various sizes and shapes; it's the *pipeline* for heat flowing into the work. For small work, a conical (pointed) tip is used, so that only a small flow of heat occurs. For large work, a large chisel tip is used, providing greater flow.

The reservoir is replenished by the heating element, but when an iron with a large tip is used to heat massive work, the reservoir may lose heat faster than it can be replenished. Thus the *size* of the reservoir becomes important: a large heating block can sustain a larger outflow longer than a small one.

An iron's capacity can be increased by using a larger heating element, thereby increasing the wattage of the iron. These two factors, block size and wattage, are what determine the iron's recovery rate.

If a great deal of heat is needed at a particular connection, the correct temperature with the right size tip is required, as is an iron with a large enough capacity and an ability to recover fast enough. *Relative thermal mass,* then, is a major consideration for controlling the heat cycle of the work.

A second factor of importance is the *surface condition* of the area to be soldered. If there are any oxides or other contaminants covering the lands or leads, there will be a barrier to the flow of heat. Then, even though the iron tip is the right size and has the correct temperature, it may not supply enough heat to the connection to melt the solder. In soldering, a cardinal rule is that a good solder connection cannot be created on a dirty surface. Before attempting to solder, the work should always be cleaned with an approved solvent to remove any grease or oil film from the surface. In some cases pretinning may be required to enhance solderability and remove heavy oxidation of the surfaces prior to soldering.

A third factor to consider is *thermal linkage*—the area of contact between the iron tip and the work.

Figure B-5 shows a cross-sectional view of an iron tip touching a round lead. The contact occurs only at the point indicated by the "X," so the linkage area is very small, not much more than a straight line along the lead.

The contact area can be greatly increased by applying a small amount of solder to the point of contact between the tip and workpiece. This solder heat bridge provides the thermal linkage and assures rapid heat transfer into the work.

From the aforementioned, it should now be apparent that there are many more factors than just the temperature of the iron tip that affect how quickly any particular connection is going to heat up. In reality, soldering is a very complex control problem, with a number of variables to it, each influencing the other. And what makes it so critical is *time*. The general rule for high-reliability soldering on printed circuit boards is to apply heat for no more than 2 s from the time solder starts to melt (wetting). Applying heat for longer than 2 s after wetting may cause damage to the component or board.

With all these factors to consider, the soldering process would appear to be too complex to accurately control in so short a time, but there is a simple solution—the *workpiece indicator* (WPI). This is defined as the reaction of the workpiece to the work being performed on it—a reaction that is discernible to the human senses of sight, touch, smell, sound, and taste.

Put simply, workpiece indicators are the way the work talks back to you—the way it tells you what effect you are having and how to control it so that you accomplish what you want.

In any kind of work, you become part of a closed-loop system. It begins when you take some action on the workpiece; then the workpiece reacts to what you did; you sense the change, and then modify your action to accomplish the result. It is in the sensing of the change, by sight, sound, smell, taste, or touch, that the workpiece indicators come in (Fig. B-6).

For soldering and desoldering, a primary workpiece indicator is *heat rate recognition*—observing how fast heat flows into the connection. In practice, this means observing the rate at which the solder melts, which should be within 1 to 2 s.

Lead   Tip   Solder "bridge"

Small linkage area   Large linkage area

FIG. B-5   Cross-sectional view (left) of iron tip on a round lead. The "X" shows point of contact. Use of a solder bridge (right) increases the linkage area and speeds the transfer of heat.

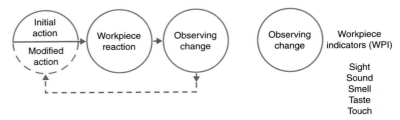

FIG. B-6 Work can be viewed as a closed-loop system (left). Feedback comes from the reaction of the workpiece and is used to modify the action. Workpiece indicators (right)—changes discernible to the human senses—are the way the "work talks back to you."

This indicator encompasses all the variables involved in making a satisfactory solder connection with minimum heating effects, including the capacity of the iron and its tip temperature, the surface conditions, the thermal linkage between tip and workpiece, and the relative thermal masses involved.

If the iron tip is too large for the work, the heating rate may be too fast to be controlled. If the tip is too small, it may produce a "mush" kind of melt; the heating rate will be too slow, even though the temperature at the tip is the same.

A general rule for preventing overheating is "Get in and get out as fast as you can." That means using a heated iron you can react to—one giving a 1- to 2-s dwell time on the particular connection being soldered.

SELECTING THE SOLDERING IRON AND TIP

A good all-around soldering station for electronic soldering is a variable-temperature, ESD-safe station with a pencil-type iron and tips that are easily interchangeable, even when hot (Fig. B-7).

The soldering iron tip should always be fully inserted into the heating element and tightened. This will allow for maximum heat transfer from the heater to the tip.

The tip should be removed daily to prevent an oxidation scale from accumulating between the heating element and the tip. A bright, thin tinned surface must be maintained on the tip's working surface to ensure proper heat transfer and to avoid contaminating the solder connection.

The plated tip is initially prepared by holding a piece of flux-cored solder to the face so that it will tin the surface when it reaches the lowest temperature at which solder will melt. Once the tip is up to operating temperature, it will usually be too hot for good tinning, because of the rapidity of oxidation at elevated temperatures. The hot tinned tip is maintained by wiping it lightly on a damp sponge to shock off the oxides. When the iron is not being used, the tip should be coated with a layer of solder.

MAKING THE SOLDER CONNECTION

The soldering iron tip should be applied to the area of maximum thermal mass of the connection being made. This will permit the rapid thermal elevation of the parts being soldered. Molten solder always flows toward the heat of a properly prepared connection.

FIG. B-7   Pencil-type iron with changeable tips.

When the solder connection is heated, a small amount of solder is applied to the tip to increase the thermal linkage to the area being heated. The solder is then applied to the opposite side of the connection so that the work surfaces, not the iron, melt the solder. Never melt the solder against the iron tip and allow it to flow onto a surface cooler than the solder melting temperature.

Solder, with flux, applied to a cleaned and properly heated surface will melt and flow without direct contact with the heat source and provide a smooth, even surface, feathering out to a thin edge (Fig. B-8). Improper soldering will exhibit a built-up, irregular appearance and poor filleting. The parts being soldered must be held rigidly in place until the temperature decreases to solidify the solder. This will prevent a disturbed or fractured solder joint.

Selecting cored solder of the proper diameter will aid in controlling the amount of solder being applied to the connection (e.g., a small-gauge solder for a small connection; a large-gauge solder for a large connection).

FIG. B-8   Cross-sectional view of a round lead on a flat surface.

REMOVAL OF FLUX

Cleaning may be required to remove certain types of fluxes after soldering. If cleaning is required, the flux residue should be removed as soon as possible, preferably within 1 hour after soldering.

APPENDIX C

SCHEMATIC SYMBOLS

TABLE C-1   GENERAL SYMBOLS

DEVICE	SYMBOL	DEVICE	SYMBOL
AC voltage source		Coil or inductance Air-core	
		Iron-core	
Amplifier		Variable	

Antenna
  General
		Powdered iron or
		  ferrite slug	

Dipole		Conductor General	
Loop		Connection	
		No connection	
Battery, cell, or dc voltage source		Current source	
Longer line positive			

Capacitor
  General, fixed
  Curved electrode is
    outside foil, negative,
    or low-potential side
		Crystal, piezoelectric	

		Fuse	

Electrolytic	or	Ground, earth or metal frame
		  Chassis or common return
		    connected to one side of
		    voltage source	

Variable	or	Chassis or common return not connected to voltage source	
		Common return	
Ganged			

964 | APPENDIX C   SCHEMATIC SYMBOLS

TABLE C-1 GENERAL SYMBOLS (CONTINUED)

DEVICE	SYMBOL	DEVICE	SYMBOL

Jack
 	
Plug for jack
	Tip
	Sleeve
		Resistor, fixed
		   Tapped
		
		   Variable	

Key telegraph		Switch, SPST SPDT 2-pole (DPDT)	
Loudspeaker, general Phones or headset		Shielding Shielded conductor	

Magnet
  Permanent
 	
  Electromagnet
	PM	Transformer
		Air-core
		
		Iron-core	

Microphone		Autotransformer	
Meters; letter or symbol to indicate range or function	A mA V	Link coupling	
Motor	M		
Neon bulb			
Relay, coil Contacts			

APPENDIX D

USING THE OSCILLOSCOPE

MAIN SECTIONS OF AN OSCILLOSCOPE

An oscilloscope is one of the most important types of test equipment for checking electronic circuits because the "scope" shows the waveform of an applied voltage (Fig. D-1). The fluorescent screen, usually green, of the cathode-ray tube (CRT) displays a graph of voltage amplitudes with respect to time. Examples of the oscilloscope display are shown in Fig. D-2 with sine waves in Fig. D-2*a* and square waves in Fig. D-2*b*. Actually, the pattern on the screen is produced by a small spot of light that is deflected vertically and horizontally to trace out the waveform.

FIG. D-1   Oscilloscope.

The vertical axis represents voltage amplitudes. More voltage applied to the vertical input terminals of the oscilloscope results in a bigger trace pattern. For horizontal deflection, the oscilloscope has its own internal sawtooth voltage generator. No external connections are used for this function. A sawtooth waveform is needed for the internal horizontal sweep because of its linear increases in amplitude. Then the horizontal axis of the display is proportional to time. The screen pattern, therefore, displays a graph of the variations of the signal input voltage, with time on the horizontal axis and voltage on the vertical axis. It should be noted that for most measurements, only the vertical input terminal is used for connections to the circuit being tested.

The number of cycles you see depends on the frequency of the input signal and the timing of the internal sweep for horizontal deflection. Usually, the horizontal sweep frequency is set for a display of two or three complete cycles of the waveform, just for convenience.

(a)   (b)

FIG. D-2 Examples of oscilloscope screen patterns. (*a*) Sine wave. (*b*) Square wave.
Vertical lines are not visible because the spot moves too fast.

Not only does the oscilloscope show the amount of voltage, as the height of
the trace pattern, but also the frequency can be checked in terms of the horizontal
time base. Furthermore, any distortion of the signal is shown in the trace pattern.

The oscilloscope is a voltmeter. You connect the cable lead from the vertical input terminal *across* a component to check the voltage. Although the oscilloscope is generally used for ac voltages, it can also indicate dc values in terms
of a steady displacement of the trace from the center position.

Figure D-3 shows the front panel of a typical dual-trace oscilloscope. The
key functional controls are indicated with an emphasis on three basic functions:

1. The cathode-ray tube (or CRT) at the left, as the visual display, shows the
    signal waveform. The CRT provides a spot of light that can be deflected up
    or down and left or right.
2. The vertical (V) deflection sections (one for each of the two channels) am-
    plify the signal applied to the V input terminals to provide enough signal
    voltage to the vertical deflection plates in the CRT.
3. The horizontal (H) deflection section has the internal sawtooth voltage gen-
    erator that is used as a time base for horizontal deflection. The H deflection
    voltage is applied to the horizontal deflection plates in the CRT.

The combined functions of these three sections result in a trace pattern on the
oscilloscope screen. From the waveform, you can measure voltage amplitude of
the V input signal, determine the period or frequency, and observe any distortion.

CRT SECTION   In Fig. D-3, note the power on-off switch for the oscilloscope. The intensity control varies the brightness of the trace. Adjust the focus
control for a sharp pattern at the desired brightness. Do not keep the brightness
high with a stationary pattern for too long, as the screen phosphor may be
"burned," which produces a permanent brown discoloration of the screen. In some
cases, the power on-off switch may be part of the brightness control.

Focus control

Intensity control

Sweep mode (X-Y switch converts channel 1 input to horizontal input)

Cathode ray tube (CRT)

Horizontal position

Time base and sweep control

Power switch

Screen graticule

Vertical attenuator (channel 1)

Channel 1 vertical input (horizontal input when X-Y switch used)

Channel 1 controls

Chassis ground

Channel 2 controls

Channel 2 vertical input

FIG. D-3 The main functional controls of a typical dual-trace oscilloscope.

The screen *graticule* is a plastic sheet over the face of the CRT to make measurements more convenient. A typical size for the graticule is 10 cm × 8 cm, with each box 1 cm high and wide. Calibrated values for the oscilloscope are often specified per centimeter.

Although not labeled in Fig. D-3, the oscilloscope also has provisions for centering the electron beam in the CRT, which positions the trace vertically and horizontally. The centering controls adjust dc voltages to leave the trace in a reference position for ac deflection by the signal voltage. If the beam should be off the screen, there will be no trace visible, but it can be returned to the screen with the V and H, or X and Y, positioning controls.

V DEFLECTION   Figure D-3 shows a step attenuator and a variable gain control to adjust the height of the trace pattern. The trace can be adjusted to fit most of the screen height in order to see the waveform better. The step attenuator cuts down the amount of signal applied to the V input terminals, often in multiples of ½, ½.₅, or ⅒. The gain control is a variable adjustment for in-between values of vertical deflection. In many oscilloscopes, the step attenuator is calibrated in units of V/cm of vertical deflection at the maximum setting of the variable gain control.

H DEFLECTION   The H deflection section is more complicated than the V section, because horizontal deflection involves timing of the internal H sweep, synchronizing the H timing to make the pattern remain still and the H amplification for the desired width of the trace pattern. For oscilloscopes with a calibrated time base, the step control is marked in μs/cm, ms/cm, or s/cm for the maximum setting of the variable timing control. Without the calibration, these controls just indicate approximate frequency for the internal time base.

The timing of the internal time base for horizontal deflection must be synchronized with the vertical input signal; otherwise, the pattern on the screen drifts to the left or right across the screen. The general procedure is to adjust the timing for two or three cycles, with as little drift as possible. Then adjust the synchronization (sync) control to make the pattern remain stationary. Always use as little sync as possible to avoid distortion of the pattern. Many oscilloscopes have an automatic sync or *trigger* level.

The pattern on the screen represents a spot of light that is moving so fast that you see the complete trace. Actually, the trace patterns are repeated one over the other, but it looks like a steady picture with the correct synchronization. Below about 30 Hz for the H sweep frequency, the brightness of the trace may flicker. At lower sweep frequencies, it is possible to see the spot moving.

In summary, then, for the general operation of using the oscilloscope to observe a signal waveform, connect the signal to the V input terminals and adjust the horizontal timing of the internal sweep generator to obtain the desired trace pattern. The H input terminals for an external input signal are only used for some special functions, such as the Lissajous patterns described at the end of this appendix. In some oscilloscopes, one of the two V inputs can be made an H input through the operation of an X-Y switch.

Y AXIS FOR VOLTAGE AND X AXIS FOR TIME

Refer to Fig. D-4, which illustrates how oscilloscope waveforms are developed. In Fig. D-4a, the spot of light at the center of the screen is produced by the CRT. It has the required electrode voltages, including high voltage for the anode. The spot is focused for the smallest size and the intensity is set for the desired brightness. Also, the spot can be centered with the positioning controls. There is no vertical or horizontal deflection as yet.

In Fig. D-4b, horizontal deflection voltage is applied to the CRT to move the spot back and forth across the screen along the x axis. There is no vertical deflection. A horizontal line is displayed because the spot repeats its motion over the same area too fast for you to see movement. Horizontal deflection is provided by the internal sweep voltage, for most applications of the oscilloscope.

With vertical deflection, but without horizontal deflection, the spot moves up and down along the y axis. This action is shown in Fig. D-4c, without any horizontal deflection. You can obtain this display by turning off the internal horizontal sweep. The vertical deflection is provided by signal voltage at the vertical input terminal of the oscilloscope.

Both vertical and horizontal deflection are used for the trace pattern in Fig. D-4d. Two cycles of sine waves show the waveform of the vertical input signal. More cycles or less cycles can be displayed according to the frequency setting of the internal horizontal sweep voltage. The complete trace pattern results from the spot of light being deflected vertically by the input signal while the spot is deflected across the screen at a uniform rate of speed.

An example of oscilloscope waveforms for the video signal in a television receiver is shown in Fig. D-5. The oscilloscope is an important instrument for adjusting and troubleshooting television receivers.

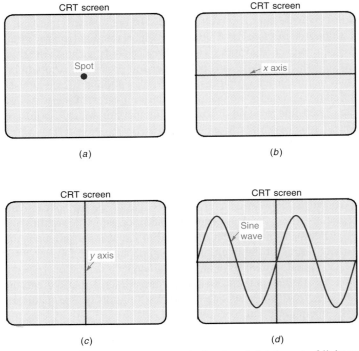

(a) (b)

(c) (d)

FIG. D-4 How an oscilloscope trace pattern is developed. (*a*) A spot of light at the center of the screen without V and H deflection. (*b*) A horizontal line produced by H deflection but no V deflection. (*c*) A vertical line produced by V deflection but no H deflection. (*d*) A sine-wave vertical input signal with V and H deflection.

CALIBRATED VOLTAGES ON THE VERTICAL *Y* AXIS

In many oscilloscopes, the step attenuator that adjusts the amount of vertical input signal is calibrated so that you can read voltage amplitudes directly from the height of the trace on the oscilloscope screen. The variable gain control must stay set at its

FIG. D-5 Oscilloscope pattern for a video signal in a television receiver. Two cycles shown.

maximum value. An example is illustrated in Fig. D-6 for a pattern with a height of six boxes equal to 6 cm. In Fig. D-6a, the horizontal deflection is turned off to show the vertical amplitude alone, whereas Fig. D-6b shows the complete trace pattern. Either way, the height of 6 cm represents the peak-to-peak voltage of the waveform. The measurement is peak-to-peak because it is between the two opposite peaks.

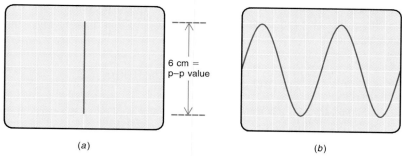

   (a)   (b)

FIG. D-6 Voltage values on the vertical axis. (a) H deflection removed to show just the peak-to-peak amplitude on the y axis. (b) Complete waveform with V and H deflection.

Assume that the vertical attenuator is at 1 V/cm. This setting means that each 1-cm-high box represents 1 V of vertical input signal. For the six boxes equal to 6 cm, the amplitude is

$$6 \text{ cm} \times \frac{1 \text{ V}}{\text{cm}} = 6 \text{ V}$$

For this example, the amplitude of the vertical input signal is 6 V p-p.

Suppose that the height of the trace is 4 cm, instead of 6 cm. For the same 1-V/cm setting, the trace amplitude is

$$4 \times 1 = 4 \text{ V p-p}$$

As another example, let the V/cm setting be changed to 0.005 V/cm. For 6 cm of deflection, the V input signal then is

$$6 \text{ cm} \times \frac{0.005 \text{ V}}{\text{cm}} = 0.030 \text{ V or } 30 \text{ mV}$$

With 4 cm of vertical deflection, the amplitude is 20 mV. The 30 and 20 mV amplitudes are peak-to-peak values.

CALIBRATED TIME VALUES ON THE HORIZONTAL X AXIS Refer to Fig. D-7 with the x axis shown 10 cm wide. Also, the calibrated H time setting is taken here as 1 ms/cm. Each box horizontally represents 1 ms of time, as shown in Fig. D-7a. The two sine-wave cycles in Fig. D-7b, therefore, take 10 ms of time. For one cycle that takes 5 boxes or 5 cm, the period T for one cycle is 5 ms.

Remember that the frequency f is equal to 1/T. Therefore, the frequency for the sine waves in Fig. D-7b is as follows.

(a)

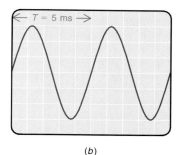

(b)

FIG. D-7 Time and frequency values on the x axis. (a) The period T of the horizontal sweep time is 10 ms. (b) One cycle of the vertical input signal has a period T of 5 ms, or f = 0.2 kHz = 200 Hz.

$$f = \frac{1}{T} = \frac{1}{5 \text{ ms}} = 0.02 \text{ kHz or } 200 \text{ Hz}$$

This value is the frequency of the vertical input signal.

Suppose that five cycles with the same time base of 10 ms were shown in Fig. D-7. One cycle would take $10/5 = 2$ ms. With T of 2 ms, the f is equal to 0.5 kHz or 500 Hz.

As another example, let the H time setting be 20 μs/cm. Then the width of 10 cm in Fig. D-7 represents $20 \times 10 = 200 \ \mu$s. For two cycles across the entire width of the screen, one cycle takes 100 μs for T of the signal input. The frequency then is

$$f = \frac{1}{100 \ \mu s} = 0.01 \text{ MHz or } 10 \text{ kHz}$$

These calculations give the frequency of the signal applied to the vertical input terminals of the oscilloscope.

For a quick, simple check of the calibrated time values, you can apply a sample of the 60-Hz voltage from the ac power line, which is an accurate reference for frequency. With the horizontal T/cm control set on 5 ms/cm there should be exactly three cycles on the screen.

COMPARISON OF H SYNC AND H SELECTOR SWITCHES

One of the most important problems in learning how to use the oscilloscope is to appreciate the difference between setting the type of deflection with the horizontal selector switch and choosing the type of sync with the sync selector switch to be used with internal sweep. The two switches have the same names for their three positions, but their functions are entirely different. In order to emphasize the comparison, Fig. D-8 shows the two switches with the name and function for each position.

HORIZONTAL SELECTOR SWITCH   In Fig. D-8a the horizontal selector switch turns on the internal sweep at the top position. This method supplies dc electrode voltages for the sawtooth generator used for H deflection. Then the sawtooth voltage output is fed to the H deflection amplifier for the horizontal deflection plates. This setting for internal sweep is the type of operation generally used for the oscilloscope to display the waveform of the vertical input signal.

On the 60-Hz position of the H selector switch, a sample of the 60-Hz ac line voltage is taken internally to be used for H deflection. The 60-Hz voltage is a sine wave.

On the "external" position of the H selector switch, the internal sweep is disconnected from the H amplifier. Without any signal connected to the H input terminals on the front panel of the oscilloscope, there is no horizontal deflection. However, any type of signal input can be connected to the external H terminals to provide signal for the H deflection amplifier.

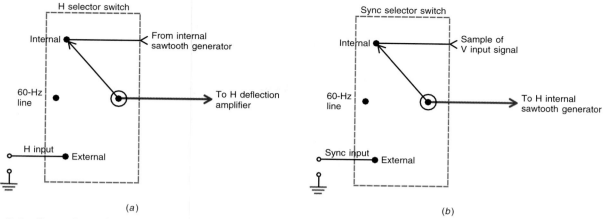

FIG. D-8 Comparison of a horizontal selector switch, shown in (*a*), with a sync selector switch, shown in (*b*).

HOW A SAWTOOTH GENERATOR IS SYNCHRONIZED

Before we consider the different types of sync that can be chosen with the sync selector switch, an illustration of synchronization with the required sync pulses is shown in Fig. D-9. Keep in mind that the sync function only applies when the internal sawtooth generator is being used to provide the internal sweep. In general, any sawtooth generator is a pulse oscillator, like the bistable multivibrator (MV). An asymmetrical type of MV circuit is used with a waveshaping capacitor to provide sawtooth voltage in the output. This type of circuit is easily synchronized by injecting pulses at the input electrode to force the oscillator to run at the frequency of the synchronizing pulses. This value is the *forced frequency,* which is locked in by the sync pulses, compared with the *free-running frequency* without sync.

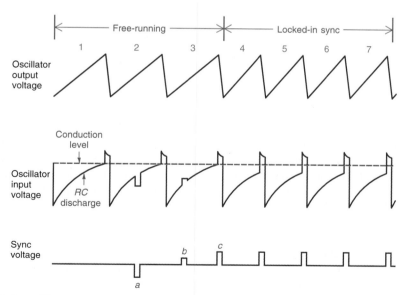

FIG. D-9 How synchronizing (sync) voltage is used to trigger a free-running pulse oscillator to lock it in at sync frequency.

The free frequency must be set a little lower than the sync frequency, thus allowing the input voltage of the oscillator to be ready for the sync voltage to produce the lock-in effect. Incidentally, synchronization of the deflection oscillator is also used in television receivers to hold the picture steady.

Refer to the waveforms in Fig. D-9. At the top is the sawtooth voltage output of the H deflection oscillator used for internal sweep. Just under the sawtooth waves are the waveforms of input voltage from the MV type of pulse oscillator. At the bottom of the figure, the pulses toward the end of the pulse train are able to lock in the oscillator at the sync frequency.

The trigger effect for controlling the oscillator occurs with the input voltage shown below the sawtooth waves in Fig. D-9. In the *RC* discharge curve, this voltage is cutting off one stage of the MV, until the input voltage approaches the conduction level. Then when one stage conducts, it cuts off the other stage.

The sync voltage is able to control when the input voltage can reach the conduction level. Consider the sync pulses at the bottom of Fig. D-9, in sequence, from left to right. First, there is no sync. Now the oscillator is free-running. Next, is the sync pulse marked *a*, but it has the wrong polarity. It cannot force the input voltage to the conduction level, and the oscillator cannot be affected. Then comes sync pulse *b* of the correct polarity but not enough amplitude. The oscillator is still free-running. During this time, the oscillator is free-running for the cycles marked 1, 2, and 3 at the top of the sawtooth waveform.

Finally, sync pulse *c* in Fig. D-9 has the correct polarity and enough amplitude to force the oscillator input voltage to the conduction level. The start of conduction corresponds to the start of retrace on the sawtooth wave.

All the sync pulses that follow *c* in Fig. D-9 also trigger the oscillator at the sync frequency, as shown for the sawtooth waves labeled 4, 5, 6, and 7 at the top of the figure. As long as the sync voltage is applied, it is able to hold the oscillator at the sync frequency.

SYNC SELECTOR SWITCH   We can now consider the different types of sync for the internal sawtooth generator. The sync section of the oscilloscope has waveshaping circuits to provide sharp pulses for exact synchronization. In many oscilloscopes, the polarity and slope of the sync pulses can be varied.

Most important is internal sync. It is used practically always with the internal sweep for horizontal deflection. The reason is that internal sync is automatically at the correct frequency for synchronizing the vertical input signal because this sync is a sample of the signal from the vertical deflection amplifier. In order to see complete cycles in the trace pattern, the sweep frequency must be at an exact submultiple of the signal frequency. As examples, for two cycles, the *V* input signal is double the H scanning frequency, and for three cycles the ratio is 3:1.

The 60-Hz position on the sync selector switch is seldom needed. One application is in the use of the oscilloscope in aligning tuned circuits.

The external sync also is used only for special applications. When necessary, though, the sync voltage must be connected to the external sync input terminal on the front panel of the oscilloscope. One application would be to display the pattern of an AM radio signal with an audio modulation envelope. In this case, the *V* input is an RF signal, but to see the envelope, the audio modulating voltage must be used as external sync for the oscilloscope.

To summarize the functions for the selector switches in Fig. D-9, remember that the sync voltage does not produce deflection. Therefore, internal sync does not mean internal sawtooth scanning. The H selector switch determines when the internal sawtooth generator is used. Furthermore, selecting the type of sync has no meaning unless the internal sweep is on. The sync has its use only for the internal sawtooth generator. In other words, the H selector switch must be set for internal sweep in order to use any type of sync.

OSCILLOSCOPE PROBES

Oscilloscope probes are the test leads used for connecting the vertical input signal to the oscilloscope. There are three types: a direct lead that is just a shielded cable, the low-capacitance probe (LCP) with a series-isolating resistor, and a demodulator probe. Figure D-10 shows a circuit for an LCP for an oscilloscope. The LCP usually has a switch to short out the isolating resistor so that the same probe can be used either as a direct lead or with low-capacitance.

FIG. D-10   Circuit for low-capacitance probe (LCP) for an oscilloscope.

DIRECT PROBE   The direct probe is just a shielded wire without any isolating resistor. A shielded cable is necessary to prevent any pickup of interfering signals, especially with the high resistance at the vertical input terminals of the oscilloscope. The higher the resistance, the more voltage that can be developed by induction. Any interfering signals in the test lead produce distortion of the trace pattern. The main sources of interference are 60-Hz magnetic fields from the power line and stray RF signals.

The direct probe as a shielded lead has relatively high capacitance. A typical value is 90 pF for 3 ft (0.9 m) of 50-Ω coaxial cable. Also, the vertical input terminals of the oscilloscope have a shunt capacitance of about 40 pF. The total C then is $90 + 40 = 130$ pF. This much capacitance can have a big effect on the circuit being tested. For example, it could detune a resonant circuit. Also, non-sinusoidal waveshapes are distorted. Therefore, the direct probe can be used only when the added C has little or no effect. These applications include voltages for the 60-Hz power line or sine-wave audio signals in a circuit with a relatively low resistance of several kilohms or less. The advantage of the direct probe is that it does not divide down the amount of input signal, since there is no series isolating resistance.

LOW-CAPACITANCE PROBE (LCP)   Refer to the diagram in Fig. D-10. The 9-MΩ resistor in the probe isolates the capacitance of the cable and the oscilloscope from the circuit connected to the probe tip. With an LCP, the input capacitance of the probe is only about 10 pF. The LCP must be used for oscilloscope measurements when

1. The signal frequency is above audio frequencies.
2. The circuit being tested has R higher than about 50 kΩ.
3. The waveshape is nonsinusoidal, especially with square waves and sharp pulses.

Without the LCP, the observed waveform can be distorted. The reason is that too much capacitance changes the circuit while it is being tested.

THE 1:10 VOLTAGE DIVISION OF THE LCP

Refer to the voltage divider circuit in Fig. D-11. The 9-MΩ of R_P is a series resistor in the probe. Also, R_S of 1 MΩ is a typical value for the shunt resistance at the vertical terminals of the oscilloscope. Then $R_T = 9 + 1 = 10$ MΩ. The voltage across R_S for the scope equals R_S/R_T or 1/10 of the input voltage. For the example in Fig. D-11 with 10 V at the tip of the LCP, 1 V is applied to the oscilloscope.

FIG. D-11   Voltage division of 1:10 with a low-capacitance probe.

Remember, when using the LCP, multiply by 10 for the actual signal amplitude. As an example, for a trace pattern on the screen that measures 2.4 V, the actual signal input at the probe is 24 V. For this reason, the LCP is generally called the "10 times" probe. Check to see whether or not the switch on the probe is on the direct or LCP position. Even though the scope trace is reduced by the factor of 1/10, it is preferable to use the LCP for almost all oscilloscope measurements to minimize distortion of the waveshapes.

TRIMMER CAPACITOR OF THE LCP

Referring back to Fig. D-10, note that the LCP has an internal variable capacitor C_1 across the isolating resistor R_1. The purpose of C_1 is to compensate the LCP for high frequencies. Its time constant with R_1 should equal the RC time constant of the circuit at the vertical input terminals of the oscilloscope. When necessary, C_1 is adjusted for minimum tilt on a square-wave signal.

DEMODULATOR PROBE

The demodulator probe has an internal diode to detect an amplitude-modulated RF signal. The output of the probe is the envelope or modulation. Polarity of the rectified dc output is usually negative. The demodulator probe can be used for signal tracing in the RF circuits of an AM

ac Abbreviation for alternating current.

active device One that can control voltage or current. Examples are transistor amplifier and diode rectifier.

acute angle Less than 90°.

A/D converter A device that converts analog input signals to digital output.

admittance (Y) Reciprocal of impedance Z in ac circuits. $Y = 1/Z$.

air gap Air space between poles of a magnet.

alkaline cell or battery One that uses alkaline electrolyte.

alpha (α) Characteristic of junction transistors. Ratio of collector current to emitter current. Value is 0.98 to 0.99.

alternating current (ac) Current that reverses direction at a regular rate. Alternating voltage reverses in polarity. The rate of reversals is the frequency.

alternator AC generator.

ampere (A) Basic unit of electric current. Value of one ampere flows when one volt of potential difference is applied across one ohm of resistance.

ampere-turn Unit of magnetizing force equal to 1 A × 1 turn.

amplifier A device that increases the amplitude of a signal.

amplitude modulation (AM) Changing the amplitude of an RF carrier wave in step with a lower-frequency signal that has the desired information.

analog circuits Circuits that use continuous variations in voltage or current, compared with digital pulse circuits.

AND gate Digital logic circuit. Produces HIGH output of 1 only when all inputs are at 1.

antiresonance Term sometimes used for parallel resonance.

apparent power The product of voltage and current VA when V and I are out of phase.

armature The part of a generator in which the voltage is produced. In a motor it is commonly the rotating member. Also, the movable part of a relay.

astable MV Multivibrator that has no stable state. Used as an oscillator to generate clock timing pulses.

audio frequency (AF) Within the range of hearing, approximately 16 to 16,000 Hz.

autotransformer A single, tapped, winding used to step up or step down voltage.

average value In sine-wave ac voltage or current, is 0.637 of peak value.

back-off scale Ohmmeter readings from right to left.

bandpass Filter that allows a band of frequencies to be coupled to the load.

bandstop Filter that prevents a band of frequencies from being coupled to the load.

bandwidth A range of frequencies that have a resonant effect in LC circuits.

bank Components connected in parallel.

battery Group of cells connected in series or parallel.

BCD Binary coded decimal. Converts a decimal number to a binary equivalent.

beta (β) Current-gain characteristic of junction transistors. Ratio of collector current to base current.

bias Average dc level of amplifier voltage or current to set operating characteristic.

binary number system Uses only two digits, 0 and 1.

bipolar transistor NPN or PNP type.

bistable MV Multivibrator that has two stable states. Used as flip-flop circuit.

bit One unit of information, either 0 or 1, in the binary number system.

bleeder current Steady current from source, used to stabilize output voltage with changes in load current.

boolean algebra Logical system of using binary information in digital circuits.

branch Part of a parallel circuit.

bridge Circuit in which voltages or currents can be balanced for a net effect of zero.

brushes In a motor or generator, devices that provide stationary connections to the rotor.

bypass capacitor One that has very low reactance in a parallel path.

byte Digital word with a string of eight bits of 0 and 1.

C Symbol for capacitance.

C Abbreviation for coulomb, the unit of electric charge.

calorie Amount of heat energy needed to raise the temperature of one gram of water by 1°C.

capacitor Device used to store electric charge.

capacitance The ability to store electric charge.

carbon composition resistors Resistors made of finely divided carbon or graphite mixed with a powdered insulating material.

carbon film resistors Resistors made by depositing a thin layer of carbon on an insulated substrate. The carbon film is cut in the form of a spiral.

cascaded amplifiers Output terminal of one stage drives input terminal of next stage.

CB circuit Common-base amplifier for junction transistors. Signal into emitter and output from collector.

CB radio Citizen's band radio, 26.965 to 27.405 MHz.

CC circuit Common-collector amplifier for junction transistors. Signal into base and output from emitter. Is emitter-follower stage.

CD circuit Common-drain circuit for field-effect transistors. Is source-follower stage.

CE circuit Common-emitter amplifier for junction transistors. Signal into base and output from collector.

Celsius scale (°C) Temperature scale that uses 0° for the freezing point of water and 100° for the boiling point. Formerly called centigrade.

ceramic Insulator with a high dielectric constant.

chassis ground Common return for all electronic circuits mounted on one metal chassis or PC board. Usually connects to one side of dc supply voltage.

CG circuit Common-gate amplifier for FETs.

cgs Centimeter-gram-second system of units.

chip Miniature semiconductor for integrated circuit.

chip capacitor A surface-mounted capacitor.

choke Inductance with high X_L compared with the R of the circuit.

circuit breaker A protective device that opens when excessive current flows in circuit. Can be reset.

circular mil Cross-sectional area of round wire with diameter of 1 mil or 0.001 in.

clamp probe Measures current without opening the circuit.

clear Same as reset on a flip-flop. Puts Q output at logic 0.

clock A device that provides timing pulses for digital circuits; it is usually a multivibrator (MV) oscillator.

closed circuit A continuous path for current.

coaxial cable An inner conductor surrounded by an outer conductor that serves as a shield.

coding of capacitors The methods used to indicate the value of a capacitor.

coil Turns of wire conductor to concentrate the magnetic field.

color code System in which colors are used to indicate values in resistors and capacitors.

commutator Converts reversing polarities to one polarity.

comparator An op amp circuit that compares the signal voltage on one input with a reference voltage on the other.

complex number Has real and j terms; uses form $A + jB$.

conductance (G) Ability to conduct current. It is the reciprocal of resistance, $G = 1/R$. The unit is the siemens (S).

constant-current source One that has high r_i to supply constant I with variations in R_L.

constant-voltage source One that has low r_i to supply constant V with variations in R_L.

continuity Continuous path for current. Reading of zero ohms with an ohmmeter.

conventional current Direction of flow of positive charges, opposite from electron flow.

corona Effect of ionization of air around a point at high potential.

cosine A trigonometric function of an angle, equal to the ratio of the adjacent side to the hypotenuse in a right triangle.

cosine wave One whose amplitudes vary as the cosine function of an angle. It is 90° out of phase with the sine wave.

coulomb (C) Unit of electric charge. 1 C $= 6.25 \times 10^{18}$ electrons.

counter Digital circuit using a flip-flop to accumulate the count of pulses.

coupling capacitor Has very low X_C in series path.

covalent bond Pairing of atoms with electrical valence of ± 4.

cps Cycles per second. Formerly used as unit of frequency. Replaced by hertz (Hz) unit where 1 Hz = 1 cps.

CRT Cathode-ray tube. A device that converts electric signals to a visual display on a fluorescent screen.

CS circuit Common-source amplifier for field-effect transistors.

current divider A parallel circuit to provide branch I less than the main-line current.

current source Supplies $I = V/r_i$ to load, with r_i in parallel.

cutoff No current in an active device such as a transistor.

cycle One complete set of values for a repetitive waveform.

D/A converter Converts digital input to analog output.

damping Reducing the Q of a resonant circuit to increase the bandwidth.

Darlington pair Combination of two transistor stages in cascade.

D'Arsonval meter A dc analog meter movement commonly used in ammeters and voltmeters.

dB Abbreviation for decibel. Equals 10 times the logarithm of the ratio of two power levels.

dc Abbreviation for direct current.

decade A 10:1 range of values.

decade resistance box A unit for providing any resistance within a wide range of values.

decibels A logarithmic expression that compares two power levels.

degaussing Demagnetizing by applying an ac field and gradually reducing it to zero.

delta (Δ) network Three components connected in series in a closed loop. Same as pi (π) network.

detector diode A device that rectifies a modulated signal to recover information in the modulation.

diamagnetic Material that can be weakly magnetized in the opposite direction from the magnetizing field.

dicing Cutting a slice of semiconductor material into tiny chips.

dielectric Insulating material. It cannot conduct current but does store charge.

dielectric constant (k) Ability to concentrate the electric field in a dielectric.

differential amplifiers An op amp circuit that amplifies differential signals but attenuates common-mode signals.

differentiating circuit An RC circuit with a short time constant for pulses across R.

digital circuit One that uses only two amplitudes for a pulse of voltage or current, either HIGH at 1 or LOW at 0.

digital IC Abbreviation for digital integrated circuit.

diode Electronic device with two electrodes. Allows current flow in only one direction.

DIP Dual inline package for the pins of IC chip.

direct current (dc) Current that flows in only one direction. Dc voltage has a steady polarity that does not reverse.

discrete component A single individually packaged component usually with two or three leads.

distributor Digital circuit to convert serial data to parallel data. Also called demultiplexer.

DMM Digital multimeter. A piece of test equipment used to measure voltage, current, and resistance in an electronic circuit.

doping Adding impurities to pure semiconductor material to provide free positive and negative charges.

double subscripts An example is V_{BA} to indicate voltage at point B with respect to point A.

DPDT Double-pole double-throw switch or relay contacts.

DPST Double-pole single-throw switch or relay contacts.

dynamometer Type of ac meter, generally for 60 Hz.

eddy current Circulating current induced in the iron core of an inductor by ac variations of magnetic flux.

effective value For sine-wave ac waveform, 0.707 of peak value. Corresponds to heating effect of same dc value. Also called rms value.

efficiency Ratio of power output to power input × 100%.

EIA Electronic Industries Association.

electricity Dynamic electricity is the effect of voltage in producing current in conductors. Static electricity is accumulation of charge.

electrolyte Solution that forms ion charges.

electrolytic capacitor Type with very high C because electrolyte is used to form very thin dielectric. Must be connected with correct polarity in a circuit.

electromagnet Magnet whose magnetic field is associated with electric current in a coil.

electron Basic particle of negative charge, in orbital rings around the nucleus in an atom.

electron flow Current of negative charges in motion. Direction is from the negative terminal of the voltage source, through the external circuit, and returning to the positive side of the source. Opposite to the direction of conventional current.

electron volt Unit of energy equal to the work done in moving a charge of 1 electron through a potential difference of 1 V.

electronics Based on electrical effects of the electron. Includes applications for amplifiers, oscillators, rectifiers, control circuits, and digital pulse circuits.

emf Electromotive force, voltage to produce current in a circuit.

emitter follower Circuit in which signal input is to base and output is from emitter. Same as common-collector circuit.

F connector Solderless plug for coaxial cable.

Fahrenheit scale (°F) Temperature scale that uses 32° for the freezing point of water and 212° for the boiling point.

farad (F) Unit of capacitance. Value of one Farad stores one coulomb of charge with one volt applied.

Faraday's law For magnetic induction, the generated voltage is proportional to the flux and its rate of change.

FCC Federal Communications Commission.

ferrite Magnetic material that is not a metal conductor.

ferromagnetic Magnetic properties of iron and other metals that can be strongly magnetized in the same direction as the magnetizing field.

FET Field-effect transistor.

field Group of lines of force; magnetic or an electric field.

field-effect transistor (FET) A device that depends on an electric field to control the current in a silicon channel.

field winding The part of a motor or generator that supplies the magnetic field cut by the armature.

film capacitor A capacitor which uses a plastic film for its dielectric.

filter Circuit to separate different frequencies.

fluctuating dc Varying voltage and current but no change in polarity.

flux (ϕ) Magnetic lines of force.

flux density Amount of flux per unit area.

flywheel effect Ability of an LC circuit to continue oscillating after the energy source has been removed.

forward voltage Polarity that allows current of majority carriers through a semiconductor junction.

frequency (f) Number of cycles per second for a waveform with periodic variations. The unit is hertz (Hz).

frequency modulation (FM) Changing the frequency of an RF carrier wave in step with a lower-frequency signal that has the desired information.

function generator A piece of test equipment which produces sine, square, and triangular waveforms. It is used when designing or testing electronic circuitry.

fuse Metal link that melts from excessive current and opens circuit.

gain (A) Also amplification. Ratio of amplified output to input.

galvanic cell Electrochemical type of voltage source.

galvanometer Measures electric charge or current.

gate Logic circuit with two or more inputs but one HIGH or LOW output for specific combinations of input pulses.

gauss (G) Unit of flux density in cgs system, equal to one magnetic line of force per square centimeter.

generator A device that produces voltage output. Is a source for either dc or ac V and I.

germanium (Ge) Semiconductor element used for transistors and diodes.

giga (G) Metric prefix for 10^9.

gilbert (Gb) Unit of magnetomotive force in cgs system. One gilbert equals 0.794 ampere-turn.

graph cycle A 10 : 1 range of values on logarithmic graph paper.

ground Common return to earth for ac power lines. Chassis ground in electronic equipment is the common return to one side of the internal power supply.

half-power frequencies Define bandwidth with 70.7 percent response for resonant LC circuit.

Hall effect Small voltage generated by a conductor with current in an external magnetic field.

harmonic Exact multiple of fundamental frequency.

henry (H) Unit of inductance. Current change of one ampere per second induces one volt across an inductance of one henry.

hertz (Hz) Unit of frequency. One hertz equals one cycle per second.

hexadecimal Number system with radix of 16.

h_{FE} Hybrid parameter for junction transistors that specifies current gain for common-emitter circuit.

holding current The minimum amount of current required to keep a relay energized.

hole Positive charge that exists only in doped semiconductors because of covalent bonds between atoms. Amount of hole charge is the same as a proton and an electron.

hole current Motion of hole charges. Direction is the same as that of conventional current, opposite from electron flow.

hot resistance The R of a component with its normal load current. Determined by V/I.

hot-wire meter Type of ac meter.

hybrid IC A device that has discrete components with an integrated circuit.

hypotenuse Side of a right triangle opposite the 90° angle.

hysteresis In electromagnets, the effect of magnetic induction lagging in time behind the applied magnetizing force.

Hz Hertz unit of frequency, equal to one cycle per second.

IC Abbreviation for integrated circuit.

I_{CB_0} Leakage current from collector to base with emitter open.

IGFET Insulated-gate field-effect transistor.

imaginary number Value at 90°, indicated by j operator, as in the form jA.

impedance matching Occurs when a transformer is utilized for its impedance transformation properties. With impedance matching, maximum power is delivered to the load, R_L.

inductance (L) Ability to produce induced voltage when cut by magnetic flux. Unit of inductance is the henry (H).

induction Ability to generate V or I without physical contact. Electromagnetic induction by magnetic field; electrostatic induction by electric field.

inductor Coil of wire with inductance.

insulator A material that does not allow current to flow when voltage is applied, because of its high resistance.

integrated circuit Contains transistors, diodes, resistors, and capacitors in one miniaturized package. Can use bipolar transistor or FET technology.

integration circuit An RC circuit with a long time constant. Voltage output across C.

internal resistance r_i Limits the current supplied by the voltage source to $I = V/r_i$.

inverse relation Same as reciprocal function. As one variable increases, the other decreases.

ion Atom or group of atoms with net charge. Can be produced in liquids, gases, and doped semiconductors.

IR drop Voltage across a resistor.

iron-vane meter Type of ac meter, generally for 60 Hz.

j operator Indicates 90° phase angle, as in $j8$ Ω for X_L. Also, $-j8$ Ω is at $-90°$ for X_C.

JFET Junction field-effect transistor.

JK flip-flop Type that has a clock input to toggle outputs between logic 1 and 0 when the J and K terminals are held HIGH.

joule (J) Practical unit of work or energy. One joule equals one watt-second of work.

k Coefficient of coupling between coils.

keeper Magnetic material placed across the poles of a magnet to form a complete magnetic circuit. Used to maintain strength of magnetic field.

Kelvin (K) scale Absolute temperature scale, 273° below values on Celsius scale.

kilo (k) Metric prefix for 10^3.

Kirchhoff's current law (KCL) The phasor sum of all currents into and out of any branch point in a circuit must equal zero.

Kirchhoff's voltage law (KVL) The phasor sum of all voltages around any closed path must equal zero.

laminations Thin sheets of steel insulated from one another to reduce eddy-current losses in inductors, motors, etc.

latch A device that remains in one stable state until activated to the opposite state. Can store binary information as logic 1 or 0. Is flip-flop in digital circuits.

leakage current Small reverse current of minority carriers across a PN junction.

Leclanché cell Carbon-zinc primary cell.

LED Light-emitting diode.

Lenz's law Induced current has magnetic field that opposes the change causing the induction.

linear IC A device that contains analog circuits, such as amplifiers, oscillators, rectifiers, and control circuits, rather than digital circuits.

linear relation Straight-line graph between two variables. As one increases, the other increases in direct proportion.

load Takes current from the voltage source, resulting in load current.

loading effect Source voltage is decreased as amount of load current increases.

loop In a circuit, any closed path.

LSI Large-scale integration for IC chips.

magnetic pole Concentrated point of magnetic flux.

magnetism Effects of attraction and repulsion by iron and similar materials without the need for an external force. Electromagnetism includes the effects of a magnetic field associated with an electric current.

magnetomotive force (MMF) Ability to produce magnetic lines of force. Measured in units of ampere-turns.

magnitude Value of a quantity regardless of phase angle.

make and break Occurs when contacts close and open.

maxwell (Mx) Unit of magnetic flux, equal to one line of force in the magnetic field.

mega (M) Metric prefix for 10^6.

memory device Digital circuit that can store information as bits of logic 1 or 0. Often is flip-flop circuit.

mesh current Assumed current in a closed path, without any current division, for application of Kirchhoff's current law.

metal film resistors Resistors made by spraying a thin film of metal onto a ceramic substrate. The metal film is cut in the form of a spiral.

micro (μ) Metric prefix for 10^{-6}.

microelectronics Microscopic components used for IC chips to miniaturize size of equipment.

milli (m) Metric prefix for 10^{-3}.

miniDIP   Miniature IC package with eight pins in dual inline form.

mks   Meter-kilogram-second system of units.

monostable   Having one stable state, as in one-shot multivibrator.

MOSFET   Metal-oxide semiconductor FET.

motor   A device that produces mechanical motion from electric energy.

multiplier   Resistor in series with a meter movement for voltage ranges.

multivibrator (MV)   Astable type of oscillator circuit to produce pulses as a clock generator for timing in digital circuits.

mutual induction (L_M)   Ability of one coil to induce voltage in another coil.

NAND gate   Logic circuit that produces a LOW output of 0 only when all inputs are HIGH at 1.

nano (n)   Metric prefix for 10^{-9}.

NC   Normally closed for relay contacts, or no connection for pinout diagrams.

neutron   Particle without electric charge in the nucleus of an atom.

nibble   Binary word with four bits, equal to one-half byte.

node   A common connection for two or more branch currents.

NOR gate   Logic circuit that produces a LOW output of 0 when any of the inputs is HIGH at 1.

Norton's theorem   Method of reducing a complicated network to one current source with shunt resistance.

NOT gate   Circuit to change binary 1 to 0 or 0 to 1. Same as inverter.

obtuse angle   More than 90°.

octal base   Eight pins for vacuum tubes. Eight digits for octal number system.

octave   A 2 : 1 range of values.

oersted (Oe)   Unit of magnetic field intensity; 1 Oe = 1 Gb/cm.

ohm (Ω)   Unit of resistance. Value of one ohm allows current of one ampere with potential difference of one volt.

Ohm's law   In electric circuits, $I = V/R$.

ohms per volt   Sensitivity rating for a voltmeter. High rating means less meter loading.

open circuit   One that has infinitely high resistance, resulting in zero current.

operational amplifier (op amp)   High-gain amplifier commonly used in linear IC chips for analog circuits.

OR gate   Digital logic circuit that produces a HIGH output of 1 when any of the inputs is HIGH at 1.

oscillator   Circuit that generates ac output from dc power input, without any ac signal input.

oscilloscope   A piece of test equipment used to view and measure a variety of different ac waveforms.

parallel circuit   One that has two or more branches for separate currents from one voltage source.

paramagnetic   Material that can be weakly magnetized in the same direction from the magnetizing force.

passive device   Components such as resistors, capacitors, and inductors. They do not generate voltage or control current.

PC board   A device that has printed circuits.

peak-to-peak value (p-p)   Amplitude between opposite peaks.

peak value   Maximum amplitude, in either polarity; 1.414 times rms value for sine-wave V or I.

permanent magnet (PM)   It has magnetic poles produced by internal atomic structure. No external current needed.

permeability   Ability to concentrate magnetic lines of force.

permeance   Reciprocal of magnetic reluctance.

phase angle   Angle between two phasors; denotes time shift.

phasing dots   Used on transformer windings to identify those leads having the same instantaneous polarity.

phasor   A line representing magnitude and direction of a quantity, such as voltage or current, with respect to time.

pickup current   The minimum amount of current required to energize a relay.

pico (p)   Metric prefix for 10^{-12}.

piezoelectric effect   Vibrations produced by some crystals compressed, expanded, or twisted, or when voltage is applied.

pinout   Pin numbers for IC package.

polar form   Form of complex numbers that gives magnitude and phase angle in the form $A \angle \theta°$.

polarity   Property of electric charge and voltage. Negative polarity is excess of electrons. Positive polarity means deficiency of electrons.

potential   Ability of electric charge to do work in moving another charge. Measured in volt units.

potentiometer   Variable resistor with three terminals connected as a voltage divider.

power (P)   Rate of doing work. The unit of electric power is the watt.

power factor   Cosine of the phase angle for a sine-wave ac circuit. Value is between 1 and 0.

power supply   A piece of test equipment used to supply dc voltage and current to electronic circuits under test.

preferred values   Common values of resistors and capacitors generally available.

primary cell or battery   Type that cannot be recharged.

primary winding   Transformer coil connected to the source voltage.

printed wiring   Conducting paths printed on plastic board.

proton   Particle with positive charge in the nucleus of an atom.

pulsating dc value   Includes ac component on average dc axis.

pulse   A sharp rise and decay of voltage or current of a specific peak value for a brief period of time.

Q   Figure of quality or merit, in terms of reactance compared with resistance. The Q of a coil is X_L/r_i. For an LC circuit, Q indicates sharpness of resonance. Also used as the symbol for charge: $Q = CV$.

quadrature   A 90° phase angle.

R   Symbol for resistance.

radian (rad)   Angle of 57.3°. Complete circle includes 2π rad.

radio   Wireless communication by electromagnetic waves.

radio frequencies (RF) Those high enough to be radiated efficiently as electromagnetic waves, generally above 30 kHz. Usually much higher.

radix Base for a number system; 10 for decimal numbers and 2 for binary numbers.

ramp Sawtooth waveform with linear change in V or I.

reactance Property of L and C to oppose flow of I that is varying. Symbol is X_C or X_L. Unit is the ohm.

read Take out digital information from a memory device.

real number Any positive or negative number not containing j. $(A + jB)$ is a complex number but A and B by themselves are real numbers.

real power The net power consumed by resistance. Measured in watts.

reciprocal relation As one variable increases, the other decreases.

rectangular form Representation of a complex number in the form $A + jB$.

rectifier A device that allows current in only one direction.

reflected impedance The value of impedance reflected back into the primary from the secondary.

relay Automatic switch operated by current in a coil.

relay chatter Describes the vibrating of relay contacts.

reluctance (R) Opposition to magnetic flux. Corresponds to resistance for current.

reset Put Q output of flip-flop to logic 0.

resistance (R) Opposition to current. Unit is the ohm (Ω).

resistance wire A conductor having a high resistance value.

resonance Condition of $X_L = X_C$ in an LC circuit to favor the resonant frequency for a maximum in V, I, or Z.

reverse voltage Polarity that prevents forward current through a PN junction.

rheostat Variable resistor with two terminals to vary I.

ringing Ability of an LC circuit to oscillate after a sharp change in V or I.

rms value For sine-wave ac waveform, 0.707 of peak value. Also called effective value.

rotor Rotating part of generator or motor.

saturation Maximum limit at which changes of input have no control in changing the output.

sawtooth wave One in which amplitude values have a slow linear rise or fall and a sharp change back to the starting value. Same as a linear ramp.

secondary winding Transformer coil connected to the load.

secondary cell or battery Type that can be recharged.

self-inductance (L) Inductance produced in a coil by current in the coil itself.

series circuit One that has only one path for current.

set Put Q output of flip-flop at logic 1.

shield Metal enclosure to prevent interference of radio waves.

short-circuit Has zero resistance, resulting in excessive current.

shunt A parallel connection. Also a device used to increase the range of an ammeter.

SI Abbreviation for *Système International*, a system of practical units based on the meter, kilogram, second, ampere, kelvin, mol, and candela.

siemens (S) Unit of conductance. Reciprocal of ohms unit.

silicon (Si) Semiconductor chemical element used for transistors, diodes, and integrated circuits.

sine Trigonometric function of an angle, equal to the ratio of the opposite side to the hypotenuse in a right triangle.

sine wave One in which amplitudes vary in proportion to the sine function of an angle.

slip rings In an ac generator, devices that provide connections to the rotor.

solder Alloy of tin and lead used for fusing wire connections.

solenoid Coil used for electromagnetic devices.

source follower FET amplifier circuit in which input is to the gate and output from the source electrode. Same as common-drain circuit. Corresponds to emitter follower.

spade lug A type of wire connector.

SPDT Single-pole double-throw switch or relay contacts.

specific gravity Ratio of weight of a substance with that of an equal volume of water.

specific resistance The R for a unit length, area, or volume.

SPST Single-pole single-throw switch or relay contacts.

square wave An almost instantaneous rise and decay of voltage or current in a periodic pattern with time and with a constant peak value. The V or I is on and off for equal times and at constant values.

static electricity Electric charges not in motion.

stator Stationary part of a generator or motor.

steady-state value The V or I produced by a source without any sudden changes. Can be dc or ac value. Final value of V or I after transient.

storage cell or battery Type that can be recharged.

string Components connected in series.

summing amplifier An op amp circuit whose output equals the negative sum of the inputs.

superconductivity Very low R at extremely low temperatures.

superposition theorem Method of analyzing a network with multiple sources by using one at a time and combining their effects.

supersonic Frequency above the range of hearing, generally above 16,000 Hz.

surface-mount resistors Resistors made by depositing a thick carbon film on a ceramic base. Electrical connection to the resistive element is made by means of two leadless solder end electrodes which are C-shaped.

surface-mount technology Components soldered directly to the copper traces of a printed circuit board. No holes need to be drilled with surface-mounted components.

susceptance (B) Reciprocal of reactance in sine-wave ac circuits; $B = 1/X$.

switch Device used to open or close connections of a voltage source to a load circuit.

switching contacts The contacts which open and close when a relay is energized.

tangent Trigonometric function of an angle, equal to the ratio of the opposite side to the adjacent side in a right triangle.

tank circuit An LC tuned circuit. Store energy in L and C.

tantalum Chemical element used for electrolytic capacitors.

taper   How R of a variable resistor changes with the angle of shaft rotation.

tapered control   The manner in which the resistance of a potentiometer varies with shaft rotation. For a linear taper, one-half shaft rotation corresponds to a resistance change of one-half its maximum value. For a nonlinear taper, the resistance change is more gradual at one end, with larger changes at the other end.

taut-band meter   Type of construction for meter movement often used in VOM.

temperature coefficient   For resistance, how R varies with a change in temperature.

tesla (T)   Unit of flux density, equal to 10^8 lines of force per square meter.

Thevenin's theorem   Method of reducing a complicated network to one voltage source with series resistance.

three-phase power   AC voltage generated with three components differing in phase by $120°$.

time constant   Time required to change by 63 percent after a sudden rise or fall in V and I. Results from the ability of L and C to store energy. Equals RC or L/R.

toggle   For digital circuits, changing between HIGH at logic 1 and LOW at logic 0.

toroid   Electromagnet with its core in the form of a closed magnetic ring.

transconductance   Ratio of current output to voltage input.

transformer   A device that has two or more coil windings used to step up or step down ac voltage.

transient   Temporary value of V or I in capacitive or inductive circuits caused by abrupt change.

transistor   Semiconductor device used for amplifiers. Includes NPN and PNP junction types and FETs.

trigonometry   Analysis of angles and triangles.

truth table   Listing of all possible combinations of inputs and outputs for a digital logic circuit.

tuning   Varying the resonant frequency of an LC circuit.

turns ratio   Comparison of turns in primary and secondary for a transformer.

twin lead   Transmission line with two conductors in plastic insulator.

UHF   Ultra high frequencies in band of 30 to 300 MHz.

unity-gain amplifier   An op amp circuit whose voltage gain is 1 or unity. It is used for buffering or isolating a low-impedance load from a high-impedance source.

VAR   Unit for voltamperes of reactive power, $90°$ out of phase with real power.

Variac   Transformer with variable turns ratio to provide different amounts of secondary voltage.

vector   A line representing magnitude and direction in space.

VHF   Very high frequencies, in band of 30 to 300 MHz.

volatile memory   Memory that loses its stored information when the power is turned off.

volt (V)   Practical unit of potential difference. One volt produces one ampere of current in a resistance of one ohm.

voltage divider   A series circuit to provide V less than the source voltage.

voltage drop   Voltage across each component in a series circuit. The proportional part of total applied V.

voltage regulator   A device that maintains a constant output voltage with changes of input voltage or output load current.

voltage source   Supplies potential difference across two terminals. Has internal series r_i.

voltampere (VA)   Unit of apparent power, equal to $V \times I$.

volt-ampere characteristic   Graph to show how I varies with V.

voltmeter loading   The amount of current taken by the voltmeter acting as a load. As a result the measured voltage is less than the actual value.

VOM   Volt-ohm-milliammeter.

watt (W)   Unit of real power. Equal to I^2R or $VI \cos θ$.

watt hour   Unit of electric energy, as power $\times$ time.

wattmeter   Measures real power as instantaneous value of $V \times I$.

wavelength (λ)   Distance in space between two points with the same magnitude and direction in a propagated wave.

wavetrap   An LC circuit tuned to reject the resonant frequency.

weber (Wb)   Unit of magnetic flux, equal to 10^8 lines of force.

Wheatstone bridge   Balanced circuit used for precise measurements of resistance.

wire gage   A system of wire sizes based on the diameter of the wire. Also, the tool used to measure wire size.

wirewound resistors   Resistors made with wire known as *resistance wire* which is wrapped around an insulating core.

word   In digital circuits, a group of bits of 0 and 1. Usually written in groups of four, eight, or sixteen bits.

work   Corresponds to energy. Equal to power $\times$ time, as in kilowatthour unit. Basic unit is one joule, equal to one volt-coulomb, or one watt-second.

wye network   Three components connected with one end in a common connection and the other ends to three lines. Same as T network.

X_C Capacitive reactance, equal to $1/(2\pi fC)$.
X_L Inductive reactance, equal to $2\pi fL$.
XNOR gate   Digital logic circuit for exclusive NOR gate.
XOR gate   Digital logic circuit for exclusive OR gate.

Y Symbol for admittance in an ac circuit. Reciprocal of impedance Z; the $Y = 1/Z$.
Y network   Another way of denoting a wye network.

Z Symbol for ac impedance. Includes resistance with capacitive and inductive reactance.

zero-crossing detector   An op amp comparator whose output switches between $\pm V_{sat}$ when V_{in} crosses zero.

zero-ohm resistors   A resistor whose value is practically $0 \ \Omega$. The 0-Ω value is denoted by a single black band around the center of the resistor body.

zero-ohms adjustment   Used with ohmmeter of VOM to set the correct reading at zero ohms.

ANSWERS TO SELF-TESTS

CHAPTER 1	1. T	5. T	9. T	13. T	17. T
	2. T	6. T	10. T	14. T	18. T
	3. T	7. T	11. T	15. T	19. F
	4. T	8. T	12. T	16. T	20. F

CHAPTER 2	1. *b*	3. *a*	5. *c*	7. *a*	9. *c*
	2. *d*	4. *c*	6. *a*	8. *d*	10. *c*

CHAPTER 3	1. 2	6. 25	10. 72	14. 0.83	18. 3
	2. 4	7. 25	11. 8	15. 144	19. 0.2
	3. 16	8. 10	12. 2	16. 2	20. 0.12
	4. 0.5	9. 0.4	13. 2	17. 1.2	21. *d*
	5. 2				

CHAPTER 4	1. *d*	3. *d*	5. *c*	7. *c*	9. *b*
	2. *c*	4. *b*	6. *d*	8. *b*	10. *d*

CHAPTER 5	1. *b*	3. *a*	5. *a*	7. *c*	9. *c*
	2. *a*	4. *d*	6. *c*	8. *b*	10. *b*

CHAPTER 6	1. *c*	3. *c*	5. *d*	7. *d*	9. *d*
	2. *c*	4. *c*	6. *b*	8. *a*	10. *d*

REVIEW: CHAPTERS 1 TO 6	1. *a*	6. *c*	10. *d*	14. *b*	18. *a*
	2. *c*	7. *b*	11. *b*	15. *a*	19. *b*
	3. *b*	8. *c*	12. *a*	16. *a*	20. *a*
	4. *c*	9. *b*	13. *c*	17. *a*	21. *b*
	5. *c*				

CHAPTER 7	1. T	3. T	5. T	7. T	9. F
	2. T	4. F	6. T	8. T	10. T

CHAPTER 8	1. *a*	3. *a*	5. *c*	7. *a*	9. *d*
	2. *c*	4. *a*	6. *c*	8. *c*	10. *c*

REVIEW: CHAPTERS 7 AND 8	1. T	4. T	7. T	9. T	11. F
	2. T	5. F	8. T	10. F	12. T
	3. T	6. F			

CHAPTER 9	1. T	3. T	5. T	7. F	9. T
	2. F	4. T	6. T	8. T	10. T

CHAPTER 10	1. T	3. T	5. T	7. T	
	2. T	4. T	6. T	8. F	

REVIEW: CHAPTERS 9 AND 10	1. T	4. T	7. F	10. T	13. T
	2. T	5. T	8. T	11. T	14. T
	3. T	6. F	9. T	12. T	15. T

CHAPTER 11	1. *a*	3. *d*	5. *b*	7. *b*	9. *c*
	2. *d*	4. *b*	6. *a*	8. *c*	10. *c*

CHAPTER 12	1. *d*	3. *b*	5. *d*	7. *a*	9. *a*
	2. *c*	4. *a*	6. *d*	8. *c*	10. *d*

REVIEW: CHAPTERS 11 AND 12	1. *d*	3. *a*	5. *b*	7. *b*	9. *a*
	2. *c*	4. *c*	6. *d*	8. *b*	10. *d*

CHAPTER 13	1. T	4. F	7. T	10. T	13. T
	2. T	5. T	8. T	11. F	14. T
	3. T	6. T	9. T	12. T	15. F

CHAPTER 14	1. F	4. F	7. T	9. T	11. T
	2. T	5. T	8. T	10. T	12. T
	3. T	6. T			

CHAPTER 15	1. T	5. T	9. T	13. T	17. F
	2. T	6. T	10. T	14. T	18. T
	3. T	7. T	11. T	15. T	19. F
	4. T	8. T	12. T	16. F	

ANSWERS TO ODD-NUMBERED PROBLEMS AND CRITICAL THINKING PROBLEMS

ANSWERS TO ODD-NUMBERED CHAPTER PROBLEMS

CHAPTER 1

1. $I = 5$ A
3. $Q = 9$ C
5. $Q = -3$ C
7. Since there are four

electrons in the valence shell, the valence is ± 4.
9. $T = 8$ s
11. (a) $R = 500\ \Omega$

(b) $R = 250\ \Omega$
(c) $R = 120\ \Omega$
(d) $R = 4\ \Omega$
13. (a) $G = 1$ S

(b) $G = 0.0001$ S
(c) $G = 0.025$ S
(d) $G = 2$ S
15. $V = 12$ V

CHAPTER 2

1. (a) $1.5\ \text{k}\Omega \pm 10\%$
(b) $27\ \Omega \pm 5\%$
(c) $470\ \text{k}\Omega \pm 5\%$
(d) $6.2\ \Omega \pm 5\%$
(e) $91\ \text{k}\Omega \pm 10\%$
(f) $10\ \Omega \pm 5\%$
(g) $1.8\ \text{M}\Omega \pm 10\%$
(h) $1.5\ \text{k}\Omega \pm 20\%$

3. (a) $470\ \text{k}\Omega$
(b) $1.2\ \text{k}\Omega$
(c) $330\ \Omega$
(d) $10\ \text{k}\Omega$
5. Reading from left to right, the colors are:
(a) brown, black, orange, and gold

(b) red, violet, gold, and gold
(c) green, blue, red, and silver
(d) brown, green, green, and gold
(e) red, red, silver, and gold

7. (a) $680,225\ \Omega$
(b) $8250\ \Omega$
(c) $18,503\ \Omega$
(d) $275,060\ \Omega$
(e) $62,984\ \Omega$
9. See Fig. 2-19b

CHAPTER 3

1. (b) $I = 15$ mA
(c) the same, 15 mA
(d) $I = 30$ mA
3. (a) $V = 36$ V
(b) $I = 150$ mA
5. (a) $V = 24$ V
(b) $P = 48$ W
(c) the same, 48 W
7. (a) $I = 300 \times 10^{-6}$ A $= 300\ \mu$A
(b) $I = 5 \times 10^{-6}$ A $= 5\ \mu$A

(c) $I = 200 \times 10^{-3}$ A $= 200$ mA
(d) $I = 300 \times 10^{-6}$ A $= 300\ \mu$A
(e) $I = 1 \times 10^{-3}$ A $= 1$ mA
(f) $I = 15 \times 10^{-3}$ A $= 15$ mA
9. (a) $R = 12 \times 10^3\ \Omega = 12\ \text{k}\Omega$
(b) $R = 3.75 \times 10^3\ \Omega = 3.75\ \text{k}\Omega$
(c) $R = 8.64 \times 10^3\ \Omega = 8.64\ \text{k}\Omega$
(d) $R = 18 \times 10^3\ \Omega = 18\ \text{k}\Omega$
11. (a) $R = 2.5\ \Omega$
(b) $V = 25$ V

(c) $P = 250$ W
15. $R = 240\ \Omega$
17. $I_{\text{max}} = 19.17$ mA
19. $I = 16.67$ mA
21. $P = 1.125$ W
23. Choose a resistor whose R and P values are $200\ \Omega$ and $\frac{1}{4}$ W respectively.
25. $R = 100\ \Omega$

CHAPTER 4

1. $I = 2$ A, $R_2 = 10\ \Omega$
3. $V_2 = 1.2$ V
5. $I = 4$ mA
   $V_1 = 8$ V
   $V_2 = 32$ V
   $P_1 = 32$ mW
   $P_2 = 128$ mW
   $P_T = 160$ mW $= 0.16$ W
7. $R_T = 2,573,470\ \Omega$
9. Each $R = 6\ \text{k}\Omega$
11. 20.7 V
13. $R_1 = 300\ \Omega$
   $P_1 = 27$ W

   $P_2 = 9$ W
15. $R_2 = 25\ \Omega$
17. $V_2 = 13$ V
19. (a) $V = 18$ V
(b) $V = 0$ V
21. $R = 60\ \Omega$
23. $V_1 = 0$ V
   $V_2 = 36$ V
   $V_3 = 0$ V
   $V_4 = 0$ V
25. $R_T = 4.5\ \text{k}\Omega$
   $I = 12$ mA

   $V_1 = 1.2$ V
   $V_2 = 2.64$ V
   $V_3 = 8.16$ V
   $V_4 = 14.4$ V
   $V_5 = 21.6$ V
   $V_6 = 1.32$ V
   $V_7 = 4.68$ V
   $P_T = 648$ mW
   $P_1 = 14.4$ mW
   $P_2 = 31.68$ mW
   $P_3 = 97.92$ mW
   $P_4 = 172.8$ mW

   $P_5 = 259.2$ mW
   $P_6 = 15.84$ mW
   $P_7 = 56.16$ mW
27. $I = 20$ mA
   $V_1 = 2.4$ V
   $V_2 = 2$ V
   $V_3 = 13.6$ V
   $V_T = 18$ V
   $R_3 = 680\ \Omega$
   $P_T = 360$ mW
   $P_2 = 40$ mW
   $P_3 = 272$ mW

CHAPTER 5

1. (b) 12 V
   (c) $I_1 = 2$ A, $I_2 = 1$ A
   (d) $I_T = 3$ A
   (e) $R_{EQ} = 4$ Ω
3. (b) 20 V
   (c) $I_2 = 2$ A
      $I_3 = 4$ A
5. (a) $I_2 = 0$ A
   (b) $I_1 = 1$ A
   (c) $I_T = 1$ A
   (d) $R_{EQ} = 10$ Ω
   (e) $P_T = 10$ W
7. (a) 7.14 Ω
   (b) 2 kΩ
   (c) 250 Ω
   (d) 54.6 Ω
   (e) 714 Ω
   (f) 5 kΩ
9. $G_T = 0.039$ S

11. (a) $R = 100$ kΩ
    (b) $R = 33.3$ kΩ
    (c) $R = 11.1$ kΩ
13. (a) 8.8 V
    (b) 8.8 V
    (c) $I_2 = 2.26$ mA
15. $G_T = 0.5$ S
    $R_{EQ} = 2$ Ω
17. $I_1 = 200$ mA
    $I_2 = 400$ mA
    $I_3 = 600$ mA
    $I_T = 1.2$ A
    $R_{EQ} = 10$ Ω
    $P_1 = 2.4$ W
    $P_2 = 4.8$ W
    $P_3 = 7.2$ W
    $P_T = 14.4$ W
19. $I_1 = 50$ mA
    $I_2 = 25$ mA

$I_3 = 75$ mA
$I_T = 150$ mA
$R_{EQ} = 60$ Ω
$P_1 = 450$ mW
$P_2 = 225$ mW
$P_3 = 675$ mW
$P_T = 1.35$ W
21. I_1 remains the same
    (50 mA)
23. $R_{EQ} = 25$ Ω
25. (a) 6 mA
    (b) 30 mA
27. (a) 42.5 mA
    (b) 157.5 mA
29. $I_T = 1.2$ A
    $I_1 = 100$ mA
    $I_2 = 900$ mA
    $R_1 = 1.08$ kΩ
    $R_2 = 120$ Ω

$R_3 = 540$ Ω
$P_T = 129.6$ W
$P_2 = 97.2$ W
$P_3 = 21.6$ W
31. $R_{EQ} = 1.105$ kΩ
    $I_T = 190$ mA
    $I_2 = 30$ mA
    $I_3 = 50$ mA
    $I_4 = 100$ mA
    $R_1 = 21$ kΩ
    $R_3 = 4.2$ kΩ
    $P_T = 39.9$ W
    $P_1 = 2.1$ W
    $P_2 = 6.3$ W
    $P_3 = 10.5$ W
    $P_4 = 21$ W

CHAPTER 6

1. (a) $R_T = 25$ Ω
   (b) $I_T = 4$ A
3. (b) $R_T = 15$ Ω
5. (a) $R = 6$ Ω
   (b) $R = 24$ Ω
7. (a) $V_1 = 2.23$ V
   $V_2 = 0.74$ V
   $V_3 = 6.7$ V
   $V_4 = 22.3$ V
   (b) $P_1 = 204$ mW
   $P_2 = 69$ mW
   $P_3 = 620$ mW
   $P_4 = 2.08$ mW

9. $V_1 = V_X = 1$ V
   $V_2 = V_S = 10$ V
   $R_X = 4.2$ Ω
11. $R_T = 10.45$ Ω
13. (a) $V_2 = 20$ V
    (b) $V_1 = V_2 = 22.5$ V
15. $R_T = 1$ kΩ
    $I_1 = 60$ mA
    $I_2 = 44$ mA
    $I_3 = 16$ mA
    $V_1 = 7.2$ V
    $V_2 = 52.8$ V
    $V_3 = 52.8$ V

$V_{AB} = -52.8$ V
17. V_{AB} increases. I_T and I_2
    both decrease, and I_3 is
    zero.
19. V_{AB} decreases to zero.
    I_T and I_3 both increase,
    and I_2 is zero.
21. $R_T = 300$ Ω
    $I_1 = 120$ mA
    $I_2 = 60$ mA
    $I_3 = 60$ mA
    $I_4 = 30$ mA
    $I_5 = 30$ mA

$I_6 = 15$ mA
$I_7 = 15$ mA
$I_8 = 7.5$ mA
$I_9 = 7.5$ mA
$V_1 = 18$ V
$V_2 = 18$ V
$V_3 = 9$ V
$V_4 = 9$ V
$V_5 = 4.5$ V
$V_6 = 4.5$ V
$V_7 = 2.25$ V
$V_8 = 2.25$ V
$V_9 = 2.25$ V

CHAPTER 7

1. $V_1 = 3$ V
   $V_2 = 6$ V
   $V_3 = 9$ V
3. $I_1 = 1$ A
   $I_2 = 2$ A
5. $V_1 = 12$ V
   $V_2 = 6$ V
   $V_3 = 10.8$ V

$V_4 = 7.2$ V
$V_{CG} = 7.2$ V
$V_{BG} = 18$ V
$V_{AG} = 24$ V
7. $I_1 = 16$ mA
   $I_2 = 8$ mA
9. $I_1 = 25$ μA
   $I_2 = 37.5$ μA

$I_3 = 12.5$ μA
$I_4 = 75$ μA
11. $R_1 = 236.8$ Ω
    $R_2 = 333$ Ω
    $R_3 = 1.5$ kΩ
    $P_1 = 342$ mW
    $P_2 = 108$ mW
    $P_3 = 54$ mW

13. $R_1 = 500$ Ω
    $R_2 = 800$ Ω
    $R_3 = 1.6$ kΩ
    $P_1 = 1.8$ W
    $P_2 = 1.62$ W
    $P_3 = 360$ mW
15. $V_{\text{load } C} = 11.21$ V

CHAPTER 8

1. (a) $R_S = 50$ Ω
   (b) $R_S = 5.55$ Ω
   (c) $R_S = 2.083$ Ω
   (d) $R_S = 0.505$ Ω
   (approximately)
   (e) Half-scale current is
   1 mA in (a), 5 mA
   in (b), 12.5 mA in

(c), and 50 mA in
(d).
3. (a) $R_{\text{mult}} = 2.95$ kΩ
   (b) $R_{\text{mult}} = 9.95$ kΩ
   (c) $R_{\text{mult}} = 29.95$ kΩ
   (d) $R_{\text{mult}} = 99.95$ kΩ
   (e) $R_{\text{mult}} = 299.95$ kΩ
5. (a) V = 4.8 V

(b) V = 3 V
(c) V = 4.77 V
7. $\dfrac{10\ \text{k}\Omega}{\text{V}}$
9. (a) $R_X = 0$ Ω
   (b) $R_X = 4.5$ kΩ
   (c) $R_X = 3$ kΩ

(d) $R_X = 1.5$ kΩ
(e) $R_X = 750$ Ω
(f) $R_X = 500$ Ω
11. $R_1 = 145$ Ω
13. 10 Ω
15. 1.1 V

CHAPTER 9

1. (a) $I_3 = 8$ A
   (b) $I_5 = 16$ A
   (c) $I_6 = 11$ A
3. (a) $V_T = 36$ V
      $R_T = 4.5$ kΩ
      $I = 8$ mA
      $V_{R_1} = 8$ V
      $V_{R_2} = 12$ V
      $V_{R_3} = 16$ V
   (b) $V_{AG} = +12$ V
      $V_{BG} = +4$ V
      $V_{CG} = -8$ V

      $V_{DG} = -24$ V
5. (a) $V_T = 30$ V
      $R_T = 25$ kΩ
      $I = 1.2$ mA
      $V_{R_1} = 12$ V
      $V_{R_2} = 6$ V
      $V_{R_3} = 12$ V
   (b) $V = +3$ V
   (c) $V = -3$ V
   (d) $V = 0$ V
7. $I_1 = 160$ mA
   $I_2 = 440$ mA

   $I_3 = 600$ mA
   $V_{R_1} = 19.2$ V
   $V_{R_2} = 79.2$ V
   $V_{R_3} = 10.8$ V
9. Answers are the same as for Prob. 7.
11. Left loop: CCW from negative terminal of V_1: -10 V $+ 16.875$ V $- 15$ V $+ 8.125$ V $= 0$. Right loop: CCW from positive terminal of V_2:

   15 V $- 16.875$ V $+ 1.875$ V $= 0$. Outside loop: CCW from negative terminal of V_1: -10 V $+ 1.875$ V $+ 8.125$ V $= 0$.
13. $I_1 = 2$ A
    $I_2 = 3$ A
    $I_3 = 1$ A
    $V_{R_1} = 30$ V
    $V_{R_2} = 30$ V
    $V_{R_3} = 10$ V

CHAPTER 10

1. $V_{TH} = 15$ V
   $R_{TH} = 3$ Ω
   $V_L = 6$ V
3. $I_S = 5$ A
   $R_S = 4$ Ω
   $I_L = 3$ A
5. R_L not open
7. $V_P = 4.2$ V
9. $V_{R_2} = 16.8$ V

11. $V_{R_2} = 16.8$ V
13. $V_{R_3} = 10.6$ V
15. See Fig. 10-31
17. (a) $V_1 = 54$ V,
       $R_1 = 6$ Ω,
       $V_2 = 72$ V,
       $R_2 = 12$ Ω
    (b) $V_{AB} = V_{TH} = -18$ V,
       $R_{TH} = 18$ Ω

    (c) $I_L = 500$ mA
    (d) $I_N = 1$ A
       $R_N = 18$ Ω
19. $V_{AB} = V_{TH} = 36$ V
    $R_{TH} = 600$ Ω
    $V_L = 24$ V
21. $V_{TH} = 36$ V
    $R_{TH} = 600$ Ω
    $I_L = 20$ mA

    $V_L = 24$ V
23. $I_N = 33.3$ mA
    $R_N = 300$ Ω
25. $I_1 = 890$ mA
    $I_2 = 522.5$ mA
    $I_3 = 1.41$ A
    $V_{R_1} = 8.9$ V
    $V_{R_2} = 20.9$ V
    $V_{R_3} = 21.1$ V

CHAPTER 11

1. (a) 1024 cmil
   (b) gage no. 20
   (c) $R = 1.035$ Ω
3. (a) 1-A fuse
   (b) 0 V

   (c) 120 V
5. $R = 96$ Ω
7. 10,000 ft
9. (a) 4.8 Ω
   (b) 4000 ft

11. 3 V
13. $I = 30$ A
15. (a) No. 14 gage
    (b) 0.25 Ω
    (c) 3.25 Ω

17. (a) 200 ft
    (b) 0.3185 Ω
    (c) 115 V approx.
    (d) 71.7 W approx.

CHAPTER 12

1. 1.5 mA
3. 600 A
5. (a) 2.88×10^5 C
   (b) 40 h
7. 20 kΩ
9. 6 Ω
11. $R_L = 1$ Ω:
    $I = 2.5$ A
    $V_L = 2.5$ V
    $P_L = 6.25$ W
    $P_T = 37.5$ W
    % efficiency = 16.67
    $R_L = 3$ Ω:
    $I = 1.875$ A

    $V_L = 5.625$ V
    $P_L = 10.547$ W
    $P_T = 28.125$ W
    % efficiency = 37.5
    $R_L = 5$ Ω:
    $I = 1.5$ A
    $V_L = 7.5$ V
    $P_L = 11.25$ W
    $P_T = 22.5$ W
    % efficiency = 50
    $R_L = 7$ Ω:
    $I = 1.25$ A
    $V_L = 8.75$ V
    $P_L = 10.938$ W

    $P_T = 18.75$ W
    % efficiency = 58.3
    $R_L = 10$ Ω:
    $I = 1$ A
    $V_L = 10$ V
    $P_L = 10$ W
    $P_T = 15$ W
    % efficiency = 66.7
    $R_L = 15$ Ω:
    $I = 750$ mA
    $V_L = 11.25$ V
    $P_L = 8.438$ W
    $P_T = 11.25$ W
    % efficiency = 75

    $R_L = 45$ Ω:
    $I = 300$ mA
    $V_L = 13.5$ V
    $P_L = 4.05$ W
    $P_T = 4.5$ W
    % efficiency = 90
    $R_L = 100$ Ω:
    $I = 142.9$ mA
    $V_L = 14.29$ V
    $P_L = 2.04$ W
    $P_T = 2.14$ W
    % efficiency = 95.3
13. $r_i = 25$ Ω
15. $R_L = 150$ Ω

CHAPTER 13

1. 5×10^3 Mx
   5×10^{-5} Wb
3. 0.4 T
5. 24×10^3 Mx

7. 300
9. 1 μWb $= 10^{-6} \times 10^8$ Mx
11. (a) 500 kG
    (b) 600 Mx

    (c) 0.25 T
    (d) 150 μWb
    (e) 40 G

13. $B = 500$ G
15. $B = 80 \times 10^{-3}$ T or 80 mT

CHAPTER 14

1. (a) 200
   (b) 500
3. (a) 300 G/Oe
   (b) 378×10^{-6} T/(A · t/m)
   (c) 300
5. (a) 126×10^{-6}

(b) 88.2×10^{-6}
7. (b) 40 V
   (c) 1000 A · t/m
   (d) 0.378 T
   (e) 3.02×10^{-4} Wb
   (f) 66×10^4 A · t/Wb

9. 14.4
11. $\mu_r = 133.3$
13. $B = 0.00189$ T or 1.89 mT
15. $\phi = 0.01$ Wb or 10 mWb

CHAPTER 15

1. 8 kV
3. (a) 2 Wb/s
   (b) −2 Wb/s
5. (a) 0.2 A

(b) 80 ampere-turns
(c) 400 ampere-turns/m
(d) 0.252 T
(e) 1.512×10^{-4} Wb

(f) See Fig. 15-7 for an example.
7. $v_{ind} = 1$ V
9. $N = 1600$ turns

CHAPTER 16

1. (a) $I = 6$ A
   (b) $f = 60$ Hz
   (c) 0°
   (d) 120 V
3. (a) $t = 0.25$ ms
   (b) $t = 0.0625$ μs
5. (a) $f = 20$ Hz
   (b) $f = 200$ Hz
   (c) $f = 0.2$ Hz
   (b) $f = 0.2$ Hz
7. (a) +10 and −10 V
   (b) +10 and −10 V
   (c) +10 and −10 V

(d) +15 and −5 V
9. $I_1 = 40$ μA
   $I_2 = 20$ μA
   $V_1 = V_2 = 200$ V
   $P_1 = 8$ mW
   $P_2 = 4$ mW
11. $I = 2.5$ A
13. (a) 27.15 V
   (b) 20.8 V
15. $I_1 = 2.553$ A
   $I_2 = 1.765$ A
   $I_3 = 5.455$ A
   $I_T = 9.773$ A

17. (a) 462.5 μV
   (b) 9.84 mV
   (c) 35.19 mV
19. (a) 7.93 Ω
   (b) 1.55 W
21. (a) 42.42 V_{rms}
   (b) 60 V
   (c) 120 V
23. 7.5 MHz, first harmonic, first odd; 15 MHz, second harmonic, first even; 22.5 MHz, third harmonic, second odd;

30 MHz, fourth harmonic, second even.
25. (a) $\lambda = 113$ ft
   (b) $\lambda = 22.6$ ft
   (c) $\lambda = 4.52$ ft
   (d) $\lambda = 1.13$ ft
   (e) $\lambda = 0.0753$ ft
   (f) $\lambda = 0.0565$ ft
27. 1.6 kHz
29. 22.5°
31. $T = 6.67$ nS

CHAPTER 17

1. $Q = 400$ μC
3. (a) $Q = 18$ μC
   (b) 9 V
5. $C = 1062$ pF
7. (a) 200 V
   (b) $Q = 200$ μC
   (c) $C = 1$ μF
9. (a) 2.5×10^{-2} J
   (b) 12.5 J
   (c) 3.2 J

11. (a) 0.06 μF
   (b) 74.2 pF
13. (a) $C_T = 0.01334$ μF
   (b) $C_T = 0.047$ μF
15. (a) 4700 pF ± 20%
   (b) 10,000 pF ± 5%
   (c) 220,000 pF ± 10%
   (d) 820 pF ± 20%
   (e) 0.0033 μF + 80%, −20%
   (f) 0.022 μF + 100%, −0%

(g) 1800 pF ± 10%
   (h) 0.0027 μF + 80%, −20%
17. (a) 56 pF
   (b) 12,000 pF
   (c) 560,000 pF
   (d) 22 pF
19. (a) 470,000 pF or 0.47 μF, ±10%
   (b) 6,200,000 pF or 6.2 μF, ±5%
   (c) 15,000,000 pF or 15 μF, ±10%
   (d) 820,000,000 pF or 820 μF, ±5%

CHAPTER 18

1. 80 pF at 1 MHz
3. (b) $I = 4.5$ mA
   (c) $f = 1$ kHz
5. (b) $I = 2$ mA
   (c) $V_{C_1} = 2$ V
   (d) $V_{C_2} = 8$ V

7. $f = 3183$ Hz
9. (a) $X_{C_T} = 200$ Ω
   (b) $C = 333.3$ pF
   $C_T = 1000$ pF
11. (a) $X_C = 300$ Ω
   $C = 8.85$ μF

(b) $C = 17.7$ μF
13. $X_C = 206.5$ Ω
15. $I = 0.78$ mA
17. $C = 422$ pF
19. See values in Prob. 21
21. See values in Prob. 19

23. (a) X_{C_T} is halved
   (b) I doubles
25. (a) I_T is halved
   (b) $X_{C_{EQ}}$ doubles
27. $C = 100$ pF

CHAPTER 19

1. (b) $Z = 50$ Ω
   (c) $I = 2$ A
   (d) $V_R = 80$ V
   $V_C = 60$ V

(e) $\theta_Z = -37°$
3. $C = 0.08$ μF at 100 Hz
   $C = 80$ pF at 100 kHz
5. At 60 Hz, $C = 26.59$ μF

At 1 kHz, $C = 1.59$ μF
At 1 MHz, $C = 1590$ pF
7. $I_C = 15$ mA
   $I_R = 20$ mA

$I_T = 25$ mA
$Z_T = 1.2$ kΩ
$\theta_I = 37°$
$V_R = V_C = 30$ V

CHAPTER 19 (*cont.*)

9. For dc or ac,
 $V_1 = 400$ V
 $V_2 = 200$ V
 $V_3 = 100$ V
11. $Z_T = 583$ Ω
 $I = 0.2$ A
 $\theta_Z = -31°$
13. $I_T = 0.466$ A

$Z_{EQ} = 258$ Ω
$\theta_Z = 59°$
15. $C_1 = 66$ μF approx.
 $C_2 = 33$ μF approx.
17. $\theta_Z = -5.7°$
19. $C = 765$ pF
21. $X_C = 31.83$ kΩ
 $Z_T = 33.37$ kΩ

$I = 3.6$ mA
$V_C = 114.6$ V
$V_R = 35.6$ V
$\theta_Z = -72.6°$
23. $X_C = 965$ Ω
 $I_C = 10.36$ mA
 $I_R = 10$ mA
 $I_T = 14.4$ mA

$Z_{EQ} = 694$ Ω
$\theta_I = 55.2°$
25. $V_{AG} = 60$ V
 $V_{BG} = 12$ V
 $V_{CG} = 1.09$ V
27. (a) $C = 1.59$ μF
 (b) 0.0106 μF or
  10.61 nF

CHAPTER 20

1. (a) 1.5 A/s
 (b) 10,000 A/s
 (c) 10,000 A/s
 (d) −10,000 A/s
3. (a) 7.5 mV
 (b) 50 V
 (c) 50 V
 (d) −50 V
5. (a) 60 Hz
 (b) 960 V
 (c) 96 mA

(d) 0.768 A
7. (a) 300 μH
 (b) 66.7 μH
 (c) 320 and 280 μH
 (d) 0.0707
9. $R = 10.52$ Ω
11. 0.243×10^{-3} J
13. (a) 80 percent
 (b) 500 W
15. 1.26 mH
17. (a) 12 V

(b) 2.4 mA
 (c) 28.8 mW
 (d) 28.8 mW
19. $V_{S_1} = 120$ V
 $I_{S_1} = 50$ mA
 $P_{S_1} = 6$ W
 $V_{S_2} = 24$ V
 $I_{S_2} = 1$ A
 $P_{S_2} = 24$ W
 $P_P = 30$ W
 $I_P = 250$ mA

21. (a) $R_L = 3$ Ω
 (b) $I_P = 2.5$ A
23. (a) $Z_P = 200$ Ω
 (b) $Z_P = 12.5$ Ω
 (c) $Z_P = 6.25$ kΩ
 (d) $Z_P = 5$ kΩ
 (e) $Z_P = 5$ Ω
25. 11.18 : 1

CHAPTER 21

1. At 100 Hz, $X_L = 314$ Ω
 At 200 Hz, $X_L = 628$ Ω
 At 1000 Hz, $X_L = 3140$ Ω
3. (b) $I = 21.4$ mA
 (c) $V_L = 16$ V
5. $X_L = 1.2$ kΩ
 $L = 3.18$ H
7. $L = 0.159$ H
 $X_L = 10$ kΩ
9. (a) $X_{L_T} = 5$ kΩ
 (b) $I = 2$ mA
 (c) $V_{L_1} = 2$ V

$V_{L_2} = 8$ V
 (d) $L_1 = 2.65$ H
 $L_2 = 10.6$ H
11. (a) $f = 0.16$ kHz
 (b) $f = 1.27$ kHz
 (c) $f = 0.4$ MHz
 (d) $f = 1.6$ MHz
 (e) $f = 16$ MHz
13. $X_L = 1628.6$ Ω
15. $X_L = 754$ Ω
17. (d) At 500 Hz,
  $X_L = 785$ Ω

$I = 12.7$ mA
19. (a) 250 μH
 (b) 125 μH
 (c) 500 μH
 (d) 25 μH
 (e) 2.5 mH
21. $X_{L_1} = 5$ kΩ
 $X_{L_2} = 10$ kΩ
 $X_{L_3} = 15$ kΩ
 $X_{L_T} = 30$ kΩ
 $I = 4$ mA
 $V_{L_1} = 20$ V

$V_{L_2} = 40$ V
 $V_{L_3} = 60$ V
23. $X_{L_1} = 1.6$ kΩ
 $X_{L_2} = 6.4$ kΩ
 $X_{L_3} = 1.28$ kΩ
 $I_1 = 20$ mA
 $I_2 = 5$ mA
 $I_3 = 25$ mA
 $I_T = 50$ mA
 $X_{L_{EQ}} = 640$ Ω
25. (a) $X_{LT} = 5.34$ kΩ
 (b) $X_{LT} = 4.08$ kΩ

CHAPTER 22

1. (a) $Z = 100$ Ω
 $I = 1$ A
 $\theta = 0°$
 (b) $Z = 100$ Ω
 $I = 1$ A
 $\theta = 90°$
 (c) $Z = 70.7$ Ω
 $I = 1.41$ A
 $\theta = 45°$
3. (b) $X_L = 377$ Ω
 (c) $Z = 390$ Ω
 (d) $I = 0.3$ A
 (e) $I = 47.8$ mA
5. $Z = 400$ Ω
 $X_L = 400$ Ω

7. $R_e = 94$ Ω
9. $Z = 566$ Ω
 $I = 0.177$ A
 $V_L = 70.7$ V
 $V_R = 70.7$ V
 $\theta_Z = 45°$
11. At 800 Hz,
 $I_R = 0.25$ A
 $I_L = 0.125$ A
 $\theta_I = -26.6°$
13. $X_L = 500$ Ω
 $L = 15.9$ mH
15. $Z_T = 583$ Ω
 $I = 0.2$ A
 $\theta_Z = 59°$

17. v_L is a square wave,
 ±160 V p-p
19. (a) 45°
 (b) 63.4°
 (c) 84.3°
 (b) 63.4°
21. (a) −45°
 (b) −26.6°
 (c) −5.7°
 (b) −26.6°
23. $X_L = 6$ kΩ
 $Z_T = 7.62$ kΩ
 $I = 3.15$ mA
 $V_L = 18.9$ V
 $V_R = 14.8$ V

$\theta_Z = 51.93°$
25. $X_L = 2$ kΩ
 $I_L = 12$ mA
 $I_R = 16$ mA
 $I_T = 20$ mA
 $Z_{EQ} = 1.2$ kΩ
 $\theta_I = -36.87°$
27. $L = 26.53$ mH
 $Z_T = 3.33$ kΩ
 $I = 4.51$ mA
 $V_L = 11.26$ V
 $V_R = 9.92$ V
 $\theta_Z = 48.6°$
29. (a) $L = 7.96$ mH
 (b) $L = 159.1$ μH

CHAPTER 23

1. (a) 0.05 s
   (b) 0.05 μs
   (c) 1 ms
   (b) 20 μs
3. (a) 4 s
   (b) 100 V

5. $\nu_C = 86$ V
7. $\nu_C = 15$ V
9. 1.4 ms
11. (a) short
    (b) short
    (c) long

13. $C = 10$ μF
15. 1.96 V
17. 0.05×10^6 V/s
19. Answer in instructor's manual.
21. (a) $V_C = 5$ V

   (b) $V_C = 10$ V
   (c) $V_C = 11.32$ V
   (d) $V_C = 13.65$ V
   (e) $V_C = 14.7$ V
   (f) $V_C = 14.93$ V

CHAPTER 24

1. (a) 100 W
   (b) no reactance
   (c) 1
3. (b) $I = 10$ A, approx.
   (c) $Z = 10$ Ω
   (d) $\theta = 0°$
5. (c) $Z_T = 500$ Ω
   $I = 0.8$ A
   $\theta_Z = 53°$

7. (a) $X_L = 0$, approx.
   $X_C = 665$ Ω
   (b) $Z_T = 890$ Ω
   $I = 135$ mA
   $\theta_Z = -47.9°$
9. (a) 180°
11. $R = 320$ Ω
13. $C = 300$ pF
15. $R = 9704$ Ω

17. $Z_T = 143$ Ω
    $I = 0.7$ A
    $\theta_Z = -36.5°$
    $\theta = 36.5°$
19. (a) $L_1 = 3$ mH
    $C_1 = 0.025$ μF
    (b) same reactances
21. $I_L = 60$ mA
    $I_C = 120$ mA

   $I_R = 80$ mA
   $I_T = 100$ mA
   $Z_{EQ} = 120$ Ω
   $\theta_I = 36.87°$
   Real power = 960 mW;
   apparent power = 1.2 W; power factor = 0.8.

CHAPTER 25

1. (a) $4 - j3$
   (b) $4 + j3$
   (c) $3 + j6$
   (d) $3 - j3$
3. (a) $5 \angle -37°$
   (b) $5 \angle 37°$
   (c) $3.18 \angle 18.5°$
   (d) $4.24 \angle -45°$
5. $Z_T = 65.36 + j23.48$
7. (a) $4.5 \angle 14°$
   (b) $4.5 \angle 34°$

   (c) $100 \angle -84°$
   (d) $100 \angle -60°$
9. $Z_T = 12.65 \angle 18.5°$
11. $Z_T = 5.25 \angle -13.7°$
13. $R = 5.08$ Ω
    $X_C = 1.27$ Ω
15. $R = 21.4$ Ω
    $X_L = 10.2$ Ω
17. $Z_T = 50 \angle -37° = 40 - j30$ Ω
    $I = 2 \angle 37° = 1.6 + j1.2$ A
    $V_R = 80 \angle 37° = 64 + j48$ V

   $V_L = 120 \angle 127° = -72 + j96$ V
   $V_C = 180 \angle -53° = 108 - j144$ V
19. $Z_T = 2.07$ kΩ $\angle 14.6°$ kΩ
    $I = 3.88$ mA $\angle -14.6°$ mA
21. $Z_T = 13.4 \angle 46.5°$
23. $Z_T = 1.28 \angle -11.3°$ kΩ
    $I_T = 18.75 \angle 11.3°$ mA
    $V_{R_1} = 13.31 \angle 56.3°$ V
    $V_{C_1} = 19.97 \angle -33.7°$ V
    $V_{L_1} = 13.31 \angle 56.3°$ V
    $V_{R_2} = 19.97 \angle 33.7°$ V

CHAPTER 26

1. $f_r = 5$ MHz
3. $f_r = 1.41$ MHz
5. $L = 35.08$ μH
7. $f_r = 5$ MHz
9. $Q = 50$
   $\Delta f = 100$ kHz
   $f_1 = 4.95$ MHz
   $f_2 = 5.05$ MHz
11. (a) $C = 202.68$ pF
    (b) $X_L = 314.2$ Ω
    $X_C = 314.2$ Ω
    $Q = 25$
    $\Delta f = 100$ kHz
13. $X_L = 785.4$ Ω

   $X_C = 785.4$ Ω
   $I_L = 1.273$ mA
   $I_C = 1.273$ mA
   $Q = 100$
   $Z_{EQ} = 78.58$ kΩ
   $I_T = 12.73$ μA
15. (a) $Z_{EQ} = 55.55$ kΩ
    $I_T = 18$ μA
    $\theta_I = -45°$
    (b) $Z_{EQ} = 55.55$ kΩ
    $I_T = 18$ μA
    $\theta_I = 45°$
17. (a) $C = 253.5$ pF
    (b) $X_L = 628.3$ Ω

   $X_C = 628.3$ Ω
   $Q = 80$
   $\Delta f = 12.5$ kHz
   $Z_{EQ} = 50.26$ kΩ
   $I_T = 19.9$ μA
19. (a) Real power = 79.62 nW; apparent power = 79.62 nW; power factor = 1.
    (b) Real power = 39.8 nW; apparent power = 56.3 nW; power factor = 0.707.

   (c) Real power = 39.8 nW; apparent power = 56.3 nW; power factor = 0.707.
21. $f_r = 3$ MHz
23. $\Delta f = 60$ kHz
    $f_1 = 2.97$ MHz
    $f_2 = 3.03$ MHz
25. $R_S = 18.85$ Ω
27. $f_r = 1$ MHz
29. $\Delta f = 4$ kHz
    $f_1 = 998$ kHz
    $f_2 = 1.002$ MHz

CHAPTER 27

1. (a) $C = 0.1$ μF
   (b) $V_R \cong 0$ V
   $V_C = 20$ V
   (c) $V_R = 7.07$ V rms value

   $V_C \cong 0$ V
3. $C = 0.64$ μF
5. (a) $f_c = 3.29$ kHz
   (b) $f_c = 5.305$ kHz

   (c) $f_c = 1.88$ kHz
   (d) $f_c = 2.39$ kHz
7. (a) $V_{out} = 10 \angle 0°$ V
   (b) $V_{out} = 9.99 \angle -2.16°$ V

CHAPTER 27 (*cont.*)

(c) $V_{\text{out}} = 7.07 \ \angle -45° \ \text{V}$
(d) $V_{\text{out}} = 2.2 \ \angle -62° \ \text{V}$
(e) $V_{\text{out}} = 1 \ \angle -84° \ \text{V}$
(f) $V_{\text{out}} = 53 \ \angle -89.7° \ \text{mV}$
9. (a) $V_{\text{out}} = 1.05 \ \angle 88.8° \ \text{mV}$
(b) $V_{\text{out}} = 26.58 \ \angle 57.9° \ \text{mV}$
(c) $V_{\text{out}} = 35.35 \ \angle 45° \ \text{mV}$

(d) $V_{\text{out}} = 46.45 \ \angle 21.7° \ \text{mV}$
(e) $V_{\text{out}} = 49.94 \ \angle 2.74° \ \text{mV}$
(f) $V_{\text{out}} = 50 \ \angle 0° \ \text{mV}$
11. (a) $N_{\text{db}} = -27.6 \ \text{db}$
(b) $N_{\text{db}} = -3 \ \text{db}$
(c) $N_{\text{db}} = -0.17 \ \text{db}$
(d) $N_{\text{db}} = 0 \ \text{db}$ (approximately)

13. $f_N = 4.42 \ \text{kHz}$
15. (a) $N_{\text{db}} = 3 \ \text{db}$
(b) $N_{\text{db}} = 10 \ \text{db}$
(c) $N_{\text{db}} = 13 \ \text{db}$
(d) $N_{\text{db}} = 20 \ \text{db}$
(e) $N_{\text{db}} = 30 \ \text{db}$
(f) $N_{\text{db}} = 33 \ \text{db}$

CHAPTER 28

1. $R = 1.6 \ \Omega$

3. $I_C = 5.7 \ \text{mA}$

5. $I_E = 50.3 \ \text{mA}$

7. $I = 20 \ \text{mA}$

CHAPTER 29

1. $A_V = 300$
$A_I = 90$
$A_P = 27,000$

3. 10,000
5. 159 Ω

7. (a) $C = 332 \ \mu\text{F}$
(b) $C = 166 \ \mu\text{F}$

9. $f_r = 1.625 \ \text{MHz}$
11. $R_L = 2.5 \ \text{k}\Omega$

CHAPTER 30

1. (a) 50
(b) 80
(c) 4000

3. 11.25
5. (a) 4 V
(b) 2 mA

7. (a) 8 V
(b) 2 mA
(c) 1 kΩ

9. (a) $\pm 2 \ \text{mA}$
(b) 50

CHAPTER 31

1. (a) 11
(b) 17
(c) 16
(d) 181
3. (a) 100000000
(b) 111100000110
(c) 1110101
(d) 1100001100111010
5. (a) 5F
(b) 5F
(c) 35
(d) B29
7.

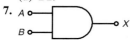

**Logic symbol for
2-input AND gate**

A	B	X
0	0	0
0	1	0
1	0	0
1	1	1

**Truth table for
2-input AND gate**

9.

**Logic symbol for
3-input NOR gate**

A	B	C	X
0	0	0	1
0	0	1	0
0	1	0	0
0	1	1	0
1	0	0	0
1	0	1	0
1	1	0	0
1	1	1	0

**Truth table for
3-input NOR gate**

11.

A	B	C	D	X
0	0	0	0	0
0	0	0	1	0
0	0	1	0	0
0	0	1	1	1
0	1	0	0	0
0	1	0	1	0
0	1	1	0	0
0	1	1	1	1
1	0	0	0	0
1	0	0	1	0
1	0	1	0	0
1	0	1	1	1
1	1	0	0	1
1	1	0	1	1
1	1	1	0	1
1	1	1	1	1

**Truth table for the boolean
expression:** $AB + CD = X$

CHAPTER 31 (cont.)

13.

$$A + B + C = \overline{X}$$

15. See Fig. 31-49.

17.

A	B	C	D	X
0	0	0	0	0
0	0	0	1	0
0	0	1	0	0
0	0	1	1	0
0	1	0	0	1
0	1	0	1	1
0	1	1	0	1
0	1	1	1	1
1	0	0	0	0
1	0	0	1	0
1	0	1	0	0
1	0	1	1	0
1	1	0	0	1
1	1	0	1	1
1	1	1	0	1
1	1	1	1	0

Truth table for the boolean
expression: $B(\overline{A} + \overline{C} + \overline{D}) = X$

19.

CHAPTER 32

1. (a) $A_{CL} = 10$
  (b) $V_{out} = 5$ V
3. $f_{max} = 15.92$ kHz

5. (a) $V_{out} = -12.5$ V
  (b) $V_{out} = +10$ V
  (c) $V_{out} = 0$ V

7. $f_c = 1.06$ kHz
  V_{out} at $0.25f_c = 24.25$ mVpp
9. $V_{out} = -10$ V

ANSWERS TO ODD-NUMBERED CRITICAL THINKING PROBLEMS

CHAPTER 1
1. $Q = 1.6 \times 10^{-16}$ C
3. $I = 0.0001$ A or 1×10^{-4} A

CHAPTER 2
1. $R = 250$ kΩ

CHAPTER 3
1. $I = 21.59$ A
3. Cost = $7.52
5. I_{max} (120°C) = 13.69 mA

CHAPTER 4
1. $R_1 = 300$ Ω
   $R_2 = 600$ Ω
   $R_3 = 1.8$ kΩ
3. $I = 35.36$ mA
5. $R_1 = 250$ Ω
   $V_T = 1.25$ V

CHAPTER 5
1. $I_T = 44.53$ mA
3. $R_1 = 2$ kΩ
   $R_2 = 6$ kΩ
   $R_3 = 3$ kΩ
5. $R_1 = 15$ kΩ
   $R_2 = 7.5$ kΩ
   $R_3 = 3.75$ kΩ
   $R_4 = 1.875$ kΩ

CHAPTER 6
1. (a) $R_1 = 657$ Ω
   (b) 2×12.9 W = 25.8 W, approx.,
      for a safety factor of 2.
   (c) $R_T = 857$ Ω
3. (b) $A(B + C) = X$

CHAPTER 7
1. $R_1 = 1$ kΩ
   $R_3 = 667$ Ω

CHAPTER 8
1. $R_1 = 40$ Ω
   $R_2 = 9$ Ω
   $R_3 = 1$ Ω
3. 10 kΩ/V

CHAPTER 9
1. $R_1 = 1.5$ kΩ
   $R_3 = 1$ kΩ

CHAPTER 10
1. $V_{TH} = 20$ V
   $R_{TH} = 12$ Ω
   $I_L = 250$ mA
   $V_L = 17$ V
3. $V_{TH} = 0$ V
   $R_{TH} = 25$ Ω

CHAPTER 11
1. Drawing provided in instructor's manual.

CHAPTER 12
1. (a) $V_L = 11.45$ V
   (b) $I_L = 1.91$ A approx.
   (c) V_1 supplies 550 mA approx.
      V_2 supplies 275 mA approx.
      V_3 supplies 1.1 A approx.

CHAPTER 13
1. (a) $B = 1550$ G or 1.55 kG
   (b) $B = 0.155$ T or 155 mT

CHAPTER 14
1. $\mu_0 = B/H{:}1 = 1$ G/10e

Since 1 G $= \dfrac{1 \times 10^{-8} \text{ Wb}}{1 \times 10^{-4} \text{ m}^2}$

$= 1 \times 10^{-4}$ T

and $10e = 79.36 \dfrac{\text{A} \cdot \text{t}}{\text{m}}$ then

$\mu_0 = \dfrac{1 \times 10^{-4} \text{ T}}{79.36 \dfrac{\text{A} \cdot \text{t}}{\text{m}}}$

$= 1.26 \times 10^{-6} \dfrac{\text{T}}{\text{A} \cdot \text{t/m}}$

CHAPTER 15
1. (a) $R_W = 1.593$ Ω
   (b) $R_T = 17.593$ Ω
   (c) $V_L = 218.3$ V
   (d) I^2R power loss = 296.5 W
   (e) $P_L = 2.98$ kW
   (f) $P_T = 3.27$ kW
   (g) % efficiency = 91.1
3. With a relay, the 1000-ft length of wire does not carry the load current I_L and thus the circuit losses are reduced significantly.

CHAPTER 16
1. (a) 65 ft
   (b) 1981 cm
3. $f = 3.9$ MHz

CHAPTER 17
1. $C_1 = 8.08$ nF
   $C_2 = 2.02$ nF
   $C_3 = 161.6$ nF
3. (a) $\mathscr{E} = 500$ mJ
   (b) $\mathscr{E} = 250$ mJ
   (c) Yes. 250 mJ of energy was lost as heat energy (I^2R) in the wire conductors when the second 100 μF was connected in part (b).

CHAPTER 18
1. Connect the unmarked capacitor in series with an ac voltage source whose frequency and output voltage are known. Measure the ac current through the capacitor. Calculate X_C as V_C/I. Next, solve for C as $C = 1/2\pi f X_C$.

CHAPTER 19

1. $X_C = 300 \ \Omega$
   $Z_T = 671 \ \Omega$
   $I = 26.83 \ \text{mA}$
   $f = 19.649 \ \text{kHz}$
   $V_T = 18 \ \text{V}$
   $V_R = 16.1 \ \text{V}$
3. $I_C = 12 \ \text{mA}$
   $I_R = 20.79 \ \text{mA}$
   $I_T = 24 \ \text{mA}$
   $X_C = 2 \ \text{k}\Omega$
   $R = 1.154 \ \text{k}\Omega$
   $C = 7960 \ \text{pF approx.}$

CHAPTER 20

1. Since $V_P = V_S \times N_S/N_P$ and $I_P = I_S \times N_S/N_P$ then $Z_P = V_P/I_P = \dfrac{V_S \times N_S/N_P}{I_S \times N_S/N_P}$
   since $Z_S = V_S/I_S$ then $Z_P = (N_P/N_S)^2 \times Z_S$.
3. (a) $Z_P = 800 \ \Omega$
   (b) $Z_P = 200 \ \Omega$

CHAPTER 21

1. $L_1 = 60 \ \text{mH}$
   $L_2 = 40 \ \text{mH}$
   $L_3 = 120 \ \text{mH}$
   $L_T = 90 \ \text{mH}$
   $X_{L_1} = 1.2 \ \text{k}\Omega$
   $X_{L_2} = 800 \ \Omega$
   $X_{L_T} = 1.8 \ \text{k}\Omega$
   $V_{L_1} = 24 \ \text{V}$
   $V_{L_3} = 12 \ \text{V}$
   $I_{L_2} = 15 \ \text{mA}$
   $I_{L_3} = 5 \ \text{mA}$
3. $L_1 = 10 \ \text{mH}$
   $L_2 = 120 \ \text{mH}$
   $L_3 = 40 \ \text{mH}$

CHAPTER 22

1. $X_L = 1.2 \ \text{k}\Omega$
   $R = 2.08 \ \text{k}\Omega$
   $L = 120 \ \text{mH}$
   $I = 15 \ \text{mA}$
   $V_L = 18 \ \text{V}$
   $V_R = 31.2 \ \text{V}$
3. $V_R = 6 \ \text{Vpp}$
   $V_{R_1} = 5 \ \text{Vpp}$
   $X_{L_1} = 833 \ \Omega$
   $X_{L_2} = 500 \ \Omega$
   $I = 6 \ \text{mApp}$
   $Z_T = 1.67 \ \text{k}\Omega$
   $L_1 = 41.67 \ \text{mH}$
   $L_2 = 25 \ \text{mH}$
   $\theta_Z = 53.13°$

CHAPTER 23

1. (a) $V_C = 30 \ \text{V}$
   (b) 7.5 ms
3. (a) 100 V
   (b) 0 V
   (c) 26.4 V
   (d) 55.37 V
   (e) 72.93 V

CHAPTER 24

1. $L = 2.98 \ \text{mH}$

CHAPTER 25

1. $V_{\text{in}} = 24 \ \angle 0° \ \text{V}$

CHAPTER 26

1. $Q = 2\pi f_r L/r_S$
   $Qr_S = 2\pi L \times 1/2\pi\sqrt{LC}$
   $Qr_S = L/\sqrt{LC}$
   $Q^2 r_S^2 = L^2/LC$
   $Q^2 r_S^2 = L/C$
   $\dfrac{X_L^2}{r_S^2} \times r_S^2 = L/C$
   $X_L^2 = L/C$
   $X_L = \sqrt{L/C}$

CHAPTER 27

1. (a) $f_c = 965 \ \text{Hz}$
   (b) $V_{\text{out}} = 3.535 \ \text{Vpp}$
   (c) $V_{\text{out}} = 68.2 \ \text{mVpp}$
3. $L = 191 \ \mu\text{H}$
   $C = 132.63 \ \text{pF}$

CHAPTER 28

1. $I_F = 150 \ \text{mA}$

CHAPTER 29

1. $V\text{dc} = 27.68 \ \text{V}$

CHAPTER 30

1. $B = I_C/I_B$
   $= \alpha I_E/I_E - \alpha I_E$
   $= \alpha I_E/I_E \ (1 - \alpha)$
   $B = \alpha/1 - \alpha$

CHAPTER 31

1.

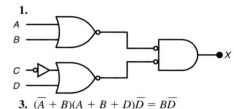

3. $(\overline{A} + B)(A + B + D)\overline{D} = B\overline{D}$

CHAPTER 32

1. $V_{\text{out}} = 2 \ \text{Vpp}$
   V_{out} is in phase with V_Y.

INDEX

Photo Credits

Cover and title page photos: Foreground: Larry Kennan Associates/The Image Bank; background: Simon Fraser/Welwyn Electronics/Science Photo Library/Photo Researchers

Pages iii, xiv: Stephen Simpson/FGP International; **Page 2:** Stephen Simpson/FPG International; **Page 3:** Bettmann Archive (Heinrich Hertz), Mark Steinmetz (Fig. S-1); **Page 5:** Science Photo Library/Photo Researchers; **Page 6:** Don Mason/The Stock Market (top), Bettmann Archive (Faraday), Courtesy of the Royal Institution (Faraday in lab); **Page 7:** Mark Steinmetz; **Page 9:** Mark Steinmetz; **Page 10:** Mark Steinmetz (Figs. S-5, S-6, and S-7); **Page 11:** Mark Steinmetz; **Page 12:** Mark Steinmetz; **Page 13:** Courtesy Fluke Corporation (Fig. S-10a), Courtesy of MCM Electronics (Fig. S-10b), Reproduced by permission of Tektronix, Inc. (Fig. S-11); **Page 14:** Phillip Hayson/Photo Researchers; **Page 18:** Bettmann Archive (Volta portrait), J-L Charmet/Science Photo Library/Photo Researchers (Volta with battery); **Page 21:** Sheila Terry/Science Photo Library/ Photo Researchers; **Page 26:** File photo; **Page 28:** Bettmann Archive (Millikan portrait and Millikan ray machine); **Page 33:** Mark Steinmetz; **Pages iv, 35:** Phillip Hayson/Photo Researchers; **Page 40:** Peter Aprahamian/Science Photo Library/Photo Researchers; **Page 45:** Mark Segal/Tony Stone Images; **Page 46:** Courtesy Harris Corporation; **Page 48:** Charles Krebs/Tony Stone Images (Fig. 2-1b), Mark Steinmetz (Fig. 2-2), P. R. Mallory (Fig. 2-3); **Page 49:** Bettmann Archive (Watt), Stackpole Corporation (Figs. 2-4 and 2-5); **Page 50:** Mark Steinmetz; **Page 55:** Mark Steinmetz; **Page 57:** Mark Steinmetz; **Page 60:** © Telegraph Colour Library/FPG International; **Page 66:** Courtesy Harris Corporation; **Page 67:** Charles Gupton/Stock Boston; **Pages v, 68:** Tom Tracy/The Stock Market; **Page 70:** Telegraph Colour Library/FPG International; **Page 77:** Bettmann Archive; **Page 79:** Bettmann Archive; **Page 80:** Bettmann Archive; **Page 82:** Telegraph Colour Library/FPG International; **Page 94:** Gabriel M. Covian/The Image Bank; **Page 95:** Matthew Borkoski/Stock Boston; **Page 96:** John Madere/The Stock Market; **Page 98:** Ben Swedowsky/The Image Bank; **Page 101:** File photo; **Page 103:** Metropolitan Museum of Art, Michael Friedsam Collection, 1931; **Page 111:** John Madere/The Stock Market; **Pages vi, 120:** Art Montes de Oca/FPG International; **Page 125:** Art Montes de Oca/FPG International; **Page 130:** Richard Pasley/Stock Boston; **Pages vii, 146:** Richard Nowitz/The Stock Market; **Page 151:** John Madere/The Stock Market; **Page 152:** Telegraph Colour Library/FPG International; **Page 157:** Richard Nowitz/The Stock Market; **Pages viii, 176:** Blair Seitz/Photo Researchers; **Page 188:** Geoff Tompkinson/Science Photo Library/Photo Researchers; **Pages xi, 194:** Joe Bator/The Stock Market; **Page 196:** Courtesy of MCM Electronics (Fig. 8-1a), Courtesy Fluke Corporation (Fig. 8-1a); **Page 197:** Weston Instrument Corp.; **Page 206:** Simpson Electric Company; **Page 215:** Courtesy of Simpson Electric Company; **Page 216:** Courtesy of Tektronix, Inc. (Fig. 8-20), Courtesy Fluke Corporation (Fig. 8-21); **Page 217:** Courtesy Fluke Corporation; **Page 223:** Alvis Upitis/The Image Bank; **Page 232:** Gary Gladstone/The Image Bank; **Page 236:** Bettmann Archive; **Page 239:** Rick Altman/Nawrock Stock Photo; **Page 240:** Charles Gupton/Stock Boston; **Page 243:** Gary Gladstone/The Image Bank; **Page 247:** Crown Studio; **Page 252:** Dick Luria/FPG International; **Page 261:** Dick Luria/FPG International; **Page 264:** SuperStock; **Pages xii, 288:** Gabe Palmer/The Stock Market; **Page 292:** L. S. Starrett; **Page 293:** Mark Steinmetz; **Page 294:** Hank Morgan/VHSID Lab/ECE Dept U of MA/Science Source/Photo Researchers; **Page 296:** Mark Steinmetz (Fig. 11-7a and b); **Page 299:** Mark Steinmetz; **Page 300:** Mark Steinmetz (Figs. 11-13, 11-14, and 11-15); **Page 305:** Bettmann Archive; **Page 306:** Gabe Palmer/The Stock Market; **Page 312:** Reproduced by permission of Tektronix, Inc.; **Page 317:** © Ken Biggs/Photo Researchers; **Page 318:** Mark Steinmetz; **Page 320:** Mark Steinmetz; **Page 321:** Mark Steinmetz; **Page 324:** Eveready Union Carbide Corporation; **Page 326:** Eveready Union Carbide Corporation; **Page 327:** Eveready Union Carbide Corporation; **Page 329:** Mark Steinmetz; **Page 330:** Exide Corporation; **Page 332:** © Ken Biggs/Photo Researchers; **Page 333:** Exide Corporation; **Page 334:** Doug Martin; **Page 335:** Mark Steinmetz; **Page 345:** Bob Daemmrick/Stock Boston; **Page 352:** Toshiba America Consumer Products, Inc.; **Page 363:** Mark Steinmetz; **Page 364:** © 1990 David A. Wagner/The Stock Market; **Page 365:** Toshiba America Consumer Products, Inc.; **Page 366:** Courtesy F. W. Bell; **Page 370:** Charles Thatcher/Tony Stone Images; **Page 375:** KS Studios; **Page 378:** Michael Gilbert/Science Photo Library/Photo Researchers; **Page 385:** Charles Thatcher/Tony Stone Images; **Page 389:** Gregory MacNicol/Photo Researchers; **Page 390:** Ralph Mercer/Tony Stone Images; **Page 402:** © Alvis Upitis/The Image Bank; **Page 405:** Mark Steinmetz; **Page 413:** Michael Rosenfeld/Tony Stone Images; **Page 414:** Tony Craddock/SPL/Photo Researchers; **Page 419:** Kim Steele/The Image Bank; **Page 445:** Mark Steinmetz (Fig. 16-22a and b; Fig. 16-23); **Page 449:** Courtesy Meteor Communications Corp., Kent, Washington; **Page 458:** Greg Pease/Tony Stone Images; **Page 469:** Mark Steinmetz (Figs. 17-4b and 17-5b); **Page 470:** Mark Steinmetz (Figs. 17-6 and 17-7); **Page 471:** Mark Steinmetz; **Page 472:** Mark Steinmetz; **Page 474:** Mark Steinmetz; **Page 483:** Bob Johnston/Texas State Technical College; **Page 489:** Bob Daemmrich/Uniphoto; **Pages x, 496:** Ken Cooper/The Image Bank; **Page 500:** Peter Scholey/Nawrock Stock Photo; **Page 507:** Ken Cooper/The Image Bank; **Pages ix, 516:** Larry Keenan Associates/The Image Bank; **Page 523:** Larry Keenan Associates/The Image Bank; **Page 526:** © 1990 Joe Robbins/FGP International; **Page 540:** © 1990 Stephen Hunt/The Image Bank; **Page 543:** Bettmann Archive; **Page 545:** Mark Steinmetz; **Page 545:** Mark Steinmetz; **Page 553:** Mark Steinmetz; **Page 559:** Mark Steinmetz; **Page 570:** Sencore, Inc.; **Page 575:** Gabe Palmer/The Stock Market; **Page 576:** Hewlett-Packard/Peter Arnold; **Page 583:** Scott Eklund/Gamma Liaison; **Page 584:** American Honda Motor Company; **Page 597:** American Honda Motor Company; **Page 597:** American Honda Motor Company; **Page 604:** Stephen Ferry/Gamma Liaison; **Page 618:** Stephen Ferry/Gamma Liaison; **Page 619:** Mark Steinmetz; **Page 630:** Eric Sander/Gamma Liaison; **Page 637:** Eric Sander/Gamma Liaison; **Page 660:** Alfred Pasieka/Science Photo Library/Photo Researchers; **Page 664:** Yvonne Hemsey/Gamma Liaison; **Page 679:** Spencer Grant/Gamma Liaison; **Page 679:** Spencer Grant/Gamma Liaison; **Page 690:** Uniphoto; **Page 705:** Courtesy of Metatec; **Page 713:** Uniphoto; **Page 719:** File photo (top left), Fred Wilson/FPG International (top right), Courtesy Apple Computers (bottom left), Davies & Starr/Gamma Liaison (bottom right); **Page 722:** Remi Benali/Gamma Liaison; **Page 730:** Remi Benali/Gamma Liaison; **Page 757:** Robert Severi/Gamma Liaison; **Page 758:** Volker Steger/Peter Arnold; **Page 766:** Volker Steger/Peter Arnold; **Page 793:** Mark Steinmetz; **Page 794:** Mark Steinmetz; **Page 794:** Mark Steinmetz; **Page 804:** Eduardo Garcia/FPG International; **Page 807:** Texas Instruments, Inc.; **Page 810:** Eduardo Garcia/FPG International; **Page 812:** Leonard Lessin/Peter Arnold; **Page 820:** Hayes Microcomputer Products; **Page 829:** DISH Network; **Page 834:** Studiohio; **Page 843:** Mark Steinmetz; **Page 849:** Mark Steinmetz; **Page 852:** Studiohio; **Page 863:** Sencore, Inc.; **Page 868:** Robert Nickelsberg/Gamma Liaison; **Page 872:** Uniphoto; **Page 892:** C. Falco/Photo Researchers; **Page 920:** C. Falco/Photo Researchers; **Page 926:** Microsoft Corporation; **Page 932:** Michael Fairchild/Peter Arnold; **Page 934:** Mark Steinmetz; **Page 940:** Michael Fairchild/Peter Arnold; **Page 967:** Reproduced by permission of Tektronix, Inc.; **Page 969:** BK Precision

Photo for Did You Know? feature: Pete Saloutos/The Stock Market; photo for About Electronics feature: Dale O'Dell/The Stock Market

Circuit board frame: Steve Allen/The Image Bank

Appendix B: Courtesy of PACE, Inc., Laurel, Maryland